"How Do We Know This?"

SUNY Series in Judaica: Hermeneutics, Mysticism and Religion
Michael Fishbane, Robert Goldenberg, and Arthur Green, Editors

HOW DO WE KNOW THIS?

MIDRASH AND THE FRAGMENTATION
OF MODERN JUDAISM

JAY M. HARRIS

STATE UNIVERSITY OF NEW YORK PRESS

Published by
State University of New York Press, Albany

© 1995 State University of New York

For information, address the State University of New York Press,
State University Plaza, Albany, NY 12246

Production by Bernadine Dawes • Marketing by Theresa Abad Swierzowski

Library of Congress Cataloging-in-Publication Data

Harris, Jay Michael, 1956–
     How do we know this? : midrash and the
fragmentation of modern Judaism / Jay M. Harris.
          p. cm. — (SUNY series in Judaica)
     Includes bibliographical references and index.
     ISBN 0-7914-2143-0. — ISBN 0-7914-2144-9 (pbk.)
     1. Jewish law—Sources. 2. Judaism—History—Modern period, 1750–
I. Title. II. Series.

1 2 3 4 5 6 7 8 9 10

To Mom and Dad,
my first teachers

CONTENTS

THE PRESENT WORK ORIGINATED IN an effort to study the ways in which Jewish intellectuals in the nineteenth century conceptualized the emergence of Pharisaic and rabbinic religion, which to them was synonymous with the term "Judaism." It is no small matter to write the history of one's cultural origins; pivotal contemporary issues of self-definition may be determined by the presentation of the past. In the case of the emergence of rabbinism, as it came to be called, the stakes were enormously high, as we shall see. Thus, I knew that it would be naïve to imagine that Jewish historians of rabbinism could actually pursue the *zwecklose Wissenschaft,* the detached scholarship, that was the historian's ideal. At the same time, I knew it would be perverse to assume that these historians were nothing more than learned but essentially crass propagandists for one cause or another. To achieve some understanding of Jewish historiography of rabbinism, one must attend to all the ideological issues, as well as the academic models that are in evidence in this historiography.

As I started to actually execute the project, I quickly became struck by the extent to which the historical debates revolved around the exegetical legitimacy and the formative role of rabbinic legal interpretation of the Bible. This issue was critical because of the recognition that the full range of Jewish praxis represents an occasional departure from, and a vast expansion of, the norms of the biblical text. As chapters 6, 7, and 8 make clear, Jewish scholars in the nineteenth century were obsessed with trying to widen or narrow the gap between ancient and modern textual assumptions, and thereby undermine or undergird the legitimacy of extrabiblical Jewish practices.[1] The nature of rabbinic exegesis and the role, if any, it played in producing the vast structure of Jewish praxis emerged as the crux in this historiographical debate. It thus soon became clear to me that a detailed discussion of the historiographical treatment of rabbinic exegesis was necessary before one could hope to write the broader history I had in mind.

I knew, however, that the nineteenth century was scarcely the starting point for such a study. Jews have been struggling with the question of the legitimacy of extrabiblical practices from their very emergence. The efforts of modern Jews to construct the proverbial "usable past" were based on the long-standing struggles of premodern Jews to comfortably respond to the question, "How do we know this?"—a question directed to the plethora of norms not explicitly mentioned in the Bible. I knew that my discussion of the modern attempts to construct models of rabbinism, with their emphasis on the role of exegesis, would have to be set against the background of ancient and medieval efforts to construct a coherent theory of the emergence of extrabiblical norms. I assumed that such contextualization would not require a great deal of original research, as the matter had been treated by a number of relatively recent scholars, who, I imagined, were largely if not completely free of the *Tendenzen* of their nineteenth-century predecessors. I quickly discovered this assumption was quite wrong. The prevailing treatments of the conceptualization of the emergence of rabbinic exegesis in recent historical work continued with many of the earlier assumptions, and for many of the same reasons; indeed, the work of these historians became part of my story, rather than the infrastructure on which I could build. It thus became clear to me that the entire question needed to be addressed anew.

Let me try to focus the issue under discussion here more sharply. In no part of the present book do I attempt to describe the historical emergence of extrabiblical Jewish practices. This is a matter for historians of ancient Judaism. A full appreciation of the modern issues, however, does demand a detailed analysis of the inner systemic understanding of the source of Jewish law—that is, the question of where ancient and medieval Jews *think* their laws come from. The first part of this book is devoted to a consideration of this matter in talmudic literature. The second part opens with a discussion of the medieval period. As we shall see, with some very important exceptions most Jews saw exegesis as playing a critical, creative role in the emergence of Jewish law. Further, as we shall see, there was certain tension between the two Talmuds—the Babylonian and Palestinian—regarding the application of a range of interpretive techniques. The second part of the book addresses the difficulties medieval and modernizing Jews had in accepting a religious legal system whose extrabiblical norms were seen as grounded in an undisciplined, unacceptable reading of the biblical text. These difficulties led some to reject the legitimacy of Jewish religious law, while it led others to reconceptualize the entire history of rabbinic Judaism, so as to make it more palatable in the modern age. The agenda for the book as a whole is governed by the modern period and the bodies of literature that shape the thinking of modernists. This fact serves to justify my ignoring kabbalistic literature, which is in any event necessitated by my limitations.[2] As I am aware that some readers may not wish to struggle through the detailed discussions of part one, I provide, at the end of chapter 3, a brief summary of the main points of this section.

While the focus of this study never strays from the conceptualization of the sources and authority of Jewish law, it does address broader themes as well. The portrait of medieval and modern Jews struggling with the burden of a cultural inheritance that has lost its self-evidence must be seen as part of a much larger chapter in the history of the transmission of cultures and traditions. After all, people change, religious needs change; sacred, canonized religious texts do not. In particular, we will have the opportunity to discern Jewish orthodoxies, which paradoxically rebel against a fundamental part of their rabbinic heritage, emerge in response to the challenges of Karaism, "Marranism," and modernity. At other times, when they were largely free of these particular cultural challenges, Jewish thinkers adjusted much more comfortably to the assumptions that were bequeathed to them.

Further, the story told here contributes to the ongoing discussion of the confrontation between tradition and modernity, and, more specifically the emergence of modern varieties of Judaism. For the weight of the burden of Jewish tradition was quite different for Jews in the Middle Ages than it has been for modern Jews. The latter have had many more social and religious options available to them; their relation to their religious past has been much more a matter of individual choice. How major religious leaders and thinkers negotiated the tensions of the modern age vis-à-vis their religious heritage is an essential part of the larger history of modern Judaism. Certainly the historical debates illuminated here played a very significant role in shaping the contours of the different denominations of Judaism that emerged in the nineteenth century.

Finally, the academy has in recent years become very interested in the limits and possibilities of language; in the nature of texts; in the (im)possibility of establishing the definitive meaning of a human communication; and in the role of the reader in shaping the significance of a text. The present work provides the literary theorist with access to an extended Jewish discussion of all these matters. This discussion represents an important part of the broader history of literary theory, of which participants in recent debates ought to be aware.

The question, "How do we know this [law]?" is asked on almost every page of the Talmuds.[3] Knowing the source of laws was obviously of great importance to the creators of these Talmuds. Despite the answers they provided, the question continued to reverberate throughout the fifteen centuries or so that separate us from the completion of these documents. For some Jews in some times and places the answer was obviously that provided in the Talmuds; for others at other times and places the answer was obviously not that provided in the Talmuds.

Either way, providing a coherent response to the question "How do we know this?" has remained an important aspect of Jewish cultural history. That is the story this work seeks to tell.

ACKNOWLEDGMENTS

IT IS A PLEASURE to acknowledge the many people who have graciously helped me to complete this book. Yaakov Elman and Michael Meyer each read an earlier version in its entirety and have provided much guidance and many corrections. I am indebted to them both. Isaiah Gafni, Benjamin Gampel, James Kugel, Peter Machinist, Bernard Septimus, Isadore Twersky, and Ruth Wisse read all or parts of the work, and provided many helpful comments of a substantive, stylistic, or bibliographical nature. I have talked through the issues of this book many times with David Weiss Halivni. Michael Fishbane and Robert Goldenberg, two of the editors of this series, have helped improve earlier versions by sharing their insights regarding substance and organization. I am grateful to all of them for their investment of time and energy in my work.

During the three years that I worked on this book, I had the honor to serve as the Harris K. Weston Associate Professor of the Humanities at Harvard. I am indebted to Mr. and Mrs. Harris K. Weston; the research assistance that accompanies the Weston chair has been invaluable to me.

To my wife, Cheryl, and my children, Elana, Rebecca and David, I give thanks for making it easy to think about things other than rabbinic exegesis and Jewish history.

I have dedicated this book to my parents, Stella and Herbert Harris, "my first teachers"; *sheli shelahem.*

1 • Introduction

R. Simlai preached: Six hundred and thirteen commandments were communicated to Moses, three hundred and sixty-five prohibitions, corresponding to the number of days in the solar year, and two hundred and forty-eight positive precepts, corresponding to the number of limbs in the body. Said R. Hamnuna, what is the biblical source for this? "Moses charged us with Torah, an inheritance etc." (Deut. 33:4). The numerical value of "Torah" is six hundred and eleven. [To this we add] "I am" and "You shall have no other Gods" (Exodus 20:2–7) which were heard directly from the mouth of the Almighty.

—Bavli, Makkot 23b–24a

THIS COMBINED HOMILY WAS, in time, to become one of the best known of all rabbinic teachings. Since the closing of the Babylonian Talmud (sixth century to seventh century) and its eventual predominance over the religious lives of premodern Jews, every Jewish child came to know that the Torah contains 613 commandments, divided into 365 prohibitions and 248 positive commandments. Given the homiletic basis of the "calculation," one may wish to question the authority of this specific number; nevertheless, a total of some six hundred biblical commandments is certainly about right, however (and whether) one chooses to actually count them.[1] And yet, these same children and their teachers knew perfectly well that the (rabbinic) Judaism they actually lived and practiced contained many, many times that number of commandments. In fact, Jewish religious practice as it developed over time and

1

as it achieved expression in the literature of the rabbis, the ancient sages and teachers of Jewish law, consists primarily of observances not explicitly stated in the Torah. This fact in turn leads to the question "How do we know this?" (more literally, "Whence do we know this?"), which is asked regarding hundreds of observances and laws, explicitly or implicitly, on virtually every page of the Talmuds, the great compendia of Jewish legal thought. That is, the question is asked, "How do we know that a particular observance is required of Jews, if it is not explicitly stated in the Bible, the revealed word of God?"

When one looks at the teachings of the rabbinic sages that spanned the first six Christian centuries, one finds two basic types of response to this question—one wholesale, in the sense that it seeks to deal with the question *tout court,* one retail, in that it seeks to provide a source for each and every law, one by one. The wholesale response is found almost exclusively within the Aggadah, or the nonlegal segments of the various documents that comprise what we call rabbinic literature, and is primarily attributed to *Amoraim,* rabbinic sages who flourished from the third to the fifth centuries of the Christian era. This response insists that virtually all extrabiblical practices[2] originate from an oral communication of God to Moses at Mount Sinai, where the Torah was given. This communication consisted of explanations of how to implement the laws actually stated in the Torah, as well as many other laws. Together, the written and oral Torahs, as they were called, represented a complete divine instruction to the people of Israel, outlining what it is that God wants of his people. In this wholesale response, everything that God actually demands was imparted at the revelation at Mount Sinai, part in writing, part orally. One rabbinic sage is quoted as having said that even the things that a student will one day bring to light were already said to Moses at Sinai.[3] Another sage is quoted to the effect that even the observances first noted in the Book of Esther— indeed, the Book of Esther itself, which relates to a time one thousand years after that of Moses—were already stated to Moses at Mount Sinai.[4] There is, of course, ample room to debate how literally such pronouncements were meant to be taken, particularly since they often depend on rather far-reaching exegeses of biblical verses. Nevertheless, there are enough such statements spread throughout the documents that comprise rabbinic literature to suggest that at least some rabbinic sages understood that together with a written Torah, God revealed a fully developed oral one as well.[5]

The retail response, which predominates in virtually all halakhic discussions in the literature, makes no such sweeping generalizations, but rather suggests that practically every law is to be derived from the written text of the Torah in some way. The answer to the question, "How do we know this?" is almost always, "We learn it from a verse." That is, the extrabiblical commandments are seen as primarily the product of exegesis. In the halakhic discussions of the Talmud, only a very small number of laws are identified as laws given to Moses at Sinai, or some other kind of tradition or decree.[6] Thus, if we collect all the responses to the question, "How do we know this?" we will note that most observances are considered the product of exegesis, while a few are categorized as laws given to Moses at Sinai or as some other form of tradition.[7] While both responses insist that God revealed laws and legal explanations orally, the retail response seems to suppose that such orally communicated laws are relatively few in number.

In my opinion, it is impossible to recover what any individual rabbi may have thought regarding the origins of extrabiblical practices, even if we were to accept all attributions at face value.[8] Both the wholesale and the retail responses might find expression in the teachings of a particular sage. The wholesale response is too readily interpreted as hyperbole to be certain just what a particular speaker had in mind. Further, the language in which the wholesale response is communicated is sufficiently pliable that it can allow for exegetical innovation in time and still claim that this represents the original intent of the divine lawgiver. We cannot, then, say anything about any particular sage and his opinion on the matter. What we can say is that whatever one wishes to do with the aggadic pronouncements that maximize what God gave and minimize the role humans play in shaping the contours of Jewish practice, the relentless insistence on the exegetical foundations of Jewish practice that dominate halakhic discussions of the various rabbinic documents leaves little doubt that, in general, these documents are informed by the belief that many Jewish practices are to be derived from the Torah exegetically.[9]

Exegesis of the Torah was the means through which the rabbis established the authority of the extrabiblical laws and practices they inherited; it was the medium they employed to create new laws in their own times; and it was the tool they used to resolve more far-reaching problems, such as contradictions within the Torah, or between the Torah and other biblical books.[10] It was, as we shall see presently, the tool they used to account for the Bible's verbosity and repetitiveness; in virtually all cases they accounted for a particular repetition by seeing it as the source of a specific law. Whatever the historian may wish to say about the origins of extrabiblical Jewish practice (a question that this book makes no effort to address),[11] the judgment of the rabbinic documents seems to me to be beyond question: the vast majority of those practices not explicitly stated in the Bible emerges through human exegesis of the Bible's language.

This may be seen most readily from the numerous rabbinic texts that contain legal exegesis of the Torah. There are, first and foremost, a series of texts sometimes called "tannaitic midrash" because, it is claimed, they derive from the time of the *Tannaim,* rabbinic teachers who flourished in the first two centuries of the Christian era. These texts are also called "midreshe halakhah" because they contain exegesis pertaining to halakhic matters, although they also contain exegesis that is not concerned with legal matters. The dates of these texts are the subject of scholarly dispute, with the third, the fourth, the fifth and the eighth centuries all receiving some support.[12] My own view is that the advocates of a third-century date, by far the majority, have made the most compelling argument. In any event, for the purposes of the present study it is not crucial that we resolve this, so long as we agree that much of the material now contained in these texts, although not necessarily all, predates the redaction of the two Talmuds and that this material was known to the Talmud's redactors and was considered by them as tannaitic. This far I think even the most skeptical of scholars will go.

The four main, apparently complete, midreshe halakhah are the *Mekhilta de-Rabbi Ishmael,* a commentary on Exodus; the *Sifra,* a commentary on Leviticus; the *Sifre Bemidbar,* a commentary on Numbers; and the *Sifre Devarim,* a commentary on Deuteronomy.[13] In addition to these and other fragmentary collections of midreshe halakhah,[14] the two Talmuds, the Bavli and Yerushalmi, contain substantial amounts of halakhic exegesis, often seeking to determine the exegetical reasoning that undergirds laws in the Mishnah, the authoritative early third-century legal collection.[15] In addition, a certain amount of halakhic midrash may be found in the Mishnah and the Tosefta, as well as the so-called aggadic midrashim. The contents of these texts, as we shall see, validate the claim that legal exegesis played a central role in the cultural orientation of early rabbinic Judaism.

Now, to be sure, exegesis of the Bible for legal purposes was scarcely an innovation of the rabbis of the first five Christian centuries. Exegesis of the Bible is as old as the biblical documents themselves, which frequently contain exegetical reworkings of antecedent biblical passages.[16] Similarly, as the nineteenth-century scholars Samuel David Luzzatto, Zacharias Frankel, and Abraham Geiger first argued, the ancient Greek and Aramaic translations of the Pentateuch exhibit intensive exegetical reflection on the Hebrew text(s) from which they were translated. Further, as Geiger argued brilliantly if not always compellingly, the Masoretic text itself may be seen as the product of politically and religiously oriented "exegesis" (read, *eisegesis*) of an antecedent Hebrew text.[17] The Samaritan Pentateuch may also reflect religiopolitical exegetical reworkings of received materials, and in any event Samaritan religion incorporates numerous exegetical extensions of the Torah.[18] The extent of the connection between these exegetical endeavors and rabbinic exegesis is subject to debate, although few would deny that there is some phenomenological overlap, if not direct historical connection.[19]

Beyond the texts and translations of the Bible, the various religiously and culturally identifiable groups that comprised the intellectual elite of the ancient world all developed systems of exegesis of important texts. The Samaritans, the Sadducees (about whose exegetical approaches we know little), the Qumran community, the Greek philosophical schools, and the early Christian communities all engaged in textual study and interpretation. Although rabbinic legal exegesis contains features that distinguish it from all these approaches, there are considerable parallels between each of them and the interpretations of the rabbis.[20] If one wishes to understand rabbinic exegesis against its historical background, one must attend to all these parallels and potential influences.

In the present work, however, I am not interested in presenting rabbinic exegesis in its appropriate historical context; indeed, in some ways, my project would be undermined by doing so. For the primary focus of the present work is the *reaction* to the existence of rabbinic exegesis and the claim advanced by its practitioners that it serves as a source of law. In trying to understand this reaction we must look at the literature as did previous generations of committed rabbinic Jews, and as did those committed to the reform or rejection of rabbinic Judaism. Among such people, rabbinic methods of scriptural interpretation were seen as sui generis; indeed, from the Middle Ages on, many Jews understood these methods as divinely revealed.[21] Others, less sympathetically inclined, saw these methods and their application as the height of absurdity and "turbidity."[22] Few of them understood rabbinic legal exegesis as reflective of a broader interpretive culture of the ancient world. Until the academic study of Judaism began to flourish in the twentieth century, the exegetical assumptions of the ancient rabbis were seen, for better or worse, as reflective of a historically unique approach to the interpretation of texts—the contrary example of the twelfth-century Karaite, Yehuda Hadassi notwithstanding.[23]

What we are interested in here is the historically repercussive approaches to Jewish exegesis and the practical conclusions that ostensibly issue from it. For in Jewish intellectual history the question, "How do we know this?"—what is the authority of the corpus of Jewish law—is frequently reopened, and numerous *Kulturkämpfe* have emerged revolving around how one answers that question. This is particularly true of the nineteenth century, since all the emerging forms of Judaism needed to address the viability of continued observance of Jewish law. The debates necessarily centered on the role and intelligibility of rabbinic readings of Scripture that seemed so foreign when judged by contemporary standards of textual meaning and linguistic significance.

To some extent the problem post-talmudic Jews faced is similar to that faced by any group whose exegetical (or any other kind of) traditions have achieved authoritative status, while exegetical assumptions change. Under such circumstances, one's sacred literature can become a distinct intellectual burden. The problem is particularly interesting in Jewish religious history in the Christian era, for rabbinic Judaism is characterized, in general, by a belief that earlier sages had greater religious authority than later ones.[24] Later authorities may not generally disagree with the *Tannaim,* who were, to repeat, the earliest rabbinic teachers, who flourished during the first two centuries of the Christian era. Furthermore, it is precisely the *Tannaim* who are viewed as the authors of the largest percentage of rabbinic legal exegesis, or midrash halakhah. Even when all acknowledge that no *Tanna* actually composed a given piece of midrash, it is often assumed by traditional students of the Talmud that the midrash accurately reflects what the *Tanna* was thinking in issuing a legal ruling without explicit exegetical underpinnings (there being little question that the ruling had such underpinnings).[25] When a law is transmitted in the name of a *Tanna* and an exegetical reconstruction of how the *Tanna* arrived at that law is offered, the midrash will be understood as the *source* of the law in question. If there are no disputes reported, the legal teaching will become normative, and the midrash will generally be considered the authoritative source of that law.

One problem faced by later generations is the fact that the midrashic literature considered tannaitic contains many disputes of an exegetical nature. To cite but one example, the Torah (Exod. 22:11) states that when an item has been entrusted to someone to guard (according to rabbinic interpretation, such a person is being paid for his services) and it is stolen, the guardian must pay compensation. The *Mekhilta de-Rabbi Ishmael,* a presumably tannaitic commentary on Exodus, asks, "Whence do we know that the trustee is liable if the item was lost," which is not stated in the Bible? It proceeds to offer two responses, in the names of two rabbis; one, an argument a fortiori, the other, an inference drawn from the use of *kefel lashon* (doubled language), here the use of the infinitive absolute with the conjugated verb. While the Talmud tries to explain the underlying dispute (Bavli, B.M. 94b), in this passage and in hundreds like it, one is left with the impression that exegesis represents nothing more than the personal preference of different sages, and, therefore, one might conclude that its results cannot be considered part of the essential message of the divine lawgiver.

Here the problem for a hypothetical post-talmudic Jew is compounded by the fact that the Yerushalmi cites yet another exegetical option from which we may learn that a lost object is the same as a stolen one in terms of liability: we have the presence of the word 'o, "or," in the verse. Now, for the rabbinic Jew living in the post-talmudic period, the law that apparently derives from this exegetical chaos is unquestionably authoritative as a biblical law. Yet, once moved to reflect on the matter, he would be quite confused as to precisely how this biblical law had been derived.

Also problematic from the perspective of post-talmudic rabbinic culture is that with the close of the Talmud (5th–6th centuries), the gates of halakhic exegesis were effectively, if not entirely, closed. That is, later authorities generally refrained from deciding legal issues by turning to a biblical text and interpreting it.[26] Thus, subsequent Jewish culture inherited a body of biblical exegesis that undergirded the ritual and legal practices that defined it; in general, it could not add to it and it could not disagree with its legal conclusions without a revolutionary reshaping of Jewish legal culture.

What happens when times change and exegetical preferences change? That is the question this book seeks to answer. In particular, we are interested in the modern period, which has seen a radical shift in textual assumptions and the perception of religious authority. However, in order to fully appreciate the issue confronting modern Jews of varying religious commitments, it is necessary to first get a sense of the role midrash halakhah played in premodern Jewish intellectual and religious history. We shall take this up in chapters 2, 3, and 4. The remaining chapters will then turn to modern times and the role the perception of midrash halakhah played in the Jewish *Kulturkampf* of the nineteenth century.

The Exegetical Problem

Before turning to that, the potential problem of midrash halakhah, the exegetical foundations of Jewish law, needs to be spelled out more concretely and in greater detail.[27] We need to understand how midrash halakhah works (or was traditionally understood to work), and to determine its implicit and explicit claim to legal creativity. Let us consider the following example. The Book of Deuteronomy (24:16) states, "Fathers shall not be put to death for sons, nor sons for fathers; a man

shall be put to death for his own sin." A modern reader, unfamiliar
with the criteria used in midrash halakhah and unfamiliar with the rest
of the Bible, will have no difficulty understanding the simple meaning
(peshat) of this verse. It means that each individual will be held ac-
countable for his or her own actions, and only he or she may suffer the
ultimate punishment, if appropriate. Guilt is not hereditary, nor is it
visited upon ancestors.[28] A reader with knowledge of the rest of the
Bible might see in this verse an admonition directed towards kings not
to visit punishment on the children of those whom the king executes,
such a practice not being uncommon.[29] None of these readers is likely
to be overly troubled by the verse's verbosity and redundancy. This the
modern reader will attribute to stylistic preference.

Those with some legal training, aware of the importance of statu-
tory construction, may, however, be troubled by these features. They
may seek to tease more meaning from the verse or they may simply
attribute the verbosity to different legal standards or, perhaps, to sloppy
construction. They might choose to argue that this is not a legal principle at all, but a theological statement, meaning that God will not
punish fathers for sons, etc., although such a claim is not justified.[30]
But what if the option of sloppy construction were not available? What
if one took for granted that the author was incapable of sloppy construction, indeed, incapable of less than perfect construction? What if
one took for granted that, even in "mere" theological statements, there
can be no redundancies in this text? One would then be forced to find
in each of the clauses a distinct statement that eliminates the redundancy, and, indeed, that is precisely what the *darshan* (the author of a
piece of midrash) in the *Sifre Devarim*, a presumed tannaitic commentary on Deuteronomy, does with this verse:

"Fathers shall not die for sons." What does this clause come to teach us? That
fathers shall not die for sons, nor sons for fathers? Does it not already say "a
man shall die on account of his own sin"? Rather [it comes to teach that]
fathers shall not die through the *testimony* of their sons, nor sons through the
testimony of their fathers. And when it says "*and* sons" (*u-vanim*) it includes
[other] relatives; and these are they: his brother, his father's brother, his mother's
brother, his sister's husband, the husband of his father's sister, the husband of
his mother's sister, his mother's husband, his father-in-law and his brother-in-
law. [When it says] "a man shall die on account of his own sin" [this means]
fathers die on account of their own transgression and sons die on account of
their own transgression.[31]

In the hands of this *darshan* the verse, apparently intended to establish
a relatively straightforward principle of human justice, becomes the source
for an important law unstated in the Torah, but of biblical authority,

namely that people may not testify against (or on behalf of) their relatives. This last point is established by the appearance of the conjunctive
"and" (in Hebrew, a one-letter prefix), also deemed superfluous. As we
shall see in chapter 4, at a later time Jews would be unable to resist asking
whether this is what the verse meant. At the same time, they were, of
course, unable and unwilling to argue against the principle excluding
relatives from bearing witness, even in formal ritual matters.

The problem is compounded because in the *Sifre Bemidbar*, a presumed tannaitic commentary to Numbers, we find a different midrash
that derives the prohibition of relatives bearing witness from another
source. Num. 35:24 states "In such cases the assembly shall decide
between the slayer and *between* the blood-avenger" (emphasis added).
The *Sifre* asks, "[W]hence do we know that relatives may not judge.
Scripture says 'between the slayer and between the blood-avenger'?"
This apparently means that the judging body must in some sense stand
between the parties, equidistant, as it were, from each.[32] Of course, to
this point all that has been established is that relatives may not be judges.
The *Sifre* goes on to establish that they may not be witnesses either, by
an argument a fortiori.[33] We should note that this passage is cited (with
variations) in the Yerushalmi (San. 3:9). Each of these midrashim takes
as its starting point the conviction that God encoded within the language of the Bible the additional information that relatives may not
serve as witnesses. Yet each sees this important information encoded
within different linguistic anomalies. Once again, our hypothetical Jew
living in the post-talmudic period would acknowledge as an undisputed
scriptural imperative the ineligibility of relatives to serve as witnesses.[34]
At the same time, he would be confronted with a problem, given the
two distinct exegeses rabbinic literature proffers. The problem becomes
more difficult when his own sense of the meaning of Scripture shifts;
then he may well ask whether either verse is an appropriate source for
the law in question. That is, he may wonder whether Scripture actually
"says" relatives may not serve as witnesses, and whether the sages who
claim it does truly thought so.

How then, we must go on to ask, did the authors of midrash
halakhah read the text of Scripture? What features triggered midrashic
comment? Attempts to answer this question usually lead to a discussion of the thirteen hermeneutical principles attributed to the *Tanna*,
R. Ishmael, and their assumptions. Such discussion strikes me as inadequate for two reasons. First, as has been noted by many, most of the
principles are rarely, if ever, actually applied in a rabbinic text. Further, even those that are used scarcely exhaust the techniques used in
rabbinic legal midrash. There are more exegetical techniques than are
encapsulated in this list of principles.[35]

Second, and more important, understanding the techniques used to interpret Scripture is only half the battle. Acknowledging that many legal passages stand *ke-feshutam* (according to their simple meaning), we must ask what scriptural problems excite midrashic interpretation. When do the rabbis comment, and when are they content to allow Scripture to stand as is?

To answer this fully, we must digress for a moment. Many scholars have argued that this is not really the right question to ask. For them, it is clear that the existing corpora of midrash halakhah are not primarily concerned with Scripture but with the Mishnah, that is, the body of law incorporated within this fundamental text. They claim that midrash halakhah represents an attempt to locate within the scriptural text sources or supports for laws that exist independently of it. In this reading, the starting point for midrash is not Scripture at all, but "traditional" law; midrash is not elicited by scriptural anomalies, but by the needs of the legal system. From this position, Jacob Neusner has gone on to locate within the so-called tannaitic midrashim, particularly the *Sifra,* a sustained polemic arguing the superiority of revelation over human logic.[36]

Neusner's position strikes me as attending only to the formal and rhetorical presentation of the midrashic passages, but not their content. Form and rhetoric are crucial, but not more so than content. Attention to content will show that neither his distinction between logic and revelation nor his reading of these passages can be sustained.[37] The overall claims regarding the relationship of the midrashim to the Mishnah needs to be taken more seriously. Certainly, the midrashim as we now have them at times take pains to indicate when the verse being explicated served as the "source" of Mishnaic law. On the one hand, some, probably most, midrashic passages strike us as inconceivable unless one assumes that the legal conclusion was already known. On the other hand, we must note that some midrashim deal with legal issues untouched by the Mishnah,[38] and the legal conclusions of others sometimes disagree with those of the Mishnah. This indicates that, while the relationship between the midrashic corpora and the legal corpora (the Mishnah and the Tosefta) is quite complex, the midrashic texts have their own integrity and direct relationship to Scripture, or, at least, to something other than the Mishnah. Furthermore, the historical issue of where Jewish law actually came from is less important for our purposes than the inner systemic judgment regarding the source of Jewish practice. Here, it seems clear to me, the texts are advancing the claim that they are interpreting the Torah with an eye to revealing all the laws encoded within its multivalent language.

Thus, even when as historians or literary critics we would insist the law is obvious and/or readily known, or explicitly stated in the Mishnah, we must note that the exegetes are still concerned with scriptural anomalies that in their view *create* law, rather than with anchoring in a scriptural passage what they acknowledge is existing law . A good example of this is the *Sifra*'s discussion of Lev. 1:3, to be treated below. However much the rabbinic exegetes may wish to anchor the Mishnah's laws in Scripture, they must operate with a theory of Scripture to achieve this. They must be able to answer the question "How do we know this" by plausibly showing that the norm in question is encoded within scriptural language; without this encoding the norm would never have been known, and would remain devoid of biblical authority. Whatever their historical point of departure, the *systemically recognized* point of departure for these exegeses is Scripture, not the Mishnah or some other source of traditional law.[39]

To return then to the issue under discussion, we must ask what scriptural anomalies elicit the use of midrashic techniques. An analysis of midrash halakhah that delves beyond the superficial form in which it is presented will not fail to note the extent to which concern for *yittur lashon*, (superfluities in language)—which, for our purposes, includes repetitions, extra words, even extra letters—is the prime mover (as in the text from Deuteronomy discussed above).[40] To the authors of this material, Scripture never says in two words what it can say in one, nor in three what it can say in two. It also never says the same thing twice. When it does, it is up to the *darshan* to show that it is not the same thing; something has been added by virtue of the repetition. In some cases the wording is slightly different, and this fact will hold the key to extrapolating a new legal result. In other cases, the wording of the repeated law is identical; then the imagination of the *darshan* must look to other possible applications of the law to explain this otherwise unacceptable anomaly.

Certainly the most famous resolution of the difficulty of scriptural repetition is the midrash halakhah that explains why Scripture says "You shall not seethe a kid in its mother's milk" three times. The first time prohibits cooking, precisely as the wording demands. The second time it cannot intend merely that, for that has already been established. Thus, Scripture must intend prohibiting consumption of a kid seethed in its mother's milk. The third time, Scripture intended to prohibit any benefit drawn from a kid seethed in its mother's milk, such as, to take a contemporary example, serving it to another in a restaurant.[41]

Another example, this time where the wording is different, may be seen in various interpretations of Leviticus 20 preserved in rabbinic sources, and today found in the printed editions of the *Sifra*.[42] As is well known, many of the prohibited sexual relationships spelled out in this chapter of Leviticus are repetitions of those stated in Leviticus 18. In the latter source a blanket punishment (namely, *karet*)[43] for all violations is given in verse 29, while in chapter 20, almost every verse carries a statement of the appropriate punishment (death, by an undefined method, or by burning). Chapter 18 is then understood as stating the prohibitions, while chapter 20 states the punishment. Indeed, an ad hoc legal principle is developed for these cases, insisting that both the prohibition and the punishment be explicitly promulgated. The blanket statement of punishment in 18:29 applies only to those transgressions not repeated in chapter 20. There is, thus, no superfluity in the text; each verse provides new legal information.

To the authors of midrash halakhah, even prepositions should not be used indiscriminately, even if that is the way people normally speak; the appearance of a preposition whose use could have been avoided calls forth a search for further meaning. For example, Lev. 1:2 and 3 make use of the phrase "from the herd" (*min ha-bakar*) in describing an animal to be brought for sacrifice. While this may appear to be a perfectly normal way of indicating what kind of animal is to be brought,[44] the interpreter(s) in the *Sifra* apparently felt that the word *min*, "from," is unnecessary; in his/their reading it is exclusionary, designed to indicate that only some from the herd may be brought as a sacrifice, while others cannot. The "from" that appears in verse 2 excludes cattle that have been used for idolatry. The *Sifra* continues:

And when it says "from the herd" below (i.e., in verse three), [this phrase is unnecessary; thus it must come to impart additional information, namely] it comes to exclude a *terefah*.[45] But would we not know this by an argument a fortiori. If a blemished animal, which is permitted [to be consumed] as *ḥullin*[46] is unfit for the altar, a *terefah* which is forbidden [even] as *ḥullin* is obviously unfit for the altar.

We must carefully attend to the force of this argument. The Torah used an allegedly superfluous word; the author states that the word is designed to exclude a *terefah* from the altar. Another voice enters the discussion and says that this is obvious. One would know this without a verse, and one has therefore not dissolved the superfluity. Note that the argument a fortiori has the same force as an explicit scriptural statement; indeed, an irrefutable argument a fortiori is sufficient to render "explicit" scriptural statements unnecessary. Thus, the superfluous *min* remains unaccounted for. The passage continues:

The fat and blood [of the animal] will show that this line of reasoning is not correct, for they are unfit for consumption as *ḥullin* but are fit for the altar.

At this point, the fat and blood of the animal show that not all things forbidden to ordinary individuals outside a cultic context are also forbidden to the altar. Perhaps the *terefah* is comparable to fat and blood, and therefore it too would be permitted to be brought to the altar. Thus, the argument a fortiori does not work, and we need the verse; it is not superfluous. The passage goes on, however:

No, if you say this in regard to blood and fat, which come from that which is otherwise permitted (namely, the healthy animal, and that is why they are permitted to the altar), can you say it with regard to a *terefah* which is entirely forbidden?

The author(s) note that the blood and fat are not really comparable to a *terefah,* even though they share the characteristic of being forbidden for everyday consumption. The blood and fat are acceptable on the altar, for they derive from an animal that is otherwise acceptable as *ḥullin*; only those particular parts are not permitted. The *terefah* on the other hand, is entirely forbidden as *ḥullin*. The point here is that blood and fat do not render the argument a fortiori unacceptable, as previously claimed. The argument remains valid, the explanation that the verse comes to exclude a *terefah* from the altar is thus unacceptable, the verse remains superfluous, and we've still got a problem. The passage continues:

[Then] the nipping [off the head] of the bird will show that this line of reasoning (the original argument a fortiori) is not correct. [For a bird killed in such a manner] is entirely forbidden [as *ḥullin*], and yet acceptable on the altar.

Yet again the *Sifra* shows that the argument a fortiori does not follow, for a bird killed by nipping off its head, which is the prescribed manner for killing birds intended for the altar (Lev. 1:15, inter alia), may not be eaten under noncultic circumstances; it is, though, acceptable on the altar. Thus, the argument is not good, and the verse is necessary to prohibit a *terefah* from the altar. The passage goes on:

No, if you say this in regard to nipping the bird, which is forbidden [as *ḥullin*] by the very act that makes it sacred, can you say it in regard to a *terefah*, which is not forbidden by an act that makes it sacred? And since it is not forbidden by any act that makes it sacred, is it not unfit for the altar?

As above, the midrash shows that the disproving case is not comparable to the case of *terefah*. Thus, the argument a fortiori remains valid, and the superfluity of the verse is unresolved. The passage concludes:

And if you reply to this, [I say] when it says "from the herd" below, this is only necessary to exclude the *terefah*.

The conclusion is perplexing, and resolving this perplexity occupies the better part of a page in the Babylonian Talmud (Menahot 5b–6a), with varying attempts to show that the argument a fortiori is not valid and therefore a verse is necessary. Whether the author of the passage in the *Sifra* had any of these arguments in mind, I cannot say. What I think can be said is that the author took for granted that the argument a fortiori that made the resolution of the superfluity unacceptable could be challenged and this was sufficient to establish the necessity of the verse.

Now what is going on here? We may take for granted, at least for the sake of argument, that the unacceptability of the *terefah* on the altar precedes this midrash; indeed, it would seem to be directly implied by the prophet Malachi (1:8). We must remember too that the Temple was no longer standing when this *derashah* was formulated. It seems most unlikely to me that in the Temple animals having the characteristics of *terefot* were sacrificed on the altar. Was the *darshan*, then, simply interested in supporting this law with a scriptural basis? Perhaps. But in the end, this could be established by the argument a fortiori; that the argument a fortiori is sufficient to provide biblical authority is, indubitably, the operating assumption of the entire passage. If establishing the biblical authority of the law excluding *terefah* from the altar were all the *darshan* had in mind, he could have relied on this argument. Rather, it seems undeniable to me that the *darshan* was perplexed here by what he considered an anomalous scriptural phrase. In his view the Torah should not have used the word *min* if its interest was simply in conveying the surface message of this verse. There must have been a deeper message; something must be excluded by the word *min*. That the *darshan* identifies an apparently well-established principle as that deeper message does not change the fact that his primary goal is to rescue Scripture from a superfluity, an imperfection. The only way for him to do that is to suggest that this superfluity exists to impart the law of the *terefah, which we would otherwise not have known*. If the *darshan* considered the unacceptability of the *terefah* to be a traditional law, this passage would be totally incoherent. Thus it is Scripture, and not the traditional law or the Mishnah, that is the exegete's point of departure, and it is the reconstruction of the creation of the law, not its ex post facto justification, that is his destination.

Let us turn again to our post-talmudic Jew, and this time he need not be hypothetical. That a *terefah* was ineligible for sacrifice was affirmed by all; it was clearly stated in the Mishnah (Zeb. 9:3, Bek. 7:7,

Tem. 6:1,5). How does one know this however? Does the word *min* in the verse actually convey this information? With the exception of Rashi, none of the major Bible commentators appears to think so.[47] To be sure, this may be because the Talmud complicates matters by introducing other verses to fully establish the point.[48] Still, the proposed meaning of "from the herd" is nowhere challenged in the Talmud. Yet later exegetes seem not to find this *derashah* so compelling as to see it as determining the meaning of the verse—not even Rashbam, who affirms the importance of *yittur lashon* as a trigger for exegetical expansion. The most radical position is that of Maimonides, who connects the unsuitability of a *terefah* to Mal. 1:8, possibly suggesting that the law is not based on the authority of the Torah.[49] Clearly, Maimonides did not find the interpretation of the *Sifra* definitive. How he and others dealt with this will be discussed more fully in chapter 4. Thus, the halakhah excluding *terefot* was affirmed by all, and, with the possible (albeit unlikely) exception of Maimonides, with the authority of the Torah. Yet, most commentators appear untroubled by the scriptural anomaly that triggered the derashah, and they therefore do not consider the midrashic interpretation of the verse definitive.

There is another, very common form of midrash in which the concern, perhaps obsession, of the authors of midrash halakhah with scriptural pleonasm and the laws that derive from it becomes clear. I wonder whether we can even call this commentarial pattern "midrash", for it seeks to draw little or no additional meaning from the scriptural text. It may leave the plain meaning of the passage intact, or it may add some piece of information that would be readily deduced anyway. While this form may not seek to add much to the text, it is troubled by the sense that there was no need for the particular scriptural statement that serves as its point of departure. It asks, "Why does this statement appear since it is superfluous, perhaps even inappropriate?" That is, a more general prohibition would appear to establish the particular point Scripture goes on to elaborate. The darshan then creates an argument, usually a fortiori, to show that the inclusion of the particular is not obvious, indeed, we would have had ample reason to think otherwise. Now, these arguments are usually thoroughly contrived; they exist for the sole purpose of removing the (justified) impression that Scripture repeats itself, or, as in the case to be cited, Scripture includes an inappropriate phrase.

To illustrate the point, let us consider the *Sifra*'s comments to Lev. 13:42.[50] The passage and our discussion of it are rather technical, and will probably be more difficult to follow that what we have seen heretofore. Leviticus 13:42-44 reads:

(42) But if a white affection streaked with red appears on the bald part in the front or at the back of the head, *it is a spreading leprosy* on the bald part in the front or at the back of the head. (43) The priest shall examine him; if the swollen affection on the bald part in the front or at the back of his head is white streaked with red, like the leprosy of body skin in appearance, (44) the man is leprous; he is unclean. The priest shall pronounce him unclean; he has the affection on his head. (Emphasis added)[51]

I think one will readily agree that the passage is quite wordy. I wish for now to focus only on the italicized portion, for it is the point of departure for the Sifra's comments on verse 42. The phrase "it is a spreading leprosy" is not appropriate here; for this verse is merely describing symptoms that may be leprous. It is only after the priest examines the patient (verse 43) that it can be determined that the patient is leprous (verse 44).[52] On the term "leprosy" in this phrase the *Sifra* comments:

A leprosy: This teaches that it [the bald spot] is rendered unclean with live flesh. For we would logically have learned otherwise: If the boil and the burning, which are unclean because of a white hair, are not unclean because of live flesh, a bald area in the front or back of the head, which is not unclean because of white hair, should certainly not be unclean because of live flesh. Scripture states "leprosy"; this teaches that it is rendered unclean with live flesh. (*Sifra, Negaim* 11:1) [53]

Given that the word "leprosy" is inappropriate in verse 42, the *darshan* argues that it was added to the verse to teach that (one of) the signs of uncleanness in bald pates is the presence of live flesh. But this adds little, since live flesh is one of the regular signs of uncleanness in scaly leprous spots on the body (see Lev. 13:9–11, 14–17; Mishnah, Negaim 3:3, inter alia), to which the condition of the bald pate is compared. (We must note that the Torah does not describe what signs the priest is looking for other than the determination that the affection resembles bodily leprosy.) We would then have little reason to think that live flesh was not a symptom of uncleanness here. The *darshan* therefore goes on to explain why this additional piece of information is significant. For, without Scripture telling us this we would have thought otherwise, even though live flesh is a normal sign of uncleanness for scaly leprous spots. For boils and burns, another category of uncleanness, do not require the presence of live flesh in order to be considered unclean (see Lev. 13:18–28; Mishnah, Negaim 3:4). They do require the presence of a white hair. Thus, "logic" demands that a possibly leprous bald head also does not require the presence of live flesh in order to be considered unclean. "Scripture states . . . ," thus showing that live flesh is (one of) the sign(s) of uncleanness on a bald pate.

Now in some sense the formal requirements for a good argument a fortiori are present here. After all, one could make the case that the fact that a white hair renders one unclean in the case of boils and burns does seem to establish that they are "severer" cases than reddish/whitish bald spots, which are not rendered unclean by the presence of white hairs. This is particularly the case once we have added one more piece of information. In addition to scaly affections to a bald head, and boils and burns, there is yet another category relevant here, namely, leprous spots on the body. These may be rendered unclean by live flesh, white hairs, or spreading flesh, while boils and burns are rendered unclean by spreading flesh or white hairs only. This seems to establish that live flesh is a more stringent requirement that in "lesser" cases may be dispensed with. The "logic" then goes as follows: (1) bodily leprous spots are rendered unclean by the presence of one of three things; (2) boils and burns are rendered unclean by one of two things, dropping live flesh as a concern; (3) reddish/whitish scaly spots on a bald head, which are not rendered unclean by one of the two conditions *included* in step (2) (namely, white hairs; this is established by the *Sifra* in 11:2), ought not to be rendered unclean by the condition *dropped* in step (2). We should, then, have three levels: bodily leprous spots, rendered unclean by any of three conditions; boils and burns rendered unclean by two conditions; and leprous bald spots rendered unclean by one condition. The conclusion we reach with this logic is that since the boils and burns are not unclean due to live flesh, neither should the leprosy on a bald head be unclean. Thus, we need a verse to teach us the opposite.

It does not, however, take much thought to realize that this "logic" is thoroughly contrived. Obviously, a bald pate cannot be rendered unclean by the presence of hairs! It is *bald,* after all![54] The only reason Scripture needs to treat the status of bald pates at all is precisely because, unlike the other forms of uncleanness dealt with in Lev. 13, they, by definition, are devoid of hairs. They are then in no sense "less severe" than boils and burns, and dropping white hairs as a sign of uncleanness scarcely makes them so; they are simply different. It is inconceivable that, had we not had an "explicit" scriptural statement, one would have doubted that live flesh is a sign of the impurity of a leprous bald head because of the absence of the white hair possibility. What the darshan has accomplished is to make a formal, ultimately contrived, case for the necessity of what would otherwise be a scriptural anomaly. This was his goal here, and this he has achieved. He has made the case by showing that this scriptural anomaly did not actually create law, but *prevented* us from erroneously creating a law based on the normally acceptable technique of *qal va-ḥomer.* That one could create laws with this technique under normal circumstances is the sine qua non for the intelligibility of this passage.

I could go on and provide hundreds of examples of the concern for repetitions and allegedly excessive wording in the scriptural text, drawn from all of the tannaitic midrashim, but it would serve little purpose. The question *lamah ne'emar* or *mah talmud lomar* (why was this word or phrase stated?) appears on virtually every page of the midrashim. Even when it is absent, as in the passage just considered, the question if often implicit. The answer is always that the anomalous phrase creates law, or redirects the creative process of deriving laws. However complex the relationship of midrash halakhah and traditional law may be, the halakhic midrashim represent a remarkably sensitive reading of Scripture, informed by a sense of verbal economy that tolerates no excess; it accounts for what would otherwise seem to be excess by seeing it as the source of law.[55]

Of course, scriptural verbosity is not the only feature that triggers midrashic comment, although it is, overwhelmingly, the most frequent. Sometimes only the most obtuse would deny that a given midrashic comment tries to resolve a conflict between the legal demands of a verse and the rabbinic sense of what justice and halakhah demands. Yet, even here the *darshan* is aided by his sensitivity to scriptural anomalies, which allows him to "derive" the law from the Bible. A case in point is Lev. 20:14. The verse states: "If a man marries a woman and her mother, it is depravity; both he and they shall be put to the fire, that there be no depravity among you." The meaning of this verse seems simple enough. It envisions a situation in which a man "marries" (Hebrew, *yiqaḥ*) a woman and her mother, and they set up a ménage à trois. This is depravity, and all three should be put to the fire. This understanding would even seem to be confirmed by a statement attributed to R. Aqiba (on which see below).

The problem with this biblical statement is that it conflicts with the laws as the rabbis develop them. For, no matter how one analyzes it, whichever woman he married first he married legally. His original relationship with her was fully licit; his continued relationship with her, while now illicit, is, in rabbinic thinking, not a capital crime. Why, then, is she to be burned? The verse cannot be allowed to stand as is; the halakhic considerations demand that the first "wife" be seen as innocent of a capital crime. Establishing a reading of the verse that conforms to this requirement is obviously the goal of R. Ishmael's exegesis (see below). Yet, even here, he takes note of, and works with, an unusual scriptural form that calls out for explanation.[56]

Literally, the verse reads "burn him and them in fire." The Hebrew word for "them" is *et-hen* rather than the more common *otan*.

Thus in a passage found in current versions of the *Sifra*[57] we find "him and them; him and one of them, the words of R. Ishmael. R. Aqiba says him and both of them."[58] It appears that R. Aqiba (a second-century *Tanna*) is simply interpreting in accord with the simple meaning of the verse. However, in the Bavli, the fourth-century sages Abbaye and Rava obviously consider such a suggestion absurd. They, each in his own way, interpret R. Aqiba's remark so that the first woman married is spared burning. The same talmudic passage justifies R. Ishmael's reading of *et-hen* as "one of them" by noting that *hen* is "one" in Greek. Thus, the word *et-hen* is here seen as a Hebrew-Greek compound indicating that only one of them—the second one on board—is subject to death by burning. As to why the Torah would speak thus, another talmudic passage notes that while only one is to be burned, in the event the court is unable to carry out the death sentence, *both* women would be prohibited from remaining with the husband. Thus, the unusual *et-hen* communicates that one is to be burned, but both are henceforth prohibited to the man. Certainly, this is a lot of mileage to get from one word.

The issues are complex, and there is a Yerushalmi version that is again different, although it too maintains one is to be burnt, while both are prohibited. What is important to note is that the exegesis of two important *Tannaim,* as their teaching was refracted through the prism of the Talmuds (which is the way our hypothetical post-talmudic Jew would look at them), completely obliterate the obvious meaning of the biblical verse.[59] It is of interest that here virtually all traditional commentators go along.[60] Even Abraham Ibn Ezra (1089/92–1164/67), generally known for his allegiance to the *peshat,* accepts that the verse intends only one of them to be burned.[61] Now, certainly here the primary difficulty is the halakhic result of letting the verse stand as is. Even so, the close attention to scriptural formulation is evident, and again the result is the notion that the acceptable legal norm is encoded within Scripture.

I have cited a number of examples designed to show the scriptural problems that elicit midrashic comment. Along the way we have seen how the midrashim resolve these problems. Often the *darshan* will indicate that the superfluous word or phrase exists to include or exclude something from the purview of the verse, and this is one way in which the *darshan* may fill the legal lacunae of the biblical text. To take the leprosy example, the Torah does not specify what symptoms the priest is looking for, other than to say a spot that resembles leprosy of the body. Which characteristics of this kind of leprosy are relevant to the bald pate is not stated. The darshan uses a scriptural anomaly as his pretext for filling in the details.[62] Similarly, Scripture nowhere specifically prohibits the sacrifice of a *terefah*; while one would have little difficulty deducing it, an extraneous scriptural phrase, which must be accounted for, will be enlisted to fill in this detail.

Sometimes, to be sure, the "filling in" of biblical lacunae seems thoroughly arbitrary, and one cannot imagine arriving at the particular conclusion if the said conclusion was not, in fact, foregone. Certainly, the ineligibility of relatives as witnesses (or judges) predates the formulation of the midrashim we examined. Still, the goal of such midrash halakhah is to account for Scripture by showing how its anomalies encode information, which the exegete must decipher. There are, however, numerous instances in which even historians standing outside the system have come to the conclusion that the legal norms do indeed emerge as a result of the midrashic exegesis.[63] Be that as it may, the impression of arbitrariness is, at times, inescapable. Occasionally the collections we have show awareness of the arbitrary character, and ask, for example, "Why have you included x and excluded y, when you could just as easily have done the opposite?" The answer will generally argue that x is better suited to the legal and/or exegetical occasion.[64] It is important for us to note here that, arbitrary or not, the response that extraneous phrase a includes/excludes x or y is the single most common retort to the question, "Why does Scripture say this?"

We have also already seen the response, "Scripture needed to say this because otherwise we would have 'logically' concluded otherwise." The logic here is scarcely impeccable. The point is to account for Scripture by showing how it governs legal options. Another possible response to the identification of a word or phrase as extraneous is to use that word in a *gezerah shavah* (a lexical comparison), one of the "thirteen principles of R. Ishmael." The force of this response is that Scripture included the word in question to call attention to a desired comparison between its legal context and some other where the word also occurs. Such instances are specifically identified in the *Mekhilta de-Rabbi Ishmael* and the *Sifre Bemidbar*; that is, these documents identify the word in question as "available" for a *gezerah shavah*; the other documents do not specify this. This has led scholars to assert that the technique is only found in these documents, and reflects only one "school" of rabbinic midrash.[65] This needs to be refined however. The *Sifra*, without specifically stating that extraneous word x is "available" for a *gezerah shavah*, occasionally accounts for such a word by using it as part of an analogy. That is, it uses the same technique without the same terminology.[66]

The sometimes arbitrary extension or limitation of a verse's purview, the explanation that a word was included to preclude a different "logical" conclusion, and that it was included to elicit a *gezerah shavah* are the most common responses to the scriptural trigger of extraneity. There are some others. Among them is the use of *kelal u-ferat (u-khelal)* and *ribbui u-miyyut (ve-ribbui)*. These have been discussed by others, and need not detain us here. It is important to note that each of these techniques is, in its own way, a response to verses, or parts of verses, that say the same thing with differing degrees of generalization and specificity. Each resolves the apparent redundancy in different ways.

A fanciful, if infrequently applied, technique that may be seen as symbolic of midrashic excess is *gor'in mosifin ve-dorshin*, (we subtract, add and interpret).[67] For example, Lev. 2:6 reads, "[you shall pour] [on it] [oil] [a meal offering] [it is]." Each phrase within brackets represents one Hebrew word, and the obviously clumsy translation reflects the word order of the verse. The antecedent of the first "it" is a meal offering prepared on a griddle, as identified in the previous verse. The problem here is obvious (I hope). The phrase "it is a meal offering" (now put into normal English) is obviously superfluous; what else would we think it was? The *Sifra* comments, "'You shall pour oil a meal offering' [note the absence of "on it" in the scriptural citation] this comes to include all meal offerings in the commandment to pour oil. Perhaps even the baked meal offering? Scripture says 'on it' [thus excluding the baked meal offering]. Perhaps I only exclude the [baked meal offering in the form of] cakes but not the [baked meal offering in the form of] wafers? (See Lev. 2:4) Scripture says 'it is' (*hi*)" (*Sifra*, Nedabah, perek 12:6).[68]

What has happened here is as follows: The *Sifra* has identified the superfluous phrase. It argues that this phrase comes to extend the commandment to all meal offerings. The problem with that is the Torah here specifies "on it," thus seeming to limit the range of the commandment only to the griddled meal offering. The darshan "subtracts" the word "on it" (*'aleha*) momentarily, so that the verse is no longer specific and is ready to be generalized to all meal offerings. However, the darshan apparently already knows that baked meal offerings do not have oil poured on them. He thus "adds," actually restores, the subtracted word "on it" to restrict the range of the verse's meaning; it now excludes the baked meal offering, even as it includes the other types.[69] The extraneous *hi* is enlisted to exclude the baked wafers as well as the baked cakes.

Assuming one were willing to follow the *darshan* this far, one would scarcely have thought that only one subcategory of baked meal offering is excluded by the verse's "on it". Again, the *darshan* works with what Scripture gives him, and here he has an extra *hi*, "it is," that demands accounting. Scripture has fortuitously divided the baked meal offering into two subcategories; our verse has two words that require accounting (once we have extended the boundary of "meal offering" to include the other meal offerings): *'aleha* and *hi*. And so a *derashah* is born. Throughout, the coherence of the *derashah* depends on the assumption that law is truly to be derived from Scripture, and is not something already known by virtue of tradition.

Often, a scriptural imperative is rendered extraneous by an argument a fortiori (*qal va-ḥomer*), as we saw above in our discussion of Lev. 1:3. The assumption here is that Scripture should not tell us what we can easily figure out on our own. The usual response to this is to show that the argument a fortiori is not valid for some reason, usually the presence of a disproving case. As we saw above, there is a particular urgency to this, and at times the argument a fortiori seems far stronger than the argument that disproves it. Even so, the disproving argument must prevail, for otherwise a superfluity remains.

Sometimes, in the *Mekhilta de-Rabbi Ishmael* and the *Sifre Bemidbar* (as well as the *Mekhilta de-'Arayot*) a different tactic is adopted. Acknowledging that the verse is superfluous because its demands are easily deduced, these midrashim state that to allow the law to rest on a *qal va-ḥomer* would entail imposing punishment based on a logical inference rather than an explicit prohibition. Thus Scripture went out of its way to teach a new principle, namely, that we do not punish on the basis of an argument a fortiori.

The issue is problematic, for as noted by Naftali Zvi Yehudah Berlin (NZIV, 1816–93), there are many instances in which we do punish on this basis in these documents.[70] To this we can add that a plurality of cases in which this solution is offered do not involve punishment at all. Further, we have one case in the *Sifre Bemidbar* in which the same argument a fortiori is adduced elsewhere. In the first case it is shown to be an invalid argument, while in the second case we invoke the "Scripture comes to teach that we do not punish on the basis of a *qal va-ḥomer*" tactic.[71] Finally, the tactic is adopted twelve times in these obviously related documents. If indeed the redactor(s) of these documents believe that punishment cannot be imposed on the basis of a *qal va-ḥomer*, how many times must Scripture tell us the same thing?

The resolution of these problems is that this is but one stock response developed to dissolve scriptural superfluities. In those cases in which the imposition of punishment is a live issue, its force is to suggest that *here, in this case* Scripture felt the need to specify what we would otherwise know so that punishment would be based on an explicitly promulgated imperative. This, despite the fact that elsewhere Scripture can live with such punishment without explicit promulgation. Once developed for this purpose, the principle is, awkwardly, extended to other cases, generally involving uncleanness, in which Scripture specifies what is unnecessary.[72] The phrase "Scripture comes to teach that we don't punish based on a *din*," (i.e., a *qal va-ḥomer*) is, then, a strictly ad hoc, ad locum response to a particular scriptural difficulty, namely, the fact that Scripture bothers to tell us what we can learn from an argument a fortiori.[73]

Indeed, virtually all midrash halakhah is in a sense ad hoc and ad locum in that there is no attempt to impose consistency within a document or across documents. As an example, within the *Sifra* we find numerous *derashot*, eleven to be precise, on the phrase *ish ish*, literally "man man," which appears primarily in the Book of Leviticus. It is used generally at the beginning of a verse, and has the force of "anyone" (who does *x*). The *Sifra*, characteristically, seeks to extract further meaning from the repetition. But within this one document the phrase *ish ish* is explained as including minors, women, or even Gentiles, but also as excluding minors, women or Gentiles. This too reinforces the picture of arbitrariness within the document, for the superfluity apparently comes to serve whatever legal purposes the *darshan* desires.

At times the sages themselves express exasperation at this apparent arbitrariness. In one of the truly great lines in rabbinic literature we find R. Ishmael reacting to what he considered a colleague's midrashic excess by exclaiming, "You say to scripture, 'Be silent until I interpret you.'"[74] That is, the speaker is, in effect, saying, "You approach Scripture as if its language had no meaning apart from that which you impose on it. You have transgressed all natural boundaries of linguistic usage; the language of Scripture is now as putty in your hands to do with what you will." While most rabbinic interpretations are not as aggressively oblivious to linguistic boundaries as is the one that elicited this comment, it still seems to me this remark says a great deal about the approach of the rabbinic exegetes to Scripture.

The approach of early Jewish *darshanim* to the legal sections of the Torah—an approach that said to the text, "Be silent until I interpret you"—struck the emerging modern mind as simply preposterous. Jews and Gentiles alike considered the rabbinic reading of Scripture to represent the epitome of intellectual decadence. Who could honestly believe that Scripture intended to prohibit selling cheeseburgers when it said, "Do not seethe a kid in its mother's milk"? Who could honestly believe that Scripture intended to exclude relatives from serving as formal witnesses at a wedding? Who could honestly believe that Scripture intended anything beyond what it actually stated and what it obviously took for granted? The answer offered by many is that no one could. The second half of this book will discuss the ideological and textual assumptions behind this rejection, and how modern but traditionally loyal scholars defend midrash in the face of it. The remaining chapters in part one will attempt to demonstrate how the Talmuds develop their own approaches to the material that was bequeathed to them, and how they, particularly the Babylonian Talmud, exacerbate the problem from a modern perspective. We will then go on to deal with how medieval scholars deal with the midrashic and talmudic material that was bequeathed to them. By the conclusion of chapter 4, we will have framed a set of "traditional" positions that shape the modern discussion and make its assumptions comprehensible.

2 • Midrash Halakhah and the Bavli

THE SUBJECT OF MIDRASH halakhah in the Bavli is, of course, vast, and well beyond the scope of the present chapter. Attention just to the midrashim that also appear in earlier (or, other) collections would require consideration of hundreds of passages.[1] If one then went on to examine all the original pieces of midrash spread throughout the Bavli, the resulting book would be enormous indeed, and quite different from this one. Let me then take a moment to explain what this chapter seeks to do.

As I already indicated in the introduction, we are in many respects working backward. We are interested in gaining an appreciation of how midrash works and of the conception of midrash that prevailed in pre-modern times, so as to better understand the nature of the issues and polemics that prevailed in the modern age. To a large extent, the questions addressed here are shaped by those that exercise moderns—specifically nineteenth-century scholars and polemicists—and are not necessarily those that ought to shape a dispassionate inquiry into the nature of midrash in the Bavli. In this chapter we are interested in ascertaining, in a general but not—I hope—superficial way, how the sages and redactors whose views are presented in the Bavli understood Scripture, its relationship to the halakhah, and the historical context of the material that was bequeathed to them.[2] But it must be remembered that the agenda for this chapter is set with a view to the post-talmudic view of midrash. Thus, the examples cited are not necessarily the best illustrations of the Bavli's approach to Scripture, they are simply among the more extreme. I do not claim that the examples adduced here are truly representative of the Bavli; supporting such a claim would require a different research agenda entirely. I do claim that my examples were seen by subsequent generations, correctly or otherwise, as representative of the rabbinic way of reading Scripture.[3]

The Bavli, or Babylonian Talmud, was to become the single most influential document in the rabbinic corpus. Its appropriation and comprehension of antecedent texts became authoritative, and its completion thoroughly reshaped the boundaries and contours of rabbinic practice and thought. Among its many distinguishing features is that, like the halakhic midrashim, it shows a keen interest in determining the scriptural origins of halakhah. It differs from the midreshe halakhah in that its organizational axis is the Mishnah, not the Torah; its point of departure is generally halakhic pronouncements contained in the former. Nevertheless, it continues with the same scriptural concerns evinced by the midreshe halakhah, and, indeed, often carries them well beyond the boundaries of the earlier documents. In general, the Bavli's pursuit of midrash halakhah is offered in response to the (sometimes implicit) question "Whence do we know this law?" The law itself is most often found in the Mishnah, but may also derive from beraitot and amoraic traditions.

The response to this question is almost always a piece of midrash. The person to whom the midrash is attributed may be a Tanna, and it is frequently the case that the said midrash is found in the current tannaitic collections. The attributed author may also be an Amora, one of the rabbinic sages of the third through fifth centuries; and sometimes the response is not attributed to anyone at all. This last type is most clearly offered by the anonymous voice of the Talmud (called the stam; I will also refer to this voice as "the redactors" in keeping with current theory),[4] although many of the teachings that involve reconstruction of the thought processes of named earlier authorities are also the product of this voice. Sometimes the Talmud will ask for the source not of an undisputed law but of two divergent legal positions, and will then wish to know why each sage rejects the exegesis of the other. Sometimes, as in the example we shall consider presently, there is agreement regarding the law but a dispute (in this case, manufactured) regarding the scriptural source. Again the Talmud will ask why each rejects the other, and may add a surprise twist to the whole discussion.

Let us consider Mishnah, Ketubot 3:1, and the relevant talmudic discussion thereto. The Torah states that a rapist or seducer of an unbetrothed virgin must pay a fine of fifty sheqalim to the father of the maiden-victim (Deut. 22:28–29 for the law of rape; Exod. 22:15–16 for seduction).[5] It also apparently presupposes that rapist and victim are legally eligible to marry one another, since it insists that they do so.

Now, the Mishnah provides information regarding the anomalous cases—those in which the parties are prohibited from marrying one another. It implicitly addresses the question whether the rapist is subject to the fine in such a case, given that the parties are forbidden to one another, and the man may be subject to a more severe penalty for his sexual relationship with the woman (thus exempting him from the fine).[6] In answering this question, the Mishnah distinguishes between the degrees of ineligibility. It gives a list of those who do pay the fine that consists of one who rapes a woman forbidden to him by a simple (noncapital) prohibition and one forbidden by a more severe prohibition, namely, one that leads to the punishment of *karet*. It exempts (at Mishnah 3:2) from the fine those whose marriage or sexual liaison is a capital crime, that is, punishable by a human court, because they are subject to the more severe penalty, and thus free of the fine.[7]

The Talmud cites the efforts of Resh Laqish (third-century Palestinian *Amora*) and Rav Papa (fourth-century Babylonian *Amora*) to determine how we know that the first two categories are subject to the fine:

Said Resh Laqish [the Torah says] "maiden, maiden, the maiden."[8] One comes [to mandate the fine] for itself [i.e., the "normal" case in which there are no prohibitions], one is for simple prohibitions, and one is for those subject to *karet*. R. Papa said [the Torah says], "virgin, virgins, the virgins."[9] One comes for itself, one for simple prohibitions, and one for those subject to *karet*.

These two exegeses call forth the question why each saw fit to reject the exegesis of the other, the implicit assumption being that of course each recognized the possibility of the other's exegesis and rejected it as inappropriate.

And Rav Papa, why did he not learn like Resh Laqish? He needs [one of the latter's verses] for what Abbaye taught, for Abbaye said, "If he came upon her and she died he is free of the fine, for it says, 'And he shall give to the father of *the maiden*' [i.e., one of Resh Laqish's verses], to the father of a maiden and not the father of a dead person."

Thus, since Rav Papa uses one of Resh Laqish's verses to learn something else, originally taught by Abbaye (fourth-generation Babylonian), he cannot use the verse for the purpose adduced by Resh Laqish.

And Resh Laqish, why did he not learn like Rav Papa? He needs [Rav Papa's verse] for a lexical analogy (*gezerah shavah*), as it is taught in a tannaitic source "'And he shall weigh out silver in accordance with the bride price for *the virgins*'[one of Rav Papa's verses]. This [the fifty specified in the rape case] shall be like the bride price and the bride price shall be like this."[10]

These distinctions fail to satisfy, because they create the impression of a legal dispute, not merely the exegetical one with which we started. That is, the reader of the passage, at this point, could suppose that Resh Laqish disagrees with Abbaye, and that Rav Papa, in turn, rejects the lexical analogy. The Talmud thus rejects this explanation and shifts gears entirely.

> But Resh Laqish also needs [his verse] for Abbaye's teaching, and Rav Papa needs his for the lexical analogy. [That is, according to the anonymous voice of the Talmud, Resh Laqish would agree with Abbaye's teaching every bit as much as Rav Papa would; similarly, Rav Papa would learn the lexical analogy just as much as Resh Laqish would]. Rather, there are six verses here. The Torah says "maiden, maiden, the maiden" and "virgin, virgins, the virgins." Two are for themselves [that is, the "normal" cases of rape and seduction], one is for Abbaye's teaching [as above], one is for the lexical analogy [as above], and that leaves two. One is for simple prohibitions, and one is for those subject to *karet*. (BT, Ketubot 29b)

Presumably, the redactor(s) of this passage had before him (them) the traditions of Resh Laqish and Rav Papa. These were themselves rather complicated exegeses of biblical verses that ostensibly sought the biblical source of the Mishnah's legal rulings. Each focused on the repetition (in Exod. 22:17, Deut. 22:29) of the terms "virgin" and "maiden," respectively, both appearing with the "unnecessary" definite article. Each teaching derived the Mishnah's position from this double "superfluity." The anonymous redactors of the passage further complicate the matter, for they wish to know why there is the divergence here. Why do these two sages disagree? The answers they offer do not satisfy, for each sage would agree with the legal point that led the other to a different exegesis. Thus, they conclude, we should combine the two teachings and derive all the necessary legal points from a total of six elements.

In considering this piece of midrash from a modern perspective, we may note, among other things, the lack of concern for history. Let us assume for the moment that two historical persons named Resh Laqish and Rav Papa offered the exegeses described (as we must if we are to think along with the redactors of the passage). The fact that these two people said what they said is, in some sense, no longer a matter of consequence; if the *stam* cannot reconcile these teachings with his/their own sense of the matter, he/they may rework the teachings until satisfied. The *stam* may say that Resh Laqish must agree with Abbaye and, ultimately, Rav Papa, even though he lived a century before them, and even though he never expressed this agreement. Given that he must agree with them, he could not have intended that we attend only to the verses he cites but to the whole set of verses utilized here.

Similarly, Rav Papa could not have intended that we ignore the lexical analogy; nor could he have thought that "the virgins" could serve further duty by also triggering the analogy. Thus, he too must have intended exegesis of all six terms, rather than the three he actually cited.

We must further note the lack of concern for the *sensus literalis* of the verses in question. From the literalist's perspective, treating the second occurrence of "virgin" and "maiden" as legally repercussive is strange enough. Isolating the definite article as yet another repercussive superfluity, triggering yet another imperative—although a midrashic commonplace—came to judged by some as downright absurd. To then put these two *derashot* together and derive six imperatives from them was seen as altogether transgressing the boundaries of disciplined thinking.

Let me review the distance we have traveled here. We start with a straightforward cluster of laws in the Mishnah; from there we get to the complex exegeses of the two *Amoraim*, Resh Laqish and Rav Papa. Viewing these exegeses ahistorically, as the Talmud does, we must say that they stand in mutual discord. In attempting to harmonize this apparent discord, the Talmud leads us to the yet more complicated sixfold exegesis with which our passage concludes. It is not incredible that many found this too great a distance to travel.

Let us consider yet another example, this time from Shabbat 132a. The Talmud has stated that all sages agree that circumcision done at the prescribed time supersedes the Sabbath; that is, the act of cutting done in circumcision would normally be prohibited on the Sabbath. But when the act is done for the purpose of circumcision on the eighth day of the child's life, all agree the act is permissible. The Talmud asks, how do they know this? It quotes two *Amoraim*, Ulla and R. Yiṣḥaq, who say it is a *halakhah*, here presumably meaning an ancient customary law (although cf. Rashi). The Talmud raises objections to this response, and then offers the attempt of another *Amora*, R. Eliezer, to respond to the question:

Said R. Eliezer, [the terms] "sign" "sign" occur [in biblical passages referring to Sabbath (Exod. 31:13) and circumcision (Gen. 17:11); encoded within these usages is the message that circumcision supersedes the Sabbath].

The Talmud objects:

But from this we would conclude that *tefillin*, which Scripture also calls a sign, supersedes the Sabbath [which we know is not so].

Another response is called for:

But "covenant" "covenant" occur [in each context; Sabbath, Exod. 31:16, circumcision, Gen 17:10. Let us learn as above].

The Talmud objects:

But from this we would conclude that the circumcision of an adult, which Scripture also calls a covenant (Gen. 17:14), supersedes the Sabbath [which we know is not so].

We try again:

But "generations" "generations" occur [in each context; Sabbath, Exod. 31:13 or 16, circumcision, Gen. 17:12, there clearly referring to the circumcision of an eight-day-old, not an adult. Let us then learn as above].

The Talmud objects:

But from this we would conclude that *tsitsit*, which Scripture also requires for all generations (Num. 15:38), supersedes the Sabbath [which we know is not so].

The Talmud responds:

But says R. Nahman b. Yishaq, we learn "sign" "covenant" "generations" from "sign" "covenant" "generations" [this teaches that circumcision supersedes the Sabbath] and excludes the other things [*tefillin*, adult circumcision, *tsitsit*] which have only one of these terms.

Although the matter appears settled, the Talmud apparently has other traditions to report. It goes on:

And R. Yohanan said, Scripture says [referring to circumcision] "*ba-yom*", "on the day" [Lev. 12:3; in English translation this will appear as the "on the eighth day"]. [Scripture emphasizes that the circumcision be performed] "On the [eighth] day" [to teach us to perform it] even on the Sabbath.

The passage proceeds to offer an objection along the lines of what we have seen ("but from this we could conclude etc."). The discussion is complex and need not detain us, since the Talmud deflects the objection to its satisfaction. It still has one more tradition to report:

R. Aha bar Ya'aqob said, Scripture said "eighth" [as in "on the eighth day," Lev. 12:3], eighth, even on the Sabbath.

It objects:

But this "eighth" we need to exclude the seventh day [it thus does not come to teach that circumcision supersedes the Sabbath; only that it may not be performed on a seven-day-old].

It responds:

The seventh!? This is excluded by [another verse, namely] "An eight-day-old shall you circumcise" (Gen. 17:12) [the "eighth" of the Leviticus verse is thus free to teach the supersession of Sabbath].

It responds to the response, thereby renewing the objection:

But we still need it [to establish the eighth day as opposed to another]. For one verse [specifying the eighth day] excludes the seventh day and one excludes the ninth day [as the commanded time for circumcision]. For if it only said one of them we would have said [it only excludes] the seventh, since its time has not yet arrived. But from the eighth day *forward* is its [commanded] time. [Thus, we need to be told "eighth" twice to fully exclude all other possibilities. "Eighth", then, is not an appropriate source for the supersession of the Sabbath.] [11]

The passage concludes:

But certainly [the scriptural source is] as [adduced] by R. Yoḥanan. And there is a tannaitic source that supports R. Yoḥanan and opposes Rav Aḥa bar Ya'aqob [which is now quoted and discussed]. . . ..

The passage is quite remarkable from a number of perspectives. Note first the structure here, in which the views of sages from different generations and countries are juxtaposed, objected to, adjusted, and recast, creating the illusion of an extended debate in an academy. The passage as we have it represents a skillful piece of knitting together these various elements. Ultimately, the redactor(s) of the passage exercises control over the finished product, determining that R. Yoḥanan's exegesis prevails.

Leaving this determination aside, we have six distinct attempts to exegetically derive that circumcision supersedes the Sabbath. We have the four lexical analogies *(gezerah shavah)*, the one offered by R. Eliezer, the two offered in the wake of the critique of his attempt, and the three-tiered one attributed to Rav Naḥman b. Yiṣḥaq. In addition we have R. Yoḥanan's *derashah*, which is based on the extraneity of the word "day," [12] and the *derashah* of Rav Aḥa bar Ya'aqob, based on

Leviticus's repetition of "eighth," made unnecessary by the verse in Genesis. In addition to all this we have two *Amoraim* apparently of the opinion that this law cannot be (or, need not be?) derived from the Bible. While the redactors have sculpted from this chaos a definitive response to the opening query, all these answers are offered in good faith, and all are theoretically acceptable. We should also note that the analogy offered by Rav Naḥman bar Yiṣḥaq, based on the appearance of the same three terms in both contexts, was definitively rejected but not actually refuted by the passage.[13]

The midrashic process here is governed by certain rules, thus allowing the passage to reject four of the tendered exegeses. Nevertheless, the fact that the passage can identify six theoretically acceptable means of deriving one law from Scripture testifies to the essential elasticity of Scripture it assumes. Attention to the formulation of the Torah's imperatives yields many possibilities to generate new meaning. From the points of view of the literalist and the cynic, though, what we have here is indicative of an inability to read intelligently or of the rabbinic manipulation of Scripture for self-serving purposes.[14] (More on this below.)

In trying to determine how these passages differ from what we find in tannaitic midrash, I would point to their chaotic nature and the activist hand of the *stam* in shaping the presentation of the positions. As a result, these passages are multitiered, and in the first case especially, do greater violence to the plain meaning of Scripture. However, none of the techniques employed is, in itself, foreign to the earlier midrashic materials. Indeed, in the *Sifra* we find the *derashah* attributed to R. Yoḥanan virtually verbatim. Similarly, the *derashah* attributed to Rav Aḥa bar Ya'aqob is found there, although it is ultimately superseded by the one corresponding to R. Yoḥanan's. The use of the *gezerah shavah* is also common coin of the midreshe halakhah, although it is primarily in the Bavli that we find the multitiered versions such as the one attributed to Rav Naḥman bar Yiṣḥaq here.[15] The Bavli, then, continues with the techniques and program of the midreshe halakhah, but does so in its own unique way. The approach of its redactors entails comparing, recasting, adjusting, rejecting, and combining the antecedent midrashic material to create a fully developed talmudic discussion.

I would like to provide one more example of midrashic excess, this time one that is not particularly technical at all. In Lev. 18:21, we find, "Do not allow any of your offspring to be offered up to Molech." The Hebrew word translated as "your offspring" should literally be translated, "from among your offspring [*mi-zar'akha*]." As we have seen, the use of "from" is interpreted as having an exclusionary force. This leads the fourth-century Babylonian sage Aḥa bere de-Rava to comment, "If he offered all his offspring to Molech, he is not liable, for it says, 'from among your offspring' [meaning some but not all]." Thus, if one offers one child to Molech one is liable to the most severe form of execution, stoning, but if one offered all one's children one is not subject to this punishment. While one is tempted to dismiss this as mere rhetoric or even play, given that it was uttered in a situation that precluded this teaching having any practical consequences, subsequent halakhists did not understand it so. If they are right, and this was intended seriously, we should pause for a moment to see where this logic could bring us. Commentators note that as soon as one offers the first child to Molech, one is immediately subject to punishment; how then could offering all one's offspring exempt one from punishment? Among the answers provided I wish to call attention to that of Joseph Karo in his commentary to Maimonides' *Mishneh Torah*.[16] Karo explains that upon offering the first child to Molech one is subject to punishment; this liability to punishment is a standing one. If the offender subsequently offers the rest of his children before the punishment is executed, however, his standing liability is removed and he is free of punishment. This creates the perverse effect of providing an incentive to someone who engages in this idolatrous rite to engage in it further.

However one chooses to understand this passage and its implications (and there is certainly more to be said here),[17] it is not difficult to see how one unsympathetic to the rabbis might react to it by thinking that the rabbinic mind has become twisted by exegetical standards that do not respect normal linguistic conventions.

I could go on citing examples of the kind already cited here, but that would scarcely advance the agenda of this particular inquiry. I think we have seen enough to say with confidence that the Bavli does nothing to mitigate whatever misgivings a medieval rationalist or modernist might have regarding the enterprise of midrash halakhah; indeed, it does much to exacerbate them.

Who Says, "The Torah Speaks in Human Language"?

I would like then to turn to a different question, one that has particularly exercised modern scholars. The question involves the historical understanding of the tannaitic midrashic materials. That is, the Talmud inherited significant amounts of earlier exegeses. Did it attempt to systematize this material, to determine who would use certain techniques and who might refrain from using those techniques? To sharpen the focus of this question, we must note that modern scholars have located a fundamental division among the *Tannaim*: There is a school, that of R. Ishmael, that insists the Torah speaks in human language (*dibrah Torah ke-leshon bene adam*), and therefore this school is more committed to simple midrash, and even to *peshat*.[18] The other school, that of R. Aqiba, insists the Torah does not speak in human language but in its own unique divine language, and is therefore not explicable in terms of human style. This school is given to extreme forms of exegesis, not unlike some of what we have seen already here.[19] Let us see how well this distinction works in the Bavli. In other words, we wish to know who says "The Torah speaks in human language" according to the Bavli. The question is particularly important, for with one exception the phrase "The Torah speaks in human language" appears in rabbinic literature exclusively in that document.[20]

The notion that the "human language" position bespeaks a general commitment to *peshat* is obviously at odds with the way the redactors of the Bavli understand the term. The phrase is used only to object to one form of midrash and one form only, and that is the use of *kefel lashon*, (immediate repetition of nouns or verbal stems). It is used to object to no other form of rabbinic midrash of any kind. Thus, it scarcely betrays a general commitment to interpreting the Torah simply or literally.

Of far greater import is the question who, in the opinion of the redactors of the Bavli—the *stam*—actually adheres to the principle "the Torah speaks in human language" and what he or they might have meant by it. This question is directed to the claim that this phrase represents the position of the school of R. Ishmael. When one examines the use of the phrase in the Bavli, it becomes clear that the attribution of this notion to the "system" of R. Ishmael, or anyone else's, is without foundation. In the picture that emerges from the Bavli, rabbinic learning in the second century, whatever its institutional locus (about which we, as yet, know little) was far more unified, on the one hand, and diverse, on the other hand, than the prevailing picture allows. It was unified in that there was a consensus regarding the status of biblical language, and all rabbis seemed to have tacitly agreed regarding the range of acceptable techniques; it was diverse, in that the techniques were applied in different ways and for different purposes, and in accord with the thinking of many of the *Tannaim,* not just Rabbis Aqiba and Ishmael. In fact, in the Bavli, the "human language position" (*dibrah*) is always used to explain an exceptional case; for the *stam,* the norm is for all sages to draw meaning from the repetitions. Thus, as we shall see below, it is not assumed that a halakhic provision based on an exegesis of a repetition necessarily carries with it a dissenting opinion. Rather, generally, such halakhot are understood as universally accepted, except when a dissenting halakhic position is actually recorded. Thus, attachment to the "human language position" is seen as an exception for all rabbis—an exception worthy of being noted.[21]

Further, in all nineteen places in the Bavli in which the "human language position" appears, save perhaps two, it is used by the anonymous redactors of the passage in question to reconstruct either the putative exegetical foundations of a legal dispute, or to explain why, in an attested exegetical dispute,[22] one side will provide an exegesis of the repetition and one side will use some other technique to arrive at the same conclusion. This latter usage is important, for it conveys the impression that implicit in any exegesis that fails to reach the desired conclusion by interpreting repetition *necessarily* is the commitment to the notion that the Torah speaks in human language. That is, one comes away from any one of the passages with the impression that the failure to interpret repetition is rooted in a principled and systematic objection to such exegesis. However, if one examines all the cases, it becomes clear that the people responsible for invoking this explanation clearly did not believe this to be the case, as they are perfectly content to attribute to anyone the position that the Torah speaks in human language, including those who are elsewhere identified as interpreting scriptural repetitions.

Thus, the use of the phrase "The Torah speaks in human language" in the Bavli is a strictly ad hoc, abstract reconstruction of a particular exegetical move (the ostensibly purposeful refusal to derive meaning from scriptural repetition), used by the redactors without concern for the person or persons to whom that move is attributed. An examination of all the passages in which the phrase appears leads to the determination that in fact no one in the Bavli consistently and systematically says the Torah speaks in human language, even if we take all attributions and reconstructions at face value. The reverse is also true: it is impossible to state on the basis of the materials we have that anyone consistently and systematically insists that the Torah does *not* speak in human language; it seems, rather, that rabbinic legal exegesis, as understood by the redactors of the Bavli, is based on the notion that the Torah in general does *not* speak in human language, and thus the meaning of repetitive phrases *can* be extended. At times, however, there will be other compelling reasons invoked to explain why one ought not to interpret the repetition in a particular case. These include the fact that the halakhic conclusion to be arrived at by such extension is unacceptable (as we shall see below), and the claim that Scripture has encoded the relevant information elsewhere, indicating that in this particular case the repetition is "revealed" to be devoid of significance.[23]

At most, what emerges from analysis of the passages is the possibility that within the rabbinic estate there were different judgments regarding which of two available techniques takes precedence over the other. Should one interpret the repetition even though there is another superfluous phrase from which one can extract the desired conclusion? Should one interpret the repetition when a *gezerah shavah* (lexical analogy) is available? How about a *qal va-ḥomer* (argument a fortiori) or a simple *diuk* (extending or excluding inference)?

In all these cases it would appear that both positions, that of interpreting repetition and the alternative technique, are assumed to be viable; the only question is one of precedence. In all cases of strictly exegetical disputes, as reconstructed by the redactors of the Bavli (as opposed to those that also split regarding the halakhic outcome), it seems that the issue does in fact revolve around the proper hierarchy of midrashic techniques. Indeed, sometimes we have the second opinion—that which does not interpret repetition—introduced with the phrase *eino ṣarikh*, "it is not necessary to employ that technique" for, it is implied, there is a better one.[24] Thus, in the Bavli, alleged commitment to the principle that the Torah speaks in human language cannot be attributed consistently to any "school" or individual "system"; there everything depends on context and result.

This fact can be illustrated in a number of ways, perhaps the simplest of which is to compare the names of the *Tannaim* to whom the "human language position" is attributed and those who supposedly interpret repetition, ostensibly indicating opposition to this position. These are the names of the people to whom the idea "the Torah speaks in human language" is attributed: (1) R. Aqiba, Berakhot 31b (in accord with the mss. and printed versions of the passage; the version of the Tosafist whose comments are found at Sotah 24a had a text in which the *dibrah* position was attributed to R. Ishmael);[25] (2) R. Eliezer, Yebamot 71a; (3) "Rabbanan", elsewhere in the Bavli and the *Sifre* identified as R. Shim'on, Ketubot 67b; (4) "man de-amar," "the one who says," Nedarim 3a; (5) "Rabbanan," Gittin 41b; (6) R. Elazar ben Azariah, Kiddushin 17b; (7) R. Elazar ben Azariah and R. Shim'on (these are recapitulations of the two already mentioned attributions in a passage we will examine in greater detail below), Baba Mezia 31b; (8) "man de-amar," Baba Mezia 94b; (9) R. Yehudah, Avodah Zarah 27a; (10) "Rabbanan," Sanhedrin 56a; (11) R. Yonatan, Sanhedrin 85b; (12) R. Ishmael, Sanhedrin 90b and Sanhedrin 64b (although *Yalkut Shim'oni* and Naḥmanides' *Torat ha-Adam* read R. El'azar ben Azariah here;[26] (13) "man de-amar," Makkot 12a; (14) R. Yosi, Zebahim 108b; (15) R. Ishmael, Keritot 11a; (16) R. Ishmael (or R. Shim'on) the son of R. Yoḥanan ben Beroqah (this is not the same R. Ishmael as above), Arakhin 3a, Niddah 32b and 44a.[27]

The following are the people who are presented as disagreeing and interpreting a biblical repetition: (1) R. Ishmael; (2) R. Aqiba; (3) R. Yehudah; (4) "man de-amar"; (5) Rabbi; (6) Rabbanan; (7) anonymous; (8) anonymous (position identified with R. Yosi ha-Gelili in the *Mekilta*); (9) R. Yosi; (10) R. Meir; (11) R. Yoshiah; (12) R. Aqiba; (13) "man de-amar"; (14) R. Shim'on; (15) R. Aqiba; (16) R. Yehudah.

As one can readily see, there is much overlap in these two lists. Further, there are many other places where those who supposedly adhere to the "human language position" interpret repetition; many of these have been collected by two different Tosafists and can be found in their comments to Sotah 24a and Menahot 17b.[28] Finally, there are many undisputed halakhot that are justified scripturally by virtue of repetition without any sense, on the part of the redactors or anyone else, that there are those who disagree with these halakhot, certainly indicating that the "human language" positions are considered ad hoc, rather than as a statement of general principles.

In dealing with the issue of who, if anyone, insists that the Torah speaks in human language, we must then deal with the ways in which later generations related to the halakhic and midrashic material they inherited, attempting to understand the principles behind it. That is, later generations, having inherited a particular exegetical or legal dispute, wished to understand why their predecessors learned the way they did. When they came upon someone who, in their view, failed to interpret repetition, they explained that the person believed that *here* the Torah speaks in human language. This in no way influenced what the redactors assumed the person would say elsewhere.

To illustrate this concretely, let us consider a couple of passages that will verify that what we have here are indeed reconstructions of putative earlier exegetical positions on the part of later redactors, and that with one possible exception, we do not have any *statement* actually attributed to a *Tanna* here.[29]

The first passage I shall examine is found at BM 31b; there we find a series of *derashot* in which scriptural repetitions are employed to indicate that various scriptural legal provisions are to be extended to situations beyond those to which they clearly apply (and certainly some of the "obvious" applications and the apparent exclusions are very much contrived). There are a total of eight such extensions; the first six are presented as universally accepted, the last two as subject to controversy. I cite these last two cases in full:

#1. "You shall surely furnish him" [the manumitted slave, with gifts] (Deut. 15:14). [From the verse] I know only that a present must be made if the [master's]

house was blessed for his sake [as implied by the rest of the verse: "as the Lord
your God has blessed you, you shall give unto him"]. Whence do we know
[that presents must be made even] if the house was not blessed for his sake?
Scripture teaches, "You shall *surely* furnish him" (*ha'aneq ta'aniq*) meaning in
all circumstances. But according to R. Elazar b. Azariah who maintained: A
present must be made if the house was blessed for his sake, but not otherwise,
what is the purpose of the pleonastic "ta'aniq," "*surely* furnish"? *The Torah
speaks in human language.*

#2. "And you shall surely lend him [sufficient for his need]" (*ha'avet
ta'avitenu*)(Deut. 15:8) [From the verse] I know only that one must lend to a
[poor person] who has nothing but does not wish to maintain himself [at
another's expense; that is, he will not accept charity]. Then Scripture says,
Lend him what he needs. Whence do I know that [one must lend to] him who
is not destitute but does not desire to maintain himself [at his own cost]. Scripture says, "You shall *surely* lend him." But according to R. Shim'on, who
maintained that we are under no obligation to the one who has his own but
refuses to maintain himself [therewith], what is the purpose of the pleonastic
"ta'avitenu" ("*surely* lend")? *The Torah speaks in human language.*

In these last two cases the field of biblical laws is extended using the
same principle as in the previous six cases, but these *laws* are disputed
by R. El'azar ben Azariah and R. Shim'on respectively. Since they do
not agree with the legal conclusions, they obviously must not agree
with the exegeses that produced them. The Talmud asks, what then do
they do with the repetition? Obviously, nothing, because the Torah
speaks in human language. This means that, according to the person(s)
responsible for this explanation, these sages are not constrained by
scriptural language to reach a legal conclusion they cannot accept. They
are, rather, free to develop the law as their own values demand.

Now clearly, as the Tosafists ad loc point out, one cannot conclude from the attribution of the "human language position" to these
sages that the redactors wish to say that they disagree with the previous six laws, nor can it be concluded that anyone thinks that they in
fact agree with one another in their respective cases. Rather, the material before us does not intend to attribute a general commitment to the
"human language position" to either figure.[30] What the redactors had
before them was actually two legal disputes, which they reconstructed
on exegetical (rather than strictly legal) grounds, in order to justify—
but not explain—Rabbis El'azar b. Azariah and Shim'on deriving different legal conclusions than those of their colleagues.[31]

The judgment that these sages would say the Torah speaks in human language is strictly that of the redactors, and is intended by them
to be understood as an ad hoc statement indicating that in the specific

cases presented each holds to this principle; there is no feeling of disso-
nance in attributing the other point of view to these sages in other
cases.

Another aspect of the ad hoc and reconstructive nature of these
usages may be seen from the following passage from Mak. 12a, referring to the phrase *yaşo yeşe* in Num. 35:26: The passage begins with
the quotation of a *baraita* that states that from the verse we can only
learn that if one guilty of manslaughter leaves the city of refuge intentionally, he can be killed; whence do we know it if he leaves unintentionally? The verse says *yaşo yeşe*, the repetition implying that under
all circumstances, leaving the city of refuge makes one subject to death
at the hands of the blood-redeemer. A *baraita* expressing the counter-
view—that leaving unintentionally does not subject one to the possibility of death—is juxtaposed to this one. The Gemara responds:

This is no difficulty;[32] this one is in accord with the one who says the Torah
speaks in human language, this one is in accord with the one who says we do
not say the Torah speaks in human language. Said Abbaye, it is more logical in
accord with the one who says the Torah speaks in human language, so that his
end should not be different from his beginning. Just as in the beginning, intentional is killed while unintentional is exiled, so too at the end, intentional is
killed while unintentional is exiled.

The Talmud dissolves the dispute regarding the disposition of the
one guilty of manslaughter who left exile accidentally into an exegetical dispute, one side interpreting the repetition and thus arriving at the
conclusion that accidental leaving nevertheless subjects the slayer to
fatal retribution, while the other side ignores the repetition and concludes that the slayer may not be killed by the redeemer. Abbaye's
statement comes to say that the latter position is more logical since
greater severity should not prevail with regard to this aspect of the case
(referred to as "his end") than prevailed at the beginning of the case.
Just as in the beginning a murderer is executed, while one guilty of
manslaughter who kills unintentionally is "exiled" (that is, is enjoined
to remain in the city of refuge until the death of the high priest), so too
at the end, if the person intentionally leaves "exile" he may be put to
death, but if he leaves unintentionally he returns peacefully to the city
of refuge.

In this passage, certainly the human-language position represents
the abstract reconstruction of the exegetical view of the second opinion. It should be pointed out, however, that the reconstruction does
not altogether *explain* the legal dispute, since commitment to the exegetical principle "the Torah speaks in human language" is nowhere

understood as *necessitating* opposition to the legal conclusion. It is simply an objection to the method used to arrive at the conclusion. The conclusion may be (indeed, usually is) maintained on other grounds—logical or exegetical. Thus, it would seem that the purpose of the reconstruction is not to *explain* the distinction in positions, per se, but rather to provide a larger context for the dispute.[33]

It is Abbaye's statement that reconstructs the legal grounds for the second position. Now, the place of Abbaye here is somewhat difficult, since, presumably, the "human language" reconstruction postdates him; however it should be pointed out that based on the continuation of Abbaye's statement, his entire remark is best understood as a direct support for the *logic* of the legal conclusion of the second *baraita* quite apart from its putative exegetical foundations. That is, Abbaye's remark (without the phrase "it is more logical in accord etc.") functions best directly appended to the second *baraita*, without the intervening discussion regarding exegetical principles. It may be that the issue of whether the Torah speaks in human language, having been raised by the redactors, is then reworked into Abbaye's remark, making it appear that he is endorsing this exegetical position.

Whatever one thinks of this conjecture, certainly the substance of Abbaye's remarks are addressed to the specific legal issue under discussion. If his remark really did contain an endorsement of the "human-language position" (that is, even if the historical figure Abbaye said all that is attributed to him as presented), it can only be seen as an ad hoc statement, suggesting that *here* this position is most logical, because it would lead to the most acceptable legal consequences, as his subsequent comment—addressing only the legal issues—makes clear. The statement, as presented, intends to suggest that the scriptural exegesis of the first *baraita* here would lead to the logically indefensible position that his final disposition is more severe than was his initial one. For this reason, the exegesis of the repetitive phrase must be rejected. This rejection does not extend beyond the boundaries of this passage.[34]

It is clear that in these two passages the "human language positions" represent the imputation of motive to earlier authorities by later ones, without concern for whether the historical person actually subscribed to this position. This pattern prevails throughout appearances of the "human language position" in the Bavli, with one possible exception.

This brings us then to the one passage in the Bavli in which it is not clear that the "human language" position represents the reconstruction of later authorities, but would appear to be a quotation of a *Tanna*. This passage, found both at San. 64b and 90b is also a direct parallel to the one instance in which the phrase "the Torah speaks in human language" appears outside the Bavli, namely at *Sifre Numbers*, par. 112. It would be helpful to consider the text and history of this *baraita,* starting with consideration of the *Sifre* version. In that version we read

That soul shall surely be cut off (Num. 15:31). "Cut off"—in this world; "surely cut off"—in the world to come. These are the words of R. Aqiba. R. Ishmael said to him, because it says "that soul shall surely be cut off"—the Torah speaks in human language. (His transgression is with him).

This is the translation of the version that appears in the British Museum MS and in the first edition. Almost all commentators agree that this formulation cannot stand as is. Thus, all other versions, from the Vatican manuscript 132 to the edition of the Zera' Avraham to that of Horovitz, amend on the basis of the Babylonian Talmud, and this emendation is supported by the commentary of Rabbenu Hillel. The Vatican MS version of the passage can be translated as follows:

R. Ishmael said to him, because it says "that soul shall be cut off" [in the previous verse] do I learn there are three cuttings off in three worlds?! [Rather] why does it say "that soul shall *surely* be cut off"? The Torah speaks in human language [and therefore we cannot learn more than one cutting off from this verse].

Despite the fact that we are dependent on some reconstruction here,[35] we must note that "the Torah speaks in human language" appears in all the text witnesses. Further, this second version is more or less the same as the two appearances of the *baraita* in the Bavli. We should note that at San. 90b, the citation of the *baraita* is preceded by a discussion between Abbaye and R. Pappa, in which the former attributes the human language position to the Kuthim (Samaritans).[36]

There is, however, strong circumstantial evidence to suggest that the "human language" portion of this *Sifre* passage is not an authentic part of the *baraita*, but is an interpolation from the Bavli, where the *derashah* originated. Such interpolations are quite common with rabbinic documents, given the centrality of the Bavli in rabbinic culture. This circumstantial evidence is as follows: in one of the Babylonian parallels to this passage (Sanhedrin 90b) it would appear that it is Abbaye who develops the notion that the Torah speaks in human language, and that Rav Pappa there clearly does not know the *baraita* and would appear not to consider the possibility that there are those who would in principle refuse to interpret repetition; that the Yerushalmi, while reporting the substance of the *derashah*, namely, that the soul is cut off in the world to come, does not attach it to this repetition at all (Pe'ah 1:1), and, therefore, it displays no knowledge of a tannaitic focus on whether the Torah speaks in human language in this matter; that the phrase does not appear elsewhere in tannaitic literature (see above, n. 6); and that the formal pattern at work in the *Sifre* closely parallels the style of these passages found in the Bavli.

Most important for our purposes is the fact that the Bavli itself does not elsewhere treat the "human language" position as part of the corpus of a *Tanna,* R. Ishmael, and cite it in his name in support of its other positions and reconstructions (as it does with other *Tannaim,* such as R. Shim'on with the concept of "davar she-eino mitkaven mutar," or R. Aqiba with the notion of "ein qiddushin tofsin b'ḥayyave la'vin," even though, according to Rashi [Ketubot 29b], he never enunciated this position this way). Further, as we have already seen, it does not associate this position with R. Ishmael to the exclusion of anyone else. Thus, in the passage from Makkot discussed above, the *baraita* that fails to explain the repetition is seen as in accord with *man deamar* (the one who says), and not R. Ishmael. That is, it is possible that the redactors of the Bavli may themselves not consider the "human language" phrase part of the *baraita* at all, as they do not feel compelled to identify this position with R. Ishmael elsewhere; this would suggest tacit acknowledgment on their part that they are responsible for the inclusion of *dibrah* in the *baraita,* although, obviously, this is an argument from silence.

No piece of this circumstantial case is sufficient to establish the point, and even all the evidence accumulated is not sufficient to establish anything, although it certainly suggests the possibility of an interpolation. Still, circumstantial evidence notwithstanding, as all versions of the *baraita* in the *Sifre* and Bavli include this passage, we cannot say definitively that the passage is not an authentic part of the *baraita.* We must note, however, that no matter how we reconstruct the passage, it appears that the objection of R. Ishmael is based on the appearance of another scriptural element (in the version cited above it is the appearance of the word "nikhretah" in the previous verse) which obviates the extension demanded by the Aqiban position, and it is this element—not some general principle—that elicits the phrase "the Torah speaks in human language." Thus, even if the "human language" portion of this passage is an authentic part of R. Ishmael's statement, we could still not conclude that he maintains this notion as a general principle of exegesis, particularly given that elsewhere R. Ishmael interprets repetition.[37] Rather, whoever is speaking and wherever and whenever he lived, no claim is being advanced for a systematic rejection of the interpretation of scriptural repetition; it is only the specific application here to which the "Ishmaelian" comment objects.

In any event, whatever historical conclusions may be justified by the *Sifre* passage, and its parallels in the Bavli, it is essential to note again that the redactors of the Bavli do not draw the conclusion that the human language position is consistently adhered to by anybody, including R. Ishmael.

In light of the foregoing, we may now answer the question with which this section began: "Who says the Torah speaks in human language" in the Bavli? As far as the redactors of the Bavli are concerned, the answer is everybody and nobody, depending on what "saying" it or not "saying it" yields, and whether there are alternative—better— techniques available. In all the cases in the Bavli, save perhaps one, we are not dealing with "quotations" of the involved parties themselves, but rather with the attempts by later generations to make sense of the chaotic world of early rabbinic legal midrash, in which many halakhot are derived by one sage on the basis of scriptural repetitions, while the same halakhah may be derived using some other technique by another sage. The idea that "the Torah speaks in human language" was developed as a stock response in order to explain why a particular sage would "abstain" from interpreting a repetition, it being assumed that such abstentions were purposeful.[38] From the Bavli, there is, however, no evidence that anyone would everywhere and always insist that immediate repetitions are devoid of meaning, nor, apparently, that anyone would everywhere and always insist that they are packed with meaning.[39] Rather, a review of the "human language" passages in the Bavli suggests that to the redactors of that document everyone operating within the world of rabbinic exegesis considers the repetitive phrases of the Bible as potential bearers of meaning. Whether that potential is translated into actuality depends on the halakhic result and/or the presence of other scriptural elements that may supersede the exegetical imperative to interpret the superfluous repetitions.

In the "human language" passages we see later generations, strongly committed to the ideology that nothing may be superfluous in the perfect Torah, attempting to explain the ostensibly purposeful refusal to interpret these phrases as not compromising on this commitment. They were content to offer the explanation that in certain places the Torah chooses to address us in the language to which we are accustomed, even as most of the time it addresses us in a language that—all sages would agree—is uniquely expressive of meaning. In this sense there are no competing systems within the world of rabbinic midrash according to the Bavli.

Other Midrashic Techniques

Students of rabbinic literature may at this point object that the focus of my inquiry is too narrow. While it may be true that there is no distinction regarding the "human language position," certainly there are distinctions between Rabbis Aqiba and Ishmael regarding other techniques. To be sure, the Bavli follows other rabbinic documents in arguing that these rabbis split on the issue of *kelal u-ferat u-khelal* and *ribbui u-miyyut ve-ribbui*, (interpreting the general and particular; or, the extending and limiting) although, as Michael Chernick has shown, the actual application of these techniques in the Bavli is scarcely guided by such considerations.

On other techniques, though, the record is considerably more murky. Consider for example the technique of *doresh vavin*, interpreting the conjunctive (or disjunctive) prefix *vav*. The Talmud in a number of places does associate this technique with R. Aqiba.[40] Further, in a passage that is often quoted by proponents of the Aqiba/Ishmael split, R. Aqiba is quoted as explicitly saying to R. Ishmael, "I interpret *bat u-vat*"—meaning, from the extra *vav* in the word *u-vat* he learns that the priest's adulterous daughter is to be burned even if she has the status of a fully married women, a *nesuah*.[41] To this R. Ishmael replies, "And because you interpret *bat u-vat* we shall take her out and burn her?!"—that is, impose a more severe form of capital punishment. This passage would seem to prove that these rabbis disagree about the technique in question (or that whoever is attributing this dialogue to them thinks they do).

It is interesting that these proponents never bother to quote the rest of the passage. Here the anonymous voice of the Talmud once again asks its standard question, "How does R. Ishmael interpret this *bat u-vat*?" That is, it is granted R. Ishmael is not willing to impose the harsher form of execution because of this extra *vav*, particularly when in his interpretation the Torah provides means of learning the opposite; but given that the *vav* is genuinely extraneous (in that it neither conjoins nor disjoins anything in particular) he must do something with it. What we see clearly here is that the redactors know of no systematic rejection of this technique on the part of R. Ishmael; indeed, they have no doubt that he would have done something with this *vav*.[42] Thus, while associating the use of this technique with R. Aqiba, the redactors do not assume that anyone else would systematically refrain from interpreting *vavin*.

Here again, the redactors deal with this technique and who uses it on an ad hoc basis. As they reconstruct the thinking of the various sages and formulate exegeses on their behalf, they assume that all sages, including, as we have just seen, R. Ishmael, could interpret *vavin;* sometimes they will "choose" not to for local exegetical or legal concerns. Thus, in a number of places Rabbis Yehudah and Shim'on are presented interpreting *vavin,* and in other places these same sages are presented as refusing to interpret them.[43] At Yoma 45a, the position of *doresh vavin* is attributed to R. Meir. Finally, there are places where a particular law is derived from a *vav,* and there is no assumption that anyone would disagree. The operating assumption is that no sage is opposed to the interpretation of *vavin* in principle.

In at least one place, Yeb. 72b, the Talmud will create, for the purposes of the passage in question, a new rule: Even those who do not interpret *vavin* interpret a *vav* and a *he,* the one-letter definite article. That the definite article is a trigger for midrashic comment we have already seen. Here its role is expanded, in that it somehow renders the *vav* more superfluous than it would otherwise be, and therefore worthy of interpretation. All this is designed to serve the needs of the particular passage, and is the creation of the *stam.* It shows, however, that for the purposes of a given passage any exegetical claim is possible; none are ruled out by systematic distinctions.

The same set of claims may be made for the technique of interpreting the inclusive "kol." As the *Tosafot* point out, despite an apparent association with R. Aqiba there is little consistency in the attribution of this technique.[44] If the give-and-take of the passage requires the assumption that R. Aqiba would disagree with an exegesis of the word *kol,* so be it. Nothing stands in the way of such an assumption.

Further, modern scholars have claimed that Rabbis Aqiba and Ishmael disagree regarding the insistence on "availability" in formulating *gezerot shavot.* They claim that R. Aqiba does not require availability in order to create an unshakable *gezerah shavah,* while R. Ishmael requires unilateral availability for a *gezerah shavah* to be beyond challenge. Now, to be sure, the Bavli assumes that R. Ishmael has a distinct position on this, namely, that only one of the two words need be available for the *gezerah shavah* to be unshakable.[45] However, it does not know of anyone who argues that the analogy can be beyond challenge without any availability. It knows only R. Ishmael's position, and the position that bilateral availability is required for the analogy to be unshakable. Further, it does not associate R. Aqiba specifically with any position. Indeed, it seems to assume that all of R. Ishmael's contemporaries, including R. Aqiba, disagree with him, and require bilateral availability to create an unshakable lexical analogy.[46] Thus, here as well, the understanding of tannaitic approaches to Scripture to be gleaned from the Bavli does not support the claims of modern scholars.

We come, finally, to the last of the exegetical techniques to be dealt with here, that of *lemed mi-lemed* (a derivation from a derivation). Modern scholars claim that R. Aqiba uses this technique, while R. Ishmael considers it inadmissible. The Bavli's position, however, seems to be that of R. Yoḥanan (third-century Palestinian Amora). He taught "everywhere we learn a derivation from a derivation other than with sacrificial matters." The Bavli then enters into a long discussion of the exegetical genus of a derivation from a derivation and its various species (e.g., a lexical analogy from something that was learned by a *hekesh*, a substantive analogy).[47] In this discussion the Bavli identifies numerous positions, almost all formulated by *Amoraim,* with one attributed to a *Tanna* of the school of R. Ishmael. The upshot of the discussion as a whole is that *lemed mi-lemed* is a universally accepted technique in nonsacrificial matters, and is accepted by many even in sacrificial matters as well. It clearly does not know of any distinction between Rabbis Aqiba and Ishmael.

From all that we have seen, it is clear that the Babylonian sages did not know of any systematic distinctions between Rabbis Aqiba and Ishmael as far as biblical exegesis is concerned. Nor were they able to discern any systematic distinctions in the material they inherited. Rather, their view, based on the way in which they reconstructed the putative scriptural bases of the disputants, seems to have been that exegetical disputes were ad hoc, ad locum affairs in which each sage evaluated all the scriptural data to determine what techniques were best suited to unlocking the Scripture's hidden meanings. To the redactors of the Bavli, the exegeses that stood behind attested or reconstructed disagreements were frequently abstracted but never universalized. Someone might not want to interpret this repetition, or that conjunction, for a given reason; but this scarcely meant that he would refrain from interpreting some other repetition or conjunction. In the hands of the redactors virtually all techniques are attributable to anyone; whatever the give-and-take of the passage demanded was perfectly acceptable. This is so because the redactors of the Bavli seem to have had more interest in generating discussion than in reaching definitive halakhic conclusions.

From the Bavli, we come away with the impression that Rabbis Aqiba and Ishmael were central figures in the tannaitic age, who disagreed about many things, legal and exegetical, sometimes consistently.[48] What is decidedly absent, however, is the notion that they were the creators of distinct and conflicting systems of interpreting Scripture, or that they dominated the exegetical landscape of the second century. For this conception modern scholars had to turn to the Yerushalmi, as we shall see in the next chapter.

The Creative Role of Midrash?

What remains to be dealt with here is the question of how seriously midrash halakhah was taken in the Bavli. As we shall see in the ensuing chapters, the question will come up over and over again in Jewish cultural history. No matter what is said here, there will be many rabbinic scholars, possessing far greater expertise than I, who will disagree. Stepping into this issue is to step into a raging controversy.

That having been said, it seems to me that the discourse of the Bavli is thoroughly incoherent unless one assumes that the redactors of the document, if not every sage cited within it, minimally saw the process of midrash as the means by which law was generated in the past, and, perhaps, could be generated in the present.

In many places in talmudic discussion, distinctions are drawn between a law that is generated by means of one verse or hermeneutic technique as opposed to another. In confronting two distinct exegeses, the Talmud may ask *mai beinaiho?* (what [legal] distinction is to be drawn from these diverse exegeses?). The answer will always be *'ika beinaiho* (there is a difference), which the Talmud will then spell out.[49] To cite but one example, at Avodah Zarah 27a, two exegeses are offered as the source of the prohibition against having a Gentile circumcise a Jew. The Talmud asks, *mai beinaiho*, and after two attempts that do not work, it answers that the acceptability of a female circumciser is at issue. Following the logic of one *derashah*, one would not permit a woman to circumcise; following the logic of the other, one would.

In my view, this discussion is incoherent if we do not understand that the *stam* assumed that exegesis generates law. Note that I am not making any claim regarding the actual historical question of whether or not women circumcisers were accepted, and, if so, when and why. What I am saying is that the redactors of the Talmud address the question only in the context of this drawing of distinctions between competing exegeses, and take for granted that the question can be answered by determining which verse governs the exclusion of the right to circumcise. Not only do the exegeses explain how we know that a Gentile may not circumcise, but the underlying logic of the exegeses can go on to generate new laws pertaining to the eligibility of other categories. As an aside, we should note that on the basis of this talmudic discussion, and the assignment to R. Yoḥanan (whose view prevails in disputes with Rav) of the interpretation that includes women as acceptable circumcisers, later Jewish decisors argue that a woman can perform circumcisions, providing that there are no qualified males.[50]

Similarly, the Talmud asks, "It is obvious! Why do I need a verse to teach me that?" It proceeds to answer that things are not as obvious as they appear, and without the verse one might have thought otherwise.[51] This is similar to the question of the *Sifra,* "Would I not know it by means of an argument a fortiori?" The answer that without an explicit scriptural statement one might have interpreted the Torah's laws incorrectly obviously presupposes that the technique of *qal va-ḥomer* can generate law. If it came to do nothing but find scriptural supports for traditional law, the whole concern evinced by the Talmud in these passages would be devoid of foundation.

To be sure, there are times in which the Talmud explicitly identifies a particular exegesis as a mere *asmakhta*—a scriptural support for a law, but not its source. In most such cases, however, the law is identified as being authoritative *mi-de-rabbanan* (on the authority of the rabbis); it is not scripturally mandatory, meaning that it is not something known by tradition.[52] Such discussions are incoherent without the understanding that the normal operating assumption of the Bavli is that exegeses of verses establish laws that are binding *mi-de-'oraita* (with the authority of Scripture).

Finally, let us recall the discussion of the passage in Ketubot at the beginning of this chapter. We end up with a multi-tiered exegesis primarily because the authors of the discussion wish to avoid creating a legal dispute that would ensue if the exegeses of the two "speakers" were not combined. Again, such a procedure would be incoherent if the discussion were not informed by the conviction that exegesis generates law.

As we shall see in chapter 4, both Maimonides and Naḥmanides provide extensive further argumentation designed to show that talmudic discourse is shaped by the conviction that most laws not explicitly stated in the Bible were generated by means of exegesis. The shapers of the Bavli were convinced that Jewish law emerged as a result of the attention to scriptural anomalies, redundancies, and superfluities.

Of course, one finds occasional reservations regarding the authority of the exegetical enterprise,[53] and one finds a few remarks suggesting that most of the extrabiblical norms originate in oral tradition, not exegesis.[54] Further, one finds many aggadic statements insisting that the entire oral Torah originates at Sinai. For all of that, when it comes time for the Talmud to answer the question, "How do we know this?" it almost always cites a verse, and always feels free to engage in the type of discussions noted above, all of which presuppose that the law or laws in question are generated exegetically. Against the thousands of exegeses offered in the Talmud to identify the source of law, neither the few expressions of reservation nor the aggadic statements measure up. To the people responsible for shaping the halakhic discussions of the Bavli, there was little doubt that law generally emerged by means of the application of exegetical techniques, and only rarely are laws identified as traditions, whether from Moses at Sinai, or from some other ancient authoritative source. It is, indeed, precisely this fact that lent such an existential urgency to subsequent discussion, as we shall see in the second part of this book.

3 • Midrash and the Yerushalmi

THE MIDRASH HALAKHAH FOUND in the Yerushalmi[1] differs little in terms of techniques and concerns from that which we have already examined. It too is concerned with the scriptural origins of the halakhah of the Mishnah and other documents,[2] and makes use of the various techniques we have seen. It too sees alleged scriptural superfluity as a trigger for midrashic comment, together with the other concerns discussed in chapter 1. Like the Bavli, its organizational axis is the Mishnah, and most of its midrash halakhah is devoted to discovering the source of Mishnaic or other tannaitic law. Unlike the Bavli it rarely engages in the "extreme" multitiered type of midrash noted in the previous chapter.[3] Still, in general, I think we can say that the Yerushalmi's reading and use of Scripture is not markedly different from that of the Bavli.[4]

The Yerushalmi, then, adds little per se to our inquiry regarding the nature of midrash halakhah. However, regarding the place of midrash in tannaitic culture the Yerushalmi has made a decisive contribution to modern scholarship, and this needs to be explored in detail. In twenty-nine different places the Yerushalmi offers an exegesis of a verse that allegedly served as the source for a tannaitic law and goes on to comment "thus far (ad kedon) according to R. Aqiba; according to R. Ishmael whence [do we know it]?" The force of this question is to suggest that these two Tannaim disagree regarding acceptable midrashic methodology.[5] Specifically, the question assumes that R. Aqiba uses certain methods while R. Ishmael rejects their suitability and grounds the law in different exegesis. It is further assumed that they agree on the Mishnaic law itself.[6]

51

The methods that R. Aqiba allegedly uses to the exclusion of R. Ishmael include the exegesis of repetitions (which, as we saw in the previous chapter, the Bavli does not associate with any individual); the derivation from a derivation; a lexical analogy where the word(s) in question are not identified as available (superfluous).[7] This position of the Yerushalmi has exercised enormous influence in modern scholarship for reasons to be discussed in chapter 7. The burden of this chapter is to show that this position represents the view of the Yerushalmi's redactors, who were attempting to impose system on the chaotic materials that were bequeathed to them.[8] With maybe one exception, *Amoraim* themselves (not to mention *Tannaim* who lived after the two rabbis), as opposed to the anonymous redactors, do not appear to know of this distinction, nor, as we shall see, was the distinction noted by the other contemporaneous Palestinian documents (*Bereshit Rabbah* and the *Yerushalmi Neziqin,* which does not derive from the same sources as does the rest of the Yerushalmi).[9] Finally, we will see that this position is not a necessary outgrowth of the material on which it is apparently based. Independent of the Yerushalmi, there is limited basis for assuming systematic exegetical distinctions between these two rabbis. To demonstrate these claims, I will discuss five of the relevant passages in detail. I will then turn to one passage that might explain where this position came from. As noted in the preface, this discussion will be quite technical, although I have saved the most technical material for the notes.

The first passage to be discussed is found at Ber. 11a (7:1): In this passage the Yerushalmi addresses the question of the source of the requirement to offer blessings before and after meals. It begins with the claim that one must make a blessing over the Torah before studying it on the basis of Deut. 32:3 "For the name of the Lord I proclaim, give glory to our God." It further claims that one must make a blessing after partaking of food, based on Deut. 8:10, "When you have eaten your fill, give thanks to the Lord your God. . . ." The question is raised, How do we know that that which applies to this (i.e., the Torah, which requires a blessing before) applies to that (food, which, to this point in the argument, has not been shown to require a blessing before)? And that that which applies to this (food, which requires a blessing afterwards) applies to that (Torah, which, to this point in the argument, has not been shown to require a blessing afterwards)? At this point, R. Shmuel bar Naḥmani, an *Amora,* quotes R. Yonatan, an *Amora,*[10] as saying we learn the mutual application from a *gezerah shavah*; the appearance of "Lord" in both verses indicates the intended mutual application of their blessing properties.[11] At this point the anonymous voice of the Yerushalmi cites the *ad kedon* formula and identifies this amoraic tradition with R. Aqiba. How then does R. Ishmael learn that foods requires a blessing before, and that Torah study requires one afterwards?

R. Yoḥanan in the name of R. Ishmael, it is an argument a fortiori. Given that food, which does not require a blessing before (i.e., Scripture does not "explicitly" ordain one)[12] requires one after, Torah study, which does require one before, must a fortiori require one after. Thus far Torah study. [How do we know that] food [requires a blessing before]? Given that Torah study, which does not require a [scripturally ordained] blessing afterwards, requires one before, food, which does require a blessing afterwards, must a fortiori require one before.

The passage proceeds to quote three other tannaitic positions regarding the requirement to offer a blessing before partaking of food (which is the real issue of our passage; the discussion regarding the blessing after Torah study is a derivative issue).

This passage sheds light on a number of the larger questions of this study. First of all, we must note that the position attributed to R. Aqiba was cited in the name of the *Amora* R. Yonatan. It was, apparently, he who created the *gezerah shavah* found in the passage.[13] The attribution of this *gezerah shavah* to the system of R. Aqiba (whatever that is intended to mean) is certainly a redactional construct, creating the context for that which is to follow. The question here is why this *gezerah shavah* is attributed to R. Aqiba. One is tempted to say that the attribution is based on the attribution of an alternative position to R. Ishmael. Given the position of the Yerushalmi regarding these two rabbis, it would be natural for it to assume that any opposition to R. Ishmael's position is grounded in R. Aqiba's "system."[14] Even if the attribution to R. Ishmael were beyond question, which it is not, this explanation would still be problematic; for throughout the Yerushalmi, as we shall see, the *ad kedon* formula is reserved for situations in which it is assumed that the argument revolves around the proper methods of scriptural exegesis. Thus, unless this passage represents an exception, one must seek a methodological issue here. This has already been recognized by the Qorban ha-Edah (David Frankel, 1707–62) and by the twentieth-century scholar, Ze'ev W. Rabinowitz, each of whom offers an explanation as to why R. Aqiba, but not R. Ishmael, would, in principle if not in fact, learn this *gezerah shavah*.[15]

The attribution of R. Yoḥanan's statement to R. Ishmael is also problematic. The statement is quoted virtually verbatim in the Bavli, Ber. 21a, but there it is attributed only to R. Yoḥanan; there can be no doubt that this reflects the Babylonian tradition in that a refutation (*tiyuvta*) is brought from a *baraita,* indicating that this is clearly an amoraic tradition as far as the redactors of the Bavli are concerned. Further, in Bavli, Ber. 48b, we have a different argument a fortiori attributed to R. Ishmael, as well as a *gezerah shavah.* Taking for granted that foods require a blessing before and after, the question is raised, how do we know about Torah study? "Said R. Ishmael, it is an argument a fortiori; one makes a blessing on temporal life (*ḥayye sha'ah* = food), how much more so [must a blessing be recited] on eternal life (= Torah)." This is followed by a *gezerah shavah* cited by "R. Ḥiyya bar Naḥmani, the student of R. Ishmael, in the name of R. Ishmael."[16]

The Babylonian tradition that attributes different teachings to R. Ishmael and R. Yoḥanan would seem to be confirmed by a passage in the *Mekhilta of R. Ishmael* (Pisḥa, 16). There the blessing after food is derived from the verse, Deut. 8:10. "How do we know that food also requires a blessing afterwards? *R. Ishmael says,* it is an argument a fortiori: if when one is already satisfied he is required to offer a blessing, how much more so when he is yet hungry." After citing two alternative positions (parallel to our Yerushalmi passage) the *Mekhilta* goes on to say, "[N]ow we know that food requires a blessing before and after; whence do we know this regarding Torah Study? *R. Ishmael says,* it is an argument a fortiori, one offers a blessing over temporal life, how much more so over eternal life."

Given the attribution in the Yerushalmi of the first teaching to *Amoraim,* and given the Bavli and *Mekhilta* passages, it would seem that the entire R. Aqiba/R. Ishmael axis here is a redactional construct. That is, it was the redactors of the passage who identified R. Yonatan's *gezerah shavah* with R. Aqiba's putative exegetical system (for whatever reason), leading in turn to the identification of R. Yoḥanan's own statement to R. Ishmael, R. Aqiba's standard opponent in the Yerushalmi.[17] One reason that they may have done this here is that otherwise we would have a passage in which five opinions are offered that disagree with one another, but two of those opinions would be those of *Amoraim.* Perhaps to lend credence to these exegetical positions it was necessary to attribute them to tannaitic systems. It seems more likely that the redactors of the Yerushalmi had reason to believe, based on their assumptions with regard to Rabbis Aqiba and Ishmael, that the first position was simply not one that R. Ishmael could endorse *in principle,* leading to the *ad kedon* formula. Be that as it may, what emerges from an analysis of this passage is that the attributions are the work of redactors, and are based on their assumptions; they cannot be independently verified, and indeed, are highly questionable.

The second passage is found at Shab. 17a (19:2). The passage comments on the Mishnah that states that one can perform all the necessities of circumcision on the Sabbath. These "necessities" include the cutting of the foreskin and the uncovering of the corona. Addressing the unstated question, "Whence do we know that both procedures are required?" the passage opens:

1. *Himol yimol* "They must be circumcised" (Gen. 17:13; new JPS) [the Hebrew verb appears twice in different forms]; from here we derive that there are two circumcisions, one referring to cutting (*milah*), one referring to uncovering (*pri'ah*), one referring to cutting, one referring to the shards that [if left behind] prevent [the circumcision from being deemed valid].[18]

From the doubled verb the passage insists that we learn the need for two procedures; this is a standard technique as we have seen. The Yerushalmi objects:

2. Thus far, according to R. Aqiba; he says (*du amar*) the [repetitions come as] extending usages (*leshonot ribuiin hen*) [which extend the meaning of the words to two different operations],

3. [But] R. Ishmael? He says (*du amar*) they are repetitive usages [that do not extend the meaning of the words], [for] the Torah speaks in its manner . . . (here we have three examples of doubled verbs, two from Gen. 31:30, one from Gen. 40:15, all drawn from the attributed speech of human beings); [thus, R. Ishmael would not derive the need for two procedures from a doubled verb; we must ask] whence does he derive [that two operations are necessary]?

4. Said R. Yudah ben Pazi, "then she said, a bridegroom of blood because of the circumcision*s*" [the Hebrew word is in the plural]; from here we learn that there are two circumcisions: one referring to cutting. . . . (as above at 1).

5. Rav (an Amora) says [the doubled language of] *himol yimol* [teaches that] if one is born circumcised, one must nevertheless draw covenantal blood from him. [Perhaps Rav, perhaps yet another voice continues, the doubled language of] *himol yimol* teaches that an uncircumcised Jew may not circumcise (others) [that is, the doubled language teaches that one must be properly circumcised in order to properly circumcise others], and it need hardly be said that a Gentile may not circumcise other (Jews). . . .

The "he said" formulae at 1 and 3 need not be understood as representing a claim that the respective sages actually said these things (*leshonot ribuiin, leshonot kefulin*), for the symmetry of the respective statements makes this most unlikely. Rather, we have here the Yerushalmi's abstraction of the method standing behind a couple of disputes between the sages (see below), leading to the conclusion that R. Aqiba will derive meaning from this kind of repetition and R. Ishmael will not. Further to be noted is the phrase "dibrah Torah kedarkah" (the Torah speaks in its manner), which in the Bavli appears as "dibrah Torah kileshon bene adam," (the Torah speaks in human language.) Both formulations represent methodological abstractions common to these documents, and need not be taken as direct quotations.

As to the attribution of the "himol yimol" *derashah* to R. Aqiba, note that the only place this *derashah* appears in tannaitic literature is in the Tosefta, Shabbat 16:6 (Zuckermandel, 15:9) where it is used to teach that a *mashukh* (one who has his prepuce drawn forward to disguise his circumcision) must be "recircumcised" as many times as is necessary. As the continuation of the passage here (5), and two passages in the Bavli indicate (A.Z. 27a, Yeb. 72a), the *Amoraim* who are quoted with an opinion on the verse do not know of any association between the *derashah* presented here and R. Aqiba, nor do they themselves associate it with two circumcisions. They feel free to use the repetition to deal with a range of issues. Further, in the parallel to this passage in *Bereshit Rabbah* (46:13, Albeck), the *derashah* is cited for the same purpose as here (namely, the two procedures), but no attribution to R. Aqiba is to be found, nor is there any methodological association of the *derashah* with R. Aqiba. Thus, in the one other contemporary source, a Palestinian one, no association is made between this *derashah* and R. Aqiba.[19]

Similarly, the alternative, presumably Ishmaelian, *derashah*, from Exod. 4:26, is here cited in the name of Yudah b. Pazi, a fourth generation *Amora*. There is no reason to suppose that R. Yudah was responding to the question posed here, "Whence does R. Ishmael learn . . . ?" rather than to the more general question, "How do we know this?" This *derashah* appears anonymously in Yerushalmi, Nedarim 3:9, with no association with R. Ishmael mentioned. Further, in *Deut. Rabbah*, we find R. Yuda(n) b. Pazi citing the same *derashah*, again with no association with R. Ishmael. Thus, it was the redactors of this passage who assumed that R. Yudah's *derashah* was "according to R. Ishmael," since we already "knew" how R. Aqiba would learn that two distinct procedures were required.

Here, then, the *ad kedon* ("thus far") identifications are redactional constructs, developed on the basis of the systematizing assumptions of the redactors of the Talmud. There is no independent evidence to indicate that the two *Tannaim* would disagree regarding the scriptural basis of the two required procedures, and certainly, no evidence may be brought from this passage to support the notion that R. Ishmael eschews interpreting scriptural repetition systematically.

The next passage is found at Orlah 62a (2:1):[20] The Mishnah states that *terumah*, inter alia, is neutralized in 101; that is, one part *terumah* to 101 parts common substance will render the common substance acceptable for use by all (less than 101 will render the entire mixture holy—that is, unfit for common use). *'Orlah* and *kil'e ha-kerem* are neutralized in 201 (as above). In the discussion relevant here, the Yerushalmi asks how we know that *'orlah* and *kil'e ha-kerem* can be neutralized at all. In response to this concern the Yerushalmi says:

1. Scripture states "fullness" "fullness" [that is, at Exod. 22:28, we read "Thou shall not delay to offer of the *fullness (me-le'atkha)* of thy harvest and the outflow of thy presses (*dim'akha*); the Yerushalmi here understands this verse to refer to *terumah*. At Deut. 22:9, we read, "You shall not sow your vineyard with two kinds of seed, lest the *fullness* of the seed be defiled." Thus we have a *gezerah shavah*, equating *terumah* with *kil'e ha-kerem*].

The Yerushalmi explains the force of this analogy as follows:

2. Just as the fullness referred to there (*terumah*) can be neutralized, so the fullness referred to here (*kil'e ha-kerem*) can be neutralized.

Of course, this analogy creates a problem since the Mishnah states that *terumah* is neutralized in 101, while *kil'e ha-kerem* is neutralized in 201. Thus further explanation is required.

3. [If that is so then] just as there [*terumah*] neutralization is with one hundred so too here [*kil'e ha-kerem*] neutralization should be with one hundred[21] [but we know that this is not so, so how can this *gezerah shavah* be the source for the neutralization of *kil'e ha-kerem*]?

The Yerushalmi responds,

4. [It can be the source for the neutralization of *kil'e ha-kerem*. As to the different ratios] since scripture doubled its prohibition [*kil'e ha-kerem* may not be eaten, like *terumah*, and one may not derive any benefit from it either] the sages changed its obligation [for neutralization].

We are thus justified in using the *gezerah shavah* for learning the "neutralizability" of *kil'e ha-kerem*. The discussion now turns to *'orlah*,

5. Thus far, [we have established the source for the neutralization of] *kil'e ha-kerem*; whence [the source for the neutralization of] *'orlah*?

6. Just as with this one [*kil'e ha-kerem*] one may not derive any benefit from it, so too with that one [*'orlah*] one may not derive benefit therefrom [thus establishing the comparison between the two things; we can then go on to say] just as this one may be neutralized, so that one may be neutralized [and in the same quantity].

At this point in the discussion we have established that *kil'e ha-kerem* and *'orlah* can be neutralized, and we have explained why its proportion is twice that of *terumah*. The discussion, should, then, be over. All the questions have been answered. However, the Yerushalmi goes on to object,

7. Thus far it [the derivation of the neutralizability of *'orlah*] is in accord with R. Aqiba. Whence [do we know this law] according to R. Ishmael?

8. R. Yoḥanan in the name of R. Ishmael: It is an argument a fortiori. If *terumah* which is forbidden to outsiders [which is a severity] may nevertheless be neutralized, *'orlah* which is permitted to outsiders [a leniency] may certainly be neutralized.

For reasons to be discussed below, the redactors of this passage assume the R. Ishmael would not accept the derivation of the neutralizability of *'orlah* presented. We are thus presented with an argument a fortiori confronted by R. Yoḥanan, "in the name of R. Ishmael." The Yerushalmi goes on to object to this argument a fortiori, as follows:

9. This is not so! If you will say [that neutralization is possible] concerning *terumah*, from which benefit may be derived (a leniency), you will say [that neutralization is possible] concerning *'orlah*, from which benefit may not be derived (a severity)?! [Quite obviously, the severe/lenient relationship cuts both ways; one cannot therefore, learn the neutralizability of *'orlah* from *terumah*. The former may be more severe than the latter, and therefore it may not be capable of neutralization. Thus, the argument a fortiori is to be rejected].

The argument a fortiori cannot work because the lenient and severe relationship can easily be turned upside down. The question is what this objection has to do with the essentially historical claim that R. Ishmael learns the Mishnah's law from the argument a fortiori (# 8). The discussion proceeds as follows:

10. R. Ḥinena [= R. Ḥanina]: [The source for the neutralization of *'orlah* is] "fruit" "fruit," *gezerah shavah* [Lev. 27:30, *terumat ma'aser*; Lev. 19:23, *'orlah*; thus the law of neutralization applies to *'orlah* just as it applies to *terumah*. Further, the logic of double prohibition, as stated above would seem to apply here as well].

The first *gezerah shavah* (1–2), determining that *kil'e ha-kerem* can be neutralized, is unattested anywhere else; it does not appear in any tannaitic source. From the structure of the passage, it would appear that this *gezerah shavah* is accepted by Rabbis Yoḥanan and

Ḥanina, both first generation *Amoraim,* since they address their attention only to *'orlah,* although this is by no means beyond doubt. Still,
the redactors of the passage have created the impression that 1–4, as
presented here, are universally accepted. It is only from 6 on that we
have divergences of opinion. In 6, the anonymous voice of the Yerushalmi
makes a comparison between *kil'e ha-kerem* and *'orlah,* claiming that
the neutralizability that applies to the former should be extended to
the latter. At this point it is objected that this is only in accord with
R. Aqiba. This assumption appears to be based on the fact that 6 entails a *lemed milemed* (a derivation from a derivation), which presumably R. Ishmael would not learn.[22] The neutralizability of *kil'e ha-kerem*
was established not by a direct scriptural statement, but by a lexical
analogy to *terumah.* It cannot then turn around and serve as the established basis of yet another analogy, namely, to *'orlah.* The question
then becomes, "Whence does R. Ishmael learn that *'orlah* can be neutralized?"

The answer to this is presumably offered by R. Yoḥanan's "quotation" of an argument a fortiori in the name of R. Ishmael. However, it
is clear that the redactors of the passage did not themselves consider
this a quotation in that they cite a refutation of this argument, and
instead offer R. Ḥinena's *gezerah shavah* as the answer to the question,
"Whence does R. Ishmael learn this law?" The result is that, according
to the redactors, R. Ishmael learns the neutralizability of *kil'e ha-kerem*
and *'orlah* from two *gezerot shavot.*[23] Now if, in fact, R. Yoḥanan's
argument was taken to be a quotation from R. Ishmael, how could the
passage go on to reject this argument as being the opinion of R. Ishmael?
If R. Ishmael said that this was his source for the neutralizability of
'orlah, the matter must end there, whatever we may think of the derivation. Rather, it is clear that the "R. Yoḥanan in the name of R.
Ishmael" formula fits into the way the redactors of the passage have
organized an essentially amoraic dispute regarding the neutralizability
of *'orlah.* That is, here R. Yoḥanan is offering his own explanation of
whence we learn the neutralizability of *'orlah.* The redactors insist that
this teaching is "in the name of R. Ishmael" since we already "know"
how R. Aqiba derives this, even though we have no reason to believe
that the historical Aqiba ever addressed this issue. This (refutable) argument *of* R. Yoḥanan's is juxtaposed to R. Ḥinena's explanation of
whence we learn the neutralizability of *'orlah,* which is also fit into the
"in the name of R. Ishmael" framework established by the redactors of
the passage. That is, this teaching of R. Ḥinena is identified by the
redactors of the passage with the position of R. Ishmael, again on the
assumption that we already "know" how R. Aqiba learns this. In fact,
we have no record here (or anywhere else) of an actual disagreement

between Rabbis Aqiba and Ishmael regarding this issue. Rather, we have three exegetical alternatives; one is attributed to R. Aqiba because it makes use of a technique that the Yerushalmi assumes only he would use,[24] while the other two are associated with R. Ishmael by default. That is, they are amoraic teachings that do not use techniques associated strictly with R. Ishmael; these techniques (argument a fortiori and *gezerah shavah*) are common coin of tannaitic exegesis. They are attributed to R. Ishmael because of the systematizing tendencies and exegetical assumptions of the Yerushalmi.[25] Thus, the Aqiba/Ishmael methodological divide is a construct of the redactors of this passage, and is not dependent on anything they actually said pertaining to *'orlah*.[26]

The next passage is found at Yeb. 7b (6:2): The Mishnah here continues the argument of 6:1, stating that we make no distinction with regard to various illicit sexual relationships, among them that of a high priest and a widow, between "normal" intercourse and "unusual" intercourse; between intended and unintended acts; or between "beginning"[27] and completing the sexual act. The passage of interest here takes up the discussion of the widow/high priest relationship. Citing the verses that contain the prohibition (Lev. 21:14–15), the Talmud poses the hypothesis that the prohibition does not apply to beginning but only to completing the sexual act. This hypothesis is refuted by noting that when the Bible says "that he may not profane his seed . . ." the Hebrew word is not YHWL but rather YHLL with the letter *lamed* doubled. This usage indicates that even beginning the sexual act is incorporated within "profanation." This position is identified, using the *ad kedon* formula, with R. Aqiba. R. Ishmael, we are told, derived the prohibition from a *gezerah shavah*. An objection to this *gezerah shavah* is raised by R. Hagi (a fourth-generation *Amora*) to which R. Yosi (a fourth-generation *Amora*) provides the response. Then R. Bun bar Bisna in the name of R. Ba bar Memel (both third-generation *Amoraim*) ostensibly responds to the objection by reworking the *gezerah shavah*, providing a different base verse. The passage closes with the citation of R. Ba bar Memel's statement quoted at 6:1, which establishes independently that beginning represents profanation.

I recognize that this summary scarcely yields a clear picture of what is going on; it is sufficient for my purposes though to focus on the alleged speakers rather than on what they said. This focus will allow us to see that we are dealing with a strictly Amoraic issue. Before going further, I should point out that R. Jacob David Willowsky (Ridbaz; 1845-1913) already commented that the Aqiban/Ishmaelian material in this passage is in fact not authentic. He states that we are not dealing here with a *baraita;* rather, these positions are constructed out of the give-and-take of the passage regarding beginning; without the statement of R. Ba bar Memel, we would indeed not be sure that there is a prohibition of "beginning" with regard to prohibited priestly sexual liaisons. The perceptive comments of Ridbaz are on target; this is an amoraic issue, designed to determine whether the Mishnayot 6:1 and 6:2 overlap completely, as 6:2 opens with "similarly" (*ve-khen*) but does not specifically state what prohibitions apply to its list of forbidden relationships. Having determined, on the basis of R. Ba bar Memel's comment that "beginning" does entail the prohibited profanation of seed, the anonymous voice of the passage wants to know how we can determine this scripturally.

The first response in the passage is to import a *derashah* known from elsewhere (see Yerushalmi, Sotah 3:7 and Makkot 1:1; see *Sifra,* Emor 2:7–8)[28] which, according to R. David Frankel (Qorban ha-Edah; at Sotah), indicates that there is more than one profanation implied by the verse, since it chose the doubled spelling.[29] In all the other places the extra profanation refers to the fact that the woman is also "profaned" in addition to the child. Here, the extra profanation refers to the act; not only is completed intercourse to be seen as a profanation, but its beginning as well.[30] Thus, in quest of the scriptural source of R. Ba bar Memel's statement, the redactors of the passage rework a *derashah* on the relevant verse. This *derashah* is identified here (but not, interestingly, at Sotah or Makkot) with R. Aqiba, since it is he who will interpret doubled phrases and letters, according to the authors of these passages.

The *gezerah shavah* attributed to R. Ishmael would appear to be the creation of the *Amoraim* of the third and/or fourth generations; it is attributed to R. Ishmael because the redactors responsible for the attribution already "know" how R. Aqiba would learn the legal principle under discussion.

The attributions and the structure of the passage accomplish a number of things. First, having used an "Aqiban" *derashah* to establish the principle, the redactors are faced with presenting R. Ishmael in disagreement with the legal principle or with the exegesis. The latter is, of course, preferable, and thus we get the *gezerah shavah.*[31] Here, as elsewhere, we see the redactors of this Talmud taking steps to ground halakhah in Scripture without concomitantly creating legal disputes, which they wish to avoid or mitigate as much as possible. Further, the redactors have succeeded in overcoming obvious historical boundaries, retrojecting to the *Tannaim* concerns that, here at any rate, first become manifest in the fourth century. In any event, certainly here the Aqiban-Ishmaelian distinctions represent a redactional overlay on the fourth-century discussion. There is no evidence that either rabbi would base the law in question on the exegeses offered, or that they ever considered the issue at all.

The fifth passage is found at Yoma 45a (8:3). The passage here is quite complex, but of great importance in illustrating the fact that the *ad kedon* passages represent the reconstructions of much later redactors, and should not be seen as reports of the traditions of Rabbis Aqiba and Ishmael or their "schools."

1. A warning against [the performing of] labor during the day [on the Day of Atonement is found in the verse] "You shall do no work [throughout that day]" (Lev. 23:28). Punishment [for transgressing this warning is stated in the verse] "I will cause that person to perish [from among his people]" (Lev. 23:30). A warning [enjoining] self-denial during the day [is found in the verse] "Indeed, any person who does not practice self-denial [throughout that day]" (Lev. 23:29). Punishment [for transgressing this warning [is found in the continuation of the above-cited verse] "shall be cut off from his kin." A warning against work on the night [of the Day of Atonement] is not found here; punishment [for performing work on the night of the Day of Atonement] is not found here. Neither warning nor punishment for self-denial at night is found. . . .[32]

Rabbinic law often requires that violations of the law be clearly stated (a "warning") and that the punishment for said violations also be stated[33] The passage here identifies the warning and punishment for work and [transgressing the demand to engage in] self-denial on the Day of Atonement. Left unspecified is the warning and punishment for work and self-denial on the night of the Day of Atonement. This latter observation becomes the point of departure for further discussion:

2. Learned R. Ḥiyya: The Torah need not have specified a punishment regarding work, for it is unnecessary. I would have learned it from [the punishment for transgressing] self-denial. With self-denial, which is lenient [in that it is not enjoined on Sabbaths and holidays], [transgressors] are liable to [the penalty of] cutting-off; does it not follow that with work, which is more severe [in that it is prohibited on Sabbaths and holidays], [transgressors] are liable to cutting-off. Thus, it only states a punishment for work [during the day] for the purpose of giving a warning for before [that is, during the night][34] [We can now learn a *gezerah shavah*]. Just as the punishment cited for work includes a warning for before [i.e., night] so too the punishment cited for self-denial contains a warning for before [i.e., night]

R. Ḥiyya responds that we do in fact have statements of warning and punishment for work and self-denial on the night of the Day of Atonement, since the statement of punishment that apparently pertains to the actual day is superfluous. It must come to provide a warning regard-

ing the preceding night. We thus have a statement of warning and punishment regarding work on the night of the Day of Atonement. The
passage continues:

3. Said R. Zeʿira, "this says that we learn a *gezerah shavah* even when it is
'available' from [only] one side [as is this one, since the verse that addresses
punishment for work is extraneous, while that which addresses punishment
for self-denial is not]."[35]

Seen in context, what has happened here is that R. Zeʿira, an *Amora,*
responds, apparently with surprise, to the teaching of R. Ḥiyya. He
notes that the *gezerah shavah* is available from only one side, and yet
this is sufficient to definitively establish the point at issue. This is noteworthy to him.

4. Said R. Yudan, "and is this not in accord with R. Aqiba, for R. Aqiba said
that we learn from a *gezerah shavah* even though [neither of the words or
phrases may be deemed] available (alternatively, even though only one side
may be deemed available)."[36]

R. Yudan, an *Amora,* responds to R. Zeʿira by stating that the authority of a *gezerah shavah* that is available unilaterally is not surprising,
but accords with R. Aqiba, who, depending on how one interprets the
statement, does not demand any availability or demands only unilateral availability. The passage then cites yet another *gezerah shavah.*

5. It was taught, R. Elʿazar ben Yaʿaqob said, "it is said 'throughout that day'
[in Scripture] regarding work, and it is said 'throughout that day' regarding
self-denial. Just as with the 'throughout that day' that is said regarding work
you make no distinctions between day and night, between punishment and
warning, so too the 'throughout that day' that is said regarding self-denial we
shall not distinguish between night and day, between punishment and warning
[thus, self-denial obtains at night and without warning].

The Talmud apparently considers this teaching of R. Elʿazar ben
Yaʿaqob as totally devoid of availability. It thus states:

6. Thus far, according to R. Aqiba. Whence [do we know that self-denial obtains at night] according to R. Ishmael?

Since only R. Aqiba would learn from a *gezerah shavah* that was not
even unilaterally available, the teaching of R. Elʿazar ben Yaʿaqob must
be according to him. Note that R. Yudan (at #4) said that only R. Aqiba
would accept this teaching; he presumably thinks that all other (at least

contemporary) *Tannaim* would disagree. The Yerushalmi, though, will automatically identify the alternative position exclusively with R. Ishmael. Thus, we find:

7. Learned R. Ishmael, "'And this shall be to you a law for all time: In the seventh month [on the tenth day of the month, you shall practice self-denial; and you shall do no manner of work . . .]' (Lev. 16:29) It compares work to self-denial. Just as [the] work which I have prohibited you is work for which you are liable to cutting off [that is, both in the day and the night], so too the self-denial which I have enjoined upon you is self-denial for which you are liable to cutting-off [which is both in the day and at night]."[37]

It has already been pointed out in the notes that the attributed sayings in this passage are all addressing an issue different from that which the redactional context of the passage projects. Thus, what we have here is an attempt by the redactors of the passage to rework material to respond to their own legal and, by extension, exegetical problem.

One of the distinctions between the "systems" of Rabbis Aqiba and Ishmael routinely cited by modern scholars is the claim advanced here that R. Aqiba learns *gezerot shavot* that are not deemed available, while R. Ishmael insists on unilateral availability.[38] The source for this judgment would appear to be the statement of R. Yudan cited here (at 4). However, we should note R. Ze'ira's statement (at 3) that expresses the noteworthiness of learning a *gezerah shavah* that is available from only one side. Now, assuming R. Ze'ira's statement was actually made in response to the *gezerah shavah* cited at 2, certainly what makes it worthy of note is that it is not available bilaterally. That is, R. Ze'ira's surprise regarding unilateral availability is in contradistinction to bilateral availability, which is apparently the norm, rather than to no availability at all. Thus, the statement at 3, whatever its context, is here used to point out that a source supports the position that, minimally, a *gezerah shavah* need be available unilaterally in order to be sustained. The author of the statement would seem not to have known of such a position, and was certainly ignorant of a position that maintained the components of a *gezerah shavah* need not be available at all. Based on the material that we have, the judgment that R. Aqiba does not require availability (or, requires only unilateral availability) in *gezerot shavot* would appear to be the opinion of R. Yudan, which the redactors of the *ad kedon* passages appear to have picked up.[39] Thus, there is little basis for the assumption that this represents an accurate portrayal of the historical distinctions between Rabbis Aqiba and Ishmael.

More interesting perhaps is the way in which the citation of R. Yudan's opinion becomes the point of departure for the citation of the "throughout that day" gezerah shavah (at 5). The context created by the redactors makes it seem as though this *gezerah shavah* is cited to respond to the fact that a *gezerah shavah* was learned that was available and the subsequent comment that this approach is that of R. Aqiba. What this seems to imply is that R. Ḥiyya's *derashah* accords with the position of Aqiba; yet the text goes on to provide another *gezerah shavah* that it identifies with R. Aqiba, this time apparently assuming that the *gezerah shavah* is not available at all. It seems to me that what we have here is a contrived context for the citation of another *gezerah shavah*, attributed to R. Elʿazar ben Yaʿaqob but judged to be in accord with the position of R. Aqiba because its components are deemed not available. (I do not think it is overly cynical to point out that viewing this *gezerah shavah* [at 5] as available would scarcely extend anyone's creative powers.)[40]

The "according to R. Ishmael" passage (7) is also of interest from our perspective. The *derashah* cited here is found in the Yerushalmi's discussion of the first halakhah of this chapter (that is, Yoma 8:1), there for the purpose of showing that the self-denial mentioned in the Torah referred specifically to refraining from eating, and not to other forms of self-affliction and denial. The Yerushalmi citation is paralleled virtually verbatim in the (presumably Aqiban) *Sifra* (Aḥare 7:1-4). In both texts R. Ishmael is quoted as *disagreeing* with the *derashah*, citing another one (Deut. 8:3) in its stead. Thus, here in our passage, we find the Yerushalmi attributing to R. Ishmael a *derashah* from which it previously claimed he demurred. Of course, the *derashot* are cited for different purposes: at 8:1, to prove that "self-denial" means refraining from food; at 8:3, to prove that "self-denial" obtains at night. Thus, one could argue, were one so inclined, that R. Ishmael accepts the premise of the *derashah* (the scriptural equation of work and self-denial) but not its application at 8:1, thus allowing him to use it at 8:3, as indicated. If this were so, however, one would expect some statement to the effect that *this*, rather than that, is the purpose of the scriptural equation. That is, there is no evidence from the *derashah* itself that it is addressing this issue or that; it is only the context in which the *derashah* is cited, for which the sage is not responsible, that indicates purpose. The decision, then, as to meaning is that of the redactors of the passage. It seems more likely to me that the redactors of this passage were unaware of, or unconcerned with, the parallels in the *Sifra* and even Yerushalmi 8:1 as we now have them, and simply applied the scriptural equation to its particular problem—namely, Whence does R. Ishmael learn, etc.? Thus, the word translated "learned" (*tani*) at 7, does not refer to a source that contains this teaching; rather, it means "would learn" or "must have learned" or something to that effect.[41] We should also note that the question is not answered as we might expect, namely, that R. Ishmael simply agrees with R. Ḥiyya, who was quoted (at 2) as having solved the problem on the basis of a *gezerah shavah* that was unilaterally available. It may be that we have two distinct sections to our passage: 1–2, and 5–7, with 3–4 representing the connecting tissue.

From this passage we see, yet again, that the *ad kedon* passages represent redactional constructs. The *derashah* representing the approach of R. Aqiba is cited in the name of R. El'azar ben Ya'aqob, and is based on the judgment of an *Amora*, R. Yudan. It is in disagreement with the judgment of another *Amora*, R. Ze'ira. The *derashah* attributed to R. Ishmael is the same as a *derashah* with which the Yerushalmi quotes R. Ishmael in disagreement. Thus, there is no basis for the judgment that either *derashah* represents part of the corpus of Rabbis Aqiba and Ishmael, respectively. Further, the unqualified judgment that R. Aqiba learns definitive *gezerot shavot* without concern for availability—the crux of this passage—is apparently the judgment of one *Amora,* and as a historical matter is, to understate the case, scarcely beyond question.

These five passages, which I regard as representative, establish beyond question that the Aqiba/Ishmael distinctions represent the reconstructions of the redactors of these passages. To buttress this claim, we should note that *Yerushalmi Neziqin,* which was redacted under different auspices, knows nothing of this distinction. In several passages, it derives Mishnaic halakhot from scriptural repetitions, and at no point do we find glosses noting that such derivations are only admissible within the system of R. Aqiba.[42] Indeed, even within the Yerushalmi proper we find exegeses that should have called forth the *ad kedon* formula but did not; we even have exegesis of repetition attributed to R. Ishmael without eliciting further comment (e.g., *Nazir* 1:1). In view of all this I would conjecture that the *ad kedon* glosses represent the incomplete work of the last redactors of the Yerushalmi. In some places they succeeded in incorporating their view of tannaitic midrash; in others, they did not. Whatever the value of that conjecture, it seems to me to be indisputable that the redactors of this Talmud, or some subgroup thereof, react to the mass of inherited material by attempting to impose some kind of system on it.

The question then becomes how they invented this particular systematization. The first part of the answer seems simple enough. The redactors obviously knew the now well-known passage in the Tosefta, *Shevuot* (1:7), which claims that R. Aqiba would refrain from employing the technique of *kellal u-ferat u-khellal,* while R. Ishmael makes use of this technique. Here we have the claim of a systematic distinction between the two rabbis, pertaining to this limited issue. The Yerushalmi's redactors have extended the range of this traditional claim to include many other principles. As to why they did this, the answer seems to be that there are after all many legal and exegetical disputes between these two rabbis recorded in the different documents. Indeed, while there are disputes between R. Aqiba and many of his contemporaries, including Rabbis El'azar ben 'Azariah, Tarfon, and Yosi ha-Galili, those between him and Ishmael far outnumber all of these. Apparently, the redactors of these passages concluded that the many Aqiban-Ishmaelian disputes are grounded in systematic and thoroughgoing distinctions rather than differing exegetical hierarchies or specific local preferences. Although there is counterevidence that gets ignored, this is not an unreasonable conclusion to draw from some of the material.

Let us consider the following passage actually found in the Yerushalmi at Pes. 29c (2:7). The passage opens with a citation of Exod. 12:9, "Do not eat any of it raw, or cooked in any way with water, but roasted. . . . over the fire." On this verse the question is asked,

1. This teaches only in water; whence do we know [that it is forbidden to cook the Passover in] other liquids?

2. Scripture teaches, *u-vashel mevushal*, "cooked in any way" [the English does not reflect the repetition of the verbal stem BSL, which forms the basis of the *derashah*], to be all inclusive.

3. Thus far according to R. Aqiba; [whence do we know this] according to R. Ishmael?

4. Learned R. Ishmael, [it is an] argument a fortiori. If with water which does not impart its taste you say forbidden, with other liquids which do impart their taste, how much more so [must they obviously be forbidden].

The issue here, as in other passages, is the repetition of the Hebrew verbal stem, the phrase translated as "cooked in any way" above. This particular passage, however, is not the invention of the redactors of the Yerushalmi, but is rather part of the material inherited from earlier generations. It reflects an actual dispute attested in the *Mekhilta* (Pisha, 6) between Rabbis Aqiba and Ishmael. Not unexpectedly, the Yerushalmi has reorganized the material to suit its preferred form of presentation.[43] The change of form is important in that it creates the impression that this is not a specific dispute between these sages regarding the issue at hand; rather, given the many other passages that utilize this form, the reworking implicitly advances the claim that the exegetical principles at work here are part of a larger systematic dispute between these sages. That is why we do not have the standard "Said R. A. . . . R. B. said" known to all the documents (including the Yerushalmi) of the rabbinic corpus.

What I am claiming is that here and in one other place (Yeb. 8c, 8:1) we have *ad kedon* passages in which the Aqiban-Ishmaelian divide does not involve amoraic traditions, but rather actual statements attributed to these rabbis that can be verified by other documents.[44] From these passages, and whatever other disputes were known to them but not cited, the redactors of the Yerushalmi have concluded that R. Ishmael would refuse to learn from scriptural repetition at all. From a few other sources they concluded that he would eschew other techniques as well. If this is correct, we can understand some of the operating assumptions of the redactors of these Yerushalmi passages. These include the notion that R. Ishmael "knew" the *derashot* of R. Aqiba and rejected them, even though he may not ever have actually heard any of them. Further, it assumes this rejection is not ad hoc or ad locum, but is based on a systematic approach to Scripture. The Yerushalmi seems not to consider the possibility that what is reflected in the *Mekhilta* tradition (which the redactors apparently knew, even if we accept that R. Ishmael was familiar with the *derashah* attributed to R. Aqiba) is a hierarchy of preferability rather than an outright systematic rejection of the alternative approach. That is, if the dispute reports are reliable, we still may have nothing more than a "statement" by R. Ishmael that a *qal va-homer* is a better means of grounding halakhic reality than is an extension based on repetition.[45] In any event, most to be noted in the Yerushalmi's reworking of the passage from the *Mekhilta* is the use of a form that is designed to communicate positions that go beyond that which the material actually supports.

Before concluding this discussion, I would like to point to one last passage, at Sot. 20a (5:1). This passage does not actually employ the "thus far" formula, but is very important in seeing how the Yerushalmi operates when confronted with an exegetical dispute. The Mishnah here reads:

As the water puts her to the proof so does it put the paramour to the proof, for it is written "[And] they shall come" "[And] they shall come" (my brackets; the verses are two of the three in Num. 5:22, 24, 27). As she is forbidden to her husband, so is she forbidden to the paramour, for it is written, "[And] she has defiled herself" "[And] she has defiled herself." (Num. 5:27, without the and, 29) So Rabbi Aqiba. . . . Rabbi says: Twice in the section of Scripture is it written, "And she has defiled herself," "And she has defiled herself"; once for the husband and once for the paramour. (Danby, somewhat revised, p. 298)

The Yerushalmi comments, "We recite 'they shall come, they shall come', while there are those who recite '*and* they shall come, *and* they shall come; the one who said the former is [in accord with (the system of?)] R. Aqiba; the one who said the latter is [in accord with (the system of?)] R. Ishmael"; similarly concerning "[and] she has defiled herself." That is, here we have the Yerushalmi identifying the *derashah* based on the repetition of the words with R. Aqiba, and the *derashah* based on the letter *vav* (= and) with R. Ishmael, on the assumption that R. Ishmael would not draw meaning from the repetition (even though it does not occur in the same verse), but would be willing to find significance in the extra *vav*. Rabinowitz switches the identifications on the basis of a generalization of the Yerushalmi's *derashot* at Sheb. 4:1 and 8:1, which suggest that R. Ishmael would not interpret the extra *vav* and (I suppose) the Mishnah at Sheb. 2:5, which suggests that R. Ishmael interprets repetition when the words appear in different verses.[46] The advantage of this emendation is that it allows the Yerushalmi to be consistent with the simple meaning of the Mishnah, which implies that R. Aqiba draws meaning from the extra *vav*. Despite the strengths of this emendation, the text as translated above is found in most versions, and is consistent with the Yerushalmi's position that in fact R. Ishmael does not (or, would prefer not to?) interpret repetition even when it occurs in different verses. Thus, no matter how our text reads, we find it attributes to R. Ishmael either the drawing of added significance from repetition or from the extra *vav*; either choice is inconsistent with other Yerushalmi passages regarding what R. Ishmael would and would not do. Further, both approaches are fully consistent with what the Yerushalmi elsewhere imagines R. Aqiba would do, and for these reasons the passage remains problematic no matter how we read it. Further, we should take note of the fact that in attributing one version to R. Ishmael, what the text is saying is that one *Tanna* taught R. Aqiba's position as being that of R. Ishmael![47] Finally, we should note that the Mishnah clearly attributes the repetition interpretation to Rabbi.[48] While there may be room to argue regarding the function of his statement,[49] it is difficult to understand how R. Ishmael enters the picture, though the Yerushalmi feels the need to introduce the name of R. Ishmael.[50] As really none of this can plausibly be attributed to R. Ishmael, his appearance in the passage shows, yet again, the extent to which Rabbis Aqiba and Ishmael are stripped of their historical personae and become, in the Yerushalmi and in the work of modern scholars, designators of diverse trends of exegesis that originate throughout the rabbinic estate.[51]

The contrast between the Bavli and the Yerushalmi is clear. The people responsible for the final form of these documents were all heirs to an overlapping but not identical mass of earlier material they considered tannaitic. Perhaps of greater import, they inherited an ideology that insisted that nothing in the Torah could be superfluous, and a methodology—midrash—that gave concrete expression to that ideology. From this common starting point they each went their separate ways. The redactors of the Bavli felt free to reconstruct the putative exegetical positions of *Tannaim* in a strictly ad hoc, ad locum manner. Thus, one rabbi could "enunciate" one scriptural principle in one place while attaching himself to the opposite position in another place. The redactors could even create entirely new concepts to which—it is implicitly claimed—the *Tannaim* must have adhered, such as the *doresh vav va-he* principle noted in the previous chapter. The important thing was to serve the needs of the passage at hand; whatever advanced the discussion and the program of the redactors of the passage was fair game. No attempt was made to impose consistency with exegetical techniques (as opposed to halakhic ones).

The redactors of the Yerushalmi, or, more likely, one subgroup thereof, saw things differently. Out of the mass of conflicting exegetical opinions and techniques they inherited, they discerned two overarching systems represented by two of the most important *Tannaim* of the early second century. This observation informed the way they constructed and/or glossed a small number of passages, which, taken together, convey the impression that the world of early rabbinic midrash is not chaotic or devoid of system. There were two distinct systems of exegesis, each capable of grounding halakhic norms in Scripture and deriving halakhic norms from Scripture, but each operating with very different ideas regarding scriptural language and the authority of derivations. What historical or textual concerns stimulated this vision I cannot say. I do not know what stake the redactors had in their acts of systematization.

I do know that whatever their efforts meant to the redactors/ glossators of these passages, their systematization was to have enormous repercussions in the modern period, in which the need of traditional loyalists to locate in the rabbinic world an ability to think systematically and read intelligently became urgent. For in answer to the question, "How do we know this?" twenty-nine passages in the Yerushalmi suggest that there are in fact two distinct ways of knowing "this," one of which could be made by apologists to appear quite compelling from a modern perspective. The glossators of the Yerushalmi laid the foundation for a fundamental reconceptualization of the history of rabbinic law and its foundations in the modern period; I cannot help but think that they had something else in mind.

Recapitulation

As noted in the preface, I recognize that there are those who may be interested in the second part of this book, but are not prepared to wade through the technical argumentation of the preceding chapters, particularly chapters 2 and 3. For that reason, I will briefly summarize the results of those chapters, so that readers will have access to the conclusions they offer, which are critical to the discussion in part two.[53]

In the rabbinic literature of the first five Christian centuries, there is perhaps no feature whose presence is as pronounced as the legal exegesis of the Torah, or midrash halakhah. In this literature, most midrash halakhah revolves around the *Tannaim*, the earliest rabbinic sages. They are either understood as the authors of much of it—whether of specific texts such as the *Mekhilta, Sifra* and *Sifre*, or the many *beraitot* contained in the Talmuds—or else the midrash is presented as the source of their particular legal opinions. In the second case, while the *Tanna* in question is not necessarily seen as the author of the exegesis, the midrash represents his thinking as reconstructed by later hands. In either case, the midrash was seen as an authentic representation of the thinking of the *Tanna* to whom it is attributed.[53]

In the tannaitic texts, we often find significant diversity regarding the meaning of a particular biblical verse or phrase, perhaps traceable to different systems of exegesis in general, perhaps to other, more local concerns. This diversity, as well as the question of what is and is not acceptable exegesis to the ancient sages, gave rise to considerable reflection, starting with the two Talmuds and proceeding up to our own day.[54]

When we examine the way the two Talmuds make use of the midrashic materials that were bequeathed to them, it is easy to discern that each takes a distinct approach. The approach of the Babylonian sages and the redactors of the Babylonian Talmud is to treat the diversity of techniques and results as, in essence, a virtue; one is left free to deal with the material as one sees fit. To take some concrete examples, in the tannaitic materials we often find sages deriving a law from a scriptural repetition. Sometimes other sages oppose the law, and therefore, it is presumed, the exegesis. Sometimes they may agree with the law, but yet reject the proffered exegesis, preferring some other to establish the point. At some moment in time, opposing the exegesis of repeated phrases was justified by the position that the Torah speaks in human language, and therefore the repetition is devoid of significance; it is merely a concession to human style. In the Bavli, as was noted by a number of medieval commentators, the position that the Torah speaks in human language is attributed to perhaps a dozen different *Tannaim*, ranging over a number of generations. Further, the same *Tanna* who in one place supposedly refrains from interpreting repeated phrases is often cited in other contexts as interpreting them. It appears, then, that to the redactors of the Bavli, everyone agrees that in general the Torah does not speak in human language; everyone also agrees that sometimes the Torah does. Thus, most repetitions are to be interpreted, but some are not.[55]

Similarly, with the technique of *doresh vavim* (that is, deriving meaning from the presence of the conjunctive *and*); while strongly associated with R. Aqiba,[56] the Talmud assumes that numerous rabbis might use this technique, and having used it in one place will yet refrain from using it in another.[57]

It seems, then, that the redactors of the Bavli took from the earlier materials the stance that there are among the *Tannaim* no systems of exegesis exclusive to an individual or a school. All techniques are available; they therefore felt free to attribute to any *Tanna* any exegetical position consistent with the legal position adopted by that sage.[58]

When we turn to the Yerushalmi, we see that the situation is quite different. While scarcely maintaining consistency throughout all the tractates, the Yerushalmi often divides the earlier tannaitic materials into two schools, that of R. Aqiba and that of R. Ishmael. Numerous times, after reconstructing the putative exegetical stance of a particular *Tanna* or *Amora,* the Talmud will state that thus far the law is grounded according to the system of R. Aqiba; it will then ask, whence do we know the law according to R. Ishmael's system? The answer to this question will always be another *derashah*. In many of these cases, it is to be noted, the midrash that is ostensibly according to the system of R. Ishmael is attributed to an *Amora* who gives no indication that he is interpreting according to anyone's system. However, because the midrash uses techniques of which R. Ishmael allegedly approves rather than those he rejects, the redactors of these passages issue the judgment that this midrash belongs to his system.[59] Thus, the redactors of the Yerushalmi react to the chaotic nature of the earlier materials by imposing system on it, arguing that there are two different approaches to Scripture that dominated the tannaitic world, one expanding the range of acceptable techniques, one resisting that expansion.

4 • Midrash in the Middle Ages

A FULL DISCUSSION OF halakhic midrash in the Middle Ages would require consideration of virtually every aspect of medieval Jewish culture. Every talmudic commentary, of which there are many, covering tens of thousands of pages, could conceivably contain relevant material. Every Bible commentary and supercommentary, of which there were scores, could conceivably contain relevant material. Every chronicle of the rabbinic tradition, every book of *kelalim*, every grammatical work and dictionary, every collection of sermons and synagogal poems can provide perspective on how medieval Jews related to the midrashic materials they inherited. While it would be presumptuous to say that such a full treatment is beyond the ken of any one person, it is certainly well beyond my abilities.

Happily, once again our inquiry is governed by a concern for the modern age, and the questions and issues that have been decisive in shaping modern discussions. This concern quickly cuts the important material down to manageable size. It is clear that the work of certain figures—Saadia Gaon (although much of the relevant material was not known to the scholarly world until the discovery of the Cairo Genizah), Ibn Ezra, Maimonides, Naḥmanides—exercised a fundamental influence in shaping the contours of modern discussion, while the works of most others were considered within these contours. Thus, it is the works of these men that will be discussed and analyzed in detail. This does not mean that all others can be ignored here, since, in addition to laying the foundation of modern discussions, we are interested in describing an important aspect of medieval Jewish culture in its own terms.

That is, we are interested in knowing how premodern Jews related to this fundamental but challenging—at times, as we shall see, embarrassing—element of their cultural heritage. Thus, even texts that were ignored by modern polemicists have some relevance here. The work of those scholars who figure most prominently in modern discussion serves as the central focus of this chapter, with the other relevant material relegated to the periphery.

Midrash and Medieval Jewish Culture

When we turn from the talmudic period to the culture of Jews in the Middle Ages, we immediately see that significant cultural shifts have taken place. New methods of biblical interpretation emerged, and new conceptions of the Jewish exegetical legacy were expressed. If talmudic Jews needed to envision their legal norms as *originating*, for the most part, from the biblical text, through extensive exegesis, Jews in the early Middle Ages, particularly within the Islamic orbit, had a different set of needs entirely. They needed to ground Jewish legal practices in the other potential source, namely, tradition. In many ways, these new needs were shaped largely by the interaction of Rabbanite Jews with Karaites and with Islamic culture and exegetical techniques. The spread of Islam allowed Jews to familiarize themselves with important textual-critical tools, and led to the hegemony of Arabic. This hegemony in turn made of rabbinically educated Jews within the Islamic orbit natural comparative Semiticists, as they became fluent in Hebrew, Aramaic and Arabic. These factors allowed Jews in the Islamic lands to understand the Bible in a new, philologically grounded way.[1]

Karaism, an amalgamation of various "heterodox" elements within the Jewish community that emerged in the eighth century under the leadership of Anan ben David,[2] provided rabbinic culture with an enormously important stimulus to reorient its approach to the Bible and rabbinic tradition. For the Karaites challenged many aspects of the rabbinic application of the Bible. What is interesting is that, for the most part, the Karaites formulated their critique of rabbinic praxis primarily with reference to the foundational claim of rabbinic Judaism to an oral tradition, which they considered fraudulent, and less in terms of rabbinic exegesis, the identified source of most extrabiblical norms. That is, the Karaites dismissed the rabbinic claim that (some of) their practices are rooted in an oral communication from God to Moses, arguing instead that such practices are *mitzvat anashim melumada* (the commandment of men, learned by rote).[3]

These "man-made" commandments are contrasted in Karaite literature with the laws of *Torat Moshe*, the Torah of Moses, i.e., Karaite practices.[4] These are derived from the self-sufficient biblical text through *ḥipus*, the thorough searching of Scripture; only through such *ḥipus* can Scripture be made to yield its manifold secrets.[5] This view is most forcefully articulated by Yehudah Hadassi, a twelfth-century Byzantine Karaite who, in his great compendium of Karaite thought, *Eshkol ha-Kofer*, repeatedly stressed the fact that proper praxis can only come about through appropriate exegesis of the biblical text, preferably with divine assistance.[6] Similarly, two centuries earlier, Salmon ben Yeruḥim, a contemporary of Saadia Gaon, argued that one can find all one needs in the Torah, and one need not turn to a so-called tradition to find out, e.g., the appropriate measure for *terumah*. There is no such measure, and the rabbinic attempt to identify one is simply fraudulent.[7] Indeed, virtually all Karaite thinkers, from Anan to Hadassi and beyond, stress this essential point. Thus the famous Karaite motto, attributed to Anan: "Search the Torah well, and do not rely on my opinion."[8] Everything is in the written Torah, and tradition is not a relevant tool in unlocking its secrets.

It is not surprising that, for the most part, rabbinic midrashic techniques are not the primary victims of Karaite attack. To be sure, Anan himself is attacked for his reliance on rabbinic techniques[9] (and indeed, there is much overlap between his exegetical principles and rabbinic ones).[10] By extension, of course, such an attack is obviously a derogation of rabbinic hermeneutic principles. Still, this attack did not deter the Karaites from developing exegetical principles that necessarily overlapped with rabbinic ones. Hadassi, for example, cited the thirteen principles of R. Ishmael; he is very critical of certain applications,[11] and after describing the techniques, paraphrases the saying of Daniel 7:15, "[M]y spirit is disturbed by them, and the vision of my mind alarmed me."[12] Yet his primary objection seems to be that these techniques are insufficient, and he proceeds to outline eighty techniques—many drawn from earlier Karaite works—that lead to proper scriptural exegesis; several of these are identical to, or extensions of, R. Ishmael's.[13] Thus, midrash halakhah, per se, was not the point of critical divide between Karaites and Rabbanites.

As Naftali Wieder has noted, it was an argument regarding the self-sufficiency of the Torah that was the crux of the debate between Karaites and Rabbanites.[14] The Karaites maintained that the written Torah contained all the information one would need to serve God, if one learned to interpret properly.[15] That Karaite midrash was not entirely congruent with rabbinic midrash either in techniques or in results does not diminish the fact that Karaism was rooted in its own brand of midrash halakhah, and was so recognized by Rabbanite opponents. Thus, the whole split could easily have become one of conflicting hermeneutic systems and applications.

That this did not ultimately happen is due largely to the efforts of R. Saadia, Gaon of Sura (882–942). Instead of fighting the Karaites on their own turf, so to speak, by engaging in interpretive jousts, Saadia changed the focus of the entire discussion. In numerous writings directed against Karaism, Saadia initiated a process of trivialization of midrash halakhah, almost completely denying it any creative role in the formation of Jewish—Rabbanite—law. Instead, in Saadia's view, the Torah's undeniable lacunae are filled, almost exclusively, by material originating in the oral tradition, whose existence is quite independent of the Torah's text, and whose provisions are not derived from it. In his commentary to the Torah, in his *Esa Meshali*—a general polemic against Karaism and defense of rabbinic tradition—and in his polemic against the use of analogy (Arabic, *kiyas*, Hebrew, *hekesh*) in interpreting Scripture, Saadia argues against the self-sufficiency of the Torah, and against the proposition that one could derive from its text all the details needed to realize its demands.

In the introduction to his Torah commentary, Saadia outlines seven reasons why the Torah would be incomprehensible without an oral tradition, implying at the same time that exegesis cannot be relied upon to provide the necessary information. As Poznanski stated long ago, these seven arguments are really one (at least, the first five are), for they are all predicated on the notion that the Torah demands compliance with various laws, without providing the slightest clue how one might actually accomplish this. Thus, for example, the Torah demands the wearing of fringed garments (Num. 15:38–39), and the dwelling in booths as part of the harvest festival (Lev. 23:42–43). The recipients of the Torah, of course, want to perform these commandments properly, but the text is silent as to the qualities these things are to have. What is the appropriate height, length and width of the booth? How many walls must it have? How are the fringes to be made? One cannot discover these things from Scripture alone. Rather, the details that govern Jewish practice are preserved in the oral tradition, and have been from the moment the Torah was committed to writing (argument #1).[16]

Similarly, the Torah is silent regarding the appropriate quantity needed to properly fulfill certain commandments, such as the *terumah* gift to the priest. How much must one give? For that matter, how many wives may a king have before violating the prohibition of not having too many wives? How many horses? How much gold and silver? (See Deut. 17:16–17) The Torah does not say, and it is impossible to derive such things from the text (#2).

How are we to know what day of the week is the Sabbath day?

How are we to know when the new month begins (#3)?[17] How do we know what is forbidden on the Sabbath? What vessels are subject to impurity (#4)? How do we know about marriage contracts, which are not even stated in the Torah? Yet all agree, Karaites and Rabbanites alike, that such a contract is necessary.[18] How do we know that we must pray? All agree that we must, yet Scripture does not specifically demand this (#5).[19] Finally, how would we know the time frame of centuries past (#6), or the nature of our expectations for the future (#7) without an oral tradition?[20]

It is clear that for Saadia none of these things can be derived from Scripture; all are the product of oral tradition. Now, to be sure, talmudic literature itself states that most of these norms are dependent on tradition, not midrash; in this respect Saadia has chosen his issues well. Still, in talmudic literature, the number of fringes and the susceptibility of vessels to uncleanness are presented as derived from Scripture.[21] Nevertheless, the Gaon insists that they cannot be derived therefrom. He obviously considers these *derashot* to be merely supports *(asmakhtot)* for what has been passed down as oral tradition from the time of Moses.

This argument was decisive for Saadia and it is repeated often in his work. His introduction to his translation of the Torah into Arabic contains a form of this argument. It is found with greater elaboration in the fragments of the *Esa Meshali* published by B. M. Lewin. In the rhymed canto that ends with the syllable *nah,* the Gaon once again asks whether one would know the dimensions of a sukkah, the amount of *terumah,* etc., for which, he informs us, there is not the slightest mention in the Scriptures (*ein le-zot be-khol ha-miqra temunah*). "All these and many others, I shall ask the readers of Scripture, is there an explanation of any of these? other than in the Mishnah and Talmud, where all this is learned, and much more."[22] Similarly, in a fragment of this work published by Shraga Abramson, the same claim is made: Scripture does not communicate what one needs to know to fulfill the commandments, and it is not possible to fulfill them without the Mishnah.[23] More than that, he claims that Karaites, by relying on their own exegesis of Scripture, their own midrash, can have neither stability nor certitude within their system of religious praxis. What is prohibited today will be permitted tomorrow. With biting sarcasm he writes, "Verily they give their lives for one of the laws; if only they had lived, it would, in time, have changed."[24] According to Saadia, when knowledge of the practical demands of the Torah is rooted in human exegesis, the system is not anchored in anything. Things change from day to day. No wonder that Saadia removed a creative role from rabbinic midrash as well. Indeed, the inability to generate acceptable meaning from Scripture alone was so clear to Saadia that he wrote, "Let us now see and investigate, whether the explanations of the commandments are written in Scripture—then we shall acknowledge that there is no Mishnah."[25]

This last remark is stunning. So much of rabbinic literature is devoted to showing that the Mishnah's rules are rooted in Scripture and to tracing how they can be derived therefrom. Saadia repudiates this entire line of rabbinic learning, apparently considering it all a post factum creation of links between two originally distinct sources of information. That is, the midrashic activity of the Talmuds merely creates supports or mnemonic devices for information actually known only through tradition, not exegesis. Now, to be sure, the notion that some exegeses are merely supports is already found in the Talmud, but in such cases it is precisely because the norms are authoritative *mi-de-rabbanan* that the verses are so identified, thus indicating the exact opposite of the position Saadia is staking out here. In the Talmud, an *asmakhta* represents an exegesis marshaled in support of a rabbinic law; a *derashah* attached to a norm that is not identified as an *asmakhta*—virtually all of them—serves as the source of an authoritative scriptural law. Saadia turns this situation on its head; all *derashot* are *asmakhtot*, but the laws remain authoritative *mi-de-oraita*.[26]

Saadia's repudiation of the exegetical aspect of rabbinic learning may be brought into sharper focus my looking at his polemic against the Karaite hermeneutic technique of analogy, or *kiyas*. As virtually all scholars who have written on Karaism have noted, the Karaites relied heavily on the notion that one could learn what is not clearly stated in the text by analogy to what is stated in the text. Thus, one would not need tradition to fill in the Torah's blanks. Saadia wrote a separate work—only pieces of which survive—and also devoted a considerable portion of his introduction to his Torah commentary to show that with the Torah's revealed commandments,[27] analogy is simply inadmissible. As Abraham Halkin pointed out, analogy here refers not only to the rabbinic principle of analogy, *hekkesh*, but also to an argument a fortiori, *qal va-ḥomer*. He notes that the Karaite Yaqub al-Qirqisani enjoyed mocking Saadia for rejecting one of the thirteen principles of R. Ishmael. As Halkin explains, the difference in Saadia's mind between Karaite analogies and rabbinic analogies is that the latter are rooted in tradition, whereas the former are not, and therefore allow for innovations in all directions.[28] Halkin is, no doubt, correct. Still, in its application, this view not only trivializes much of rabbinic activity, but also seems to do violence to its basic assumptions.

In his polemic Saadia turns to the Karaite justification of *kiyas*, which was rooted in the analogy the Torah itself makes at Deut. 22:26. The verse, referring to a betrothed rape victim, reads, "But you shall do nothing to the girl. The girl did not incur the death penalty [for adultery], for this case is like that of a man attacking another and murdering him." The Karaites saw in this verse a case of the divine author drawing an analogy between different cases, thereby authenticating the procedure for them. In a fragment of Saadia's polemic against this reasoning preserved in Qirqisani, Saadia shows that in fact the two cases are not genuinely comparable, and "therefore, their claim that [this verse] represents an analogy is groundless (*batel*)."[29] In this polemic against the *kiyas* of the Karaites, Saadia ends up totally distancing himself from the Karaite explanation of the verse. In so doing he has, for polemical advantage, fully repudiated, not only this explanation, but also the interpretation of the verse found in the *Sifre Deut.* (ad loc.) and the Bavli (Sanhedrin 73a), which see analogies in all directions here, and from which we learn the important law that just as one may save a maiden from rape at the cost of the rapist's life, so too one may save someone from murder at the cost of the murderer's life.[30]

No doubt, Saadia would explain that the *Sifre* and Bavli passages do not contain an authoritative and legally creative exegesis of the verse, that they do not actually serve as the source of the law in question. However, not only must he deny the authority of this particular reading of Scripture, but he ultimately rejects the very premise on which it is based—namely, that there is a clear analogy drawn between murder and rape victims in this verse. That is, not only is the *derashah* a phenomenon of secondary importance legally, but the very claim it advances is incorrect. Yet again, Saadia would, probably, dismiss this whole discussion in the *Sifre* and Bavli as merely a convenient—and in this instance, imprecise—way of communicating elements of the tradition. The authors of the passage did not actually learn anything from Scripture; they merely played "connect the dots" with various pieces of information already known from elsewhere. Still, to do so, they advanced a claim that, to Saadia, was manifestly false. Now, some modern scholars may wish to endorse the notion that rabbinic midrash halakhah is not genuinely creative, historically, and in my view such a position is partially justified. Yet there can be no denying that such a historical stance is thoroughly at odds with the self-understanding that emerges from countless, albeit not all, talmudic discussions, which see midrash halakhah as an indispensable means of realizing the will of the Creator.[31] Nevertheless, in Saadia's oeuvre, we find a marked distancing from this aspect of rabbinic thinking and learning.

I have no doubt that Saadia's rejection of creative midrash was fueled by Islamic exegetical works, and is rooted in his interest in grammar and philology, and his overall interest in *peshat*. Yet the existential urgency of his rejection is ultimately rooted in his battle with

Karaism. For some of Saadia's claims are simply too extreme, *given his fealty to the rabbinic tradition,* for them to have emerged from any dispassionate analysis of the material. This is particularly the case with the calendar, where Saadia's claims are thoroughly inconsistent with numerous Mishnaic and talmudic passages.[32] Further, Saadia's arch-traditionalism led to his implicit denial of the generally recognized distinction between the language of the Scriptures and the language of the sages; for Saadia, the lion's share of the Mishnah was itself revealed at Sinai, although he acknowledges that its formulation was not necessarily preserved verbatim. Still, in his Torah commentary and in a distinct work devoted to explaining biblical *hapax legomena,* Saadia often explains obscure biblical words on the basis of the language of the Mishnah. Thus, not only does the Mishnah provide the traditionally sanctioned interpretation, but it provides an important linguistic source for understanding the *peshat* of the biblical text. Although he was excoriated by Dunash ibn Labrat for this reliance on the language of the Mishnah,[33] in Saadia's own terms the procedure makes sense. What better corpus of linguistic information could there be than the Mishnah for the elucidation of the language of the Hebrew Bible?[34] This traditionalism cannot be explained as simply a commitment to *peshat,* or as the result of the influence of Islamic hermeneutic techniques. On the contrary, it seems that his interest in *peshat* was more an outgrowth of his battle with Karaism. For a real understanding of *peshat* would indicate just how much is left unsaid in the Torah, and demonstrate that it is impossible to derive definitive, legally and linguistically valid extensions of Scripture's formulations in order to fill in these lacunae. Fealty to *peshat* makes clear how fully dependent one is on tradition if one wishes to fulfill the demands of the Torah.[35]

In attempting to demonstrate that one simply cannot make Scripture whole from within itself, Saadia hoped to deal a fatal blow to Karaism. In the process, he trivialized an enormous chunk of rabbinic endeavor—the putatively creative halakhic midrash. (We shall encounter this strategy again in our consideration of the modern period.) In this, he pioneered a new orientation towards Scripture and tradition that was to exercise enormous influence on the direction of Jewish exegesis for the next three centuries, and beyond.

It seems likely that Saadia's view was able to exercise such influence on others, not only because of the challenge of Karaism, but also because some midrashic passages were far-fetched and offended the developing exegetical sense of those within the Islamic orbit. The two factors together allowed questions to be raised regarding some of these unlikely exegeses. Let us consider a question addressed to Rav Hai

(939–1038), Gaon of Pumbedita: "Whence do we know that a master, who attempts to evict a slave whose term of servitude is over and thereby injures him, is exempt from compensation? The Torah says, 'Nor may you accept ransom . . . to return' (Num. 35:32). For one who has returned." (Bavli, BK 28a) The questioner wants to know what kind of proof that is. The force of the question seems to be that the verse in question has absolutely nothing to do with tort law, but with the disposition of the one guilty of manslaughter. Further, the verse does not speak of "one who has returned," as the *darshan* would have us believe. Thus what proof can this verse offer that the master is exempt from the normal compensation due an injured party?

Hai responds that we see "that it is not a proof but a midrash [*delav ra'ayah hi 'ela midrash hu*], and the matter is actually a received law . . ."[36] That is, the midrash establishes nothing and proves nothing. We know this law by virtue of the received tradition, not from exegesis. Still it is clear that the Gaon thinks the *derashah* has its own logic, and can be used as a secondary support for this legal ruling. What we must note is that for Hai Gaon the Talmud's presentation of a law as derived from scriptural exegesis is not decisive; the *derashah* is readily transformed into an *asmakhta*. Indeed, in general, Hai's view seems to be that traditionally sanctioned practice is decisive, not talmudic discussion and certainly not talmudic exegesis.[37]

A similar view seems to have been held by his father, Sherira Gaon, who, in his famous *Epistle,* wrote of the *Sifra* and *Sifre* that they contain "*derashot* on the biblical verses, and show where allusions to the halakhot are found in scripture."[38] That is, these works take the existing halakhot, transmitted by tradition, and locate allusions to them in the Scriptures. As he notes, this was the primary direction of study in Temple times. Thus, in all likelihood, he too was of the opinion that tradition was the source of those laws not stated explicitly in the Bible, not exegesis.

Another important voice in favor of this view is the author of the "Mevo ha-Talmud" attributed to Shemuel ha-Nagid. The author, either an eleventh-century Spaniard or a twelfth-century Egyptian, stated matters most succinctly and unambiguously:

And you should know that all that our Rabbis, may their memory be for a blessing, upheld as the halakhah with regard to the commandments came directly from Moses, our teacher, may he rest in peace, who received it directly from the all-powerful—do not add to it or subtract from it. But as to their explanations of the verses, each one [explained] as it occurred to him, and as things appeared to him. We accept all that seems reasonable from among these explanations, but as to the remainder, we do not rely on them.[39]

One can ask for no clearer a statement of the matter. It should be noted that this statement is appended to the author's explanation of the term "Haggadah" (or "Aggadah"), of which, he informs us, one should also study only that which appears reasonable. The two forms of midrash are treated as representing essentially identical intellectual processes, and it is clear that the author intends to suggest that midrash halakhah (although not the halakhah itself) is of no greater authority than rabbinic Aggadah. Like Aggadah, none of it serves as a binding source, and much of it is contrary to reason and therefore unworthy of study.

Similar arguments are presented by R. Yehudah Halevi, who directs his remarks against the methods of the Karaites. He repeats the same arguments we found articulated by Saadia, to the effect that the Torah simply cannot be comprehended without being supplemented by an oral tradition. The calendar and its basis would be incomprehensible, as would all the details of the myriads of laws unexplained in the written Torah, like the sukkah, the proper way to make fringes, the proper way to circumcise, etc., etc.[40] Further, he follows Saadia in noting that the Karaite way of searching the Scriptures leads to anarchy and the breakdown of religious certitude, since everyone applies the method of *hekesh* in his own way, without boundaries and guidelines.[41] The midrashic methods of the Karaites are thoroughly arbitrary and they are exegetically and religiously unacceptable.

It will come as no surprise then that Halevi, too, denies to rabbinic halakhic midrash any creative role in the fashioning of the halakhic system. Rather, he argues, the rabbis offered their midrashic readings as an *asmakhta*, a support, for something that was known through the tradition. The purpose of fashioning these supports was to "facilitate remembering the commandments."[42] Thus, while their *derashot* may seem far-fetched and their exegetical methods beyond understanding, this is of little consequence. To know the law, "we must rely on their tradition, since we are certain of their wisdom, piety and extraordinary efforts to ascertain the truth. . . ."

In the two introductions to his Torah commentary, Abraham ibn Ezra (1089/92–1164/67) expressed a similar line of thought. He too finds the Karaite approach devoid of certitude. Things change from day to day, and one can never be certain of fulfilling the wishes of the Creator.[43] Further, their work is based on faulty grammatical theories, rendering it of even less value. Like Saadia and Halevi, he insists that the Torah is not self-sufficient, and without tradition we could never understand it properly.[44] He too insists that the rabbis are the reliable and true recipients of the tradition, to which they have not added or subtracted anything, "God forbid."[45] He too wants to explicate the

Scriptures in terms of their *peshat*, insisting that many of the midrashic interpretations are not sufficiently grounded in the text.

Thus, at first glance, it seems that Ibn Ezra has nothing new to offer. Yet as the most comprehensive Hebrew commentary produced within the Islamic orbit (or, more accurately, by someone influenced by this cultural world) up to his own time, Ibn Ezra's work provides important illustrations of just how one would read the Bible, verse by verse, when informed by the view outlined above. Further, Ibn Ezra has provided us with an important theoretical statement of what all this means in his work, *Yesod Mora*. There he writes,

There are commandments that are explained in the Torah, and there are those for which we only know their true interpretations through the holy traditers, who have received them, son from father and student from teacher. If not for the tradition one could interpret them differently. Further, there are commandments that we have received that are not mentioned in the Torah at all. I will tell you—were it not for the Men of the Great Assembly, and the men of the Mishnah and Talmud, the Torah of our God would be lost, and its memory forgotten, God forbid. For they clarified everything, and explained the commandments properly, and all the laws as they received them. And [among these explanations] there are those that are clearly attested in the Torah, and there are those presented midrashically (*derekh derash*), and there are those presented by way of support (*asmakhta be'alma*). Anyone with a mind can discern when they are expounding midrashically, and when they are expounding in accord with the plain sense of scripture, for they do not always speak in one manner. . . . And I have already explained that [the rabbinic interpretation of the phrase] "And he inherits it" (Num. 27:11) is merely a support.[46]

According to this, the source for Jewish laws not explicitly stated in the Torah is tradition, not exegesis. Yet these explanations rooted in tradition are presented in relation to the Torah text in rabbinic literature. In this presentation we must distinguish among those that are clearly attested in Scripture, those that are the product of midrash, and those that are simply supports. The distinction between the latter two categories seems to be that midrashic interpretation has some basis in the wording of the text, or at least does not do violence to it, whereas "supports" represent verses connected to laws in defiance of the meaning of the verse. Ibn Ezra's example of the latter is the phrase "and he inherits it" (*ve-yarash otah*), which the rabbis read as if it said, "and he inherits her," meaning a man inherits his wife's property. To Ibn Ezra, this is a gross misreading of the text that could not have been intended seriously. Rather, that a man inherits his wife's property is a received law that has no connection to any verse. The rabbis connected it to this (superfluous) phrase to provide support for the law.[47] There are other examples of this kind of connection between biblical verses and received laws.

When the rabbis are speaking midrashically, the verse that is connected to the received law has a more direct connection, although other possibilities are plausible, and the latter are sometimes more in accord with the plain meaning. In such cases the tradition provides us with the correct interpretation of the verse. Ibn Ezra's explanation of Exod. 16:29 (in the short commentary) may serve as an example. The verse reads, "Let everyone remain where he is; let no man leave his place on the Sabbath day." Ibn Ezra comments, "We need the tradition to know the [correct] interpretation of 'where he is' and also 'his place'. Similarly, [we need tradition to know] how much [is intended] by Isaiah's words (58:13), 'If you refrain from trampling the Sabbath', and what are 'your affairs'(ibid.). And all this is explained in our Talmud. May the Lord double the reward of the sages, who removed all doubt and established all things as they should be. The *peshat* of the verse is that the commandment 'let every man remain where he is' means that they should not go out to collect [manna] as they did." Thus, here the *peshat* of the verse is clear. But the tradition provides another *interpretation* of the verse that is sound and true. This interpretation is not congruent with the *peshat*, but it is a legitimate interpretation of the words of the verse all the same. It is not an *asmakhta*. Still, one could not authoritatively extract this interpretation from the verse without tradition. Without tradition, there would be no reason to prefer this interpretation to the *peshat* for legal purposes. Thus, midrash halakhah cannot provide the means to establish the relevant legal norms, but they can provide insight into the meaning of biblical verses.

A particularly interesting illustration of Ibn Ezra's thought on this subject emerges from a comparison of the two commentaries on Exod. 13:9. The verse reads, "And this shall serve as a sign of your hand." In the short commentary, which he wrote first, Ibn Ezra notes that two interpretations are possible. The first is to interpret the verse metaphorically, as one should interpret Prov. 3:3. The other is to interpret the verse literally as demanding the wearing of *tefillin*. He decides in favor of the second explanation since this accords with the tradition of the sages, and therefore the "first explanation is void." In the longer commentary he writes, "[T]here are those who disagree with our holy ancestors, and have said that 'sign' means reminder, in accord with Prov. 1:9 ... [he provides other examples of metaphorical usages drawn from the Book of Proverbs; the Hebrew for Proverbs can also mean parables]. But this is not the correct path. For at the beginning of the book [Proverbs] it says 'the parables of Solomon,' indicating that all that is mentioned is parabolic. But it is not written in the Torah that it is parabolic, God forbid. Rather, it is to be taken literally, and therefore we should not remove it from its *peshat*, for understanding it literally is not illogical, as is, by contrast, the verse 'and you shall circumcise the foreskin of your hearts' (Deut. 10:16) where reason demands that we understand it metaphorically."

Now, in both cases he opts for the traditional explanation, demanding the wearing of *tefillin*. Yet the criteria for the choice have changed. In the first comment, each explanation is equally plausible; there is no way to choose between them without tradition. In the second case, we have a literal interpretation that does not offend against reason, and therefore, we cannot allow any other explanation. Here, we invoke tradition to support the literal interpretation. The proper law is explicitly stated in the text, and the rabbis, the authentic bearers of tradition, are speaking in accord with the *peshat*, as in the citation from *Yesod Mora* above. While we can only speculate what occasioned the shift,[48] we can see here the distinction between tradition providing the proper interpretation when more than one is plausible, and tradition simply upholding the *peshat* against other less compelling alternatives. In any event, it is noteworthy that for Ibn Ezra midrashic principles are rarely, if ever, invoked to provide the proper interpretation. Thus, tradition can have important midrashic consequences; it can establish the appropriate interpretation of the verse.[49] In contrast, midrash halakhah as the Talmuds seem to recognize it, namely, creative human exegetical endeavor that goes beyond *peshat*, does not establish the meaning of the Torah. Thus, here again, midrash halakhah, so central to talmudic learning, is a trivial or secondary enterprise in which one reinforces tradition by finding scriptural triggers to state what one already knows. Whether this enterprise is designated *derash* or *asmakhta* seems to depend on its proximity to the meaning of the verse. The source of the interpretation, though, is always tradition. Thus, like Saadia, Ibn Ezra goes out of his way to note that some of the things earlier sources ground in midrash, such as the proper identification of vessels subject to impurity, actually depend on tradition, thereby implicitly repudiating the midrashic constructions.[50]

As we have seen, by the 1160s, a substantial "tradition" had developed within the Babylonian/Spanish orbit that largely trivialized, if not repudiated, the ubiquitous halakhic midrash of the earlier rabbinic sources. They ascribed to it no creative power; no new information was generated through it. They did so to combat Karaism and to accommodate their developing sense that rabbinic midrash stood at a great distance from the real significance of the biblical text. In this respect, there was great existential urgency to resolve important religious problems. After all, people change and ideas shift. If talmudic Jews needed to envision their legal system as *originating* from the biblical text by way of exegesis, Jews within the Islamic orbit, combating Karaism, had the directly opposing need. They could not come to terms with the exegetical contortion needed to ground rabbinic praxis in the biblical texts, nor could they differentiate it from Karaite exegesis without the epistemological boundaries of tradition. What made this position so paradoxical is that to "save" the Talmud its defenders ended up repudiating a substantial portion of its efforts. While rabbinic praxis was now properly grounded and justified, what of the tireless efforts on the part of the earlier sages to ground large portions of the law in the scriptural text? To bring the question into sharper focus, we must remember that all the figures discussed so far were rabbinic Jews, indeed, rabbinic leaders, fully committed to the authority of the Talmud and rabbinic law. Yet their sense of midrash and its place in the halakhic system is difficult to reconcile with the nature of talmudic discourse. The give-and-take of a substantial chunk of talmudic discussion, not to mention the documents of tannaitic midrash, revolves around the exegesis of Scripture and the conviction that Jewish law is derived from it. How does one make sense of the Talmud and the *Sifra* if midrash is a secondary, supportive discipline? How does one justify studying this largely trivial material?

It is important that we bear these questions in mind as we come to chronicle the next important chapter in this story. For in the work of Maimonides (1135–1204) we find an attempt to largely continue with the tradition discussed so far, while at the same time restoring some genuinely creative element to rabbinic midrash that would help account for a substantial part of rabbinic literature. Accomplishing this led Maimonides to such radical conclusions that, ironically, he heralded the decline of the tradition that extended from Saadia Gaon to his own efforts.

Moses Maimonides lived his entire life within the Islamic cultural field, first in Spain, then Morocco, and finally Egypt. He was familiar with all the major currents of Islamic and Jewish culture within that world, although there is some question regarding how familiar he was with the work of Ibn Ezra. In any event, there is no doubt that he was familiar with the direction of Jewish thought on the question of midrash outlined above, and in many respects he—and his son, Abraham[51]—were fully in agreement with it.

In the introduction to his *Commentary on the Mishnah*, his first major halakhic work, Maimonides describes five distinct categories into which the many laws are divided. He starts with the usual supplementary materials that God communicated to Moses at Sinai, which comprise a very substantial portion of the extrabiblical laws of Judaism. These divinely communicated explanations and definitions find allusions in the Scriptures, or can be related thereto by means of the hermeneutic principles. The distinguishing feature of this category is that there are no disputes regarding them, and they are rooted in the traditional passing down of this communication. "As soon as someone says, 'I have received such and such' all contention ends." An authentic tradition precludes dispute; thus, wherever a dispute is recorded, there can be no authentic tradition regarding the matter in question.[52]

The next category is the *halakhah le-Moshe mi-Sinai*, a law of Moses from Sinai. This is a law without a scriptural source, and again, there are no disputes surrounding such a law.[53] An example would be the requirement that the straps of the *tefillin* must be black.[54] Although Scripture demands the wearing of *tefillin*, it provides no description at all. Thus, the *halakhah le-Moshe mi-Sinai* fills the gap. Thus far, there is little deviation from the earlier participants in the discussion; the one important exception to this is the emphasis on the absence of dispute. Unlike Saadia, and like many Karaites, Maimonides could not reconcile "authentic tradition" with legal or exegetical disputes.[55]

This inability to reconcile disputes with tradition was no doubt a critical factor in the innovation Maimonides introduced with his next category. This category includes those things actually derived from the various hermeneutic principles and not grounded in tradition. Here disputes are possible and frequent.

Disputes and discussion are only possible with those things that are not received by tradition. Everywhere in the Talmud we find examination of the thought processes that led disputants to opposite positions; they ask "what is the point underlying their dispute" (*be-mai ka mipalge*), or "what is the reason of R. So and So" or "what is the distinction between them" (*mai beinaihu*).[56]

Further on, explaining how these disputes emerged, Maimonides recapitulates the standard talmudic treatment of the matter. He writes that after the time of Hillel and Shammai, when students were less distinguished than their predecessors, and different modes of learning spread,

disputes emerged among them in their deliberations (*masa u-matan*) regarding many issues, for each one reasoned according to his own intellectual capacity and the principles known to him. And we cannot fault them for this, for we cannot force two disputants to deliberate on the intellectual level of Joshua and Pinḥas. Nor may we cast doubt on the substance of their disagreement simply because they are not like Shammai and Hillel, or superior. For God, may he be exalted, did not demand this of us. Rather he demanded that we heed the sages of a given generation. . . . In this way disputes emerged, not because one or the other erred regarding the tradition.

Maimonides appeals directly to talmudic discourse to deny that all the exegeses of the sages are really the products of tradition. The give-and-take of talmudic discussion makes clear that different sages understood the Torah differently, as their minds worked in various ways, in accord with different intellectual capacities. For Maimonides, disputes, by definition, are incompatible with authentic traditions. Yet, rabbinic literature records hundreds of disputes, rooted in differing exegeses. The Talmuds, in particular, take these disputes very seriously, attempting to understand their underlying principles, and often attempting to limit and even dissolve the disputes. What emerges from this is the undeniable fact that these exegeses are not shaped by tradition, but are the result of the rabbinic manner of reading the Torah.

The presence of disputes and the nature of talmudic discourse made it impossible for Maimonides to consider the laws (presented as) derived from exegetical principles as part of the authentic tradition that God communicated to Moses. At the same time, these same disputes, and Maimonides' own sense of the meaning of the biblical text, made it impossible for him to consider these exegeses as actually unlocking the secrets of Scripture. They were the reading of one or more people, a reading ultimately confirmed by the majority (theoretically, anyway),[57] but one could not definitively affirm that they are part of Scripture's message. Other exegeses are theoretically possible. These exegeses are, thus, neither the product of tradition, nor the decoding of the actual meaning of the Torah; and yet they comprise, in the aggregate, a massive portion of rabbinic endeavor. How then are they to be understood?

The effort to sort out the difficulties of the previous paragraph is what led Maimonides to the radical formulation found in the second principle of his methodological introduction to his *Book of the Commandments*. There Maimonides states that all laws derived from the exegetical principles of the rabbis are of rabbinic authority (*mi-derabbanan*), rather than of scriptural authority (*mi-deoraita*).[58] They are not to be included in the enumeration of the 613 commandments, nor are they subject to the more severe limitations pertaining to laws of scriptural authority. They are simply of a different quality. Maimonides states emphatically that he does not intend to suggest that the exegetical principles, and the derivations they produce, are not true. They certainly are; they simply do not produce laws that are authoritative *mi-deoraita*.[59] This statement has perplexed his interpreters, starting with Naḥmanides. Yet its import seems clear. The exegeses are serious and legally repercussive, as any reader of the Talmud can see. They are not an ex post facto drawing of connections between traditional laws and verses.[60] Thus, they are important tools in applying Scripture. Yet, because they are the product of human intelligence, because they are subject to dispute, and because they are often quite distant from the plain meaning of Scripture,[61] they simply cannot have the authority of laws explicitly stated in Scripture, or laws that are part of the tradition originating from Sinai. They are, therefore, of rabbinic authority.

As stated thus far, there is still considerable distance between Maimonides' formulation and talmudic discourse. For, as every reader of the Talmud knows, many laws derived from exegetical principles are specifically identified as authoritative *mi-deoraita*, or are clearly subject to certain punishments applicable only to laws bearing that authority. To account for these, Maimonides insists that whenever the Talmud identifies something as part of Torah, it does so on the strength of tradition, not exegesis. That is, the same old argument reappears, but its scope is radically limited. Exegeses presented in rabbinic texts, whose "results" nevertheless have the status of *mi-deoraita* are, ipso facto, part of tradition. The exegeses are simply supports, concocted by humans (and thus subject to dispute) to display the wisdom of Scripture. They cannot produce laws of scriptural authority.

With this last proviso, Maimonides is readily seen to be part of the tradition extending from Saadia to Ibn Ezra. He too insists that human exegetical endeavor cannot produce *divinely mandated* observances. The source of knowledge of the Torah is the plain meaning of its text and the tradition extending from Moses at Sinai. There is no other source. Unlike them, however, Maimonides will not deny midrash halakhah a central place in the Jewish legal system. Its centrality in rabbinic literature was too great for this thoroughly systematic mind to ignore. For Maimonides, human exegetical efforts do create laws that are binding on all Jews. What makes these often disputed laws authoritative, however, is the approval or acquiescence of the majority of rabbinic scholars. This approval is sufficient to make a law legally binding; it is insufficient to make it part of the Torah. Therefore, all laws that are truly the product of exegesis are *mi-derabbanan*. They have authority, and they are an essential part of the system, but they are not Torah.

While Maimonides' approach is more readily rooted in rabbinic literature than was the position of his predecessors, his radical reshaping of the contours of the Jewish legal system drew an immediate reaction. For Maimonides expanded the range of rabbinic law far beyond any previous conceptualization, and, obviously, greatly limited the range of biblical law. While the practical consequences of this are probably far less significant than the reaction might lead one to believe,[62] it is clear that with this conception Maimonides touched a theological nerve, and still failed to account for rabbinic discourse as understood by many. There ensued a reaction that was so strong and overwhelming that in a short time the tradition we have surveyed became very much a minority view until the seventeenth century in Western Europe and Italy, and until the nineteenth century in Central and Eastern Europe.[63]

While he was not the first to react negatively to Maimonides' conception, certainly Naḥmanides' challenge to it was to become the most powerful, and most influential. Moses Naḥmanides (1194–1270) lived in Christian Spain, where Karaism did not represent a particularly strong challenge to rabbinic Judaism. To be sure, an aggressive Christian community presented Spain's Jews with formidable challenges; these challenges largely revolved around the validity of Jewish praxis of any kind, proper interpretation of the prophetic portions of the Bible, and the aggadic portions of rabbinic literature. Thus, the theological challenges he faced were quite different from those confronted by his predecessors in the Islamic world.

He was one of the first Spaniards to be influenced by the dialectical methods of Talmud study that came to prevail in France and Germany a century earlier. These methods assumed the enormous authority of talmudic discussions and exegeses, and subjected talmudic inferences and distinctions to detailed analysis and comparison. For the most part, the Franco-German school took talmudic exegeses very seriously, seeing them as the creative sources of rabbinic law.[64] Naḥmanides thus approached the issue from a cultural perspective that differed significantly from what we have already seen.

To Naḥmanides, Maimonides' conception threatened to destroy the Talmud as an authoritative source of Jewish law. Anyone who could read and understand the Talmud could see the error of Maimonides' way. It at best trivialized, and at worst distorted, literally hundreds of talmudic passages. Furthermore, it denied what, to Naḥmanides, was axiomatic: the hermeneutic principles that the rabbis used to interpret the Torah were themselves imparted by Moses at Sinai.[65] That is, the oral tradition itself contained these principles. While for Naḥmanides, the oral tradition contained a certain amount of concrete legal information, its principal demand of the Jewish people was to search the Torah and interpret it. Maimonides' position was simply intolerable, "for if we say that hermeneutic principles were not received from Sinai [then] we were not commanded to interpret and apply the Torah with them. They are thus untrue, and the truth rests with the plain sense of the meaning of Scripture, not the product of exegesis. . . . [We have then] uprooted our tradition of the thirteen hermeneutic principles, and the majority of the Talmud that is founded on them."[66]

He proceeds to cite numerous talmudic passages that demonstrate that the products of exegesis are authoritative *mi-deoraita*, and are to be taken seriously as the source of law. All these passages demonstrate that Maimonides is simply wrong. Even those things learned by a *gezerah shavah*, which is often connected to tradition, are, according to Naḥmanides, the product of exegesis, not tradition.[67] As for the fact that rabbinic exegesis often seems at some distance from the plain meaning of the text, Naḥmanides is untroubled. He notes that verses can carry more than one meaning. "When the rabbis say that no verse may be removed from its plain meaning" this does not imply that no other interpretation can be valid. Rather, "it also can sustain a midrashic reading together with the plain sense, and it is not removed from either one of them, but Scripture can bear all, and both senses are true."[68] Thus, talmudic discussion makes plain that to the sages the "hermeneutic principles [and their resulting laws] are as matters explicitly stated in the Torah, and they interpret on the basis of their own understanding (*mi-da'atam*)" not on the basis of tradition. Much of what is considered scriptural law is actually produced by creative human exegesis, circumscribed only by the authoritative exegetical principles imparted at Sinai.[69] When for some reason a given exegesis is not considered as genuinely creative of scriptural law, the Talmud will so specify, identifying the exegesis as *asmakhta*. In the absence of an explicit talmudic identification of *asmakhta*, all exegeses and their resulting legal norms are considered of scriptural origin.

Unlike Maimonides, Naḥmanides is not even troubled by the presence of disputes, and the obviously real possibility of error that necessarily accompanies a system of law resting on human exegesis. In his Torah commentary on Deut. 17:11 ("you shall act in accordance with the instructions given you . . . you must not deviate from the verdict that they announce to you either to the right or to the left"), he writes,

"To the right or to the left." Even if they say regarding your right that it is left, or your left that it is right [listen to them]. These are the words of Rashi. This means that even if you think that they are in error, and the matter is as clear to you as the difference between right and left, do as they command; do not say "how can I eat this forbidden fat or execute an innocent person." Rather should you say, thus have I been commanded by the master, who has commanded all the precepts, that with all the commandments I should do as instructed by those who stand before him in the place that he has chosen; the Torah was given to me on the basis of their understanding, even if they err. This law is urgently needed because the Torah was given in writing, and obviously not all will agree regarding issues that will come up in the future; disputes would increase and the Torah would become several Torahs. Therefore scripture explicitly demands that we abide by the high court, that stands before God in the chosen place, in all that they say regarding the meaning of the Torah; the Torah is given on the basis of their understanding of it. . . .[70]

Naḥmanides had no doubt that extrabiblical law was derived from Scripture and that the Torah was given by God with the full understanding that it would be interpreted and mediated by religious authorities who might err at times. In no way did this fact compromise the religious significance of the Torah.

From the many talmudic passages he discusses, and the many more that he knows "contradict the words of the rabbi" (i.e., Maimonides), Naḥmanides concludes that Maimonides' position is thoroughly wrong. He concludes acerbically that "this work of the rabbi is sweet and delightful, except for this principle which uproots great mountains in the Talmud, and fells fortified walls in the Gemara. To students of the Talmud this matter is evil and bitter; it should be forgotten and never said."[71]

Naḥmanides' attack on Maimonides' position is punctuated with numerous talmudic references and with insightful discussion of certain talmudic passages. It is clear that Naḥmanides' treatment is much more in keeping with talmudic discourse, and the "intent" of the talmudic compilers than are the earlier treatments from Saadia through Maimonides. Thus, the position of Naḥmanides quickly came to prevail among Talmudists everywhere. Indeed, as Jacob Neubauer has chronicled, a veritable industry started up, extending from the fourteenth to the nineteenth century, devoted to proving that in actuality Maimonides agreed with Naḥmanides on the substance of the issue. Needless to say, such a position entailed considerable distortion of the relevant Maimonidean texts. Neubauer actually categorized the positions by virtue of their level of distortion. Whatever the level of distortion, all the sources examined by Neubauer find the simple meaning of Maimonides statements to be unacceptable. These statements, so understood, simply cannot be reconciled with the conception of Jewish law that prevailed in the rabbinic world of the Middle Ages. I do not intend here to repeat Neubauer's work, but I do think it would be helpful to provide the names of some of the figures discussed in his book: Simon ben Zemach Duran, Bezalel Ashkenazi, Samuel de Medina, Moses Isserles, Shabtai ha-Kohen, Malachi ha-Kohen, and Akiva Eger, inter alia. Indeed Neubauer provides a study of some the most important rabbinic figures of the fourteenth through nineteenth centuries, none of whom could accept what Maimonides was saying at face value.

One need not look only to sources that explicitly discuss the dispute between the two giants, as Neubauer does, to demonstrate the near-total victory of Naḥmanides' position. In the post-Naḥmanidean *responsa,* commentarial and even sermonic literatures, which were shaped by increased fealty to the direction of talmudic discourse to the exclusion of other considerations, the creative exegetical power of midrash halakhah went largely unquestioned. From R. Solomon ibn Adret[72] through the Ḥatam Sofer (1762–1839)[73] and beyond, the position represented by Naḥmanides, and the Tosafists who preceded him, reigned supreme, with few exceptions. There was a certain amount of information that God imparted to Moses orally, in order to facilitate performance of certain commandments, but the bulk of Jewish observance is derived from exegesis, commanded by God, on the basis of principles imparted by God. In particular, this view came to prevail within rabbinic circles in Ashkenaz.

Given that I seek to build here on what Neubauer has already done, it will suffice to provide two examples. The first is drawn from the talmudic commentary of one of the pillars of the sixteenth-century Polish Jewish community, Solomon Luria. In his commentary, *Yam Shel Shelomo,* Luria quotes Maimonides' opinion that we know that physical damage leads to monetary compensation even though the Bible reads "an eye for an eye" because it is a *halakhah le-Moshe mi-Sinai.* Maimonides writes, "Even though these things appear to be so from the written Torah, and they were all explicated by Moses at Mount Sinai, they are all *halakhah le-Moshe mi-Sinai* to us, and so it was seen by our ancestors, judging in the court of Joshua and Samuel, and in every court that arose from the days of Moses until our day."[74] To this Luria responds, "I do not understand his, for there are several *gezerot shavot* and several verses that the Talmud interprets regarding this matter. And why do we need a tradition handed down from one to the other in an unbroken chain? Perhaps it was difficult for him to strip the verse, 'an eye for an eye,' of its plain meaning on the basis of midrash, for in so doing one would provide an opening to heretics and Sadducees, and therefore he said it was a tradition (and this is the opinion of Ibn Ezra in his commentary); if so, in vain have they striven, for how can we say that an eye for an eye is to be taken literally?" For Luria it was clear that no one who knew the Bible well would take the verse literally. Luria proceeds to show why this is so, offering an interpretation of the Bible that he considers a persuasive explication of its true meaning, although the Talmud (BK 84a) objects to this exegesis. This objection, he claims, is based on the Talmud's desire to further refine the matter, but it does not truly overwhelm the exegesis. Even if it does, he continues, "If we believe in the objection of the Talmud let us then also perforce believe in its response [in which it establishes the point] by means of *gezerot shavot* and scriptural extraneities. Thus it is clear that *the words of the sages are sufficient without any tradition.*"[75]

Luria's retort to Maimonides is telling. He surmised that the latter, and Ibn Ezra as well (and he was no fan of Ibn Ezra's, as is well known),[76] was led to claim that monetary compensation was made a tradition (which Luria equates with *halakhah le-Moshe mi-Sinai*) by the desire to suppress any opportunities for Karaites (= Sadducees) or other heretics to say that Jewish law distorts the Bible. In so doing, however, Maimonides and Ibn Ezra in essence asserted that the extensive exegetical efforts of the talmudic sages were of no genuine value; the talmudic discussion is trivial, teaching nothing. This Luria cannot accept. From the relatively insulated cultural perspective of the sixteenth-century Polish rabbinic elite,[77] repudiating talmudic discourse to respond to the cultural irritation of Karaites or Muslims is self-defeating. The words of the sages are Torah, and one should not claim "tradition" when the Talmud explicitly provides exegetical foundations for a given law. To be sure, Luria himself seems to feel that the talmudic discussion is not completely on the mark, in that the Talmudists, in their interest to fully discuss all possibilities, do not consider monetary compensation to be the *peshat*; nevertheless, the fact that they provide various exegeses to establish the point makes one thing crystal clear: They did not have a tradition concerning monetary compensation. Thus the efforts by Ibn Ezra and Maimonides to claim that they did are in vain and lead to conclusions that are insupportable. For Solomon Luria no apologies for midrash halakhah are needed, and any effort to make the foundations of Jewish law more "rational" by eliminating the creative power of rabbinic exegesis must be vigorously combated.[78]

Our second example comes from the work of R. Yeḥezkel Landau (1717–93) of Prague. Writing some two centuries after Luria, Landau stated with equal force his belief that exegesis not tradition must be seen as the primary source of extrabiblical Jewish law. In the introduction to his talmudic commentary, *Ḥiddushe ha-Ṣelaḥ*, Landau engaged in a playful *pilpul* designed to explain why the oral law began with the tractate *Berakhot*. Within the context of this broader *pilpul*, Landau addressed the question of the source of the oral law. He wrote,

Perhaps it begins with the tractate *Berakhot* to connect the end of the written Torah with the beginning of the oral Torah, for they are integrally connected. The foundation of the oral law is the thirteen principles with which the Torah is interpreted, for on the basis of these principles the sages of Israel derived all the teachings of the oral law, with the exception of those that they received as a *halakhah le-Moshe mi-Sinai*—but the majority [of the teachings were derived] by means of the thirteen principles.[79]

He goes on to discuss the unique qualities of the Hebrew letters in numerological terms, apparently indicating the ease with which these letters accept multivalence.

To describe, then, the state of the question as we approach the modern period, I think we can say that the trivialization of midrash halakhah, represented by Saadia and Ibn Ezra, and the diminution of its authority, advanced by Maimonides, were definitively rejected by the vast majority of rabbinic scholars. As Jews became increasingly isolated from the philological challenges of Islam, and the religio-legal challenges of the Karaites, they felt free to return unabashedly to the dominant talmudic view of the emergence of Jewish law. Their interaction with Christians led to other important cultural shifts, but as regards the response to the question, "How do we know this?" they did not need to resort to apologetics. As we leave the Middle Ages, I think it is clear that the position I have called Naḥmanidean, which was shared almost unconsciously by his Ashkenazic predecessors, was clearly the traditionally sanctioned one on the question of midrash halakhah.

The Bavli and the Yerushalmi

Before proceeding to address the question of the place of midrash halakhah in modern Jewish culture, we should first examine the reception accorded the differing views of the Bavli and Yerushalmi on the place of midrash in tannaitic culture in the medieval period. This will allow us to frame a "traditional" view of the matter as we head into the modern period. It will come as no surprise to students of rabbinic literature that the Bavli's approach, which, as described in chapter 2, did not discern any distinctions between the systems of Rabbis Aqiba and Ishmael except as it pertains to *kellal u-ferat,* etc., came to prevail, without exception. Given the extent to which the Bavli dominated rabbinic learning in the Middle Ages, this is to be expected. It is nevertheless surprising that other than a stray reference here and there, the Yerushalmi's notion of the distinct exegetical systems of Rabbis Aqiba and Ishmael vanished as though it never were. Not only do medieval rabbinic scholars not accept the Yerushalmi's view, but they do not even attend to it.

There are at least four distinct bodies of literature that substantiate this claim. We shall turn first to the various chronicles of the rabbinic tradition, which emerged as a very important genre of Jewish literature as early as the tenth century and have remained so to this very day. We search this literature in vain for any reference to a systematic exegetical distinction between Rabbis Aqiba and Ishmael. Many of the references to these rabbis note that each is the *bar pelugta* (the frequent disputant) of the other, although Maimonides, in his survey of the tradition, seems to think that R. Ishmael was a student rather than a colleague of R. Aqiba.[80] In any event, it was generally recognized that these two rabbis were contemporaries, and often disagreed with one another. None of these chronicles notes that they assumed distinct approaches to Scripture, however. From the tenth-century *Seder Tannaim ve-Amoraim* and *Iggeret R. Sherira Gaon* on through the *Sefer Yuḥasin* of Abraham Zacuto (sixteenth century) to the *Seder ha-Dorot* of Yeḥiel Heilperin (seventeenth century) and the *Shem ha-Gedolim* of Ḥayyim Yosef David Azulai (eighteenth century), no awareness of this alleged distinction is exhibited. Now, some of these chronicles merely list names, and thus nothing can be argued from their silence. But others, such as the *Yuḥasin* and the *Seder ha-Dorot* give relatively lengthy reports of the lives of both Rabbis Aqiba and Ishmael, and review elements of their teaching. Even these either do not know the Yerushalmi's position or reject it to the point of considering it unworthy of mention.[81] Here the silence is telling.

The closest we may come to the Yerushalmi's position is the claim by Maimonides, in the brief chain of tradition with which he opens his *Mishneh Torah*, that both rabbis authored a *Mekhilta* on the entire Torah. Still, Maimonides does not claim that they were divided along the lines of distinct exegetical systems, and from elsewhere in his work, it is clear that Maimonides did not understand the distinction between the two *Mekhiltas* in this way.[82] I should add that, if Isaac Hirsh Weiss's conjecture is correct, Maimonides may have been preceded in this claim by the *Mevo ha-Talmud* attributed to Shmuel Ha-Nagid.[83] In any event, there is nothing in the remarks of Maimonides or, possibly, the Nagid, to indicate acceptance of—or even awareness of—the Yerushalmi's view of early tannaitic midrash. This claim of Maimonides was picked up by later Jewish bibliographers, but again with no sense that methodology was a fundamental dividing point between the *Mekhiltas*.[84]

Overall, the main concerns that animated the treatment of Rabbis Aqiba and Ishmael in the various chronicles that go beyond lists were identifying the students of Aqiba, and the relationship, if any, between R. Ishmael, Aqiba's contemporary, and R. Ishmael ben Elisha the High Priest, who presumably lived before the Temple's destruction in 70 C.E. The latter was considered by some to be the same person as the former, by others his grandfather. This question in turn led to extensive examination of the possible priestly descent of R. Ishmael.[85] These extended discussions make clear that the relationship between Aqiba and Ishmael's methods, and "schools," if indeed they had any, was simply not a major concern of the creators of this literature.

While the absence of any discussion of our issue in the chronicles literature may be due to a different agenda on its part, the same cannot be said for another body of literature that emerged in the Middle Ages. In this period, a number of works devoted to the principles undergirding rabbinic learning (*sifre kelalim*) were composed. The most significant of these that deal with rabbinic midrashic techniques (and not all do) is surely the *Sefer Keritut* of R. Samson of Qinon (fourteenth century).[86] Here the author deals with the techniques used in rabbinic literature to interpret Scripture (i.e., the so-called thirteen principles of R. Ishmael, as well as all the others). In this work, he devotes an entire chapter to a discussion of the acceptability of *lemed mi-lemed*, a derivation from a derivation. This discussion is nothing but a review of a lengthy passage in the Bavli, without the slightest hint that the Yerushalmi views the matter differently, claiming that R. Ishmael always regards such a derivation as illegitimate.[87]

Similarly, R. Samson treats the issue of availability in the formulation of lexical analogies from a perspective informed wholly by the Bavli. As discussed in chapter 2, the Bavli (Niddah 22b and ff.) identifies various positions on this issue, never entertaining the notion that one can create a decisive lexical analogy without at least unilateral availability (that is, the superfluity of at least one of the words forming the basis of the analogy). The Yerushalmi, on the other hand, conveys the impression that R. Aqiba does not require any availability in order to fashion an analogy beyond challenge. Again, R. Samson's work takes no note of this at all.[88]

Perhaps most telling is his treatment of the principle "the Torah speaks in human language." This principle is invoked to explain why a particular scriptural repetition is not interpreted as extending the purview of a given commandment. Now, the Yerushalmi claims that R. Ishmael categorically refuses to interpret such repetitions, while R. Aqiba insists that we must, although we should note that the Yerushalmi does not actually use the phrase, "the Torah speaks in human language." As we have seen, the Bavli's position on this is quite different; here the principle is attributed to various *Tannaim,* and to none of them consistently and systematically. R. Samson's treatment is guided exclusively by the Bavli; he seeks to make sense of the apparent inconsistencies in the Bavli's attribution of this principle to many different figures. Again here, he shows absolutely no awareness of the Yerushalmi's position.[89]

It cannot be said that this approach was in any way limited to scholars in Ashkenaz. Spanish scholars also followed the Bavli—and thoroughly ignored the Yerushalmi—in all these matters. This can be seen from the *Halikhot 'Olam* of Yehoshua ben Yosef Halevi, a North African scholar who studied in Castile in the time of Yiṣḥaq Kampanton.[90] The discussion of scriptural exegesis in this work basically follows the pattern set by *Sefer Keritut*, and as pertains to our issue does so without deviation.[91] This work has been published accompanied by two commentaries deriving from Spanish circles, one, *Kelale ha-Gemara* by Joseph Karo, and one, *Yavin Shemuah*, by Shelomo Algazi. In these commentaries as well, there is no deviation from the vision of the Bavli as it pertains to the distinction between Rabbis Aqiba and Ishmael. In addition, we should consider the work of Aharon Ibn Ḥayyim, a Moroccan Jew who flourished at the turn of the seventeenth century, whose edition of and commentary on the *Sifra*, *Qorban Aharon*, has become classic. He prefaced the commentary with a separate work devoted to a discussion of the thirteen principles of R. Ishmael entitled *Midot Aharon*. Here again, we find no concern with the Yerushalmi's distinctions, even though Ibn Ḥayyim was well aware of disputes surrounding the hermeneutic principles. Even the dispute concerning *kelal u-ferat/ribui u-miyyut* is seen by Ibn Ḥayyim as a divergence of opinion between R. Aqiba and R. Eliezer, not Ishmael.[92] Further, Ibn Ḥayyim states categorically that everyone agrees that a *gezerah shavah* cannot be definitively learned when neither of its components are deemed available, despite an explicit statement in the Yerushalmi that R. Aqiba does indeed disagree.[93]

The *Yad Malachi* of Malachi ben Ya'aqob ha-Kohen, an eighteenth-century Italian Jew, while devoted primarily to halakhic rather than exegetical rules, nevertheless contains reflections on some of the latter as well. Here, again, there is no mention of any of the Yerushalmi's claims regarding availability and *gezerot shavot*, the disagreement regarding *lemed mi-lemed*, nor the Yerushalmi's view that only R. Ishmael claims *ein onshin min ha-din* (one cannot be punished on the basis of an argument a fortiori).[94] For the purposes of this work's discussion of these principles, the Yerushalmi might well not have existed.[95]

In addition to the chronicles and *sifre kelalim*, the various Hebrew bibliographies that emerged in the late Middle Ages also contribute to our story. Specifically, the various entries on the *Mekhilta*, *Sifra* and *Sifre* show once again the extent to which the view of the Yerushalmi and of modern scholars was ignored by the medievals. Modern scholars have argued, on the basis of the Yerushalmi, that we must distinguish among these presumably tannaitic texts. For the *Mekhilta* of R. Ishmael and the *Sifre Numbers* allegedly reflect the system of R. Ishmael, while the majority of the *Sifra* and *Sifre Deuteronomy* reflect the system of R. Aqiba. The bibliographies show that the medievals knew nothing of this. This fact is not by itself surprising; but the bibliographies show more, for they indicate that their authors were not at all concerned with any distinctions between the rabbis in question.

The *Sifte Yeshenim* of Shabtai Bass, for example, notes that the *Sifra* was attributed by some to the *Amora* Rav, and by some to the *Tanna*, R. Yehudah.[96] It in any event reflected the views of R. Aqiba's students, who, he claimed, used the principles of R. Ishmael to interpret Scripture.[97] Similarly, his entry for the *Sifre* argues that it was authored by R. Shim'on, a student of Aqiba.[98] He shows no sense that the *Sifre Numbers* and the *Sifra Deuteronomy* are qualitatively distinct; both are seen as representing the students of R. Aqiba interpreting the Torah on the basis of the principles of R. Ishmael. Certainly, someone whose thinking was shaped in any way by the Yerushalmi could be expected to raise questions regarding such a description. Yehiel Heilperin, in the bibliographical section of his *Seder ha-Dorot*, follows Bass quite directly in his entries for these works, as indeed he does with most bibliographical matters. Further, while Azulai, following *Yad Malachi* (# 256), recognizes that the matter is more complex than Bass and Heilperin allow, he too notes no distinction between the two *Sifres,* nor between the systems of Rabbis Aqiba and Ishmael that supposedly are reflected in them.[99] Finally, the *Rav Pe'alim* of R. Abraham, the son of the Gaon of Vilna, also shows no awareness of any distinctions among these texts.[100] Thus, in the more important bibliographies produced by the world of traditional rabbinic scholarship up to the threshold of the modern age, there is no attention given to the Yerushalmi's view of Rabbis Aqiba and Ishmael.[101]

We come finally to the commentarial literature. The literature is too vast for me comfortably to make any definitive statement without qualification. Still, whatever the limitations of my own expertise here, the authors of the various works referred to above all claim a high level of expertise in the commentarial literature, and yet none of them comes away with any concern for the Yerushalmi's view of our issue, as we have seen. This fact gives me greater confidence in saying that the Yerushalmi's position had a negligible impact on the commentarial literature that shaped the medieval world's understanding of rabbinic culture. Indeed, the only important comment with which I am familiar is that found in the *Tosafot Hadashim*[102] on Keritot 11a, which argues that whenever the Bavli refers to "one who says" (*man de-amar*) the Torah speaks in human language, it always intends R. Ishmael, and whenever it speaks of "one who says" the opposite, it always intends R. Aqiba. This identification is made explicitly on the basis of the Yerushalmi, and represents the Tosafist's effort to reconcile the two Talmuds as much as possible. But this comment was itself unknown or ignored, and exercised no influence on anyone's thinking about the issue of "the Torah speaks in human language," or on any other aspect of rabbinic hermeneutics.[103] To provide but one example beyond those found in the notes to chapter two of this book, R. Yom Tov al Ishbili (Ritba) explains R. Aqiba's exegesis of the phrase *ish ish*, noting that it is based on a particular assumption. Were that assumption not sustainable, R. Aqiba would have to learn something else from the repetition, or he could simply say, "the Torah speaks in human language."[104] The recent annotator of Ritba's work, Raphael Aaron Yaphan expresses his perplexity at this remark, since he knows that Aqiba would not adhere to the principle that "the Torah speaks in human language," and states that Ritba's remark "requires investigation."[105] As far as I can see, the comment requires no investigation at all. Ritba's understanding is fully shaped by the Babylonian tradition, which assumes as a matter of course that R. Aqiba would say, "the Torah speaks in human language." The comments in the *Tosafot Ḥadashim* stand alone and ignored; the comment of the Ritba represents the nearly unanimous opinion of medieval commentators. While I do not doubt that others more expert than I can identify a few more stray remarks like those of the *Tosafot Ḥadashim*, I am confident in saying that they exercised little or no influence on the thinking of Talmudists before the rise of *jüdische Wissenschaft*.

Now, the fact that the Bavli's view came to prevail is in no way surprising. After all, the Bavli's view on just about everything prevailed over the Yerushalmi's. Further, while the debate regarding how well known the Yerushalmi really was within the world of rabbinic learning goes on, there is no doubt that the Yerushalmi was much less studied and generally known than the Bavli was. If Solomon ibn Adret exaggerated when he said that there was but one a generation who had expertise in the Yerushalmi's textual traditions,[106] certainly there is ample reason to question how well known the document in its entirety actually was, and whether complete texts of it were generally available to scholars before the introduction of printing. Furthermore, the Yerushalmi was generally studied for the purpose of shedding light on the Bavli, and not as an independent document worthy of study in its own right.[107] Thus, we would expect the Bavli to prevail.

That having been said, it is still surprising that the Yerushalmi's understanding is so universally *ignored*, as opposed to rejected. After all, while less popular and probably less available, the Yerushalmi was certainly known throughout the Jewish world in the Middle Ages.[108] The explanation for the near-total absence of consideration of the Yerushalmi's view must go beyond the factors mentioned in the previous paragraph. I would tentatively suggest that this near-universal ignoring of the Yerushalmi is related to the increasingly discernible need on the part of many rabbinic scholars to argue that all the hermeneutic principles of the rabbinic tradition are *halakhot le-Moshe mi-Sinai*, laws of Moses from Sinai. Already Rashi (1040-1105) articulates this view in his commentary to Bavli, Pesachim (24a), inter alia.[109] Similarly, this view was maintained by such luminaries as Maimonides,[110] Nahmanides,[111] R. Samson of Qinon,[112] Joseph Albo (c. 1380–c. 1444),[113] and R. David ibn Zimra,[114] on through the Gaon of Vilna, and many others.[115] As such, disagreements regarding these principles and their applications must be dissolved.[116] Even the disagreement between Rabbis Aqiba and Ishmael regarding *kelal u-ferat u-khelal*, which is well attested in the Tosefta and both Talmuds, is diminished or ignored in the literature we have surveyed. The introduction of the Yerushalmi's conception, with its assumption of a clear dispute regarding numerous principles and their applications, even for the purpose of rejecting it, might have been seen as creating serious theological problems.

Be that as it may, if we wish to frame a traditional view of the issue as we head into the modern age, there can be no doubt that in pre-modern rabbinic scholarship Rabbis Aqiba and Ishmael, while seen as frequent disputants, were not seen as separated by the methodological divide the Yerushalmi posits. This view simply disappears from the landscape of rabbinic learning. Just as Nahmanides prevailed over Maimonides, the Bavli prevailed over the Yerushalmi, and far more completely.

5 • At the Dawn of a New Age

THE UBIQUITY OF MIDRASH halakhah in rabbinic documents played a significant, often unrecognized, role in the processes of modernization affecting the Jews. In saying this I do not mean in any way to downplay the various factors—political, economic, intellectual, cultural or social—to which Jewish historians have pointed in their descriptions of modern Judaism. Nor do I think it can be said with certitude that the Jewish paths to modernization would have been significantly different had rabbinic Judaism somehow developed all its practices and beliefs without even one instance of "peculiar" exegesis. For, clearly, the modernization of Jewish societies, as with non-Jewish ones, came about as a result of the complex interplay of the many forces enumerated above, with some displaying greater strength in one place and time, while others seem to dominate the process elsewhere. In sorting out the relative weight of these various factors, it is certainly difficult to determine what role was played by the intellectual forces that called much that was previously sacred into question. It is more difficult yet to determine the extent to which discomfort with rabbinic exegesis played a genuinely creative role in the religious shifts of the period. Thus, in discussing midrash halakhah and modernity, I do not claim that Jewish modernity was necessarily fashioned by the intellectual challenges of distinctly nonmodern forms of exegesis. What is undeniable, however, is that many modernizing Jews who consciously moved away from "tradition" as they understood it—even if only to restore a more authentic tradition—routinely justified this path, as had other "heretics" before them, by claiming that Jewish praxis and social ideals were rooted

103

in a defective reading and application of the Bible, and therefore ought
to be rejected or recast. That is, whatever concerns may have shaped
their thinking and behavior, when it came time to explain them they
turned to the claim that extrabiblical Judaism was without proper foundation. Neither the historical claim that the written revelation was accompanied by an oral one, nor the stance that the biblical text could be
interpreted by the hermeneutic principles of the rabbis was seen as particularly compelling.

While the foundations of extrabiblical Judaism had been challenged
before, as we have seen, most scholars agree that a new kind of challenge emerged in the seventeenth century, primarily in England, Italy
and Holland, and in some parts of France and Germany as well. The
seventeenth century in general witnessed major intellectual shifts in
scientific and historical thinking, shifts that would inevitably have had
an impact on those Jewish communities in which familiarity with the
general environment was not unusual.[1] In addition to these general
shifts, the seventeenth century saw the return of many Marranos to
Jewish communities, Amsterdam in particular,[2] as well as the rise of
Sabbatianism.[3] Beyond that, in the Italian communities, the residual
intellectual effects of Renaissance humanism were still to be felt.[4] This
meant that many individuals who approached Jewish sources did so
from a variety of perspectives, which often challenged prevailing assumptions.

Most scholars would agree, I think, that the impact of returning
Marranos was of enormous importance in shaping new intellectual
challenges for the "established" Jewish communities and their leaders.
As Yosef Hayim Yerushalmi put it, "By virtue of the years each had
spent in the Peninsula, these former Marranos constituted the first considerable group of European Jews to have had their most extensive and
direct personal experiences completely outside of the organic Jewish
community and the spiritual universe of normative Jewish tradition."[5]
They came with various levels of Judaic knowledge, but it is safe to say
that few, if any, came with extensive knowledge of postbiblical Jewish
practices and beliefs. While it appears that most did successfully integrate within their new Jewish communities in Amsterdam, Hamburg,
London, Venice, and Verona, and elsewhere, there were some who
simply could not make the transition from overt Catholicism/crypto-
Judaism to overt Judaism with all its detailed practices and beliefs.

The oft-cited description of the situation by Isaac Orobio de Castro
(c. 1617–87), himself an ex-Marrano, anticipates the claims of modern
scholars in seeing in the Marrano experience the source of heresy. He
indicates that while some Marranos fully returned to the faith of their
ancestors, others who had studied "various profane sciences" were too

proud and haughty to accept instruction in anything. "It seems to them that their reputations as learned men will diminish if they allow themselves to be taught by those who are truly learned in the Holy Law." Within this second group he goes on to delineate three distinct forms of religious doubt. There are the "unspeakable atheists" who deny Sacred Scripture; there are those who believe in God and acknowledge the sanctity of Scripture but deny the oral law, understood as the explanations of the law that God himself has imparted; and there are those who believe in both the written and oral laws, but deny the various "fences" that the rabbis have constructed around the law.[6] This last category, Orobio asserts, is itself quite dangerous, in that the onset of denial of rabbinic authority grows in time, such that those in the third category eventually move "up" into one of the other categories. In the end, "atheism" awaits all these heretics.[7] Yet, for all that modern scholars have echoed Orobio's view regarding the source of heresy, and for all that they have focused on the questions surrounding the oral law, the extent to which discomfort with midrash played a role in the intellectual rejection of rabbinic Judaism has gone unnoted. It is the intent of this chapter to demonstrate that a fundamental part of the debates of the seventeenth century revolved around the viability of a religious praxis rooted in rabbinic exegesis.

Uriel da Costa

In describing the heretical tendencies among ex-Marranos, scholars have pointed to the life and writings of Uriel Da Costa as paradigmatic. This is so despite the fact that we confront serious difficulties in determining precisely what Da Costa actually wrote and what he actually experienced. Until recently it was assumed that we had three works detailing Da Costa's views and attitudes, namely his autobiography, *Exemplar Humanae Vitae*, his "Theses Against the Tradition," and his argument against the belief in the immortality of the soul preserved in Samuel da Silva's polemical response to it. Questions have been raised regarding all of them. The autobiography may actually be a biography by another hand, and in any event is certainly not entirely accurate on the basic point of how much Da Costa actually knew upon his return to Judaism.[8] The "Theses" may or may not have been written by Da Costa; they may have been written by the author of the Hebrew work *Magen ve-Tsinnah*,[9] who may or may not have been the Venetian rabbi Leone de Modena. Similarly, the specific arguments against the immortality of the soul may not be fully and faithfully preserved by da Silva.

What emerges from this recent research is that we can no longer accept at face value a claim made in Da Costa's alleged autobiography. Upon arriving in Amsterdam, he says,

I had not been there many days, before I observed, that the customs and ordinances of the modern Jews were very different from those commanded by Moses. Now if the law was to be strictly observed, according to the letter, as it expressly declares, it must be very unjustifiable in the Jewish doctors to add to it inventions of a quite contrary nature. This provoked me to oppose them openly, nay, I looked upon it as doing God service to defend the law with freedom against such innovations.[10]

It is now quite clear that Da Costa knew perfectly well that "modern" Judaism entailed practices that went beyond the letter of the biblical text before he arrived in Amsterdam. He was thus no more shocked to find rabbinic (i.e., extrabiblical) practices going on in Amsterdam than Captain Renault was to discover gambling going on in Rick's Casablancan café. Nevertheless, Yirmiyahu Yovel is no doubt justified in claiming that Da Costa would certainly have been unaware of the extent to which practices not directly referred to in the Bible had come to dominate the nature of Jewish praxis.[11] Thus, it was not the fact that they were doing things not expressly commanded in the Bible that probably perplexed Da Costa, but rather the extent to which they were doing scarcely anything that was "expressly stated" in the Bible, in the manner that was "expressly stated" in the Bible. Further Yovel makes a strong case that Da Costa expected to find a Judaism more easily reformed than the seventeenth-century Catholicism from which he defected. He thought he would find Jews to be more reasonable than the Catholics, and in this expectation he was disappointed.

Nevertheless, we must note that whatever he expected, his objections to what he saw are presented in terms of a biblical literalism that Jews had abandoned. To Da Costa, it was clear that Jews had moved far beyond what God had commanded; they had interpreted the text in a manner that violated what the text itself "expressly declared." Indeed, for Da Costa, at least when, as a Judaizer,[12] he first encountered Judaism, the literal sense of the Torah governed all, including apparently what other books were authentically part of Sacred Scripture.[13] This literalism was not viewed by Da Costa as one important level of meaning; the literal meaning was the only level on which one could legitimately read the Bible. That is, Da Costa's literalism presupposed that the biblical text communicated its ideas in a manner consistent with other texts, namely in human language; one could assert that it "expressly declared" not only its rules and imperatives, but even the

manner in which it was to be understood. It was an "expressly declared" imperative of the biblical author that the text be interpreted
literally. The rabbis, or more accurately, the Pharisees,[14] failed to understand this, and produced a Judaism that was theologically and practically absurd.[15]

Whether or not they fully reflect the thoughts of the same person
described in the *Exemplar*, the same point appears in the arguments
against the immortality of the soul attributed to Da Costa. There the
argument is advanced that nowhere does the Torah mention this doctrine, and nowhere does it speak of any kind of afterlife. The rewards
and punishments envisioned by the Torah are all this-worldly. Thus,
only the position attributed to the Sadducees, who allegedly denied
any such doctrines, could be accepted. Da Costa acknowledged that he
could say nothing of the Sadducees that was historically verifiable, but
even without   historical evidence he could determine what biblical
works and ideas they rejected by evaluating the material itself from a
"Sadducaic" perspective.[16] Thus, in this challenge to the belief in the
immortality of the soul, we find a starkly literalist approach to the
Pentateuch that allows for nothing not explicitly stated therein to be
granted any legitimacy as a doctrine of faith or practice.

Similarly, in the "Theses Against the Tradition" we find, yet again,
a strongly literalist approach that rejects all rabbinic expansions of the
field of biblical law. The seventh thesis provides the most general enun-
ciation of the principle:

It is by itself enough to cause the destruction of the fundament of the Torah if
one says we should interpret the ordinances of the Torah according to oral
deliveries and that we must believe in the latter as one believes in Moses' Torah
itself and to hold them to be true and hereby creating changes to the Torah and
creating a new Torah *opposing to the real one.* It is impossible that a verbal
Torah exists for the following reasons:

1. From the Torah one cannot perceive that another Torah exists. . . . Even
if some word in the Torah would let us think so, it would not prove it. . . .

2. It appears from the Torah that there is but nothing besides the Torah
itself and that we have to go by the words of it and by nothing else. . . .

After we have now explained that no other Torah and no other commentary but the written ones came from God, the so-called verbal deliveries in
regard to the above-mentioned can only have been man-made. Setting aside
that it means an important breach if one would give to people occasion to
deviate from Moses' Torah, to explain and offer man-made explanations instead of the ones given by God to teach and proclaim, . . . it would mean a
great denial. It would make the word of God equal to that of man by saying
that we are obliged to keep all the Laws of the Talmud as the Torah of Moses.[17]

According to this, no expansion of the biblical text, whether on the basis of tradition or exegesis, can have any religious legitimacy. And indeed, in the other theses we find the author challenging a range of practices and interpretations that run counter to the literal meaning of the text. Among these are the standard rabbinic opinion that "an eye for an eye" intends monetary compensation; that circumcision requires two distinct procedures;[18] and that the sign referred to in Exodus 13, Deuteronomy 6 and Deuteronomy 13 actually refers to something physical, namely *tefillin*. All these interpretations and others are denied by the author of the "Theses," since they all run counter to the plain meaning of Scripture. Note that to the author of the "Theses" the clear meaning of Scripture in the case of the "sign upon your hand" is the metaphorical.

Thus, whatever the number of hands involved in the production of the "Da Costan" texts, the same basic stance is visible throughout. "Modern" Judaism represents a serious betrayal of the identifiable biblical legacy. Adherence to rabbinic practices represents a denial of the divine lawgiver's wishes, and should be resisted. Only conformity to the clear meaning of Scripture can be regarded as genuine divine service.

Before leaving Da Costa, it may be useful to note, in anticipation of what is to come, and mindful of Isaac Orobio's claim that one heresy leads to another, the next stages of Da Costa's spiritual odyssey. After discovering the full nature of the divergence between Judaism and biblical religion, Da Costa's journey continued:

Some time after this, as age and experience are apt to occasion new discoveries to the mind of man, and consequently to alter his judgment of things. . .; it was some time after this, I say, that I began to question with myself, whether the law of Moses ought to be accounted the law of God, seeing there were many arguments which seemed to persuade, or rather determine the contrary. At last I came to be fully of the opinion, that it was nothing but a human invention, like many other systems in the world, and that Moses was not the writer; for it contained many things contrary to the law of nature. And God, who was the author of that law, could not contradict himself, which he must have done, had he given to men a rule of obedience contrary to that first law.[19]

This determination took him full circle. He reasoned that since none of the religious systems available in Europe had any truth, he might as well return to the Jewish community for social reasons. He would observe the law, which he regarded as nonsense, on the grounds, "When in Rome, do as the Romans do." In the end he was unable to do this, and eventually, after suffering much indignity, took his own life.

Kol Sakhal

The challenge to rabbinic tradition emerged not only from ex-Marranos like Da Costa, who were devoid of significant rabbinic learning, but also from people who could claim substantial rabbinic erudition. In particular, the author of *Kol Sakhal*, an Italian Jew writing in the first quarter of the seventeenth century, was clearly a person of considerable learning, and yet was one of the most inveterate opponents of rabbinic exegesis and praxis. The entire second and third sections of this three-part work were devoted to showing the extent to which rabbinic interpretations and practices led one away from the proper realization of the Bible's meaning.

The author of this work—often thought to be the Venetian rabbi, Leone da Modena[20]—makes clear that he considers the biblical text to have been revealed by God to Moses. This is the only way that God's subjects could have known what the Divine Master wanted, "for the human intellect lacks the capacity to order human conduct by itself, to excel in its reflections and discern the good. . . . Therefore, it was necessary for God to reveal to people the proper way to conduct themselves under all circumstances" and to make clear the various rewards and punishments that accompany fulfillment of, or rebellion against, the divine will."[21] While the author goes on to question whether the biblical text has survived through the centuries fully unscathed, he nevertheless seems to feel that the Torah as we have it substantially represents God's revelation to his people.

The question that the bulk of *Kol Sakhal* wished to investigate is whether the "followers of the sages of the Talmud" actually observe these commandments as intended, or whether perhaps "we have deviated from the proper path."[22] He notes that there are many nations, and Karaites as well, that insist that they observe the Mosaic law properly; yet, each of them has developed its own system of observance and praxis, and all quite distant from what the Mosaic law actually intended to impart.

The author takes as his starting point the fact that on numerous occasions Moses refers to his teaching as *devarim* (words), intending to teach that one should interpret his text as one understands language generally—in accord with accepted linguistic convention, in conjunction with one's rational faculty. To the author of *Kol Sakhal*, the biblical text expressly states that it speaks in human language. What this means to our author is not that the text accommodates human limitations in such a way that its secrets need to be encoded within the text, requiring detailed philosophical or mystical hermeneutics on the part of specialists to locate its underlying message. On the contrary, this standard assumption of medieval Jewish thinkers contributes greater distance between the intent of the lawgiver and the understanding of the receiving community. Nor does his adoption of the notion that the Torah speaks in human language mean one should refrain from one form of midrash, as in the Talmud, thereby tacitly agreeing that everything else is fair midrashic game. To the author of the *Kol Sakhal* the fact that the Torah speaks in human language means that there is a simple and accessible interpretation available for almost all of the Torah's imperatives. It does not contain secrets that are concealed from the simple reader. Rather, it consists of simple "words" no different from those used in everyday speech. (That the belief that Torah speaks in human language necessitates a conventional linguistic approach is something that we shall encounter again.)

Further, not only does the Torah make clear that it is presenting its ideas in the form of simple speech, but it also insists that no one add or detract from these simply formulated imperatives. It forbids deviation from these imperatives to the left or the right. And yet, remarkably, not one of three major interpretive communities discussed—Rabbanite, Karaite, and Christian—has successfully achieved the appropriate interpretation of Scripture.

The Karaites have failed, for they ignore language's natural capacity to bear various tropes; they thus fail to understand basic nuances of the text. It is, writes the author, "like one whose father sees him wandering about and tells him 'do not move from your place' [and] who then wishes to stay in that place forever."[23] On the other hand, the Christians have failed to properly follow Scripture, for they tend to allegorize or "typologize" (*le-vaer derekh ṣurah*) everything. They thereby annul all that is difficult for them, stating that with the practical imperatives of the Torah the hidden meaning is sufficient and the manifest one makes no claim.

The rabbinic sages combine these two flaws, sometimes interpreting like the Karaites and sometimes like Christians. We see them interpreting like Karaites in their failure to discern that the "sign upon your hand" is to be understood as a metaphor, something that even the Karaites themselves, despite their general tendency, could figure out. We see them interpreting like Christians when they exempt themselves from the full range of difficult observances such as the fringes (*tsitsit*). The Bible demands that one place them on all one's garments, makes no temporal distinctions, and insists that they be blue. Yet the rabbis have interpreted the verses as requiring fringes only on four-cornered garments, and then only when the garments are worn during the day; they have also exempted one from dying the threads blue, claiming that the intended dye is no longer accessible. Furthermore, our author claims, they insist it is sufficient to fulfill the commandment if the fringes are worn only during prayer. They thus completely change the entire imperative under the guise of acting as interpreters and protectors of the biblical commandments.

From here he goes on to argue that through rabbinic interpretations of Scripture, dozens of clear biblical commandments, like *tsitsit*, have been thoroughly changed from the lawgiver's intent. Had the divine lawgiver intended what the rabbis say he intended, he would have said so explicitly, for he "had a full mouth to speak and a strong hand to write, and extensive wisdom to formulate commandments and express them in words that facilitate the achievement of the perfection of his matter and form . . . and not these childish, difficult observances that are derived from the text through forced interpretations that strive to serve absolutely no purpose."[24] In particular, chapter 3 of the *Kol Sakhal* reviews numerous rabbinic deviations from the proper interpretation of biblical commandments, acerbically claiming that these deviations lengthen the exile, and make it far more difficult to bear.

Now the author of the *Kol Sakhal* is sufficiently schooled in rabbinic apologetics to know that an attack of this kind on rabbinic midrash is usually met with the claim that all these interpretations are actually grounded in the imperatives of the oral tradition, handed down from Moses to Joshua and on and on, until "this very day." They are not really *interpretations* of scriptural language at all, and certainly these supplements to biblical commandments do not owe their origins to a reading of Scripture that is in any way comparable to Karaite or Christian appropriations of the Scriptures. We have already encountered a number of adherents to this position in chapter 4.

The author of *Kol Sakhal*, however, is not prepared to treat such claims with any more respect than he accorded rabbinic exegesis. For, in his view, a survey of the history of the Jewish religious tradition reveals plainly that there is simply no evidence for such an oral tradition extending back to Mosaic times. The Bible itself amply attests to the fact that the *written* Torah was largely forgotten in First Temple times, making it quite impossible that a putative oral one was successfully transmitted. Further, a review of Ezra's activity and the nature of Jewish sectarianism in Second Temple times reveals yet again that there was no oral tradition. Yet further, the fact that there are disputes on fundamental issues within the rabbinic estate indicates that the rabbis could not have been bearers of an authentic tradition that contained the various "explanations" of biblical commandments that characterize rabbinic Judaism. Indeed, even as late as the time of the talmudic commentators Rashi and Rabbenu Tam (eleventh and twelfth centuries), there was a fundamental dispute regarding the placement of the scriptural portions within the *tefillin*. How then could one claim that rabbinic Judaism was the expression of an ongoing tradition from Sinai? In addition to all this, our author takes note of the observance of ritual hand-washing, which Jesus obviously considered an innovation of the rabbis and therefore not binding on him.[25] That Jesus could have been so cavalier regarding this ritual indicates that in his time it was not generally accepted among the Jews. The fact that the rabbis felt the need to respond to such challenges, and that, alluding to Jesus, they could say, "all who mock [the commandment of ritual] hand-washing will be uprooted from this world" (Bavli, Sotah 4b), provides an important clue to the motives for the creation of the fiction of an oral tradition. For it is clear that things that are weak and prone to be seen as of limited authority need to be strengthened, and thus the rabbis were more stringent regarding these innovations than they were with what was actually stated in the Torah "in order to strengthen the belief in the hearts of the people that these things were from Sinai." For this reason we find them imputing to biblical figures a range of recently developed observances such as the *eruv tavshilin*, a device designed to permit cooking on the Festival days for the Sabbath.[26]

The point is clear. For the *Kol Sakhal*, there was no oral tradition extending back to Sinai; this was merely a convenient political myth designed to augment the authority of rabbis as they went about their rebuilding of Judaism. While there may well be a few traditional laws that are worthy of respect,[27] the basic source of Jewish praxis derives from a gross misappropriation of the Torah and the unharnessed rabbinic imagination, and therein lies the problem. If we may speak unhistorically, we can say that, for the *Kol Sakhal*, this misappropriation takes the worst that Karaism and Christianity have to offer. It thoroughly destroys the clear and accessible message of the biblical text and creates a legal system that is oppressive and contributes to Jewish misery in the exile.

David Nieto

The kinds of challenges adumbrated in the works of Da Costa and in *Kol Sakhal* naturally led to an extensive literature, much of it in Spanish, Portuguese and Latin, designed to respond to this and to defend the rabbinic tradition. Much of this literature has been surveyed by Shalom Rosenberg.[28] What emerges from Rosenberg's essay is that while there were some who defended rabbinic tradition by favoring the exegetical grounding of rabbinic law, most seem to have argued that the primary source of extrabiblical Jewish praxis is the tradition extending back to Sinai. That is, they seem to have accepted the linguistic critique of people like Da Costa and the author of *Kol Sakhal*, which stripped the biblical text of the capacity to be interpreted midrashically, or, at least, to produce definitive and binding conclusions. On the other hand, they seem to have felt that the historical critique, which challenged the claim to an authentic tradition, was far more vulnerable. This is demonstrably the case with someone like Isaac Orobio de Castro, who explicitly affirms that words do not carry the kind of multivalence necessary to extract the oral law from the written one. To claim otherwise would be contrary to the rules of linguistic convention and common sense.[29] To Orobio it was certain that the perfect God has perfectly revealed a perfect law—clear, comprehensible and absolute.[30] No ambiguities, no flaw. There is, thus, no basis for creative midrash. At the same time, he was quite emphatic that the extrabiblical norms of Judaism must surely have been communicated by God orally, the claims of Da Costa and *Kol Sakhal* notwithstanding. To be sure, Orobio's interest in denying the creativity of rabbinic midrash went beyond his desire to rest Jewish praxis on a linguistically acceptable and historically viable foundation; in denying any creative role to midrash, Orobio was certainly motivated by a desire to challenge the christological reading of Scripture that served, in his opinion, as a fundamental—and fraudulent—basis of Catholicism.[31] Just as those who, in an earlier age, wished to undermine the exegetical foundations of Karaism had to distance themselves from rabbinic midrash, so too did Orobio, in attempting to undermine the exegetical foundations of Catholicism, distance himself from this aspect of his rabbinic heritage.

The need for a historically sound response to the challenges of the seventeenth century was fully recognized by David Nieto (1654–1728), rabbi of the Spanish and Portuguese congregation in London, who wrote at the beginning of the eighteenth century.[32] In his *Ha-Kuzari ha-Sheni, hu Matteh Dan*, which was first published in 1714 and was written, like the first *Kuzari* of Halevi, in the form of a dialogue, he too rejected the path of seeing rabbinic midrash as the source of law. He saw in its deviance from the meaning of the biblical text an insufficient basis for defending the extrabiblical patterns of Jewish life. This is not to suggest that Nieto had sympathy for the position of the stark literalists. On the contrary, he notes that if one were to be too strict in one's insistence on literalism, one would have to allow the murderer of a woman to go free, since Scripture uses the word for man in stating the punishment for murder.[33] No, literalism is not acceptable, for it undermines the natural flexibility of language; it fails to recognize obvious tropes, and therefore misunderstands the Bible. Of course, Nieto is largely arguing against a straw man here, for it was the "literalists" like Da Costa and the author of the *Kol Sakhal* who insisted that the rabbis failed to recognize obvious metaphors, such as "And you shall bind them for a sign upon your hand." Be that as it may, Nieto is clearly sensitive to the natural boundaries of biblical language, and is not prepared to defend traditional rabbinic exegesis as the basis of Judaism.

Perhaps of greater importance, Nieto saw the danger in perceiving rabbinic midrash as a source of law, for such a view would mean Jewish law developed over time, and was shaped by the differing exegetical skills of the sages. In response to the argument by the as yet unconvinced Kazar that a particular remark by Maimonides suggests that "he believed that everything the sages said in interpreting the Torah derived from them, and not from a tradition from Moses at Sinai," the Ḥaver (Nieto) replies, "God forbid that a great sage in Israel would believe and say such a thing!"[34] If one looks at the history of Jewish practice, it is inconceivable that norms originated with the exegesis of a particular sage sometime in the early Christian centuries. Responding to the Kazar's claim that such a conclusion seems to follow from Maimonides, Nieto insists:

Even though Maimonides, of blessed memory, wrote that new laws were created by means of the hermeneutical principles that were not learned by means of tradition, do not think that those things learned by means of the hermeneutic principles were in fact innovations. On the contrary, in the vast majority of cases the legal norm was of great antiquity; the tannaim and amoraim simply learned the law that was known and performed from the time of the giving of the Torah through one of the hermeneutic principles. Consider the example cited previously of the Day of Atonement. It is inconceivable that from the time of Moses our teacher, may he rest in peace, it was unknown to all Israel what kind of "affliction" scripture demanded. Nevertheless, if you attend to the baraita [in which the manner of affliction demanded is derived from Scripture] would you say that it was unknown until the tanna who taught the baraita came and determined it? This is impossible. Thus, we must say that just as with the affliction of the Day of Atonement, which was long-established, the tanna wrote as if it were new, so too most of the things that are learned by the hermeneutic principles.[35]

Nieto goes on to address the exegesis designed to prove that the "fruit of a goodly tree" (Lev. 23:40) means an *etrog* (citron). It is impossible that this was unknown until the second Christian century, and therefore, once again, we must see the exegesis as a secondary phenomenon (a claim with which, in this case, Maimonides and most commentators would agree).

Within his frame of reference, Nieto's arguments are quite strong here; certainly the notion that these basic matters of Jewish law were undetermined until the tannaitic period is incredible. Whether the same argument actually can apply to "most of the other things learned by the hermeneutic principles" is another matter. The talmudic "evidence" for this claim is weaker, and Nieto himself acknowledges that perhaps they did learn something through exegesis, but even then such learning involved recovery of what was forgotten rather than something original.[36] In general, though, Nieto insists that what the sages "learned" through their hermeneutic principles was in fact received at Sinai, and transmitted from one generation to the next.[37]

Like the medievals before him, to make this argument work Nieto had to show historically that this was a credible view of the origins of extrabiblical practices. Rather than recapitulating the chain-of-tradition type of argument that had dominated this discussion, Nieto focuses on biblical "data" that ostensibly demonstrate the existence of an oral tradition. These include the presence of pre-Sinaitic laws, such as circumcision, that were orally transmitted until the time of Moses. At that point brief references were possible, for the orally transmitted laws would fill in the details. Other "proofs" include citations from Jeremiah (17:21), Ezra (10:3) and Nehemiah (10:30), inter alia, that display familiarity with norms not expressly stated in the Torah, and the presence within the Torah of norms that could not possibly be implemented without additional information. Having shown that there must have been an oral tradition, Nieto proceeds to show that the Mishnah represents that tradition. He works hard to limit the scope of rabbinic controversies and of sectarian disputes.[38] In all, it is clear that he felt the kinds of historical arguments advanced against rabbinic tradition could be effectively countered; it was thus not historically correct to see Jewish praxis as rooted in biblical exegesis.

From Nieto's point of view, however, negating the creative power of the vast majority of rabbinic exegeses did not make the phenomenon trivial. For these exegeses were needed to allow knowledge of the system to continue long after much of it was no longer practiced, i.e., after the destruction of the Temple and the exile from the land. What was known to the people who lived in the time of the Temple would have been forgotten by those who lived after it if the sages had not developed a means of preserving what was known and retrieving what was forgotten. Midrash halakhah was that means. Thus, while they did not create law, the exegeses of the rabbis helped preserve it intact.[39]

By arguing that the hermeneutic principles of the rabbis could allow for retrieval of that which was forgotten, Nieto is implicitly conceding that the exegetical method itself is capable of unlocking the

Torah's hidden significance, while at the same time maintaining that those hidden meanings are fully in accord with the tradition handed down from Moses to the ensuing generations. It is clear that, more than anything else, he wished to show that there was no innovation on the part of the rabbis.

Given that the hermeneutic principles played a critical role in preserving the oral Torah, they were of great importance, and needed to be shown respect. In an effort to uphold their dignity, Nieto closes his defense of the oral law with a brief commentary on the thirteen principles of R. Ishmael. Here he again insists that these principles do not create law, but that they are critical to fully understand the Bible. The point is summed up nicely by the Kazar, who is finally convinced:

Now I know that it is impossible to fully understand the Torah without these thirteen principles, and I also know that you were correct in what you said, that what appears to us as an innovation of the sages is not genuinely new; for there are many, many laws that are learned by means of the thirteen principles that perforce had to have been implemented immediately after the giving of the Torah.[40]

The Kazar closes by expressing his anger at those who mock the teachings of the sages of Israel; if only they were willing to consider these teachings dispassionately, he says, they would understand their truth and profundity and their doubts would evaporate.

In Orobio and Nieto, then, we find a revival of the kind of rabbinic apologetic characteristic of the encounter between Rabbanites and Karaites. Although more careful to create room for midrash halakhah as an important part of rabbinic culture, Nieto's reading of the theological needs of his day made it impossible for him to acknowledge even the possibility that Jewish law underwent changes in time. If the rabbis applied the exegetical techniques to the Torah for the purpose of determining law, the claims of the critics of rabbinic law would have historical foundation. Responding to cultural pressure, Nieto, like Saadia, felt the need to disinherit the exegetical process in order to uphold the legal norms that defined rabbinic Judaism.

Menasseh ben Israel

As the strand of Jewish apologetics culminating with Nieto was once again emerging in the seventeenth century as a powerful force, it seems to me that there were at least two individuals, Saul Morteira and Menasseh ben Israel, who arrived at the interesting conclusion that in looking to save the oral law by insisting on oral traditions from Sinai, one has in fact contributed to the undermining of the written law. That is, in accepting, at least tacitly, the linguistic critique of people like Da Costa and the author of the *Kol Sakhal*—a position that in essence states that the Torah speaks in human language, and therefore rabbinic Judaism must be understood as the biblical text supplemented by tradition—one exposes the biblical text to the dangers of criticism. Without an extensive hermeneutic apparatus, grounded in the conviction that the Torah does *not* speak in human language, the Torah, and the Hebrew Bible generally, appears as a text replete with contradictions, indeed, as a text that is incoherent.[41] The most comprehensive statement of this position was advanced by Menasseh ben Israel.

Menasseh ben Israel was born in Portugal in 1604. Escaping from the Iberian peninsula with his parents, he came to Amsterdam, there to take up traditional Jewish life, eventually coming to serve as a community rabbi. Defending the major tenets of Judaism became a central focus of much of his activity; nowhere is this better exemplified than in his *Conciliador*, designed to reconcile the contradictions in Scripture. While Menasseh ben Israel had other motives for writing his *Conciliador*,[42] certainly the primary one was to defend the biblical text against those who would attack it on the basis of its many contradictions, for, the "freethinkers, 'lovers of novelty' as Menasseh ben Israel called them, missed no opportunity of pointing out the contradictions in the Old Testament, and of casting doubt on the unity of the writing of the Pentateuch."[43] The work consists of four parts, the first appearing in 1632, the last in 1651. It was written in Spanish, with a Latin translation appearing almost immediately; an English translation of the entire work appeared in 1842. The book collects the many passages in which the Bible either openly contradicts itself or seems inconsistent in its approach to matters legal, cosmological, historical, and theological. In attempting to serve as the conciliator of these passages, Menasseh draws on a wide range of Jewish and non-Jewish literature; certainly, the former predominates, and serves Menasseh's secondary goal of displaying the power of Jewish wisdom before the Gentiles.[44]

From an examination of Menasseh's treatment of the legal contradictions and inconsistencies, it becomes clear that he could not countenance an approach to Scripture that did not recognize its distinct divine nature, and therefore the unique multivalence of its language. Neither the Torah nor rabbinic tradition could stand if each was perceived as a discrete corpus of information, simply supplementing the other. To be sure, Menasseh, like all rabbinic Jews, affirms an oral tradition from Sinai; he suggests that many of the extrabiblical observances of Judaism derive from it. But seeing the biblical text as devoid of multiple meanings rendered its understanding shaky, and seeing Jewish praxis as originating simply in the oral law represents a lower level of understanding. Rather the integrity of both written and oral laws depended on the authoritative exegeses of the rabbis, which allowed the Torah the flexibility to stand in the face of criticism and safeguarded the divine integrity of rabbinic praxis.[45]

This claim may be illustrated by examining his efforts at reconciling legal contradictions and inconsistencies. Like many before him, he notes that Exod. 13:7 and Deut. 16:3 demand that unleavened bread be eaten for seven days. On the other hand, Deut. 16:8 says, "Six days shalt thou eat unleavened bread." The reconciliation of this contradiction begins with this explanation:

Where contradictions occur in distinct and remote passages of the production of a human author, it may be attributed in some measure to his having forgotten what he had previously written, but such variations are never found in close approximation to each other. This being the case, how can such an error be applied to laws dictated by the Spirit of God? The admission of their unerringness requires, therefore, some explanation to reconcile these verses.[46]

Menasseh's explanation is clever in that while he obviously assumes divine authorship, he begins by showing that the nature of this contradiction and the proximity of the verses renders it impossible that a human author would have done something like this.[47] The very occurrence of the contradiction is only explicable if there is a divine author, incapable of truly contradicting himself.

In attempting to reconcile the verses, Menasseh cites five different possible explanations, two drawn from medieval commentators, one from the *Sifre,* one found in the *Yalkut Shim'oni,* and one that he apparently developed on his own. He sees the first reconciliation, drawn from the commentary of Isaac Abravanel, as the best. This explanation notes that the "seven day" imperative is given in the context of preparing the Passover sacrifice, while the "six day" imperative is addressed to the remainder of the holiday. It is as if the verse (16:8), coming after the description of the sacrifice, had said, "for the remaining six days . . ."

His reconciliation drawn from the *Sifre* is interesting and perplexing. He writes,

It is inferred in the Siphre, from these two passages, that the obligation of eating unleavened bread is only imperative for the first night of the seven days, but in regard to the others, the obligation was fulfilled by not eating leaven, and it was optional to subsist on any thing else. This is also conformable to the letter; although the first reason [that of Abravanel] seems the best.[48]

The explanation of the *Sifre* is the only one that has any normative force in Jewish law, and is clearly considered an acceptable reconciliation—that is, the multivalent language of the text can support it. Given that Menasseh's primary task is to reconcile the contradictions of Scripture, however, the normativity of the conclusion is not decisive in rating the potential reconciliations. In Menasseh's opinion, this is not the best reconciliation of the problem, but it will do. At the same time, of course, Menasseh affirms the normative judgment of this reconciliation. Be all that as it may, the passage serves as a good example of the way in which midrashic sources and methods provide Menasseh with ammunition in his battle to rescue Scripture.

Similarly, in focusing on the contradiction between Exod. 20:5, which states that God visits the iniquity of the fathers upon the children, and Deut. 24:16, which states (as we have had occasion to see before) that fathers shall not be put to death for children, nor vice versa, Menasseh considers a number of possible reconciliations. In this instance he is more enthusiastic in his endorsement of the normative conclusions—discussed above in chapter 1—drawn midrashically from the latter text.

But the other passage, saying the fathers shall not die for the children, nor the children for the fathers, they dogmatize differently, explaining it that the fathers shall not die by the hand of justice on the testimony of their children, nor the children on the accusation or testimony of their fathers, because it is unnatural, for as Don Isaac Abarbanel observes, nature prompts the parent to advocate the cause of the child, and the child that of the parent, therefore neither should be condemned on the forced testimony of the other; and it is added in the Siphre that the same rule holds good in respect of other near relations. This conciliation is very appropriate to the text. . . .[49]

While there are other ways of reconciling the two texts, the legally normative one has achieved an important insight into the nature of the parent-child relationship, and is therefore very appropriate to the text. Note that Menasseh does not feel constrained by the absence of any explicit reference to testimony or judicial proceedings, whereas many who are sympathetic to what he is trying to accomplish (and, it scarcely needs to be said, those who are antipathetic to his project) would no doubt retort that the words do not bear this interpretation.

The justification for this type of scriptural reading is provided by Menasseh in question 132 of the *Conciliador*. Here he juxtaposes the two clauses of Exod. 34:27, which reads, "Write these words, for by the mouth of these words . . ." This is a hyperliteral translation of the verse, and is inspired by a discussion in the Bavli (Gittin 60b). In this reading the two clauses contradict each other, for the first clause implies that the law was written, while the second (understood hyperliterally) implies that the law was transmitted by word of mouth. In the Talmud, the "contradiction" is reconciled, as we would expect, by invoking the two distinct laws, the oral and the written, and seeing this verse as proving the existence of the oral law. Further, the Talmud interprets the verse to mean that God commanded Moses to write only certain words to the exclusion of all others ("these" being an excluding term), while communicating other things, which may not be written.

Based on this talmudic passage, Menasseh sees the two parts of this verse as contradictory and reconciles them by citing the solution of the Talmud. He goes on, lest his audience regard the reconciliation as too facile, to explain more fully what this oral law is, how it functions, and why it is necessary.

He begins by noting that all other languages, having human origins, are necessarily monosemic. The Hebrew of the Bible, on the other hand, had the "Lord for its author and framer, and is thence called the holy tongue, as it proceeded from that consummate wisdom which is infinite; each word in itself contains the profoundest mysteries, so that it is impossible to be clearly comprehended."[50] The Bible is *not* written in human language, then, and cannot be understood within the normal linguistic framework pertinent to other documents in other languages. This leads Menasseh to construct a hierarchy of students of the Bible. The lowest level represents those who

attain the mere outward shell, that is, the superficial history, and occupy themselves in the endeavour to learn how things happened according to the literal record. . . .

Others employ themselves in studying the explanation of the precepts ceremonies, that is, the knowledge of the "Mishna" . . . called by some the Oral Law. . . .

And lastly, many aspire to the highest contemplation of the mysteries contained in the words, letters points and musical accents used in the construction of the text of the Law.[51]

He goes on to note that there are two divisions within the concept of an oral law, namely the Mishnah, which describes the concrete results of investigation, and the Kabbalah, encompassing the halakhic, aggadic, and mystical teachings inherent within the divine language of the Bible. Here the term "Kabbalah" includes two of the meanings that it carries in Jewish sources, namely rabbinic tradition and mystical tradition, as both are the product of the investigation of the unique language of Scripture. He proceeds with a detailed exposition of thirteen rules of mystical interpretation, which parallel the thirteen rules of halakhic interpretation.[52]

Menasseh has thus acquainted his reader with the method of the sages. He has shown to his satisfaction that "their knowledge is not only founded on reason, but deduced from the plain texts of Scripture, whence they collect, that there is no science or knowledge whatever that is not contained in the Law; from it, as from a summary of the whole, they derive and collect everything, and, by the grace of God, the reader will understand that not only these excellencies are spiritual, but that the Law comprehends and includes even others unknown."[53]

For Menasseh ben Israel, to see in the language of the Bible the language of human beings was to render the Bible incoherent. It would be replete with contradictions, which no sensible human could possibly reconcile. Only if we start from the assumption that the Bible communicates in its own unique language can it be understood, on all its various levels of meaning. Indeed, without the assumption that the Bible speaks in the language of God, it cannot even be understood literally. It would simply be incomprehensible. However, once we acknowledge that the Bible speaks in the language of God, it not only yields a coherent literal meaning, but allows for a far deeper understanding, whether halakhic or kabbalistic, of its words and letters. The oral law, understood as encompassing the entire range of Jewish learning, was founded on the exegetical skills of the rabbinic sages, and only on the basis of this oral law could the written law be comprehended and appropriated.

Benedict de Spinoza

Menasseh ben Israel's *Conciliador* represents a magisterial effort to keep the floodgates of criticism from opening. It never had a chance. Though many scholars, Jewish and Gentile, were highly impressed with it and recommended it with enthusiasm,[54] its a priori theological and linguistic assumptions could not hope to sway those committed to what at the time seemed a more rational and less metaphysical approach to texts and language. Indeed, as Anthony Grafton has put it, the seventeenth century was witness to an exegetical revolution;[55] this revolution stripped the Bible of its sacredness and perfection, leaving behind a flawed, at times incoherent, document. Desperate defenders of the text may have found Menasseh's arguments compelling, but to those prepared to subject the biblical text to criticism, its assumptions were passé. Obviously, if the Bible was no longer sacred, any exegesis grounded in the assumption that it was would appear as sheer nonsense.

In 1641, the midway point in the publication of the four parts of the *Conciliador*, Isaac La Peyrere, possibly an ex-Marrano, completed his *Prae-Adamitae*, a work devoted to showing that there were people before Adam, and that the Bible in fact does not provide a history of the entire world, but only of the Jewish people. This, for La Peyrere, was the only way in which numerous biblical passages could be understood in light of internal inconsistencies, and in light of other chronologies that extend much further back than the biblical one.[56] Furthermore, on the basis of the many inconsistencies in Scripture, La Peyrere concluded that Moses could not have written the Pentateuch; rather, "These things were diversely written, being taken out of several authors."[57] While these several authors made an honest effort to transmit accurately a genuinely divine revelation, copyists and scribes rendered the text hopelessly inaccurate.

Now, as our previous discussion has made clear, La Peyrere was scarcely the first to recognize the inconsistencies and discrepancies that led to his conclusions. What stands out in his work is the unwillingness to rely on the kinds of conciliatory exegeses that characterize the work of Menasseh ben Israel, and, indeed, virtually all traditional exegetes over the previous millennium and a half. For La Peyrere, however much the message may be infused with divinity, the biblical text represented the language of humans, a language ultimately corrupted by copyists and scribes. These conclusions are grounded in the exegetical revolution of the century, and in turn helped to advance that revolution. From within this revolution, rabbinic legal exegesis could only appear as foolish and unfounded.

In 1651, the year in which the last volume of the *Conciliador* appeared, Thomas Hobbes (1588–1679) published his *Leviathan*. While better known for its contribution to political theory, the third part of the work contains important reflections on the nature of the Bible and its origins.[58] Here Hobbes, too, insists that in interpreting the Bible, we are constrained by the normal patterns of language, and cannot try to read into the text philosophical or logical truths its language cannot sustain.[59] Acknowledging that discerning the political lessons of the Bible is critical to his enterprise, he states that he must attend not only to the natural word of God, namely, human reason, but also to the "prophetical" word (i.e., the Bible) as well.

Nevertheless, we are not to renounce our Senses, and Experience; nor (that which is the undoubted Word of God) our naturall Reason. For they are the talents which he hath put into our hands to negotiate, till the coming again of our blessed Saviour;. . . For though there be many things in Gods Word above Reason; that is to say, which cannot by naturall reason be either demonstrated or confuted; yet there is nothing contrary to it; but when it seemeth so, the fault is either in our unskillfull Interpretation, or erroneous Ratiocination.

Therefore, when any thing therein written is too hard for our examination, wee are bidden to captivate our understanding to the Words; and not to labour in sifting out a Philosophicall truth by Logick, of such mysteries as are not comprehensible, nor fall under any rule of naturall science. . . .

But by the Captivity of our Understanding is not meant a Submission of the Intellectual faculty, to the Opinion of any other man; but of the Will to Obedience, where obedience is due. For Sense, Memory, Understanding, Reason and Opinion are not in our power to change; but alwaies, and necessarily such, as the things we see, hear and consider suggest unto us; and therefore are not effects of our Will, but our Will of them. We then Captivate our Understanding and Reason when we forebear contradiction. . . .[60]

For Hobbes, the kind of exegesis so prevalent in rabbinic literature, as well as that which dominated medieval Jewish rational and mystical works, represented a failure to "captivate the understanding"—that is, to obey the inescapable demands of rational reflection on the meaning of a text. While, to be sure, Hobbes's polemical thrusts were scarcely aimed at Jews or Jewish literature, they nevertheless played an important role in defining the Bible as a document formulated in the normal patterns of human speech, rendering it immune to the kinds of interpretation that defined Jewish exegesis. The methods of reconciling contradictions that are necessary if one is to maintain the divinity of the text require a hermeneutics that extends the significance of words beyond their ordinary boundaries; only thus could one maintain the unity of, say, the Pentateuch. Hobbes would have none of this, and thus goes on to challenge the traditional assumptions regarding the authorship of many of the books of the Old and New Testaments. Hobbes' whole endeavor here depends on the notion that no reconciling hermeneutic that failed to respect the boundaries of language is admissible. He thus set the stage for the work of Benedict de Spinoza (1632–77), who in many respects completed the exegetical revolution of the seventeenth century.

On 28 January 1665, Spinoza wrote to the "very learned and distinguished" Willem van Blijenbergh, a believing Christian who had taken an interest in his work, "I confess, clearly and without circumlocution, that I do not understand Sacred Scripture, though I have spent several years on it."[61] What he did understand at that time, as he had written in a letter to the same Van Blijenbergh some three weeks earlier, is that "Scripture, since it is intended mainly to serve ordinary people, continually speaks in a human fashion."[62] It is clear that at this stage of his intellectual development Spinoza understood the notion that the Torah speaks in human language primarily in accommodationist terms.[63] As the last citation continues,

For the people are not capable of understanding high matters. Therefore, I believe that all the things which God has revealed to the prophets to be necessary for salvation are written in the manner of laws. And in this way the prophets wrote a whole parable. First, because God had revealed the means to salvation and destruction, and was the cause of them, they represented him as a king and lawgiver. The means, which are nothing but causes, they called laws and wrote in the manner of laws. Salvation and destruction, which are nothing but effects which follow from the means, they represented as reward and punishment. They have ordered all their words more according to this parable than according to the truth. Throughout they represented God as a man, now angry, now merciful, now longing for the future, now seized by jealousy and suspicion, indeed even deceived by the devil. So the Philosophers, and with them all those who are above the law, i.e., who follow virtue not as a law, but from love, because it is the best thing, should not be shocked by such words.[64]

In early 1665, Spinoza was still prepared to entertain the notion that the biblical prophets deliberately shaped their discourse to serve the needs of the masses.

For this reason he was unwilling to attribute to Scripture, he said, "that Truth which you [Van Blijenbergh] believe to be in it." Nevertheless, he continued, "I believe that I ascribe as much, if not more, authority to it, and that I take care, far more cautiously than others do, not to attribute to it certain childish and absurd opinions. No one can do this unless he either understands Philosophy well or has Divine revelations."[65] The import of this last sentence seems to be that one needs to be a philosopher to identify that which is absurd, and to know thereby what opinions *not* to attribute to Scripture, whatever the connotation of its language. For, Spinoza says, "I have never seen a Theologian so dense that he did not perceive Sacred Scripture very often speaks of God in a human way and expresses its meaning in Parables."[66] Interpreting the messages that were intentionally committed to parabolic form required an awareness of what was precluded by rational speculation; otherwise, one would attribute to Scripture "childish and absurd opinions."

While it is clear that by this time Spinoza had long since abandoned the metaphysical beliefs of medieval Jewish philosophy,[67] he was, it seems, still attracted to the essential strategic dogma of the world of medieval religious philosophy, namely, that wise prophets, who knew better, spoke in parables to accommodate the needs of the masses. They did not themselves actually believe that God is jealous, for such would be a philosophical absurdity, and yet they felt some useful divine purpose would be served by representing God this way.[68] Thus, at this stage of his career, Spinoza still seems to have felt that philosophy had an important role to play in shaping the interpretation of Scripture. On the other hand, it was already clear to him that Scripture could teach the philosopher nothing. "As for me, I have learned no eternal attributes of God from Sacred Scripture, nor could I learn them."[69] Philosophy shapes the contours of scriptural interpretation, but Scripture teaches the philosopher nothing at all.

Some time in the early fall of the same year, 1665, Spinoza resolved to write a work dedicated to explicating his conception of Scripture. As he explained, his hope was (1) to expose the prejudices of the theologians that hindered the spread of philosophy, and thereby to lead the intelligent away from them; (2) to disabuse the public of the notion that he was an atheist; (3) to argue for the freedom to philosophize and to express what one thinks.[70] Yet, in the four years that it took him to complete this project, Spinoza's thinking was to undergo a complete transformation.

The intensive study of Scripture to which he (re-?)turned in his effort to explain his conception of Scripture to the public led him to conclude that in fact the Bible contains much that is repugnant to reason. That is, it contains the many "childish and absurd opinions" that he was not prepared to attribute to it some four years earlier. Therefore, no system of hermeneutics, save a dishonest one, could allow it to appear otherwise.

Whereas in 1665 he could see the biblical claim that God is a jealous god as an accommodation to the lack of intelligence of the masses, by 1670, when he published his *Theologico-Political Treatise*, he could not. In arguing the absurdity of the position of "R. Jehuda Alpakhar [*sic*]," Spinoza writes:

Perhaps it will be answered that Scripture contains nothing repugnant to reason. But I insist that it expressly affirms and teaches that God is jealous (namely, in the decalogue itself, and in Exod. xxxiv. 14, and in Deut. iv. 24, and in many other places), and I assert that such a doctrine is repugnant to reason. It must, I suppose, in spite of all, be accepted as true [if the position of Alpakhar is accepted—JH]. If there are any passages in Scripture which imply that God is not jealous, they must be taken metaphorically as meaning nothing of the kind. So, also, Scripture expressly states (Exod. xix. 20 &c.) that God came down to Mount Sinai, and it attributes to Him other movements from place to place, nowhere directly stating that God does not move. Wherefore, we must take the passage literally, and Solomon's words (1 Kings viii. 27) "But will God dwell on the earth? Behold the heavens and the earth cannot contain thee," inasmuch as they do not expressly state that God does not move from place to place, but only imply it, must be explained away till they have no further semblance of denying locomotion to the Deity. So also we must believe that the sky is the habitation and throne of God, for Scripture expressly says so; and similarly many passages expressing opinions of the prophets or the multitude, which reason and philosophy, but not Scripture, tell us to be false, must be taken as true if we are to follow the guidance of our author. . . ."[71]

Now, to be sure, the notion that we must interpret some verses metaphorically to resolve contradictions represents Spinoza arguing according to the alleged position of his opponent; he himself would recognize different authors with different points of view. Still, the notion that Scripture clearly teaches things repugnant to reason is certainly Spinoza's attitude. "We ought not to be hindered if we find that our investigation of the meaning of Scripture thus conducted shows us that it is here and there repugnant to reason. . . To sum up, we may draw the absolute conclusion that the Bible must not be accommodated to reason, nor reason to the Bible."[72] Once God's jealousy represented a metaphor to Spinoza; now it is clear to him that some biblical authors certainly believed that the God of Israel was indeed a jealous God.[73]

In 1665, Spinoza claimed that he could not really understand Scripture. By 1670, however, he was quite certain that he knew precisely how to interpret it. Obscurities would remain, but all the nonsense maintained by the theologians to the detriment of humanity would be banished from intelligent discourse. For, in a frequently quoted passage, he informs us that "the method of interpreting Scripture does not differ widely from the method of interpreting nature—in fact, it is almost the same." He goes on to explain that in interpreting nature one examines its history and derives from it definitions of natural phenomena, based on certain fixed axioms.[74] Applying the principle to Scripture, the only hermeneutics one can apply to the text come from within Scripture itself. One cannot employ reason to shape the contours of one's exegesis. Whereas once he encountered absurd notions in the Bible and assumed that the prophets accommodated their message to the intellectual level of the masses, he now banishes reason from the discussion. He thus realizes that the prophetic message is not accommodated simply to the intellectual level of the masses, but is in fact "adapted to the opinions of the prophets."[75] The prophets were actually quite ignorant of many things,[76] and in no position to accommodate their message to anyone.[77] The primary faculty on which they relied was their imaginations; their message was refracted through the prism of this faculty, each prophet formulating his message according to it. These prophets, "endowed with unusually vivid imaginations and not with unusually perfect minds,"[78] routinely contradicted one another. "It therefore follows that we must by no means go to the prophets for knowledge, either of natural or spiritual phenomena."[79]

In his insistence that one interpret Scripture as one interprets nature,

Spinoza was led to the conclusion that one may legitimately attend only to the actual and conventional meaning of the words, as established by a study of the overall linguistic data of the text. One had to interpret the biblical text literally, unless there was internal evidence to suggest that a particular passage was to be taken as a metaphor.[80] No matter how repugnant to reason or to accepted truths a particular passage might be, it could not be deprived of its literal meaning on those grounds. Indeed, if we admit the right of the interpreter to bring extra-textual concerns to bear, "we may as well shut our Bibles, for vainly shall we attempt to prove anything from them if their plainest passages may be classed among obscure and impenetrable mysteries, or if we may put any interpretation on them which we fancy."[81] The notion that the text can be twisted to bear any interpretation demands the presence of commentators endowed with religious authority. But these commentators, in addition to their total disrespect for truth, can accomplish nothing of value, for in reality, in ancient times, the "unlearned people" understood perfectly well "the language of the prophets and apostles."[82] That is, the Bible is not really a sophisticated text at all; it is readily accessible to anyone who understands the significance of language. Spinoza considers it a distinct virtue of his method of reading Scripture that it dispenses with the need of the masses to "follow the testimony of commentators."[83]

The historical and exegetical argument of Spinoza's *Theologico-Political Treatise* indicates what happens to the biblical interpreter when he or she is, in principle, deprived of the ability to shape the meaning of the text. When a single definitive, usually literal, meaning is all one can posit of the text (acknowledging that the actual meaning of a particular passage may be metaphorical—this too allows for only one interpretation to the exclusion of all others) accommodation, in the medieval sense of the term, is impossible. Contradiction thus reigns supreme, precisely as Menasseh ben Israel understood and feared. From the presence of these contradictions that cannot be honestly reconciled, we learn that the Pentateuch had different authors living at different times; that many of the other biblical books are also composites, and were not written by the people to whom authorship is traditionally ascribed; that the Bible can impart no speculative truths; that in biblical terms, Israel's election consisted only in "temporal happiness and advantages of independent rule;"[84] that the ceremonial law of the Pentateuch was designed to help attain that temporal happiness; and that, as we have seen, the prophets were largely ignorant people with imaginations working overtime. Indeed, virtually the entire treatise is devoted to explicating the teachings of the Bible appropriated without the distorting effects of traditional exegesis. It is for this reason that Spinoza often engages in theological discourse that is quite distant from what he actually believed.

When the Bible is explicated without presuppositions, all the cherished assumptions shared by Jews and Christians emerge as untenable. For all these assumptions presuppose that the Bible contains some hidden message. But the text of the Bible—its manifold contradictions, its philosophical primitivity—does not admit of such hidden messages. Spinoza is, of course, aware that there are those who would argue that the true meaning of Scripture is preserved in extratextual traditions. But he can find little reason to accept the validity of these claims.

But as we can never be perfectly sure, either of such a tradition (i.e., the alleged Pharisaic tradition) or of the authority of the pontiff, we cannot found any certain conclusion on either: the one is denied by the oldest sect of Christians, the other by the oldest sect of Jews. Indeed, if we consider the series of years (to mention no other point) accepted by the Pharisees from their Rabbis, during which time they say they have handed down the tradition from Moses, we shall find that it is not correct, as I show elsewhere. Therefore such a tradition should be received with extreme suspicion. . . .[85]

There is then no legitimate exegesis nor legitimate tradition that can rescue the Bible from the legal and theological difficulties presented by what it really says. The Bible does indeed speak in human language, and it is time that people grow up and face what this really means. The Bible was written by human beings, and is formulated in their own words.[86] The legal system envisioned by the Bible is, *in biblical terms,* obsolete, and its theological views are, in our terms, primitive.

Now, to be sure, having arrived at the conclusion that the Bible is devoid of divinity, Spinoza's rejection of midrash is scarcely surprising. However, we must recognize that for Spinoza, the Bible, while devoid of metaphysical significance, nevertheless must remain the central document in the construction of an axiological system suited to the masses. In Spinoza's thinking, the Bible remains a critical document. The enduring importance of the Bible is its ability to teach much regarding politics, and the political role of religion. We can derive from the Bible certain basic dogmas that are politically useful, in that they promote obedience and, if *stripped of their ecclesiastical interpretations,* would undermine the religious divisiveness that challenges the harmony of the state.[87] Here, as well, Spinoza's hostility to the established religious communities is visible, in that he would negate the significance of all that is distinctive to any of them. Thus, the Bible remains of value; its accepted interpretations do not. Certainly, for Spinoza, rabbinic interpretations and enactments betray the true meaning of the biblical text, and contribute to the deadly disharmony that plagues human society. In one of the *Treatise*'s most acerbic passages he identifies the exegetical activity of the ancient and contemporary rabbis, inter alia, as sacrilegious and criminal:

When people declare, as all are ready to do, that the Bible is the Word of God teaching man true blessedness and the way to salvation, they evidently do not mean what they say; for the masses take no pains at all to live according to Scripture, and we see most people endeavouring to hawk about their own commentaries as the Word of God, and giving their best efforts, under the guise of religion, to compelling others to think as they do: we generally see, I say, theologians anxious to learn how to wring their inventions and sayings out of the sacred text, and to fortify them with Divine authority. Such persons never display less scruple or more zeal than when they are interpreting Scripture or the mind of the Holy Ghost; if we ever see them perturbed, it is not that they fear to attribute some error to the Holy Spirit, and to stray from the right path, but that they are afraid to be convicted of error by others, and thus to overthrow and bring into contempt their own authority. But if men really believed what they verbally testify of Scripture, they would adopt quite a different plan of life: their minds would not be agitated by so many contentions, nor so many hatreds, and they would cease to be excited by such a blind and rash passion for interpreting the sacred writings, and excogitating novelties in religion. On the contrary, they would not dare to adopt, as the teaching of Scripture, anything which they could not plainly deduce therefrom; lastly, those sacrilegious persons who have dared, in several passages, to interpolate the Bible, would have shrunk from so great a crime, and would have stayed their sacrilegious hands.[88]

The rabbis, like the popes, have been blinded by ambition, and, in the name of safeguarding Scripture, have totally betrayed its meaning and message. They have failed to see what Scripture really is, and have concocted theories regarding its origins that permit them to strip the Hebrew of the Bible of its meaning. The future harmony of human society depends on once and for all eliminating the rabbinic and papal approaches to Scripture; this would allow the appropriate axiological significance of the Bible to be manifest to all.

The question that the *Theologico-Political Treatise* leaves largely unanswered is how to recapture the true meaning of the biblical text. Spinoza tells us in general terms how to read Scripture. But how is one actually to go about determining the meaning of the actual words? He acknowledges that we must rely on "pharisaic" tradition for this, since only there are the plain meanings of the words preserved, before their contextual significance is subverted. This reliance on the traditions of the Pharisees does not trouble him greatly, as "no one has ever been able to change the meaning of a word in ordinary use, though many have changed the meaning of a particular sentence. . . . Further, the masses and the learned alike preserve language. . . . For these and such-like reasons we may readily conclude that it would never enter into the mind of anyone to corrupt a language, though the intention of a writer may often have been falsified by changing his phrases or interpreting them amiss."[89] Thus, the basic reliability of the received traditions regarding the significance of words can be affirmed, even as the claim to a broader interpretive tradition is viewed as groundless.

The real problems one faces in attempting to interpret the words of Scripture according to his method revolve around the absence of an ancient grammar, and the apparent chaotic nature of Hebrew tenses and vocabulary. Indeed, one can get the impression from the *Treatise* that Spinoza, for all his emphasis on discerning the literal meaning of the text and for all his insistence that in most cases this can be done[90] actually despaired of ever grasping the Hebrew language sufficiently.[91] There appeared to be no rules that properly governed the language.

Whether or not he did so despair before 1670, when the *Treatise* appeared, we know that by the end of his short life in 1677 he was certain that he could formulate the basic rules of the Hebrew language. At the time of his death he was working on a Hebrew grammar, which was published, unfinished, posthumously. There Spinoza strove to establish the basic normativity of the Hebrew language, which, he insisted must be distinguished from the language of Scripture.[92] The work is highlighted by discussions of Hebrew letters and vowels; nouns, which he considered the basic unit of the language;[93] pronouns, adjectives and adverbs; "infinitive nouns"; the many conjugations of active and passive verbs, composite verbs, deponent verbs, nominative participles—everything one would expect in a grammar.

The point of the *Grammar* is to explain all the rules that govern the use of Hebrew, including the explanation of what appear to be exceptional forms. Everything that can be is subordinated to a rule. The philosophical significance of this work has been discussed at length by Ze'ev Levy in a recent book;[94] the focus here will be on what Spinoza wanted to accomplish and how he went about establishing the rules of the Hebrew language.

The work, as noted, is unfinished, and a full evaluation of its goal and its success in meeting it is impossible. Still, it seems clear enough that Spinoza wished to provide the grammatical basis for implementing the revolutionary exegetical demands of the *Treatise*. While he could not hope to illuminate every obscure passage, with the norms of Hebrew grammar more firmly established than had hitherto been the case one could hope to approach Scripture and apply his methodology. With the proper understanding of Hebrew grammar, the plain meaning of the text emerges—with exceptions—obviating the need for unscrupulous commentators. Further, by subsuming allegedly anomalous cases under discernible rules, Spinoza deprived the commentator of the "hook" on which he or she could hang his or her manufactured interpretations.[95] With these rules Spinoza could identify scribal errors in the text, and exegetical/grammatical errors of the interpreters and grammarians.[96]

Spinoza's *Hebrew Grammar* is, I believe, the first Hebrew grammar that, with one exception, never refers to rabbinic understanding of the biblical text. The implicit message seems clear enough. The interpretive traditions of the Jews are of no value in determining the significance of Scripture. One does not turn to them, and one does not learn from them. Now, de facto, Spinoza's *Grammar* is thoroughly dependent on the Masoretes, whose pointing and punctuation often reflect midrashic exegeses; nevertheless Spinoza does not acknowledge the debt, and denigrates the Masoretes, calling them lazy.[97] The one exception involves his endorsement of the rabbinic position (which he identifies as such) that the word *aḥare* indicates "long after" while *aḥar* connotes "shortly thereafter."[98]

The *Hebrew Grammar* completes the exegetical program of the *Theologico-Political Treatise*.[99] Together they establish the general comprehensibility of the Bible in its own terms. It can be appropriated without fanciful exegesis or fraudulent traditions, without contemptible commentators or ambitious rabbis and priests. A definitive determination of the significance of the text was possible, and all traditional explanations that deviated from that definitive significance were now to be rejected. Together, the two works argue that the Torah speaks in human language in a way that negates all the textual assumptions undergirding rabbinic midrash halakhah.

Midrash Halakhah and Gentile Scholars

Our discussion of the challenges to traditional rabbinic assumptions would not be complete without at least a brief discussion of certain important Gentile scholars. For various reasons, the intellectual revolution of the Renaissance, and the religious/intellectual revolutions of the Reformation and Counter-Reformation, led gentile scholars to search the rabbinic writings. This search in turn gave rise to a considerable literature in Latin and the vernaculars, devoted to bringing different aspects of rabbinic learning to light. Some of the greatest scholars of Europe, and many of the not-so-great, turned to rabbinic learning. Some, like Peter Christfels,[100] did so to continue long-standing debates; others, more important, did so to expand the field of human knowledge; some did so for polemical purposes, some for ecumenical purposes.[101] For the most part the attitude of these Gentile scholars to rabbinic exegesis, halakhic and aggadic, and to rabbinic Judaism generally, was rather negative; they are important here because they exercised considerable power in shaping the discomfort of some modern Jews.

Richard Simon, the seventeenth-century pioneer of biblical criticism and a Catholic priest, approached the issue of the Bible from a different perspective than did La Peyrere, Hobbes and Spinoza. He saw in biblical criticism a powerful weapon with which he could attack the fundamental Protestant notion that Scripture could be interpreted from within itself, without benefit of Catholic tradition. It was clear to Simon that the text of the Bible was the product of many hands, professional scribes and public writers, and has come down to us having been ravaged by careless copyists. The text is filled with obscurities beyond redemption; without the guidance of Catholic tradition it would be incomprehensible. How sincere Simon was in this stance can be debated. What is beyond doubt is that he sets out to show that Scripture can simply not be interpreted, *fully and completely*, from within itself.[102] At the same time, Simon insisted that many passages can and should be understood literally (thereby leading some to question the sincerity of his insistence on the authority of Catholic tradition). Thus, when he comes to discuss Jewish interpreters of the text, he denigrates the classical exegesis of the rabbis, and applauds those Jews who learned how to read the Scriptures free of rabbinic tradition. For Simon needed to direct his scholarly contempt toward rabbinic exegesis every bit as much as towards the Protestant notion of *sola scriptura*. Simon was certain that the rabbis had not unlocked the secrets of Scripture, and to show it enjoyed using the insights of Abraham Ibn Ezra, Isaac Abravanel, and Elias Levita that ran counter to traditional interpretations.[103]

Before issuing his judgment regarding the value of rabbinic exegesis, he felt the need to note the hypocrisy of the Jews, who rely on the literal sense when they dispute with Christians, but on "something quite different in their ancient biblical commentaries, such as allegories, intellectual games, stories manufactured to suit one's whim. It is rare that they endeavor to determine the literal sense: their minds are fully inclined towards the invention of parables and allegories."[104] "One can rightly neglect the ancient scriptural commentaries of the Jews, for they contain almost nothing of value; these include the Zohar, the midrashim or *Rabbot*, and several other works that the Jews respect due to the great antiquity which they attribute to them."[105] Clearly, Simon's scorn is primarily directed towards kabbalistic and aggadic exegesis and the fact that Jews distance themselves from it when debating with Christians; yet, rabbinic halakhic exegesis fares little better:

The talmudists also possess a method for interpreting scripture, quite similar to that used by the allegorists, found primarily in the Gemara, where they are much freer than in the Mishnah. The latter is like the text of the Talmud, to which the Gemara serves as a kind of gloss or commentary. The most ridiculous and absurd things that one can imagine are found in these variegated glosses, to which they grant authority in the name of their fathers, for the purpose of facilitating their imposition on the people, under the pretext that they are only passing on the unadulterated doctrine of their ancestors. While the Mishnah is purer, scriptural passages are almost never explained according to their literal sense. They are accommodated to the prejudices of the tradition, to give authority to the decision of their sages. In truth, one would have to be pretty disturbed [préoccupé] to believe that the authors of scripture had ever thought that which is attributed to them in the Talmud.[106]

Thus, for Simon, midrash halakhah is a largely fraudulent tool the rabbis use to grant biblical authority to their teachings, themselves rooted in ridiculous glosses fraudulently attributed to ancient sages. In other words, Simon had nothing but contempt for rabbinic scriptural reading.

While Simon's idiosyncratic synthesis of Catholicism and criticism was to deprive him of any disciples, certainly the critical side of his enterprise exercised considerable influence on how the Bible was understood. For he provided yet more philologically grounded evidence that the Bible is written in human language, and must be interpreted within the framework of normal linguistic conventions. That such an interpretation would yield an, at times, incomprehensible text apparently troubled him, and led to his call for reliance on Catholic tradition; those who came after him and learned from him were not similarly troubled by the resulting incomprehensibility of the Bible.[107]

Among other scholars who expressed an opinion on this subject, mention should be made of Jacques Basnage, the Huguenot historian of the Jews, whose history remained the only full-length historical synthesis for over a century. In the course of his discussion of the distinctions between Karaites and Rabbanites, Basnage noted that rabbinic midrash, which entailed the abandonment of the literal meaning of Scripture, was directly responsible for the multiplication of Jewish practices. The result, he insisted, was a religion that enslaved, rather than saved.[108]

Denis Diderot, a leading figure of the French Enlightenment, noted that rabbinic midrash could be very helpful in recovering the meaning of the ancient scriptural text, particularly so since Jews remain obligated to perform "certain ceremonies of the law." However, this is mitigated by the fact that "often, instead of seeking the literal sense of Scripture, they seek the mystical sense, which causes the obfuscation of the intent of the writer, itself sufficiently obscure."[109] While Diderot's comments are directed primarily against aggadic interpretation, halakhic midrash is also included in the indictment. I consider Diderot's remarks particularly important because he had no access to any of the material in the original, nor does he seem to have worked his way carefully through the various Latin compendia of rabbinic learning that were available to him. He was, rather, simply parroting the accepted wisdom of the age among people in his enlightened circle. He thus provides a very useful snapshot of how Judaism was viewed by the philosophes.[110]

Even figures otherwise sympathetic to Jews could muster little tolerance for midrash halakhah or for the rabbinic culture that proceeded from it. Gotthold Ephraim Lessing, perhaps the most significant figure in the German Enlightenment, and certainly a friend of the Jews, explains the providentially ordained shift from the Old Testament, the first stage in human education, to the New Testament, a higher stage of human education, as follows:

Every primer is only for a certain age. To delay the child, who has outgrown it . . . is harmful. For to be able to do this in a way that is at all profitable, you must insert into it more than there is really in it, and extract from it more than it can contain. . . . This gives the child a petty, crooked, hairsplitting understanding: it makes him full of mysteries, superstitious, full of contempt for all that is comprehensible and easy. The very way in which the Rabbis handled *their* sacred books. The very character which they thereby imparted to the spirit of their people! A better instructor must come and tear the exhausted primer from the child's hands. Christ came.[111]

The Jews in refusing to advance beyond first grade, as it were, had no choice but to find all kinds of new meanings in their Dick and Jane stories. Accomplishing this required adopting a ridiculous hairsplitting method that read into the text far more than it could reasonably bear.

Johann Gottfried Herder, another figure often sympathetic to Jews, noted that upon the return of the Jews from the Babylonian exile, "Their religion was pharisaism; their learning a minute nibbling at syllables, and this confined to a single book."[112] Elsewhere, he was to accuse the rabbis of arrogance in assuming the divine character of biblical Hebrew.[113] As Herder never tired of insisting, the language of the Bible was human, for only in human terms, and through the medium of human language, could God be revealed to humanity. Further, the Bible was essentially a book detailing the history of humanity, written by humans "for the purpose of expressing in poetic-historical terms the ways of God through the course of human history."[114] From this assumption, Herder went on to develop a detailed poetic hermeneutics that brought the biblical message alive for him. He was no literalist, for he saw in human language, particularly in the earliest stages of its "oriental" form, a deeply poetic structure. This position left ample room for interpretation. Nevertheless, he insisted that the (arrogant, rabbinic) assumption that the Bible spoke in divine language made it impossible to properly discern the true messages of the work. What such an assumption leads to is a childish nibbling at syllables that obscures the poetic majesty of the text.[115]

One could collect many more such denigrations of rabbinic scriptural reading, but such a collection would serve little point. For in the end, these denigrations are part of a much larger assault on rabbinic Judaism that also focused on aggadic passages displaying all kinds of "reveries" and on the alleged immorality of the contemporary rabbinic Jew.[116] The effect of this broader assault, of which the attack on midrash was but a part, led to a strongly held belief on the part of certain would-be enlightened ones (as Solomon Maimon called them) that they had to distance themselves completely from the legacy of rabbinism, and it is in that context that the attacks on midrash halakhah, and halakhah generally, are relevant to our story.

By the end of the eighteenth century, then, the exegetical revolution had penetrated deeply into the European intellectual consciousness. While some Bible scholars could continue to find divinity within the biblical text, midrash halakhah demanded far more. To sustain midrash halakhah one had to affirm that the Bible was given by God to Moses, however that was understood; that it was formulated in distinct divine speech demanding not just multivalence, but the hermeneutic significance of even prepositions, syllables, and letters; that this speech was preserved in its pristine purity throughout some three millennia; that the hermeneutic techniques developed by the rabbis (or handed down by God to Moses at Mt. Sinai) represent the tools needed to expose the multiple meanings of the text; and that the applications of those techniques by the rabbis are authoritative and correct. I think it is safe to say that no Jew who engaged the emerging modern world could comfortably affirm all these propositions. Like a small group of their medieval predecessors, they could perhaps affirm some, but not all. Like their medieval predecessors, such Jews also confronted intellectual

challenges to the notion of an unbroken tradition. Unlike their medieval predecessors, they came to have the freedom to be transformed by
these challenges, as we shall see in the next chapter. We can see from
their experiences that, in the late eighteenth and early nineteenth centuries, rabbinic Judaism was to face its most formidable challenge, at
the heart of which stood the question of the viability of rabbinic
hermeneutics. It is to this that we now turn.

6 • Midrash and Reform

IN THE HEARTLAND OF Ashkenazic talmudism—the German lands, Bohemia, Moravia, Poland and Lithuania—the Jews were largely insulated from contact with the exegetical revolution of the seventeenth century. Yet, while they did not have to face the intellectual challenges that revolution brought with it, the period from 1650 to 1750 was scarcely one of spiritual calm within this world. For various reasons—some valid throughout all these areas, some unique to specific locations—traditional Jewish society was in decline and subject to frequent internal critiques. While I think Jacob Katz is essentially correct that throughout this period the traditional center was able to hold,[1] it cannot be gainsaid that the forces leading to its demise were gaining momentum.

This is a story that has been told before and need not detain us here.[2] What is of significance for us here is the fact that much of the internal critique revolved around the educational defects of pilpulistic Talmud study, which had emerged as the dominant form of study in these lands.[3] The opposition to such study often called for increased attention to the Hebrew Bible and biblical grammar, and independent Mishnah study, as well as occasionally calling for greater Jewish awareness of "outside" sciences. While such calls for educational reform[4] seem to have had limited social impact, they did set in motion, among the intellectual elite, a concern for Hebrew grammar and the plain meaning of the biblical text, which obviously had an impact on the way the Bible was received. In addition, the new awareness of the limitations of contemporary Talmud study gave rise to a process of questioning the

137

nature of talmudic discourse and the extent to which it lent itself to the casuistry of the pilpulists.

These tendencies are most evident in the work of Israel ben Moshe Zamosc (1700–1772), a teacher of Moses Mendelssohn; he is generally mentioned as a proto-maskil, whatever that means.[5] His work of talmudic novellae, *Netzaḥ Yisrael*, published in 1741 (the same year he moved to Berlin from his native Galicia), is generally described as a pioneering work in integrating European sciences within the world of Talmud study. To be sure, this description is largely accurate, as Israel insisted that all talmudic opinions be sensible and comprehensible, and often, he claimed, it is only the sciences that can explain what a particular sage had in mind.[6] But the use of the sciences to explain rabbinic passages—and Israel, in an understatement, claims that he only rarely has the need to employ such explanations[7]—is but one of two strategies Israel promoted for the purpose of reordering Jewish learning and freeing it from pilpul.

The other strategy was to sever any connection between Jewish law and theology, on the one hand, and Jewish exegesis, whether halakhic or aggadic, on the other. For him, it was crucial that the modern student of the Talmud recognize that the midrash halakhah of the rabbis is to be wholly understood as *asmakhta*, supports and mnemonic devices for laws originating in tradition, while midrash aggadah is to be understood as *meliṣah*, here meaning the appropriation of scriptural language to impart ideas having no actual connection to Scripture. Regarding the former, Israel writes,

As for the substance of the *asmakhta*, it is when sometimes the Talmud will extrapolate some teaching from some verse on the basis of some inference they drew from scripture; even when the verse is not the least bit difficult, and is readily understood from the perspective of its essential *peshat*, they nevertheless made the verse appear as if it were problematic in order to relate it to the law received by tradition or established by logic. Therefore these laws are *mi-derabbanan*, unless they specifically say that the law is *mi-deoraita*, in which case they definitely had a tradition. . . . It is not that they thought, or wanted to convince others, that the verse intended to teach the law that was "derived" from it, for, from the perspective of the *peshat*, there is no indication of this [derived meaning]. And in some cases, what is derived is very distant indeed from the *peshat*. In all cases the point was to relate the law to the language of scripture, to serve as a reminder so that the law would not be forgotten.[8]

Clearly, Israel is thoroughly dependent on Maimonides here. The latter, Israel proceeds to argue, was undoubtedly correct in his dispute with Naḥmanides; he thus enters into a long discussion of the legal status of monetary betrothal—a major fly in the Maimonidean ointment[9]—to show that it is indeed rabbinic in nature. But, while Israel Zamosc was one of the very few to accept and defend Maimonides' position without deviation, the eighteenth-century Berliner (by way of Galicia) had a very different agenda from that of the twelfth-century Egyptian sage.

With the publication of his *Netzaḥ Yisrael* in 1741, Zamosc was arguing for no less than a reform of the rabbinic mind. The disease of the age, as diagnosed by Israel, was that the pure and appropriate methods of study of an earlier age have been "sealed off and filled with dust" by people who, caught in the dire economic straits of the exile, could not make sufficient livings by being recognized as merely accomplished Talmudists. They felt the need to display new intellectual skills. Thus, in his day the tendency of Talmudists, he said, was

to dishonest creations, fabricated from their belly-thoughts,[10] and to counterfeit and false investigations. They wholly occupy themselves with puny and shriveled inferences.[11] They are shirkers, shirkers.[12] On something with no substance they imagine they have established stones on top of stones [i.e., a structure resting on a firm foundation].[13] . . . Regarding the Talmud they invent slanderous claims. . . . They have wandered through and collected introductions to all the books, and accumulate them in big piles.[14] The least of them still manage to accumulate ten piles. And they weave some of them together into a tapestry of thorns, which they treat as clothing in which to dress the *gemara* and *tosafot*; and ten people hold onto one corner of inferences. This corrupts the simple meaning, and confuses the thought processes.[15]

The point of this rambling passage, with its confused and mixed metaphors, is to indicate the extent to which Talmud study has been completely corrupted by people more interested in "finding" something that had never been said before than in understanding the given text properly. It was Israel's goal to root out these methods of learning and inference-gathering. Towards that end it was critical that he impart a proper appreciation of rabbinic exegesis, for it was a failure to properly conceptualize this exegesis, he thought, that contributed to the intellectual corruption of the age. After all, if the rabbis really thought a particular verse, interpreted midrashically, created law, they would be indicating that meaning was not circumscribed by language or normal interpretive conventions. Such an understanding of rabbinic exegesis would lead one to believe that the sages had no respect for the limits of the clear meaning of the words. Further, such an interpretation of rabbinic exegetical activity would corrupt proper thought processes. Why shouldn't a student take liberties with the clear meaning of the talmudic text, since the talmudic rabbis seemingly took such liberties with the biblical text? Why should one refrain from making words mean whatever one wishes them to mean, or from adding ideas to which the language of the text never alludes?

For Israel Zamosc, then, stripping midrash halakhah of its honored place within the rabbinic corpus was critical to his project of reforming the Ashkenazic talmudic mind of the eighteenth century.[16] It was imperative that one recognize that neither the halakhic nor aggadic "exegeses" of the rabbis were really understood as emerging from the verses in question. The ancient sages never thought that, and those who would understand rabbinic reasoning properly must recognize this essential fact. Once it becomes clear that the rabbis actually did have respect for the linguistic boundaries of the biblical text, modern pilpulists would (theoretically) be forced to confront the defects of their method; they would find no support for it in rabbinic exegesis.

In many respects, Zamosc must be seen as a transitional figure. He was well aware of the deficiencies in Talmud study in his day, and he was also an ardent supporter of cultivating concern for Jewish philosophical discourse. At the same time, he was not able to fully free himself from the intellectual traditions he inherited. Despite his bold introduction, his talmudic novellae read like those of his contemporaries, his frequent recourse to scientific explanations notwithstanding. He could engage in lengthy pilpulistic discussions of why a particular verse is necessary to establish a law, a question he had no business asking had his work been fully shaped by the thinking laid out in his introduction.[17] From the work of Israel Zamosc, as from that of so many others, we see how seductive pilpulistic reasoning can actually be. Even for one who has concluded that succumbing to the temptation is wrong, the lure is too great. Thus, in Israel's case, as in that of so many others, the polemic against *pilpul* is actually a polemic against everyone else's *pilpul*. One's own brand is, of course, straight thinking. Be that as it may, it remains important to note the critique of rabbinic exegesis that assumes a central role in Israel's polemic against the Ashkenazic talmudic mind. For Zamosc, midrash halakhah, if taken seriously, could only lead to intellectual corruption. This claim was to be frequently repeated over the next century and a half.[18]

Israel Zamosc's criticism of Polish talmudism found echoes among other members of Germany's intellectual elite in the middle of the eighteenth century.[19] It is part of the response of this elite to perceived flaws within the world of traditional learning. Yet, Zamosc's response shows little awareness of, or concern for, the judgment of the outside world. While he will draw what he can from that world's scientific learning, I can see no concern for that world's view of Jews and Judaism. For Zamosc, cleansing talmudic learning of its *pilpul* was seen as the pressing need of the day; in that effort, recourse to "outside" sciences was necessary. Otherwise, the wisdom and prejudices of Gentiles were simply not a concern, as far as I can see.[20]

The Early Haskalah

For the next generation of Germany's intellectual elite, things would be infinitely more difficult. Numerous factors, the precise identification and weight of which historians continue to debate, came together to produce a group of intellectuals who were fully at home in European languages and learning. They were aware of, and attracted to, what Western thought could offer them, and they were well aware of what Western thinkers had to say about Jews and Judaism. They knew what Spinoza, Simon, the philosophes, Lessing and Michaelis were saying about rabbinic exegesis and thought. They also knew what Leibniz and, later, Kant were writing in the realms of metaphysics and ethics. The encounter between these Jewish intellectuals and Western wisdom and prejudice could not help but give rise to important reflections on the nature of Jewish life and law, the origins of the Jewish legal system, and the political and social aspirations that emerge from that system.

Within the framework of this encounter, the question of the legitimacy of Polish talmudism paled by comparison to the far more fundamental question of the legitimacy of Judaism. While, to be sure, Polish (and Bohemian)[21] Talmudists were routinely vilified in Hebrew satires of the 1790s, these satires represented an act of distancing oneself from what was acknowledged by all within the circle to be defective and useless.[22] The more lasting issues confronted by the Berlin *haskalah* (Enlightenment) went to the very heart of the continued viability of rabbinic Judaism; here the question of rabbinic exegesis would become central.

It is a standard of Jewish historiography relating to the Berlin *haskalah* that its earliest devotees, represented by Moses Mendelssohn (1729–86) and Naftali Herz Wessely (1725–1805), were relatively conservative and traditional, remaining observant of Jewish law and substantially affirming the basic belief structure of traditional Judaism. The next "generation" of *maskilim* (devotees of *haskalah*) are generally depicted as being far more radical in their approach to rabbinic texts and practices, even as they proclaimed their fealty to the ideals of Mendelssohn.[23] While there may be those who wish to challenge parts of this picture,[24] as far as the attitudes of the *maskilim* to rabbinic exegesis and law are concerned, the standard approach seems to me to be wholly justified. For there is a world of difference between the positions of Mendelssohn and Wessely and those of the next generation of German *maskilim*.

Mendelssohn and Wessely represent the first generation of Ashkenazic Jews to confront the criticisms of rabbinic exegesis and law advanced by Spinoza, ex-Marranos and Gentile scholars of various orientations. Unlike those who came after them, their reaction to the intellectual challenges was to defend rabbinic exegesis, just as they defended the reliability of the Masoretic text of the Bible in the face of burgeoning criticism of this text.[25] To them, while there were many aspects of Jewish social and educational life that needed reforming, challenges to the fundamental structure of Judaism had to be combated.

As Edward Breuer has argued, it is against the backdrop of the intellectual challenges to tradition that we must view the emergence of the German translation of the Bible by Mendelssohn, and the *Biur*, or commentary on the Bible, produced by Mendelssohn and a number of others, including Wessely. By all accounts this edition and commentary was an epoch-making event in Jewish intellectual and educational history,[26] and its approach to the question of rabbinic exegesis was of great significance. Both Mendelssohn and Wessely clearly understood rabbinic exegesis to be a problem in light of recent standards of interpretation, and each took divergent paths to resolve the problem.

Wessely's contribution to the *Biur*, the commentary to Leviticus, was motivated throughout by a desire to explain the Bible in a way that was philologically sound, but that presented the interpretations of the rabbis as indispensable in realizing that task.

It was Wessely who introduced into Jewish exegetical discourse a redefinition of the notion of *'omek ha-peshat*, the profound plain sense. To its twelfth-century devotee, Samuel ben Meir (Rashbam), the quest for *'omek ha-peshat* referred to a recovery of the appreciation of the *peshat* (the plain sense of Scripture), which, he felt, had been severely compromised by the overwhelming power of midrashic exegesis. To Rashbam, people, including his own grandfather Rashi, no longer had an appreciation of the true *peshat*. One needed to delve deeply into the wording of the text in order to restore it to its rightful place alongside midrashic readings. Thus, to Rashbam, *'omek ha-peshat* represented the *peshat* stripped of all midrashic accretions; it was the theoretical negation of midrash.[27]

Wessely, however, was not fighting Rashbam's fight. He was not struggling for the recognition of *peshat*, but rather to prevent the burgeoning appreciation of *peshat* from overwhelming the integrity of midrashic readings. For him *'omek ha-peshat* is opposed, not to midrash, but to simple *peshat*, or, rather, to the superficial understanding of the plain sense that, he felt, had previously dominated notions of *peshat*. In other words, what to Rashbam represented the profound plain sense (in contradistinction to midrash), to Wessely represented a superficial appreciation of the language of the Bible. This superficial understanding of the plain sense certainly made rabbinic exegesis seem far-fetched, but the fault lay not with the rabbis, who worked tirelessly to discern the more profound *peshat*, but with those who were incapable or unwilling to go beneath the surface. Were they to delve more deeply into the Bible's language they would see just how close midrash and *peshat* actually are.

As he explained in the introduction to his commentary to Leviticus, his goals in writing the commentary were twofold:

> that I should not deviate from the trusted path of the tradition of our ancestors, and secondly, that I not deviate from the path of clear, sensible *peshat*, "that the two of them shall come together at the top." (Exodus 26:24) And if one treads a narrow path in seeking to bridge the gap between the *peshat* and the midrash that seem far from one another, I have said that there is hope only if God favors me with the ability to discern the meaning of the roots with clarity. For if we determine their meaning, it will become clear that the midrash is nothing other than the profound *peshat* of scripture; those that were distant shall be brought together.[28]

Thus, for Wessely, a profound understanding of the language of Scripture would eliminate any sense that the rabbis were deficient readers. Rather, one would see that the rabbinic interpretation was based, not on exegetical deficiencies, but on the basis of a profound understanding of the language. Of course, as with the commentary of Meir Leib Malbim in the next century (which will be discussed in chapter 8), this whole argument becomes circular, since it is the rabbinic texts themselves that serve as the primary source for determining what is the "profound *peshat*." Thus it is scarcely surprising that rabbinic texts are found by Wessely to incorporate this "profound *peshat*." Be that as it may, the notion of profound *peshat*, grounded in the heightened linguistic sensitivity of the rabbis, became a critical means of responding to challenges to rabbinic exegesis. It is, thus, not surprising that Wessely's commentary on Leviticus is far more dependent on the *Sifra* than any of the commentaries produced by Mendelssohn and the other commentators depended on the midrashim relevant to the other books of the Torah. For Wessely, one could not discern *peshat* without recourse to rabbinic insights, and therefore halakhic midrash became an indispensable tool in the effort to understand the Bible.

Wessely's commentary on Leviticus, published in 1783, was hardly his first effort at identifying the exegesis of the rabbis with the deep meaning of scriptural language. Already in 1755, with the publication of his *Gan Na'ul*, a work devoted to a study of Hebrew synonyms, Wessely had made clear his commitment to the notion that rabbinic midrash represented "absolute *peshat*" (*ha-peshat ha-gamur*), and that it testified to the reality of the tradition from Moses at Sinai.[29] This had gone unrecognized before him, he claimed, because previous commentators simply had not penetrated to the full profundity of the Hebrew language. The superficial understanding of the biblical text was the result of a carelessness that failed to discern critical nuances in the Hebrew language, and, in particular, took for granted the possibility of total synonymity. To Wessely it was clear that no two words ever convey exactly the same thing, and he provides the "evidence" for this claim in the massive *Gan Na'ul*. From this study it becomes clear to him that "our ancestors and predecessors, the teachers of the Mishnah and Talmud, may their memory be for a blessing, knew the foundations of the language, and clearly understood the meaning of its forms of expression (*meliṣotav*), and based their teachings and exegeses on the firm foundations that were known to them."[30] Rabbinic exegesis was not the product of syllable-nibbling fools, but of people who were fully cognizant of the unique features of the Hebrew language, which they laid bare for all those with eyes to see.

For Wessely, then, there was no actual distinction between rabbinic midrash and the profound *peshat* of the biblical text. Philology—however contrived it must appear to us today—became the answer to the long-standing discomfort with Jewish scriptural reading. For philology, in Wessely's hands, showed that the rabbinic interpretations were not fantastic, eisegetical creations, but represented the true and profound meaning of biblical language.

Mendelssohn, for all his sympathy for Wessely's goals, was not able to fully share his colleague's approach to the challenge. For Mendelssohn was not convinced of the qualitative uniqueness of the Hebrew language, nor was he convinced that rabbinic midrash could be reduced to "profound *peshat*." Further, he could not fully accept Wessely's views on synonymity.[31] At the same time, Mendelssohn was not prepared to trivialize rabbinic midrash and rely completely on tradition from Sinai, as so many Jewish intellectuals of an earlier age did (and as so many of a later age would do). This is not because Mendelssohn doubted the possibility of an ongoing tradition in principle (he clearly affirms the unbroken transmission of the *Mesorah*)[32] but rather because such a position cannot adequately account for the activity of the sages. For Mendelssohn the answer to the problem lay in understanding the nature of language generally, and the way in which words function as signifiers.

His first important effort to deal with the problem can be found in his introduction to his translation of and commentary on Ecclesiastes, published in 1770. There he noted that in the normal course of linguistic interaction, people speak with concern for conveying a particular idea; the actual words used are often of less importance. For, the

natural speaker generally pays attention to the sense and not the words. And likewise a prophet or one speaking with divine inspiration. To convey his primary meaning he will attend to the sense with particular care. He arranges the words according to the beauty of the language, its purity of expression, and its poetics, without attaching particular significance to, or intending to impart additional substance by means of, every linguistic shift.[33]

All speakers, prophets included, intend to convey something when they speak, and linguistic shifts are not self-conscious attempts to convey secondary meanings, but to conform to aesthetic standards. It is therefore quite reasonable and appropriate to look at, say, Ecclesiastes from this perspective, in order to elucidate the primary intent of the author. Here one must be ever conscious of the syntax of the verse and the context in which its wording is embedded. The goal is to convey what the speaker *intended* to say, without taking apart every turn of phrase.

However, human beings do not always communicate in this way. Sometimes they are quite painstaking in their choice of words. They carefully choose a specific word that most closely approximates the intended significance, not some other that appears to be almost synonymous. This choice is governed by the speaker's desire to communicate more than he or she can or wishes to convey with language. In this case the careful choice of words may provide an allusion to the intended matter, a secondary but intended meaning. Thus,

There is no doubt that prophetic or inspired speech will not [generally?] be devoid of particular significance. If the speaker chooses a particular word or expression from among several possibilities he does so intentionally and wishes to signify some matter. And thus he does not attend only to the general sense [of the words], but to the degrees of overlap and distinction [among the possible choices]. Here, every linguistic shift, whether large or small, is consciously directed to conveying the secondary meaning, even if, at times, it is far from the primary meaning. The explanation of this secondary meaning is called *derash*.[34]

He goes on to explain that the linguistic shift observed in the two Decalogues in the Torah from "remember the Sabbath day" in Exodus, to "observe the Sabbath day" in Deuteronomy—which, from the perspective of the *peshat*, or primary significance, conveys nothing, as the words are essentially synonymous—was not inadvertent. "For the supernal wisdom does not do anything without purpose."[35] Thus, the shift certainly was intended to convey something beyond the simple meaning of the words to the recipient of this speech. This being so, "the sages, may their memory be for blessing, did well in interpreting the shifts between the two Decalogues, on the basis of the traditional exegetical principles."

As we have seen, Mendelssohn was not troubled by the fact that the secondary meaning was often very far from the primary meaning. For the primary meaning, syntax and context are critical, whereas the actual use of a particular word is not. To discern the secondary meaning, by contrast, one focuses on specific words or morphemes (sometimes less than a complete word), and not on the flow of the verse or the larger context. This is the method employed by the sages in their midrashic interpretations; they took each phrase and sought its secondary meaning, and this is perfectly legitimate and appropriate, for, "it is the way of the supernal wisdom to direct one act towards several purposes."[36] As Breuer put it, rabbinic midrash illuminates the "intended linguistic possibilities that in some structural or philological way resisted complete assimilation to contextual considerations."[37]

Mendelssohn, thus, argues for the inherent multivalence of language—all language—that, in turn, fully legitimizes rabbinic exegesis. This legitimization emerges from the fact that, for Mendelssohn, linguistic multivalence does not lead to abrogating the connection between meaning and authorial intent. The careful writer (and the divine writer of the Torah was certainly careful) exercises control over meaning by virtue of conscious choices that convey a desired secondary significance. This secondary intent can be identified by means of a disciplined hermeneutics that is attuned to the unique features of a text's linguistic peculiarities. Thus, rabbinic interpretations, which are the result of this disciplined hermeneutics, are not arbitrary, but authoritative.[38]

Because rabbinic elucidations of the secondary intent of the author were authoritative, on the one hand, and sometimes quite distant from the primary significance, on the other, Mendelssohn confronted a problem of just how he should proceed to translate the biblical text. One could not reproduce in another language the linguistic materiel that could signify an identical secondary intent. The translator had, therefore, to choose. No matter what he did, something would be lost. In response to this quandary, in the introduction to his Torah commentary Mendelssohn worked out a compromise position. When the *peshat* and midrashic interpretation were complementary, he would translate only according to the *peshat*, for this was a legitimate level of meaning. When, however, the midrashic interpretation conflicted in some way with the *peshat*, Mendelssohn would abandon the latter and translate in accord with the former.[39] While in practice such instances were few in number[40]—and at times Mendelssohn seemed unable to make up his mind when the midrashic interpretation conflicted with the *peshat*[41]— this procedure, when followed, lent greater force to his theoretical discussion. The midrashic interpretation was an authoritative and genuinely exegetical elucidation of the meaning of the biblical text.[42] Critics of rabbinic exegesis, Jewish and Gentile, were thus off the mark in seeing distance between the rabbis and sound interpretation.

Wessely and Mendelssohn were as committed as Israel Zamosc to the reform and expansion of the Jewish curriculum, and to the destruction of *pilpul*. Unlike Israel, they could not agree that Maimonides had properly conceptualized rabbinic midrash, and they therefore could not view it as a secondary phenomenon. At the same time, they knew full well that without some philological or philosophical reconceptualization, midrash halakhah stood as Judaism's weak link in light of the prevailing theories of textual signification. Each tried in his own way to present a new understanding of rabbinic exegesis that would withstand the scrutiny of a skeptical age.

The Haskalah: The Next Generation

Just as the efforts of Menasseh ben Israel in his *Conciliador* a century earlier never had a chance of succeeding, so too the efforts of Wessely and Mendelssohn to defend rabbinic exegesis, and, by extension, rabbinic law never had a chance of convincing their successors among the intellectual elite of Germany. For one thing, there was an inevitable imbalance in Mendelssohn's work in particular. Despite his expressed fealty to rabbinic exegesis, which I regard as genuine and sincere, we must recognize that Mendelssohn's introductions do not merely establish the legitimacy of rabbinic *derash*; they also affirm the legitimacy of *peshat* as an independent, indeed the primary, level of meaning. Mendelssohn's translation and his commentaries are thoroughly guided by the desire to demonstrate the latter point. Further, the actual execution of his commentary gave far greater emphasis to the aesthetic and moral features of the biblical text, thereby granting the Bible authority as a guide to behavior and taste, quite distinct from the oral law or rabbinic exegesis. Finally, the universal ideals of natural religion play a central role in his apologia for Judaism, *Jerusalem*, leading some of

Mendelssohn's disciples to conclude that they represented the core of Mendelssohn's thought, whereas the claims regarding biblical and rabbinic law in that work and in the Bible project were secondary and dispensable.[43]

Beyond this, the successors of Wessely and Mendelssohn were fully imbued with the spirit of the more radical *Aufklärung* and the progressive historical views and deistic theology of Lessing, Reimarus, and others. They did not and could not share the theological and metaphysical assumptions that undergirded Mendelssohn's weltanschauung. (Somewhat paradoxically, this attachment to progress went hand in hand with a vision of the gradual corruption of the original ideals of Israelite religion or early Judaism. This parallels precisely the view of the philosophes that the Middle Ages represented a period of frightful decadence, but that there was an earlier age—that of classical Greece and Rome—to which one could turn for inspiration in the struggle to progress beyond them.)[44] For however one understood the emergence of language, without belief in a divine revelation of positive law the text could have all the levels of meaning imaginable. It still would not be able to exercise authority. Under such circumstances, the vast expansion of biblical law by means of exegesis became once again the focus of criticism and discontent.

While some of the *maskilim* began by ignoring talmudic literature, others felt the need to ridicule it or subvert it. The *Lebensgeschichte* of Solomon Maimon (c. 1753–1800) represents an important example of one who turned to ridicule, while the *Besamim Rosh* of Saul Berlin (1740–94) exemplifies the effort at subversion.

Besamim Rosh is the title given by Berlin to a collection of *responsa,* most allegedly originating from the pen of R. Asher ben Yehiel (c. 1250–1327; he was known by the acronym "Rosh"), that he claimed had been preserved in manuscript. He published it in 1793. The *responsa* were accompanied by Berlin's own commentary, given the rather odd title of *Kasa de-Harsana*[45] Although there remain some who even today argue that the work is genuine,[46] it is generally regarded as a clever forgery by Berlin, an accomplished rabbinic scholar.[47]

Berlin's intent in forging this volume was to subvert the demands of the rabbinic tradition from within, for, as Louis Jacobs has written, "practically every Responsum in the volume contains a thinly disguised attack on Rabbinic Judaism."[48] Drawing on the prestige and authority of the Rosh and other medieval Talmudists, Berlin argued for the relaxation of numerous elements of Jewish law, downgrading many of them, such as the washing of hands before meals, to the status of mere custom,[49] while downgrading others, that previously had been seen as obligatory from the Torah, to the level of rabbinic ordinances.

The latter task Berlin accomplishes wholesale by invoking Maimonides' principle, discussed at length in chapter 4, that all laws created by means of the rabbinic exegetical principles are to be considered of rabbinic authority.[50] While the practical consequences of this principle in Maimonides' hands were limited, in Berlin's hands they are enormous. For, in the *Besamim Rosh*, once a law had been determined to be rabbinic, it was easily discarded in the name of some greater concern. We should note that in the *Besamim Rosh*, all laws, biblical and rabbinic, are theoretically subject to abrogation if they fail to promote happiness.[51] Still, virtually the only laws he actually recommends relaxing are those identified as rabbinic or customary. Thus, Berlin's acceptance of the Maimonidean principle became an important tool in his efforts to reform Jewish law.

Furthermore, the fact that rabbinic interpretations were subject to dispute and therefore were incapable of establishing any principles with certitude is cited by Berlin as a partial justification for two of his most far-reaching pronouncements: (1) that there exist no impediments to the marriage of a Jew to a Karaite; (2) that the talmudic demand that one accept martyrdom rather than transgress the prohibitions of idolatry and adultery no longer applies. In the first case, Berlin has R. Asher send the questioner the response of Baruch of Mayence,[52] which he just happens to have. In the *responsum* "Baruch" argues that "Sadducees" (= Karaites) who disagree with rabbinic laws should not be seen in a different light than rabbis who argue about the products of midrashic exegesis. So long as they do not reject what is explicitly stated in Scripture , they remain within the community for purposes of marriage.[53] Rejecting this exegetically derived law or that one has no effect on their status, even though this may lead them to practices that in rabbinic law are seen as conducing to *mamzerut*, a status that precludes entry into the community. Hillel and Shammai had different standards, and Rabbanites and Karaites have different standards, he proclaimed. Just as the former intermarried,[54] so too the latter may intermarry.

The argumentation surrounding the second issue is more complicated, and has been summarized in English by Louis Jacobs.[55] What is of concern to us here is that in reflecting on the varying conclusions reached by different rabbinic courts, Berlin compares the matter to the application of the technique of *qal va-ḥomer*, which cannot serve as the basis for punishment. This is because, he argues, the application of this technique is thoroughly subjective; one man's logical extension of Scripture is another man's nonsense. Similarly, the judgment of different courts in applying the basic principles of Jewish law will differ; one court's certainty may be totally devoid of foundation to another court. Regarding the issue of "accepting martyrdom rather than transgress," the matter appears to be clear and settled, but if we consider the variability in court judgments and also look at talmudic discourse generally, and talmudic exegesis in particular, we discover that there is nothing so clear that it cannot be reinterpreted and subverted. One should not therefore forfeit one's life on the basis of talmudic discussion in the absence of a clear scriptural statement.[56] The absence of certitude makes martyrdom a foolish and unjustified act. It may not be accidental that Berlin's argumentation here echoes the polemics of Saadia, Halevi and Ibn Ezra against the exegesis of Karaites.

From these and other *responsa* it is clear that for Berlin rabbinic Judaism has produced numerous ordinances that no longer address the situation of modern Jews. The rabbinic reading of the scriptural text and the rabbinic claim to exclusive authority in implementing the norms of the biblical text have led to the multiplication of rituals and the drawing of unnecessary social boundaries.[57] These rituals and boundaries no longer serve to promote the best interests of the Jews, and substantial changes are in order.

If, in looking to reform the practice of Judaism, Berlin chose the path of subverting from within, Solomon Maimon chose the path of ridiculing from without. In his autobiography, Maimon felt compelled to provide his readers with a brief description of the Jewish religion from its origins to modern times, in order for them to fully understand the world in which he originated. After a brief discussion of different types of religion, Maimon proceeds to inform his reader that originally Judaism was a natural, true religion, sharply distinguished from paganism—equally natural, but apparently not true. Instead of numerous conceivable gods, Judaism was characterized by the unity of one inconceivable God, the cause from which all effects issued.

From its status as a natural religion, in time Judaism was transformed into a positive religion, characterized by its blending of religious and political interests in a theocracy. This theocracy rested on the principle that within this true, rational religion civil and private interest must exist in harmony. Tellingly, he notes that at this stage, the Jewish religion posited no mysteries in the actual meaning of words.

With the fall of the Jewish state, the religion was once again transformed, for it lost its essential political connection, and now existed only for the purpose of existing. "Driven by hatred against those nations that had destroyed their state and by concern that the fall of the state not succeed in bringing about the demise of their religion," the Jews developed means of preserving and spreading their faith and norms. The primary means of doing this was to develop the pretense that they had a method of interpretation handed down from Moses to explicate the laws, and apply them to specific cases. He notes "this method is not that demanded by reason to update the laws in accordance with their purposes, but rather rests on certain rules in the examination of scriptural expression." The application of these rules continued on through the different periods of Jewish history, one culminating with the completion of the Mishnah (end of the second century), another with the completion of the Talmud (end of the fifth century). The last one began in the immediate post-talmudic period that continues to this day, and will continue until the Messiah comes. It was during these historical epochs that Judaism was progressively distorted (*missbraucht*), resulting in the emergence of a monstrous number of rules and rituals.

A Jew should neither drink nor eat; neither sleep with his wife, nor attend to his most urgent needs, without therein observing a monstrous number of laws. One could fill an entire library, which would certainly rival the ancient Alexandrian one, with books regarding ritual slaughter (the conditions of the knives and the investigation of the internal organs). And what can I say regarding the monstrous number of books that concern laws that are no longer practiced, such as the laws of sacrifice, purity and the like? The pen falls from my hand as I recall that I, and many like me, spent our best years, when the faculties are the strongest, in this intellectually stultifying pursuit (*geistestötenden Geschäft*), staying up nights in order to: bring meaning where there was no meaning; exercise our wit to discover contradictions where there were none; use our acumen to remove them where they were obviously to be met; grasp at shadows through a long chain of inferences; build castles in the air.[58]

Rabbinic Judaism represented a distortion of the earlier forms of Judaism, in that it was so obsessed with surviving intact that, in monstrous fashion, it kept expanding and growing until it was filled with contradictions. It then devoted its energies to removing the contradictions, and then it needed to create new contradictions so that it could resolve them, too. This stifled the spirit, and robbed each generation of its youth.

How did this gross distortion of the original religion come about? For Maimon the answer is clear. The primary factor is the exercise of an "artificial method of scriptural interpretation" that is readily distinguished from any rational one. This more than anything else contributed to the growth of the intellectually stifling culture of rabbinism. Like Israel Zamosc, Maimon believed that rabbinic exegesis established a pattern of thought that progressively diminished the rationality of Jewish intellectual energy and moved it further away from reality. Unlike Zamosc, though, Maimon did not believe that this was a recent development, rooted in the economic privation of the intellectual class. Rather, the irrational, artificial intellectual underpinnings of rabbinic law began to eat away at Jewish rationality from the beginning. The problem was not Polish talmudism, but rabbinism in general; for the latter was energized from the beginning by unacceptable exegesis.

For Maimon, further, there was a certain dishonesty about the whole thing, since, realistically, the artificial method of the rabbis is only a means of creating an external connection between the new laws, demanded by changes in time and circumstance, and the old laws, grounded in the biblical text. He informs us that no rational rabbi would actually say that the sages' exegeses represent the meaning of Scripture; rather he would say that these new rules are necessitated by the time, and are connected to a particular verse on imaginary grounds. However, such "rational rabbis" were to become few and far between, to say the least. The effort to create connections where none existed overwhelmed the awareness of what one was doing and why, and led people to actually believe in the creative prowess of the exegetical principles. In this way Judaism came to be dominated by irrational rabbis, who actually believed in a connection between law and exegesis, and thus went about creating the monstrous number of laws of which Maimon complained.[59]

Maimon's importance for our story derives primarily from the fact that his work, written in German, was read widely and helped fuel the movement for reforming Jewish practice on the grounds that its foundations were not properly established. Maimon himself, though, was not actually interested in reforming Judaism. He did not conclude from his sketch of Jewish religious history that Judaism needed to be reformed. On the contrary, Maimon recognized but two choices confronting the contemporary Jew: to continue to live a fully committed Jewish life, or to recognize the perversion that Judaism represented and abandon it. Reform is dishonest and unworkable. Thus, the perverse nature of rabbinic exegesis is, for Maimon, an indisputable fact, but not one that called for rethinking the connection of the modern Jew to his rabbinic heritage. Rather, it called for the abandonment of that heritage. Nevertheless, the arguments presented by Maimon would resurface in the work of committed Jewish reformers of one kind or another.

Maimon's work is important to our story for another reason as well. His digression on the nature of Jewish history reveals a vision of a tradition in decay. To Maimon, the earliest manifestations of Judaism represented a great intellectual breakthrough in moving beyond paganism's fragmented view of natural causality. Even in its second stage, Judaism incorporated an important political vision. Only with the destruction of the Jewish state did the perversion of its religion begin.

While Maimon eschewed drawing the conclusion that the proper path for the contemporary Jew was to attempt to restore the glory of bygone days, many others who shared his general historical vision, if not its particulars, did not. From the 1790s through the 1830s and, in some cases, beyond, Jewish thinkers routinely saw rabbinism as a decadent form of religion that traduced the ideals and values of the earlier Mosaic revolution. The answer for many of them was a return to Mosaic values, bypassing rabbinism altogether.

The determination of what these "Mosaic ideals" actually were depended on the ideologies of the authors of these works. At different times and in various works, Mosaism was equated with deistic natural religion, Kantian ethics, Hegelian metaphysics, and with the radical egalitarianism of the French Revolution. Some ignored the ritual and cultic elements of the "Mosaic constitution" entirely; some acknowledged them grudgingly; and some saw in them the genius of Moses in accommodating his message to his time, while insisting that they were totally inessential to the true Mosaic frame of mind. What these works had in common was the belief that the contemporary Jew could successfully reorient him- or herself only by the removal of the influences of decadent rabbinism. Even among those "Mosaists" who did not reduce Mosaism to a single principle—monotheism—and its ethical message, rabbinic interpretations and pronouncements were of little value.

One example should suffice to illustrate the point. In his multi-volume *Histoire des Institutions de Moïse et du peuple Hébreu* (1828), certainly the most comprehensive reconstruction of the Mosaic legacy produced by an identifying Jew in this period, Joseph Salvador argued fervently for the political genius of Moses (as he had done in his previously published *Loi du Moïse* [1822]). In marked contrast to the political thinking that prevailed in France until the eighteenth century, most fully adumbrated by Louis XIV's famous dictum *L'état c'est moi*, the Mosaic constitution was founded on the principle *L'état c'est Israël, c'est le peuple.*[60] Anticipating Rousseau, Moses recognized that "there is only a people where there is a law, and that, to generate this law, one needs a general will, a general consensus, freely and clearly expressed."[61] In this construct, Moses seems to play the role of Rousseau's legislator.[62] From here Salvador goes on to discuss the entire range of Mosaic institutions and their applicability. He makes clear at the beginning, however, that rabbinic interpretations and traditions can be used only when they seem to conform to the natural extension of the institutions in question; otherwise they are to be seen as the opinions and aberrations of a later age. While he acknowledges that the historian of the Mosaic age must occasionally fill in lacunae, this is best done by the educated speculation of one who has engaged in lengthy study, rather than by reliance on these "opinions and aberrations" of rabbinic scholars.[63]

Whatever the merits of such a position, the work of Salvador, which was one of the least hostile to rabbinism in this genre, and the other "Mosaists" represented a fundamental challenge to the continuity of rabbinic Judaism. If they did not frame their disavowal of rabbinic Judaism strictly in terms of rabbinic exegesis, it was nevertheless quite clear that they thought rabbinic interpretation was of no value in interpreting the Mosaic texts. (Then again, in some cases, the Mosaic text itself had very little to do with their conceptions of Mosaism.) The demand of these works was that Jews, in searching for historical models for contemporary reform or *régénération*, bypass the previous two millennia entirely, and devote themselves to reappropriating prerabbinic ideals.

I wish to make clear that the issue here, as I see it, is not one of appropriate methodology in the reconstruction of "Mosaic" institutions. The very notion of a single unified cultural and legal system that can be called Mosaic is highly dubious. Enough was known or theorized by the early nineteenth century to at least raise questions about the legitimacy of the "Mosaist" enterprise, whatever one's attitude to rabbinic exegetical and legal materials. That Jewish scholars chose to ignore these questions had much to do with their contemporary struggle for recognition, and little to do with scholarly methodology. These Jews were committed to showing their essential place in the history of Western culture, and, by extension, their rightful and equal place in society. Towards this goal, the ethnically distinctive and exegetically aberrant rabbinism needed to be jettisoned in favor of a pure Mosaism, the bedrock of Western civilization.

A fabricated Mosaism was but one of the cultural alternatives posited by disaffected Jewish intellectuals in this period, and, as noted, was often combined with some of the others. Spinozism, Kantianism, Hegelianism, and Enlightenment liberalism all found their partisans. What united this group was an unremitting hostility to rabbinic Judaism, a hostility shared by most German intellectuals of the period.

The *Verein für Cultur und Wissenschaft der Juden*, founded at the end of the second decade of the nineteenth century, for example, consisted of German-Jewish intellectuals of different backgrounds and ideologies. One of their common elements was a commitment to the "destruction of rabbinism."[64] Similarly, the historian Isaak Markus Jost, briefly associated with the *Verein*, devoted considerable energy to the undermining of rabbinic Judaism in his multivolume *Geschichte der Israeliten*, published through the 1820s.[65] Sometimes the focus of these challenges was on the inadequacy of rabbinic exegesis, but more often it was not. Still, it is against the backdrop of this broad hostility to rabbinism, together with the challenges discussed in the previous chapter and the failure of Wessely and Mendelssohn to deflect them, that we must view the sustained controversies surrounding rabbinic exegesis that emerged in Germany in the early 1840s and continued throughout the century.

Before moving on to that story, we must note that the attack on midrash was not limited to historians and scholars. Missionaries of various sorts, posing as scholars (or perhaps the other way around) also got into the act. They too directed their activity to displaying the foolishness of rabbinic Judaism, which would, they hoped, facilitate their claims that Christianity was a more rational and religiously compelling alternative. Luigi Chiarini (1789-1832), an Italian abbot and a professor of Oriental languages at the University of Warsaw in Poland, was hired by the Russian government to translate the Talmud into French, primarily for the benefit of missionaries who could then direct the attention of Jews to various passages. The assumption here was that once Jews had unmediated access to this document they would of course recognize how ridiculous it was, and how far it stood from the message of Moses' Torah.[66] He prefaced his translation with a two-volume work entitled *Théorie du Judaïsme*, in which he notes among many other things the distorting nature of rabbinic legal interpretation. Similarly, the British missionary Alexander McCaul, whose *Old Paths* created quite a sensation in the middle of the nineteenth century. First published as a book in English in 1837, it was almost immediately translated into Hebrew (by the apostate Stanislaw Hoga), and German; it subsequently appeared in French as well. The primary target of McCaul's pen was the superstition and immorality of the aggadic section of the Talmud that found expression in the liturgy. By focusing on the liturgy, McCaul cleverly insulated himself against the counterclaim that the aggadic passages in question were not meant to be taken seriously. If, after all, they found expression in the *piyyutim* of the synagogue service, they must have been taken literally and seriously. In any event, although very much a secondary target, midrash halakhah also does not fare well in McCaul's treatment. Many halakhot derived from Scripture are derided by McCaul as obviously false readings, the result of rabbinic lack of charity and inability to read the Scriptures correctly.

While these works are no longer of any significance, each of them obviously proved embarrassing to Jewish intellectuals, as each elicited a number of vehement responses. As might be expected the responses focused on the motives and sources of the authors, which would lead one to question their impartiality, and also on the issue of Aggadah, which served as the primary point of attack of both Chiarini and McCaul. The relative ease with which the Jewish respondents dispensed with Chiarini in particular may well indicate the extent to which the abbé did not really understand the Jewish community of Poland; he made clear that his critique was based on the assumption that virtually all Polish Jews believed in the literal meaning of the Aggadah.[67] In the end, Chiarini could do no more than attack Judaism at what he considered its weakest, most ridiculous point, and the same is true for McCaul. Thus, we have a missionary attack focusing primarily on Aggadah. Yet, despite the esteem with which Aggadah was regarded by many segments of Polish Jewry, an insider would know that only by striking at the foundations of halakhah could one hope to truly undermine traditional Judaism.

It is not surprising that when a Jewish missionary, Abraham Buchner, a teacher in the government sponsored rabbinical school in Warsaw[68] who was far more at home in—if no more sympathetic to— the living Judaism of Poland, came to try to undermine Judaism, he did so by means of a frontal assault on the halakhic tradition and the exegetical principles that undergirded it, rather than Aggadah. Abraham Buchner never converted to Christianity, although his two sons did. He helped Chiarini prepare his *Théorie du Judaïsme* in the late 1820s, but until 1848 otherwise exhibited himself as an enlightened defender of talmudic Judaism. After a career disappointment, which he blamed on the Jewish communal leaders of Warsaw, Buchner reversed his course and took his pen in hand to compose a work, *Der Talmud in seiner Nichtigkeit (The Worthlessness of the Talmud)*, which was published in two short volumes by the Missions-Druckerei of Warsaw in 1848. The point of the work was to estrange Jews from their customs (*abwendig zu machen von Gebräuchen*) by showing that there could be no oral tradition from Moses, and more to the point, that rabbinic explanations (*Erklärungen*) of the Scriptures were totally absurd. The book is replete with descriptions of rabbinic exegesis as laughable, disgracing human reason (*den Menschenverstand entehrend*), eccentric (*wunderlich*), a distortion of the divine word (*Entstellung des göttlichen Wortes*), and so on.[69] Jewish Sabbath law and the Jewish means of reckoning time are singled out for particular ridicule; each is depicted as being devoid of all foundation, since the exegeses the undergirded them represented ludicrous readings of Scripture.[70]

In the end, Buchner's work, while strategically superior to those of Chiarini and McCaul, was seen for what it was, and exercised little influence on Polish Jewry. To my knowledge, the book elicited but one response, an insignificant work entitled *Der Talmud in seiner Wichtigkeit*.[71] Clearly, Buchner's efforts to demonstrate the worthlessness of the Talmud by attacking its historical and exegetical foundations cannot be considered successful in any way. Yet, the work does demonstrate the extent to which the exegetical foundations of rabbinic law were subject to challenge in the nineteenth century; at least one knowl-edgeable missionary felt that these foundations could easily be stripped of their self-evidence in the Jewish community, and with that the edi-fice of rabbinic Judaism would fall. For us here, the work of Abraham Buchner provides yet another illustration of the stakes involved in the Jewish community surrounding the question of rabbinic exegetical ex-pansion of Scripture. More generally, the missionary activity of Chiarini, McCaul, and Buchner must be seen as part of the background of the religious polemics that shaped the ideologies of the major institutional manifestations of Judaism in the nineteenth century.

Abraham Geiger

As many segments of German Jewry were becoming increasingly es-tranged from traditional Judaism, other elements, lay and rabbinic, emerged that tried to harness this alienation through a positive pro-gram of religious reform. The early efforts of the Reformers were char-acterized by liturgical modernization, and, increasingly, the relaxation of norms that no longer addressed the needs of modernizing Jews. Until the 1830s, these attempts at Reform were not part of any organiza-tionally or ideologically coherent movement. From this decade forward, we find increasing efforts to enunciate a clear ideological basis for the reform of traditional Jewish life.

The single most important voice in the development of the ideol-ogy of the Reform movement in Germany belonged to Abraham Gei-ger (1810–74). Many of the theorists of Reform who preceded him argued their case in terms of the inherent flexibility of halakhic sources. Men such as Aaron Chorin, Eliezer Liebermann, and, to a far lesser degree, Michael Creizenach, all argued that rabbinic sources had suffi-cient flexibility to allow for the implementation of numerous reforms including prayer in the vernacular and organ music in the synagogue. Such an approach was certainly limited, as Creizenach, most of all, realized. While the sources may have been flexible enough to justify changing this or that religious practice, they could not provide the in-tellectual moorings for the extensive changes that the times demanded. Further, the vast majority of those committed to the authority of the rabbinic sources—the only ones who might be concerned with talmudic justification—vituperatively challenged the reasoning and motives of Chorin and Liebermann. Those unconcerned with the authority of the rabbinic sources—laypeople and disaffected intellectuals—were com-mitted to a far broader program of change than someone like Liebermann could possibly justify from rabbinic sources.[72] While as late as 1851 the Galician reformer Yehoshua Heshel Schorr continued to polemicize against the effort to reform with concern for halakhic justification (perhaps in response to local versions thereof), by the late 1830s such justification was no longer necessary or decisive in Germany.

That the Talmud could not serve as an authoritative source for Reformers became clear. What was not clear was precisely what role the Talmud should play as Reformers tried to develop a coherent program. On the one hand they realized they could not, and should not, adopt a submissive stance vis-à-vis talmudic demands. Neither they, nor the laity they wished to serve, had any interest in such a stance. On the other hand, they seem to have recognized intuitively that the hostility to rabbinism of someone like Jost was not something on which to build. It involved disinheriting nearly two millennia of Jewish intellectual effort—not only its substance but its animating spirit as well. Indeed, for reasons that cannot distract us here, Jost himself recognized that his early stance on rabbinism could lead just as readily out of Judaism as it could to some kind of purified Judaism, and one confronts considerable moderation of his hostility in his later work.

It is not surprising that, instead of leading to a definitive response to the problem, this quandary should have led to a high level of ambivalence toward rabbinic Judaism in the thinking of early Reformers. Nowhere is this ambivalence more in evidence than in the early work of Abraham Geiger. (By early work I mean here his writings until 1855.)[73]

On the one hand, Geiger saw in the Talmud the embodiment of the principle of tradition, which represents the ongoing reinterpretation and updating of the Bible in the spirit of succeeding ages. As he wrote in one of his earliest published pieces, which appeared in 1835,

The principle of tradition, to which the entire talmudic and rabbinic literature owe their emergence, is nothing other than the principle of constant advance and timely development. It is the principle not to be subservient to the letters of the Bible, but rather to continuously generate anew in accordance with its spirit and the genuine religious consciousness that has penetrated the synagogue. Thus, Judaism fully acknowledges the role of an oral teaching, which in accordance with the spirit and time, is always able, by means of its particular spirit, to revive, restore and regenerate the written word, which would otherwise grow pale with the steady stagnation of death.[74]

The principle of the oral law, which animates the Talmud, is, for Geiger, a central model on which modern Reformers can build. It represents a critical historical example of infusing an ancient text with new life and meaning. This does not mean, of course, that Geiger considered himself bound by the actual teachings of the talmudic rabbis. Even the rabbis themselves admit, he insisted, that the authority of their teachings depended not on tradition per se, but on their acceptance by the whole community. A new generation that no longer accepts these teachings may change them. It does mean, though, that Geiger saw rabbinic Judaism as encompassing wide-ranging religious changes that were understood as "tradition" in the sense that they sought to revive and regenerate the ancient inheritance.

On the other hand, five years earlier, when he was twenty years old, Geiger noted in his diary that already at the age of seventeen he realized that the later *Tannaim* and (especially) the *Amoraim*, were not content with the doctrine of an oral law that could supplement and effectively change the demands of the earlier written law. Rather, they eventually came to the conviction—partly visible in the Mishnah, and fully developed in the Gemara—that everything needed to be grounded in the Bible, which could only lead to artificial exegeses.

Already at that time it became clear to me that just as the spirit of the Talmud thoroughly differs from that of the Bible, so too, the two parts of the Talmud, the Mishnah and Gemara, stand at considerable distance from one another. For, while both of them proceed from the primary goal of applying the biblical law to every possible case by means of their explanations, yet, the Mishnah displays a firm grasp of the earlier (i.e., the Bible) and the assertion that the laws and ordinances it lays down are either grounded in the Bible itself,[75] or that God communicated them to Moses, and from him they were handed down to those who came after him. On but rare occasions do we find in the Mishnah sophistic biblical interpretations or the assertion that a specific law was a tradition, although the beginnings [of these tendencies] lie therein.[76]

However, the seventeen-year-old thought on, the Mishnah's reliance on ancient forms and traditions and reasonable biblical interpretations became unworkable with the political turmoil of the first two Christian centuries and the rise of Christianity. This had minimal impact on the Mishnah itself, because most of its teachings were formulated in the pre-Christian period (thus Geiger's view that the Mishnah, redacted in the early third century, firmly held fast to the inherited traditions), or in Christianity's earliest stages, and therefore, in general, it does not reflect the need of Jews to defend their way of life from Christian challenge. The *Amoraim*, by contrast, read every teaching of the Mishnah into the Scriptures, giving rise to absurd (*verkehrte*) interpretations. Such methods of interpretation then became the basis for the appropriation of the Mishnah's laws and gave rise to further legal expansion. When a biblical "interpretation" was impossible, the *Amoraim* simply advanced the peremptory claim that their particular view was actually a tradition.[77]

For the youthful Geiger, then, only the Mishnah, in the earliest stages of its formation, represented the concept of an adaptive oral law. The later stages of the Mishnah, and especially the Gemara, represent a marked cultural decline, for they are distinguished by perverse biblical exegesis and dubious claims to possession of individual traditions. These developments are understandable, given the political and religious challenges of the age; they are no less regrettable, however, and scarcely provide a model for contemporary Reform.

If we piece together the different aspects of Geiger's thought early in his career, we see that he could relate with sympathy and understanding to the earliest stages of rabbinic Judaism, in which the spirit of the age dominated the approach to the outmoded biblical legacy. These early rabbis, the bearers of the oral law, served him as theoretical models for his own work. The later stages in the emergence of rabbinic Judaism, by contrast, are characterized by an unwillingness to honestly confront change, resulting in the need of the rabbis to perversely locate every response to their "modernity" in the linguistic interstices of the Bible. This aspect of the rabbinic legacy seems to be an embarrassment to Geiger.

For the most part, these early negative thoughts remained private, consigned to a diary never meant for publication. Through the 1830s, while serving as a rabbi in Wiesbaden, Geiger's published work was replete with calls for small changes, and these were often justified in terms of the spirit of rabbinic literature.[78] His already developed views regarding the absurdity of rabbinic exegesis find little expression in these pieces. He seems to have felt that he would have undermined his role as a spiritual leader if he had given full voice to his innermost thoughts. To be sure, already in this decade much of his work is devoted to a lifelong interest in medieval Jewish biblical commentators who had an appreciation for *peshat*.[79] Implicit in these pieces is his sense of the superiority of *peshat* to rabbinic exegesis. Further, Geiger was scarcely reluctant to express his contempt for the emptiness of religious formalism.[80] Still, through his thirtieth birthday, Geiger was able to hold his pen back from an open attack on rabbinic exegesis. However, in 1841, at the height of an ugly controversy surrounding his recent appointment to the rabbinate in Breslau,[81] Geiger could hold back no longer. Perhaps his expressed anger at the anti-intellectual nature of his adversaries got the better of him; perhaps other factors came into play.[82] Whatever the reasons, Geiger let loose with what is probably the most thorough, sustained, and acerbic—if not altogether original—attack on rabbinic exegesis and its related law ever written to that time.[83]

"Das Verhältnis des natürlichen Schriftsinnes zur thalmudischen Schriftdeutung" (The relationship of the natural meaning of Scripture to talmudic scriptural exegesis) appeared some time in 1841.[84] It begins with a consideration of exegesis in the Mishnah, and on this point, Geiger echoes his earlier views that the Mishnah begins on the right path. Here, however, he seems to feel that the Mishnah went astray at an earlier point, and to a far greater degree, than he had previously thought. A particular crux is visible in Mishnah, Chagigah 1:8, which notes that the laws of annulling vows hover in the air, since they have no scriptural support; certain other laws are like mountains hanging from a thread, with extremely limited scriptural support, and others are fully supported by Scripture. On the one hand, this passage indicates that the sages did not think that all law was created in connection to Scripture, but it also shows that at a certain time this came to be considered a problem. Other passages from the Mishnah, such as Sotah 5:2, indicate that already in the time of Yoḥanan ben Zakkai, fear was expressed that a lack of scriptural foundation would lead to the subversion of law. Thus, with the destruction of the Temple the Mishnaic authorities initiated the profound cultural shift to a thoroughly exegetical legal system. Geiger characterizes this as a retrogression to Sadduceeism in spirit, albeit not in substance.

When we look to the Talmuds, we are immediately struck by how fully they absorbed this tendency of the later Mishnaic authorities. Particularly telling is the talmudic discussion of the above-cited Mishnah in Chagigah, which challenges the Mishnah's assertion that a cancellation of vows is devoid of any scriptural support! The notion that anything could be devoid of support was anathema to the Talmudists. What in the Mishnah was only

gently begun now completely and totally overran the ground of healthy exegesis, of which not a trace remained. Words and letters were interpreted in the most arbitrary way, analogies were found in the most accidental and contingent similarities, which then justified the complete transference of legal consequences from one legal text to another. One literally set out to look for, and to some extent produce, anomalies and superfluities in the relevant passages, in order to connect them with interpretations to which they could not truly be related, even if there really were an anomaly present.[85]

Geiger's conclusion was that rabbinic exegesis manifested a "turbid" (indeed, a defective) exegetical sense. For, everywhere midrash halakhah was infected with a ridiculous *Buchstäblichkeit*, here meaning an excessive concern with words, half-words, even letters, ripped from their context and natural meaning.

Geiger was aware that there were places in the Talmud that seemed to question certain midrashic applications, such as the principle that the Torah speaks in human language. But, he correctly argues, these represent exceptional cases, in which people who otherwise support these applications resist a given interpretation for one reason or another. Similarly, the principle that a verse never departs from its *peshat* scarcely means that one must always sustain the "simple meaning of the words" (*einfachen Wortsinne*), since the rabbis had only a dim sense (*dunkle Ahnung*) of what that was. The thousands of instances in which the rabbis show no concern whatsoever for the *peshat* overwhelm the few instances in which they actually take note of the fact that the exegeses in question bear no relation to it. In particular, Geiger notes that at Shabbat 63a, R. Kahana reacts to the claim that no verse can depart from its *peshat* by exclaiming, "By the time I was eighteen I had studied the entire Talmud, and I did not know that a verse does not depart from its *peshat* until today." Such a declaration on the part of an important talmudic sage is evidence enough that one is scarcely dealing with a general principle here.

Throughout the essay the exegetical sense of the rabbis is described as *getrübt* (turbid), and is contrasted with views that are *gesund* (healthy). The rabbis, impelled by the perceived need to ground everything in Scripture, lost their ability to read Scripture intelligently.

Geiger, like the author of the *Kol Sakhal*, is sufficiently schooled in Jewish apologetics to know that the response to his broadside will be that the rabbis did not really mean it—that their exegesis had no relation to the norms they produced, or, rather, tradited. For this reason a central focus of the essay is to show that this position is nonsense. Without addressing the question of a tradition at all, Geiger showed to his satisfaction that the rabbis obviously took their exegeses extremely seriously, and understood them as the basis of law. Numerous passages from the Mishnah and the Gemara are noted, each one of which would be devoid of meaning if the rabbis in question did not believe that the exegeses they proffered were authentic readings of Scripture that produced law.[86]

It is important to understand what is at stake here. Geiger is not actually addressing the historical question of whether rabbinic law proceeded from rabbinic exegesis. Indeed, in the early work under consideration at the moment, he seems to suggest on a number of occasions that most of it did not. The laws contained in the Mishnah emerged before the misguided effort to ground them in Scripture. To be sure, once the exegetical imperative came to dominate rabbinic thought, new laws did emerge as a result. Still, the historical question was not the issue. For Geiger the question was one of inner-systemic description, that showed clearly that the rabbis truly thought that the basic extrascriptural laws emerged from the imagined anomalies of scriptural language, even though he was prepared to state that historically most of them did not. Because the later *Tannaim* and *Amoraim* truly thought this, they imparted to their laws a level of authority and a sense of eternal validity they did not deserve.[87] They made it seem as if God had intended all their modifications, and that he intended for these modifications to be valid forever. For Geiger, then, the issue was not the law's emergence, but the authority granted that law.[88]

Geiger's point was clear. The fundamental norms of rabbinic Judaism, produced in the early rabbinic period, came about as scholars tried to apply biblical laws, in spirit if not to the letter, to the demands of developing religious life. Their efforts were progressive and conditioned by time and place, and for that reason had unquestioned legitimacy at that time. Later scholars, particularly those who lived after the completion of the Mishnah, were driven by a sense of insecurity and felt compelled to enhance the level of authority of these laws and norms. They thus began a misguided effort to ground these laws in Scripture, doing violence to the meaning of the latter while extinguishing the progressive spirit of the former. Their exegeses were increasingly more turbid, defective, and devoid of a healthy interpretive sense. All this being so, the demands of the age are clear. A proper historical conceptualization of the emergence of Jewish law is required, so that its essential temporally conditioned nature will be recognized. Once this is accomplished, Judaism can be put back on the proper path as a religion with a progressive dynamic, able to respond to the demands of time.

Geiger's argument here is actually rather subtle, and even moderate. However, his aggressive tone, and the accusations of turbidity, defectiveness, and unhealthiness overwhelmed the ability of any traditionally-oriented reader to discern the nature of the argument. Further, the fact that the piece was published at a time of heightened tension between the Orthodox and Reform segments of the Breslau Jewish community (and the tension spilled well beyond Breslau) meant that such readers would not even try. What they saw in this piece was a claim that all Jewish law is created by turbid exegesis, and therefore devoid of any legitimacy at any time. Such views were indubitably heretical,[89] and provided the Orthodox with further confirmation that Geiger was unfit to be a community rabbi. Thus, the argument of this essay was attacked together with other aspects of Geiger's work in a general indictment prepared by Solomon Tiktin, the Orthodox rabbi of Breslau, with the participation of other Orthodox spokesmen.[90]

What is of interest in this response is the extent to which (implicitly, of course) the Orthodox writers essentially agreed that Jewish exegesis could not serve as an acceptable basis for Jewish law. In response to the age-old question, "How do we know this?" the writers of this work would respond, "From a communication given by God to Moses and successfully transmitted throughout all the generations." Exegesis had nothing to do with the promulgation of the laws. In support they cite Halevi, Maimonides (which represents, in my opinion, a very sloppy reading of Maimonides' work), and Mendelssohn's introduction to Ecclesiastes. The last source is surprising for two reasons: first, that they quote Mendelssohn at all; and, second, that they cite a text that seems to argue for precisely the opposite position. In any event, the polemical response to Geiger goes so far as to accuse him of having insulted the reputation of the rabbis and having demonstrated that they were ignorant by stating that they truly believed in the creative power of their exegesis, when, in fact, the authors claimed, they did not.

The attack of the Orthodox gave Geiger a chance to respond in turn. Here he accused his opponents of ignorance and of an inability to properly read the Talmud. He seemed to revel in pretending that he was being attacked for finding rabbinic exegesis to have been seriously intended, and sarcastically wonders whether his opponents would consider Naḥmanides a heretic as well. For Naḥmanides had fully and completely refuted the position of Maimonides, and, by extension, the position that the Orthodox spokesmen were now advocating.

This whole exchange, while not advancing understanding one iota, is of interest in demonstrating the shifts that had taken place in Orthodox historical views within one to two generations. An insulated Orthodox, or, rather, traditional, rabbinate, feeling no pressing need to defend the validity of the oral law, could confidently appropriate the traditional vision of most medieval rabbinic scholars; a defensive German Orthodoxy, by contrast, could not. Its spokesmen saw that the traditional vision would undermine rather than support adherence to the oral law, and thus begins a shift in understanding that led Orthodox rabbis and historians in the modern period to insist that the entire oral law was revealed by God to Moses at Sinai. As we have seen, such a position is not new by any means, and was, on the explicit basis of talmudic discourse, rejected by Naḥmanides and virtually all who followed him. Yet it re-emerges in full force among the Orthodox in the nineteenth century directly in response to the work of people like Geiger.[91]

The response of Tiktin and some of his colleagues was not the only response elicited by Geiger's essay. Geiger obviously heard from others, who pointed out to him that he had ignored important counter-evidence, particularly, the differing conception of the Yerushalmi. This more thoughtful response led to Geiger's second essay on rabbinic exegesis,[92] which contained detailed discussion of the Yerushalmi's views, as well as consideration of various passages in which rabbis rebel against what appears to them as unsupportable exegesis. Geiger demonstrates to his satisfaction that these all represent exceptions, for even the rabbis in question in other places engage in the same kind of exegesis that they attacked in the exceptional case. His point is once again to affirm the claim that the later talmudic sages really believed that most Mishnaic law could be exegetically derived from the Torah, and this fact led them to a defective exegetical sense, and to wildly inaccurate claims regarding the authority of the oral law. In the position of Geiger's opponent(s) here, we see the beginnings of a yet another traditionally oriented historical response to the problem of the foundations of Jewish law: one which sees the Yerushalmi's views on Rabbis Aqiba and Ishmael as being of central importance. This will be the focus of the next chapter.

Geiger's two essays were hardly his last offerings on the subject. In numerous works he continued to demonstrate the vast distance that separated rabbinic exegesis and healthy interpretation; he showed that talmudic halakhah could not truly be grounded in any kind of reasonable reading of Scripture.[93] Rabbinic norms were products of a time and place, not eternally valid laws encoded within a revealed and timeless text. On this point Geiger never wavered.[94] In addition, he continued to document the rebellion against rabbinic exegesis from within, that is, the medieval commentators who pioneered philologically based appreciations of the plain sense of Scripture. These commentators, he thought, represented a considerable cultural advance, which should be fully appreciated by the modern Jew.[95] Yet the many reactions to his work, which will be discussed in the next chapter, raised some serious challenges to the particulars of Geiger's argument. It is a sign of Geiger's maturity and honesty as a scholar that the many reactions to his work led him to rethink certain issues, and, in his *Urschrift und Übersetzungen der Bibel in ihrer Abhängigkeit von der innern Entwicklung des Judenthums*, published in 1857, to advance a conception of Jewish law and exegesis that broke important new ground. While full discussion of this work must be postponed to later in this chapter and again in the next chapter, I wish to note here that Geiger's rethinking seems to have had an important impact on his Reform colleague Samuel Holdheim, to whom we now turn.

Samuel Holdheim

The learned Samuel Holdheim (1806–60) was the product of a traditional Polish talmudic education. A restless and mercurial spirit, in less than a decade he went from serving as a traditional rabbi in Frankfurt-on-the-Oder to championing the cause of radical Reform.[96] His developed vision of Reform demanded the abrogation of all ceremonial laws, and all civil laws that applied only to the ancient Jewish theocratic state. For Jews today anything recognized by the secular civil law as valid had authority for the Jew as well, regardless of what traditional Jewish sources had to say on the matter. Thus, Holdheim could sanction a mixed marriage, since in Judaism marriage is a civil matter, whose jurisdiction now passed to the state. In short, the absolute and pure *religious* elements of the revealed Mosaic legislation remain eternally binding; the rest no longer applies.

As far as Holdheim's attitude to rabbinic literature is concerned, one can discern a clear development in his thinking. In one of his earliest works as a Reformer, written in 1842 at the height of a controversy regarding a new prayer book in Hamburg, he followed Geiger in making a clear distinction between tradition and Talmud. Unlike Geiger, however, he asserted that he believed fully in the former. He understood tradition to mean "an orally transmitted explanation of the holy Scriptures, for without this the Scriptures would, on the one hand, be incomprehensible and incapable of practical realization . . . and, on the other hand, the spirit would be enslaved to the letters, and these alone would dominate."[97] However, the tradition does not consist of substantive conclusions, for one could hardly exhaust all the interpretive possibilities. Rather, the tradition consists of the hermeneutic rules themselves, which seek to draw meaning from the most allusive of scriptural phrases. While the exegetical method represents tradition originating from Sinai, the content that emerges from applying the rules is authoritative for the interpreter but not for others who may apply the rules differently. For one can apply them in an erroneous manner. The content represents the fallible human side, and is subject to dispute; it is not necessarily binding. In support of this position he, like so many before him, quotes the second principle of Maimonides' *Sefer ha-Mitzvot*.[98]

Holdheim would quickly abandon the effort to retain the interpretive techniques of the past; he believed they related to the legal sections of the Bible in a manner that was ultimately based on a complete misunderstanding of the verdict of Jewish history. In time he arrived at the conclusion that after the destruction of the Jewish state, the Mosaic law could no longer have any validity, however one chose to interpret it. Only the few basic, eternally valid principles of the Torah could continue to speak to Jews in the messianic age that was now approaching.[99] To the Talmud he denied all authority; ultimately, as Michael Meyer notes, for Holdheim, all authority rested in reason and conscience alone.[100] From the perspective of reason and conscience he polemicized frequently against talmudic norms, sometimes with such vehemence and exaggeration as to call forth negative reactions from those otherwise sympathetic to him, such as David Einhorn,[101] who himself was certainly not reluctant to express his contempt for rabbinic interpretation.[102] Nevertheless, through most of his career, Holdheim seems to have been guided by the assumption that the rabbinic legislation represented an honest, if misguided, effort to meet the religious needs of his day. His oft-quoted remark that "The Talmud speaks out of the religious consciousness of its age and for that time it *was* right; I speak out of the higher consciousness of my age and for this age I *am* right"[103] is an expression of this attitude. While less in need of historical role models than other Reformers, Holdheim still seemed to feel that the Talmud does involve a certain effort to address the changed situation of its day. Its teachings and methods are irrelevant, but its reformist example is worthy of note.

In addition to showing a certain appreciation for the efforts of the rabbis, Holdheim's dictum betrayed his confidence that the path of Reform was right and destined to triumph. What he did not expect in 1845, I imagine, was the emergence of a conservative scholarship (as opposed to Orthodox polemics) and an aggressive political reaction that would challenge that confidence. But that is precisely what the 1850s were to bring. As Ismar Schorsch has noted, the decade saw the publication of four works that forcefully challenged the prevailing notions of rabbinism in liberal religious circles. The first two, Nachman Krochmal's *More Nevukhe ha-Zeman* (*Guide of the Perplexed of the Time*), and the fourth volume of Heinrich Graetz's *Geschichte der Juden*, which appeared in 1851 and 1853 respectively, and the fourth, Zechariah Frankel's *Darkhe ha-Mishnah*, which appeared in 1859, were works of conservative scholarship that sought to fashion a scholarly framework in which rabbinic Judaism could be seen as the embodiment of authentic Jewish tradition.[104]

The third work to appear in the decade, Geiger's *Urschrift*, published in 1857, while scarcely conservative in any way, also reconceptualized the history of rabbinic Judaism. In Geiger's view, the dispute between the Pharisees and Sadducees was a dispute between progressive and conservative forces, respectively. Here the Pharisees, led by Hillel, and some of their rabbinic successors, led by Aqiba, emerged as the leaders of the people in the fashioning of a new law. Perhaps more surprising in light of Geiger's previous work is his claim that they were able to accomplish this progressive reform through the means of biblical exegesis. To be sure, Geiger still considered the method artificial,[105] but now he saw it as the means through which the biblical text (which, he now understood, was always tied to the internal development of Judaism anyway) could continue to reflect the inner religious consciousness of the age. The Sadducees and some of the more conservative rabbinic sages, by contrast, were unable to adapt to the inevitability of change, and history has passed them by.[106] In the *Urschrift*, even the Babylonian Talmud gets favorable notices, as opposed to the Yerushalmi, which is shaped too much by the older material.[107] Thus, while scarcely conservative, Geiger's work is devoted to rehabilitating the Pharisees and rabbis in the face of the negative portrait of them in works of Christian historiography,[108] and involves a positive reconceptualization of rabbinic exegesis, albeit one that argues for its legitimacy because of its subversive political potential rather than its actual interpretive insights.

In the face of this scholarship, Holdheim was moved to write what was to be his last work, *Ma'amar ha-Ishut*; it was written toward the very end of his life, and was published posthumously. While ostensibly a study of Rabbanite and Karaite marital law, it is actually two intertwined polemics. The first is against the new scholarship; conservatives like Krochmal, Graetz, Frankel, and also Shlomo Yehudah Rapoport are explicitly criticized,[109] and Geiger in particular is bludgeoned throughout the work,[110] often on the basis of his earlier essay attacking rabbinic exegesis, which Holdheim turns against his more recent work. The second polemic is against virtually every legal institution ever established by Pharisees and rabbis in the realm of family law and beyond; these institutions are routinely contrasted with those of the Sadducees and Karaites, who always got it ethically and textually right.

The Pharisees and rabbis routinely missed the mark, because their legal thinking was always guided by, mirabile dictu, perverse exegesis. No matter how clear it was that a particular rabbinic pronouncement violated an explicit scriptural imperative, the rabbis would not yield.[111] They therefore constructed a system of family law that defied what was clearly God's message. They allowed divorces when they should not have, and turned the sacred and loving institution of marriage into a loveless contract. The Sadducees and Karaites, by contrast, committed themselves to implementing the wishes of the divine lawgiver and constructed a system far more in tune with the exalted values of the Bible.

Holdheim was well aware that the Karaites were not always literalists; they too often interpreted the Bible in ways contrary to *peshat*.

Yet, even when they did so they were guided by an entirely different ethos:

> The differences between Karaites and rabbanites is not just the difference between *peshat* and *derash*; it is also the difference between *derash* and *derash*. For the Karaites follow a midrashic path that is essentially different from that of the rabbanites. The rabbanites delve into the meaning (*kavvanat*) of the writings; the Karaites delve into the intent (*kavvanat*) of their writer. The rabbanites struggle to know their substance; the Karaites seek the will and desire of their giver. The rabbis are concerned with the law; the Karaites, with the legislator. The rabbis will interpret the Torah employing principles that are external to it; the Karaites will interpret on the basis of the Torah itself, employing the principles on which it is founded. . . .[112]

For Holdheim, the Sadducees and Karaites were devoted to God and God's word, not to perverting the language of a text. The Pharisees and rabbis, by contrast, transgressed the boundaries of linguistic convention and common sense. They had no compunction against attributing to God anything that occurred to them, to their contemporaries, or even to the Gentiles among whom they lived. It is no wonder that "wise sages who know the Torah" rose up against them and refused to accept their dishonest interpretations.[113]

In 1845, Holdheim could say that the Talmud was right in its day, confident that such a pronouncement would never impede his efforts at Reform; for his day he was right, and that was all that mattered. In 1859, however, he was not so sure. He was thus led to the insistence that the rabbis were *not* right in their day or any day. They were not people committed to the needs of the time, they were not students of the spirit of the biblical text using their ingenuity to keep it alive; if only they had been, he said, "I would not pour scorn on them. On the contrary, I would say that God should bless them for this. For they would have been midwives to Israel, who preserved the children who were born and sired by their wisdom and understanding, in their discernment of the inner idea of the giver of the Torah. . . ."[114] But they were nothing of the kind! They were perverters and distorters, whose exegesis destroyed the inner idea of the giver of the Torah. Their triumph has impeded the spiritual development of the children of Israel, and they deserve his contempt.

Holdheim, too, knows the nature of Jewish apologetics, and thus attacks Ibn Ezra and Maimonides, who deny the creative power of midrash in fashioning Jewish law. They have falsified the record in so doing, and even more in positing that the ancient rabbis truly understood the distinction between their interpretations and the natural significance of the Bible's language. This is a distinction the later thinkers created; it does not have any role to play in understanding the classical rabbinic texts.[115] This fact was understood by Rashi and Naḥmanides, who were more honest in asserting that the *derashot* of the rabbis represent their actual understanding of the meaning of the text.

Equally galling to Holdheim was the attempt by apologists to suggest that the rabbinic system itself acknowledges the right to interpret the biblical text in a manner that differs from that of the rabbis, so long as exercising this right does not impinge on the halakhah. That is, these apologists grant that the text does not mean what the rabbis say it does; yet, they would have Jews conduct themselves in conformity to a law that was created by distorting the meaning of the text. This position, whose modern representative Holdheim takes to be Rapoport, is thoroughly dishonest. The ancient rabbis who created this perverse system are guilty of inadvertent error; they simply could not read any better. But if we attempt to perpetuate this error, now that we recognize it as such, it is no longer an inadvertent offense. It is an active commitment to falsehood, which we would continue to bequeath to our children. This cannot be tolerated.[116]

Soon after committing these thoughts to paper, Samuel Holdheim was dead. When he died, his was probably the only significant voice (at least in Germany) among those committed to the continuity of the Jewish religion in some form that saw its future ensured by a complete and total break with rabbinic exegesis and authority. Not even David Einhorn or Kaufmann Kohler, who were otherwise quite sympathetic to Holdheim's practical vision of Reform, could envision a Judaism that completely severed its connection to its rabbinic antecedents. Holdheim's *Ma'amar ha-Ishut* was written in the spirit of rebellion that characterized certain German Jews in the preceding decades; by his time, however, German Reform, led by Geiger, was moving beyond the rebellious stage, to selectively reclaim elements of the rabbinic past.[117] Yet Holdheim's work assumes an important and radical place in the history of the constant Jewish grappling with the exegetical foundations of rabbinism. For Holdheim, in 1859, depriving rabbinic norms of any vestige of historical legitimacy was critical if Reform was to continue on its proper path. Attacking the exegetical foundations of these norms, and the integrity of the exegetes, represented the means to accomplish this. Perhaps few, if any, could find interest in his resolution of the problem; yet he articulated the issues with a brutal honesty that brings home just how overwhelming the weight of the irrationality of Jewish exegetical assumptions could become. For Holdheim all previous efforts to find some place for rabbinic midrash within a rational cultural vision were doomed by their dishonesty. Even Geiger's vision, in addition to being historically unfounded, depicts a kind of *mitzvah ha-ba'ah be-'averah*—an achievement of spiritual progress through a dishonest appropriation of the authority of Scripture on the part of the Pharisees and rabbis. Holdheim would have none of it. Distorting a text could never lead to anything but error. Apologizing for the distortion or creating demonstrably false historical models compounds the error. Perhaps naïvely, he seems to have felt that one cannot re-write one's past to suit contemporary needs (although he seemed to have little difficulty creating a usable Karaite past); nor may one say of one's spiritual ancestors that they did not mean what they obviously did mean. The historical legacy of rabbinic exegesis was clear; nothing could be salvaged from it.[118]

With Holdheim a "tradition" of cultural parricide comes to an end in Germany. As with all parricidal dramas, this one brought with it demonstrable liberating effects. Attacking the legitimacy of rabbinic Judaism was palpably cathartic for someone like Solomon Maimon and for the many others who followed him up to Samuel Holdheim. Shedding the burden of rabbinic religion was, for them, a sine qua non for a happy existence; given their orientation, such relief required ideological justification.

Yet, as with all parricides, the result is orphan status and, often, overwhelming guilt. Maimon was prepared, at least consciously, to accept this status and become a citizen of the cosmopolitan philosophical realm he imagined was emerging in his time. Others who came after him were less intellectually bold and/or politically naïve. They needed to replace or compensate for the loss of the rabbinic parent. Eschewing conversion, they wished to remain Jews, and imagined that they could dislodge the exegetical culture of rabbinism and replace it with a prophetic Judaism cleansed of rabbinic accretion. In Germany, the relentless attacks on rabbinism eventually petered out, largely, I suspect, for two reasons. First, because a de-rabbinized, prophetic Judaism led just as readily out of Judaism as to its reform;[119] in particular, it could lead just as readily to liberal Protestantism as to a reformulated Judaism.[120] Second, like the earlier deistic attacks on revealed religions, mutatis mutandis, all participants had but one theme to play that allowed for a limited number of variations. In time, if one wished to disinherit the products of rabbinic exegesis, there was nothing left to say that had not been said before.[121]

Subsequent Reformers recognized that they could not break completely with earlier Jewish traditions and still create a compelling historical vision that would support continued Jewish identification. They needed to find a way of reconnecting with the parent culture without submitting to its demands. Most of them found the means to create the compelling vision they required through the researches of Heinrich Graetz, (to be discussed in the next chapter), the later Geiger, and the Hungarian Reformer, Leopold Löw.[122] In Graetz's *Geschichte der Juden* and Geiger's *Urschrift* they found a historical portrait of Pharisaism and rabbinism that allowed for a vision of the past with which Jews could continue to identify. They were able to reclaim rabbinic sources as *part* of their heritage without traducing their modern sensibilities.[123] The earlier efforts at killing the parent culture were necessarily rejected.[124]

While in time the positions of the early Geiger and Holdheim were modified, their influence on the Reform movement in the 1840s and 50s was substantial. In particular, Geiger's influence—both reputed and real—loomed large and opponents felt his work required response. His vision of Jewish exegesis took center stage in the larger criticism of rabbinic culture that emerged with such force in the modern period. His position as a rabbi, as an editor of an important journal, and as the emerging chief spokesman for the Reform movement in Germany, made it impossible to dismiss him as peripheral, and his substantial learning rendered the inevitable charges of ignorance dubious. His essay challenged the foundations of traditional Judaism, and could not be ignored. It was only a matter of time before scholars with different orientations would enter the fray.[125]

7 • The Traditionalists Strike Back

As WE HAVE ALREADY seen, attacks on the legitimacy of the oral law could not go without response. The very existence of traditional Judaism depended on a viable conception of the origins of Jewish praxis. Yet the responses of the nineteenth century, which originated primarily in the German and Habsburg lands, could not simply echo those of earlier times. What could plausibly be seen as a defense of traditional Judaism in the tenth or eleventh century, or even the seventeenth, looked unrefined in light of the challenges of the nineteenth century, for several reasons. In many cases, the attacks on midrash halakhah, and the oral law generally, routinely included a detailed rejection of the responses of earlier Jewish apologists. Certainly this was the case with Geiger and Holdheim, as we saw in the previous chapter. For this reason alone, a simple restatement of past apologetics would scarcely do.[1]

The situation in the nineteenth century was different for other reasons as well. The new intellectual options pioneered in the previous centuries were now joined by new social alternatives that significantly weakened essential centripetal forces. Not only could one question or reject the norms of traditional Judaism, one could now continue to do so while remaining within the organized and recognized Jewish community; one could also stake out a middle ground between wholesale acceptance and rejection of these norms. One had far greater flexibility in how one behaved and in the way in which one's history was appropriated. One could question the divine provenance of the Pentateuch without abandoning Judaism, an option essentially unavailable to an ex-Marrano like Juan de Prado or to Baruch Spinoza.[2] Thus, the black-

and-white alternatives of the past were replaced by the ability to carve out one's own niche within the Jewish community, if that is where one wished to remain. This being the case, reflections on the nature of Jewish law and exegesis that were geared to the times had to be more subtle and complex than previous responses had been.

Further, Jewish thinkers of the nineteenth century were influenced by the intellectual disciplines that emerged in Germany and elsewhere. The German academy, in particular, was dominated by competing historical visions, and these in turn demanded considerable subtlety on the part of those who would offer a historical response to the challenges of Reform. In addition, as we shall see, while some among the Orthodox retained essentially fideist readings of the Jewish past and the place of the oral law within it, they too had intellectual disciplines on which to draw in their efforts to defend the legitimacy of their way of life, particularly philology.

The new social options and academic disciplines meant that the terms of the debate simply could not be the same as in previous encounters between rabbinic exegesis and its critics. The times called for more creative responses, and the call did not go unheeded. The nineteenth century was witness to substantial reflection on the nature of Jewish law and exegesis emanating from those who were vigorously opposed to the lessons of history learned by Reformers.

While those committed to retaining traditional Jewish practices and norms responded to the challenges with vigor, they did not do so with anything approaching conceptual harmony. Some were prepared to fully engage historical thinking and fashion a response from within it. Others turned to philology and new exegetical theories to confront the problem. In the end, the traditionalist camp came to be divided into two mutually hostile groups. One group posited a development of Jewish law over time and in response to changing moral, religious, and cultural values, while the other insisted on retaining what they identified as the traditional approach. The latter affirmed either a comprehensive revelation that fully encompassed problematic extrabiblical norms, or, alternatively, that all laws that emerged over time were as intended at the beginning. The first group was thoroughly historical in motivation, if not always in execution, for its essential traditionalism often clouded historical judgments. The second was profoundly ahistorical, coming ultimately to see efforts to defend tradition by recourse to history as more damaging than the efforts of Reformers to undermine it. Historical defenses, as opposed to dogmatic or textual-exegetical approaches, served to relativize the tradition by seeing it as a response to contingent circumstance. Coming from defenders of tradition, observers of Jewish law, this relativism had a much greater chance of infiltrating traditional self-perceptions than did the more radical Reform challenges, which were far more easily recognized as compromising the essentials of the faith. Thus, by the middle of the nineteenth century a new *Kulturkampf* had emerged, pitting the Orthodox and the so-called historical school against one another, even as both groups were working hard to combat Reform.[3]

THE HISTORICAL SCHOOL

Heinrich Graetz

The "historical school" refers to a group of conservative scholars who, despite many differences, were committed to the notion that the Jewish present and future must be continuous with the essential patterns of the past. It included such men as Nachman Krochmal (1785–1840) and Shlomo Yehudah Rapoport (1790–1867) of Galicia (although Rapoport served as a rabbi in Prague from 1840); Samuel David Luzzatto (1800–1865) of Padua; Zechariah Frankel (1801–75); Heinrich Graetz (1817–91) (ultimately) of Breslau; and Isaac Hirsh Weiss (1815–1905) (ultimately) of Vienna.[4] As a rule, they were quite traditional in their view of revelation, and largely deferential to the halakhic rulings of the rabbis. What distinguished them from the Orthodox was their commitment to *Wissenschaft,* and their conviction that Jewish law and praxis have undergone lengthy processes of development, which can be illuminated by historical research. For the purposes of this chapter, we will focus primarily on Frankel, Graetz and Weiss, as their work broke new historical ground in creating constructs of rabbinism and also provides the best opportunity to understand the tremendous intellectual difficulties presented by rabbinic exegesis. Although he was the youngest of the three, we will turn first to Graetz.

He was born into a working-class Jewish family in Posen in 1817, and was educated in a traditional manner. By the age of twenty he found himself in the throes of a spiritual crisis; his reading of Samson Raphael Hirsch's *Neunzehn Briefe über Judentum* had a profound impact on him, and he went to Oldenburg to study with Hirsch, the leading voice of the emerging modern Orthodoxy in Germany. Graetz was not to remain in Oldenburg (or in Orthodoxy) for long. He moved on to the university of Jena, where he received his Ph.D. In time he found his way to another mentor, Zechariah Frankel, and soon after it was founded (1854) he became a professor of history at the Jewish Theological Seminary of Breslau.

By his own admission, in the middle 1840s Heinrich Graetz was an ambitious and restless man, anxious, among other things, to deflect the momentum of Reform.[5] He was driven by an "irrepressible attachment to the divine and revealed Judaism, as opposed to the empty deism or even the deification of humanity,[6] as it is preached by the newest philosophy. . . ."[7] He identified the latter tendency with Abraham Geiger, and it was Graetz's greatest hope to be able to turn the Jewish community away from it.[8] His motives were not entirely noble; he confided to his diary that he felt moved to act not only by his allegiance to traditional Judaism but also by a personal hatred (*Privathass*) for Geiger, partly rooted in the latter's disrespect towards Graetz's erstwhile teacher, Samson Raphael Hirsch.[9] Thus, for religious, scholarly and personal reasons Graetz was driven to challenge Geiger's reading of Jewish history, and to develop an understanding of that history that displayed the power of Jewish tradition.

He was thus most gratified when Michael Sachs (1808–64) published his *Die Religiöse Poesie der Juden in Spanien*, which took up the question of rabbinic exegesis from a traditional but scholarly perspective. Sachs, originally of Prague, where he studied with Rapoport, was trained in classical philology at the University of Berlin.[10] An inveterate opponent of Reform, Sachs included a brief overview of the development of Jewish religion in his study of medieval Spanish poetry. Here he noted the central role played by the Bible in legitimizing Jewish religious activity; to keep the Bible ever present, though, required intensive scholarship and reflection on its meaning. "The word, inherited from the past, should not confront the present as something historical and transient, foreign and indifferent to it. Thus, the life of the present was set into the letters of the past, and one can hardly distinguish in this unique treatment of the ancient scriptural word between exegesis and eisegesis. The sacred books as such were the ever present, certain point of unity, the banner around which the generations could rally."[11]

Viewed from this perspective, rabbinic midrash becomes the method through which the Jews can sustain their immediate and real relationship to the Sacred Scripture. The interpretations were rooted in the spirit of the people, and display a concern with the immediacy of God, not with the rules of grammar. Sachs thus laid the foundation for an attack on Geiger's view of rabbinic midrash. Sachs proclaimed that when Geiger finds a turbid exegetical sense in rabbinic literature he betrays his own turbid sense of the characteristics of these works. He does not understand what motivates the rabbis, nor can he appreciate the theological underpinnings, which see each letter of an expression of divine thought as its own "independent organism" giving rise to new meanings. It is absurd to expect that textual and linguistic research of the modern kind can be a concern for the living forces that produce religious thought; when the creative juices of a religion still flow, such research can only impoverish and impede.[12] A modern sense of linguistic boundaries could emerge only after the dawn of a new age; in the case of the Jews this occurred with the rise of Islam and Jewish contact with it. For Sachs the period in which reflection—a function of distance—sets in is even later than that posited by Hegel. To the scholar of Jewish poetry, the owl of Minerva does not spread its wings with the falling of the dusk, but must rather awake with the rooster to herald a new day, a more distant age in which one can reflect on the past. For Sachs, Minerva's owl can spread its wings only after immediacy and creativity are already completely gone; reflection is the outgrowth of a historical process and signifies that something has been irredeemably lost.

Sachs's vision made a deep impression on Graetz when it appeared in print in 1845. In his first published attack on Geiger's work, Graetz challenged the Reformer's views on rabbinic exegesis primarily by quoting Sachs. The latter had "bestowed lustre on the truth"; it was "no small merit . . . of the ideas-rich writer on religious poetry that he demolished the insipid arguments in support of the turbid exegeses of the talmudists."[13] Elsewhere in the same attack, Graetz also cited the objections of Rapoport, who expressed the standard apologia that the rabbis did not generate law by means of exegesis, but rather merely sought supports for the tradition within Scripture.[14] From the fact that Graetz can do no more than quote Sachs and Rapoport against Geiger in this early piece, we can see that he had not yet developed a genuinely historical vision of rabbinic law and its emergence. He knew that Geiger had to be wrong, but had not come up with a compelling competing vision on this issue.[15] Yet, the man who would go on to become the greatest and most widely read Jewish historian of the century could remain content neither with Sachs's romanticism nor with Rapoport's apologetics, let alone both together. As he prepared the first volume of his monumental history of the Jews, he would return to the matter, ultimately to initiate a new paradigm of rabbinic exegesis and law that continues to reverberate in academic circles and beyond to this day.

Unlike the other members of the historical school, Graetz's work was not primarily monographic, but synthetic.[16] His multivolume *Geschichte der Juden* focused on all periods of Jewish existence; it represents an effort to create a national history that concentrates on Jewish intellectual and political achievement, and Jewish suffering. The history of rabbinic literature and law was not an all-consuming passion for him, as it was for his teacher Frankel. Nevertheless, the first task Graetz set for himself in writing his history was to address the historical emergence of rabbinic law and literature, and to explain the role of midrash in that historical process.

As is well known, Graetz chose to begin his history with volume 4 (1853), which was devoted to the history of the Jews after the destruction of the Second Temple in 70 c.e. The choice may indicate the author's sensitivity to the academic polemics of his own age, which were, in turn, rooted in long-standing Christian interpretations of the existence of the Jews.[17] The destruction of the Temple here represented the final dissolution of the vital existence of the Jews. Henceforward they existed as fossils or shadows, as a people whom history had passed by. In many ways the academic vision of the continued existence of the Jews resembled, in properly secularized form, the long-standing view of the Church Triumphant, which saw the continued existence of the Jews as a witness to the greatness of Christ, and to the depravity of those who reject him; Jews as such had no independent value. While not all who addressed the matter would have identified the year 70 as the great turning point—many saw it coming far earlier[18]—most agreed that with the events of that year, Jewish religion took a substantial turn for the worse. As we saw in the previous chapters, such a reading of Jewish history was scarcely confined to non-Jews; it found a rather comfortable place within Jewish intellectual circles as well. It was already a basic assumption of Spinoza that the destruction of the Temple and the Jewish state rendered Judaism obsolete, and that continued adherence to it was contrary to what the Bible expressed as God's will. From that point forward more and more Jews came to see the culture produced after the year 70 as a betrayal of the biblical heritage; among them were many early spokesmen for Reform. The belief that such theories had a genuinely deleterious effect on the survival of the Jews in the modern world made it particularly urgent that they be exposed as historical errors.

Graetz, in starting his *Geschichte der Juden* at precisely the point at which many would have claimed there was no longer a vital history of the Jews, defiantly challenged this approach. He was committed to showing the essential continuities of the post-70 culture of the Jews with that which preceded it. This did not mean that there were not substantial changes from the earlier period, but rather that these changes flowed rationally and logically from the legacy of the Pharisaic leaders of the pre-70 Jewish community.[19]

Further, starting his history in the middle, at the point of greatest controversy, made manifest Graetz's conviction that history represented the indispensable medium by means of which one could address the religious and political challenges of the age. Specifically, if in confronting the mass of talmudic law one is moved to ask, "How do we know this?" the answer for Graetz cannot be confined to an exposition of exegetical principles or the assertion of an unverifiable tradition from Sinai. It must rather extend to a consideration of the living and breathing people who are depicted in the literature as active creators of this system of law. We must ask, Who were they? What were their essential characteristics? Why did they do what they did? His history starts out by focusing on the major personalities of the rabbinic movement: Rabban Yoḥanan ben Zakkai, Rabban Gamliel, Rabbis Eliezer, Joshua, Aqiba, and Ishmael. It was from the interaction of these strong personalities, their strengths and weaknesses, that rabbinic Judaism was created.

Graetz understood that his readers could make no sense of what he wanted to tell them here unless he moved back a little bit first. For however much these individuals, who flourished from 70 to 135 C.E., shaped rabbinic Judaism, they were, after all, heirs to the teachings of earlier sages, which they had to take into account in their own work. Furthermore, reading the literature as Graetz did,[20] it was clear that these people did not entirely originate the exegetical methods manifest in their work. Therefore, some foundation, some broad summary of what preceded their work, was necessary for a comprehensible picture to emerge.

That foundation was provided in an article published in 1852, innocuously entitled "Jüdisch-Geschichtliche Studien," with which Graetz helped inaugurate the *Monatsschrift für Geschichte und Wissenschaft des Judenthums*, which was to become perhaps the most important periodical devoted to Jewish studies. The second installment of the article depicts the activities of the Pharisaic sage, Hillel, whom Graetz describes as representing a "decisive turning point in the formation of Jewish law [*Lehre*]." For "Hillel laid the foundation stone for the monumental structure [*Riesenbau*] of the Talmud; one can almost say that he transformed tradition into investigation [*man kann beinahe sagen, er verwandelte die Überlieferung in Forschung*]."[21] What did Hillel do that changed the course of Jewish religious history, according to Graetz? He introduced seven hermeneutic techniques that allowed the received laws to be grounded in Scripture, and allowed subsequent sages to derive new laws from the biblical text.[22]

In Graetz's reconstruction, the historical background to this was as follows. Long before Hillel, a controversy broke out between two groups, who came to be called Pharisees and Sadducees. The controversy surrounded the authority of the received laws, which represented the teachings of earlier authorities, known as scribes or *Soferim*. The dispute, he claims, was not over whether these laws were from Sinai; all agreed they were not. The controversy surrounded whether they had any authority at all. Before the disputing sides had an opportunity to settle the matter in a scholarly way, political contention reared its ugly head, and created further divisions between these two groups. In this politically charged atmosphere, it was impossible for intelligent scholarly debate to proceed. There the matter stood for over a century, from the reign of John Hyrcanus in the second pre-Christian century, until the reign of Herod at the end of the first pre-Christian century. Herod was sufficiently disliked by all to be able to bring about political rapprochement between the factions, and thus, they were finally able to get around to the scholarly debate that politics had postponed for over a century.

It was in the context of this scholarly debate that Hillel introduced his seven rules before the Bene Bateira, who apparently exercised some leadership role. His aim was noble; he wished to demonstrate to the satisfaction of his opponents, who insisted on following only biblical commandments, that these scribal rules were indeed biblical laws. In this way he hoped to remove them from controversy, and put an end to the religious contentiousness of the age. Despite these noble efforts, the Bene Bateira, his first interlocutors, were not receptive, and the desired peace was never achieved.[23]

From the time of Hillel forward, the parties to the dispute were further fragmented, with the Pharisees now divided into two groups: Hillel and his followers, who applied hermeneutic techniques to the Torah, and Shammai and his followers, who relied strictly on the literal meaning of the biblical text and what was bequeathed to them in the name of tradition. The latter therefore possessed no means to generate new laws and respond to new circumstances; the former, by contrast, were seen by Graetz as progressive forces, possessing the means to respond authoritatively to new challenges.

What Graetz has done here is actually quite clever. He has painted a portrait of the development of Jewish law that sees it as rooted ultimately in the ancient enactments of the *Soferim,* who themselves had responded to the spiritual needs of a community returning from exile. When, centuries later, the authority of these laws were challenged, and only then, the hermeneutic rules were developed; they were designed to grant authority to existing laws, on the assumption that they must have had a biblical basis, but they also provided the means to develop new laws. In Graetz's reading of Jewish spiritual history, claiming that everything extrabiblical was the product of tradition was to ordain paralysis; Hillel saw this. He knew that only midrash could grant authority to existing tradition and also provide the flexibility required if Judaism was to remain viable. This flexibility that Hillel bequeathed to the progressive wing of the Pharisaic party was to become even more critical as the rabbinic leaders sought to rebuild after the destruction of the Temple.

From this starting point, one can now make sense of the early history of post-70 rabbinism as Graetz describes it in volume 4 of his *Geschichte*.

This history begins with the activity of Yoḥanan ben Zakkai, described here as the quintessential man of peace. A follower of Hillel, he distinguished himself in all areas of rabbinic learning, including scriptural interpretation, the authority of which remained controversial, with the Hillelites affirming and the Shammaites rejecting.[24] He had many students, some of whom remained loyal to Shammai despite studying with Yoḥanan. Two of his contemporaries were particularly significant for the development of the oral law: Naḥum of Gimso and Neḥuniah ben Hakanah. The latter was an enthusiastic devotee of Hillel's hermeneutic rules, while the former pioneered new methods of exegesis in addition to those of Hillel. These included attaching significance to various linguistic particles, which either extended or limited the range of a particular scriptural imperative. His contribution to the development of Jewish exegetical principles is described by Graetz as a "fruitful addition to Hillel's interpretive rules."[25] The important point is that each was committed to the basic principle that Scripture required legal interpretation, and each attracted important disciples. Thus, each played a role in the progressive development of Judaism.

The next generation of sages were led by the patriarch Rabban Gamliel, a descendent of Hillel. In Graetz's *Geschichte* he is depicted as a man of controversy whose primary goal, paradoxically perhaps, was to achieve peace and harmony among the various sages. While not successful, due partially to his overbearing nature, he did manage to get most of his generation's scholars to accept Hillel's approach, including the hermeneutic rules and their actual exegetical applications.[26] In so doing he played a critical role in the normalization of Hillel's revolution.

Beyond the patriarch, the central figures of this generation were Rabbis Eliezer and Joshua. The former is described by Graetz as a rigid conservative, one of the last Shammaite hold-outs. Unlike the followers of Hillel, who recognized two sources of extrabiblical laws—tradition and exegesis—he recognized only one source, namely, tradition.[27] For this reason, he was incapable of responding to new problems; if he did not have a tradition regarding the matter, he would simply reply, "I have not heard this." He stood alone in his generation; his contemporaries were fully committed to the Hillelite approach. They did not aspire to simply retain what was received, but rather they were committed to interpreting and developing the laws of the Torah and the received tradition.[28]

The portrait of Eliezer, drawn by selective citation of talmudic passages, is critical to Graetz's challenge to Reform historiography.

For Eliezer was the one who rejected the hermeneutic principles, and it was he who was incapable of movement and change. The equation is clear: midrash halakhah meant progress and development within the limits of biblical law and soferic tradition; literalism, traditionalism, or whatever else, meant stagnation. To be sure, centuries earlier the *Soferim* had assumed the authority to develop new norms in response to the needs of the time, without explicit recourse to midrash. But due to the challenges and controversies that ensued, their approach was no longer viable. Development had to be tied directly to Scripture to find acceptance; the progressively minded understood this and responded accordingly. By contrast, the Sadducees, Shammaites, and now Eliezer, could not adjust, and ultimately lost the battle. Given the contentiousness of the age, midrash was the only means of moving forward while still remaining true to the traditions of the past.

This was understood by Eliezer's contemporary, Joshua, who is depicted here as a moderate in all things. He understood the need to balance competing forces, and thus accepted the new methods of midrash while also remaining loyal to tradition. He opposed the burgeoning tendency to midrashic excess; Hillel's rules were important tools, but not if they made a mockery of Scripture by overinterpreting it.[29] Again, the message is clear enough. This moderate and intelligent man, who rejected the severities of Shammai as well as miraculous interventions in legal decisions[30]—thus, no fool he—nevertheless saw the need for the judicious application of the exegetical principles of Hillel. If we judge ideas by the company they keep (and Graetz seems to want us to), certainly the intellectual commitment to midrash represents moderation, intelligence, and good judgment. All the good guys, the progressive forward-thinking types—Hillel, Yoḥanan ben Zakkai, Joshua—do it; the bad guys, the rigid, severe conservatives—the Sadducees, the Bene Bateira, Shammai, and Eliezer—do not. It is, thus, perverse to view Jewish spiritual history as going wrong with the introduction of midrashic techniques.

Up to this point Graetz has shown the necessity for the development of midrash, and the progressive purposes it served. Since, however, in Graetz's reading, midrash is sometimes creative, not merely supportive, one still confronts the problem of its excess. Joshua may have known to avoid it, but clearly not all did. In particular, we must recall the activity of Naḥum of Gimso, who sought to draw meaning from all kinds of particles and innocuous usages in Scripture. This lent to Scripture a greater flexibility than did Hillel's rules; indeed, it allowed one to say to Scripture, "Be silent until I interpret you."[31]

In response to this concern, Graetz introduced a third school of thought that was emerging with great force at this time. The first, that of Shammai and Eliezer, eschewed using midrash to respond to new needs and challenges; the second, that of Yoḥanan ben Zakkai, Neḥuniah ben Hakanah, and Joshua, was committed to a level-headed and balanced application of Hillel's techniques; the burgeoning third position built on the methods of Naḥum of Gimso, which, while "fruitful" in the sense of legally productive, did not always respect the boundaries of scriptural language or healthy human understanding. The first position was destined to lose, and as we enter the third generation of rabbinic sages it essentially disappears. The battle in this generation was to be between the second and third positions—between the disciples of Neḥuniah ben Hakanah and Naḥum of Gimso. That the range of scriptural law needed to be expanded was no longer a matter of contention. The question was whether the plain meaning of scriptural language would exercise any control over the way in which the Torah was interpreted.

The champion of the negative response to this question, in Graetz's telling, was R. Aqiba; the positive response was developed by R. Ishmael. The evidence for this firm distinction is drawn almost exclusively from the Yerushalmi.[32] Thus, it was in the work of Heinrich Graetz that this ancient Palestinian conception returned to Jewish historical consciousness. Graetz informs us that Aqiba pioneered new methods of interpretation that went well beyond those of Hillel, and even beyond those of his teacher and inspiration, Naḥum of Gimso. Indeed, in Graetz's telling, he was the creator of an entire system of exegesis, hitherto unknown in Jewish history.

The animating principle of this system was the belief that the "existing material of the oral law was not a dead treasure, incapable of growth and enrichment, nor, as in the view of R. Eliezer, was it the object of mere memorization. Rather it comprised an eternal source, from which new treasures could be obtained by the proper application of the proffered means."[33] It was the conception of R. Aqiba that nothing in the Torah should be seen as a concession to style or form. The language of the Torah was sui generis, and should be approached in a manner that was sui generis. No word, no letter, no unusual expression could possibly be devoid of significance. Furthermore, any deduction once derived from Scripture could be turned around and become the basis of yet another new deduction.[34] Thus, the existing material was readily supported by Scripture, and new interpretations always available. The system he developed became a source of wonder and amazement on the part of his contemporaries, but it also generated opposition.

Basing his claims almost exclusively on the Yerushalmi, Graetz proceeds to note that the opposition was spearheaded by R. Ishmael, who believed that the Torah speaks in human language; here, that is translated into a belief that Scripture is generally to be approached in the manner employed in the interpretation of all other documents. It contains numerous expansive elements that are indeed devoid of significance; they are concessions to human style and nothing more. This basic commitment to the notion that the Torah speaks in human language becomes the cornerstone for all of Ishmael's exegetical judgments. In a lengthy note, Graetz cites one Yerushalmi passage after another, rehearsing all the principles that Ishmael supposedly rejects; all of them are ultimately conditioned by his insistence that the Torah speaks in human language.

The language of Graetz's description of Ishmael's system is particularly worthy of note, for it evokes quite consciously Geiger's essay of a decade earlier that created so much commotion. In the very title of Geiger's essay, a clear contrast is drawn between the natural meaning of Scripture and talmudic exegesis. As the essay explains, there is virtually no relationship between the two. Yet, in describing Ishmael's system, Graetz states that "in the interpretation and exegesis of scriptural law it represents the natural meaning" of Scripture.[35] Thus, according to Graetz, an integral component of early halakhic exegesis is grounded in the natural meaning of the text, and is in no way discordant with it. Further, Geiger had argued that rabbinic exegesis failed to express a healthy understanding of biblical language, and insisted that rabbinic exegesis was guided by a "turbid" exegetical sense; by contrast, Graetz here insists that Ishmael's system represents *den gesunden Menschenverstand* (healthy human understanding), once again locating within the rabbinic world precisely what Geiger said it lacked. (To Geiger, all "healthy" exegesis represents an exceptional case that is strictly ad locum, and not indicative of broader rational approaches.) Finally, by claiming that R. Ishmael always insists that the Torah speaks in human language, Graetz was able to locate a general and consistently applied commitment to this logical principle where Geiger had insisted that it represented a rare exception to that otherwise turbid sense which dominated all rabbinic exegesis. In short, all the positives that Geiger said rabbinic exegesis generally lacked, and all the negatives that he insisted it possessed, are turned on their heads by Graetz, who finds in the Yerushalmi's conception of the matter the means to combat Geiger's attack on midrash halakhah. Indeed, in R. Ishmael one "recognizes an enlightened spirit" who proceeded as an exegete with scrupulous caution (*gewissenhafter Vorsicht*)—a far cry indeed from the muddled, irresponsible exegesis posited by Geiger.[36]

How does this resolve the problem of midrashic excess? We must note that, for Graetz, the practical significance of the dispute between the two sages is rather limited, since the lion's share of their efforts was to ground in Scripture material preserved by tradition. Graetz reconstructs the essential difference between the two sages as follows. Ishmael's "views regarding the connection of the traditional law to the language of Scripture were distinguished by a sensible uncontrived approach [*eine verständige ungekünstelte Haltung*], and seem to have been especially directed against R. Aqiba's artificial [*künstliches*] system."[37] For Ishmael it was important that the traditional laws not be grounded in an exegesis that failed to respect the language of Scripture; Aqiba, in locating scriptural sources for these laws, did not feel bound by any such considerations.

The point here is that in *most* of their disputes the two rabbis in question agreed regarding the law; only the exegetical foundation of the law was a matter of controversy. This distinction becomes the cornerstone of a new historical construct, on the basis of which Graetz has returned to the familiar claim that midrash did not generally create law, even if some talmudic authorities thought it did. He is no longer confronted by the difficulty of talmudic discourse, as were his predecessors who advanced this line of argument. For one thing, his attitude to the reliability of the exegetical reconstructions of the Bavli is necessarily skeptical. For another, in challenging this operating assumption of the Talmud, he has relied on a conception that he has drawn from the Yerushalmi—a conception that was almost universally ignored by his predecessors. However problematic his claims are in light of the Bavli, they work fine in light of the small group of Yerushalmi passages that posit systematic exegetical but not legal distinctions between the two second-century sages. No matter how one slices it, there is tension between the two Talmuds; Graetz gives preference to (his interpretation of) the Yerushalmi, and thus can provide what he considers historical support to the notion that most Jewish law is not rooted in exegesis.

To be sure, in Graetz's view not all disputes between Aqiba and Ishmael revolve around the exegetical foundations of received law. These distinct systems of exegesis did occasionally lead to halakhic disagreements, such as whether the appearance of an extra *vav* can lead to a severer form of punishment.[38] Such legal disputes notwithstanding, the main point of contention was in locating sources for the traditional material, and here each of these two sages embarked on his own path, guided by his own intellect. Thus, neither the thought processes guiding midrashic exegesis nor the consequences of that exegesis were necessarily as described by Geiger.

To put the final piece in place, we must note that for Graetz, the competing rational system of R. Ishmael's was not some ineffective call for exegetical sense; it was not a rare manifestation of exegetical responsibility. It was rather an alternative approach to Scripture that found a very comfortable place within the larger rabbinic world. For R. Ishmael, while certainly less popular than Aqiba, nevertheless founded his own school, which became known as the *Be R. Ishmael*, the house [of learning] of R. Ishmael. The teachings of this school are found in both Talmuds, and form an integral component of the overall rabbinic legacy. Furthermore, Ishmael expanded Hillel's seven exegetical rules into thirteen, and these thirteen rules have become an authoritative list of rabbinic techniques. Authoritative, but not exhaustive, and that is the point; neither the system of Aqiba nor that of Ishmael ever succeeded in suppressing the other. "The thirteen principles of Ishmael were acknowledged as an integral standard, without thereby suppressing the partially competing system of R. Aqiba's; both were used with equal acceptance by later authorities (*beide blieben als gleichberechtigt bei den Späteren im Gebrauch*)."[39] Thus, both these exegetical systems were used by later authorities in their limited efforts to apply exegesis to the production of new norms, and in their more extensive efforts to ground existing norms in Scripture. Neither the artificial approach nor the healthy approach ever fully dominated rabbinic exegetical endeavors. The progressive possibilities of rabbinic midrash were strengthened by Aqiba's aggressive approach to scriptural language, while the more temperate and rational perspective of Ishmael served to harness his opponent's excess. Contra Geiger, concern for the natural meaning of Scripture was never absent from the second-century rabbinic academy.

The opening chapters of the first published volume of Graetz's monumental history are devoted primarily to a discussion of the emergence of rabbinic exegetical principles.[40] No other issue was as central to the Jewish historian committed to establishing a historical understanding of Jewish law that would not allow it to be undermined by a system of exegesis that seemed so foreign by nineteenth-century standards. I do not consider it an exaggeration to say that in some respects the legitimacy of the whole history he would ultimately write depended on a successful treatment of the emergence of rabbinic law and midrash. After all, so much of subsequent Jewish intellectual activity was devoted to the study and development of that law, and perhaps none before him was as committed to telling the story of that activity as was Graetz. The most important task facing an intellectual of Graetz's existential commitments was to respond forcefully and historically to the challenges to the legitimacy of Jewish learning and exegesis—challenges that were a commonplace of German and German-Jewish reflections on Jewish history. Thus, the history as a whole opens with a discussion of rabbinic personalities in which the question of exegetical principles and the circumstances surrounding their emergence assumes center stage.

For Graetz, midrashic principles emerge against a background of strife and contention; they are pioneered by Hillel in an effort to bring peace to Israel. They are also the product of Hillel's progressive vision, and ultimately become the key to the survival of Judaism after the destruction of the Temple. That they did not immediately bring peace cannot overshadow the fact that in the long run Judaism survived by applying these techniques, allowing its adherents to understand the origins of their laws and to develop new laws. The commitment to midrash halakhah in general ultimately led to dissension within the rabbinic movement, culminating in the arguments of Aqiba and Ishmael. Yet, later rabbinic authorities were able to effect compromise by adopting both systems in their exegetical efforts.[41] Most importantly, the lion's share of Jewish observances are rooted in a long-standing tradition, going back many centuries before the rabbis of the first two Christian centuries; midrash granted this tradition authority. It allowed its bearers to move through time and enabled them to generate new laws, precisely as they imagined their predecessors had done.

Thus, any effort to discredit rabbinic Judaism because of its exegeses is turned by Graetz into a reactionary reading of history—precisely the opposite of what Reform critics intended. The tradition was progressive, the exegesis that emerged to buttress it was progressive, and the new norms the exegetes produced were. . . progressive. The task of the current age was to continue in the pattern of the ancient sages: to accept the traditional material, reflect on it, fine-tune it, develop it further, and perhaps change this or that. Wholesale changes, however, were clearly devoid of historical precedent. For, it was decidedly contrary to the verdict of history to see the rabbis as people who betrayed their heritage by failing to interpret it correctly or responsibly, as Reformers had done in seeking to justify the effort to effect broad changes in contemporary Jewish life.

It is one of the ironies of Jewish intellectual history that the opening chapters of the *Geschichte*, designed to counter Reform conceptions of history and to bolster tradition, should in fact have found a receptive audience among most Reformers, Geiger among them, and should have drawn the angriest response among the Orthodox. Samson Raphael Hirsch (1808–88), Graetz's former mentor to whom he dedicated the published version of his dissertation, was so outraged by Graetz's efforts in this area that he wrote detailed challenges to every one of Graetz's claims discussed above. Together they totaled more than two hundred pages.[42] For Hirsch the very notion of historical development was anathema. The notion that the exegetical principles emerged in time and in response to specific circumstances totally undermined their legitimacy. Hirsch preferred to argue that the exegetical principles of the rabbis were in fact given at Sinai, and they have always been considered as originating there.[43] Further, they were never employed to generate law, but merely to locate scriptural sources for oral traditions from Sinai.[44] The notion that Shammaites or Eliezer actually disputed the applicability of the hermeneutic rules was also vigorously challenged by Hirsch, as was the distinction between Aqiba and Ishmael.[45]

Much of Hirsch's critique is trenchant; Graetz does interpret certain passages in a rather questionable manner, to state the matter charitably. But just as often, Hirsch's critique is beside the point; it is grounded in fideistic postures that have no historical validity. Further, as regards the distinction between Aqiba and Ishmael, Hirsch must perforce become a rather clumsy reader of the Yerushalmi, arguing that it does not say what it appears to say, and at other times suggesting that, even if it says it, it does not mean it. Further, Hirsch is not above partial quotation or misrepresentation in describing Graetz's historical portrait.

In challenging the Aqiba/Ishmael distinction, Hirsch resorts to citing counterevidence from the Bavli, without recognizing that Graetz has assumed a rather critical posture towards the reconstructions of the exegetical foundations of Mishnaic law in that document. Thus, what Hirsch treats as a genuine expression of, say, Eliezer's or Ishmael's thought, is discounted by Graetz. That the latter did not bring the same critical attitude to the discussions of the Yerushalmi is to be explained by his a priori sympathy to what the Yerushalmi had to say, and the greater popularity the Yerushalmi enjoyed among scholars who could not accept the way the Bavli interpreted the Mishnah. Finally, Hirsch did not see the extent to which Graetz was trying to combat Reform by turning its "counterhistory" on its head. What Hirsch saw is that, whatever his intent, Graetz in fact conceded too much to the Reform point of view; ultimately Jewish law came to rest far too fully on the personality quirks and intellectual preferences of a small number of rabbinic sages—hardly the basis for continued commitment in the modern world.

Hirsch's reactions were fully predictable; far more surprising was the reaction of Abraham Geiger, who, while no fan of Graetz's *Geschichte* overall, nevertheless drew a great deal from the opening chapters. As we saw above, Graetz wanted nothing more than to refute Geiger's vision of rabbinic exegesis, and to lead him and his followers away from their understanding of Jewish law and its exegetical foundations. What happened can only call to mind the adage that one should be careful what one asks for; one may just get it. For, as the Galician scholar Zvi Menaḥem Pineles recognized long ago, Geiger's attitude to rabbinic exegesis and law as articulated in the *Urschrift* owes much to Graetz's distinction between the schools of Rabbis Aqiba and Ishmael,[46] and, more generally, his view of midrash as a progressive response to the exigencies of history. Yet, Geiger was not prepared to see the distinctions between these two schools within the same larger historical framework developed by his challenger. He had absorbed far too much from the New Testament critic, David Strauss, from the so-called Tübingen school of New Testament scholarship, and from Theodor Mommsen's *Römische Geschichte*, to accept the naïve conception of Graetz.[47]

Nevertheless, with Graetz's help he now perceived a progressive element in midrash halakhah. Unlike Graetz, however, he was not prepared to stop at the progressive; for him, midrash halakhah of the Aqiban variety could only be conceptualized as religiously subversive, precisely because of its exegetical absurdity. In Geiger's new reading, the exegetical revolution of the first and second centuries, pioneered by Hillel and fully executed by Aqiba, completely overturned the "old" halakhah and replaced it with one that was fresh and new. This revolutionary activity became necessary because Jews were no longer in a position to "correct" the very words of the Bible, as previous generations of Jews had done; they thus had to "correct" the significance of the old words, so that they now meant something entirely new. In Geiger's *Urschrift* midrash is seen as the means through which Aqiba overthrew the old law; Ishmael and his contemporaries, by contrast, emerge as stodgy conservatives, futilely holding on to the old ways. Thus, in a near total transformation of his earlier thinking, Geiger now saw an inextricable link between the natural sense of Scripture and the stultifying conservatism of a portion of the rabbinic elite of the second century. As Geiger saw matters in 1857, the creative power in Judaism had always been expressed by controlling the text of Scripture, with different groups, upon achieving power, changing the names and words of the text to suit their preferred reading of history. At a certain point it became impossible to continue to exercise that power; yet to relinquish power over the text and submit to the old norms would be to commit cultural suicide. It was the revolutionary vision of Hillel and Aqiba that saw that controlling the text did not necessarily entail controlling the wording; controlling the socially accepted meaning was equally effective. They were thus able to save Judaism—for a time— from suffering stultification and stagnation by generating new linguistic assumptions that subverted the received meaning of the biblical text. As exegesis, what Aqiba said was absurd; as religious politics it was brilliant. Thus, Geiger and many other Reformers[48] accepted part of Graetz's vision without ever being deterred from their broader program; Hirsch would not have been surprised.

Finally, we should note, in anticipation of what is to come, that on the basis of Graetz's revival of the Aqiba/Ishmael competition, i.e., the Yerushalmi's conception, Geiger went on to identify important distinctions among the early rabbinic documents, seeing the *Mekhilta* of R. Ishmael and the *Sifre* as reactionary documents, while insisting that the *Sifra,* which utilizes the techniques of Aqiba, represents the new, revolutionary halakhah.[49] This claim represents the first step in the emergence of a new historical consensus regarding these documents that culminated with the publication of the views of David Zvi Hoffmann (1843–1921), an Orthodox rabbi from Berlin (on which see below.)

Zechariah Frankel

Zechariah Frankel, born and educated in Prague, received his Ph.D. in 1831, and served in Dresden as the chief rabbi of the German state of Saxony from 1836 to 1854, when he became the head of the Jewish Theological Seminary in Breslau. He was the pioneer of a middle path in German Judaism, demanding halakhic observance while accepting the possibility of minor modifications,[50] and intellectual openness, except with regard to the Pentateuch.[51] Frankel, in many respects Graetz's teacher and mentor but also his student (as we shall see), provides us with yet another example of a Jewish intellectual who expended enormous energy trying to fashion a cogent and compelling response to the question, "How do we know this?" Like Graetz, his scholarship was devoted to developing a portrait of Judaism that would challenge the denigrating models that prevailed in the German academy, and that would negate the historical justification of Reform as well.[52] Like Graetz, he was deeply committed to the idea that *Wissenschaft* was necessary for the continuity of Jewish identity in the modern world. Unlike Graetz, Frankel limited his scholarly activity almost exclusively to elucidating the history of Jewish law, seeing in that project the great challenge of the day. From one of his earliest scholarly works, the *Vorstudien zu der Septuaginta,* published in 1841, to his last, *Mevo ha-Yerushalmi,* published in 1870, Frankel was committed to unpacking the history of halakhah, laying out its various stages of development. As he put it in *Vorstudien,* the task entailed undertaking

an analysis that would show how the individual elements of the halakhah came into being, and how the halakhah itself grew from a trickle into a rich and raging river; an investigation through which we would come to know what belongs to each period, and further, what sprang from the needs of the day and what owed its existence to uninhibited study; an inquiry into the study techniques of different periods and how one derived from the other and then intermingled with each other through the ages, and finally, how the diverse conglomeration of techniques was forged into a single system.[53]

This historical program was self-consciously offered as a polemical corrective to the views of others; as he put it, actually accomplishing what he set out to do would demand classical study of the Talmud, so that he could "obviate superficial judgments as well as many immature views."[54]

While Frankel's commitment to the history of halakhah was lifelong, his actual presentation of that history must be divided into two distinct periods. The first, extending through the 1840s, was characterized by a highly romanticized picture of the emergence of Jewish law in accordance with the spirit of the *Volk* and its leaders. The second period, beginning in the 1850s, shows the influence of Krochmal's *Guide of the Perplexed of the Time* and the first published volume of Graetz's *Geschichte*. In Frankel's first stage, biblical exegesis scarcely plays any creative role at all; in the second stage, Frankel is led by Krochmal to emphasize the exegetical activity of the *Soferim,* and by Graetz to differentiate between distinct stages and schools of rabbinic exegesis. Common to both stages is a clear rejection of any reading of Jewish history that challenged the antiquity of its norms or the rationality of the process that produced those norms.

Frankel begins the task in the *Vorstudien,* there outlining the various sources that attest to early observance of extrabiblical prescriptions. For example, Josephus, the first-century historian, attests to observances that were in place in the time of Antiochus Epiphanes, in the early second pre-Christian century. According to Frankel, these observances "emerged quite silently [*geräuschlos*], they came to life gradually [*nach und nach ins Leben getreten*], and should be seen not as the law's explanation, but as its natural corollary."[55] Indeed, many practices eventually emerged as normative, without recourse to "higher authority. They emerged from the [demands of] ordinary life, from that which the piety of the people had elevated to a guiding principle; because they had struck such roots, they achieved lasting validity."[56] Thus, extrabiblical laws did not, for the most part, emerge as a result of academic discussions or contrived exegeses, but rather by means of the creative responses of living communities to the challenges of life.

We can learn a great deal about Frankel's existential commitments from his remark that in approaching the Septuagint for the first time, he was struck by how much overlap there was between its explanation *cum* translation of the Bible's laws and the ordinances of the rabbinic documents. This overlap fit nicely with the view of Judaism he wished to develop; its halakhot were norms clearly extending back into antiquity, guiding the religious lives of Jewish communities the world over. When driven by his sense of integrity to pursue the matter more fully, he realized that "a substantial portion of [his] earlier perceptions had dissipated." He now recognized the Septuagint as a composite document, betraying different hands with varying attachments to the developed halakhah. Thus, he saw that there was substantially less harmony between the two bodies of literature. Still, a great deal remained of his earlier sense of things, and he rejoiced in the firm scholarly basis he could now provide for it.[57] His joy was rooted in his desire to show that the halakhah had undergone a lengthy process of emergence, that it was rooted in popular piety, and that little of it depended on the activity of professional legal experts or exegetes.

Particularly telling, for our purposes, is his discussion of midrash and the Septuagint. While acknowledging that sometimes new prescriptions flowed from the careful study of Scripture that was the hallmark of postbiblical Jewish piety, most newly developed practices represented responses to changed circumstances; as these responses became normative, they were preserved as part of the orally transmitted legal culture of the people, and only later they came to shape the legal interpretation of the biblical text.

The [biblical] law was explained in terms of its current applications, while understanding the literal sense of scripture . . . was of secondary interest. Thus, the halakhah and halakhic exegesis take shape as reciprocally conditioned entities. And even when, at another time, different exegetical conceptions appear, the halakhic product that emerged at this time remained unchanged, for it was drawn from [the demands of] life, and was upheld by general consensus; only in a case in which the halakhah did not achieve general currency was it subject to alteration.[58]

Thus, halakhic change was never dependent on shifting exegetical taste, but on the broad-based desuetude of a given practice. Frankel does what he can to mitigate the role that exegesis and jurisprudential expertise play in creating law; law emerges positively by virtue of a response of the living spirit of the people to the demands of time. The newly created laws are then read into the biblical text, but in no way does the law's legitimacy depend on the acceptance of such "exegesis." Rather, the response to the demands of life draws its legitimacy from the general approbation of the Jewish community. The extent to which the post factum exegesis is seen as compelling is largely irrelevant. It is for this reason that later generations, having very different exegetical tastes, do not challenge the validity of the laws or their connection to the Bible; they simply offer alternative readings that may make better sense of the Bible. Such interpretations can never attain normative power, nor detract from an existing norm's legal force, because they do not represent the immediate and creative response of a living community to changed circumstances, because no consensus regarding their validity has ever emerged, and because they are not grounded in long-standing custom. They may lead to a more refined understanding of the Bible, but they never produce norms incumbent on the community.

There is no doubt in my mind that Frankel's conception here was developed under the influence of the legal theories of Friedrich Karl von Savigny and G. F. Puchta, then the dominant voices among the conservative practitioners of *Rechtswissenschaft* in Germany.[59] By adapting their theories to the history of Jewish law, Frankel could respond to the challenges of Reform and academic anti-Judaism at one and the same time.[60] Savigny's theories granted legitimacy only to those norms that emerge over a lengthy period of time—norms that originated in the customary practices of the people and were preserved in oral form before they were subject to the jurisprudential scrutiny of legal scholars. Further, Savigny vigorously protested against the introduction of sudden changes in a legal system in the name of "rational" and "universal" considerations. This intellectual structure served Frankel well in his efforts to combat Reform and to paint a portrait of Jewish legal history without an overwhelmingly large exegetical infrastructure. Armed with this explanatory model, he was ready to approach and interpret the historical data.

This is where the Septuagint enters the picture. For, the fact that many extrabiblical norms are recorded in both the Septuagint (the second-century B.C.E. product of the Alexandrian Jewish community) and rabbinic literature (the product of Palestinian and Babylonian communities over the first five Christian centuries) provides the historical "proof" for the claim of a long-standing halakhic tradition not tied to complex exegetical methods of the rabbis. Many of the norms of rabbinic literature were clearly very old, and most did not derive from exegesis of the biblical text. Once accepted by the people, they endured over significant spatial and chronological expanses. While developments are visible across these expanses, sudden and extensive shifts are not.

Frankel's reliance on the theories of Savigny is particularly to be seen in his study from 1846, *Der gerichtliche Beweis nach mosaisch-talmudischen Rechte* (The judicial process in Mosaic-talmudic law).

Here Frankel's preference for dealing with rabbinism in the larger context of *Rechtswissenschaft* is made clear. Here too, Frankel argues that Jewish law grows organically out of the real-life situations of the Jews, and, furthermore, that this organically grown law is faithfully recorded in the talmudic documents. He argues that some of the material in rabbinic documents derives, for example, from Maccabean times—long before the emergence of rabbinic exegetical techniques.[61]

Aside from the appeal to antiquity, the influence of Savigny and Puchta is discernible in Frankel's understanding of the nature of rabbinic documents. He insists with great urgency that none of the rabbinic documents qualifies as a code that is designed to have the final word regarding Jewish law. Rather all the documents draw their material from the norms of the living Jewish communities, and apply juristic expertise to it post factum, ultimately determining what is generally accepted and thus authoritative, and what is not, precisely as envisioned by Savigny and Puchta.[62] The documents remain open and subject to interpretation and modification, while at the same time always showing respect for the legal products of the past. Not only can no rabbinic document be considered a definitive code, but for Frankel the classical rabbinic documents scarcely exhaust what he considers the sources of Jewish law. He argues that the student of Jewish law must turn to the Apocrypha, New Testament, and Josephus, in addition, of course, to the Septuagint, for yet more examples of a living legal tradition in action. To a lesser degree, one must turn to Philo and other Alexandrian writings. All of this without an appreciation that there may be many different legal systems at work in these documents. For Frankel, the purview of "Mosaic-talmudic law" takes all this material in, and serves to prove the antiquity, vitality, and continuity of the tradition. In this discussion virtually no role whatever is ascribed to midrash, for creative midrash would posit the existence of juristic experts fashioning law for the people from a text, rather than abstracting norms from the accepted customary practices of the people. Furthermore, positing a creative role for midrash would lead Frankel to portray Jewish law as dependent on irrational exegeses.

It is worth digressing for a moment to note that Frankel's adoption of Savigny's approach was designed to craft a response not merely to Reform Judaism but also to the general scholarly environment; this may be seen from his apologia for the Mosaic materials, which he insists must *not* be seen within the larger context of ancient Near Eastern cultures with their subservience to despotic kings, human or divine. The contrary opinion was a commonplace of Hegelian historiosophy, but is scarcely represented among Jewish reformers. Clearly, however, Frankel felt the need to respond. He insisted that the Mosaic law cannot be seen as the imposition of the supreme lawgiver, which would render it despotic from Hegel's point of view (and juridically suspect from Savigny's). He asserts that the Mosaic law "is not an external, arbitrary impulse; rather it possesses its own inner necessity; it finds its authorization in the human spirit. Through divine prescriptions it is transferred into human consciousness."[63] The divinely revealed Mosaic legal system should not be understood as imposed obligation,[64] but as divine direction of the human spirit grounded in recognition of human need. Thus, not only postbiblical law, but the law of the Bible itself, takes shape within human consciousness in response to human needs, and grows over time. We can see, then, just how thoroughly apologetic this work is; it takes its place alongside an earlier work devoted to Jewish oaths as part of Frankel's efforts to present a historical Judaism that was academically respectable and was yet capable of displaying continued vitality.

Against this backdrop, his effort to minimize the role of midrash in the emergence of Jewish law was perfectly understandable. After all, as we have seen, there was nothing academically respectable about midrash. Furthermore, laws actually created by means of midrash would represent the efforts of legal scholars to shape norms not necessarily in keeping with the long-standing customary practices of the people and their spirit. Thus, while acknowledging that sometimes laws are drawn from the intensive study of the Bible,[65] generally he imagines laws emerging as a response to new circumstances and only later achieving authority by means of the sanction of the highest court, the Sanhedrin. The latter will often feel compelled to draw a connection to the Bible, although not always. In this reading of Jewish legal history, midrash is a decidedly secondary phenomenon.

All of this having been said, one aspect of this work remains striking, and indicates the length to which this essentially conservative writer would go in distancing himself from rabbinic exegesis. The discussion of the nature of Jewish law in *Der gerichtliche Beweis* is accompanied by a brief discussion of the sources relevant to a proper evaluation of talmudic criminal and civil law. The list includes the Mishnah, the *baraitot* of Rabbis Hiyya and Oshaya, and the Talmuds, as well as the commentaries and *responsa* of the Geonim, the early medieval authorities, and later medieval and early modern writers of codes, commentaries and *responsa*. The section closes with a footnote calling attention to various Christian writers on the subject. Totally absent from the discussion of the sources of talmudic law are the midreshe halakhah. The *Mekhilta*, which one would think was a highly relevant source, is mentioned in a note that essentially dismisses its reliability; similarly, the *Sifra* and *Sifre*, each of which contain important material.[66] Thus, not only is the midrashic process denied a role in the formation of Jewish law, but the midrashic texts are considered devoid of legal-historical value, as well. Frankel, apparently, has no interest in presenting these texts as sources of Jewish law. They draw connections between the new and the old, but their methodology is so suspect that they can teach nothing of value that is not in the Mishnah or some other document.[67]

The conception of Jewish law that dominated Frankel's thinking in the 1840s was to produce little of lasting value from either an intellectual or social viewpoint. Frankel's early work is of interest for what it says about Zechariah Frankel, the man often seen as the founder of modern Conservative Judaism. While his conception of the history of Jewish law changed significantly, his basic existential orientation did not. In time, he saw that the issues needed to be rethought; his traditionalist motivation remained constant.

The impetus for the shift in Frankel's historical thinking seems to be related to the three major Reform conferences in Germany (1844–46) and the political events of 1848. In the wake of these events, Frankel began to rethink his rather syrupy, romantic presentation of the history of Jewish law. While never wavering in his commitment to its roots in hoary antiquity, he began to insist on a much more substantial and creative role for the religious and juristic leaders of the people, and this meant, among other things, a new understanding of the historical place of rabbinic midrash. In his publication of 1851, *Über den Einfluss der palästinischen Exegese auf die alexandrinische Hermeneutik*, Frankel makes clear that the direction of Palestinian intellectual activity in the centuries before the Septuagint (i.e., from the fifth to the third centuries B.C.E) was not to find a foundation for the laws originating in "life"; rather, "The teachers and students of the law strove essentially to determine how life was to be regulated according to it [i.e., scriptural law], how the law was to be preserved and carried out: 'knowledge should lead to action.'"[68] These teachers and students turned to exegesis to regulate behavior in the face of new circumstances; their goal was to find a way to keep the Bible alive as a source of law and knowledge. He acknowledges that we know next to nothing about the actual activity of these Palestinian exegetes, but says that, happily, significant portions of their efforts can be reconstructed from the translations of the Septuagint.[69] Let us leave the problems with this construct aside; what is important for us here is to recognize that where Frankel once envisioned a legal system that largely worked from the bottom up he now described one that worked primarily from the top down. Whatever once drew him to the romantic theories of Savigny was now gone. Scholars, not the "people," shaped Jewish praxis; the response to the new challenges of life were wholly informed by the text of the Bible, not the other way around.

Perhaps the euphoric events of 1848 and their disappointing aftermath brought on a sense of despair about whether the Jews would ever attain equality in Germany and a recognition of the hopelessness of ever convincing the German academic world of the integrity of the Jewish legal system. Perhaps he perceived the extent to which Savigny's theories worked against the contemporary legal and political aspirations of Jews, since those theories saw the unique spirit and history of a particular people as the only legitimizing factors in creating appropriate legal norms, thus effectively excluding Jews from participation. Perhaps he saw the extent to which theories of law developing as a silent, natural response to the challenges of life serve equally well to buttress Reform, whose direction, the conferences made clear, he could not control, and whose numbers were rapidly increasing.[70] Perhaps the shift resulted from conversations he had with Graetz. We can only speculate. The shift in views is clear; the reasons for it are not.

In his articles and addresses throughout the decade of the fifties, the shift in Frankel's views was spelled out more clearly. In particular, in an address, delivered in 1854 at the opening of the new Jewish Theological Seminary in Breslau, of which he was the first director, Frankel once again returned to the subject of Palestinian and Alexandrian exegesis. Here he focused on the different phases of Jewish exegetical activity, starting with that of the *Soferim,* who related immediately to Scripture and produced new explanations of its norms. The *Soferim,* or *Schrifterklärer,* had taken over the role once assumed by the people in Frankel's thinking. With the close of the period of the *Soferim,* a new period of independent study began, the age of the *Tannaim.*[71] Here the focus was not so much the exegesis of the Bible as the ordering and shaping of the expanded corpus of law itself. That is, Jewish intellectual energy was now expended on gathering the laws together into coherent and easily remembered units, without citing their scriptural sources. Scripture now became the infrastructure on which the laws were built, although they did not formally relate directly to it.[72] This does not mean that midrash ceased to be an essential method of learning. Here he left no doubt that an essential part of the activity of the *Tannaim* was to generate new laws by means of biblical exegesis.[73] It simply means that it was not considered essential to preserve the connection between the law and its exegetical foundation in the early tannaitic period. Only later was it recognized that this formal severing of the connection between law and its foundations in Scripture did not achieve the desired goal, and thus the effort began to reconstruct the exegetical assumptions that informed the preserved laws. This reconstructive exegesis was designed to supplement the norms ordered in the earliest versions of the Mishnah, whose organization represented the primary focus of learning in this period. Thus, in the tannaitic period, we confront two types of exegesis: one that generates law, and one that hypothetically reconstructs the exegetical basis for existing law.

The first kind of exegeses of the *Tannaim*, those that produced halakhot, were, for the most part, simple and reasonable, and stand in marked contrast to the more far-fetched interpretations that characterize the second kind. Further, Frankel claims that most of the second kind of exegeses were actually the product of the *Amoraim;* the latter did not engage in genuinely creative exegesis but merely sought to continue with the reconstructive project that emerged in the later tannaitic period. That is, these exegetes sought to ground Mishnaic imperatives in Scripture.[74] Already in 1854, then, Frankel was differentiating between two types of tannaitic exegesis, and between tannaitic and amoraic exegesis, attributing most of the bizarre interpretations to the latter group, who did not produce any laws but merely justified the existing tannaitic laws. Thus, there were really no practical consequences from the bizarre exegesis that unquestionably characterized amoraic—specifically, Babylonian—exegesis. The majority of the exegeses that really created laws were simple and defensible; the creative midrash halakhah of the *Tannaim* was no weak link in Jewish legal history. Such exegesis was no longer to be judged on the basis of the supplementary, largely inconsequential interpretations of the later sages. This distinction between tannaitic and amoraic midrash was to be part of the picture that he painted a few years later, with the publication of his influential magnum opus, *Darkhe ha-Mishnah*, in 1859.

The *Darkhe ha-Mishnah* was written in Hebrew, and the choice of linguistic medium suggests that Frankel had despaired of ever getting a hearing among a broader German audience. He seems to have directed his book to those who continued to study classical Jewish texts, but who may have been confounded by the historical and/or exegetical underpinnings of the world of rabbinic literature.

In the *Darkhe ha-Mishnah* we find a full articulation of Frankel's mature view of the emergence of Jewish law and the role of exegesis in it. Here the influence of Krochmal and Graetz is clear and obvious. Like them, and consistent with his earlier views, he continues to insist on the antiquity of the fundamental core of extrabiblical practices. They are rooted in the enactments of the *Soferim,* whose activity is described as "explaining to the people the laws of the Torah, and what is the intent of a particular law; for example, [when] the Torah prohibits work on the Sabbath, [the *Soferim* come and explain] what forms of labor come under this category. . . . Secondly, they issued decrees and protective ordinances in accord with the needs of the time. . . .For, as is known, in the course of time new matters appear that were not foreseen by the earlier authorities. . . .and people have need of new laws and mores (*nimusim u-mishpatim ḥadashim*)."[75] These latter ordinances were developed without recourse to Scripture; later generations attributed great authority to these. Yet, as Frankel now tells the story, the first function described is primary; the Soferim were the authoritative interpreters of Scripture, establishing the basic norms of Judaism as we know it.[76]

As we noted above, Frankel saw the period of the *Tannaim* as quite distinct from that of the earlier period. Now he was more secure in asserting that midrash halakhah played a critical role in the activity of the *Tannaim*. Referring directly to the controversy between Maimonides and Naḥmanides (see chapter four above), Frankel notes that the whole matter has been the subject of contentious disputes for a long time, but this is largely a function of distance. Since post-talmudic Jews no longer engaged in midrash halakhah, its method of reading became increasingly foreign and led to claims that the earlier rabbis could not have meant for their exegeses to be taken seriously. If we train ourselves to think historically, to recognize the difference between them and us, we will recognize that while we cannot see how they read in such a way, for them, particularly R. Aqiba, such methods of reading presented no problem. If we learn to think historically, we will have no problem understanding rabbinic activity.[77]

In our efforts to comprehend the work of the early sages, he insisted, we must learn to distinguish between what the rabbis themselves intended as *asmakhta* and what they intended seriously. That is, if we develop sufficient critical faculties, we will see that some of the proffered interpretations of Scripture were never intended to be seen as genuine sources of law, while others were. Thus, neither the broad generalizations of Maimonides nor of Naḥmanides are acceptable. Sometimes the *Tannaim* created "scriptural" law through exegesis; sometimes they simply enlisted the support of the verse for the purpose at hand.

Furthermore, we must learn to distinguish between the exegesis of the *Tannaim*, which was partially creative, and the exegesis of the *Amoraim*, which was almost exclusively supportive, post factum. If we succeed in making all these distinctions properly, we can arrive at a historically grounded understanding of the emergence of Jewish law.

As we have seen, the *Tannaim* engaged, some of the time, in creative biblical exegesis. When their efforts were directed to developing the laws of Scripture exegetically, they were guided first by the seven

principles introduced by Hillel, and later expanded to thirteen by
R. Ishmael.[78] These principles are wholly logical, and their application
produces simple interpretations, which represent rational extensions
of the purview of scriptural law.

Frankel's reliance on Graetz here is clear,[79] and like Graetz he confronted the problem that the tannaitic texts themselves contain exegeses that are rather far-fetched. While in his view most of such exegeses
are to be found among the *Amoraim,* and they are readily explained as
post factum supports, there is no denying the fact that the texts generally considered tannaitic are filled with such exegeses as well. He has
already explained that these interpretations were not intended seriously,
and that in most cases they, too, like the *derashot* of the *Amoraim,*
represent post factum reconstructions. What was needed now was some
evidence. How do we know that the rabbis were not guided by far-
fetched exegetical assumptions? On what basis can we say that they
are simply creating supports for existing norms?

In resolving the problem, Frankel once again follows Graetz's lead.
Relying almost exclusively on the Yerushalmi, Frankel too puts forth
the argument that R. Ishmael followed an independent exegetical path
opposed to that of R. Aqiba.[80] While acknowledging that sometimes R.
Aqiba's position appears more committed to *peshat,*[81] Frankel says that
in general R. Ishmael was devoted to *peshat* and it was R. Aqiba and
his disciples who often pursued far-fetched interpretations.[82] R. Ishmael
insisted that the Torah speaks in human language, and he therefore
refrained from fanciful exegeses. Like Graetz, Frankel extends far beyond the limits of its usage in the Talmud the principle that the Torah
speaks in human language . There it refers strictly to refusal to interpret repetitions; for Frankel and Graetz, it embodies a general commitment to natural, healthy exegesis.[83] Thus, once again, we find a scholar
of *jüdische Wissenschaft* locating a basic concern for *peshat* in the heart
of the emergence of rabbinism. Rabbinic scriptural reading did not
develop in an arena thoroughly devoid of an appreciation of the plain
meaning of Scripture.

Further, Frankel makes explicit what in Graetz was merely implicit. In the disputes of Rabbis Aqiba and Ishmael he finds incontro-
vertible evidence that the issue surrounded the exegetical foundations
of existing law. He notes that in the majority of the controversies
between these two sages, the actual norm itself is never contested; the
discussion involves the exegetical foundation of the law, not the law
itself. Given the substantial differences that govern their exegetical
systems, such extensive agreement regarding norms suggests that the
establishment of the laws themselves preceded their disputes. They,
therefore, must have been traditional laws, that is, laws established by

the *Soferim* or by sages in the early tannaitic period, in which, as we have seem, the legal results were formally severed from their scriptural sources.[84] To be sure, some new ordinances emerged as a result of Aqiba's approach, and these met with opposition; still, the majority of the disputed exegeses and, by extension, the remaining far-fetched exegeses in tannaitic literature involve the search for scriptural support for existing laws, which Frankel has already explained can lead the searcher in all directions. We may find such interpretations absurd; in no way, however, can we see them as compromising the rationality or integrity of rabbinic law, which rests on rational exegesis or long-standing traditions.

For Frankel, then, the position taken by Naḥmanides that virtually all rabbinic exegeses are to be taken seriously as legally creative efforts must be rejected. Yet, Frankel cannot endorse Maimonides' position entirely either, and for two reasons. First, he acknowledges that many of the tannaitic exegeses really did create what was considered scriptural law; second, like Graetz, he cannot affirm that the halakhah not dependent on exegesis extends back to Sinai. He insists, however, that it is the product of a long organic process of growth rooted in the life of the Jews and their leaders, the *Soferim*, extending back into antiquity. Some of these laws are connected to Scripture, post factum. Others, the so-called *halakhot le-Moshe mi-Sinai*, are not. Either way, neither extrabiblical laws nor the guiding exegetical principles are seen by Frankel as deriving from an oral divine communication.

It is perhaps ironic that in the work of Frankel and Graetz—men trying to uphold the practical demands of the historical Jewish tradition—one encounters a rejection of the two main features of the earlier traditional consensus. In that consensus the perspective of the Bavli totally overwhelmed that of the Yerushalmi, while that of Naḥmanides prevailed over that of Maimonides. Frankel and Graetz reject the "traditional" positions, developing a modified Maimonidean conception and relying heavily on the Yerushalmi. They were driven to this by Geiger and Holdheim, inter alia, each of whom upheld the traditional consensus, for it made the halakhic tradition a much easier target. A system of behavior based on ridiculous exegesis is far more readily overturned than is the more subtle vision of the history of the Jewish legal system put forward by Frankel and Graetz, who manage to relegate far-fetched and creative exegeses to a relatively insignificant position in the emergence of Jewish law. Only Aqiba and his disciples engaged in such exegeses, and more often than not these interpretations did not generate law. The remainder of the more significant rabbis, particularly in Graetz's version, eschewed such exegeses, and in particular Ishmael, a central figure in the tannaitic period, presents himself as the model of judicious *peshat*-oriented exegesis. In Ishmael, Graetz and Frankel had found their champion.

Isaac Hirsch Weiss

Isaac Hirsch Weiss was author of the first comprehensive history of the Jewish tradition, written in Hebrew and carrying the Hebrew title *Dor Dor ve-Dorshav* and the German title *Zur Geschichte der jüdischen Tradition*.[85] It is a remarkably rich and detailed study of the different stages of Jewish halakhic and aggadic development. It brings together the many insights and discoveries of Krochmal and Frankel (and Graetz to a lesser extent), and adds enormous documentation, together with the substantial refinements and correctives of the author. It was a monumental work, which saw many editions, as well as an abridged Yiddish translation.[86] I cannot imagine it was read by many,[87] but it obviously was one of those works that a certain class of people wanted in their libraries. In any event, while it represented a far more synthetic treatment than did the researches of Frankel, and provided a far more detailed discussion of the stages of Jewish legal development than did Graetz's *Geschichte*, it does not advance the discussion of our issues much beyond the contributions of the Breslau scholars, and need not detain us long. However, we must stay with him long enough to get a sense of the development of his thinking—to see, once again, the extent to which the question of Jewish exegesis and its history provoked anxiety among the traditionally oriented historians of the nineteenth century. Spending a few moments on Weiss adds to our picture because Weiss's path to a satisfactory resolution of the problem of midrash went along different lines than did that of Frankel and Graetz. He did not have the university training and doctoral degrees of the latter two; he was largely an autodidact, and was fundamentally unfamiliar with (or indifferent to) the academic trends that shaped the thinking of the German scholars (indeed, of Krochmal, as well). The nature of his work, the nature of this thinking, differed significantly from that of Graetz and Frankel; yet, somehow he ended up in basically the same place.

In the eightieth year of his long life, Isaac Hirsch Weiss published his memoirs; there he recounted his youth in the yeshivot of Moravia and Hungary, and the different styles of biblical and talmudic study and the varying attitudes to "scientific" knowledge that prevailed in the two domains. If we are to believe the recollections of the elderly scholar, early in his life he was led to the awareness that there were different ways of approaching the Bible and Talmud in Jewish life. Early on he developed a certain contempt for the insulated world of the

Hungarian yeshivot, and early on, he tells us, he "had a passion to investigate the history of the sages of our nation"—for, he claimed, from that one could arrive at an appreciation of the history of the people as a whole.[88]

Whatever we are to make of this last claim, and however much he may have been interested in the lives of the sages, it seems clear enough that Weiss's path to the historical school was not the culmination of some lifelong passion, but actually represented a rather abrupt conversion. When, as a man of forty-seven in 1862, Weiss published his edition of the *Sifra*, his first lasting scholarly contribution, he was yet a strong opponent of the historical approach to halakhah. The work is prefaced by an introduction in which Weiss insists on a tradition that extended back to Sinai. In particular, he asserted that the various hermeneutic principles of the rabbis must have been revealed by God to Moses. Were this not so, one could not begin to explain how it is that Jewish law can demand corporal and capital punishment for transgressions derived exegetically from the biblical text.[89] Whatever merits such arguments might have, they scarcely indicate historical consciousness. Indeed, his first two footnotes indicate just how strongly opposed he was to the historical school. These notes forcefully criticize the author of the *Darkhe ha-Mishnah* for failing to properly appreciate the true nature of Jewish exegetical principles, for he had conceded far too much to history. I think it is safe to say that the author of this introduction would have been far more at home in the orthodox *Rabbiner-seminar* soon to be founded in Berlin[90] than he would have been at the Jewish Theological Seminary of Breslau.

Beyond the introduction, the semiotics of presentation in this edition exhibit a strong attachment to traditional learning and a desire to address an audience untouched by modernity. A folio volume, the upper part of the page presents the text of the *Sifra* in square letters; underneath we find the commentary of Abraham ben David, "published in its entirety for the first time," transcribed from an Oxford manuscript, and presented in "Rashi" script. Underneath this we find Weiss's original contribution to the volume his "Mesoret ha-Talmud," which notes the parallels between the *Sifra* and other rabbinic documents. It is published in yet smaller "Rashi" script. Unlike his *Mekhilta* edition, to be discussed presently, this edition was constructed in accord with traditional patterns of presentation of such works; it has found its place in Orthodox circles, and has been reprinted there with but one deletion: the name Isaac Hirsh Weiss.

Three years after the publication of his *Sifra* edition, Weiss brought out a new edition of the *Mekhilta* with a commentary he entitled *Midot Soferim*. The title of the commentary is sufficient to tell us that we now

confront a very different man—one who now sees the hermeneutic principles deriving from the period of the *Soferim,* rather than from the
revelation at Sinai.[91] Weiss included a much lengthier introduction to
this work, in which it becomes clear that the man who in 1862 vilified
Frankel was now, in 1865, his staunch supporter. I do not know precisely what explains this transformation; the memoirs do not even acknowledge it.[92] The transformation does coincide with Weiss's appointment as an instructor of Talmud in the newly established *Beit Midrash*
in Vienna in 1863.[93] There he would have come into contact with other
figures sympathetic to the approach of Frankel and Graetz, who may
have persuaded him of the legitimacy of their methods and conclusions. Be that as it may, Weiss's intellectual efforts in the early sixties
make clear enough that Weiss was drawn to a study of midrashic texts;
that he understood their intellectually problematic nature; that he wished
to address this problematic nature; and, clearly, that he simply could
not sustain his fideism as he delved more deeply into the matter, and
tried to resolve its difficulties.[94]

The "conversion" to the historical school did not mean that Weiss
had managed to arrive at a consistent approach to the literature. As he
made clear in article published a few months before his *Mekhilta* edition, the conception of the tradition that had been with him since youth
did not withstand challenge easily. Thus, at this time, he still wished to
uphold traditional conceptions of rabbinic history as much as was possible.[95] His commitment to *Wissenschaft* was now such, however, that
if the evidence forced the matter in the other direction, he felt he had
no choice but to follow it. One method Weiss devised for mediating the
tension was to challenge previously held beliefs that he now saw as
unsustainable, while at the same time looking to explain the errors of
the past so as not to impugn the integrity or intelligence of the sages.
For example, this time around he acknowledged that he had been wrong
in asserting that the hermeneutic principles could be traced back to
Sinai.[96] At the same time, he wished to explain why so many important
rabbinic scholars were led to that erroneous belief. The best he could
do was to suggest that the principles all provide for thoroughly rational deductions from Scripture. Such deductions, by virtue of their rationality, were always available, and must have been freely drawn
throughout the ages. Thus, while the principles were not identified and
systematically applied until a later period, it is not improper to imagine
them as originating with rational reflection on the Torah, which is to
say, from the day the written Torah was given (an issue on which he
maintained thoroughly traditional views).

Weiss's introduction to his edition of the *Mekhilta* laid the foundation for what would appear six years later in the first two volumes of

Dor Dor ve-Dorshav. Both works display the marked influence of Krochmal and Frankel in their emphasis on the exegetical efforts of the *Soferim,* the period of organizing halakhot without scriptural sources, the return to midrash, and, once again, the distinction between Aqiba and Ishmael. *Dor Dor ve-Dorshav* added enormous documentation for these claims, and refined them in certain ways, but the basic structure of the later multivolume work was established in his *Mekhilta* introduction. The historical picture pioneered by Krochmal, Frankel, and Graetz, slightly modified, served to satisfy the Viennese historian of the rabbinic tradition. The introduction, then, adds little to the historical picture pioneered by the historical school; it speaks volumes about Isaac Hirsch Weiss, however.

Before leaving Weiss's introduction to his *Mekhilta* edition, I wish to note one other scholarly aspect of it. Here he continued developing the insight of Geiger that the *Mekhilta* and *Sifra* clearly derived from different schools—the former from the school of Ishmael, the latter from the school of Aqiba. Similarly, *Sifre Numbers* and *Sifre Deuteronomy* each derived from these same two schools, respectively. He thus became the second link in the emerging scholarly construct—soon to become a consensus view—regarding these documents, a construct that was thoroughly at odds with the assumptions of the medievals.

In *Dor Dor ve-Dorshav* Weiss recapitulates the arguments of his introduction at greater length. What is new in this work regarding our issues is his insistence that R. Ishmael's commitment to the principle that the Torah speaks in human language extends, beyond a general commitment to *peshat,* to a rejection of anthropomorphism. The idea is that the Bible spoke of God in human terms because the Bible addressed human beings within the limitations of their language. The adoption of this principle to explain anthropomorphic usages in the Bible became a staple of medieval Jewish thought; such an adoption is unattested before the tenth century.[97] Weiss, however, reads it into R. Ishmael's alleged system, thereby portraying him as deeply committed not only to rational exegesis but to rational theology, advancing his stock that much further. Thus, Weiss too joined in the effort to locate a moderate, almost modern consciousness within rabbinic Judaism at its formative stage. He, more than his colleagues, saw in Ishmael a model for those who would remain committed to traditional Jewish practice while seeking a rational understanding of its (largely secondary) exegetical foundation.

On the other side of the equation, we should note that in Weiss, far more than in Graetz or Frankel, we find genuine anger at R. Aqiba for developing his far-fetched exegetical system; this anger, it seems to me, is eloquent testimony to Weiss's embarrassment at midrashic excess.

This anger is rooted in Weiss' evaluation, contrary to Graetz and Frankel, that in the battle for the hearts and minds of Jews between Aqiba and Ishmael, the former clearly won. From this time forward, Judaism would be shaped by the assumptions—exegetical and theological—of the Aqiban school[98] While he too sees the Aqiban/Ishmaelian disputes as proving that most of the fundamental laws of Judaism were not the product of truly corrupt exegeses,[99] this fact has been lost on students of Talmud for generations, and for that Judaism has paid a high price.[100] It is, it seems, his hope that a genuinely historical understanding of the emergence of the Aqiban system and, more generally, of the nature of Jewish learning in the second century could redound to the benefit of those committed to Jewish tradition in the nineteenth century. For such an understanding would show that an essential assumption of Reform historians—which was, after all, based on the natural assumptions of Ashkenazic traditionalists—was simply false. The halakhah was not, for the most part, created by outlandish exegeses, despite what the Babylonian Talmudists thought. They were seduced by the Aqiban system, but the norms they sought to uphold were actually the products of the simpler exegeses of the *Soferim,* whose approach was understood and continued by Ishmael.

CLOSING REFLECTIONS

The arcana surrounding the exegetical systems of two second-century rabbis is scarcely awe-inspiring stuff. Some are no doubt thinking that the historical vision of the traditionally oriented historical school must have had more to offer than just this. After all, this inchoate "school" did eventually provide the intellectual foundations of the Conservative movement. Indeed, the historical school had much more to offer than what I have described. The constructs of rabbinism pioneered by the historical school were certainly directed to more important questions than who will interpret a biblical repetition and who will not. They addressed the very viability of rabbinism in the modern world, and created a portrait of its richness and vitality that had a significant impact on Jewish consciousness. But all constructs must be erected piece by piece, starting, as the cliché would have it, with a strong foundation. I have tried to demonstrate here that the traditionally oriented historical school could not allow rabbinism to rest on the foundation of talmudic exegesis, for, with the shifts in perception and exegetical taste that characterize modernity, nothing resting there could continue to stand. The first step in creating a compelling portrait of rabbinism was to resolve the problem of far-fetched midrash. Every member of this school worked to resolve this problem; the existential urgency of the matter for them is palpable. The most lasting strategy devised by the historical school to alleviate the tension created by rabbinic midrash was to revive an ancient, long-ignored model, and greatly exaggerate its historical reliability and significance. The Aqiba/Ishmael distinction became the critical piece of "evidence" in support of the thesis that "far-fetched" exegeses played a negligible role in the formation of rabbinic Judaism. That these second-century exegetes spent so much of their time finding scriptural supports for existing law upheld the proposition that the laws antedated them by centuries, for the laws had already achieved authority, and yet their scriptural sources had been long lost.

As I have noted already, this specific historical claim eventually achieved virtual consensus in the Jewish academic world. Scholars of ancient Judaism of all ideological stripes came to take for granted that rabbinic halakhic midrash emerged from two distinct schools, and that this fact lent credence to the ultimately more important claim that most rabbinic exegesis was intended to find the connection between ancient traditions and Scripture. It did not generate law. This small matter, in and of itself, has engaged academics for over a century.

But the stakes here went well beyond the still rather arcane question of what function midrash served. One does not build broad religious movements nor impress laypeople on the basis of such issues. But rationalizing the nature and function of midrash was the critical first step in the broader rehabilitation of Pharisaic rabbinic Judaism in the face of political and historical constructs that would identify it as the incarnation of foolishness and immorality. Rescuing the ancient rabbis from the caricatures of Gentile and Jewish scholars was deemed an urgent need by conservative religious leaders, and in this they came to be followed by liberal Jews as well. Portraying the rabbis as intelligent readers, progressive minds, and judicious legislators came to dominate public lectures and sermons and the popular Jewish press, as well as scholarly periodicals. Committed Reform and Conservative Jews today, whatever their level of practical observance, often claim to be motivated by the belief that historical Judaism represents a progressive ethical force in world history.[101] I submit that this confidence in the vitality of the rabbinic tradition is the result of the efforts of the historical school and the adoption of many of its conclusions by Reform and Conservative Jews alike. To be sure, debates regarding the limits of change go on, just as they did between Geiger and Frankel a century and a half ago. To be sure, debates go on regarding which of the two alleged approaches—that of Ishmael (allegedly traditional but progressive) or that of Aqiba (allegedly subversive)—is most appropriate in the face of contemporary challenges. But the historical school succeeded in banishing the antirabbinic animus of much German and early Reform scholarship from *Jewish* consciousness, allowing liberal Jews to appropriate the rabbinic heritage without shame. Descriptions of the ancient rabbis as foolish readers whose inability to read led to the monstrosity known as rabbinic Judaism, descriptions which were common 150 to 200 years ago, no longer resonate within the Jewish community. In bringing about this shift in Jewish consciousness, the work of Graetz, Frankel, the later Geiger, and others, and their hundreds of students and disciples in the rabbinates of Germany and the United States, was critical. While the alleged activity of the *Soferim,* the methods of tannaitic learning, and the alleged differences between Aqiba and Ishmael are scarcely known in the broader Jewish community, what ideological historians have constructed out of these arcane matters has penetrated deeply into Jewish consciousness. By reconceptualizing the nature and function of midrash, these historians resolved to their satisfaction the question of rabbinic intelligence and honesty; they could then present to the public glorified images of Hillel, Yoḥanan ben Zakkai, Joshua, Ishmael and, sometimes, Aqiba. They could favorably contrast the teachings and accomplishments of these men with those of Jesus and the early Church leaders, confronting Protestant triumphalism with Jewish triumphalism. Understanding the motivations of the major historians who brought about this shift in Jewish consciousness and evaluating the bases of the historical constructs are, I believe, critical to our understanding of the emergence of modern Judaism.

To be sure, there is a gulf that separates liberal Jewish intellectuals in the last decade of the twentieth century from their nineteenth-century forebears. Today it is increasingly popular to return to an earlier view of rabbinic patterns of reading texts, albeit with an inverted evaluation of what this means. That is, today more and more people are quite comfortable viewing the rabbis as people who intentionally subverted the meaning of the biblical text, not as an act of dishonesty or stupidity, but in brilliant recognition of the fact that the Bible, like any text, does not in fact have a definitive meaning anyway. The properties of language and the nature of texts make it quite absurd to talk about *peshat* as earlier generations have done. Today, many would see the rabbis as doing precisely what Spinoza claims they did; but to contemporary critics, the rabbis were right and Spinoza, with his sense that one can establish the definitive, natural meaning of the text, was wrong.

We must remember that from the seventeenth to the early twentieth century very different standards prevailed in the academic world. It was believed that the definitive meaning of a text could be established with philological precision. Despite the efforts of people like Mendelssohn and Wessely to partially challenge this construct, the views of the philologists came to prevail. From this perspective, as we have seen, rabbinic patterns of reading seemed irredeemably foreign and inferior; such a vision of one's cultural heritage cannot help but erode one's sense of attachment and belonging. Many Jews in these centuries came to feel alienated from rabbinic Judaism, a feeling aided by an intolerant German academy. This alienation went beyond a sense that certain rituals no longer seemed relevant; it involved a sense that rabbinism itself was perverse—that it took the sublime demands of the Bible and extended them in totally arbitrary and unjustifiable directions. Today's religious leaders no longer confront a religious alienation rooted in such concerns. For this reason, perhaps, the teachings of men like Geiger and Frankel ring hollow. However, it is important to understand that they faced different challenges, different cultural irritants. To judge by the extent to which the problem was treated in the literature, the problematic nature of rabbinic exegesis was, in the nineteenth century, a major concern for all those who wished to remain committed to some form of Judaism. As we shall see in the next chapter, this was true for the Orthodox as much as for the more liberal branches of Judaism that emerged in the nineteenth century. All of them felt compelled to create a vision of the cultural past that continued to speak to their present.

In some ways, I cannot help but feel that the historical school did its work too well; out of all the detailed discussion of rabbinic exegesis and law, it created a usable past with which people could comfortably live. Comfort stifles curiosity; the mythical glorifications of the past replace genuine inquiry into it. Paradoxically, perhaps, this makes their inquiries, which created the constructs that dominate Jewish self-understanding, seem distant and irrelevant. I would argue that while liberal Jews no longer confront the problems these nineteenth-century scholars did; while contemporary intellectuals may be comfortable with a picture of the rabbis as subversive readers; while the laity may not care about how rabbis read anything, the comfort of liberal Jews with their collective past is the result of the efforts of people like Graetz, Frankel, and Geiger. The concerns of these men no longer matter because they successfully resolved them.

Finally, we must note the extent to which the works of the traditional historical school, opposed to Reform as they were, shook the foundations of the world we have come to call Orthodox. Already in this chapter we have noted the reaction of Samson Raphael Hirsch to the work of Graetz, and in the next chapter I will try to more fully describe and assess the Orthodox response to the challenges of the historical school as well as the Reform movement. There I will argue that important aspects of Orthodox ideology develop because of the need to provide firm foundations for extrabiblical Jewish law in the face of the criticism of rabbinic exegesis and the emergence of scholarly models that historicized it.

Providing a stimulus to ideological retrenchment on the part of the Orthodox was, however, only one element of the *Nachleben* of the work of Graetz, Frankel and Weiss. Not all of their readers emerged with their faith intact, ready to do battle with them. Many of the youthful Jewish elite of Eastern Europe were led away from traditional Jewish observance by their discovery, through the works of the historical school, that Jewish law was not insulated from the laws of history. Moshe Leib Lilienblum, for example, recounts his "path to heresy" in his memoirs, there noting the effect of reading works that historicized the halakhah. Micha Yosef Berdichewski in his recollections of life in the yeshiva of Volozhin, the leading higher academy of Talmud study in Jewish Lithuania, notes over and over again how students were "led astray" by reading Graetz's history, Frankel's *Darkhe ha-Mishnah* or Weiss's *Dor Dor ve-Dorshav*.[102] In time, the destructive role of these works became almost a cliché, with the blame for the breakdown of tradition in the modern world laid squarely at the feet of their authors. In the summer of 1939, as European Jewry stood on the brink of disaster, Elḥanan Wasserman, one of the leading figures in the Lithuanian yeshiva world (much of which was transplanted to Poland), could see in the works of Graetz, Geiger, and Weiss the "torah of Satan" that led to the falsification of the Torah of God, and was leading Jewish youth to catastrophe.[103] Whatever one thinks of Wasserman's historical judgment, there is little doubt that he was reflecting a common perception among the rabbinic elite of Europe, who saw, not without cause, the works of the historical school leading to a new conception of Jewish law that did not lead to a more sophisticated attachment to it—as was intended—but to its abandonment. While a few older *maskilim*, such as Samuel Joseph Fuenn,[104] could adopt the conservative stance that Graetz and Frankel's historiography was designed to uphold, most of the younger readers of these works in Eastern Europe were led to more radical conclusions than their authors intended.

In the end, then, we must say that the traditional historical school was quite successful in its efforts to rehabilitate the reputation of the rabbis as readers and jurists; they were much less successful in promoting continued attachment to a historicized rabbinic tradition in the modern world.

8 • Midrash and Orthodoxy

THE GERMAN ORTHODOX

As in all cases of religious change, the new varieties of Judaism included within the term "Reform" naturally called forth a shift in the consciousness of those who would remain uncompromisingly loyal to traditional patterns of life. Such people went from an unreflective traditionalism[1] to a self-conscious orthodoxy[2] within a generation or two of the rise of liberalizing tendencies. A range of factors influenced how that orthodoxy would actually be defined in the different areas of Jewish settlement in Europe. The program of the Reformers and the policies of the various governments, particularly pertaining to questions of education, combined with the distinct social and religious ethos of the different traditional communities to produce a variety of orthodoxies within Europe in the nineteenth century. By the middle of the century, specific patterns of orthodoxy were discernible in many places in Europe; most significant for our purposes here are the Orthodox communities of the German lands and Lithuania.[3] Seeking to impede the spread of reforms, the Orthodox embarked on a program of differentiation and counterattack that in turn changed the face of Jewish tradition. Since religious liberalization and institutionalized Reform began first in Germany and made greatest advances there, the Orthodoxy that emerged there confronted a far more developed and advanced liberal program. It is therefore not surprising that the German patterns of Orthodoxy would distinctly differ from those that arose in other parts of Europe, and would display the most extensive grappling with the actual theological and historical foundations of organized Reform.[4]

211

As we have seen in the previous chapters, attacks on rabbinic midrash like those of Abraham Geiger were subject to immediate counterattack by partisans of Orthodoxy of Germany. The nature of some of these early responses, however, indicate that their authors did not really understand the problems that made rabbinic exegesis such a difficult issue to modern Jews. Thus, we find a response on the part of Solomon Plessner that amounts to nothing more than citations from Gentile scholars in support of a long-standing talmudic tradition.[5] Plessner's work indicates that he did not at all comprehend the extent to which rejection of rabbinism was rooted in a sense that its norms derived from foolish readings of the Bible, and a new historical consciousness that could not be impressed by a Renaissance Hebraist's stray remark regarding talmudic tradition. From a different perspective, we find the response of Salomon Tiktin and his colleagues, which essentially sought to revive the position staked out by Saadia and Ibn Ezra. This response argued that the exegeses of the talmudic sages never were employed to generate law, and in no way reflect what the rabbis really thought the Bible meant. The problem here was, as in the Middle Ages, that this conception stood at such odds with talmudic discourse. It was quite simple for Geiger to refute these claims, relying explicitly on Naḥmanides and his far more compelling and honest accounting of talmudic discussions.

The more insightful among the Orthodox recognized early on that the responses generated by an earlier age, when it too came under cultural pressure, would not be effective in the nineteenth century without considerable refinement. We thus find that as the century wore on, a marked shift is discernible in the attitude to the Bible, its language, and rabbinic exegesis among a small group of Orthodox commentators. While never wavering in their commitment to certain basic metaphysical and historical beliefs, the authors of these works pushed the contours of rabbinic learning in new directions.

The oldest of the major German commentators and scholars to be discussed in this section was Jacob Zvi Meklenburg (1785–1865). A student of Akiva Eger, the chief rabbi of Posen, Meklenburg eschewed the rabbinate, preferring a career in business. Only with the failure of his business in 1831 did he assume a rabbinic position in Königsberg, a position that he held until his death. By temperament and training, he may be described as a rabbi of the old school. However, his years as a businessman provided him with a thorough command of the German language, giving him access to the full range of German-Jewish writing, including Bible translations, Reform catechisms, and synthetic works like Creizenach's *Schulchan Aruch*. It is thus not surprising that during his many years in this rabbinate he took it upon himself to vigorously oppose the burgeoning Reform movement, and, unlike his teacher, Eger, to do so by responding directly to their understanding of halakhah and its origins.

To fully understand what motivated Meklenburg's activity, it is worth digressing for a moment to consider the religious conditions he witnessed in Königsberg, and how he reacted to them. Despite Meklenburg's strenuous opposition to Reform, Königsberg in the 1830s and 1840s was not as deeply divided by the bitter disputes between the Orthodox and Reform that came to characterize other German cities (such as Breslau) at this time. This was due, in part, to the efforts of the Prussian government to suppress Reform (relevant elsewhere, of course), and, in part, to the religious moderation of the leading spokesman of Reform in Königsberg, Joseph Levin Saalschütz.[6] As far as we know, Saalschütz remained committed to the observance of Jewish law, and certainly his program for Reform was limited to increased decorum in the synagogue, the introduction of a choir, a weekly sermon in German, and the like. (Meklenburg opposed even these minor changes, but the community avoided major division.)[7] Saalschütz's continued respect for rabbinic tradition is evident from his scholarly work. While he too made an effort to reconstruct the system of Mosaic law, his efforts, unlike most others, explicitly relied on rabbinic judgments to supplement the biblical materials.[8] Saalschütz, then, was decidedly not among those who justified their commitment to Reform by attacking rabbinic exegesis as a gross misappropriation of the biblical message.

Thus, the impetus for Meklenburg's work was not in his personal confrontations with the local Reform rabbi. Still, we should not turn away from local considerations in trying to understand Meklenburg. It is almost certain that the Jewish laity of Königsberg did not share the moderation of Joseph Saalschütz. While detailed information on the Jewish laity of Königsberg in the 1830s is difficult to come by, I can see no reason to think that the behavior of the Jewish bourgeoisie there differed significantly from that of other Prussian cities such as Breslau and Berlin; after all, Königsberg had been a center of *haskalah* a generation earlier. Further, there seems little doubt that the rates of conversion to Christianity among the Jews of Königsberg were comparable to those in the other Prussian cities.[9] If, in fact, the behavior of the city's Jews was similar to that of Berlin and Breslau, Meklenburg would certainly have been witness to extensive violations of Jewish law among the laypeople of Königsberg.

Whether or not my assumption of extensive violation of Jewish law in Königsberg is correct, it is beyond dispute that the Orthodox rabbi of the city was deeply troubled by what he perceived as an abandonment of Jewish tradition, whether in his immediate environment or

elsewhere in the German lands. One might expect that the local conditions would have led Meklenburg to the realization that Reform
ideologues and ideologies were not the primary causes of the religious
liberalization he so vigorously opposed. Yet, Meklenburg, given his
own assumptions regarding traditional culture, could not imagine that
the deviance of the laity was not grounded in an ideological rejection
of Jewish law as formulated by the intellectual leaders; that is, he assumed
"official" Reform ideology and rhetoric was responsible for the breakdown of traditional Jewish life, for Jews, in his imaginary universe, did
not act en masse without rabbinic approval. With this assumption in
place, Meklenburg would naturally be drawn to the question of the
nature and authority of rabbinic exegesis, which, as we have seen, was
the primary point of attack of Reform ideologues.

His unyielding opposition to Reform ideology provided the impetus for his major work, *Ha-Ketav ve-ha-Kabbalah*, a commentary on
the Torah whose title may be translated *Scripture and the Tradition*.
The first edition appeared in 1839, with a second revised edition appearing in 1853. To this second edition was added a German translation of
the biblical text; the intent of this translation was to more accurately
reflect the traditional interpretations of the Torah than did the prevailing German translations prepared under Jewish auspices, including
Mendelssohn's. A third revised edition appeared in 1857, and a fourth
revised edition appeared posthumously in 1880.[10]

Ha-Ketav ve-ha-Kabbalah represented the first in a series of Bible
commentaries to emerge from the German rabbinate whose expressed
purpose was to unify the written and the oral Torahs.[11] In Meklenburg's
case, the strategy was to explain the Torah according to its *peshat* and
thereby unify it with the oral law.[12] That is, the commentary was guided
by the conviction that a proper understanding of the language of the
Bible would allow one to discern its more profound meaning, which
corresponds to the teachings of the oral law. In some respects, this was
a return to the strategy pioneered by Naftali Herz Wessely, although as
we shall see, there are important differences.

Like Saadia, Meklenburg's approach rests on the assertion that the
entire corpus of extrabiblical laws that are considered of scriptural
authority (*mi-de-oraita*) was received orally by Moses at Sinai, and has
been handed down generation to generation from that time forward.
To a greater extent than Saadia, though, Meklenburg was guided by
the conviction that a full understanding of the complexity of biblical
language would allow one to see encoded within it the many laws of
the oral Torah. In Meklenburg's opinion, this was vastly different than
saying that the whole Torah consists of two corpora containing distinct and mutually complementary material. Rather, the two corpora

together form a larger unity, whose components are comparable to a body and its soul.[13] This is Meklenburg's starting point, but it is scarcely an adequate response in and of itself. It represents little more than standard rabbinic platitudes, with a dash of Wessely thrown in. Meklenburg obviously felt that there were more questions to be answered, and went on to explain precisely why the Bible is formulated in language that is often ambiguous, why it demands a unique form of exegesis, and how his understanding of the matter—resting as it does on a claim for a comprehensive tradition—accounts satisfactorily for talmudic discourse.

According to Meklenburg, the divine author of the Bible purposely expressed his wishes in an ambiguous form, so as to increase the difficulty of compliance. For to comply with rules and norms one fully understands demands but one act of will; one need simply decide that, despite one's inclination to the contrary, this norm will be abided by. When however the formulation of the norm allows for other interpretations, the decision to comply with the only one that is identified as authoritatively expressing the will of the legislator requires much greater self-control. For one can easily justify acting in an entirely different manner by appeal to the language of the norm in question. Thus, complying with the laws of the Torah as God wants them observed requires suppressing one's intellectual independence and submitting to the one interpretation preserved by tradition that definitively represents what God desires.[14] By presenting his norms in such a way, God provides more fully for the development of the strength of character humans need to lead full ethical lives, and greatly enhances the reward that is due to those who follow on the difficult path he has set before them. Thus, the ambiguity of the Bible is seen by Meklenburg as a product of God's love of humanity.

Knowing how to interpret the Bible correctly is, as we have seen, a function of submitting to the demands of the tradition. This does not mean that there is not an integral relationship between the language of Scripture and the demands of tradition, however. For, Meklenburg tells his readers, as all its students know, Hebrew is the most excellent of languages, whose system of grammatical roots allows for fullest and broadest expression of different ideas within a single expression or word. This inherent multivalence allows for the expression of various thoughts in a single word or phrase.[15]

The language of the Bible is, then, both ambiguous and multivalent,[16] and we must appreciate the distinction to see what Meklenburg is trying to say. As I see it, Meklenburg is suggesting that the language of the Torah is intentionally ambiguous, but in the same sense that all languages are sometimes ambiguous. Any particular combination of words can be interpreted in more than one way, perhaps by rearranging the punctuation, perhaps by virtue of the fact that a particular word encompasses more than one meaning (and sometimes these meanings may be quite distant from one another). What makes this ambiguous, rather than multivalent, is that one can say that all but one of the meanings is wrong; it is not intended by the speaker. To one who cannot appreciate the profundity of biblical language, Scripture will appear ambiguous, perhaps leading him or her away from the intended behavior. Because of this danger, the intended meaning of the text must be controlled, and this can be done only by means of tradition. It is tradition that will come and say, "The words in question demand x, and do not demand y."

Given the unique properties of the Hebrew language, the formulation of the Torah's norms is also multivalent, in that it comprehends more than one *intended* meaning. These intended meanings are not necessarily tied to context or syntax, and they may be indicated by use of an unusual word or form. The determination of these intended meanings, what we call midrash, represents, for Meklenburg, the effort to show that what was received by tradition is also encoded within the linguistic materiel of the written text, and in fact represents the profound *peshat* of scriptural language.[17] Tradition rescues us from the problems of ambiguity, while at the same time allowing us to fully appreciate the multivalence of the text, a testament to the genius of the divine legislator.

One example of how this works should suffice. As noted in chapter 1, Lev. 1:2–3 discusses the animals acceptable for sacrifice. Verse 2 states that sacrificial animals are to be drawn "from livestock (*min ha-behemah*), [i.e.,] from cattle (*min ha-baqar*) and from sheep (*min ha-ṣon*)." The following verse repeats the phrase "from cattle," or "from the herd." The *Sifra* on these verses notes that the phrases come to exclude a number of types of cattle and sheep, such as those that have had sexual encounters with humans, those that have been employed in idolatrous rites, and the *terefah*. The usual understanding of these exclusions is that they derive from the effort to account for the superfluous preposition "from." By insisting that each use of "from" comes to exclude some kinds of sheep and cattle, rather than representing biblical style, the ancient rabbis have successfully attached a function to each word of the verse. Given this interpretation of the passage, the specific exclusions appear arbitrary, and the "from" that excludes *terefot* could just as easily have been invoked to exclude one of the other categories, and vice versa. Further, given the ambiguity of the word *min*, one could well be led to claim that there are no intended exclusions present within the verse at all. In either case, one would readily conclude that there is no relation between the *peshat* of the verse and the midrashic understanding.[18]

Meklenburg insists, however, that these exclusions are not arbitrary, and do not emerge from an effort to account for superfluous prepositions. Rather, leaving the word *min* aside, Meklenburg engages in a thorough examination of the semantic field of each of the words, *behemah, baqar, şon*; understanding their full range of meaning in turn precludes certain possibilities specifically related to each word. For example, the word *baqar* does not simply designate cattle, but rather indicates the capacity for plowing; a sickly animal, or *terefah*, incapable of plowing is excluded from the semantic field of the word *baqar*. Similar claims are advanced regarding the words *behemah* and *şon*. "I have treated this matter at some length," he writes, "to show that the rabbis of blessed memory derived their explanation from the roots of the words themselves and not from the exclusionary force of the word 'from'."[19] In Meklenburg's interpretation, there is nothing arbitrary in the midrashic explanation, and in fact, this explanation represents the profound *peshat* of the biblical text.[20] For the words *behemah, baqar*, and *şon* are multivalent; their conventional meanings scarcely exhaust their potential significance. The rabbis, uniquely talented readers and linguists, were, by means of their insight into the roots of the Hebrew language, able to show that the traditional laws rendering certain animals sacrificially ineligible are actually promulgated in Scripture.

There is, perhaps ironically, considerable overlap between what Meklenburg is suggesting here and what Wessely (and, to a lesser extent, Mendelssohn) had to say on the subject. The fundamental difference is that Meklenburg insists that rabbinic interpretation, however much it illuminates the profound *peshat* of Scripture, is ultimately predetermined, and is confined within the boundaries established, a priori, by a comprehensive tradition; it represents the search for a scriptural foundation for information received independently of Scripture. Thus, in the example above, the unacceptability of the *terefah* is ultimately established by received tradition, and is not dependent on human recognition of the technical meaning of *baqar*; nevertheless, a proper understanding of this word will show how the traditional norms are encoded within Scripture. For the Berlin *maskilim*, by contrast, the interpretations of the rabbis are the product of the independent, rational application of their linguistic expertise.[21] Meklenburg's position was to become increasingly prominent among the Orthodox in the nineteenth century, as they feared any historical picture that portrayed the rabbis freely and independently interpreting Scripture. This was the image of the rabbis cultivated by many Reformers; and while some of the latter judged the results negatively and others did not, all saw the rabbis determining the meaning of Scripture to suit their tastes, and the Reformers argued that they possessed the same right. Although not all Orthodox rabbis went in Meklenburg's direction—some acknowledged that not all extrabiblical laws originated in tradition—most did, and they did so as a way of deflating the arguments put forward by Reformers and, later, members of the historical school.

As I have already noted at other points in this book, the claim that rabbinic exegesis was primarily interested in creating mnemonic devices for traditional laws did considerable violence to talmudic discourse. The give-and-take of passage after passage suggested that the talmudic redactors saw something both serious and creative in the sages' exegetical endeavors. Meklenburg seems to have intuitively recognized the problem, and was far less prepared than was Saadia or Nieto to trivialize talmudic discourse in the pursuit of constancy and certitude. To deal with the problem, Meklenburg introduced a distinction between two types of mnemonic devices, for which he used the German terms *Denkmal* and *Merkmal*. The *Denkmal* represents a strictly external connection that one draws between things to aid one's memory. One might set a connection to rhyme, or focus on the same first letter or some other contingent feature shared by two items that can help one remember something that otherwise eludes memory. If we were to view rabbinic exegeses as *Denkmale*, we would have serious difficulties with talmudic discourse, since such *Denkmale* could scarcely be considered serious or worthy of the frequent disputes to which rabbinic interpretations are subject in the Talmud.

The *Merkmal*, however, is something entirely different. This is a form of mnemonic in which one identifies an essential feature of a given item or thought, and connects it in one's mind to something that shares that essential feature. The connection does not only help one remember something important, but actually increases one's insight and understanding regarding both sides of the nexus. In the case of midrash, drawing a connection between scriptural language and a traditional law allows the Jews to more fully appreciate the profundity of the scriptural message, the importance of linguistic minutiae, and the full range and authority of traditional laws. Seen as *Merkmale*, rabbinic interpretations do indeed represent something serious and important, and aid in a very real way in understanding Scripture and upholding traditions. Further, determining which unusual turn of phrase or verbal root signifies an essential relationship to a traditional norm is certainly a serious matter: it can illuminate features of each, and is therefore worthy of the time and effort it takes to reach a definitive resolution of the question of which verse actually communicates the connection between Scripture and tradition.

Further indicative of the religious and exegetical importance of rabbinic exegesis, even though it does not generate law, is the fact that God imparted to Moses various hermeneutic techniques designed to determine the appropriate *Merkmal* for a given traditional norm.[22] Finding *Merkmale* for traditional laws in Scripture, then, represents the fulfillment of an implicit divine command, one that enhances our understanding of Scripture by identifying the intended significance of a scriptural norm. More than that, it allows us to see how the entire traditional oral law is encoded within the language of Scripture—provided, of course, that we learn to appreciate its profundity.

From Meklenburg's perspective, the argument he has presented profoundly challenges the Reform understanding of the *peshat* of the Torah that was so frequently invoked to justify the relaxation of the demands of rabbinic interpretation. It is, of course, based on assumptions not shared by Reformers, and he could scarcely have hoped to deter them from their ways. He seems rather to have hoped to keep from succumbing to heresy those who were learning the Torah with the help of German translations and those who were exposed to the interpretations of various Reformers, but who had not yet abandoned traditional Judaism. He wanted his reader to know that those who had approached the Bible from a perspective other than the rabbinic one had grossly distorted its meaning, precisely because they did not rely on tradition. In a number of places he refers to the interpretations of Reformers (without naming them, of course), claiming that his interpretation shows just how foolish they actually are.[23] Clearly, Meklenburg read the literature produced by Reformers, and in particular seems to have regarded the *Schulchan Aruch* of Michael Creizenach as paradigmatic of what happens when one thinks that there is a gulf between rabbinic interpretations and *peshat*.[24] Similarly, he takes on Mendelssohn and other translators for trying to translate in accord with the *peshat* without realizing that it cannot be distinguished from traditional interpretations.[25]

Meklenburg's commentary represents a pioneering effort to redefine what "orthodoxy" means in the face of the problem of midrash halakhah. It markedly distances itself from the traditionalism of premodern Ashkenazic Jewry, which was quite comfortable acknowledging that only a small portion of rabbinic law derived from tradition, while a much larger proportion was produced by means of exegesis. This traditionalist conception was all too readily adopted by Reformers to justify their challenge to rabbinic laws and practices. Like Saadia confronting Karaism and Nieto confronting Marranism and Spinozism,

Meklenburg was pushed to reject the predominant talmudic response to the question "How do we know this?" in favor of one that could hope to strengthen the larger structure of Jewish law and observance.

It is difficult to determine what impact Meklenburg's commentary may have had on traditional Jews of a scholarly bent; it is clear that it could not hope to exercise influence on Jewish laypeople or liberal intellectuals. The spread of Reform Judaism continued apace. In the years 1844-46, Reform leaders convened three conferences to develop coherent ideological principles, an important step in the coalescence of the movement. The first of these conferences was held in the German city of Braunschweig, and it (far more than the next two conferences) elicited extensive Orthodox reaction. The Orthodox reacted against Reform attacks on the tradition, the rejection of a personal messiah, the conferees' endorsement of the permissibility of marriages with Christians, and the possibility of civil divorce, among other things. For the most part the Orthodox responses cast doubt on the religious integrity and the intelligence of the Reformers, arguing that they were motivated by material and political rather than spiritual concerns, and that they were largely ignorant of rabbinic tradition. Jacob Katz, who has described the Orthodox reaction in detail, is certainly right in his claim that the Orthodox were unwilling or unable to "confront the intellectual convictions, and the claims of rational and historical criticism, which serve, at least post factum, to justify the cessation of observance among those [accused] of materialistic motives."[26] Yet this was not true of all Orthodox rabbis incensed by the decisions of the Reformers at Braunschweig. At least one, Meir Leibush Malbim, saw the need to undermine the intellectual foundations of the basic orientation of the Reformers.

In many ways Malbim (1809–79) had little in common with Jacob Zvi Meklenburg. Where the latter's rabbinical career was the model of stability, the former's was anything but. Never settling in comfortably anywhere, he went from place to place—from Poland to Prussia to Romania to France to Russia.[27] He was a contentious and impatient man who never backed away from a quarrel; in many respects his most interesting work was the result of his efforts to defend Orthodoxy from the challenges of Reform. For the aspect of his work most relevant here, his years as a rabbi in the Prussian town of Kempen (1841–58) were decisive, as they placed him in the front row of the arena in which Reform was solidifying its hold in various Prussian communities.[28]

As he himself attests, the results of the first Reform rabbinical conference in Braunschweig in 1844 filled him with an irrepressible anger that provided the impetus for a Bible commentary that would show the unity of the written and oral Torahs. He understood the connection between the behavior of these "few evil men in Germany" and their sense that the norms of Judaism were grounded in the foolish interpretations of men incapable of appreciating the *peshat* of the Torah. (Like Meklenburg, he assumes that these ideologues and intellectuals were responsible for the extensive abandonment of Jewish traditional praxis in the German cities and towns.) To combat these "evil men" Malbim felt compelled to show that the interpretations of the rabbis in actuality represented the *peshat*; it was the Reformers who were the ignoramuses, content with the most superficial comprehension of the Torah. "The *peshat* that accords with the true and clear rules of language is only to be found in [what we conventionally refer to as] the *derash*";[29] the interpretations that the Reformers consider *peshat* are nothing but superficial readings of the text.

For Malbim, this was not some glib response to the challenge of Reform. He recognized full well that he was making a momentous claim, one that challenged the understanding of rabbinic exegesis that prevailed among many important medieval commentators. He knew full well that many Jews of previous generations could not reconcile themselves to rabbinic readings of Scripture. He knew that the distinction between *peshat* and *derash* had been a standard of Jewish thinking for centuries. But he also knew that those of an earlier age who could not treat midrashic interpretations as authentic readings of the Torah nevertheless remained fully observant of Jewish laws and practices. They alleviated the tension of this position by insisting that *derashot* represented fanciful readings of different individuals and had no generative power. The laws were traditions from Moses; the *derashot* were dismissed as *asmakhtot*, and nothing more.

Malbim felt compelled to reject such a vision of rabbinic exegesis, as it simply did not accord with talmudic discourse (that Reformers were not buying such apologetics may also have had something to do with his rejection). Anyone who studies the Talmud, he insisted, will immediately see that the exegetical discussions therein obviously presuppose that laws are generated by exegesis. The number of laws that can be classified as laws given to Moses at Sinai is small indeed; "the remaining myriads of laws are learned from Scripture, and their foundation is in the written Torah."[30] Thus, it is impossible to claim that most of the specific laws of Judaism were received as traditions;[31] rabbinic literature testifies to the contrary. Without recourse to a detailed, comprehensive tradition, however, one is left with the problem that led earlier scholars to develop such a view of tradition in the first place— namely, the distance that separates rabbinic interpretations from the language of Scripture. Now, to be sure, in an earlier age, many Jews were untroubled by the gap they perceived between *peshat* and *derash*;

it was clear to Malbim, however, that new textual assumptions had emerged. The perception of a gap between *peshat* and *derash* threatened to become a chasm separating Jews from *miṣvot*.

Like Wessely and Meklenburg, Malbim saw the solution to the problem in the concept of a profound *peshat*. Appreciation of this profound *peshat* depended on a denial of genuine synonymity, as with Wessely, and, more importantly, on discerning the true grammatical rules that governed scriptural language. Towards that goal, Malbim prefaced his commentary, entitled *Ha-Torah ve-ha-Miṣvah*,[32] with a grammatical treatise entitled *Ayelet ha-Shaḥar*, which presented 613 rules of usage and spelling that govern biblical Hebrew. As has been noted by many, the very number itself testified to the total artificiality of Malbim's conception,[33] particularly when one considers that he divides these 613 rules into 248 that govern usage and 365 that govern the use of verbs and (apparent) synonyms.[34]

Malbim drove home the point in the commentary itself, which was unique in the history of Jewish Bible exegesis. It was not an effort to explain the biblical text per se; rather, Malbim juxtaposed the text of Leviticus to the *Sifra,* its tannaitic commentary. (In subsequent volumes he would do the same with Exodus, Numbers and Deuteronomy and their respective tannaitic midrashim.) He divided the *Sifra* into specific, numbered units of thought, each of which embodied a distinct linguistic principle. To these discrete units of the *Sifra* was juxtaposed, in turn, Malbim's commentary, which identified the linguistic link between the two antecedent texts, adding, where appropriate, discussion of the talmudic sources relevant to the issues at hand. Malbim was quite conscious of the semiotics of this form of presentation. The Torah and its rabbinic interpretation stand next to one another as two columns upholding a single unified structure, the sacred *mishkan* or tabernacle,[35] which is recognized as such on the basis of the linguistic insights afforded by his commentary.[36]

Like Meklenburg, then, Malbim was pressed by the challenges of the age to insist that the written and oral laws were one contiguous whole, negating the distinction between *peshat* and *derash*. Unlike Meklenburg, however, he was not moved to insist that all the norms of the oral law originate in divine oral communications to Moses; rather they emerge from the revealed written text with the application of the received hermeneutic and grammatical rules. The essential point is that the Reformers were wrong in claiming that these norms are the product of defective exegesis, for they represent standards fully embedded in the linguistic structure of the scriptural text. The ancient rabbis who gave formal articulation to these norms were simply uncovering the definitive grammatical significance of Scripture's words and phrases;

far from distorting Scripture, they kept alive its deeper significance, which would otherwise have fallen into oblivion as its language grew old.

Meklenburg and Malbim were each rabbis of the old school in many respects. Although the former was fluent in German and the latter could manage it, neither had formal secular education, and neither knew how to speak the "language" of acculturating Jews in the nineteenth century. While each was aware of how profoundly midrashic exegesis compromised the coherence of rabbinic religion among the learned elements of the liberal camp, neither was able to fashion a response that could extend beyond the boundaries of his own community. Each did much to invigorate the intellectual life of German Orthodoxy for a time, but neither could address the needs of even Orthodox laypeople, let alone the non-Orthodox. While their works have been frequently reprinted and remain readily available, they are studied (perhaps consulted would be a better word) primarily by those of East European origin, and their larger systematic visions have never caught on in any identifiable community. While Meklenburg and Malbim are interesting as commentators and as historical phenomena, German Orthodoxy was not to be led by such figures. For German Orthodoxy to coalesce and emerge as a significant presence, a new type of rabbinic leadership was necessary.

Samson Raphael Hirsch

This new type of rabbinic leadership was probably best represented by Samson Raphael Hirsch (1808–88),[37] rabbi of a number of German cities, most importantly Frankfurt-am-Main (1851–88), as well as the Moravian city of Nikolsburg.[38] Unlike Meklenburg and Malbim, he represented the new type of rabbinic leader emerging in Germany in the first half of the nineteenth century. Secularly educated—as were his teachers Jacob Ettlinger and Isaac Bernays—and politically active, Hirsch was more at home communicating in German than in Hebrew, and was far more aware of the full range of Reform thinking than were either Meklenburg or Malbim. He was in many respects far more a theologian than a scholar of classical rabbinic texts. By the 1830s Hirsch had achieved prominence as a spokesman for the new Orthodoxy, arguing for its continued cogency in the modern world. In two works, *Die Neunzehn Briefe über Judentum* (1836) and *Horeb: Versuche über Jissroels Pflichten in der Zerstreuung, zunächst für Jissroels denkende Junglinge und Jungfrauen* (1837), Hirsch pioneered a symbolic, ethical understanding of the commandments, which showed how attuned he was to modern sensibilities. However, his concessions to the intellectual demands of modernity came to an abrupt halt at the border of the dogmatic and behavioral structure of Jewish Orthodoxy, a few minor divergences notwithstanding.[39] For Hirsch, nothing could be allowed to shake the foundations of that structure, for it represented the product of divine revelation; nothing the human mind could attain could challenge that. In these works and others[40] he made clear his rejection of the exegetical assumptions that he perceived in the work of the Reformers.

Still, in these early works the focus of Hirsch's attention was not really on the Reform critique of rabbinism per se. After all, many of the practices that liberalizing Jews were abandoning, or considering abandoning, were clear biblical requirements.[41] For Hirsch in his anti-Reform works of the thirties and forties, the paramount issue would appear to be the indispensability of halakhah in the realization of the complete human ethical potential (the divine source of halakhah was assumed). That is, Hirsch accepted from his Reform-minded contemporaries that religion must represent a force promoting the ethical sensitivity of the human being. However, in a cogent challenge to the often facile Kantianism that prevailed among Reformers, he insisted that only through the externally imposed discipline of halakhah could this possibly be achieved. Thus, Hirsch chose to engage Reform on a different level than did Meklenburg and Malbim; taking for granted that we indeed know what the law is, Hirsch focused on the need to observe it. The question "How do we know this?" that had engaged Jewish thinkers for centuries was a minor issue in Hirsch's early work; for Hirsch the question was, "Why should we do this?" and the answer was, "Because God commanded it to lead humanity toward ethical perfection."

As we have already seen, in the 1850s he added the work of the newly emerging historical school to his list of targets. In some ways the emergence of this school frightened him more than Reform, for this group threatened to make inroads into a community that heretofore had resisted the more radical program of the Reformers. This group proclaimed its fealty to halakhah and its faith in the divine origins of the Torah; however, its understanding of the historical emergence of halakhah threatened to relativize it by showing it to be a system of law originating in divine revelation, but carried forward over time by human intelligence in response to changing circumstance. In his battle with the historical school the question "How do we know this?" became paramount. As we have seen, in his fight with this school, Hirsch attacked the historical conclusions regarding the birth of Jewish exegesis and extrabiblical norms. For Hirsch, Jewish law was the product of a comprehensive tradition originating at Sinai; the hermeneutical principles "preserve and regulate" the laws, but do not produce them. They also originated at Sinai.[42] Thus, like many before him, he responded to what he perceived as challenges to the immutability of the halakhah by insisting that it did not emerge over time through human agency, but rather by means of a single comprehensive divine revelation. Like everyone else who advanced such a position, he insisted that the *derashot* were merely mnemonics. Like many who maintained this position, he ignored the difficulty of talmudic discourse, choosing instead to focus on the aggadic statements that lent support to the notion that everything was communicated to Moses at Sinai.

While his polemical responses to the work of the historical school served to highlight his understanding of Jewish law and exegesis, they were not the appropriate forum in which to address dispassionately the question of the *derashot* and their role in Jewish intellectual history, and they were not to be Hirsch's final or most original word on the matter. Like Meklenburg and Malbim before him, Hirsch provided his most complete statement of these matters in his translation of and commentary on the Pentateuch, composed in the 1860s. Although he claims to have compiled the published commentary from the class notes of his students over the years, he oversaw the entire production and saw it through to press; in my view, it thus carries weight as the definitive statement of the issues, free of the admixture of a student's erroneous perception that otherwise raises questions about works compiled from students' notes.

Unlike his predecessors, he does not preface his work with an introduction that spells out the operating assumptions of the commentary. This is done in the commentary itself, particularly in his remarks to Exod. 21:2. There he writes,

The written law is to be to the oral law in the relation of short notes on a full and extensive lecture on any scientific subject. For a student who has heard the whole lecture, short notes are quite sufficient to bring back afresh to his mind at any time the whole subject of the lecture. For him, a word, an added mark of interrogation, or exclamation, a dot, the underlining of a word, etc. etc., is often quite sufficient to recall to his mind a whole series of thoughts, a remark etc. For those who have not heard the lecture from the Master, such notes would be completely useless. If they were to try to reconstruct the scientific contents of the lecture literally from such notes they would of necessity make many errors. Words, marks, etc., which serve those scholars who had heard the lecture as instructive guiding stars to the wisdom that had been taught and learnt, stare at the uninitiated as unmeaning sphinxes. The wisdom, the truths, which the initiated reproduce from them (but do *not produce* out of them) are sneered at by the uninitiated as being merely a clever or witty play of words and empty dreams without any real foundation.[43]

Before proceeding to discuss this passage, we must understand what elicited it here to fully appreciate Hirsch's apologetic. Exod. 21:2 initiates a discussion of the laws of slavery: "If you acquire a Hebrew servant. . ." This discussion comes at the beginning of a group of laws pertaining to civil and criminal matters, "which quite naturally deals with the rights of man," Hirsch declares. Given that this treatment of human rights begins with the owning of slaves, Hirsch is moved to comment, "What an unthinkable enormity if actually this 'written word' of the 'book of law of the Jewish nation' should really be the one and only sole source of the Jewish conception of 'rights.'" Thus, he continues,

What a mass of laws and principles of jurisprudence must have already been said and fixed, considered, laid down and explained, before the Book of Law could reach these, or even speak of these, which, after all, are only quite exceptional cases. And it is with these sentences, the contents of which deny and limit the very holiest personal right of man, the right to personal freedom, that the Law *begins*. But it is quite a different matter if the written word, the "Book" is *not* the real source of the Jewish conception of rights, if this source is the traditional law, which was entrusted to the living word to which this "book" is only to be an aid to memory and reference, when doubts arise; if, as indeed is stated in the "book" itself, the total and complete Law had been given over to the people in its complete form, and had been impressed upon them, and explained to them, and lived by them for full forty years, before Moses, just before his death, was to hand them this written book. Then we can well understand that it is just the exceptional cases which principally come to be described, so that just from them, the normal general principles of justice and humanity may be more strikingly realized. . . . Then we can understand how the language used in this "book" is so skillfully chosen that often by the use of a striking expression, an unusual or altered construction, the position of a word, a letter etc., a whole train of ideas of justice and human rights is indicated. *After all, it was not out of this book that the law was to be acquired.* This book was to be given into the hands of those who were already well informed in the Law, simply as a means of retaining and reviving ever afresh this knowledge which had been entrusted to their memories; and also to the teachers of Law as a means of teaching to which the students can go for references to the traditional actual laws, so that the written sentences lying before them would make it easy for them to recall to their minds the knowledge they had received orally.[44]

The conception here represents a remarkable reversal of centuries of Jewish thought on the nature of Jewish law. However one chose to answer the question, "How do we know this?" all theorists began from the assumption that the oral law came to supplement the written law in some way; it filled in its lacunae and made it practicable. For Hirsch, by contrast, the written Torah never existed as a distinct source requiring supplementation and explanation. There was one sweeping, comprehensive oral revelation of all the laws incumbent on Jews by divine command, a small number of which, usually exceptional or otherwise distinctive cases, were set to writing, and were formulated in linguistically unusual ways. For Hirsch, then, the ubiquitous talmudic question, "How do we know this?" is not asking for the source of the law under discussion. The answer to such a question is obvious, and the same for every law in the Mishnah, save for what are acknowledged to be rabbinic decrees. Rather, the question must mean something like, "What written verse or part thereof calls attention to the larger constellation of laws of which the law under discussion is an integral part?" We wish to know the answer to this question so that we can more readily preserve the entire corpus of traditional laws. As with many others who have recast the issue, the responses and controversies the question elicited in rabbinic literature are extremely problematic from Hirsch's point of view.[45] Nevertheless, as with those others, Hirsch was undeterred. His commentary itself seeks to provide answers to this expanded question, often relying on contrived etymologies and metatheses to identify the words that embody some aspect of the oral Torah; such "scientific" and "philological" "discoveries" supplemented the midrashic readings offered in classical rabbinic literature, and, he hoped, gave them greater credibility.[46] In this commentary, Hirsch subtly and implicitly distances himself from earlier rabbinic patterns of reading, which did not succeed in identifying the etymological basis of its exegetical endeavors (which were in any event secondary phenomena).

Hirsch's view of the relationship between the written and oral laws is, as far as I can see, unprecedented.[47] This unprecedented traditionalism—an oxymoron if there was one—is in some ways comparable to Saadia's in the extent to which it breaks with what it comes to defend. For Hirsch as for Saadia, the authority of talmudic give-and-take is readily sacrificed to the larger goal of maintaining the integrity of halakhah. Like Saadia, Hirsch is driven to his extreme position by outside forces, in this case the liberalizing trends of the nineteenth century. But he is also driven by his own absorption of the Western concept of human rights that makes certain biblical institutions, such as slavery, offensive to his moral sensibilities.[48] He could not live with the plain sense of the biblical text for moral reasons, nor could he live with the notion that human exegesis cleansed the Bible of its morally questionable norms for theological reasons. He was thus led to a radical reformulation of the entire relationship between the oral and written laws, one that preserved the divine authority of the entire body of Jewish law and vitiated any effort to historicize it.[49]

It seems to me that Samson Raphael Hirsch, the great defender of

Jewish tradition, is actually to be seen as a man in many respects profoundly ill at ease regarding this tradition. Neither the teachings of the
biblical text nor the traditional means of interpreting that text were
acceptable to Hirsch as they were. He thus radically reinterprets the
nature of the biblical teachings, treating them as exceptional so to not
mitigate the moral force of a divine law whose purpose is the moral
instruction of humanity. His discomfort with rabbinic exegesis as traditionally understood was equally profound; he thus pioneered his own
method of interpreting the language of Scripture in an effort to display
the full range of legal and moral teachings to which the biblical text
alludes. While his vision overlaps substantially with those of Meklenburg
and Malbim, he is, in my view, much less comfortable with rabbinic
exegesis, and he has absorbed much more from his intellectual surroundings, and thus has a very different existential stake in the position he advanced. To the age-old question, "How do we know this?"
and to his own, "Why should we do this at all?" the only answer was
that God had so commanded for the moral betterment of humanity,[50]
and there was no other appropriate response from humans than obedience.[51]

David Zvi Hoffmann

As we have seen, the members of the historical school and the Orthodox
went their separate ways in trying to develop a vibrant and relevant
view of the Jewish legal tradition. Even as each struggled to combat
Reform, their respective partisans could not live with what the other
side produced. To the historical school, the expansion of the scope of
Sinaitic tradition to encompass virtually all halakhah was grounded in
a set of assumptions that historical consciousness could not accept.
Efforts at collapsing distinctions between *peshat* and *derash*, making it
appear as if all of what rabbinic Judaism considers scriptural law actually emerges naturally from the language of Scripture, were viewed as
equally unsupportable. On the other side, the Orthodox could not accept that their sacred laws emerged many centuries after the initial revelation of the Torah at Sinai; they could not countenance the notion
that for centuries the religious behavior of Jews was entirely different
than the Judaism they knew and practiced; they could not accept that
the basic norms of Judaism emerged as a response to contingent circumstance. To them, such views could not truly challenge Reform, for, in
many respects, the historical views of Graetz and Frankel were indis-
tinguishable from those of Reformers. To the Orthodox, the historical
school differed from the Reformers only in terms of the conservative

lessons they drew from their tradition's history. They granted to history a continued voice in shaping the present, but the Orthodox were not prepared to rely on their idiosyncratic conservatism. Thus, rather than turn to history as a source of intellectual support, the German Orthodox turned to (an often contrived) philology to buttress their a priori acceptance of a comprehensive tradition from Sinai.

Yet not all among the Orthodox were prepared to concede the territory of history to their opponents. The leaders of the Orthodox *Rabbinerseminar* in Berlin, Azriel Hildesheimer (1820–99) and David Zvi Hoffmann (1843–1921), insisted that historical *Wissenschaft* and Orthodoxy were not incompatible.[52] Hoffmann, in particular, devoted most of his considerable energy to the creation of an Orthodox historiography. In his Bible commentaries, his historical monographs, editions of rabbinic texts, and his detailed challenge to Julius Wellhausen's classic of biblical criticism, *Prolegomena zur Geschichte Israels*,[53] he combined fideism with a keen historical sense, laying the foundation of subsequent Orthodox historiography.[54]

Hoffmann, a native of Hungary, where he was a student of Moses Schick and Esriel Hildesheimer, received his doctorate from the University of Tübingen. In 1873, he joined Hildesheimer on the faculty of the *Rabbinerseminar*, where he taught and, from 1899, served as rector until his death. Unlike the other German rabbis discussed, he did not serve as a community rabbi (although he did emerge as the leading rabbinic decisor among German Jewry), but rather as a professor of Bible and Rabbinics. Further, it worth noting that Hoffmann was younger by a generation or two than the others; in his time, Reform remained a force to be combated, but the terms of the battle were different. Reform communities were well-established throughout Germany. Orthodoxy could no longer dream of eliminating Reform as a religious option, but rather had to consider how to live with it. Principally, they had to consider whether the Orthodox could remain in a single unified community now that the German *Reichstag* had allowed the creation of separate communities (1876), and whether they could join with Reformers in pursuing broader Jewish interests, such as combating anti-Semitism. How the Orthodox communities answered these questions is not at issue here. What is of importance is that by the time Hoffmann reached adulthood, the agenda of the Orthodox community had changed. The existence of the Reform movement was an irreversible fact, as was the solidification of Orthodox communities throughout Germany. Reform continued to provide social, halakhic and intellectual challenges, but the urgency of combating Reform had diminished.

Hoffmann further stands apart from the other German rabbis in that perhaps his most significant intellectual stimulus emerged from outside the Jewish community. After a period of some three decades in which conservative forces had the upper hand in the major German universities, free critical study of the Bible reemerged in the German academy, providing people of all biblical faiths with keenly felt challenges.[55] To someone absorbing the lessons of the German Bible critics, the authority of rabbinic law and its relation to Scripture was moot. The Pentateuch itself was now to be seen as a document produced by people over many centuries, with different religous views, responding to different political and cultural realities. Hoffmann was ever so aware of the challenge of Bible criticism; in defending his Orthodoxy he had to respond to it directly. At the same time, he also felt compelled to address the questions that engaged his Orthodox predecessors surrounding the issues of rabbinic law and exegesis. Ultimately, the two tasks coalesced as one in Hoffmann's written corpus.

Throughout his life Hoffmann was a partisan of the comprehensive Sinaitic tradition position; that is, he insisted that both the written and oral Torahs were revealed in their entirety at Sinai. His history of the Mishnah and the midreshe halakhah were informed by this position, as was his Bible commentary. Although published last, I would like to turn to the Leviticus commentary first, for, he claims, it represents ideas formulated some thirty years before its publication, in German, in 1905. In this commentary on Leviticus Hoffmann categorically affirmed what he calls the position of Maimonides, to the effect that the Torah was accompanied by a comprehensive oral tradition, which filled in all the Bible's lacunae.[56] For Hoffmann, this was not only or even primarily an attempt to challenge Reform models; rather, its primary focus was providing the grounds for a total rejection of the documentary hypothesis of biblical authorship, and complements his direct attack on the hypothesis' primary contemporary spokesman, Julius Wellhausen.[57] The seams that Wellhausen detected in the biblical text, which led him to identify different sources, do not indicate shifts of voice, but direct the reader to different aspects of the oral tradition. The two are equal parts of a single revelation; without taking account of the oral tradition's resolution of textual problems, any treatment of the biblical text must be ill-informed and inadequate. Like Menasseh ben Israel at the dawn of the age of criticism, Hoffmann saw that the biblical text itself could not withstand criticism without an authoritative basis for resolving its manifest textual difficulties. For Menasseh, the answer resided in traditional exegesis; for Hoffmann, in seeing the Pentateuch as the written part of a broader, indivisible, revealed Torah.

The desire to insulate the Pentateuch from criticism led Hoffmann to reject any creative role for rabbinic exegesis, since he needed to argue that "rabbinic" norms actually represent a contemporaneous legal supplement to the Pentateuch. At the same time, he advanced the argument, now becoming a commonplace of German Orthodox Bible study, that these supplementary norms were actually encoded within the profound *peshat* of the biblical text. Much of the commentary is devoted to showing how the "extrabiblical" laws fill in the seams of Scripture and actually make manifest the linguistically precise significance of scriptural formulations. Thus, while his motivations are broader, he ultimately continues very much in the tradition of Meklenburg.

Unlike Hirsch, Hoffmann believed that within the framework of a revealed tradition there was ample room for historical investigation of rabbinic literature (even as there was none for investigation of the Torah). Dating texts, identifying accretions, collating variants—all the work that textual historians do—can be done without in any way diminishing the authority of the tradition whose precepts these texts embody.[58] In some respects, the historical work can actually serve to buttress traditional claims, particularly as regards the midreshe halakhah, to which Hoffmann devoted a substantial portion of his scholarly attention.

In 1886, Hoffmann published his *Zur Einleitung in halakischen Midrasch*, in which he confronted the conclusions of Graetz and Frankel, accepting some and rejecting others. Specifically, he rejected the notion that the hermeneutic principles originated at the time of Hillel, or even centuries earlier. He insisted, rather, that they originate at Sinai, and that this claim is easily supported by many talmudic passages. It is worth noting that this is one of Hoffmann's few claims regarding what we can learn from the Talmud that carries no footnote, no citation of talmudic sources, with which the book otherwise abounds.[59]

The historical school's effort to uphold the independence of the vast majority of halakhot from far-fetched exegeses, by contrast, struck Hoffmann as compelling. Like them, albeit for different reasons, Hoffmann too wished to diminish, indeed eliminate, any creative role for rabbinic midrash. He thus became the most enthusiastic supporter of the distinction between the two ancient sages, Aqiba and Ishmael, assiduously collecting evidence to support the distinction while ignoring or explaining away the counterevidence. Whereas Hirsch feared that this distinction diminished the integrity of rabbinic learning, Hoffmann, like Graetz and Frankel, saw that this historical distinction could be invoked to demonstrate that the halakhah was not dependent on midrash, but on tradition; the midrashic efforts of the second-century rabbinic schools were designed simply to connect tradition to Scripture. Further, like the historical school, Hoffmann sometimes engaged in his own far-fetched exegeses to show that R. Ishmael was really a partisan of *peshat*.[60] For the latter insisted that the Torah speaks in human language, which once again is interpreted as a general commitment to simple exegesis.[61]

Hoffmann was not content to simply argue for a systematic exegetical distinction between Rabbis Aqiba and Ishmael. He went on to insist that all rabbinic midrash should be seen as deriving from one of these two schools. Thus, he continued to develop the position pioneered by Geiger and Weiss regarding the connection between the *Mekhilta* and *Sifre Numbers*. Far more systematically than his predecessors, Hoffmann argued that they are both the products of R. Ishmael's *beit midrash*. This identification is based almost entirely on the Yerushalmi's conception of the Ishmaelian techniques, now applied to the presumably tannaitic documents; in addition, following Weiss, Hoffmann took note of the fact that the students of Ishmael appear in these documents frequently, unlike the other tannaitic works. Similarly, he insisted that the *Sifra* and *Sifre Deuteronomy* were the product of R. Aqiba's *beit midrash*.[62] Hoffmann gathered a great deal of evidence to complete this revolutionary historical conception, which has become the consensus among scholars of midrash, despite a judicious (and, in my view, correct) critique by Hanokh Albeck, among others.[63] Hoffmann's claims have roots in the scholarly work of the Reform and historical school movements; they have found acceptance among Jewish intellectuals of all stripes as they have a strong appeal to those who wish to present the rabbis as intelligent jurists and exegetes. In Hoffmann's view, R. Ishmael's position—the one modern traditionalists like—is not a dissenting voice in a literature dominated by R. Aqiba's less appealing midrash, but is, rather, an equally dominant voice. In this view, fully half of the major bodies of halakhic midrash displayed a commitment to upholding the *peshat* of Scripture.[64]

Finally, as we might expect in light of his categorical endorsement of Maimonides' position, Hoffmann views midrash halakhah as having played a primarily supplementary role in the development of Jewish practice. Both Rabbis Aqiba and Ishmael were attempting to support this practice by connecting it to Scripture. In this activity, R. Ishmael was guided by exegetical assumptions quite hospitable to the modern mind. When we put the pieces of this whole construct together, we see that for those who accept Hoffmann's dogmatic presuppositions the Pentateuch is fully insulated from criticism; further, we see that the halakhah is not the product of twisted exegetical minds, as many of its opponents would insist. It is the product of revealed traditions, and supported by two distinct exegetical systems, one of which was devoted to simple, logical deductions from the biblical text. To those who could accept this construct, what better answer could there be to the question, "How do we know this?"

Under the leadership of people like Hirsch, Hildesheimer, and Hoffmann, German Orthodoxy succeeded in building important institutions and establishing itself as a viable and significant religious option in Germany. It did not succeed in eliminating the other religious tendencies (as it once hoped to do), nor could it have. Yet, building on a traditional dogmatic infrastructure, it was able to fashion a coherent and impressive response to the intellectual challenges of the day, including the question of the authority of rabbinic law. I do not claim that the laity fully delved into or were interested in all the particulars. But I would claim that the fact that rabbinic leaders could directly confront the critics and could fashion such a response had its social importance. People do not necessarily need to be able to articulate a response to challenge, so long as they have an authoritative source to which they can confidently refer for such a response.

In my judgment, a case in point is the popularity of the *Dorot ha-Rishonim* of Isaac Halevy (1847–1914). Halevy, an accomplished Lithuanian Talmudist who relocated frequently, came to Germany around the turn of the century. He had already embarked on his multivolume history of rabbinic tradition, working backwards from Geonic times. The work was designed to refute the conclusions of the historical school and to establish the foundations of a synthetic Orthodox *Wissenschaft*.[65] I do not intend to discuss this work at any length since, in terms of the issues of this book, Halevy broke little new conceptual ground; on some matters he was at one with Hirsch, on others he stood closer to Hoffmann.[66] What is of interest here is the fact that Halevy's work generated considerable enthusiasm, and seems to have sold quite well. Indeed, it remains in print today and is readily available. It is my impression that this work was often to be found in the libraries of German Orthodox Jews. And yet, I cannot imagine that Halevy's massive work was actually read very widely in this community; much of the German Orthodox community did not possess the linguistic and talmudic skills to navigate through Halevy's volumes. Rather, Halevy was important for the development of German Orthodoxy, because as Mordechai Breuer has written,

his arrival in Germany powerfully strengthened the self-assurance of the Orthodox intelligentsia because of the joyful discovery that it now had its "own" Jewish *Wissenschaft*. His call, "*Wissenschaft des Judentums* is ours" set minds on fire and brought his admirers to a pitch of activity. In 1902 the *Jüdisch-Literarische Gesellschaft* was established in Frankfurt. Its program referred

specifically to Halevy: "Already the first beginnings of strictly scientific research, based on adequate knowledge, *have yielded excellent results that con-
firm our tradition on all sides.* Along this path, we will and must continue to
walk."[67]

Clearly, Halevy's work—the massive multivolume synthetic history,
written by a traditional Talmudist—struck a resonant chord among
the German Orthodox. In different measures the same may be said for
the work of the other Orthodox intellectuals discussed here. For traditional Jews, confronting a world in which the self-evidence of their
weltanschauung was under attack from various quarters, the existence
of learned responses confirming their tradition was critical to their ability
to retain their orientation. Such responses had to address the question
of midrash in order to provide compelling answers to the age-old question, "How do we know this?"

LITHUANIAN ORTHODOXY

The social and cultural history of Jewish Lithuania still awaits synthetic presentation; and this is particularly the case with regard to
Lithuanian Orthodoxy. We do not yet have the kinds of information
and interpretation regarding this community that is available to students of German Jewry. A book that focuses on a specific aspect of
culture and its role in shaping identity, such as this book, cannot compensate for this deficiency. It is nevertheless important that we examine aspects of Lithuanian Orthodox culture to provide a contrast with
developments in Germany; this will illustrate just how substantial the
·ideological adjustments were there. At the same time, the question of
the authority of rabbinic law and the nature of midrash were major
concerns of a number of intellectual leaders in Lithuania, and their
contribution to the ongoing Jewish discussion of this matter is worthy
of study in its own right, even in the absence of broader scholarly
contextualization. For, while a major reconsideration of halakhic first
principles is, with but one exception known to me, not to be found
here (at least, not in the nineteenth century), important shifts of emphasis are, and these cast substantial light on the nature of traditional,
elite Lithuanian Jewish culture.

In consideration of what is to come it is important, first, to note
the obvious: Russian Jewry faced social, economic, cultural, and political conditions that differed radically from those confronted by most
Jews in the German lands. Second, traditional Jews in Lithuania did
not confront a Reform movement that is in any way comparable to

that of Germany. To be sure, a *haskalah* emerged in the Russian lands through the 1830s and 1840s that was increasingly seen (with but some justification) as a powerful force.[68] This *haskalah* was interested in reshaping the educational, occupational, and linguistic profiles of Russian Jewry, but was not, for the most part, interested in religious Reform.[69] Indeed, a recent study of the *haskalah* in Vilna makes very clear that its early adherents were very much integrated into traditional society.[70] I do not mean to suggest that there were no tensions between *maskilim* and "traditional" elements of the community, but rather that these tensions were not by themselves the cause of a social rift in Lithuanian Jewry, nor were they much of a cultural irritant for traditional Jews at this time. Further, we must note that the early *maskilim,* with rare exception, did not engage in wholesale attacks on rabbinic literature, and did not denigrate rabbinic patterns of reading. Indeed, some actually felt compelled to defend rabbinic literature and exegesis against the attacks coming from the West.[71] As I shall discuss below, much of this was to change after 1860, but certain patterns of thought on our issue were already in place before that.

Given the very different social and political situations of the two Jewries, and the slacker pace with which modern thought came to the Russian lands, one could scarcely be surprised that the entire dynamic of traditional culture in Lithuania traveled a different course than it did in Germany. Yet these external factors do not tell the entire story.

For, more than by the external cultural forces the Lithuanian rabbinate was to face in the nineteenth century, Lithuanian Orthodoxy was shaped by the internal revolution wrought in the eighteenth century by Elijah ben Solomon Zalman (1720–97), known as the Gaon of Vilna, or Vilna Gaon. Long before the rise of *haskalah* in Eastern Europe, and even before the rise of Hasidism—a thoroughly corrosive force in the minds of the Gaon and his followers—the Gaon of Vilna was challenging the unreflective traditionalism that prevailed among Lithuanian Jewry. Deeply committed to the authority of sacred texts, the Gaon challenged the legitimacy of many of the time-honored customs of Eastern European Jewry, which were, he insisted, contrary to the demands of the basic texts that comprise the halakhic "canon."[72] While the practical effects of these challenges was limited to a small circle of disciples, there is no gainsaying the fact that the Gaon redefined the range and purpose of rabbinic learning in Lithuania for generations to come, leading to the emergence of a social substratum thoroughly committed to the overriding significance of Torah study.[73]

No rabbinic text escaped the Gaon's scrutiny, and all the *midreshe halakhah* were subjected to intensive textual study and "correction" by the Gaon. Frequently, these "corrections" meant bringing the texts of the midreshe halakhah into conformity with the teachings of the Mishnah or the Bavli;[74] sometimes the corrections were designed to yield a text that made sense.[75] Such work, in addition to producing what he considered better texts, gave voice to the Gaon's conviction regarding the interrelationship of all rabbinic documents, and the thoroughly intertwined nature of the oral and written Torahs—a conviction that comprised a central part of the Gaon's thought.[76] His ingenuity in finding connections between the written and oral laws was to become central to his reputation and a topos of Eastern European folklore.[77]

Particularly significant for our purposes is the Pentateuch commentary of the Gaon, known as the *Aderet Eliyahu*, parts of which are little more than paraphrases of the *Mekhilta* and *Sifra,* and his commentary on Proverbs. The first, like all the works of the Gaon, was published posthumously (1804); it has all the hallmarks of a composite text[78] and I am unaware of any way of dating its components.[79] The tendency of the work is clear; it is to show the inextricable link between the oral and written Torahs. Apparently, the Gaon felt that Jewish Bible commentary, which for centuries had stressed the literal or homiletical significance of the text, had weakened the sense that rabbinic exegesis had determined the definitive meaning of the text, and that this significance was integrally related—but not identical—to the *peshat*. The Gaon, then, was thoroughly committed to depicting rabbinic midrash as creatively and rationally interpreting the linguistic peculiarities of the biblical text to determine its definitive applied significance. He did not deny the legitimacy of identifying other levels of meaning beyond those of the *peshat* and the *derash*; as a kabbalist, he actively cultivated such activity, especially with regard to the tabernacle.[80] Yet, in dealing with the halakhic sections of the Torah, he wished to restore the primary and normative interpretation of the text as the central focus of Bible study, thereby, presumably, buttressing the authority of rabbinic law.

The Gaon's project was, then, in many ways similar to that of the nineteenth-century exegetes we have already discussed. Yet the Gaon's work, preceding as it does the onset of *haskalah*, displays a different apologetic than that of the Germans. Clearly the Gaon felt the need in his day to forcefully address the question of the authority of rabbinic law and the subtle relationship of the two Torahs. Yet, to the extent that the Gaon's work was stimulated by external irritants, these must be identified as pilpulistic talmudism, under whose weight rabbinic culture was collapsing; a crisis in the Vilna rabbinate and community structure; according to one biographer, a resurgent Lithuanian Karaism;[81] and, perhaps, Wessely's work.[82] None of these—not even contemporary Karaism—provided the kind of direct frontal assault on the rationality and authority of rabbinic midrash as did later Jewish reformers in the West. The Gaon was, thus, not pushed by his surroundings to radically reevaluate the nature and authority of *derashot*. Rather than seeking to collapse the distinction between *peshat* and *derash* in order to elevate the grammatical and linguistic coherence of the latter, as did the Germans who came after him, the Gaon insists on maintaining and intensifying this long-standing distinction.[83] For the various levels of meaning discernible in the Torah represent its greatness and energize the commandment to study it in order to produce a *ḥiddush* (an innovative interpretation) that is latent in the written text.[84]

Of particular relevance in this regard are the Gaon's comments to Prov. 8:9.[85] The verse reads, "They are all evident to one who understands; and right to those who have attained knowledge." This appears in a series of verses that the Gaon identifies with different texts of Jewish learning.[86] Verse 9, he claims, corresponds to "midrash, such as Sifra, Sifre etc."

For they [the *derashot*] are surprising for two reasons: 1. They determine the meaning of the law [to be a certain way], even though the Torah explicitly states that the law is otherwise, as in "an eye for an eye" etc. 2. They determine the meaning of the verse, such as "'*and if*' (Lev. 1:3) to include the substitute" (Sifra, ad loc.), etc., when this meaning is not at all evident from the verse. Regarding that which is not evident from the verse he [the author of Proverbs] said: "They are all evident", that is that all these things correspond to the true intent of the verse; regarding those things that are not implied by [the language of] the verse he said "to one who understands"; they are understood only by those who understand the inner significance of things (*she-hem muvanim rak lemi she-mevin davar mi-tokh davar*).[87] "And right": That is, that which [the rabbis taught which] he imagines is not right, he [the author of Proverbs] said that they are "right" but only "to those who have attained knowledge," that is to one who has knowledge of Torah.

In the Gaon we encounter, yet again, a vision of the controlled multivalence of the biblical text. The *peshat* of "an eye for an eye" is clearly not pecuniary compensation; nevertheless, to those who understand the Torah, the rabbinic interpretation demanding compensation is clearly "right," for it reveals the deeper significance of the verse. Similarly, the inclusion of the substitute is not implied by the *peshat* of Lev. 1:3; nevertheless, to those who understand the inner significance of the Torah, that interpretation is quite evident. The Gaon is not suggesting that rabbinic readings represent a profound *peshat*; such a position at least theoretically precludes the creativity of the sages and subsequent learners of Torah in discerning law, and that is contrary to the Gaon's view of the purpose of Torah study. Rather, appropriating the deeper significance of the Torah depends not on tradition, nor on understanding *peshat*, but on the cultivation of human understanding, and, as we know from elsewhere, on herculean human toil in applying it.[88] What a truly understanding person finds in the Torah is genuinely there, but it is but one aspect of the multivalent text, whose different layers of meaning remain latent until the intellect uncovers them.[89]

A powerful attestation of the centrality of applied human rationality in determining the true legal significance of the biblical text is to be found in the Gaon's comments to Prov. 2:3, which reads, "If you call to understanding and cry aloud to discernment." (The apodosis is found in verse 5, "Then you will understand the fear of the Lord and attain knowledge of God.") The Gaon comments,

[J]ust as there is discernment (*tevunah*) in wisdom (*ḥokhmah*), which entails understanding wisdom in its utmost clarity, there is discernment in understanding (*binah*);[90] this involves understanding the object of understanding with utmost clarity, that is, how this [insight produced by the faculty of] understanding depends on this particular fine point of wisdom. For example, [the midrash] "'and from the sheep' to exclude the gorer" (Sifra ad Lev. 1:2) is based on the extra letter *vav*. [The ability to grasp this practical] exclusion is called "understanding" and it is incorporated within wisdom; and "discernment" is to know why this extra *vav* specifically excludes the gorer.

Knowledge depends on the broad category of wisdom (= pure reason), but correct human behavior depends on the cultivation of understanding (= practical reason). Yet within both faculties a higher level of insight, "discernment," is possible. Applying the rational faculty of understanding to the biblical text will yield the necessity to assign meaning to the extra *vav* (even after the *darshan* has assigned meaning to the superfluous *min*, "from") and will determine what is to be excluded from the altar; yet without discernment in understanding one will not know why this letter excludes a gorer, as opposed to something else. Only discernment in understanding makes clear that specifically the gorer is excluded by this particular biblical extraneity.

In my judgment, it cannot be definitively determined whether the Gaon is describing the intellectual forces at work in the original formulation of this midrash, or whether he is addressing the intellectual faculties needed for the contemporary student to penetrate its secrets. I do not see any reason why the Gaon could not have intended both, as each is consistent with his general approach.[91] If so, he is suggesting that the *darshan* (whoever he is and whenever he lived), endowed with substantial powers of "discerning understanding," could discover the practical demands of the Torah by discerning the exclusion encoded within the superfluous letter. Having done this, he has bequeathed to subsequent students of Torah the task of reconstructing this process of understanding and discernment in order to fully appreciate the profundity of Torah.

For the Gaon of Vilna, then, midrash halakhah represents the greatness of the sages of Israel (rabbinic or pre-rabbinic), for—in the first example—it was they who attained sufficient powers of discernment to know that monetary compensation was the "right" application of the words "an eye for an eye," even though these words obviously signify something else.[92] Thus, unlike the German rabbis of the nineteenth century, the Gaon of Vilna did not shy away from attributing to Torah scholars throughout the generations an essential role in determining the latent significance of the written Torah. Clearly, in his time he sensed a need to address the question "How do we know this?" but he was not pressed by circumstance to radically mitigate the effects of the standard talmudic response; on the contrary, he accentuates the role of the rational human interpreter in establishing meaning and controlling the applied significance of the text.

In many respects the Gaon's views on the matter of midrash do not differ significantly from the traditional view of Ashkenazic scholars. However, the force of his intellect and/or external irritants led him to focus on the matter, theoretically and practically, in a more intensive way than did his predecessors. His vision of the all-encompassing and multivalent nature of the written law combined with his view of the power of the properly engaged human intellect to produce a vision of midrash as the process by which discerning minds generated textual meaning. He had not encountered Jewish reformers who would conclude that this gave them license to change the meaning the sages generated, but I doubt it would have mattered if he had. His vision of midrash in no way relativized the end product, for, like many Western rationalists, the Gaon believed that understanding, properly and painstakingly applied, led to unshakable truth, in this case the truth approved by the divine author of multivalent Scripture and the creator of the human intellect.[93]

Naftali Zvi Yehudah Berlin

Energized by his deep personal commitment to the toil of expounding the Torah, the disciples of the Gaon went on to enrich the world of Jewish learning with books in all areas of rabbinic intellectual activity. Noteworthy is the Bible commentary of the Gaon's student and colleague, Dov Ber Treves (d. 1803), entitled *Revid ha-Zahav*, whose expressed purpose was to "link and join the two Torahs, the written and the oral."[94] In addition, in the first half of the nineteenth century Lithuanian rabbis produced new editions of the *Sifra*, with commentaries, and displayed renewed and acute interest in the Yerushalmi. These works testify to the influence of the Gaon's views of the religious centrality of Torah study, and to the belief in the power of the human mind to generate authentic *ḥiddush*. At the same time, the ideals of the Gaon were given institutional expression with the establishment in 1803 of a new type of yeshiva in Volozhin under the leadership of the Gaon's disciple, R. Ḥayyim.[95] This was followed by the establishment of many other such institutions throughout the nineteenth century.[96]

Of the various Lithuanian intellectuals who came of age in the middle of the century, none more closely approximated the ideals of the Gaon of Vilna (despite the absence of a commitment to study of kabbalah) than R. Naftali Zvi Yehudah Berlin (1816–93), head of the Volozhin yeshiva from 1853 to 1892. The range of his work includes a lengthy commentary on the *Sifre*; a commentary on the Pentateuch; two commentaries on the Song of Songs; a remarkable commentary on the *She'iltot*, the first post-talmudic rabbinic work; commentaries on various tractates of the Bavli and Yerushalmi; *responsa*; a commentary on the *Mekhilta*; notes on the *Sifra*; various ephemera including correspondence pertaining to the early Zionist movement; and an essay explaining the causes of modern anti-Semitism, stimulated by the outbreak of pogroms in 1881. Other than the last category, the list of works characterizes someone who had fully imbibed the program of the Gaon of Vilna. The interest in the relationship of the oral and written laws, so central to the Gaon, dominates virtually all of Berlin's work and led to his distinct focus on midrash halakhah.

His commentary on the *Sifre* was Berlin's first written work, although it remained unpublished until 1959.[97] According to legend, it was the means by which he showed his father-in-law, R. Yiṣḥaq ben Ḥayyim of Volozhin, that the latter had not made a mistake in allowing his daughter to marry him. Until he read the commentary, the story goes, he did not think his son-in-law was fully aware of what was going on in the yeshiva. The commentary convinced him otherwise; it is, indeed, a testimony to Berlin's remarkable expertise in rabbinic literature. It was designed to show, among other things, how the midrash serves as the "accessible path" connecting the written Torah and the laws of the oral one included in the Mishnah; it also made an effort to come to terms, as best a yeshiva student could, with the fact that the Bavli often departed from this path.[98]

More than the *Sifre* commentary, Berlin's mature views on our subject are spelled out in his Pentateuch and *She'iltot* commentaries. When one looks at the title page of the Pentateuch commentary, one can get the impression that this is yet another effort to collapse the distinction between *peshat* and *derash*, such that the latter is identical to the former, and the objections to its irrationality are dissolved. For Berlin states that the commentary, entitled *Ha-'amek Davar*, will delve into matters to show that the *derashot* of the sages are illuminated by the *peshat* when its full profundity is appreciated. Study of the work itself, however, makes clear that this is not entirely the case; the commentary of Berlin differs significantly from those of the German apologists. As Berlin makes clear on numerous occasions, he will not come to defend rabbinic midrash by saying it is identical to *peshat*. To be sure, the two overlap far more than superficial readers appreciate and are often identical, but Berlin insists that what emerges from *derash* is not always identical to the *peshat*.[99] The matter is complicated further by his denial that a particular verse even sustains a single identifiable *peshat*; no speech is wholly reducible to a single accepted significance.[100] To the difficulties in identifying a single *peshat* for many scriptural words and phrases must be added the fact that Scripture is not to be seen as a transparent work of prose. Rather the divine speech of the Torah, identified as a "song" in rabbinic literature, must be approached as if it were poetry, filled with the many tropes to which the poetic soul resorts. The most sacred of all commandments, studying Torah, is itself rooted in the reality of the poetic structure of the Torah. For a poem can be best appreciated by someone fully at home in the poet's thought world. Only such a person can understand why the poet utilized a particular expression. Someone uninitiated who seeks to comment on the poem's style can only fabricate explanations from within his own mind, which may have nothing to do with what the poet intended. When one comes to explicate as complicated a poetic structure as the Bible (not just the Torah), one must be guided by a thorough familiarity with all its linguistic peculiarities; in addition, one can only hope to succeed if one opens one's mind to the guidance of the tradition received from Sinai.[101]

Now, as we have seen, the introduction of the category of tradition often creates problems even as it solves others. For the notion of a comprehensive tradition creates distance between the defender of talmudic norms and the methodology used in the Talmud to account for the origins of such norms. But Berlin, unlike Meklenburg and Hirsch, is not insisting on an all-encompassing oral tradition. In numerous places he makes clear that many of the norms of Judaism proceed from the independent intellectual endeavor of the student of Torah. Further, he challenges the long-standing position that, at the very least, the hermeneutic principles were given at Sinai and preserved by tradition. They too are the product of human intellectual endeavor.

Tradition for Berlin represents a concrete but limited body of norms transmitted by God at Sinai and preserved orally throughout the generations. These norms are designed to supplement the Torah, providing the details it lacks. At the same time, every one of these norms is encoded within the text of the written Torah.[102] Already Moses himself and the sages who succeeded him, generation after generation, engaged in determining the connections between these norms and the written text; by reflecting on these connections these sages were able to produce exegetical principles that in turn would guide the production of new halakhot by students of Torah. In marked contrast to the long-standing medieval tradition that insisted the hermeneutic principles were revealed to Moses, Berlin writes, "At first there were seven principles that Hillel brought with him as it is stated in the Tosefta Sanhedrin and other places. After him, the *Tanna de-be R. Ishmael* added other principles. This [expansion of principles] is done by means of renewed study in every generation."[103] Yet elsewhere he insists that various rabbinic sages, foremost among them Hillel, established a range of hermeneutic principles to fill in the legal lacunae where they had no tradition.[104] Thus, for Berlin, the hermeneutic principles that expanded the range of halakhah were the product of deep and rational reflection on the oral traditions entrusted to Moses and their connection to Scripture. As with the Gaon before him, Berlin did not see in this historical understanding any relativization of the halakhic system.

In his comments to Deut. 1:3, he explicates his understanding of the process more fully. Already in Moses' lifetime, he writes, Torah learning emerged as the central defining characteristic of the Jews. Basing himself on a specific talmudic passage, and talmudic discourse generally, Berlin argues that this learning involved midrash, for clearly the divine lawgiver intended for laws to be derived from Scripture by means of specific hermeneutic principles. Originally, only Moses was entitled to engage in such creative study; all others could do no more than rely on the traditions they had received. To resolve issues for which they had no tradition they could only rely on analogies to what was received, but could not turn to the text of the Torah itself, until, at the end of his life, Moses taught the people the exegetical means to create halakhah where they had no traditions or appropriate analogues.[105] From that time forward, the sages of Israel have, through intensive study and reflection, discerned many new halakhot by using the principles that "create law" (*midot she-ha-torah nehqeqet bahen*).[106]

Berlin's Torah and *She'iltot* commentaries were already written by 1860, at a time when Eastern European *haskalah* was perceived (with some justification) as a powerful force,[107] although its adherents were just beginning to express some of the radical challenges to rabbinic tradition that had become common coin in the West.[108] Nevertheless, despite its relative moderation to this point, the direction of this *haskalah* was already clear enough, and it was sufficiently feared that one cannot say that Berlin was insulated from any external pressures to either accommodate or challenge modern sensibilities.[109] Like his colleagues in the German lands, he knew full well that the foundations of the traditional world he inhabited were being shaken. He knew that there were those—whom he dismissed as heretics—who insisted that the Bible be appropriated without the mediation of rabbinic tradition.[110] Like the Germans, he too responded by seeking to expand the range of traditionally transmitted law. Like them, he too wished to identify many rabbinic *derashot* as the profound *peshat*.[111] Unlike them, however, he was not prepared to save rabbinic Judaism by distorting it. The people of Israel may have received many traditions at Sinai, but, he insists, anyone who studies Talmud and all the post-talmudic commentaries can see that it is abject foolishness to insist that the entire structure rests on traditions preserved throughout the generations.[112] It is obvious to anyone with eyes to see that many practices have emerged over time by means of human intellectual endeavor, whether midrash halakhah or analogous methods of interpreting the Mishnah and Gemara.[113] To be sure, inherited traditions are more reliable, and it would be wonderful if the entire structure could stand on them. And, indeed, much of it does; but essential components do not. Similarly, a profound comprehension of biblical language will make clear that many of the *derashot* do conform to the *peshat*. But, once again, Berlin saw that one can take this theory only so far, and that one pays a heavy price for it, namely, reducing the uniqueness of the Jewish appropriation of Scripture.[114]

Berlin recognized the need for a restatement of principles in his age, and he did perhaps shift some emphases to challenge the modernists. In the end, though, Berlin, in his Lithuanian environment through the 1850s, seems to have had greater confidence in the ability of Orthodoxy to withstand the challenges of the "heretics" and hold onto its core than did his German colleagues. From this position of confidence, he could respond to the question, "How do we know this?" with greater intellectual honesty than could the Germans. He remained a partisan of an Orthodoxy that was uncompromising in its commitment to the absolute centrality of Torah study and *ḥiddush;* he would not seek refuge for this Orthodoxy in an all-encompassing tradition he knew did not exist, and which devalued the most important of human activities: engaging in *pilpulah shel Torah* (assiduous Torah study) to produce *ḥiddush*. To be sure, within the next twenty-five years his confidence was shaken as he came to confront *haskalah* and "heresy" more and more, especially in his own yeshiva, but he took up the battle within the framework of politics, Zionism, and practical halakhah, not Bible commentary and talmudic history.

Yiṣḥaq Ya'aqob Reines

Neither the Gaon nor Berlin (at the time at which he wrote his commentaries) directly confronted contemporary acerbic attacks on the Talmud or rabbinic exegesis. Yet in the decade after Berlin completed his Torah and *She'iltot* commentaries, major controversies—revolving more around the contemporary rabbinate than rabbinic Judaism, per se—broke out in the Hebrew press that serviced the Russian lands, particularly *Ha-Meliṣ*, *Ha-Shaḥar*, and *Ha-Levanon*. From a conceptual point of view most of the attacks and the Orthodox responses contained little of lasting value. From a social point of view, the extended battles, particularly in the years 1868–71, did serve to heighten the consciousness of traditional elements and made them more sensitive to their vulnerability and ever more vigilant in guarding their way of life. Yet, unlike the Orthodox of Germany, the Lithuanian Orthodox produced little that can be characterized as a direct challenge to the crisis of faith in the authority of rabbinic law during the last four decades of the century. That is, they produced little that attempted to respond directly to the content of the modernizer's critique.[115] To be sure, there were responses to the historical conceptions of Weiss and Graetz, and polemical responses to the local critics and satirists, but these broke little new conceptual ground, and, in some cases, relied more on name-calling than on intellectual discourse. When they attempted to engage in the latter, they often could do little better than simply assert that which had been challenged, such as that the Talmud was not subject to scholarly criticism as were all other books because it was divinely inspired.[116]

There were, at the very least, two works that are obvious exceptions to the above generalizations. One, the *Torah Temimah*[117] of Baruch Halevi Epstein (1860-1942), may be described as yet another Bible commentary, although together with Epstein's comments the work provides a compendium of classical interpretive teachings on each verse. The idea was to demonstrate that the two Torahs are one complete

Torah (hence the name, *Torah Temimah*). Although perhaps the most useful of the Lithuanian Torah commentaries, it breaks the least new conceptual ground, and, with its rhetoric of creating one complete Torah, never really challenged the critics of rabbinic Judaism.[118] The dismissive and disdainful review by Micha Yosef Berdichevski (1865–1921)—the greatest of the Eastern European rebels against rabbinic Judaism—demonstrates the size of the chasm that separated Epstein from those who challenged the exegetical integrity of rabbinic halakhah.[119]

The other work worthy of mention in this connection is the *Hotam Tokhnit* of Yiṣḥaq Ya'aqob Reines, rabbi of a number of communities (he is best known as the founder of the Orthodox Zionist movement, *Mizrachi*, and a yeshiva that provided instruction in secular studies in Lida, the place of his last rabbinical position).[120] Reines, a product of the Lithuanian *yeshivot*, was the closest thing to a modern Orthodox rabbi Lithuania was to produce.

Hotam Tokhnit was the name given by Reines to a work he published in 1880, which was a distillation of the arguments of the first three parts of his larger work, *Derekh ba-Yam*. Due to the substantial financial investment publication of this massive work would have required, it was never published; it seems to have been lost, as it is not to be found among the many manuscripts of Reines's work now housed at the Yad Harav Maimon Library in Jerusalem.[121] Reines was persuaded to publish instead the *Hotam Tokhnit*, a smaller book that contained examples from the larger work. Reines's full treatment of the question of midrash was part 6 of the lost work. Still, from the few references in *Hotam Tokhnit* to what was contained in part six of *Derekh ba-Yam*, and his general epistemological statements, one can reconstruct at least the general contours of Reines's thought. Further, while the former work does not contain Reines's fully developed thoughts on our issues, it does contain a very important statement of the problems and their potentially destructive impact on Torah learning and halakhic living.

More than perhaps any Lithuanian rabbi, Reines was aware of the extent to which defectors from rabbinic Judaism from among the learned class were alienated by a sense that rabbinic expansions of the written law were exegetically and linguistically unsustainable. He knew that this alienation had started in the West and had moved East, and was a very real problem for an Orthodoxy seeking to retain its best and brightest. As he wrote,

The voice of the heretics gets stronger every day; many shepherds have destroyed the talmudic vineyard. They have trampled on the oral Torah, and mercilessly destroyed the fortresses of the traditional Torah. . . . They strive to show the weirdness of the *derashot* of our sages, may their memory be for a blessing; they labor to demonstrate that their *derashot* have no lot among the laws of rationality, and no inheritance in the ways of clear thinking. They display outright contempt for those who study them—they have profaned the temple of the oral Torah—and they strip them of any respect. Their intent is to completely win over the hearts of the Jewish people, so that not even a spark of the purified faith remains.[122]

Reines makes it very clear that the views of these "heretics" are grounded in ignorance and bad faith; they are hunters intent on destroying Judaism. At the same time he painfully acknowledges that they have made significant inroads among the learned classes. "Every day the number of those who study [Torah] decreases."[123] The Torah itself has been so debased that it must cry out for help. If no one comes to its aid, he writes "a great destruction will occur to me and to you. [Therefore], build a powerful fortress for those who seek me; reveal to all my justice and uprightness, my wisdom and understanding that are stored within me."[124]

The task of saving the oral Torah was urgent. While Reines was prepared to dismiss the critics of rabbinic law as ignoramuses, he was also honest and/or self-important enough to insist that the precise relationship of the oral Torah to the written one—and *the* foundation of the former is its conjunction with the latter—remains inadequately articulated after all these centuries. He dismisses the recent tendency to legitimize the exegetical expansions of law by recourse to grammatical rules, which served to collapse the distinction between *peshat* and *derash*. This tendency, he thinks, relies too heavily on grammatical principles; when they "reach *derashot* that cannot be explained on the basis of known grammatical rules, they have seen fit to create new ones in an effort to demonstrate that the understanding of Torah is governed by grammatical rules, and the source of every midrash is the *peshat*." In response to such activity, the critic has the right to ask for proof of the concrete existence of the proffered grammatical principle; that such a principle may be shown to be logically necessary is irrelevant, "for grammatical principles are not always rational, but are rooted in the unique properties of each and every language." In response to such a request, one could only point to the rabbinic midrash as the sole embodiment of the principle, and the circularity of the process is obvious.[125]

To Reines, then, the problem of midrash was the central intellectual thorn in Orthodoxy's side. Yet the Torah scholars had either ignored the problem or responded inadequately. This allowed heresy to flourish to a critical point. The times and circumstances demanded a comprehensive assessment of the foundations of rabbinic law, which, in turn, required rejecting linguistics and embracing epistemology. For the key to understanding the entire oral Torah is insight into the nature of category formation and its reverse, the derivation of logically coherent particulars from general categories.

The cornerstone of the entire oral Torah and its relationship to the written Torah is the ability to determine the inner sustaining forces [of a particular norm]. This involves making generalizations from the particulars. It is analogous to the synthetic and analytic judgments regarding physical things. The foundation of synthesis and analysis is the abstracting of the internal sustaining forces of particular things, and their subsequent application to other things. In terms of their external form all physical phenomena simply exist and do not produce anything new. Only by knowing this science [of abstracting the inner sustaining forces of phenomena] have the intelligent succeeded in penetrating into the innermost depths of every phenomenon, observing its constituent parts and the different principles that are embodied and united within it; they know how to separate these principles from the observed phenomenon and to manufacture new syntheses. There is no limit to the value this manner of thinking has brought to the world of science and technology. Every day new machines are created; there is no end to the innovations and discoveries that derive from such thinking. Yet all these innovations are only new in terms of their external manifestation, but they are ancient in terms of the sustaining forces on which they rest, for they represent but a partial apprehension of the secrets inherent since the time of the creation in existing, created phenomena...This science may be called the "transformation of particulars into general categories." Without this we would think that just as every phenomenon is particular in terms of its external manifestation, so too in terms of its sustaining forces and properties, [we would think that] they inhere only in [the given phenomenon], and cannot be transferred to other things. But on the basis of this science the wise have shown that the internal sustaining forces may be transferred and successfully applied to other matters, such that all the sustaining forces of particular phenomena are universal. The purpose of this creative insight is to observe that the relationship of the oral Torah to the written Torah is also to be understood in these terms. For the written Torah contains an epitome of all the laws and knowledge; and the generalizing function of the oral law is to abstract the internal ideas of the particular laws [of the written Torah] and extend them into generalized principles. For the entire expansion of laws that is seen throughout the oral Torah represents matter synthesized by means of the principles hidden within the written Torah. Every norm written in the Torah is, in its external manifestation, but a particular norm; yet in its spiritual sense each norm represents something all-encompassing. The purpose of the hermeneutic principles transmitted to Moses at Sinai is to instruct in the ways of deriving the internal ideas, and how to make generalizations from particulars. With this knowledge they penetrated to the variegated core of each and every norm and derived from them many other norms. For by means of these principles they transformed the particulars into general rules.[126]

Just as more than two centuries earlier Spinoza invoked the philosophical and epistemological foundations of scientific discourse and method to challenge the coherence of the exegetical traditions of the "Pharisees," Reines invokes such discourse and method (as best he understood them) to defend those traditions. For as more recent philosophy had shown, category formation and the determination of the universal properties of specific phenomena represent an essential component of human intellectual activity. Thus, in looking at the relationship of the biblical text and the vastly expanded range of Jewish law—where Spinoza could see only caprice and dishonesty—Reines could see the proper application of intellectual insight and energy.

The rest of the work is designed to illustrate this philosophical apologia for the oral Torah; the different possibilities available to the student of the written law as illustrated by talmudic literature are laid out and explained in accord with the epistemological vision outlined in the above quotation. Unfortunately, the full explication of midrashic principles and how they work was included in the part of the work now apparently lost. Thus, we can only imagine how Reines would have worked out all the particulars, although there are sections of the existing work that can direct the imagination.[127]

Reines's work was sui generis, and, not surprisingly, was best received among the modern Orthodox of Germany.[128] It could not appeal to the Torah scholars of Lithuania, for its manner of discourse was simply foreign.[129] That it could not redirect the thinking of the rebels is also clear, and due to two factors. The first is that they did not share his dogmatic presuppositions regarding the revelation of the hermeneutic principles; of course, many did not believe in any kind of revelation anymore. The second reason is that Reines' work in some ways betrays a time lag; the critique of rabbinic midrash no longer revolved exclusively around its exegetical coherence. With the spreading influence of the work of the historical school in Eastern Europe, the critique was now firmly historical in nature. The fact that rabbinic norms could be shown to be responsive to particular historical situations and, as Graetz and others argued, directly related to the personalities of the sages was largely unaddressed by Reines. Even if the results of rabbinic exegetical endeavors were philosophically coherent and compelling, the historical circumstances of their emergence militated against endowing them with unquestionable authority.[130]

Unlike the other works we have examined here, which, while they did not make an appreciable dent in the spread of liberal forms of Judaism (nor could they have), contributed to a reinvigorated Orthodoxy, Reines's work exercised little influence on either group. Yet his work illustrates the extent to which the matter of midrash was central to the religious commitments of the learned classes of Eastern Europe (although most seem to have been comfortable remaining within the framework established by the Gaon). Further, his work illuminates the philosophical path otherwise not taken by Orthodox intellectuals, and the limits of modernity among the Torah scholars of Eastern Europe.

CLOSING REFLECTIONS

The discussion of the differing approaches to the problem of midrash in Germany and Lithuania[131] sheds light on the nature of the two distinct Orthodoxies that emerged in these centers of Jewish culture. It is no accident that precisely in Lithuania we find a vision of the rabbinic past in which rabbis engaged in assiduous Torah study, ultimately coming to control texts and their meanings. This reflects the social and cultural ideals of Lithuanian Orthodoxy itself. Lithuanian Orthodoxy could never compromise on the importance of Torah study as a creative enterprise; here, the stated purpose of life was to engage in 'amalah shel Torah, intellectual toil devoted to understanding and innovation. While as a practical matter the vast majority of Lithuanian Jews did not engage in such toil, throughout the century thousands did in the various institutions that were created for this purpose.[132] More important, the centrality of Torah study was demonstrably a broad-based cultural ideal, affecting marital and occupational choices and aspirations throughout Jewish Lithuania. As Berlin, especially, recognized, such an ideal demanded a conceptualization of the emergence of Torah rooted at least partially in such intellectual toil. Indeed, in Berlin's historical view, Moses himself and all who came after him engaged in pilpulah shel Torah, in the deep, dialectical reflection on the meaning of every word of the text, in order to generate meaning; it is by means of these efforts that halakhah emerged from the text of the Torah.

In contrast to the Germans, the social and cultural reality of the Lithuanian Orthodox demanded a vision of the religious past that affirmed the perfection of the Torah, while acknowledging, with less paradox than one might suppose, that this theoretically perfect Torah is never practically complete. Previous and contemporary culture are then understood as the sacred religious task of generating ḥiddush. A vision of the sages of Israel as passive recipients of a comprehensive tradition, by contrast, would have undermined the contemporary cultural aspirations of traditional Jewish Lithuania; it would have created a theoretical gap between the scholarly activity demanded and energized by the Gaon and his followers, on the one hand, and the activity of the venerated sages of old, on the other. Presenting the ideal of assiduous, *creative* Torah study as a historical constant came to Berlin naturally; it reflected his own world and cultural values, and what he mediated to the students who came to study with him. In Berlin's view, by actualizing this defining ideal, students of Torah continue a process that extends back to Moses, and give meaning and purpose to their lives. The cultural pressure to once again address the question "How do we know this?" gave him and many others in Lithuania the opportunity to reshape a religious foundation myth to suit their specific cultural needs.

German Orthodoxy, by contrast, had little choice but to give voice to very different cultural aspirations. Its educational efforts were not, for the most part, devoted to producing great Torah scholars, but rather halakhically observant *ba'ale batim* (householders or laypeople). Its educational institutions, from its elementary schools to its rabbinical seminary, were not created to produce such Torah scholars, nor could they have been. Thus, beyond playing into the hands of Reform, a vision of scriptural law rooted in ongoing exegetical creativity would have created a gulf between the adherents of Orthodoxy in Germany and their religious tradition. They could only live an Orthodoxy that was apodictic and fixed; it is thus not surprising that, with the exception of Malbim (who was the least at home in Germany, anyway), German Orthodox thinkers envisioned a religio-legal past that was fixed and apodictic. All law of scriptural authority was conceived as the product of a single revelation in time, and was passed from generation to generation. The rabbis were the recipients and transmitters of this scriptural law, who felt free to tinker at the margins, creating "fences" around the law, but *creating* nothing more.[133] This certitude—this projected closing of creativity and active participation in the formation of the historical Jewish legal system—reflected the reality of a German Orthodoxy consisting of laypeople (and even some rabbis) who could live the halakhic life, but not master halakhic discourse.[134] Thus, the vision of the comprehensive tradition was invoked to insulate German Orthodoxy from the challenges of the liberals, but it also reflected the social and cultural reality and limitations of that Orthodoxy.

In examining these two patterns of Orthodoxy, then, we can see how, yet again, the response to the question "How do we know this?" helped form and also reflected a central component of religious identity.

9 • Conclusion

IT IS ONE OF the ironies of Jewish cultural history that the talmudic quest for epistemological and legal certainty has led to divisive and rancorous debate. By providing what, in their cultural contexts, they considered compelling midrashic responses to the ubiquitous question, "How do we know this?" the talmudic sages supposed they were establishing a firm foundation for extrabiblical Jewish praxis, enabling Jews to live their religious lives confident they were fulfilling divine mandates. As discussed in the first part of this book, their search for certitude led them to take what appear to be considerable liberties with the language and letters of the biblical text; they constructed a system of legal interpretation that, when carried to extremes, could be characterized as saying to the biblical text, "Be silent until I interpret you."[1]

Beyond taking liberties with the biblical text, the talmudic exegetical writings give the impression of legal chaos and arbitrariness, as the same law may be presented as deriving from different biblical verses by different exegetes. Similarly, the same phrase in the Bible may be interpreted in different ways even in the absence of any textual mandate. In one place a given sage may draw significance from a particular linguistic feature, and refrain from doing so elsewhere. The talmudic redactors saw fit to extend and rearrange the exegetical traditions under discussion in a given passage. The sages "removed and added" words to serve their exegetical needs. This image of arbitrariness was enhanced by the fact that, with the exception of an unidentifiable voice that overlays some passages in the Yerushalmi (see chapter 3), no one overtly discerned any consistent pattern in the application of techniques on the

251

part of any individual sage. It seemed that any sage might interpret the text in whatever way struck his fancy[2]—all of this in answer to that fundamental question, "How do we know this?"

As we have seen throughout the second part of this book, for many Jews, throughout the generations, the sages' efforts to provide a firm foundation for extrabiblical law have done precisely that. For others, however, the midrashic method has served to undermine their confidence as they confronted a complex web of extrabiblical praxis demanded by rabbinic literature, but whose epistemological foundation was less than self-evident to them.

The reasons for these differing reactions to the exegetical activities of the rabbis of antiquity are tied to the very nature of midrash itself. The coherence of midrash, not merely as a means of reading but of authoritatively establishing norms, depends on one's ability to share in a particular weltanschauung that incorporates distinct views regarding the controlled polysemic nature of the language of the biblical text. To the people who produced the halakhic midrashim and the Talmuds, the polysemy of the legal texts was an obvious outgrowth of its divine origins. As a divinely revealed text, the Torah must be perfect. Yet judged from the perspective of human linguistic conventions, it appears to be anything but. Repetitions, partial repetitions, partially contradictory repetitions; lengthy, verbose treatment of some matters and frustrating reticence regarding others; syntactically or contextually inappropriate phrases—all these would all compromise the perfection of the text were they not intended to encapsulate information or preclude erroneous conclusions. The rabbis of antiquity went further still. To them, the notion that the Torah was a perfect text meant that not only the apparent imperfections required explanation; in a divine text nothing, not even prepositions or conjunctions, could be haphazard or unintended. Thus, throughout rabbinic literature, we find laws that, it is claimed, were encoded within the biblical text's use of a conjunctive or prepositional prefix.[3] While as a practical matter much remains unexplained, and while occasionally one finds theoretical doubts expressed in classical rabbinic literature, the entire text of the Torah was generally conceived, theoretically, as being extraordinarily elastic and replete with meaning.

At various stages in Jewish history the implications of this weltanschauung became terribly problematic. With the emergence of new textual assumptions in the tenth through thirteenth centuries in the Islamic lands, many Jewish intellectuals could no longer find in talmudic exegesis a reliable rendering of the meaning of the biblical text. While the intellectual standards of the world in which they lived led to discomfort with their rabbinic exegetical heritage, these standards did not, with few exceptions, lead to a rejection of the Torah itself, or to its practical expansion in talmudic literature. The challenge for these Jewish intellectuals, then, was to uphold the demands of the halakhah even when they could not accept the dominant talmudic conception of its source. The Talmud claimed that we "know" hundreds of unwritten laws, because that information is encoded within the linguistic peculiarities of the Torah. This explanation was not acceptable to these intellectuals, because it implied that a change of practice had occurred (or could have occurred) from the time that the written text was revealed until it was interpreted to yield law X, and because their own sense of language led them to reject the linguistic assumptions that supported the rabbinic interpretation. Yet they could not and did not wish to reject the halakhah as established in the Talmud; they simply insisted that the laws must derive from a different and time-honored source, namely revealed tradition. By shifting the epistemological foundations of their legal system from the talmudic emphasis on exegesis (with a minority of laws identified as traditional) to a comprehensive revealed tradition, these scholars replaced the talmudic path to halakhic certitude with one that was more culturally and existentially appropriate. In the process they markedly distanced themselves from the "irrational" exegetical discourse of the Talmud, the legal prescriptions of which they were seeking to uphold.

Other Jews, living primarily within the Christian *Kulturbereich*, were not so troubled by the distance between the simple and applied meanings of the Torah. This is not because they were somehow less aware of this distance. Certainly Rashi, his grandson, Samuel ben Meir (Rashbam), and Naḥmanides, among others, recognized that the rabbinic legal applications often had little relation to the *peshat* of the verse; indeed, on rare occasions, one can even find them rejecting the midrash offered in rabbinic literature as the source of law.[4] Nevertheless, they were all decidedly more comfortable attributing multivalence to the language of the Bible and thus with the results of the rabbinic quest for certitude. They therefore insisted that the *peshat* represented but one level of significance—an important one, to be sure—that scarcely precluded other levels of meaning that were legally repercussive.

It seems to me that there are two essential points of difference that are noteworthy here. The first is the very different nature of the external cultural pressures. There was an absence of a strong Karaite presence, and the Christian attacks focused on other issues, or on issues of which Franco-German Jews may have been unaware. To be sure, until the thirteenth century, Christian attacks on the Talmud did indeed focus on its exegetical distortion of the "Old Testament" and its "heretical" preference for laws made by humans over divine mandates.[5] Yet the Tosafists were not Latin readers, and I wonder how aware they were of all this.[6] In any event, by the thirteenth century the grounds of the polemics shifted, since as Amos Funkenstein points out, the Church could hardly have argued for a *sola scriptura* position. I would add that in some sense focusing on the talmudic applications of biblical mandates was to lose sight of the larger point of contention. After all, the Church argued against the religious viability of the Old Testament law, however one chose to interpret it. To challenge the interpretation and not the obstinate subordination to "the law" was to focus on secondary matters. Further, in time Christians came to see the Talmud as a useful source in their polemics against Jews.[7] Thus throughout most of the time frame I have explored, Jews in Christian lands rarely experienced direct challenges to their system of *legal* exegesis—although their traditional exegeses of the narrative and prophetic portion of the Bible were subject to extensive debate—and almost never in a language they could understand.

Second, as the sixteenth-century Polish rabbi, Solomon Luria, understood, the whole issue could be reduced to the degree of pious confidence one had in the authority and exegetical skill of the ancient rabbinic sages. For someone like Maimonides, the rabbinic sages interpreted as best they could, but, as he put it, they were not necessarily the equivalent of "Joshua and Pinḥas." Thus the disputes and the possibility of error made it impossible for Maimonides to consider the exegetical readings of the rabbis as scripturally authoritative. For Naḥmanides, and Luria, and hundreds of others, by contrast, the sages who interpreted were inspired by the holy spirit, and their teachings carry a different authority than the interpretations of those Jews who came after them. While Saadia and Ibn Ezra would see the greatness of the sages in the fact that they assiduously and impeccably transmitted the traditions they received, those from the Christian *Kulturbereich* (with exceptions to be sure) saw the sages' greatness in their actively determining the meaning of the Scriptures. For whatever the reason, they were able to maintain far greater confidence in the exegetical greatness of their rabbinic predecessors.

By the seventeenth century modern textual assumptions were emerging that necessarily and fundamentally challenged the weltanschauung that gave coherence to midrashic patterns of reading. At the same time, the advent of modern historical consciousness provided a formidable challenge to the credibility of a comprehensive, orally transmitted tradition. These cultural shifts were accompanied by the beginnings of a broader pattern of secularization that undermined the power of the centripetal social and religious forces that limited the range of expression of medieval skepticism. Over the next two centuries numerous students of rabbinic literature came to the conclusion that rabbinic readings were the absurd fancies of men either dishonest or foolish, and they felt perfectly free to express this understanding. Such published conclusions naturally led to calls for the reform or disappearance of traditional Judaism. In the early part of this time frame, the calls for change issued from scattered individuals. In time, however, the numbers calling for—and implementing—religious change became much greater. There were many forces that led to this increase; in chapters 5 and 6 I show that the ideological justification that accompanied these changes frequently revolved around the "irrational" textual assumptions that shaped the Jewish legal system. In the nineteenth century, a Reform movement emerged that sought to give shape, and sometimes rein in, the impulse to modify Jewish religious praxis. In the early stages of this movement, disenchantment with rabbinic midrash continued to provide justification for religious shifts rooted in the quest for modernization (and Westernization). In time, though, even the more radical Reform intellectuals saw the need to forge a reconciliation with their parent culture; here the exegetical freedom manifest in rabbinic midrash is invoked in an effort to cast the ancient rabbis as reformers who put the demands of life ahead of the demands of text.

As is to be expected, both the attacks on rabbinic midrash and the liberating reconciliation to it stuck in the craw of traditionalists of different types. Thus, in the nineteenth century both religiously conservative and Orthodox Jews were driven to address the origins of rabbinic midrash in historical and/or exegetical terms. The traditionalist historical school developed a new picture of the emergence of rabbinic Judaism that depicted the rabbis and their predecessors as judicious legislators and exegetes. Building on earlier, neglected traditions, they portrayed Jewish praxis as having but shallow roots in far-fetched exegeses; for the most part it emerged over time, in response to various needs, through rational and logical extensions of the biblical law codes that, despite a few exceptions, continue to speak to contemporary society.

The Orthodox, in Germany in particular, were led to challenge the historical and exegetical conclusions of the traditionalists as well the Reformers. They insisted that no extrabiblical law to which scriptural authority is imputed ever emerged as the result of exegesis. Rather they asserted that all laws of scriptural authority not specifically written in the Bible were revealed by God to Moses orally at the same time as the written Torah was revealed. I have discussed in chapter 8 the various ways they justified this claim. Here I wish simply to emphasize the extent to which this construct was crafted in response to cultural challenge. As with the earlier efforts to identify extrabiblical law as originating in a single revelation, the Orthodox participants in this discussion have distanced themselves considerably from the thought-world of the ancient rabbis and of their more recent Ashkenazic predecessors. In other words, they have felt compelled to reshape traditional self-understanding in order to rescue its practical demands.

It should come as no surprise that in the history of the so-called people of the book so much energy has been expended trying to determine the socially accepted meaning of the book. After all, any socially important text, and especially a sacred canonical text that does not allow for addition or formal amendment, is inherently culturally limiting. Controlling its socially accepted meaning is, by contrast, potentially liberating and empowering. It harnesses the power of the sacred text to the thought world of the exegetes.

Nor should we be surprised that, historically, once the midrashim and Talmuds constructed what was to become the socially accepted meaning (at least for practical purposes), this too would come to be seen at specific times as a culturally limiting, even undermining, force. The textual assumptions, the apparently arbitrary application of hermeneutic techniques, and the apparent manifestations of change severely shook the religious confidence of Jews at various times in Jewish history. For those committed to halakhah, the option of trying to establish a different socially accepted meaning was not viable, a priori. All they could do was try to establish a different foundation for the established meaning. That is, they could craft a different response to the question "How do we know this?" than did their rabbinic predecessors, one that removed the exegetical taint from Jewish law and, to those who accepted this response, restored the divine imprimatur to the full range of Jewish praxis to which biblical authority is imputed.

Those who felt free of the constraints of halakhah, by contrast, could reopen the question of authoritative meaning; they could seek to define anew what the Torah meant. At the most fundamental level they could address the question of whether the Torah ever intended to speak in practical terms to all subsequent generations, and, whatever its intent, whether this was possible from their newly controlling point of view. They could determine what resemblance, if any, their religious lives would bear to those of their ancestors. As we have seen, the efforts to reopen the question of the accepted meaning had first to reject and ridicule the talmudically established significance of the text, as well as the alternative foundation of Jewish praxis—tradition—determined by those who remained committed to halakhah but felt compelled to reject rabbinic patterns of reading. In time the Reformers came to look on their predecessors' exegetical endeavors more benignly, and sometimes with considerable enthusiasm.

In the adherents of the historical school, we find the middle ground. Their faith and sense of Jewish religious history led them to embrace halakhah, but their sense of language precluded them from finding certitude in halakhic midrash, and their vision of history prevented them from believing in a comprehensive oral tradition that was transmitted intact through some three millennia. In the nineteenth century they chose, for the most part, not to challenge the socially accepted legal significance of the text. Yet, try as they might, they could not fully replace the lost sense of certitude with their historical constructs. With considerable ingenuity they developed arguments for the antiquity and continuity of Jewish law; for them that was sufficient to establish its authority. Yet, answering the question "How do we know this [law]?" with "It is a demonstratively ancient and time-honored practice that has helped to define what Judaism has been historically" does not establish contemporary relevance, nor does it address the full import of the question. For the question seeks to determine that we know this law to be a divine mandate; its demonstrative antiquity and time-honored observance beg the question. It is thus not surprising that there were many who found their historical constructs compelling but did not find the practical religious demands they endorsed as useful or authoritative.

What emerges from a study of all of these groups in the nineteenth century is the centrality of the question of rabbinic midrash and the authority of Jewish law. Spokespersons for any form of Judaism that engaged modernity on any level had to explain the basis for their rejection or continued acceptance of the authority of rabbinically developed law. Inevitably and invariably, this need led them to address anew the long-standing questions regarding midrash and the expansion of the legal codes of the Bible. Modern textual assumptions allowed little room for doubt that learned and critical historical and/or linguistic analyses could determine *the* definitive meaning of a text. In the face of such assumptions, rabbinic patterns of reading and applying the Bible appeared misguided and in need of full or partial rejection or explanation in order to sustain some kind of Jewish religious commitment in the modern world.

In the three previous chapters I have told this story in terms of the emerging denominations of modern Judaism in the nineteenth century. I wish here to briefly direct attention to the individual, existential aspects of the confrontation of rabbinic and modern textual assumptions. Dismay, anger, disgust, and, perhaps most of all, embarrassment are all visible in the writings of the various scholars, rabbis, publicists, and historians who addressed the way in which rabbinic Judaism appropriated Scripture. Whether one chose, with Reines, to argue that rabbinic readings were actually an unappreciated, brilliantly crafted application of universal epistemological techniques; or, with Hirsch, that they were legally trivial and of limited cultural importance; or, with Graetz, Frankel, and Weiss, that they were historically conditioned, progressive, and often legally secondary; or, with Wessely, Meklenburg, or Malbim, that they revealed the profound *peshat* of Scripture; or with the early Geiger and Holdheim, that they were absurd and reflective of turbid minds; or, with the later Geiger and other Reformers, that they represented deliberately and brilliantly subversive readings of the Bible—all were motivated by the conviction that the new cultural contexts rendered it impossible to go on with the traditional consensus that prevailed in premodern Ashkenaz and elsewhere. For all of them, in their struggle for recognition and some form of religious continuity, the inherited literature and patterns of thought proved to be a considerable burden. The inheritance could not be accepted without theoretical and, in many cases, practical, modification. Ultimately, their sense of who they are and what they can be was linked to their ability to confidently appropriate or justifiably reject all or part of their rabbinic heritage. Addressing the question of how or whether to remain connected to this heritage was existentially urgent for these scholars. This need proved to be a major cultural stimulus for Jews in the nineteenth century.

The Twentieth Century

In the twentieth century the problem of midrash halakhah has ceased to be a public issue. I do not mean to suggest by this statement that, as a point of debate, it was ever an issue dealt with by the Jewish public at large. However, in the nineteenth century it was debated *before* the Jewish public at large. That is, many of the writers who addressed the issue were engaged in a battle for the hearts and minds of Jews in the modern world; their treatments of the rabbinic past were aimed at the proverbial intelligent layperson. The German-Jewish journals, such as Frankel's *Monatsschrift*, Geiger's *Wissenschaftliche Zeitschrift für jüdische Theologie*, or Hirsch's *Jeschurun*, were geared to sympathetic, educated laypeople. The lecture series, sermons, histories and Bible commentaries (at least the German ones) that treated the matter also hoped to reach this audience. Graetz's *Geschichte der Juden* was probably the most widely read German-Jewish book of the nineteenth century (although, admittedly, its success was scarcely due to his portraits of the ancient rabbis alone). The Jewish reading public of the nineteenth century, particularly in Germany, was well aware of the Talmud's image problem, and had ample opportunity to know that rabbinic exegesis played a fundamental role in this problem.

In the twentieth century, while the adjectives "pharisaic" or "talmudic" continue to be used as pejoratives, primarily by non-Jews who have never opened a Talmud, the Jewish community no longer feels the discomfort of the previous century. As I suggested in the closing section of chapter 7, I believe that for the non-Orthodox this is because the more liberal defenders of the Talmud have done their jobs well. Jewish readers of works like Graetz's Geschichte, or Geiger's lecture series, Das Judentum und seine Geschichte (1863–64), gained confidence in the progressive possibilities of rabbinic Judaism, and they and their successors have been able to comfortably dismiss what they considered the outdated parts as historically conditioned; that is, they may no longer address our needs, but they were perfectly understandable and acceptable in their own time, place, and cultural and political context. This confidence has been transmitted to those Jews who still actively embrace some form of Jewish religious observance, though they may no longer know of the underlying issues. Similarly, for the Orthodox for whom midrash emerged as a problem, the works of Hirsch, Hoffmann, and Halevy serve as a source of confidence that those who "know" history as well as the heretics have successfully established firm foundations for belief in a comprehensive revealed oral tradition.

The fact is that most Jews no longer study the Talmud, and are in no position to be made uncomfortable by its rhetoric or exegeses. They are therefore more dependent on the religious professionals to mediate its contents to them. I am in no position to judge with what accuracy this is done, but I know from my own experience teaching and lecturing to adults that people who have never opened a Talmud readily opine that it represents a remarkable compendium of pious and ethical extensions of the biblical law. Liberal Jews today see in the application of the biblical "an eye for an eye" to pecuniary compensation a remarkable ethical advance; that similar patterns of reading and legislating could exempt someone who offers all his children to Molech from punishment remains unknown to them. The linguistic and cultural distance that separates the majority of Jews from detailed talmudic learning has defused the urgency of reconciling this learning with modern exegetical and ethical assumptions.

Whereas it was once common to find Jews publicly attacking and ridiculing the Talmud, today it is rare indeed. One hundred and seventy years ago, the *Oberrabbiner* of the German city of Emden, Abraham Loewenstamm, felt compelled to write a book entitled, *Der Talmudist, wie er ist; oder wir sind alle Menschen* (Emden, 1822). I have already described the circumstances that could lead such a person to write such a book—one whose content evokes a greater sense of pathos than does its title. Today it is difficult to imagine someone feeling the need to write such a book.

In the 1850s, men like Graetz and Geiger had to marshal all their considerable historical and polemical talents to create images of the Pharisees to which Jews could relate positively. Today all the major denominations proudly claim to be heirs of the Pharisees.

In the early decades of the nineteenth century in Germany, and in the last decades of the century in Eastern Europe, there were still many Jews raised in the rabbinic tradition who, upon discovering new cultural possibilities, felt an almost adolescent need to rebel in the strongest possible terms against the traditional culture in which they were raised. At these times in these places, there was yet strong centripetal social pressure that collided with what, in some cases, were even stronger centrifugal political and intellectual forces; this volatile mix did not readily lead to moderation. In time, the political and intellectual challenges of modernity became more routine (or were neutralized through emigration from Eastern Europe to the West), and the religious choices of parents were largely decisive for their children. In urban areas, at least, the intense traditional centripetal forces were thoroughly weakened. As a result, Jews escaping tradition found it easier to fashion their religious identities without the need to publicly rebel against and seek to undermine the traditional culture that once nurtured them.[8]

As the various denominations emerged in the nineteenth century, each could, for a time, maintain the ambition to be the dominant, if not the only, form of Judaism that would survive in the modern world. For this reason, each had a strong need to try to negate the teachings of the others. As I have argued in the previous three chapters, this competition was to prove to be a major stimulus of Jewish thought and historiography. By the end of the century, at least in Germany, it was clear to anyone with eyes to see that none of these groups would supersede the others. While questions of cooperation and communal integration remained, each, de facto, accepted the existence of the others. The polemics either ceased or shifted to other grounds. Each group had fashioned its own "usable past" that served its needs; as these "pasts" were fashioned out of the polemics of the century, it is not surprising that they were, for the most part, mutually incompatible. It is also not surprising that, in time, each community gave preference to internal consolidation over externally directed polemics. The question of rabbinic reading and midrash halakhah largely receded into the background, as each community had fashioned a picture of rabbinic religion that could support its contemporary aspirations and goals.[9]

That the problematic nature of midrash is no longer a public issue does not mean that it has ceased to be an issue at all, or that it has ceased to be a stimulus for Jewish cultural creativity. From among the Orthodox of Eastern European origins has come the greatest Torah commentary of this century, the *Meshekh Ḥokhmah* (1927) of Meir Simḥah Ha-Cohen of Dvinsk (1843–1926), which continues with the agenda of the Gaon of Vilna and Naftali Berlin, and is very attuned to the question of the relation of Jewish law to the biblical text. The magisterial *Torah Shelemah* of Menaḥem Mendel Kasher (currently forty-three volumes) represents a massively expanded cultural offshoot of Epstein's *Torah Temimah*. Yet other lesser-known figures have continued the effort to explain the exegetical principles of the rabbis.[10]

But it has been primarily the heirs of the historical school who have kept the issue alive in this century. We must divide this group into two: those who remained overtly attached to the religious dimension of the traditional historical school, and those who, whatever their religious commitments may be, remained devoted to the research program of the historical school, without drawing any overt religious conclusions from this research.

To the first group belong various ideologues of the American Conservative movement. In particular, the central focus of Louis Finkelstein's (1895–1991) work has been the development of Jewish law and the role of midrash. Like most who have addressed the question in this century, he has argued for the division of the rabbinic estate in the second century into two schools headed by Rabbis Ishmael and Aqiba. He has argued for important exegetical and theological distinctions between these schools. At the same time he has been the primary advocate of the antiquity of the Jewish legal process, arguing for its roots in prophetic times.[11]

Finkelstein's work developed in tandem with that of the leading theologian of the Conservative movement, Abraham Joshua Heschel (1907–72). The latter's *Theology of Ancient Judaism* (3 vols., 1962–90) is a theological tour de force predicated on the fundamental divide within the rabbinic estate in the second century. Heschel builds on the theories of the nineteenth-century historians of midrash halakhah to construct two distinct theological systems that carry forward throughout Jewish history. As Arnold Eisen has argued, Heschel's project is, among other things, an effort at reclaiming the place of Ishmael in Jewish tradition—an effort, that, as we have seen, has roots in nineteenth-century *jüdische Wissenschaft*.[12]

To the second group belongs the work of Saul Horovitz (1859–1920) of Breslau, whose edition of the *Sifre Be-Midbar* was prefaced by an introduction in which Horovitz continued with the claims of Weiss and Hoffmann regarding the sources and authority of Jewish law. I should note that in his notes to the *Sifre*, Horovitz's commitment to the two-system hypothesis led him to sometimes suggest emendations to dispose of texts that he surmised, ex hypothesi, could not be as transmitted.[13]

Ya'aqob Naḥum Epstein (d. 1950), doyen of the Talmud scholars of the Hebrew University, also continued with the historical schema of the *Wissenschaft* scholars.[14] With erudition, he argued for the Ishmaelian provenance of the *Mekhilta de-Rabbi Ishmael* and *Sifre Be-Midbar* and parts of the *Sifre Devarim* and *Sifra*; and the Aqiban origins of the *Sifre Devarim* and *Mekhilta de-Rabbi Shim'on bar Yoḥai*.[15]

The attachment of these scholars to paradigms pioneered by the *Wissenschaft* scholars of the nineteenth century is not of much interest in and of itself. What is noteworthy is that these scholars were drawn to these constructs for essentially the same reason as their predecessors, namely, that these constructs help diminish the legal and historical significance of rabbinic patterns of reading. The distance between rabbinic and modern textuality was simply too great for these scholars to seriously countenance the possibility that the rabbis really read Scripture as the rabbinic documents suggest they did. Whatever their own religious agenda may have been, the rabbinic writings formed a central part of the cultural legacy they were instrumental in recovering; as such they were driven to retrieve rabbinic culture in a manner that diminished its apparent irrationality.

These scholars were driven by the modern assumption that the definitive meaning of a text can be established; since the rabbinic reading was quite distant from the "definitive" meaning of the Bible, modern textual assumptions would render the practical component of rabbinic Judaism devoid of foundation. By showing, through historical and philological investigation, that Jewish laws transmitted in rabbinic texts did not generally or ever originate in preposterous exegesis, the scholars of the twentieth century have carved out their own place in the ongoing Jewish struggle with the question, "How do we know this?"

A recent example of a scholar who has grappled with this question is David Weiss Halivni (b. 1928). His work is much more self-aware than is that of his modernist predecessors, and he has formulated the problem in overtly religious terms.[16] He too cannot accept that the rabbis could change the unmistakable meaning of divine imperatives and still command religious allegiance. He thus offers a theory of the restoration of the original meaning of the text to resolve the religious problem. What is of note for us here is that once again a work of scholarship and theology is motivated by the distance that separates modernist and rabbinic textuality. Halivni is, I would guess, the last of the major Jewish scholars who would formulate the problem as he does.

In the past several decades new theories of textuality have emerged that have come to be called—in a triumph of meaninglessness—postmodern. Students of postmodern or poststructuralist textuality have rebelled against the notion that texts have definitive and timeless meanings unrelated to the consciousness of the reader and/or the self-referential character of language. Scholars who have engaged post-modern textual assumptions have come to see rabbinic midrash, whether halakhic or (especially) aggadic, as precursors in some sense, whose textual insight has been ignored or suppressed by the triumph of other cultural systems. Daniel Boyarin, for example, has explicitly announced his ongoing "intellectual/cultural project of inserting rabbinic textuality into critical discourse and critical discourse into the scholarship of rabbinic literature."[17] A generation ago, or a century ago, the last thing a Jewish scholar would have been comfortable doing is inserting rabbinic textuality into critical discourse. The former stood at such distance from what was then the latter that Jewish scholars spent their efforts undermining rabbinic textuality so as to provide a culturally respectable foundation for rabbinic religion and culture. This is clearly no longer the case. Today, the scholarly pendulum has swung in the opposite direction, providing scholars of rabbinics with new vocabularies and theories through which they can understand talmudic exegesis. Where these theoretical shifts will take the story of this book, and what impact, if any, they will have on living Judaism, remains to be seen. I think it is safe to say that the apologetics of the Reform, historical and Orthodox schools of the nineteenth century and their twentieth-century offshoots, as well as the attacks of the Reformers and Eastern European rebels, will be sublated by the new theoretical discourse. It is equally safe to say that the question of the nature of rabbinic midrash will remain alive among those who continue to take this ancient culture seriously, and that new responses remain to be offered to that ubiquitous rabbinic question, "How do we know this?"

Preface

1. The phrase "extrabiblical" practices or laws, as well as the phrase "rabbinic law" used throughout this book, refers to those laws that are not explicitly stated in the Bible but are regarded by the rabbinic legal system, the halakah, as having the authority of a scriptural law. From the perspective of their authority they are biblical laws; in terms of their textual origins, however, they are extrabiblical, and, in most cases, are first attested to in one rabbinic document or another.

2. For discussion of kabbalistic exegesis, see Gershom Scholem, *On the Kabbalah and Its Symbolism* (New York: Schocken, 1969); Moshe Idel, *Language, Torah and Hermeneutics in Abraham Abulafia* (Albany: SUNY Press, 1989); idem, "Midrashic versus Other Forms of Jewish Hermeneutics: Some Comparative Reflections," in Michael Fishbane, ed., *The Midrashic Imagination: Jewish Exegesis, Thought, and History* (Albany: SUNY Press, 1993), pp. 45–58; and Elliot R. Wolfson, "Beautiful Maiden Without Eyes: *Peshat* and *Sod* in Zoharic Hermeneutics," in Fishbane, *Midrashic Imagination*, pp. 155–203.

3. The question may be more literally translated as "Whence do we know this?" (= *mina lan;* other versions include *minayin* or *mina hani mili*).

Chapter 1. Introduction

1. For a discussion of this number and its authority, see Naḥmanides' "Hassagot" to Maimonides' *Sefer ha-Mitzvot*, first principle.

2. I use the phrase "extrabiblical" to refer to any laws that are not explicitly stated in the Bible but which are regarded by the rabbinic legal system as having biblical authority. That is, I am referring to those laws considered as being obligatory *mi-de-oraita* (from the Torah), but which are not actually stated therein.

3. Yerushalmi, Pe'ah 2:6, Hagigah 1:8. See also Bavli, Megillah 19b.

4. Yerushalmi, Megillah 1:5.

5. For further discussion, see Peter Schäfer, *Studien zur Geschichte und Theologie des rabbinischen Judentums* (Leiden: E. J. Brill, 1978), pp. 153–97. To be sure, in his classic description of the Pharisees Josephus claims that they preserved traditions of the fathers not written in the Torah (*Antiquities* 13.9.6); however, this is scarcely the same thing as an oral tradition from Sinai.

6. An extensive literature exists regarding the law of Moses from Sinai (*halakhah le-Moshe mi-Sinai*) that details the many disputes regarding the

identification of what laws are to be so categorized, and what such an identification actually means. See most recently, Shmuel Safrai, "Halakhah le-Moshe Mi-Sinai—Historia 'o Teologia," in Yaakov Sussmann and David Rosenthal, eds., *Meḥkere Talmud* (Jerusalem: Magnes Press, 1990), pp. 11–38. Safrai reviews the earlier literature, to which one should add Yehoshua Heshel Schorr's important study, "Halakhah le-Moshe mi-Sinai," *He-Haluṣ* 3.

7. That throughout rabbinic literature the two are distinct, rather than complementary, sources of authority is manifest from discussions in different rabbinic documents; see, e.g., *Sifra*, Ṣav, pereq 11:4-6; Bavli, Moed Katan 3b–4a.

8. Compare Abraham Joshua Heschel, *Torah min ha-Shamayim be Aspaklaria shel ha-Dorot*, 3 vols. (vols. 1–2: London: Soncino Press, 1962–65; vol. 3: New York, Jewish Theological Seminary, 1990)

9. For further discussion, see most recently David Weiss Halivni, "On Man's Role in Revelation," in Jacob Neusner et al., eds., *From Ancient Israel to Modern Judaism: Essays in Honor of Marvin Fox* (Atlanta: Scholars Press, 1989); Yoḥanan Sillman, "Torat Yisrael le-'Or Ḥiddusheha—Beirur Phenomenologi," PAAJR 57 (1990–91). One rabbinic source attempts to bridge the gap between the wholesale and retail responses by suggesting that God communicated all the ancillary information needed but much of this was forgotten during the period of mourning following Moses' death. This material was reconstructed dialectically by Othniel ben Kenaz, suggesting that God revealed a perfect Torah—written and oral—whose results can also be reconstructed by human intellect working from the written text alone. As with all the other pronouncements on the subject, one cannot know what authority to attach to this teaching. See Bavli, Temurah 16a.

10. For example, readers familiar with rabbinic texts know full well that at least some rabbis, living sometime during the first six centuries of the Christian era, expressed the thought that the Book of Ezekiel should be withdrawn from circulation; they apparently were uncomfortable with the canonical status of the Book of Ezekiel, because it blatantly contradicts the Pentateuch in a number of places. The remedy for their discomfort became exegesis. Thus, according to a report in the Talmud, the discomfort created by the Book of Ezekiel was relieved by the herculean exegetical efforts of Ḥanina (or Ḥananiah) b. Ḥizkiah. (See Bavli, Shabbat 13b, Ḥagigah 13a, and esp. Menahot 45a. It is striking that the Talmud does not record Ḥanina's exegeses, although Rashi, commenting on the Shabbat passage, identifies some of the Talmud's reconciliations between Ezekiel and the Torah, found in the Menahot passage, as being those of Ḥanina. It seems the very fact that someone with appropriate status resolved the difficulties was sufficient.) The historical veracity of such a report is not particularly important for our purposes; the claim stands as an important cultural marker quite apart from whether it happened. For, it makes the point that it is through exegesis that a culture can resolve difficulties and continue to grow and develop.

11. For a review of recent literature on this matter, see, H. L. Strack and Gunter Stemberger, *Introduction to the Talmud and Midrash* (Minneapolis: Fortress Press, 1992), pp. 141–45.

12. Most scholars advocate a mid-third-century date for these texts, primarily on philological and, it must be admitted, traditionalist grounds. Jacob

Neusner is the primary advocate for a fourth-century date, on the grounds that the message he discerns in these texts is most readily correlated with a Christianity triumphant, i.e., that of the fourth century. Leaving aside the question of whether Neusner has correctly reconstructed the message of these texts, the correlation of this message with Christian triumph and dating of the texts accordingly is strikingly reminiscent of the questionable methods of Krochmal and Graetz in their dating of biblical books. It is most surprising to see this rather unhistorical, essentially intuitive approach from Neusner. The primary advocate of the fifth century is Ḥanokh Albeck, who argues from the fact that the Talmuds did not cite these texts when they "should have," thus proving they did not know them in their present form. This, in turn, proves the texts did not exist until the fifth century at the earliest. Such a claim strikes me as rather dubious and unhistorical, as it argues ex silentio and presses an almost theological claim far beyond its appropriate limits. See his *Untersuchungen über die halakischen Midraschim* (Berlin, 1927), 87–120. The only advocate of an eighth-century date, for the *Mekhilta d'Rabbi Ishmael* at least, is Ben Zion Wacholder. See his "The Date of the *Mekhilta de-Rabbi Ishmael*," *Hebrew Union College Annual* 39 (1968): 117–44. For a reply, see Gunter Stemberger, "Die Datierung der *Mekhilta*," *Kairos* 21 (1979): 81–118.

13. For basic information on all of these texts and those mentioned in the next note, see Strack and Stemberger, *Introduction*, pp. 269–99.

14. Such as the *Mekhilta de-Rabi Shim'on bar Yoḥai* or the so-called *Midrash Tannaim 'al Sefer Devarim*.

15. See chapters 2 and 3 below.

16. See especially Michael Fishbane, *Biblical Interpretation in Ancient Israel* (Oxford: Clarendon Press, 1985), pp. 91–277.

17. Geiger, *Urschrift;* more recently, see Fishbane, *Biblical Interpretation* and Emanuel Tov, *Textual Criticism of the Hebrew Bible* (Minneapolis: Fortress, 1992), pp. 199–285, esp. pp. 262–75. Most of Tov's examples pertain to the non-Pentateuchal parts of the Hebrew Bible.

18. For a review of the literature on Samaritan exegesis, see Reinhard Pummer, "Einführung in den Stand der Samaritanerforschung," in Ferdinand Dexinger and Reinhard Pummer, eds., *Die Samaritaner* (Darmstadt: Wissenschaftliche Buchgesellschaft, 1992), pp. 34–37.

19. See Fishbane, *Biblical Interpretation*, pp. 157 n. 36, 247–50, 273–77.

20. The most extensive presentations of purported Sadducean exegesis are to be found in rabbinic literature. Given the rabbinic tendency to present even Gentiles as arguing with the rabbis by using rabbinic techniques to achieve different results, one should attach little or no historical value to its presentation of Sadducean exegesis. Its presentation of basic legal disputes between Sadducees and Pharisees may be of greater value. If Lawrence H. Schiffman is correct that the acceptable teachings of the Qumran scroll 4QMMT reflect the teachings of early Sadducees, we may be better able to reconstruct Sadducean exegetical approaches. The problem with Schiffman's identification is that it is based on the Mishnah's attribution of certain opinions to the Sadducees. It seems clear to me, however, that at a certain point "Sadducee" in rabbinic literature became a generic designation, much like our use of the term "Protestant." On the sole

basis of a seventeenth- or eighteenth-century Catholic polemic against a set of ideas identified as Protestant, one could not say that the ideas in question reflect the teachings of, say, Luther and his followers. See Lawrence H. Schiffman, "The Sadducean Origins of the Dead Sea Scroll Sect," in Hershel Shanks, ed., *Understanding the Dead Sea Scrolls* (New York: Random House, 1992), pp. 36–49; see also Ya'aqob Sussmann, "History of Halakhah and the Dead Sea Scrolls—Preliminary Observations on *Miqṣat Ma'aseh ha-Torah* (4QMMT)," *Tarbiz* 59 (1989–90): 11–76. On the Qumran community, see Michael Fishbane, "Use, Authority and Interpretation of Mikra at Qumran," in Martin J. Mulder, ed., *Mikra: Text, Translation, Reading and Interpretation of the Hebrew Bible in Ancient Judaism and Early Christianity* (Assen: Van Gorcum, 1988), pp. 339–77; Steven D. Fraade, "Interpretive Authority in the Studying Community at Qumran," in *Journal of Jewish Studies* 44 (Spring 1993); Lawrence H. Schiffman, *The Halakhah at Qumran* (Leiden: E. J. Brill, 1975), pp. 22–76, 84–136; idem, *Sectarian Law in the Dead Sea Scrolls: Courts, Testimony and the Penal Code* (Chico, Calif.: Scholars Press, 1983), pp. 4–17. On the methods of the Greek schools, see the classic article by Saul Lieberman, "Rabbinic Interpretation of Scripture," in idem, *Hellenism in Jewish Palestine* (New York: Jewish Theological Seminary, 1962), pp. 47–67.

21. See below, chapters 4 and 7.

22. See below, chapter 7.

23. See Lieberman, *Hellenism in Jewish Palestine,* p. 55.

24. It is not crucial that we be able to date at what point this position became dominant. The problem we seek to investigate involves the difficulty facing those who accept the authority of the midreshe halakhah and the Talmuds; certainly such people accepted this position as axiomatic. For a discussion of this phenomenon, see S. Z. Havlin, "Al 'ha-Ḥatimah ha-Sifrutit' ke-yesod ha-Ḥalukah le-Tequfot be-Halakhah," in *Meḥkarim be-Sifrut ha-Talmudit* (Jerusalem: Israel National Academy of Sciences, 1983), pp. 148–92. Furthermore, in saying rabbinic Judaism is characterized by this belief is not to claim that there was unanimity regarding it. I simply claim here that in the culture shaped by rabbinic Judaism this position became a commonplace, although I cannot specify when.

25. This aspect of Jewish learning will be dealt with in chapters 3 and 4. For our present purpose, one abstract example should suffice. Rabbi X is quoted in the Mishnah (the product of the *Tannaim*) to the effect that Y is prohibited. The Gemara, the product of later sages, asks how he knows this. The answer will almost invariably be a midrash. Now in this situation the *Tanna,* Rabbi X, did not actually compose the midrash; traditional students of the Talmud would normally assume that nevertheless the midrash is an authentic reflection of his exegetical thinking.

26. There are, to be sure, exceptions to this. These, and the principle generally, are discussed by Malakhi ben Ya'akov ha-Kohen in his *Yad Malakhi,* par. 144. See also Yiṣḥaq D. Gilat, "Midrash Ketuvim ba-Tequfah ha-batar-talmudit," in idem, *Peraqim be-Hishtalshelut ha-Halakhah* (Ramat Gan: Bar Ilan University Press, 1992), pp. 374–93; Avraham Grossman, *Ḥakhme Ashkenaz*

ha-Rishonim (Jerusalem: Magnes Press, 1981), pp. 154–57. Note that we are talking about definitive and binding legal rulings; it is these that were no longer drawn midrashically from the biblical text. I do not mean to imply that the Bible itself ceased to serve as an important focus of study, or that commentary came to a halt. Quite obviously, this is scarcely the case. In 1840, Isaac Reggio could count well over 140 Pentateuch commentaries composed by Jews since the onset of the Middle Ages. With all that have been discovered and written since then, I am confident the number must approach 300. If we then add all the commentaries to other books of the Bible, the overall number of Jewish Bible commentaries is well into the hundreds, if not thousands. The Bible, thus, remained very much a source of study and reflection throughout the ages, although more in some places and times than others. The point here is that these commentaries were never intended to create new halakhic rulings on the basis of the biblical text.

27. In the last two decades or so, scholars have paid substantial attention to rabbinic exegesis and have developed various theories regarding it. In what follows I ignore this literature entirely. In no way do I intend to suggest any judgment of this work; it is simply that for the purposes of this book, this important scholarly literature is irrelevant. The conceptualizations of midrash formulated therein are all of recent vintage, and have not yet had any historical repercussions. The difficulties confronted by medieval and modern Jews were based on different assumptions entirely.

28. Such an understanding of the plain meaning of the verse is not limited to modern readers. Biblical commentators themselves insist that this is the meaning. See inter alia the comments of Gersonides to 2 Kings 14:6. See further Moshe Greenberg's "Some Postulates of Biblical Criminal Law," in Judah Goldin, ed., *The Jewish Expression* (New Haven: Yale University Press, 1976), pp. 29–34.

29. This would be in accord with 2 Kings 14:6 and 2 Chron. 25:4; see the comments of Ovadiah Seforno to Deut. ad loc.

30. See the comments of Ibn Ezra, ad loc. See Greenberg, "Postulates," pp. 29–30.

31. Finkelstein, ed., *Sifre Devarim*, piska 280, p. 297.

32. So Naftali Zvi Yehuda Berlin. Others explain that a relative of the blood-avenger would himself be a (potential) blood-avenger, and the verse demands judgment between slayer and blood-avenger, indicating that the latter may not serve as judge.

33. Berlin cleverly argues that this applies only to relatives of the blood-avenger (who may also be relatives of the victim). He is undoubtedly motivated by reducing the tension between this passage and the one previously discussed, although he is aware that they disagree regarding judges. In any event, it is clear that the Yerushalmi did not understand the passage this way; it saw it as an alternative way of excluding witnesses of the accused, and by extension all litigants (see San. 3:9)

34. The only exception known to me is the anonymous questioner to whom R. Solomon ibn Adret responds in his *Responsa*, vol. 1, no.1185.

35. This was noted already by R. Sherira Gaon, who in his famous *Epistle* gives an extended, although not exhaustive, list of rabbinic exegetical techniques.

36. See most recently the introduction to his *Sifra: An Analytical Translation* (Atlanta: Scholars Press, 1988), esp. p. 31, (where, in note 11, he claims the same program motivates the *Sifre Bemidbar*) and pp. 46–53. On p. 31 he claims that the *halo din hu* passages of the *Sifra* serve no purpose other than to argue for the supremacy of revelation over logic. But as we shall see below, they serve the important function of accounting for scriptural excess. They point to instances in which Scripture states more than is necessary, for we could easily learn the conclusion without a verse. Other times, as in the discussion of Lev. 1:3 below, they impose a certain discipline on a *darshan*, for one should not account for scriptural excess or anomalies by saying they come to teach the obvious. It is important to show that what they teach is not obvious. Thus, we have the introduction of an argument a fortiori that must then be unraveled in order to show that Scripture is not excessive. See below and next note.

37. A reading of midrashic passages that attends to their content will allow us to see the dialectical relationship of these categories. On the one hand, as the *Sifra* itself often notes, the revelation itself depends on the logic of the human reader to determine. Thus when the text includes X and excludes Y, the question is asked, "Why have you done so when you could have done the opposite?" It will then provide some response showing why the presented way is superior. Sometimes these can be quite involved, as in the *kelakh bederekh zu* passages. Thus, "revelation" can scarcely be seen in the *Sifra* as independent of human logic; the demands of revelation are determined by human logic. Similarly, to refer to the process of extending scriptural imperatives as "logic," as though it were an independent exercise of human thought, is scarcely adequate. The "logic" that exists here is not an independent human jurisprudential exercise, but an attempt to draw logical connections between scriptural facts—connections that the *Sifra* is quite happy to make when it suits its purposes. When, however, such connections render Scripture superfluous they cannot be allowed to stand. See the discussion of the *Sifra* to Lev. 1:3 below. Although I provide but a single example in the text, one could readily add dozens more. It should be noted that a position on the matter that overlaps partially with that of Neusner's may be found in the Gaon of Vilna's biblical commentary, *Aderet Eliyahu*, to Deut. 11:32.

38. With remarkable erudition, R. Yitzhak Hutner collected all the halakhot whose source is the *Sifra* (that is, those not dealt with in the Bavli; most of these are not treated in the Mishnah); he counts 325 of them. R. Hutner's comments to these laws make clear the extent to which Maimonides relied on the *Sifra* in codifying many areas of Jewish law, as other sources were unavailable to him. See his *Quntres Osef ha-halakhot ha-mehudashot ha-nimsaot ba-Sifra asher lo ba Zakhran ba-Talmud Bavli* appended to Shachna Koloditzky's edition of the *Sifra im Perush Rabbenu Hillel*. To be sure, some these identifications are questionable, for they rely on a particular interpretation of a medieval commentator, and other interpretations are possible. Even so, if only half stand up under

scrutiny—and I believe the number would be much higher—we would still have a large body of laws that are independent of other rabbinic documents. I cannot provide figures for the other midreshe halakhah. My intuition is that none provide anywhere near this number of "new" halakhot; still, all of them deal with numerous issues not dealt with fully or at all in the Mishnah.

39. I am aware of the fact that in a number of places in tannaitic documents, laws that are regarded by certain rabbis such as Yoḥanan ben Zakkai or Tarfon as devoid of scriptural foundation (and thus subject to forgetting) are subsequently identified by Aqiba as being derived from a verse. This, in my view, does not challenge the claim I am making here. That is, the texts do not understand Aqiba as having connected traditional law to a verse; rather they understand Aqiba as having revealed the actual scriptural *source* of laws whose scriptural source had been forgotten. Otherwise he would have accomplished nothing other than establishing a mnemonic; this would scarcely have relieved the concern of Ben Zakkai that the law would one day be abrogated because its scriptural source was unknown. See Mishnah, Sotah 5:2.

40. Even many of the so-called thirteen principles of R. Ishmael are, in the end, attempts to deal with scriptural redundancies and superfluities. The various techniques for dealing with the *kellal* and *perat* are responses to the fact that Scripture, having provided a general prohibition, proceeds, apparently unnecessarily, to enumerate particulars. Explaining that the particulars serve a purpose removes their apparent superfluity. Even the *gezerah shavah* often starts with a word superfluous in context, and explains its appearance as intending a comparison with some other place where the word occurred. In light of what is to follow, I should point out that this technique appears in all of the tannaitic texts, although only the *Mekhilta de-Rabbi Ishmael*, the *Sifre Bamidbar* and the so-called *Mekhilta d'Arayot* (see note 42) actually identify the word as superfluous. Cf. *Sifra*, Emor 14:9.

41. In his memoirs, Chaim Tchernowitz recalls the first piece of "heresy" (*apikorsut*) that he heard in his youth from a particular Abraham Hirshl, an older boy who had already abandoned traditional patterns of thought if not behavior. "I recall the first piece of heresy I heard from his mouth, regarding the *derashah* of R. Ishmael, why it says 'do not seethe a kid in its mother's milk' three times—one to prohibit cooking, one to prohibit eating, one to prohibit deriving any benefit—which pricked my heart like a needle in live flesh, until I got used to his mockery. Thus he would joke: Moses knew that the Jews are shrewd, and their way is to distort the meaning of the scriptures, and to remove them from their simple meaning. They would thus come to interpret 'a kid in its mother's milk' as applicable broadly, implying all meat in milk. He therefore repeated himself and wrote a second time explicitly 'do not seethe a kid in its mother's milk,' to specifically exclude a kid, specifically in its mother's milk. [He thought] maybe two times is not enough; he thus taught a third time, specifically prohibiting a kid in its mother's milk, and not all meat in milk. What did R. Ishmael do? He came and interpreted the threefold appearance of 'do not seethe,' as 'the verse comes to be inclusive; one appearance prohibits cooking . . . to teach you that all meat in milk is prohibited.' In this way he would mock

serveral *derashot* of the sages." Chaim Tchernowitz, *Pirqe Ḥaim* (New York: Bişaron, 1954), p. 16. The second half of this book will deal with the emergence of this Abraham Hirshl's form of heresy. I cite this here as it relates to the talmudic passage under discussion.

42. See H. L. Strack and Gunter Stemberger, *Einleitung in Talmud und Midrasch* (Munich: C. H. Beck, 1982), pp. 245–46 for explanation.

43. For explanation of this punishment in the Bible, see Baruch Levine, *The JPS Torah Commentary: Leviticus,* "Excursus One," pp. 241–42.

44. We should note that Abraham Ibn Ezra understands the preposition to indicate that the animal must be selected "from" the superior animals, indicating that the preposition must have some exclusionary intent, albeit not the one the midrash will identify.

45. A *terefah* is an animal that suffers from a serious disease of its organs; such an animal is unfit for consumption, and, as this passage indicates, for the altar as well.

46. That is, the ordinary meat one would normally eat as opposed to that of an animal prepared for sacrifice on the altar, regarding which higher standards prevail. An animal with a blemish is considered kosher, and may be consumed.

47. We should note that Ibn Ezra seems to accept the underlying reasoning when he comments that the word *min* indicates that the animal should be *mi-nivḥeret* (from the best). If we accept the assumption that the preposition *min* is not innocuous, certainly Ibn Ezra's explanation is simpler than that offered by the *Sifra.*

48. See Bavli, Men. 6a, Bek. 57a, Tem. 29a.

49. Maimonides, *Mishneh Torah,* Issure ha-Mizbeach, 2:10, and the comments of R. Joseph Karo, *Kessef Mishneh,* ad loc. It is to be noted that Maimonides in his *Sefer ha-Mitzvot* lists the unsuitability of a blemished animal but not a *terefah.* It is possible that Rashbam intended something similar, although this is not altogether clear from his comment on the verse.

50. I have chosen this passage because it is treated by Jacob Neusner as a prime example of the polemic he locates in the *Sifra.* Attention to the scriptural trigger for this comment, to the contrived logic involved in it, and to the fact that what "revelation" says is ultimately bound up with the reasoning of the exegete, would negate his interpretation. See his *Midrash in Context* (Philadelphia: Fortress Press, 1983), pp. 38–39, and see below.

51. I have followed the New JPS translation except for the italicized portion, where the translator, in trying to resolve the problem of the *Sifra,* translated the word *şara'at* (leprosy) differently than in two other places where the word, or a form of it, occurs. That is, in verse 42 the word is translated as a descriptive term, whereas in verses 43 and 44 it is translated as a technical term. This procedure is wholly justified in translating the Bible. It does not provide adequate understanding, though, of the way the rabbis read the verse.

52. See the comments of Meir Malbim (1809–79) to this verse.

53. I should note that the *Sifra* goes on to discuss the word "spreading"— also inappropriate for the same reason—in the same manner, and also the word *hi,* "it is."

54. See *Sifra,* Negaim 10:6, which defines these spots as incapable of growing hair. Thus, it is clear, we are talking about spots that are fully smooth, devoid of any hair.

55. For some reason, Neusner considers the *Sifra*'s constant repetition of the question "Why does Scripture say so?" unimportant. In my reading, the question is central. In any event, I do not want to imply that the *Sifra* is unconcerned with grounding traditional law in Scripture. Clearly it does this over and over again. I simply claim here the primary polemic of the document surrounds the perfection of Scripture, not legal origins of the Mishnah.

56. The word in question, *et'hen,* does appear elsewhere in the Bible; indeed it appears thirteen times. Still, it is unusual, and becomes the basis for the legally acceptable reading.

57. The passage comes from the so-called *Mekhilta de-'Arayot;* see Strack and Stemberger, *Einleitung,* pp. 245–46.

58. I have followed the version of the ms., which is supported by the version of Rabbenu Hillel and the emendation of the Gaon of Vilna. The printed versions have been emended to conform with the conclusion of Rava in the Bavli as to the meaning of R. Aqiba's statement. See Bavli, San. 76b.

59. I have not dealt here with other instances in which rabbinic *derash* uproots the plain meaning of a biblical verse, as opposed to adding to it. For a discussion of this phenomenon, see Halivni, *Peshat and Derash.*

60. The only one, to my knowledge, who may be called traditional who does not go along is the nineteenth-century Italian exegete Samuel David Luzzatto, who explains that the first woman is punished for remaining in a marital threesome with her husband and mother or daughter.

61. See his comments ad loc. For further discussion of Ibn Ezra, see below, chapter 4.

62. Actually, in the full passage all three inappropriate words—*zara'at porachat hi*—come to fill the lacuna, the *porachat* indicates that a "spreading" is also a disqualifying symptom, while *hi* indicates that a white hair is not.

63. See, e.g., the discussion of the location of the altar in *Sifra,* Nedabah, 7:1–2, where clearly the issue revolves around how the .words "before the Lord" are to be interpreted. Note that the historical issues, the *realia,* are insignificant.

64. See, e.g., *Sifra,* Shemini 6:4. A study of these passages by Eliezer Diamond will be forthcoming.

65. For full discussion, see chapters 7 and 8.

66 The full relevance of this observation will become clear in chapter 7.

67. The technique is used most, although still infrequently, in the Bavli. See e.g., Baba Batra 111b, and parallels cited there. See also Aruch, s.v. "gara," as noted by the *Masoret ha-Shas.*

68. See the version in Finkelstein's edition, 2:82, and the variants he collects ad loc. Some versions have the word *'aleha* in the scriptural citation, others do not. Obviously, the *Sifra* operates here on the understanding that *'aleha* is temporarily removed from the verse.

69. For the identification of the technique at work here, see Yerushalmi,

Sotah, 5:1. There one can find a far more surprising use of the technique *gor'in mosifin ve-dorshin,* attributed to *Amora* R. Yoḥanan. I should also add here that Maimonides, in codifying the absence of oil-pouring on baked meal offerings, cites Lev. 2:4 in support and not this verse (2:6), despite the *Sifra* passage and its quotation by the Bavli at Menahot 75a and the Yerushalmi in several places. See Maimonides, *Mishneh Torah,* Hilkhot Maʿaseh ha-Qorbanot 13:8.

70. Naftali Zvi Yehudah Berlin, *Birkat ha-Neziv* (Jerusalem, 1980), pp. 238–39.

71. Compare *Sifre Bemidbar,* pisqa 124, s.v. "ve-ha-soref otah, etc." (ed. Horowitz, pp. 156–57) with ibid., s.v. "ve-khibes ha-'osef, etc." (p. 159).

72. I am in the process of preparing a separate study of this matter now.

73. Students of the Bavli will, of course note the echo of that Talmud's response to this problem, namely "milta de-atya be-qal ve homer, tarah ve-katav lah qera." This is quite intentional, for, in my view and that of Berlin, the principles are related; indeed, I would say they are essentially identical.

74. *Sifra,* Tazriʿa 13:2.

Chapter 2. Midrash Halakhah and the Bavli

1. See the collection of Ezra Zion Melamed, *Midreshe Halakhah shel ha-Tannaim be-Talmud Bavli* (Jerusalem: Magnes Press, 1988).

2. As already indicated in the introduction, I find a third-century date for the midreshe halakhah the most compelling of the dates that have been proposed. One need not accept this claim entirely for the purposes of this chapter. All that one needs to accept is that the redactors (*stam*) of the Bavli had before them much of the same material that appears in our midreshe halakhah and that *they* considered it tannaitic.

3. Full support for this claim will be provided in the second half of the book.

4. See, most recently, Richard Kalmin, *The Redaction of the Babylonian Talmud: Amoraic or Saboraic?* (Cincinnati: Hebrew Union College Press, 1989).

5. There are differences in the law between rapists and seducers; see the biblical texts. I am, in the interests of brevity, conflating the two cases where they overlap in this and other talmudic discussions. See Halivni, *Meqorot u-Mesorot,* ad loc.

6. In rabbinic law people subject to more severe penalties, i.e., corporal or capital punishment, are generally exempt from monetary payments, whether compensatory or punitive.

7. An example of the first category is a *mamzeret,* a maiden conceived through an adulterous or incestuous relationship. She is prohibited from marrying into "the community of the Lord" (the Jewish people). An example of the second category is one's sister; this incestuous relationship is, in rabbinic thinking, punishable by *karet.* Raping one's sister when she is a *naʿarah* (a certain age), and a presumptive virgin, renders one subject to the fine. An example of the last category (drawn, actually, from the next mishnah) is one's daughter. This incestuous relationship is subject to the capital jurisdiction of the court, overriding the fine.

8. That is, in Deut. 22:28 we find the word *na'arah*. In the next verse, we have *ha-na'arah* (the *ha-* represents the definite article). The force of the remark attributed to Resh Laqish is that both the word *na'arah* and the prefix *ha* in verse 29 are extraneous. Each of these two "words" is there to add information, as the continuation of the passage indicates.

9. Much like the Resh Laqish's *derashah*, there are actually two words here; one is doubly extraneous and thus becomes two words for the *darshan*. Exod. 22:15 contains the word *betulah* (virgin). This word is needed. The next verse contains *ha-betulot*. Both the *betulot* and the definite article *ha* are considered extraneous here. Thus they are adduced to provide information, as the passage indicates.

10. That is, we learn that the bride price is fifty by comparing the seduction case, where no amount is specified, to the rape case where fifty is specified. On the other hand, we learn that in the rape case the payment is made in *sheqalim* (the verse merely states fifty of silver) from the seduction case, where the root for the term translated "he shall weigh out" is *sql*, the same as *sheqalim*.

11. Although not directly relevant to the passage under discussion here, it may be of interest to note that the author(s) of the Book of Jubilees felt the need to specify that the commandment to circumcise on the eighth day precluded both an earlier or later performance, although, of course, he or they did not enter into a complex exegetical discussion, as the Talmud does here. See Jubilees 15:25 (Charlesworth edition, p. 87).

12. That is, instead of writing *u-vayom ha-shemini* the Torah "should" have written *u-vashemini* if it did not intend to impart more information than the surface meaning.

13. But cf. the comments of the *Tosafot*, s.v. "tanya kavvate de-R. Yoḥanan, etc."

14. It may be of more than passing interest to note that R. Saadia Gaon (882–942) apparently found none of these *derashot* and explanations acceptable, for he entirely ignores this talmudic passage and explains that circumcision supersedes the Sabbath because its commandment in the Torah appears before the commandment to observe the Sabbath. See his *Emunot ve-De'ot* 3:9 (Rosenblatt edition, p. 169) and also the fragment attributed to him by S. Poznanski in "Anti-Karaite Writings of Saadia Gaon," *Jewish Quarterly Review*, o.s. 10:270–73. For further discussion of Saadia, see chapter 4.

15. Compare, e.g., the *gezerah shavah* developed by the *stam* at Meg. 23b (*tokh, tokh, edah, edah*) with Yerushalmi, Ber. 7:3 and San. 1:4. See also Eruvin 51a, to which compare *Mekhilta*, Mishpatim 4.

16. *Hilkhot 'Avodat Kokhavim*, 6:4.

17. Explanations include the notion that the Bible only punishes for "normal" Molech worship, and this consists of offering some but not all of one's children; and the characteristically ethically oriented comments of Moses of Coucy in his *Sefer Miṣvot Gadol*, to the effect that punishment constitutes expiation *(kaparah)*, and one who offers all his children is so monstrous as to be undeserving of the expiation effected by punishment.

18. Abraham Joshua Heschel in particular sees this alleged aspect of R. Ishmael's "system" as decisive; all other elements proceed from this notion.

See his *Torah Min ha-Shamaim be-Aspaklariah shel ha-Dorot,* vol. 1, through-out.

19. For full discussion, see below chapter 7.

20. The one exception is *Sifre Numbers,* par. 112, which will be discussed below. In the printed editions of the *Sifra* the phrase appears two times but both are later additions. Some printings contain the phrase at Ked. 5:2, but it is not found in either Vatican manuscript (nos. 31 and 66), and it is clear from the commentaries of Rabad and (attributed to) Rash of Sens that they did not have the phrase in their editions. It is cited by Rabbenu Hillel as the correct version, although his comment makes clear that he knows of another version in which the phrase is not found; he prefers the version with the phrase on the basis of its appearance in the Bavli, Hor. 11a, but there is little doubt that the Bavli is, in fact, the source of the addition. The other appearance is at Ked. 10:1, and again the mss. do not contain it, and the commentary of Rabad indicates that he does not have the phrase in his version. The phrase is in any event totally inappropriate here as R. Yosi's point is precisely the opposite of what *dibrah Torah* usually conveys. The Yerushalmi does not know this phrase at all; as an equivalent, it uses *dibrah Torah k'darkah* (the Torah speaks in its way) and in one place in the Leiden ms. (Shabbat 19:2) *ribtah Torah k'darkah* (the Torah extends in its way), although the *ribtah* was emended (perhaps hastily?) to *dibrah* in the margin, and subsequent editions of the Yerushalmi have contained both words. See Saul Lieberman *Yerushalmi k'fshuto,* ad loc. The Yerushalmi's position requires separate treatment. See next chapter.

21. This point was already made long ago by Abraham Geiger in his acidulous "Das Verhältnis des natürlichen Schriftsinnes zur thalmudischen Schriftdeutung," *Wissenschaftliche Zeitschrift für jüdische Theologie* 5 (1844): 78–80; and more recently by Yitzhak Heinemann in his *Darkhe ha-Agada,* p. 12 and note 106 on p. 201. Heinemann correctly notes that the explanation is offered to take account of exceptions to the normal patterns of rabbinic midrash, in which all agree that that Torah speaks in its own unique language. He fails to take note of the fact that these "explanations" are never those of *Tannaim,* however. See below.

22. By legal dispute I mean that the rabbis in question are only quoted as disagreeing regarding the law—whether something is permitted or prohibited, for example, or whether one is liable for damages or not. The different exegeses are then used to provide what the redactors consider the likely explanation of the source of the legal disagreement. In the passages that concern us here, the form will be, "Why does Rabbi X decide what he does? Scripture says, [repetitive phrase from a verse]; and what does R. Y do with this phrase? He says [it is devoid of significance because] the Torah speaks in human language." By exegetical dispute, I mean that the rabbis in question are quoted as agreeing concerning the law but as disagreeing regarding the biblical source of that law. The form will be, "Whence does [the author of the law] know it? R. X says [repetitive phrase]; R. Y says [some other technique]. Why does R. Y. not learn as does R. X. [He says], the Torah speaks in human language." (There will also usually be a question of why R. X. does not learn as does R. Y.)

23. As we shall see below, the Bavli, and, indeed, all the rabbinic documents that contain legal exegesis, with the partial exception of the Yerushalmi, are quite sanguine regarding this ad hoc approach to scriptural exegesis. The explanation that sometimes the repetition is not exposited because Scripture has revealed that it is devoid of significance was already offered in a somewhat different fashion in the *Sefer ha-Keritot* of R. Samson of Qinon, part 5, 1:30.

24. See, e.g., the parallel passages at Arakhin 3a, Niddah 32b and 44a. After the extension of impurity to infants on the basis of the repetitive "ish, ish" (Lev. 15:2) we find R. Ishmael b. R. Yoḥanan b. Beroqah saying "eino ṣarikh" (we can learn this principle from elsewhere). "Eino ṣarikh" implies here that R. Ishmael b. R. Yoḥanan b. Beroqah accepts the validity of exegeting phrases such as "ish, ish" but considers the technique weaker than the one he offers, namely the exegesis of the otherwise superfluous "le-zakhar vela-neqevah" (Lev. 15:33). Wilhelm Bacher associates the phrase "eino tzarikh" with the "Ismael'schen Midrasch"; see his *Die exegetische Terminologie der jüdischen Traditionsliteratur* (1899; reprint, Hildesheim: Georg Olms, 1965), 1:165.

25. This version is supported by the parallel at Sotah 26a. In this passage it is abundantly clear that neither R. Aqiba nor R. Ishmael was interpreting the repeated phrase. The whole passage is the creation of the *stam*.

26. *Kitve Ramban*, Chavel edition, 2:300.

27. We should note in particular the presence of R. Aqiba and his students, Rabbis Shim'on and Yehudah, on this list.

28. See also the passage in the *Sefer ha-Keritot* referred to in note 23. The Tosafists offer differing solutions to the problem. The one whose comments are recorded at Sotah 24a, s.v. "v'Rabbi Yonatan etc." attempts to provide all kinds of distinctions between the places in which a given *Tanna* will supposedly say *dibrah* and when the same *Tanna* will explain repetition, based on whether the conclusion may be considered within the meaning of the verse, rather than involving an extension of the verse beyond its meaning (*im ein inyan l'gufe*, etc.). While ingenious, this approach is unconvincing. The Tosafist at Menachot 17b, s.v. "Mai he'akhel ye'akhel etc.," is less ambitious, and provides the more general response that no one is committed to *dibrah* always, but that any *Tanna* will say it if he has any reason not to explain the repetition. He bases this, inter alia, on the passage from Makkot that we will discuss below.

29. The exception is San. 90b and parallel. This passage is parallel to the *Sifre* passage mentioned in note 20 above. I should point out that there is one passage in which the *dibrah* position may have been part of a statement attributed to Rav Yosef, the third generation *Amora*, although I believe, there as well, that the *dibrah* Torah phrase is an addition of the redactors and is not part of their "quotation" from Rav Yosef. The discussion is at Gittin 41b; the statement attributed to Rav Yosef need not have included the "human language position." The relationship between this passage and the one from Ker. requires further study. In addition, in the passage at San. 90b, the "human language position" is attributed to Abbaye, and there it is clearly the point of the statement and cannot be understood as an addendum; of course, one can and should question whether the historical figure Abbaye actually said it. This one, or

possibly two, attributions of the idea to an *Amora* does not affect the basic contention of this chapter, since clearly both passages represent a reconstruction of the exegetical positions of *Tannaim* by authorities living much later. The only issue affected would be how to assign the date of the first appearance of the concept in Babylonia; if the attributions are correct, then this explanation of why, in a particular case, a particular *Tanna* does not interpret repetition first gained currency in the early to middle fourth century. If they are not correct, then the explanation would have to be assigned to the redactional layer of the document, in which case the explanation would have first gained currency in the middle to late fifth century, at the earliest.

30. Heschel would have us believe that the passage here indicates a general commitment to the human language position on the part of R. Shim'on, in order to facilitate his own imposition of system on the rabbinic materials. See *Torah min ha-Shamayim*, 1:207.

31. For the R. Shim'on case, see Tosefta, Pe'ah 4:12 for a presentation that does not presuppose the exegetical context of the discussion. Of course, one would not expect the Tosefta to deal with the exegetical issues, although such treatment would not be foreign to the document. In any event, given the direction of rabbinic legal midrash, one need only explain the repetition if one is comfortable with the conclusion reached.

32. The phrase "this is no difficulty" does not come to introduce a harmonization of the sources, as it often does, but rather comes to dissolve only one element of the difficulty, by maintaining that each source may be treated as a legitimate tannaitic teaching (rather than allowing the existence of one source to challenge the legitimacy of the other). That is, the "lo qushya" here moves the locus of the discussion from exile to a well-known (to the Bavli) dispute regarding exegetical techniques. In this sense, each source retains its legitimacy even though no harmonization is achieved.

33. See previous note.

34. The notion that Abbaye's staement is ad hoc and not general is found in the *Tosafot* to Menachot 17b, s.v. "Mai he-akhel ye'akhel etc."

35. See, however, the commentary of Naftali Zvi Yehudah Berlin (NZIV; 1816–93); he does not add anything to the text but merely repunctuates, as it were, so that the phrase "his transgression is with him" becomes the source of the cutting off in the world to come. That is, the phrase "hikaret tikaret" teaches that the transgressor is cut off in this world, while the phrase "avonah bah" indicates that the transgression remains with him after he has been cut off, suggesting that he is cut off in the world to come as well. The notion that the phrase "avonah bah" is the basis of extending the punishment to the world to come is supported by the Yerushalmi, Pe'ah 1:1. See also the remarks attributed to R. Shim'on b. El'azar at the very end of par. 112 of the *Sifre Numbers*.

36. The printed texts read "Ṣedokim" (Sadducees), which led Lauterbach to the absurd claim that the principle originated with the Sadducees. However, the ms. evidence favoring "Kutim" (Samaritans) is strong, and certainly the overall context, suggesting a fraudulent text, makes more sense when directed against Samaritans. For discussion, see David Zvi Hoffmann, *Melamed Le-Ho'il*, 3:79, p. 125.

37. See *Sifre Numbers,* par. 157. Horovitz points to the tension of this passage and a similar *derashah* in the Yerushalmi in which R. Ishmael appears to take the opposite position (Sotah, 7:5, 24d). He presupposes that the printed versions, which do not accord with the Leiden ms., are correct. There can be little doubt, however, that the printed texts are emended to accord with the general position of the Yerushalmi that R. Ishmael does not explicate repetition. The ms., on the other hand, preserves the exegeses in accord with the position of the *Sifre,* and the reason for its emendation is clear. Only after the passage is emended to make it accord with the general position of the Yerushalmi is there tension between the *Sifre* and Yerushalmi passages. (See Leiden MS, 3:86; the passage in the body of the ms. is defective, and the reconstruction in the margin—which presupposes a *homoieteleuton*—is plausible. The interchange there between the names "Shim'on" and "Ishmael" is quite common.) Further, it should be pointed out that in the version of the Bavli parallel to the passage under discussion here (San. 90b), found in the editio princeps Yalkut Shim'oni, the position of *dibrah* is attributed to R. El'azar ben Azariah, rather than R. Ishmael. Similarly, in the *Torat ha-Adam* of Naḥmanides (Chavel edition, p. 300).

38. A similar situation exists in the Bavli in regard to expositing the conjunctive *vav,* in which, again, the same sage is placed on different sides of the issue in different places. On this see *Tosafot,* Menaḥot 51a, s.v. "vav lo darish," and *Tosafot,* Mo'ed Qatan 8a, s.v. "mai u-vayom." Again, the answer is that these are the putative positions of the sages in question, reconstructed by others in a strictly ad hoc manner, with no attempt to impose consistency throughout the document. See below.

39. In this respect, the medieval commentators, especially R. Samson of Qinon and the Tosafist, whose position is recorded at Menahot 17b, were much more insightful than modern scholars have been.

40. See Yeb. 68b.

41. In this passage this status stands in contrast to that of an *arusah* (one who is betrothed). A *nesuah* is a woman who is fully married. R. Ishmael's contention is that the punishment of burning demanded in Lev. 21:9 only applies to an *arusah,* not a *nesuah,* while R. Aqiba's position is that it applies to both because of the conjunctive "and" (the letter *vav*). I should note that in a private communication, Prof. Shama Friedman has told me that he considers this part of the passage, which ostensibly quotes Aqiba directly, to be actually of later Babylonian origin.

42. I ignore the second response of the *Tosafot* at Yeb. 68b, s.v. "ke-man ke-Rabbi Aqiba"; it is devoid of foundation.

43. See the *Tosafot* at Mo'ed Qatan 8a, San. 14a, and Men. 51b. Each of these sources collect the places that stand in tension.

44. See *Tosafot,* Pesachim, 43b, s.v. "man de-lo darish."

45. See Bavli, Niddah 22b.

46. This follows the explanation of R. Nissim Gaon, Shabbat 131a. Modern scholars such as Epstein insist that the Bavli only identifies R. Eliezer as requiring bilateral availability, but this seems motivated more by his insistence on an Aqiban/Ishmaelian distinction than on a reading of the relevant passages.

47. Bavli, Zevaḥim, 49b–51b. The results of this discussion are summarized in the *Sefer Keritut*, chap. 3. He notes that people did not study these matters, and therefore he devotes a chapter specifically to them.

48. See the discussion at Sotah 3a-3b, regarding *reshut* and *ḥovah*. While the discussion presupposes a consistently different approach to certain issues, it makes an effort to limit the applicability of these approaches to three verses. I do not believe that one could, on the basis of this passage, challenge the larger picture I have drawn.

49. See, e.g., Pesaḥim 41a, Rosh ha-Shanah 20b, and Yoma 5a, 55a, 60b, inter alia.

50. See *Kefef Mishnah* to Hilkhot Milah 2:1.

51. See, e.g., Pesachim 96b, 97a; Kiddushin 78b; Baba Kamma 66b, 67b; Avodah Zarah 38a; Bekhorot 41b; Niddah 35a.

52. See David Weiss Halivni, *Peshat and Derash: Plain and Applied Meaning in Rabbinic Exegesis* (New York: Oxford University Press, 1991), pp. 13–16.

53. As at Kiddushin 24b.

54. As in the statement of R. Yoḥanan, Gittin 60b, which is juxtaposed to that of R. El'azar, insisting the opposite is true (I am following Rashi's interpretation here; I do not see any other way to make sense of the passage). Compare Yerushalmi, Pe'ah 2:6, Ḥagigah 1:8.

Chapter 3. Midrash and the Yerushalmi

1. This title has been variously translated as the Palestinian Talmud, the Jerusalem Talmud, and the Talmud of the Land of Israel; the second is the most literal but least accurate historically. It is generally assumed that this Talmud was redacted prior to the Bavli, sometime around the year 400 of the Christian era.

2. See Jacob Neusner, *The Talmud of the Land of Israel*, vol. 35: *Introduction: Taxonomy* (Chicago: University of Chicago Press, 1983), pp. 52–56.

3. This and other distinctions between the Bavli and Yerushalmi have already been noted by Zechariah Frankel in his *Mavo ha-Yerushalmi* (Breslau: 1870), p. 31b. See also Saul Lieberman, *Hellenism in Jewish Palestine* (New York: Jewish Theological Seminary, 1952), p. 61.

4. For a discussion with somewhat different emphases, see Frankel's *Mavo ha-Yerushalmi*, pp. 31b–32a.

5. As we shall see, one commentator, Moses Margolies, author of the commentary *Pene Moshe*, often sees this question as indicating different sources rather than different midrashic methodologies. Even he, though, acknowledges that the question often indicates the latter. Indeed, the Yerushalmi itself often makes this plain. On this see below. It is my contention, and certainly that of modern scholarship generally, that the force of this quesion is always to suggest different methodologies, whether or not different sources were available to the person(s) formulating this question.

6. A discussion of this form may be found in Gary G. Porton, "According to Rabbi Y: A Palestinian Amoraic Form," in William Scott Green, ed., *Approaches to Ancient Judaism: Theory and Practice* (Missoula, Mont.: Scholars Press, 1978), pp. 173–88. My own understanding of these passages differs significantly.

7. For a more extensive list and discussion, see Hoffmann, *Einleitung*, pp. 5–12.

8. Gary Porton, in his work, leaves the question of origins open, suggesting—implausibly in my view—that at least some of the passages derive from the Tiberian academy of R. Yoḥanan.

9. See, most recently, Yaacov Sussmann, "Ve-shuv le-Yerushalmi Neziqin," in *Meḥqere Talmud*, pp. 55–133.

10. For identification of these figures, see Hanokh Albeck, *Mavo la-Talmudim* (Tel Aviv: Dvir, 1969), p. 167.

11. This seems to me to be the simple explanation of the *gezerah shavah*. However, in the parallel to this passage, Megillah 4:1 (74d), the Qorban ha-'Edah explains that the *gezerah shavah* is based on the appearance of the totally extraneous "your/our God" in the two verses. I suspect this is because he too is perplexed as to why the redactors proceed to identify this hermeneutic device, cited in the names of *Amoraim*, with R. Aqiba (to the exclusion of R. Ishmael), and so turns it into a case of *kefel lashon* (on which see below). This position makes sense given the position of the Bavli regarding R. Aqiba and the learning of the *gezerah shavah*. (According to it only R. Ishmael thinks that one can learn an unchallengeable *gezerah shavah*, even if only one of the two words or phrases is deemed extraneous; see Niddah 22b and 23a and the comments of R. Nissim Gaon on Bavli, Shabbat 131a. But cf. Epstein, *Mavo'ot*, p. 523, who thinks that only R. Eliezer demands that both words or phrases must be extraneous to be unchallengeable. This seems to me to be an overly narrow and credulous reading of Bavli, Shabbat 131a and Yebamot 70b.) But the position does not accord with the Yerushalmi's position on this at all (according to which R. Aqiba demands no extraneity at all; indeed, Rabinowitz plausibly explains the identification of this *gezerah shavah* with R. Aqiba as based on the understanding that the *gezerah shavah* of "Lord/Lord" is not at all extraneous. See, Rabinowitz, *Sha'are Torat Ereṣ Yisrael*, p. 15). On this, and the entire issue, see below.

12. This explanation follows that of Rashi on the parallel version in the Bavli, Ber. 21a; an alternative explanation is offered by Elijah ben Loeb Foulda in his commentary on the Yerushalmi, ad loc.

13. I see no reason to question the attribution here, since I can discern no reason whatsoever that someone would attribute this teaching to this *Amora*, while, given the structure of the *sugya*, I can think of at least two reasons why someone would want to attribute the teaching to someone else, preferably a *Tanna* and a student of R. Aqiba. Alternatively, one might wish to cite the teaching anonymously (as many of the "Aqiban" positions in fact are), so as to strengthen the attribution to R. Aqiba.

14. Already medieval students of the Babylonian Talmud recognized that at

times positions were attributed to the standard opponent of a particular figure, even though that figure did not make the statement in question. For an example regarding the *Amoraim* Abaye and Rava, see *Tosafot*, Baba Kamma 73b, "amar leh Abaye."

15. See above, note 7. The position of the Pene Moshe here, although not totally unambiguous, would seem to reject this approach, as he does in many places. That is, he does not view this as an argument in principle, but rather that R. Ishmael simply derives the principle from a *qal va-ḥomer* rather than a *gezerah shavah*, for whatever reason. But it apparently would be wrong, according to him, to conclude that R. Ishmael would not learn this *gezerah shavah* in principle. For other explanations of the issue here, see the commentaries of Solomon Sirillo (c. 1530), Joshua Benvenisti (c. 1590–c. 1665), *Sedeh Yehoshua*, and Elijah ben Loeb Foulda (ca.1660–1720), ad loc., the latter two under the influence of the Bavli. See also the convoluted explanation of Ridbaz, ad loc.

16. The *gezerah shavah* involves the use of "give" in Deut. 8:10 (regarding food), and the use of "give" in Exod. 24:12 (regarding the tablets with "the teaching and the commandments").

17 That the "R. Yoḥanan in the name of R. Ishmael" formula does not necessarily denote quotation from the point of view of the redactors of the text can be seen from our analysis of the passage from *Orlah*, below.

18. As to the difficulty that there appear to be two things being derived from this repetition, see the "Shi'are Qorban," ad loc.

19. The exact relationship between the Yerushalmi and *Bereshit Rabbah* is complex; see, Albeck's introduction, pp. 66–84, and esp. 71–72, for a brief comparison between the Yerushalmi and BR passages relevant here. Albeck concludes that the passage in BR drew on an different version of our *sugya* (to be more precise, on a different version of the Yerushalmi) but not our *sugya* as is. In general, I am very skeptical of such pronouncements, as they are based on the judgment (essentially religious in nature) that the compiler of BR should not be "suspected" of the arrogance required to create anew in the name of others, but rather he "certainly found the *sugyot* in this language [in which they are cited in BR] in the Talmud which he used" (ibid., p. 71). Here, however, it may well be the case that BR drew on an earlier version of this *sugya*, since it seems that the *ad kedon* material dates from the period of the final redaction of the Talmud, for so many of its judgments seem unknown to (or unaccepted by) relatively late *Amoraim* such as R. Yudah B. Pazi, and to late documents such as *Devarim Rabbah*.

20. I have deviated from the order of the tractates in the belief that the discussion of the Shabbat passage was easier to follow than the ensuing discussion of the *Orlah* passage.

21. The Talmud throughout ignores the one, and refers simply to one hundred and two hundred. This may be a form of shorthand, or simply due to the fact that one hundred and two hundred accurately express the difference between substances in the mixtures in question.

22. So Rabinowitz, *Sha'are Torat Ereṣ Yisra'el*, p. 135, and Epstein, *Mavo'ot*, p. 524 n. 47. The Pene Moshe does not relate the "according to R. Aqiba" judgment to the issue of *lemed milemed*; this is in accord with his usual ap-

proach of viewing the *ad kedon* passages as being based on different sources rather than as being based on the give-and-take of the redactors. Thus, here he feels that the *ad kedon* is elicited by "R. Yohanan in the name of R. Ishmael. . . ." It should be pointed out that in a number of cases, as we shall see, the Yerushalmi actually states that its objections are in fact systematic and methodological. See, e.g., Shabbat 19:2 (just discussed) and Kiddushin 1:2 (59a). The Pene Moshe seems to feel that when the Yerushalmi does not explicitly state that the *ad kedon* is elicited by the assumption that R. Ishmael would not learn said *derashah*, it must be elicited by a different *baraita*, which contains a conflicting view in the name of R. Ishmael. As we shall see, this position is untenable, and was implicitly recognized as such by the Qorban ha-'Edah. See also the comments of the Gaon of Vilna, ad loc., who thinks that the *ad kedon* objection is based on the assumption that Ishmael disagrees with the position that there is a prohibition regarding deriving benefit from *'orlah*. Thus, he too discerns no claim regarding methodological differences between the schools in this passage.

23. David Zvi Hoffmann cites the fact that R. Aqiba learns from a *gezerah shavah* while R. Ishmael learns from a *qal va-homer* as an example of the greater simplicity of the latter's approach to Scripture ("während R. Ismael dieselbe Lehre durch einen einfachen logischen Schluss"). Given the particular *qal va-homer* offered, it is difficult to see how it has the advantage of simplicity. Further, since in any event you must say that, as far as this *sugya* is concerned, R. Ishmael learns the first *gezerah shavah*, the whole "simplicity" argument here is thoroughly unconvincing. Thus, he apparently reads the *sugya* as offering no solution to the question of how R. Ishamel would learn the neutralizability of *kil'e hakerem*, nor to the untenability of R. Yohanan's argument. This reading of the *sugya* is simply unacceptable; it obviously motivated by taking the "in the name of" formula too seriously, and by certain preconceived notions regarding the greater simplicity of R. Ishmael's approach to Scripture. See D. Hoffmann, *Zur Einleitung in die halachischen Midraschim* (Berlin: 1886–87), p. 6.

24. See esp. Yerushalmi, Kiddushin 59a, (1:2).

25. See above, "Introduction," pp. 7–24.

26. As to the source of the Yerushalmi's assumption that R. Ishmael will not learn a *lemed milemed*, see Rabinowitz, Sha'are,' who cites a *baraita* in the *Sifre Numbers*. Note though that the Yerushalmi never actually refers to this source, and it is not clear that it knew this *baraita*. In any event, detailed analysis of the *baraita* in question does not support the notion tha R. Ishmael would everywhere reject a *lemed mi-lemed*.

27. See Lev. 20:18. The Yerushalmi explains what this actually means at Yeb. 6:1. According to one opinion this refers to the point at which the penis may be seen between the vaginal labia, while according to another opinion this refers to the insertion of the corona. It is contrasted with finishing the act, which is defined either as ejaculation or as the insertion of the corona (obviously in disagreement with the position that such insertion represents the beginning and not the completion); obviously, the discussion seeks legal definitions.

28. The printed editions of this *Sifra* passage all read as the Bavli (Qiddushin

67b); however, *Codex Assemani* 66, the Rabad, and Rabbenu Hillel have the Yerushalmi's version. The printed editions must have been "corrected" to correspond to the Bavli's reading.

29. See also Malbim to Lev. 21:15.

30. The paradigm of the *Sifra*, Sotah, and Makkot passages leads me to think that the emendation of the text suggested by Qorban ha-'Edah is preferable to that of Rabinowitz, in that with Qorban ha-'Edah's emendation the word YHLL is only used to extend the prohibition to beginning and not to rape; Rabinowitz's emendation has YHLL extending the prohibition to both. I think that the tight reading of this extension (indicating a doubling of the prohibition rather than any plurality) is preferable, in particular given the ordering tendencies of the Talmud.

31. I should point out that this *gezerah shavah* is paralleled at Bavli, Yeb. 55a, where it is neither explained nor challenged in any way. There is no indication that the redactors considered it a *baraita*.

32. The ellipsis includes a discussion by various sages regarding how such a warning would be formulated. Clearly, these sages do not think that the source cited contains a warning for self-denial; rather they assume, with the *Sifra* (see below) and the Bavli, Yoma 81a, that there is in fact no warning in the Torah enjoining self-denial, for the verse cited (Lev. 23:29) is understood as merely offering the punishment, not the warning against transgressing. Thus, the sages here discuss how such a warning ought to be phrased—indeed, whether such phrasing is even possible. I have not filled in the words of the ellipsis because, for our purposes, they are not relevant. I have noted them because they establish immediately that there are different assumptions at work in this *sugya*.

33. See above, chapter 1, pp. 11–12.

34. This material in brackets follows the explanation of Qorban ha-'Edah, who seems to be correct in his understanding of R. Hiyya's words in their redactional context. The explanation of the Pene Moshe fits the words of R. Hiyya far better, but does not account for what they are designed to prove here, which is that work and self-denial apply at night, and transgressions that occur then are punishable. The statement of R. Hiyya, viewed apart from its context here in the Yerushalmi, also assumes that we have no warning for self-denial, and argues that this warning is established by the extraneous report of punishment regarding work. This argument, in its appropriate context, is found, with linguistic variations, in the *Sifra*, Emor 14:9. It is only the Yerushalmi that understands the biblical phrase "throughout that day" as excluding the night of the tenth of Tishre, the Day of Atonement. All other sources understand the phrase as excluding the additional parts of the day (i.e., the evening before; see Lev. 23:32) from punishment, but never consider that the night, which is part of the twenty-four-hour day, can be excluded by this phrase. Because the redactors of this passage understand the issue under discussion differently, all the sources will be reworked by the redactors to fit the context they have established.

35. "Available" in the context of a *gezerah shavah* means that the word or phrase denoted as such may be deemed extraneous in its own context and thus

is a signal that it may be used for a *gezerah shavah*. As for the bracketed "only," see below.

36. I have translated in accord with Qorban ha-'Edah; Pene Moshe insists here that R. Yudan means to suggest that the Aqiban position is that unilateral availability is required. Thus, he is compelled to explain the objection in a way that is forced. I believe that he explains as he does here because of the assumptions of the Bavli regarding this issue, as well as the context, and the fact that the subsequent *gezerah shavah* can be readily judged as available. See below.

37. Again here, I am following the Qorban ha-'Edah, again because he explains in accord with the context of this passage. I have ignored Rabinowitz's extensive emendations of this passage (*Sha'are*, p. 260), as they are unattested elsewhere, and are too clever and convenient.

38. See Hoffmann, *Einleitung*, p. 6; Horowitz, *Sifre al Bamidbar*, "Einleitung," p. vi; Epstein, *Mavo'ot*, pp. 522–24. I should point out that here again these systematizers run into trouble by claiming that R. Ishmael insists on availability in *gezerot shavot* and yet at the same time maintains the principle "that *all* passages which are stated in one place and repeated in another were only repeated to fill in that which was absent"; or, as the Bavli puts it, they "were only repeated for that which was newly-stated [in the second passage]." One of the primary ways of establishing availability in the exegetical texts is by claiming that the law was already stated in some other passage. Thus, in the *Sifra* to Lev. 20 (attributed to the Ishmaelian "school") there are *gezerot shavot* learned, whose availability is established by virtue of the fact that almost all the laws of Lev. 20 were previously stated in Lev. 18. Thus, according to this "Ishmaelian" text, the repetition is not for the novel law, but to establish availability. (See e.g., *Sifra*, Kedoshim 10:9) In fact, the ad hoc and ad locum nature of rabbinic exegesis allows both principles to stand simultaneously (although "all" in such passages refers to the actual passage under discussion and nothing more. Similarly, the phrase, "ein x ela y," although stated in an unqualified manner, always refers only to the word defined in the specific case).

39. Epstein, *Maro'ot*, supports this judgment by pointing out that only the "Ishmaelian" midrashim do we find the phrase *mufneh lehakish veladun gezerah shavah*. But this need be nothing more than a redactional distinction. The real issue is how the documents actually construct *gezerot shavot*. The *gezerah shavah* found in this *sugya* (at 2) is in fact found anonymously in the "Aqiban" portion of the *Sifra*, Emor 14:9. It is quite clear that the author of this passage was very concerned to establish the extraneity of one of the verses pertaining to work, so as to apply it, through the medium of a *gezerah shavah,* to self-denial. Thus, the absence of the phrase *mufneh lehakish*, etc., is not decisive.

40. The Bavli reckons this *gezerah shavah* available in its way. See Yoma 81a. One could simplify the matter by pointing out that the phrase actually occurs twice in relation to work (Lev. 23:28, 30), and one of them could, by rabbinic standards, be judged available. The point, however, is that the redactors have no interest in pursuing the matter in this direction, for when all is said here, they have succeeded in providing three different scriptural justifications for the law under discussion, which seems to be the passage's primary interest.

41. Albeck already recognized that the use of "tani R. Ishmael" in the Yerushalmi does not imply the citation of an actual source that quotes R. Ishmael, albeit for different reasons. See his *Meḥqarim be-Vraita ve-Tosefta ve-Yaḥsan La Talmud* (Jerusalem: Mossad ha-Rav Kook, 1969), pp. 43–44.

42. See e.g., Baba Kamma (BK) 5:8, *hashev teshivem* and *'azov ta'azov;* BK 7:1, *himatze timatze,* BK 8:2, *verapo yerape;* Baba Meziah (BM) 9:12 *havol tahbol.* In addition the Talmud takes no note of the Mishnah's *derashah* at BM 2:10, to which compare Yerushalmi, Sotah 5:1

43. But compare Bavli, Pes. 41a, where the dispute is recorded in the names of "Our Rabbis" (= the position attributed to R. Ishmael here) and Rabbi (Judah the Prince).

44. I am assuming the reliability of the *Mekhilta* tradition here. We should not overlook the possibility however that in fact this passage of the *Mekhilta* was influenced by the Yerushalmi's *derashot* and identification of the authors of these *derashot.* That is, the form of the *sugya* (based on almost all the others) suggests that the Yerushalmi is not reporting traditions here, but rather constructing positions based on its assumptions. In the absence of any other evidence to support this position, it seems preferable to accept the reliability of the *Mekhilta* passage and see it as one of the few foundation stones of the Yerushalmi's generalized conclusions regarding Rabbis Aqiba and Ishmael.

45. On this see the discussion of the Bavli material above. I should point out here that once again the assumptions of Hoffmann and Epstein collide with one another. On the basis of the *Mekhilta* passage and the Yerushalmi's generalization from it, they both assume that R. Ishmael would not expound repetition. They also assume that the *Mekhilta,* among other documents, provides a good reflection of R. Ishmael's method. Yet the immediately previous passage in the *Mekhilta* anonymously expounds the same repetition, for another purpose, without any methodological objection being raised. So too with the immediately following passage (where the *derashah* is cited in the name of Rabbi). In fact, this phenomenon is also to be found in the other supposedly "Ishmaelean" midrash, the *Sifre Numbers.* It is further to be noted that with one (in my view unreliable) exception (on which see above, chapter 2), nowhere do we find R. Ishmael raising a methodological objection to the exposition of repetition in the tannaitic stratum, even though such objections are to be found (such as the "dayo" principle associated with the *qal va-ḥomer*).

46. See further Albeck's supplementary notes to this mishnah in *Shisha Sidre Mishnan: Seder Nashim,* p. 384.

47. Epstein, *Mavo,* p. 83, understands the Yerushalmi as quoting a separate *baraita* rather than quoting differing versions of the Mishnah. I believe that he does so because of the problem pointed out in the text, but I do not think that this understanding is justified.

48. Because of the difficulties Rabbi's presence in the mishnah creates, Epstein, *Mavo,* p. 84, posits that the Yerushalmi did not have the "Rabbi" passage in its Mishnah, although it is found in the Palestinian Mishnah manuscripts (Kaufmann and Lowe). Given the way in which the Yerushalmi operates regarding Rabbis Aqiba and Ishmael, this hardly seems necessary. The fact that

the Rabbi passage is not cited does lend support to Epstein's interpretation of the Mishnah, which is similar to that of Rabinovitz.

49. In accord with the version of the Yerushalmi I have presented, Rabbi is seen as arguing with R. Aqiba. In accord with Rabinovitz's emendation, Rabbi is in fact merely commenting on the position of R. Aqiba. See Albeck, *Seder Nashim*, p. 384.

50. This is not to suggest that there is no reason to think that R. Ishmael was involved in this issue; see *Sifre Numbers*, Naso, 7, where it is apparent that R. Ishmael learns that she is prohibited to both her husband and paramour from the repetition of "she has defiled herself"; so too does R. Aqiba there.

51. See, further, Yerushalmi, Sotah 7:5, where the verse (Num. 13:2) "one man, one man per tribe" is understood, "according to the opinion of R. Aqiba," as implying that in fact the spy delegation consisted of twenty-four rather than twelve spies, while "according to the opinion of R. Ishmael" there were twelve. The surrounding context leaves little doubt that these claims derive from the amoraic or (post-amoraic?) redactional stratum of the text; the authors have adopted what they believe to be exclusively Aqiban methodology to explicate the repetition of the verse.

52. The presentation that follows is largely taken from my article "Between Tradition and *Wissenschaft*: Modern Students of Midrash Halakhah," in Jack Wertheimer, ed., *The Uses of Tradition: Jewish Continuity in the Modern Era* (New York: Jewish Theological Seminary, 1992), pp. 261–78, and is reprinted here by permission.

53. For the purposes of this book it makes little difference how we date this material. My own view is that the *Mekhilta, Sifra,* and *Sifre* are products of the first half of the third century. In any event, I take for granted that, whenever these specific texts emerged, much of the material contained therein was known to the redactors of the Talmuds, and was considered by them to be legitimately tannaitic.

54. This diversity of opinion may result in an exegetical dispute, in which the principals agree regarding the law but disagree regarding its biblical "source," or it may result in an actual legal dispute in which the principals disagree regarding the legal contours of the verse(s) in question.

55. See the comments of the Tosafists at Bavli, Sotah 24a, s.v. "ve-Rabbi Yoḥanan," etc. and at Bavli, Menahot 17b, s.v. "Mai he'akhel ye'akhel," etc. See also Samson of Qinon's *Sefer ha-Keritot*, pt. 5, 1:30.

56. See Bavli, Yebamot 68b and the parallels noted there.

57. See the *Tosafot* at Bavli, Menahot 51b, s.v. "vav lo darish" and the parallels noted there. See also Bavli, Yebamot 72b, where the anonymous voice of the Gemara (the *stam*) states that even those who do not interpret *vavin,* interpret *vav ve-he,* again indicating how the redactors are prepared to attribute techniques to *Tannaim* to suit their own needs.

58. The one exception concerns the use of the techniques of *ribui u-mi'ut* and *kelal u-ferat.* Already the Tosefta (Shevuot 1:7) associates the former with R. Aqiba and the latter with R. Ishmael, and this position is echoed by the Talmuds. See the discussion in Michael Chernick's *Hermeneutical Studies in*

Talmudic and Midrashic Literature (in Hebrew) (Haberman Institute: 1984). Even here, as Chernick makes clear, the distinction is often blurred.

59. One example is the passage at Yerushalmi, Shabbat 19:2. Here the Talmud asks whence we know that both *pri 'ah* and *milah* are required for an acceptable circumcision. It cites a scriptural repetition (*himol yimol*, Gen. 17:13) and comments that this *derashah* is in accord with the system of R. Aqiba, who interprets such repetitions. Whence, the Talmud goes on to ask, do we know the law according to the system of R. Ishmael? It then cites the *derashah* of R. Yudah b. Pazi, an *Amora*, who interprets the plural word *lamulot* as signifying the requirement in question. Now, the first, allegedly Aqiban, *derashah* is found in *Bereshit Rabbah* (46:13, Theodor-Albeck, 1:468) without any mention of R. Aqiba. As to the second *derashah*, nowhere does R. Yudah indicate that his interpretation is in accord with the system of R. Ishmael; nor does he indicate that he is opposed, in principle, to the allegedly Aqiban *derashah*. This is also the case in the parallel passage found in *Devarim Rabbah* (very beginning of parshah 6, p. 111d in the Vilna edition) in which both *derashot* are presented but there is no mention of Rabbis Aqiba and Ishmael at all. Finally, it is to be noted that same *derashah* is presented at Yerushalmi, Nedarim 3:9 anonymously, again with no mention of its place in R. Ishmael's system. It is the redactors of this passage who link R. Ishmael to this *derashah*, on the assumption that he would oppose the "Aqiban" *derashah*, but still agree with the legal requirement of *pri'ah* and *milah*.

Chapter 4. Midrash in the Middle Ages

1. For a much more detailed discussion of the influence of Islam on the exegesis of R. Saadia Gaon and R. Shmuel b. Ḥofni Gaon—the two most prominent early commentators within the Islamic world—see Moshe Zucker, *Perushe Rav Saadia Gaon le-Vereshit* (Jerusalem: Jewish Theological Seminary, 1984), pp. 35–69.

2. Although see now Haggai Ben-Shammai, "Between Ananites and Karaites: Observations on Early Medieval Jewish Sectarianism," in Ronald L. Nettler, ed., *Studies in Muslim-Jewish Relations*, vol. 1 (Chur, Switzerland: Harwood Academic, 1993), pp. 19–29.

3. The phrase is found at Isaiah 29:13; obviously the phrase was meant to direct one to this verse and the consequences of adhering to such *mitzvot* are spelled out in the next verse—the loss of wisdom and understanding. By following the oral law, Rabbanite Jews lose their ability to properly understand the Bible, which is sufficient to teach the word of God to those who know how to read it properly.

4. See Naftali Wieder, *The Judean Scrolls and Karaism* (London: East-West Library, 1962) p. 71. Especially instructive are his citations from al-Qumisi, who writes, "[W]e have abandoned the Torah of Moses to go astray after the commandments of men, learned by rote"; and Yehudah ibn Qoreish, who asks, "[W]hy should we accept the word of Ravina and Rav Ashi [the presumed compilers of the Bavli] when we have the Torah of Moses?"

5. See ibid., pp. 73–77.

6. See ibid., pp. 82–85.

7. See Salmon ben Yeruḥim, *Sefer Milḥamot Hashem,* ed. Israel Davidson (New York: Jewish Theological Seminary, 1934), pp. 47–50. Salmon proceeds to argue that one does not need an oral tradition in order to know the times for the Sabbaths and holidays—indeed, rabbinic halakhah, particularly as articulated by Saadia, has clearly corrupted the Bible's message—nor for anything else. The messianic age is adequately described in the prophetic books, and here again recourse to the "tradition" leads one astray.

8. For discussion of this motto, and various scholarly opinions pertaining to its Ananite provenance, see Wieder, *Judean Scrolls,* pp. 88–89. Cf. Haim Hillel Ben-Sasson, *Perakim Be-Toledot ha-Yehudim Bime ha-Beinaim* (Tel Aviv: Am Oved, 1977), p. 163, and Ben-Shammai, "Between Ananites," p. 22 and n. 34 there and the literature cited there.

9. See Leon Nemoy, *Karaite Anthology* (New Haven: Yale University Press, 1952), pp. 8–9.

10. See A. A. Harkavy, *Sefer ha-Mitzvot le-Anan ha-Nasi* (St. Petersburg, 1903), pp. xi–xii.

11. See Yehudah Hadassi, *Eshkol ha-Kofer,* (1836) alphabet 162, mem.

12. Ibid., alph. 163, aleph.

13. Ibid., 163–74. See especially alphabets 170 and 171, where Hadassi discusses *kellal u-ferat* and *binyan av,* expanding each category beyond what is offered in the "Baraita de-Rabi Ishmael," but clearly dependent on it.

14. See esp. Wieder, *Judean Scrolls,* p. 74.

15. There are, of course, rabbinic precedents for this position, the best known being the statement of Ben Bag Bag in Avot 5:22. Of course, in rabbinic parlance such descriptions of the "Torah" are inherently ambiguous, since the term "Torah" may refer to the entire Torah, oral and written. And, in any event, it is not at all clear precisely what the phrase *hafokh bah* actually means.

16. It is clear that for Saadia the Torah was first committed to writing in the fortieth year of Israel's sojourn in the desert; prior to that time the "written" Torah was also transmitted orally. See Zucker, *Perushe,* p. 185, and note 101 there.

17. As has been noted by many, Saadia, in his polemics against the Karaites, insisted that the institutionalized calendar in use in his day was part of the oral tradition and had always been in place. Karaites delighted in pointing out the numerous places in which the Talmud contradicted this claim, and other flaws in this theory as well. See Salmom ben Yeruḥim, *Milḥamot,* cantos 4–8, esp. 5–6.

18. See Zucker, *Perushe,* p. 184 n. 96 for a review of the different positions in rabbinic literature regarding this matter. Saadia's presentation is interesting, since in general it seems that the Bavli considers the contract a decree of the sages, while the Yerushalmi considers it *de-oraita,* of scriptural origin.

19. As Isadore Twersky points out, in the introduction to his *Siddur* Saadia advanced a position generally associated with Maimonides, namely, that prayer is commanded *mi-de-oraita.* Obviously, such a view informs Saadia's discussion here. See Isadore Twersky, *Introduction to the Code of Maimonides (Mishneh Torah)* (New Haven: Yale University Press, 1980), p. 225 n. 79.

20. Salmon b. Yeruḥim in turn rejected all these as necessitating an oral tradition (see *Milḥamot*, pp. 47–50), as did Yaqub al Qirqisani (Zucker, *Perushe*, p. 181 n. 86).

21. For fringes see Bavli, Menahot, 39b; see the Tosafist there, s.v. "Vehahi gedilim leminyana," who, with his last question, makes clear that he does not consider the matter a piece of oral tradition. For vessels, see the extensive discussion in the *Sifra*, Shemini, parsha 6 and perek 8.

22. B. M. Lewin, ed., *Esa Meshali* (Jerusalem: Mossad ha-Rav Kook, 1942), pp. 46–47.

23. Shraga Abramson, *Inyanot be Sifrut ha-Geonim* (Jerusalem: Mossad ha-Rav Kook, 1974), p. 52, lines 13–14 and notes thereto.

24. Lewin, *Esa Meshali*, p. 32, lines 9–10.

25. Ibid., p. 45. Naftali Wieder also emphasizes the importance of this stanza. He writes, "Here we see Sa'adya actually staking the whole cause of the Oral Law on this argument; it stands and falls with it (Wieder, *Judean Scrolls*, p. 74). The argument referred to is that Scripture is not self-sufficient, and cannot generate from within itself a complete understanding of its provisions.

26. See Halivni, *Peshat and Derash*, pp. 13–16.

27. On which, see *Emunot ve-De'ot*, chap. 3.

28. Abraham Halkin, "Mi-Petiḥat Rav Saadia Gaon le-Ferush ha-Torah," in *Sefer ha-Yovel Likhvod Levi Ginzberg* (New York, 1946), p. 132 n. 19.

29. Ibid., p. 155.

30. It is important to note that in the Bavli, this is not a matter of logic but rather the result of a direct scriptural analogy, which comes to obviate the need for relying on logic, for (some say) we may not punish on the basis of an argument a fortiori. Here we rely on an explicitly identified *hekkesh* (analogy) to learn the law in question.

31. See above, chapter 2. In light of all this, I would disagree strongly with the description of Saadia's thinking in Yeruham Fischel Perla's *Sefer ha-Mitzvot le-Rasaq*, who argues that Saadia would not count in the 613 commandments anything that derives from the thirteen principles if it involved the filling in of details, but would if it were an independent principle in its own right. In particular, his claim that Saadia felt that "anything learned from one of the hermeneutic principles is as though it were specified in the Torah for all purposes" seems unacceptable. Saadia would deny that anything is actually learned this way. As for his commentary on the *baraita* of R. Ishmael, there is nothing here that challenges the interpretation offered. The *baraita* was a rabbinic source—an oft-quoted one that required explanation. Saadia's commentary makes no claim regarding the source of apparently derived laws, but merely explains how the principles are applied. An analogous procedure is followed by David Nieto in his *Mateh Dan;* Nieto explicitly denies the creative force of midrash, but feels the need to explain the *baraita* anyway. See below, chapter 5.

32. As for how Saadia would deal with this, see S. Poznanski, "Anti-Karaite Writings of Saadiah Gaon," *Jewish Quarterly Review,* o.s. 10:264–73. For sources that might be seen as supporting Saadia and a full discussion of the issues, see M. Kasher, *Torah Shlemah*, 13:40–66.

33. See *Sefer Teshuvot Dunash Halevi ben Labrat al Rabi Saadia Gaon,* ed. Robert Schroter (rpt., Jerusalem, 1971), esp. nos. 3, 8, 12, 15, 19, 45, 59, and 62, inter alia.

34. The claim here is not merely that the Mishnah explains obscure biblical words on the basis of tradition. It is that these obscure words are part of the living linguistic material from which the Mishnah is constructed. Thus, to take the most interesting and obviously mistaken example, the word or phrase *lig'e yonim* (Ps. 123:4) is explained by Saadia as the Mishnaic word *ligeyon,* which in fact comes from the Latin "legion." (Dunash jumps all over him for this, and even Ibn Ezra, who generally defends Saadia from Dunash's attacks, agrees that Saadia has this one wrong. His consolation seems to be that Dunash got it wrong as well.) In any event, for Saadia, given his sense of the historical place of the Mishnah, this procedure makes sense. Where should one turn if not the Mishnah, whose contents were largely contemporaneous with the Bible?

35. A similar argument, mutatis mutandis, is offered by the seventeenth-century Catholic biblical critic Richard Simon, who argued that an appreciation of the true meaning of Scripture would fully reveal the latter's inadequacy, creating the need for authentic Catholic tradition to create a comprehensible and authoritative understanding of the document. See below, chapter 5, and references there.

36. *Ozar ha-Geonim,* Baba Kamma no. 68 (to BK 28a)

37. See ibid., Rosh Hashanah no.117 (to RH 33b). Part of this *responsum* is cited in English translation by Zvi Groner in his *Legal Methodology of Hai Gaon* (Chico, Calif.: Scholars Press, 1985), pp. 16–17.

38. Lewin, ed., *Iggeret Rav Sherira Gaon,* chap. 5.

39. "Mevo ha-Talmud," in Vilna ed. of Bavli, Berakhot, p. 46a of second pagination.

40. See *Kuzari,* 3:35 (ed. Even-Shemuel, p. 125–26).

41. Ibid., 3:39, 41, 49, 50 (pp. 127–28, 130, 134, 136).

42. Ibid., 3:73 (p. 149). See also the comments of Yehudah Moscato to these passages in his *Qol Yehudah,* printed in "traditional" editions of the *Kuzari.*

43. See the "regular" introduction in Asher Weisser, *Ibn Ezra al ha-Torah,* 3 vols. (Jerusalem: Mossad ha-Rav Kook, 1977), 1:2.

44. Ibid., p. 5; see also his "other" introduction in ibid., p. 138.

45. Ibid., p. 138.

46. Abraham Ibn Ezra, *Yesod Mora ve-Sod Torah,* chap. 6, in *Kitve R. Avraham Ibn Ezra* (Jerusalem: Makor, 1970), 2:9–10.

47. For other examples, see his comments to Exod. 21:8, esp. in the short commentary. Ibn Ezra's discussion was evoked by the fifteenth-century Karaite Eliyahu Bashyatchi in his *Sefer ha-Mitzvot Aderet Eliyahu* (1966), p. 4. His comments are interesting: "And our tradition (*ha'atakah*) is not like the tradition (*qabbalah*) in which they believe because they add and detract from Scripture, and say that the tradition will prevail [over arguments in opposition] (*ha-qabbalah tenatzeach*) while the Scripture screams 'Do not add to that which I have commanded you.' Now if their intent is to interpret the words of prophecy

they should not say the tradition will prevail. As when they say, 'You shall smite him forty times' means forty less one, or when they say that the husband inherits his wife's property from the verse 'and he shall inherit it/her,' although a few of them have said that this is only an *asmakhta be'alma*. . . . And they have added to Scripture and said that a husband inherits his wife. Indeed, the tradition (*ha'atakah*) of all Israel acknowledges this, and does not stand against that which is stated in Scripture."

48.   See Weisser's note 21 to chapter 13 of the long commentary.

49.   Again, this is different from *asmakhta*, where the tradition has nothing to do with the interpretation of the verse. There it is merely attached to the verse for mnemonic or some other concerns.

50.   See Ibn Ezra to Lev. 11:32. Other relevant comments are found at Exod. 21:2, 14; Lev. 7:20, 20:19, 21, 21:2, 23:11; Num. 27:11; Deut. 12:15, inter alia.

51.   Strange as it may seem, it appears to me that Abraham Maimuni was actually closer to the conception of Saadia and Ibn Ezra than to that of his father. See his comments to Exodus 20, verses 7, 9, 13, 14; Exodus 21, verses 1, 16, 24; Exodus 22, verses 4, 13, inter alia, in his *Perush al Bereshit Shemot* (London, 1958).

52.   Maimonides, *Commentary on the Mishnah,* ed. and trans. Yosef Kafiḥ, 3 vols. (Jerusalem: Mossad ha-Rav Kook, 1976), 1:11. See also *Mishneh Torah*, Mamrim, 1:3.

53.   Maimonides, *Commentary*.

54.   Ibid., p. 10.

55.   Ibid., p. 11. Maimonides argues against "one who thought that even laws that are disputed are part of the tradition from Moses." No doubt he had Saadia, inter alia, in mind. See Saadia's introduction to his Torah commentary, in Zucker, *Perushe,* 187–88.

56.   Ibid.

57.   Ibid.

58.   For a discussion of the legal distinctions, see Menahem Elon, *ha-Mishpat ha-'Ivri,* 2 vols. (Jerusalem: Magnes Press, 1978), pp. 194–207.

59.   *Sefer ha-Mitzvot,* ed. Chavel (Jerusalem: Mossad ha-Rav Kook, 1981), p. 48

60.   For this reason, the explanation of the Yad Halevi, cited by Chavel, needs to be refined. Maimonides is not saying that these exegeses are really *asmakhtot,* in the exegetical sense that they do not produce the laws. They are real readings of Scripture, that genuinely produce law. They are, however, *asmakhtot* in the legal sense, in that they do not produce laws that are binding *mi-deoraita.*

61.   See esp. ibid., pp. 45–46, and David Weiss Halivni, *Peshat and Derash: Plain and Applied Meaning in Rabbinic Exegesis* (New York: Oxford University Press, 1991), pp. 83–88. One should not conclude on the basis of Maimonides' concern for the plain meaning of the text that he was in fact committed to *peshat.* Clearly his whole philosophical enterprise is built on the assumption that the Torah communicates metaphysical knowledge, while at the same time it speaks in human language. This means that the Torah accommodated its

message to its audience, hiding its secrets for only the initiated to discover. See Amos Funkenstein, *Theology and the Scientific Imagination in the Seventeenth Century* (Princeton: Princeton University Press, 1986), pp. 213–43; Stephen D. Benin, *The Footprints of God: Divine Accommodation in Jewish and Christian Thought* (Albany: SUNY Press, 1993), pp. 139–67. The same position stands behind Saadia's philosophical work. Even Ibn Ezra, while ostensibly objecting to the esoteric exegesis that animates this approach (in his description of the third method of exegesis; Weisser, *Ibn Ezra al ha-Torah*, 1:6–7), nevertheless engages in such exegesis himself.

Certainly, Maimonides was not committed to a text that only carries a plain meaning. Nevertheless, in halakhic matters, the plain meaning of the text was paramount. In the introduction to the *Guide of the Perplexed* he clearly differentiates between the parabolic and allegorical significance of the nonhalakhic parts of the Torah and the laws of sukkah, lulav and the like, which are intended to convey the necessity to perform these commandments, and nothing more. Similarly, when discussing the significance of the laws in the third part of the *Guide,* Maimonides once again limits his understanding of many of these laws to their plain meaning. See, e.g., *Guide,* 3:41. On this see Ya'aqob Levinger, *Ha-Rambam ke-Filosof u-khe-foseq* (Jerusalem: Mossad Bialik, 1989), pp. 56–66; also his earlier work, *Darkhe ha-Maḥashavah ha-Hilkhatit shel ha-Rambam* (Jerusalem, 1965). See also the important comments of Gerald J. Blidstein, "Where Do We Stand in the Study of Maimonidean Halakhah?" in Isadore Twersky, ed., *Studies in Maimonides* (Cambridge: Harvard University Press, 1991), pp. 14–15.

62. In addition to the material to be cited below and that cited by Neubauer (see below), see, e.g., Yair Bacharach's *Ḥavvot Yair* no. 192, who commends Maimonides for trying to build a reinforced barrier around the oral law, by insisting that it is not subject to forgetting or disputes; yet he loses more than he gains by saying that "all the disputes of the sages, which represent the vast majority of the oral law and the orders of the Mishnah are not at all from Sinai" (p. 102b).

63. It was maintained by Abraham Maimonides, Yehudah Moscato, Joseph Ibn Kaspi, Yosef Bonfil, Don Isaac Abravanel, and others.

64. There are exceptions to this generalization, to be sure. A number of them have been collected by Urbach in his *Ba'ale ha-Tosafot,* 2:701–2, esp. notes 17 and 18. There are occasions in which Rashi also feels compelled to categorize a talmudic *derashah* as an *asmakhta* (see Sotah 24b, s.v. "ana de-amre afilu ke-Rabbi Yonatan"; Sotah 25a, s.v. "u-Shmuel de-amar ana de-amre afilu le-Rabbi Yoshayah"; Kiddushin, 57b, s.v. "Rava amar"; BM 92a, s.v. "ka nasiv"; and AZ 48b, s.v. "ve-avar taḥteha"). In all these cases the *derashot* are so categorized because of the impact of the talmudic discussion, or, in the last case, because the law is identified elsewhere as being *mi-derabbanan.* They are not considered *asmakhtot* because they offend against the sense of how Scripture should be read, as is the case with, say, Ibn Ezra. Compare Rashi, *Berakhot* 11a, s.v. "midrash." The one exception regarding a halakhic midrash known to me is at *Ketubot* 45b, s.v. "petaḥ mi-petaḥ u-petaḥ mi-sha'ar." As for Rashbam,

his position is well known; for all his interest in *peshat*, he insisted that the *derash* is primary (*'ikkar*). See his comments to Gen. 37:2, and see Halivni, *Peshat and Derash*, pp. 27–28.

65. In truth, Maimonides affirmed this principle in the introduction to his Mishnah commentary. It seems to me, however, that he understood the meaning of this proposition in entirely different terms. For Naḥmanides, the fact that the hermenutic principles were given by God at Sinai, which was actually a rather recent claim, granted a higher level of integrity to the interpretive process. It did not preclude disputes but made it easier to regard the product of rabbinic exegesis as genuinely reflective of the divine will. For Maimonides, by contrast, the fact that the hermeneutic principles had divine sanction could not change the fact that the exegeses were still the product of human reason, and subject to dispute. Using these divinely ordained techniques to interpret the Torah may fulfill a divine imperative, and grants the exegeses produced authority; the exegeses themselves still cannot be considered as definitively reflective of the divine will .

66. *Sefer ha-Mitzvot*, p. 31.

67. Ibid., p. 42.

68. Ibid., p. 45.

69. Responding to his reading of Maimonides, which insists that everything not explicitly identified as a law *mi-deoraita* is an *asmakhta*, Naḥmanides writes that "on the contrary, everything exegeted in the Talmud with one of the thirteen exegetical principles is *mi-deoraita* until we hear them saying that it is an *asmakhta*" (ibid., p. 34). For further discussion of Naḥmanides, see Bernard Septimus, "'Open Rebuke and Concealed Love': Naḥmanides and the Andalusian Tradition," in Isadore Twersky, ed., *Rabbi Moses Naḥmanides (Ramban): Explorations in His Religious and Literary Virtuosity* (Cambridge: Harvard University Press, 1983), pp. 11–34; Elliot R. Wolfson, "By Way of Truth: Aspects of Naḥmanides' Kabbalistic Hermeneutic," *Association for Jewish Studies Review* 14, no. 2 (Fall 1989): 103–78.

70. Naḥmanides goes on to note that the holy spirit rests on the servants of the Lord, guarding them from error. I do not take this to mean that Naḥmanides precludes the possibility of error from ever creeping into rabbinic decisions and deliberations. Even if he does, each person is instructed to accept the teachings of the authorities even if he or she thinks they are in error; thus, objective error may be precluded, but the subjective sense of error is always possible.

71. *Sefer ha-Mitzvot*, p. 51.

72. See his *Responsa*, vol. 1, no. 1185, where, quoting Alfasi, he affirms that "all that is derived from midrash is *de-oraita*." The context is a challenge to the scriptural status of the disqualification of witnesses based on Deut. 24:16, on which see chapter 1. See also Menahem ha-Meiri, *Beit ha-Behirah al Masekhet Avot* (Jerusalem: Makhon ha-Talmud ha-Yisraeli ha-Shalem, 1964), pp. 9–32, esp. 20–21.

73. See his *Derashot*, vol. 1, 19b, 38a, 41b, 71a, 81a.

74. Maimonides, *Mishneh Torah*, Hilkhot Ḥovel u-Maziq, 1:6. Cf. ibid, 1:5, where Maimonides provides a biblical justification for compensation rather

than actual talion (one that, as *Leḥem Mishneh* notes, is not found in the talmudic discussion at BK 83b–84a). Despite this apparent illumination of the plain meaning of the Torah as it relates to *ḥaburah,* Maimonides writes at 1:6 that the law of monetary compensation is not drawn from the Torah. This is so, perhaps, because in the end the teaching at 1:5 involves extending a principle established for *ḥaburah* to the other forms of injury noted in the Torah. Such an extension could only be justified if it were a *halakhah le-Moshe mi-Sinai* that all bodily injury results in monetary compensation.

75. Solomon Luria, *Yam Shel Shelomoh Baba Kamma,* 8:1. See Halivni, *Peshat and Derash,* p. 201 n. 77. I have highlighted the phrase "the words of the sages are sufficient without any tradition" to draw attention to the fact that this question was the crux of the whole matter. At different times and places rabbinic Jews felt confidence that the teachings of the sages were sufficient, even if that meant that law developed and changed over time. At other times and places, rabbinic Jews had no such confidence.

76. See *Yam shel Shelomoh,* BK, introduction.

77. On which see Jacob Elbaum, *Petiḥut ve-Histagrut* (Jerusalem: Magnes Press, 1990).

78. See also *Yam shel Shelomoh,* Yeb. 1:2, where Luria takes Maimonides to task for abandoning a talmudic midrash and replacing it with one of his own. He insists that Maimonides' midrash could lead to unacceptable halakhic conclusions, thus indicating that, as far as he is concerned, midrash creates law, and that the midrash of the Talmud is superior, halakhically, to that of Maimonides. For a discussion of the attitude of Moses Isserles, Luria's contemporary and frequent disputant, on the issues under consideration here, see Yonah Ben-Sasson, *Mishnato ha-Iyyunit shel ha-Rema* (Jerusalem: Israel Academy of Sciences and Humanities, 1984), pp. 184–91.

79. Yeḥezkel Landau, *Ḥiddushe ha-Ṣelaḥ,* p. 2b. As for what the thirteen principles have to do with connecting the two Torahs, one must consider the following "facts" found throughout the various rabbinic documents: The written Torah ends with the words "before the eyes of all Israel." What occurred before the eyes of all Israel? Moses' shattering of the first tablets. How did Moses know that he could shatter the tablets? He derived it from a *qal va-ḥomer.* What is the first of the thirteen principles? A *qal va-ḥomer.* What is the first tractate in the Mishnah? Berakhot. How do we know that one must make *berakhot* (blessings) before eating? We derive this from a *qal va-ḥomer.* Thus the written Torah ends with a *qal va-ḥomer;* the thirteen principles begin with a *qal va-ḥomer;* the first tractate in the oral Torah founded on the thirteen principles bases one of its central requirements on a *qal va-ḥomer.* And thus, in this beautiful *pilpul,* the two Torahs are connected. That is why the Mishnah begins with *Berakhot.*

80. He writes, "And R. Aqiba b. Yosef received [the tradition] from R. Eliezer the Great [i.e., Eliezer ben Hyrcanos], and Joseph his father was a righteous convert. R. Ishmael and R. Meir, the son of a righteous convert, received it from R. Aqiba." This would imply that Ishmael was Aqiba's student. He goes on though and claims, "R. Meir and his colleagues also received it from

R. Ishmael," thus implying that Ishmael assumed a teaching status before Aqiba's other students, and in the latter's lifetime. See his introduction to the *Mishneh Torah;* see also his *Commentary on the Mishnah,* Eduyyot, chapter 2. Virtually all other chroniclers disagree with Maimonides' claim. See esp. Abraham Zacuto, *Sefer Yuhasin,* ed. H. Filipowski (Frankfurt a.M., 1924), p. 25.

81. See especially *Sefer Yuhasin* and the *Seder ha-Dorot,* each of which engage in extensive discussion of who this R. Ishmael was (assuming there were others). In attempting to locate him in time, surely the position of the Yerushalmi would have been relevant, for it presents them in ostensibly direct discussion and as the dominant exegetical voices of their age. And yet no mention of this position is to be found in their work.

82. See Maimonides' introduction to his *Mishneh Torah.*

83. Isaac Hirsh Weiss, "Mavo'ot ha-Talmud ve-Toldotehem," in *Beit Talmud,* 1:87. If the author of this work was Shmuel ibn Hannaniah Nagid, the Egyptian Nagid of the twelfth century (rather than the better known Spanish scholar of the previous century), the question of precedence becomes murky, as the *Mevo ha-Talmud* may have been written after 1160, as claimed by Mordecai Margoliot in the introduction to his *Sefer Hilkhot ha-Nagid* (Jerusalem: 1962), pp. 72–73. See, in general, Weiss, "Mavo'ot," pp. 68–73.

84. Obviously, a *Mekhilta* of R. Shim'on was known to Maimonides, who, as M. Kasher has shown, drew from it. See his *Ha-Rambam ve- ha-Mekhilta d'Rashbi;* cf. Solomon Zeitlin's review "Maimonides and the Mekilta of Rabbi Simon ben Yochai," reprinted in his *Studies in the Early History of Judaism* (New York: Ktav, 1978), 4:337–39. Further, it is clear that the compilers of the *Midrash ha-Gadol,* whose relationship to Maimonides has yet to be sorted out, also knew of this text, as they frequently cite it. Whether Maimonides considered this to be the *Mekhilta* of R. Aqiba remains an open question. The later bibliographers, though, combine the two and claim that this *Mekhilta* of R. Shim'on was compiled by "Shim'on b. Azzai [*sic*] in the name of his teacher R. Aqiba. [It starts with] Leviticus and runs through the end of the Torah" (*Seder ha-Dorot,* "Shemot ha-Sefarim," s.v. "Mekhilta").

85. See esp. the treatment of R. Ishmael in *Sefer Yuhasin,* pp. 25 32.

86. For a brief discussion of this work, see E. E. Urbach, *Ba'ale ha-Tosafot* (4) (Jerusalem: Mossad Bialik, 1980), 2:720–22.

87. See above chapter 2, p. 46, and chapter 3, pp. 58–59. See *Sefer Keritut,* pt. 2.

88. See *Sefer Keritut,* pt. 1, "house" 2, "rooms" 6–8.

89. See ibid., pt. 5, "gate" 1, par. 30.

90. See Daniel Boyarin, *Ha-Iyyun ha-Sephardi* (Jerusalem: Makhon Ben-Zvi, 1989), p. 20 n. 63.

91. See, e.g., his discussion of *gezerot shavot,* pp. 26a–b, and his discussion of *dibrah Torah keleshon bene adam,* p. 49b.

92. Aharon Ibn Hayyim, *Midot Aharon* (Venice, 1609), p. 22a. For a response to some of Ibn Hayyim's claims, see Yair Bacharach, *Havvot Yair,* no. 192.

93. Aharon Ibn Hayyim, *Midot Aharon,* p. 17a.

94. See Yerushalmi, Yeb. 11:1 (p. 11d).

95. *Yad Malachi,* rules no. 3, 50, 125–27.

96. For a review of these positions see, Azulai, *Shem ha-Gedolim,* s.v. "Sifra, Sifre." The first position, held by Maimonides, inter alia, is based on the names, *Sifra d'Be Rav, Sifre d'Be Rav* that appear in the Talmud. The latter position is based on the report in Bavli, San. 86a.

97. To be sure, the fact that all known versions of the *Sifra* open with a list of the R. Ishmael's thirteen principles no doubt contributed to this impression. Cf. the opening lines of R. Abraham b. David of Posquières to his commentary on the *Sifra.*

98. This too is based on the Bavli, San. 86a.

99. Azulai, *Shem ha-Gedolim,* s.v. "Sifra".

100. I recognize that my treatment of Azulai and R. Abraham as medieval figures is not without controversy. But if one prefers to consider them "early modern" in some qualitative sense, it merely strengthens the claim I am advancing here. The traditional rabbinic world simply would not accept the Yerushalmi's view of any distinction between Rabbis Aqiba and Ishmael, whether informed by some modern sensibility or not. See also the still later Ḥayyim Ḥizkiah Medini's *Sedeh Ḥemed,* s.v. "dibrah Torah ke-leshon bene adam."

101. That the medievals did not discern any distinctions between the different midreshe halakhah and their techniques may also be seen from the commentarial literature. The many comments of Rashi and Rashbam explaining the talmudic phrase *Sifr(e)(a) de-be rav* indicate that they too know only the conception that emerges from the Bavli, namely that all the documents are the product of R. Aqiba and his students. See e.g. Rashbam to Baba Batra 124b, s.v. "ve-sha'ar sifre de-be rav."

102. See Urbach, *Ba'ale ha-Tosafot,* p. 672 for this title and the provenance of these *Tosafot.*

103. Urbach, in ibid., states that these *Tosafot* were unknown to R. Bezalel Ashkenazi, the compiler of *Shitah Mekubetzet.* They were apparently first printed with the Frankfurt printing of the Talmud (1722). See R. N. Rabinowitz, *Ma'amar al hadpasat ha-Talmud: Toledot hadpasat ha-Talmud* (Jerusalem: Mossad ha-Rav Kook, 1952), p. 111; on this printing of the Talmud in general, see H. Pick, "Aktenstücke zur Geschichte der Talmudausgaben Berlin-Frankfurt an der Oder," in Simon Eppenstein et al., eds., *Festschrift zum siebigsten Geburtstage David Hoffmanns* (Berlin, 1914), 1:175–90). Only from there forward could one expect them to be known to Talmudists generally.

This comment is not the only one to take note of the Yerushalmi's position; it is merely the only one of which I am aware that makes a real effort to reconcile the Bavli and Yerushalmi in some way. Rabbenu Ḥananel refers to the Yerushalmi's distinction, but not with any comments or effort to integrate it into his understanding of the history of rabbinic midrash. (See Rabbenu Hananel to Bavli, Shabbat 134a.) Similarly, the *Ittur* of R. Yitzḥak b. Abba Mari cites the passage from Yerushalmi, Shabbat 19:2 cited in chapter 3. Yet he writes that the argument is between R. Aqiba and R. Yosi. As noted by the editor, Meir

Glanouski, in all likelihood the version from which he worked read "RY" (that is, "resh" "yod") and he assumed that these initials referred to R. Yosi, no doubt on the basis of the Bavli, AZ 27a. If so, then we have yet another example of a rabbinic scholar deciphering a Yerushalmi passage on the basis of the Bavli. Here it is more telling than elsewhere, given that the Yerushalmi knows no argument on this other than between Rabbis Aqiba and Ishmael. Were R. Yitzḥak really at home with the Yerushalmi's understanding, he would not have deciphered the initials as he did. Thus, while he is familiar with the Yerushalmi, he does not cite it correctly, nor does he note any tension between it and the Bavli. (*Sefer ha-Ittur* [Vilna, 1875], 2:100.)

104. Yom Tov al Ishbili, *Ḥiddushe ha-Ritba: Masekhet Yebamot,* vol. 2 (Jerusalem: Mossad ha-Rav Kook, 1992), pp. 795–96 (comments to Yeb. 70a).

105. Ibid., p. 796 n. 64.

106. *Teshuvot ha-Rashba ha-Meyuḥasot la-Ramban,* no. 96.

107. For discussion, see Isadore Twersky, *Rabad of Posquières: A Twelfth-Century Talmudist* (Cambridge: Harvard University Press, 1962), pp. 206–13, and the literature cited there. See also Avraham Grossman, *Ḥakhme Ashkenaz ha-Rishonim* (Jerusalem: Magnes Press, 1981), pp. 424–35.

108. Twersky, *Rabad of Posquières.*

109. It cannot be claimed, as is so often the case with Rashi, that his comments represent his understanding of the Talmud, ad locum, and are not necessarily his own understanding of the matter generally. Here the comment is a gratuitous addition to a comment that explains the talmudic passage in question.

110. See above note 65.

111. See his animadversions to the second root of Maimonides' *Sefer ha-Mitzvot,* Chavel edition, pp. 31ff.

112. See the comments with which he opens the third section of his *Sefer Keritut.*

113. Joseph Albo, *Ikkarim,* 3:23.

114. See *She-elot u-Teshuvot Radbaz ha-Shalem,* no.1303.

115. Lists of others who maintain this view may be found inGottlieb Fischer's response to Zechariah Frankel's *Darkhe ha-Mishnah,* printed in *Collected Writings of Samson Raphael Hirsch* (New York: Feldheim, 1988), 5:240–60; Isaac Hirsh Weiss's introduction to his edition of the *Mekhilta* (Vienna, 1865), pp. ii–iii; Abraham Joshua Heschel, *Torah min ha-Shamyim be-Aspaklariahshel ha-Dorot,* vol. 2 (London: Soncino, 1965), p. 229 n. 3 (Heschel considers the attribution of this position to R. Ishmael in the medieval compendium, *Midrash ha-Gadol,* to be authentic; I see no compelling reason to think so); and Louis Finkelstein, "Ha-De'ah ki 13 ha-Middot hen Halakhah le-Moshe mi-Sinai," in Shama Friedman, ed., *Sefer ha-Zikaron le-Rabbi Shaul Lieberman* (New York: Jewish Theological Seminary, 1993), pp. 79–84.

116. Even Aharon Ibn Ḥayyim, who acknowledges disputes regarding the principles insists that they are *halakhot le-Moshe mi-Sinai.* Again, see *Ḥavvvot Yair* no. 192 for a reaction. In general, the *Ḥavvot Yair* is the most important exception to the generalization I have made here.

Chapter 5. At the Dawn of a New Age

1. For a discussion of these shifts and their impact on religious thought, see Amos Funkenstein, *Theology and the Scientific Imagination* (Princeton: Princeton University Press, 1986); see also Richard H. Popkin, *The History of Scepticism from Erasmus to Spinoza* (Berkeley: University of California Press, 1979), pp. 129–248.

2. On Amsterdam (and Holland generally) at this time, see Salo Baron, *A Social and Religious History of the Jews* (New York: Columbia University Press, 1973), 15:3–73; more briefly, Henry Méchoulan and Gérard Nahon, *Menasseh ben Israel: The Hope of Israel* (Oxford University Press for the Littman Library of Jewish Civilization, 1987), pp. 1–22.

3. See Gershom Scholem, "Redemption Through Sin," in idem, *The Messianic Idea in Judaism* (New York: Schocken, 1971), pp. 78–141; Elisheva Carlebach, *The Pursuit of Heresy: Rabbi Moses Hagiz and the Sabbatian Controversies* (New York: Columbia University Press, 1990), pp. 100–101.

4. For an appreciation of the full range of Renaissance approaches, see Anthony Grafton, *Defenders of the Text: The Traditions of Scholarship in an Age of Science, 1450–1800* (Cambridge: Harvard University Press, 1991), pp. 23–46 and passim.

5. Yosef Hayim Yerushalmi, *From Spanish Court to Italian Ghetto* (New York: Columbia University Press, 1971), p. 44.

6. The citations come from Yerushalmi's translation in ibid., pp. 45–46. To these three categories of Orobio, Yerushalmi notes yet one more, namely, those who found their "deepest spiritual affinity with Jewish mysticism." Yerushalmi also notes (p. 47) that we must take Orobio's explanation of the cause of these deviant forms with a very large grain of salt, always mindful of the polemical context in which they were formulated. Other discussion of this passage may be found in Yovel, *Spinoza and Other Heretics*, pp. 52–54; I.S. Revah, *Spinoza et Juan de Prado* (Paris: Mouton, 1959), pp. 14–16; José Faur, *In the Shadow of History: Jews and Conversos at the Dawn of Modernity* (Albany: SUNY Press, 1992), pp. 110–13; Yosef Kaplan, *Mi-Natsrut le-Yahadut: Ḥayyav u-Fa'alo shel ha-Anus Yitzḥak Orobio de Castro* (Jerusalem: Magnes Press, 1983), p. 130. Kaplan's work (esp. pp. 98–155) provides the larger context of Orobio's statements and gives a good description of the larger issue of "doubt and certainty" among the ex-Marranos. Revah's work, p. 126, contains excerpts of the original text.

7. The last type is dangerous because, he writes, "[E]l discredito a las prohibiciones o Vallados de nuestros Doctores para la mas perfecta observancia de la Ley tacitamente los conduce al desprecio de la Tradicion y, despues, de lo Escrito, passando ultimamente al Atheismo. . . ." (Revah, *Spinoza et Juan de Prado*, p. 127).

8. See the summary of research into this matter by Yirmiyahu Yovel in his *Spinoza and Other Heretics* (Princeton: Princeton University Press, 1989), 1:42–45, 207–9; see also Faur, *In the Shadow of History*, pp. 113–27. The accuracy of Da Costa's autobiography has relevance beyond this point as the ordeal he

describes suffering at the hands of Amsterdam's rabbis played an important role in efforts to portray Judaism as an inquisitorial religion. See, e.g., Alexander McCaul, *Israel Avenged* (below n. 31), introduction; Fritz Mauthner, *Der Atheismus und seine Geschichte im Abendlande,* vol. 2 (Stuttgart, 1922), p. 348.

9. See Jean-Pierre Osier, *D'Uriel da Costa à Spinoza* (Paris: Autre Rive, 1983), pp. 219–51.

10. Uriel Acosta, *A Specimen of Human Life* (New York: Bergman Publishers, 1967), pp. 13–14.

11. Yovel, *Spinoza and Other Heretics,* pp. 46–50.

12. See Osier, *D'Uriel da Costa,* p. 33. He concludes his discussion of Da Costa as a Judaizer with the pithy remark, "Uriel judaisant, voilà pourquoi Uriel ne pouvait se faire Juif!"

13. See Carl Gebhardt, *Die Schriften des Uriel da Costa* (Amsterdam: 1922), pp. 85, 95; Osier, *D'Uriel da Costa,* p. 53.

14. On Da Costa's use of this term, see Faur, *In the Shadow of History,* pp. 129, 139.

15. In his discussion of the mortality of the soul, he writes of the Pharisees (in Gebhardt's translation): "denn diese Menschen sind von der Art, dass sie aus Beruf oder aus Narrheit unternehmen, Worte zu vertauschen, abzuändern, zu verdrehen, zur Bestätigung und Bekräftigung ihrer verworrenen Träume die Schriften verkehrt auszulegen, um durch diese falschen Mittel sich Unterstützung zu verschaffen. Wenn sich die Unwahrheit der angeführten Stellen nicht von selbst zeigte—erscheint doch die ganze pharisäische Lehre im Gegensatz zur Lehre des geschriebenen Gesetzes in jenem Buche unter der Namen der Prophetie zur Täuschung des Volkes und zur Bestätigung der falschen Predigt— . . ." (Gebhardt, *Schriften,* p. 95).

16. Gebhardt, *Schriften,* p. 85; Osier, *D'Uriel da Costa,* p. 53.

17. "Uriel Acosta's Eleven Theses Against the Tradition," in Uriel Acosta, *A Specimen of Human Life,* pp. 59–62. I think one could translate the Hebrew version—perhaps the original—in a somewhat different manner, but none of the essential points would be affected. See Abraham Geiger, ed., *Magen ve-Tzinnah* (Breslau: 1856), pp. 2b–3a.

18. See above, chapter 3, pp. 54–56.

19. Da Costa, *Specimen,* pp. 18–19.

20. For discussion of the history of the work's attribution to Modena, see Talya Fishman, "Kol Sachal's Critique of Rabbinic Tradition: A Solution to the Problem of Galut" (diss., Harvard University, 1986), pp. 1–13.

21. Isaac S. Reggio, *Beḥinat ha-Kabbalah* (Gorizia, Italy, 1852), p. 12.

22. Ibid., p. 21.

23. Ibid., p. 22. No doubt, the author is mocking the Karaite interpretation of Exod. 16:29, "Let everyone remain where he is; let no man leave his place on the seventh day." The author obviously thought that the proper interpretation of this verse is not the literal one, but one that takes account of the metaphorical susceptibility of language.

24. Ibid.

25. See Mk., 7:1–8; Matt. 15:2.

26. Reggio, *Beḥinat ha-Kabbalah*, pp. 23–28. Citations from p. 27.

27. See the discussion in Talya Fishman, "Kol Sachal's Critique," pp. 98ff. I have had access to Dr. Fishman's forthcoming mongraph on the *Kol Sakhal*, and have learned much from it.

28. Shalom Rosenberg, "Emunat Ḥakhamim," in Isadore Twersky and Bernard Septimus, eds., *Jewish Thought in the Seventeenth Century* (Cambridge: Harvard University Press, 1987), pp. 285–341.

29. Rosenberg, "Emunat Ḥakhamim," in ibid., p. 322.

30. I cite from the published French translation of his work entitled *Israël Avengé*. He writes, "Cette loi si sainte est aussi parfaite que la source d'où elle est sortie: cette volonté de Dieu si clairement enoncée dans le Pentateuque, les commandements aussi absolus qu'irrevocables prononcés avec tant d'energie et de bonté sur la montagne de Sinai et reiterés sans la moindre alteration sur celle d'Horeb, sont les regles qu'Israël doit suivre à perpetuité entre toutes les nations de l'univers pour mériter les effets des promesses de ce divin legislateur." Isaac Orobio de Castro, *Israël Avengé* (London, 1770), p. 6. On this translation, see Kaplan, *Mi Natsrut le-Yahadut*, appendix 6, pp. 393–99.

31. He writes, "C'est en vain que les Chrétiens prétendent trouver dans les Prophéties des obscurites qu'ils éclairissent à leur manière pour detruire l'unité de Dieu et l'observation de sa loi. . . . Des intentions perverses soutenues par les artifices affreux peuvent seules déterminer à faire des suppositions contraires à une vérité si évidente et c'est se déclarer ouvertement le fauteur des erreurs les plus grossières, que de s'attacher ainsi à un mot vague, à une syllable, pour prouver une opinion qui répugne au bon sens et à la raison, comme sont des disputeurs de profession qui prétendent annuller un acte authentique en prenant d'une periode un mot qui convient à leur dessein, mais qui n'a ni rapport ni liaison avec ce qui ou ce qui suit cette période" (*Israël Avengé*, pp. 9–10.). Of course, all that Orobio described as characteristic of Christian exegesis represented standard complaints against rabbinic exegesis. When, in response to an English translation of Orobio's work, the nineteenth-century British missionary, Alexander McCaul, wrote a response to Orobio, it required little effort to turn Orobio's arguments against rabbinic literature—or more accurately, to turn rabbinic literature against Orobio. See Alexander McCaul, *Israel Avenged by Don Isaac Orobio: Translated and Answered* (London, 1839), pp. 70–132.

32. For a recent discussion of Nieto, see David B. Ruderman, "Jewish Thought in Newtonian England: The Career and Writings of David Nieto," *Proceedings of the American Academy for Jewish Research* 58 (1992): 193–219. For further bibliography, see ibid., note 1.

33. David Nieto, *Matteh Dan* (Jerusalem: Mossad ha-Rav Kook, 1958), 2:30 (p. 28).

34. Ibid., 2:69–70 (pp. 32–33).

35. Ibid., 3:14 (p. 58)

36. Ibid., 3:160 (p. 89)

37. Ibid., 3:158, 160 (pp. 88–89).

38. For discussion of this aspect of the *Matteh Dan*, see Jacob J. Petuchowski,

The Theology of Haham David Nieto: An Eighteenth-Century Defense of the Jewish Tradition (New York: Ktav, 1970), pp. 69–98.

39. *Matteh Dan*, 3:10,12 (pp. 57–58).

40. Ibid., 3:183 (p. 94).

41. On Morteira, see Rosenberg, "Emunat Ḥakhamim," p. 324. Morteira's interest in this issue seems to be directed more towards the aggadic elements of the tradition.

42. Se Aaron L. Katchen, *Christian Hebraists and Dutch Rabbis* (Cambridge: Harvard University Press, 1984), pp. 128–44; Noah H. Rosenbloom, "Discreet Theological Polemics in Menasseh ben Israel's Conciliador," *Proceedings of the American Academy for Jewish Research* 58 (1992): 143–91.

43. Henry Méchoulan and Gérard Nahon, eds., introduction to *Menasseh ben Israel: The Hope of Israel* (Oxford: Oxford University Press for the Littman Libary of Jewish Civilization, 1987), p. 29.

44. See Katchen, *Christian Hebraists,* pp. 128–30.

45. Compare this to the introduction of Rabbi Moses Coucy to his *Sefer Mitzvot ha-Gadol.*

46. Menasseh ben Israel, *The Conciliator: A Reconcilement of the Apparent Contradictions in Holy Scripture* (London: 1842), question 86, p. 135.

47. A similar argument regarding the rather chaotic nature of the Book of Daniel and its divine inspiration may be found at *Bereshit Rabbah* 85:2 (ed. Theodor-Albeck, p. 1033).

48. Ibid., p. 136.

49. Menasseh, *Conciliator,* question 104, pp. 165–66.

50. Ibid., p. 207.

51. Ibid.

52. Ibid., pp. 208–13. He concludes the section by stating, "The foregoing observations will give an idea what is Cabala; its division into two parts . . . and its thirteen rules; similar to the same number by which Talmudists draw their conclusions on the texts of Scripture, and the Cabalists also use to explain the mysterious meaning of various matters in Holy Writ." (p. 213)

53. Ibid., p. 213.

54. See Rosenberg, "Emunat Ḥakhamim," pp. 299–301; Katchen, *Christian Hebraists,* p. 140ff. As Katchen makes clear, not all Christians were impressed with the work.

55. Grafton, *Defenders of the Text,* p. 205. Grafton notes that in 1582 a schoolmaster named Noël Journet was burned for heresy for questioning details of biblical stories and concluding that Moses could not have written Deuteronomy. In 1692, on the other hand, Pierre Bayle could publish similar conclusions, and live to tell about it. The century in between was, obviously, decisive for the history of the Bible in the West.

56. See Richard H. Popkin, *Isaac La Peyrere, 1596–1676: His Life, Work and Influence* (Leiden: E. J. Brill, 1987), pp. 42–49, and passim. See also idem, *Scepticism,* pp. 214–28; Grafton, *Defenders,* pp. 204–13.

57. Popkin, *Isaac La Peyrere,* p. 49.

58. This is not to suggest that the two parts are not integrally related. For

discussion, see Henning Graf Reventlow, *The Authority of the Bible and the Rise of the Modern World* (Philadelphia: Fortress Press, 1985), pp. 194–222.

59. Regarding contact between La Peyrere and Hobbes, and possible influences, see Popkin, *Isaac La Peyrere*, p. 49; idem, *Scepticism*, p. 215.

60. Thomas Hobbes, *Leviathan* (New York: Penguin Books, 1968), pp. 409–10.

61. Letter 21 in Spinoza, *The Collected Works of Spinoza*, edited and translated by Edwin Curley (Princeton: Princeton University Press, 1985), 1:375–76.

62. Spinoza, letter 19 in ibid., p. 360.

63. On accommodationism, see Funkenstein, *Theology and the Scientific Imagination*, pp. 213–71.

64. Letter 19, in Spinoza, *Collected Works of Spinoza*, p. 360.

65. Letter 21, in ibid., p. 380.

66. Letter 21, in ibid., p. 381.

67. Ibid., pp. xiii, 349–50, 405–7.

68. Compare Maimonides, *Guide of the Perplexed*, 3:26.

69. Letter 21, in Spinoza, *Collected Works of Spinoza*, p. 381.

70. Letter 30 in Carl Gebhardt, ed. and trans., *Spinoza Briefwechsel* (Leipzig: Verlag von Felix Meiner, 1914), pp. 141–42.

71. Benedict de Spinoza, *A Theologico-Political Treatise*, trans. R. H. M. Elwes (New York: Dover Publications, 1951), p. 193.

72. Ibid., p. 195.

73. See also ibid., p. 102.

74. He was not the first to invoke this argument. He was preceded by a number of others, most importantly Francis Bacon. See Sylvain Zac, *Spinoza et l'interpretation de l'écriture* (Paris, 1965), pp. 29–33. See also Panajotis Kondylis, *Die Aufklärung* (Stuttgart: Klett-Cotta, 1981), pp. 113–16.

75. Spinoza, *Treatise*, pp. 40, 100.

76. Ibid., p. 35

77. To be sure, Spinoza occasionally backtracks from this position, arguing that some prophets, particularly Moses, do accommodate their message to the masses (see, e.g., ibid., p. 77). In no way does this change the fact that each of the prophets formulated his message in terms of his own actual beliefs, and was not accommodating anyone when, for example, he represented God as a human.

78. Ibid., p. 27.

79. Ibid., p. 40.

80. Ibid., p. 102.

81. Ibid., p. 33.

82. Ibid., p. 116.

83. Ibid.

84. Ibid., p. 47. Note that this is presented as the true biblical view of the matter. For the philosopher, of course, the notion that God could enter time to select a particular people for any purpose is a total absurdity. See below, n. 99.

85. Ibid., p. 107.

86. See Funkenstein, *Theology and the Scientific Imagination*, p. 220.

87. See Spinoza, *Treatise*, chap. 14.
88. Ibid., p. 98.
89. Ibid., pp. 107–8.
90. Ibid., p. 112 bottom, and p. 270 n. 8.
91. See the catalogue of difficulties facing the would-be interpreter of the biblical text in ibid., pp. 108–11.
92. Baruch Spinoza, *Hebrew Grammar [Compendium Grammatices Linguae Hebraeae]*, trans. Maurice J. Bloom (New York: Philosophical Library, 1962), p. 36. For a discussion of this distinction, see Ze'ev Levy, *Baruch or Benedict?: On Some Jewish Aspects of Spinoza's Philosophy* (New York: Peter Lang, 1989), pp. 174–77. What the distinction meant in practical terms is that Spinoza could assume the existence of forms that are not to be found in the Bible, but which conform to the norms he can establish. See e.g., *Hebrew Grammar*, p. 59.
93. On the philosophical significance of this, see Levy, *Baruch or Benedict?* pp. 177–82.
94. See note 83 above.
95. He writes that because the grammarians did not understand the unique nature of the Hebrew noun, "they considered many words to be irregular which according to the usage of the language are most regular, and they were ignorant of many things which are necessary to know for a proper understanding of the language" (Spinoza, *Hebrew Grammar*, p. 28). It need hardly be said that these grammarians stood firmly within the broad framework of rabbinic learning.
96. See ibid., pp. 87, 148.
97. See Levy, *Baruch or Benedict?*, pp. 161–62.
98. Spinoza, *Hebrew Grammar*, p. 59. See *Bereshit Rabbah* 44:5, and *Esther Rabbah* 5:2. In these sources the matter is actually subject to controversy, for one rabbi explains as Spinoza does, the other explains that *aḥar* means "long after," while *aḥare* means "shortly thereafter."
99. I have not focused on the *Ethics* here, even though that work supports Spinoza's challenge from a metaphysical and logical point of view. This is particularly so regarding book 1, which makes absolutely clear that a divine revelation in time is an absurdity. I have not done so because, while many Jews grappled with the metaphysics of the *Ethics*, in my view the work exercised far less influence in general in the Jewish community. It was certainly a limited factor in the story I wish to tell, for many people found Spinoza's biblical criticism compelling even when they did not share his metaphysics at all.
100. See his *Gespräch in dem Reiche der Todten über die Bibel u. Talmud zwischen dem seeligen Herrn Doctor Luther u. dem berühmten jüdischen Ausleger, namens Raschi* (1737). I mention this work by name because it is not discussed in Manuel's book (see next note), and is certainly unusual in its choice of protagonists. As one might expect, the debate revolves around Isaiah 52–53 more than anything else.
101. For full discussion, see now Frank E. Manuel, *The Broken Staff* (Cambridge: Harvard University Press, 1992).
102. On this see Paul Hazard, *The European Mind: The Critical Years,*

1680–1715 (New York: Fordham University Press, 1990), pp. 180–97. For further discussion, see Auguste Bernus, *Richard Sion et son histoire critique du Vieux Testament: la critique biblique au siècle de Louis XIV* (Lausanne, 1869); Maurice Olender, *The Languages of Paradise* (Cambridge: Harvard University Press, 1992), pp. 21–27; Jean Steinmann, *Richard Simon et les origines de l'exégèse biblique* (Desclée de Brouwer, 1960); Jean Robert Armogathe, ed., *Le grand siècle et la Bible* (= *Bible de tous les temps,* vol. 6), pp. 193–231.

103. Richard Simon, *Histoire critique du Vieux Testament* (Rotterdam: 1685; Geneva: Slatkine Reprints, 1971), pp. 373–75, 535–39.

104. Ibid., p. 371.

105. Ibid.

106. Ibid., p. 372.

107. See John D. Woodbridge, "German Responses to the Biblical Critic Richard Simon: From Leibniz to J. S. Semler," in Henning Graf Reventlow et al., eds., *Historische Kritik und biblischer Kanon in der deutschen Aufklärung* (Wiesbaden, 1988), pp. 65–88.

108. See his *L'histoire et la religion des juifs depuis Jesus Christ jusqu'à present* (1709), tome neuvième, première partie, p. 257.

109. Denis Diderot, *Oeuvres complètes,* ed. J. Assezat, vol. 15 (Paris: Garnier, 1876), pp. 372–73.

110. For further discussion, see Arnold Ages, *French Enlightenment and Rabbinic Tradition,* Heft 26 (Frankfurt am Main: Analecta Romanica, 1970).

111. G. E. Lessing, "The Education of the Human Race," in Henry Chadwick, ed. and trans., *Lessing's Theological Writings* (Stanford, Calif.: Stanford University Press, 1956), p. 91.

112. J. G. Herder, *Ideen zur Philosophie der Geschichte der Menschheit,* in B. Suphan ed., *Herders Sämtliche Werke* (Berlin: Weidmann, 1877), 14:62.

113. Ibid., 6:275.

114. Wulf Koepke, "Truth and Revelation: On Herder's Theological Writings," in B. Suphan, ed., *Johann Gottfried Herder: Innovator through the Ages* (Bonn: Bouvier, 1982), p. 145. See also Thomas Willi, *Herders Beitrag zum Verstehen des Alten Testaments* (Tübingen: J. C. B. Mohr, 1971), pp. 3–14, 26–53.

115. In this context, it may be worth noting the words of Johann David Michaelis of Göttingen in his study of Mosaic law, *Mosaisches Recht.* In explaining the sources on which he would rely in reconstructing Mosaic law, Michaelis notes that in no way would he turn to the Talmud for any information. "Die mündlichen Überlieferungen zum Theil unwissenden Rabbinen, die man im Thalmud gesammelt antrifft, können uns das gewöhnliche Recht der Juden zu der Zeit, da diese Männer lebten, nicht aber den Sinn Mosis lehren." Reasonable enough. He continues, though, "Seine Gesetze würden zum Theil ein sehr wunderliche figur machen, wenn man sie so verstehen wollte, als die Pharisäer thaten, deren Auslegungen nach Christ ausspruch oft das gerade Gegentheil von dem waren, was Moses befühlen hatte" (*Mosaisches Recht* [Biehl: 1777], 1:44). Clearly, the "pharisaic" understanding of the Mosaic law bears little relation to that law, and comparison of pharisaic exegesis to that of

Jesus makes clear just how off the mark their interpretations were. It is worth noting that elsewhere he remarks that he cannot mention the names of those Jews who have freed themselves from the intellectual fetters of rabbinic interpretation, such as Ibn Ezra and David Kimchi, without expressing admiration. See his review of Christian Wilhelm von Dohm's *Über die bürgerliche Verbesserung der Juden* (Berlin: 1781; repr., Hildesheim: Georg Olms, 1973), included in volume 2 of that work, p. 42.

116. Johann David Michaelis even calculated that Jews, informed by the rabbinic tradition, were twenty-five times as immoral as their Christian counterparts, although, to be sure, he did not think much of Jews who abandoned rabbinic tradition, either. See Dohm, *Verbesserung,* 2:34, 37. Although far more forgiving, Dohm himself was not overly impressed with the development of Jewish law and practice (primarily in the post-talmudic period), which was characterized by "spitzfindigen Speculationen" (ibid., 1:143)

Chapter 6. Midrash and Reform

1. Jacob Katz, *Out of the Ghetto* (New York: Schocken, 1973), p. 41.

2. See Haim Hillel Ben-Sasson, *Hagut ve-Hanhagah* (Jerusalem: Mossad Bialik, 1959); Jacob Katz, *Mesoret u-Mashber* (Jerusalem: Mossad Bialik, 1958); Gershom Scholem, *Sabbatai Sevi* (Princeton: Princeton University Press, 1973), pp. 77ff.; Azriel Shohet, *Im Hilufe Tekufot* (Jerusalem: Mossad Bialik, 1960); Bernard D. Weinryb, *The Jews of Poland* (Philadelphia: Jewish Publication Society, 1972), pp. 179–261. For a discussion of the place of books and printing as potential agents of cultural change in this period, see Menahem Schmelzer, "Hebrew Printing and Publishing in Germany," *Leo Baeck Institute Yearbook* 33 (1988): 369–83.

3. For an early review of the anti-pilpulistic literature, see Yair Bacharach's introduction to his *Yair Netiv* printed in *Bikkurim* 1, (1864): 4–26, esp. pp. 4–7. In addition to this introduction, Bacharach's own repudiation of *pilpul* may be found in his *Havvot Yair,* nos. 123, 124. Further documentation may be found in David Rappel, *Ha-Vikuah 'al ha-Pilpul* (Jerusalem: Devir, 1980). For discussion, see now Elhanan Reiner, "Temurot bishivot polin ve-ashkenaz beme'ot ha-16-17 ve-ha-vikuah 'al ha-pilpul," in Yisrael Bartal et al., eds., *Ke-Minhag Ashkenaz u-Folin: Sefer Yovel le-Chone Shmeruk* (Jerusalem: Zalman Shazar, 1993), pp. 9–80, and the bibliography collected there in note 3.

4. For the purposes of this chapter, "reform" refers to any effort to significantly reshape the nature of Jewish spiritual and cultural life. It will not be used only for those who were formally identified with the Reform movement of the nineteenth century, and for that reason will not be capitalized except when referring to that movement.

5. On him, see Raphael Mahler, *Divre Yeme Yisrael: Dorot Aharonim* (1956), 4:26–30.

6. See his *Netzah Yisrael* (Frankfurt on the Oder, 1741; xerographic repr., Brooklyn, N.Y., 1991), p. 1b. For examples of Israel's "scientific" explanations

of difficult rabbinic passages, see pp. 16a, 23b, 40a, and esp. the *kunteres aḥaron*.

7. Ibid., p. 3b.

8. Ibid., p. 1b.

9. See Neubauer, *Ha-Rambam al Divre Soferim.*

10. *Sevarat keresam,* meaning an "idea" without any rational or intellectual foundation. See Eliezer Ben Yehuda, *Dictionary of the Hebrew Language,* 8 vols., s.v. "keres." The phrase inspired a Yiddish equivalent, *boykh sevares.*

11. The insult works far better in the Hebrew, *dikdukim dakim u- shedufim,* designed to call to mind the ears of corn in Pharaoh's dream, Gen. 41:6.

12. Exod. 5:17.

13. Cf. Bavli, Zevahim, 61b.

14. *Ḥamarim ḥamarim;* a play on words, leading us to think of the people doing this as asses, or ass-drivers.

15. Zamosc, *Netzaḥ Yisrael,* p. 2a.

16. Nothing that I have said here should be interpreted as suggesting that Israel of Zamosc opposed talmudic dialectics. On the contrary, his whole work is based on the validity of such dialectics, and his intellectual heroes include the Tosafists and R. Samson of Qinon, master dialecticians all.

17. Zamosc, *Netzaḥ Yisrael,* p. 15a.

18. We should note that the *Netzaḥ Yisrael* was not republished until 1991, and no doubt had limited circulation. However, part of the introduction containing the gist of Israel's polemic against midrash halakhah was reprinted by Aaron Jellinek in the periodical *Bikkurim,* vol. 2, 1866. He reprinted it in an effort to show that even among Polish Jews one can find those with a proper appreciation for correct methodology, that is, people who rejected pilpulistic reasoning.

19. See David Sorkin, *The Transformation of German Jewry, 1780–1840* (New York: Oxford University Press, 1987), pp. 51–54.

20. The absence of any concern for Gentile disdain for rabbinic learning allowed Zamocz to approach the matter in a forceful way, without a hint of the defensive postures assumed by Naftali Herz Wessely and Moses Mendelssohn. See immediately below in text.

21. I have in mind here primarily Yeḥezkel Landau; it seems that Landau was targeted more because of his opposition to the *Biur* and Wessely's program of educational reform outlined in *Divre Shalom ve-Emet,* than for *pilpul,* of which he was a master practitioner.

22. Moses Mendelssohn, as well, felt the need to distance himself from *pilpul,* in all likelihood, under the influence of Israel of Zamosc. See Michael Meyer, *The Origins of the Modern Jew* (Detroit: Wayne State University Press, 1967), p. 22. As for Mendelssohn's familiarity with *Netzaḥ Yisrael,* see Meir Gilon, *Kohelet Musar le-Mendelssohn 'al Reka' Tequfato* (Jerusalem: Israel National Academy of Sciences, 1979), p. 42 n. 19.

23. See Isaac Eisenstein-Barzilay, "The Treatment of the Jewish Religion in the Literature of the Berlin Haskalah," *Proceedings of the American Academy for Jewish Research* 24 (1955); Jacob Katz, *Out of the Ghetto,* pp. 124–41;

Meyer, *Origins;* Isaac Samuel Reggio, *Ha-Torah ve-ha-pilosofia,* 1828, 143–63; David Sorkin, "From Context to Comparison: The German Haskalah and Reform Catholicism," in *Tel Aviver Jahrbuch für deutsche Geschichte* 20 (1991): 23–41; idem, "Jews, the Enlightenment, and Religious Toleration—Some Reflections," *Leo Baeck Institute Yearbook* 37 (1992).

24. See Moshe Pelli, "The Attitude of the First Maskilim in Germany towards the Talmud," *Leo Baeck Institute Yearbook* 27 (1982).

25. See Edward Breuer, "In Defense of Tradition: The Masoretic Text and Its Rabbinic Interpretation in the Early German Haskalah" (diss., Harvard University, 1990).

26. For a recent description of the project and its publication history, see Werner Weinberg, "Les traductions et commentaires de Mendelssohn," in Yvon Belaval and Dominique Bourel, *Le siècle des lumières et la Bible* (= *Bible de tous les temps,* vol. 7) (Paris: Beauchesne, 1986), pp. 599–621. See also S. M. Lowenstein, "The Readership of Mendelssohn's Bible Translation," *Hebrew Union College Annual* 53 (1982).

27. David Rosen, *Perush ha-Rashbam ha-Shalem al ha-Torah* (Breslau, 1882), comment to Gen. 37:2. I would emphasize the word "theoretical" in this last sentence, since in no way did Rashbam intend to actually negate the importance and centrality of rabbinic midrash.

28. *Netivot Shalom,* Leviticus (Vienna, 1846), 4:1.

29. Naftali Herz Wessely, *Gan Naul* (Vienna, 1829), 1:3b. I interpret this to mean the exegetical tradition, rather than the fully developed legal tradition. If Wessely meant to say that rabbinic exegesis indicated the existence of a comprehensive set of norms handed down from generation to generation, then rabbinic exegesis again becomes nothing more than *asmakhta.* Yet that is not what Wessely appears to believe from his various comments elsewhere. Thus, I assume he means to suggest that there was a traditional manner of reading Scripture that goes back (literally or metaphorically) to Moses. See the discussion in Breuer, "Defense of Tradition," pp. 240–48.

30. Wessely, *Gan Naul,* p. 20b.

31. He did, however, partially accept them. See below.

32. See also his *Jerusalem; or, On the Religious Power and Judaism* (Hanover, N.H.: University Press of New England, 1983), pp. 127–28.

33. Moses Mendelssohn, *Megillat Qohelet,* in *Netivot ha-Shalom* (Vienna, 1846), 9:206b. The translation is by Edward Breuer, "Defense of Tradition," p. 266, revised by me.

34. Ibid.; Breuer, "Defense of Tradition," pp. 268–69, significantly modified.

35. Ibid., p. 207a.

36. Ibid.

37. Breuer, "Defense of Tradition," p. 277.

38. It is interesting to note that Mendelssohn's introduction to Ecclesiastes was cited as an example of a work showing that rabbinic exegesis did not draw meaning from the biblical text, but rather simply served to connect it to tradition, by the Orthodox apologist M. Deutsch, in Tiktin, *Darstellung* (below n. 90).

39. *Netivot* (Vienna, 1846), 1:xxvi–xxvii. See Halivni, *Peshat and Derash*, pp. 29–30.

40. See Peretz Sandler, *Ha-Biur la-Torah shel Moshe Mendelssohn ve-Siyyato: Hithavuto ve-Hashpa'ato* (Jerusalem: Reuven Mass, 1984), pp. 52–54.

41. See e.g., his translation of Lev. 7:18, where he translates first according to the *peshat*, and then, in parentheses, according to the midrashic interpretation; the two are linked with the word *oder*. (Here it seems to me that the *peshat* and midrashic interpretations are mutually exclusive; Mendelssohn apparently could not make up his mind on this matter.) When the same law is repeated in abbreviated fashion at Lev. 19:7, Mendelssohn translates according to the *peshat* alone.

42. It seems to me that there is actually considerable tension between Mendelssohn's discussion of *peshat* and *derash* in the introductions to his edition of Ecclesiastes and the Pentateuch on the one hand, and the discussion of language, scripts, and laws in his Jerusalem, on the other. See his *Jerusalem; or, On Religious Power and Judaism* (Hanover, N.H.: University Press of New England, 1983), pp. 104–20. This is not the place to deal with this matter.

43. Meyer, *Origins*, pp. 61–62.

44. See Peter Gay, *The Enlightenment* (New York: Norton, 1966), 1:31–71.

45. The phrase appears in the Babylonian Talmud in a few places, and appears to mean something like "ground fish-meal" or "fish hash." I do not think it is overinterpreting to suggest that the double entendre of these words indicates that Berlin was well aware of the destructive nature of his project. In this regard it is worth noting that Berlin ultimately despaired of his place within the Jewish community and asked to be buried outside a Jewish cemetery.

46. See, e.g., Reuven Amar, "Yafeh le-Besamim," introduction to *Besamim Rosh*, 1984. In my study of the *Besamim Rosh* I have been aided by a research paper written by my student, Joshua Levisohn.

47. See the bibliography collected by Louis Jacobs, *Theology in the Responsa* (London: Routledge and Keegan Paul, 1975), p. 347, to which add Raphael Mahler, *Divre Yeme Yisrael, Dorot aharonim* (Merḥavia, 1954), 2:77–79, 336–42; Moshe Samet, "Besamim Rosh shel R. Shaul Berlin: Bibliografyah, Historyografyah, ve-Ideologyah," *Kiryat Sefer*, 1973, 509–23; and esp. Leopold Zunz, *Der Ritus des synagogalen Gottesdienstes* (Berlin, 1859), pp. 226–28.

48. Jacobs, *Theology*, p. 352.

49. *Besamim Rosh*, no. 325.

50. Ibid., no. 17.

51. Ibid., no. 251.

52. On him, see Urbach, *Ba'ale ha-Tosafot*, 1:425–29.

53. *Besamim Rosh*, no. 220.

54. This is based on Mishnah, Yebamot 1:4. Cf. the talmudic discussion ad loc.

55. Jacobs, *Theology*, pp. 351–52.

56. *Besamim Rosh*, no. 301. Incredibly, José Faur seems to consider this *responsum* to be the genuine product of the pen of R. Jacob Mekhiri, the

responsum's signatory, who would have lived in the time of Naḥmanides and his student, Solomon ibn Adret. He then goes on to cite this *responsum* as a classic example of the deleterious historical effects of the penetration of Ashkenazic casuistry on the mentality of Spain's Sephardim. It may well be that that is precisely the conclusion Berlin wished his readers to draw, but it is nothing short of irresponsible to cite this *responsum* as actual historical proof of the matter. See Faur, *In the Shadow of History*, p. 227 n. 82.

57.   We should note, however, that Berlin is scarcely calling for a return to a literal interpretation of the biblical laws, as such an interpretation also can lead to unacceptable legal consequences. See *Besamim Rosh,* no. 325.

58.   Solomon Maimon, *Lebensgeschichte* (1792; Frankfurt am Main: Insel Verlag, 1984), pp. 222–23.

59.   Ibid., pp. 219–26. In addition to scriptural exegesis, Judaism was perverted by the need to adopt the customs of the peoples among whom they were dispersed. See Eisenstein-Barzilay, "Jewish Religion," pp. 63–64. It is interesting to note that after this polemic Maimon goes on to assert that many of the contemporary charges against rabbinic Judaism leveled by Christians and would-be enlightened Jews were unfounded. Indeed, an entire book would be needed to fully refute all these canards. It seems then that for Maimon rabbinism represented the mindless multiplication of rules and rituals that robbed life of its vitality and the mind of its rationality, but that never traduced the basic moral values that animated the system from its inception.

60.   Joseph Salvador, *Histoire des institutions de Moïse et du peuple Hébreu* (Paris, 1828), 1:70.

61.   Ibid., p. 103.

62.   Jean-Jacques Rousseau, *The Social Contract,* bk. 2, chap. 7.

63.   Salvador, *Histoire*, p. xvi. Yet another Frenchman worthy of note here is Olry Terquem. See the discussion of his work in Jay R. Berkovitz, *The Shaping of Jewish Identity in Nineteenth-Century France* (Detroit: Wayne State University Press, 1989), pp. 129–39. On *jüdische Wissenschaft* in France in general, see Perrine Simon Nahum, *La cité investie: La "Science du judaïsme" français et la République* (Paris: Cerf, 1991).

64.   Hanns Günther Reissner, *Eduard Gans: Ein Leben in Vormärz* (Tübingen: J. C. B. Mohr, 1965), p. 52. In general see, Sinai Ucko, "Geistesgeschichtliche Grundlagen der Wissenschaft des Judentums," reprinted in Kurt Wilhelm, ed., *Wissenschaft des Judentums in deutschen Sprachbereich: Ein Querschnitt,* vol. 1 (Tübingen: J. C. B. Mohr, 1967); and Ismar Schorsch, "Breakthrough into the Past: The Verein für Cultur und Wissenschaft der Juden," *Leo Baeck Institute Yearbook* 33 (1988); and Rachel Livné-Freudenthal, "Der 'Verein für Cultur und Wissenschaft der Juden' (1819–1824) zwischen Staatkonformismus und Staatskritik," *Tel Aviver Jahrbuch für deutsche Geschichte* 20 (1991): 103–25.

65.   See Ismar Schorsch, "From Wolfenbüttel to Wissenschaft—The Divergent Paths of Isaak Markus Jost and Leopold Zunz," *Leo Baeck Institute Yearbook* 22 (1977): 114–21; idem, "Scholarship in the Service of Reform," *LBIY* 35 (1990): 74–78. See also Reuven Michael, *I. M. Jost* (Jerusalem, 1983).

66. Of course, the choice of French rather than German (or Yiddish) for the purpose would have undermined the entire project even if Chiarini had not died so soon after beginning it, and this fact was recognized by the Polish authorities. In 1834, the administrative board of the Ministry of Religion and Education in Poland approved the importation of Jost's German translation of the Mishnah, which, it had been assured, would be of greater benefit to Reform-minded Jews in Poland. See Jacob Shatzky, *Yiddishe Bildungs-palitik in Poilin fun 1806 biz 1866* (New York: YIVO, 1943), pp. 212–15.

67. Luigi Chiarini, *Théorie du Judaïsme*, 2 vols. (Paris, 1830), 2:51.

68. On this school, see Sabina Levin, "Beit-hasefer le-Rabbanim be Varshe, 1826–1863," *Gal-Ed* 11:35–58.

69. A. Buchner, *Der Talmud in seiner Nichtigkeit* (Warsaw: Missions Druckerei, 1848), 1:17, 23, 32, 35. See in general pp. 30–40, and 2:1-71, where Buchner takes on the hermeneutic principles one by one. For more on Buchner, see Raphael Mahler, *Hasidism and the Jewish Enlightenment: Their Confrontation in Galicia and Poland in the First Half of the Nineteenth Century* (Philadelphia: Jewish Publication Society, 1985), pp. 214–20; Jacob Shatzky, *Yiddishe Bildungs-palitik*, pp. 199–208.

70. Shatzky, *Yiddishe Bildungs-palitik*, p. 206 approvingly cites the opinion of the Polish Jewish writer M. Mieses to the effect that notwithstanding its provocative title, Buchner's work is actually a work of "objective research in the spirit of Isaac Hirsh Weiss." Only someone who has not read either Buchner or Weiss could utter such nonsense. Shatzky takes Joseph Klausner to task for judging the book by its title; but Shatzky and Mieses seem to have judged the book by its introduction, which is indeed a moderate description of the Talmud. The body of the work, however, is as I have described it in the text, and is not in the spirit of Weiss (on whom, see next chapter).

71. M. Tannenbaum, *Der Talmud in seiner Wichtigkeit* (Magdeburg, 1849); Tannenbaum wrote the work in Hebrew and it was translated by his son-in-law, H. Nussbaum of Warsaw. On Tannenbaum, see Mahler, *Hasidism*, pp. 222–33.

72. See Meyer, *Response*, pp. 50–53. See also the anonymously published "Der Mangel an Glaubensinnigkeit in der jetzigen Judenheit: Bedenken eines Laien," *Wissenschaftliche Zeitschrift für jüdische Theologie* 1 (1835): 141–50.

73. See Meyer, *Response*, p. 91; for discussion of Geiger and his work during this period, see ibid., pp. 89–99; Susannah Heschel, "Abraham Geiger on the Origins of Christianity" (diss., University of Pennsylvania, 1989), pp. 39–80; Max Wiener, *Abraham Geiger and Liberal Judaism* (Philadelphia: Jewish Publication Society, 1962), pp. 3–80, esp. 3–17; and for the subject under discussion here, see especially Ismar Schorsch, "Scholarship in the Service of Reform," *Leo Baeck Institute Yearbook* 35 (1990): 83–91.

74. Abraham Geiger, "Der Kampf christlicher Theologen gegen die bürgerliche Gleichstellung der Juden, namentlich mit Bezug auf Anton Theodor Hartmann," *Wissenschaftliche Zeitschrift der jüdische Theologie* 1 (1835): 349. I am grateful to Professor Michael Meyer for his help in rendering this passage into English.

75. Here he apparently intended to suggest that they were grounded in the Bible without need to resort to forced interpretations. Otherwise what comes next would be incomprehensible.

76. Abraham Geiger, *Nachgelassene Schriften,* vol. 5 (Berlin, 1878), p. 13.

77. Ibid., p. 14.

78. On Geiger's attitude during this period, see Max Wiener, *Abraham Geiger and Liberal Judaism,* p. 16; Meyer, *Response,* 90–91.

79. See, e.g., his "Die wissenschaftliche Ausbildung des Judenthums in den zwei ersten Jahrhunderten des zweiten Jahrtausends bis zum Auftreten des Maimonides," *Wissenschaftliche Zeitschrift für jüdische Theologie* 1 (1835), esp. pp. 13–20, 307–26.

80. See his "Der Formglaube in seinem Unwerth und in seinen Folgen," *Wissenschaftliche Zeitschrift für jüdische Theologie,* 1839, pp. 1–12.

81. On the so-called Geiger-Tiktin affair and its background, see Ludwig Geiger, *Abraham Geiger: Leben und Lebenswerk* (Berlin, 1910), pp. 50–95; Meyer, *Response,* pp. 110–12; David Philipson, *The Reform Movement in Judaism* (New York: Macmillan, 1907), pp. 72–101; Wiener, *Geiger and Liberal Judaism,* pp. 24–33.

82. See his letter to Leopold Zunz dated 4 March 1841, in *Nachgelaßene Schriften* 5:155–56; English translation in Wiener, *Geiger,* p. 110. There he notes that the only way out of Judaism's inner confusion is schism (although, in general, he was opposed to this; see Meyer, *Response,* p. 91), and his conviction to make history rather than write it. Later in the letter he claims that Orthodoxy, like Catholicism, must ultimately erode, while the other parts of the Jewish and Christian communities will have a share in the dominion of *Wissenschaft.* The latter fate awaits Protestants, and ought to await "biblischen Judenthums"—a phrase noteworthy more for what it excludes than what it includes—to an even greater degree. Certainly for Geiger the battle with Orthodoxy and rabbinic Judaism needed to be raised to a higher level.

83. As we shall see in the next chapter, part of its path-breaking character is due to the direct responses it elicited.

84. In *Wissenschaftliche Zeitschrift für jüdische Theologie* 5:53–81. Although the volume is dated 1844, its component parts appeared over a period of four years, and this essay of Geiger's was already in circulation before 1842. See L. Geiger, *Abraham Geiger: Leben und Lebenswerk,* pp. 74–75; Neubauer, *Ha-Rambam al Divre Soferim,* p. 165, and Ismar Schorsch, "Emancipation and the Crisis of Religious Authority: The Emergence of the Modern Rabbinate" in Werner Mosse et al., eds., *Revolution and Evolution: 1848 in German-Jewish History* (Tübingen: J. C. B. Mohr, 1981), p. 224 n. 60. Actually two essays with the same title appeared in this volume; although continuing installments of articles is quite common in nineteenth-century periodicals, here we have two distinct essays that do not entirely agree with one another. Clearly, the second was written in response to criticism, which led Geiger to evince awareness of subtle differences between the Bavli and Yerushalmi, while at the same time maintaining the basic thesis without reservation. The second essay is found in *WZJT,* 5:235–59.

85. Mosse, *Revolution and Evolution,* p. 70.

86. Ibid. See esp. pp. 62–68 for a sustained discussion of the Mishnaic sages.

87. Regarding the Mishnah he wrote, "Bald nach dem Abschlusse erstarkte seine Autorität zu einer bindenden, fesselnden, so daß es in dieser beziehung ebenbürtig neben der heiligen Schrift stand. Wenn man nun dieser, als Gottes Worte, die Autorität zuerkannte, so musste man eine gleiche Berechtigung auch bei der Mischnah suchen. Den Standpunkt der Mischnah, welche im guten Glauben war, vollkommen in biblischen Sinne die Gesetzweiterung zu unternehmen, wenn auch nicht das biblische Wort immer sie belegt, und damit dem fortschreitenden religiosen Leben und dessen Vertretern wolle Macht einräumte (Sanhedrin 11, 3), konnte man nicht ganz festhalten, da hiemit wohl eine zeitliche Autorität der Mischnah begründet, aber nicht eine ewige zugeben wäre, indem im Gegentheile die weitere Entwicklung des religiösen Lebens sich der Mischnah gegenüber hätte geltend machen können, die Mischnah aber als für ewige Zeiten verbindlich betrachten wurde. Man musste daher einen Rückschritt zu den Saducäern hin machen und die Autorität aller gegebenen Bestimmungen möglichst auf das Schriftwort zurückführen, die Bedeutung des nicht darauf Zurückgeführten wirklich geringer stellend" (ibid., pp. 68–69).

88. I must disagree mildly with Ismar Schorsch ("Scholarship in the Service of Reform," p. 87) who sees the polemical intent to be a suggestion that the halakhah rests on error. It seems to me that Geiger is not suggesting this. For Geiger the halakhah of the Mishnah represents a progressive response to the conditions of a time and place that have long since vanished. The *authority* granted halakhah is what rests on error and impedes reform. With the proper historical understanding this impediment will be removed, and then rabbinic norms may be evaluated in terms of the spirit of the new age. Some of these norms may indeed be retained.

89. I do not mean to suggest that had they properly discerned what Geiger was saying they would have considered it any less heretical. The substance of the response would have been different, though.

90. It was published by Tiktin under the title, *Darstellung des Sachverhält-nisses in seiner hiesigen Rabbinats-Angelegenheit* (Breslau, 18420). Geiger's lengthy response to this attack can be found in *Nachgelaßene Schriften* 1:52–112.

91. For fuller discussion, see below, chapter 7.

92. See above, note 84.

93. For discussion, see Schorsch, "Scholarship in the Service of Reform," pp. 87–89.

94. See, e.g., *Nachgelaßene Schriften* 2:53ff., for a discussion of the matter in Geiger's public lectures delivered in the last two years of his life.

95 See his "Die nordfranzösische Exegeten-Schule im 12 Jahrhundert" in S. L. Heilberg, ed., *Nit'e Na'amanim* (Breslau, 1847) and *Parshandata* (Breslau, 1855; repr., Jerusalem: Makor, 1971); see especially pp. 6–8 of the German section of the latter work.

96. See Meyer, *Response,* pp. 80–84; Jakob J. Petuchowski, "Abraham

Geiger and Samuel Holdheim—Their Differences in Germany and Repercussions in America," *Leo Baeck Institute Yearbook* 22 (1977); Schorsch, "Scholarship in the Service of Reform," pp. 95–97; Max Wiener, *Jüdische Religion im Zeitalter der Emanzipation* (Berlin, 1933).

97. Samuel Holdheim, *Verketzerung und Gewissensfreiheit* (Schwerin, 1842), p. 78.

98. Ibid., pp. 80–81.

99. See Petuchowski, "Abraham Geiger," pp. 142–44; Kaufmann Kohler, "Biographical Essay," in *David Einhorn Memorial Volume* (New York: Bloch, 1911), pp. 420–21.

100. Meyer, *Response*, p. 81.

101. Kohler, "Biographical Essay," pp. 419–20.

102. See David Einhorn, *Das Princip des Mosaismus und dessen Verhältnis zum Heidenthum und rabbinischen Judenthum* (Leipzig, 1854), pp. 82–89, 94, 106, and passim. See also his "Stellung des neueren Judenthums zum Thalmud," *Sinai* 1, nos. 1–3 (1856). For discussion see Meyer, *Response*, pp. 244–50 and index, and Gershon Greenberg, "Mendelssohn in America: David Einhorn's Radical Reform Judaism," *Leo Baeck Institute Yearbook*, 1982, 281–93.

103. Quoted in Meyer, *Response*, p. 83.

104. On this aspect of Krochmal, see Jay M. Harris, *Nachman Krochmal: Guiding the Perplexed of the Modern Age* (New York: NYU Press, 1991), chap. 5; on Graetz, see Ismar Schorsch, "Ideology and History in the Age of Emancipation," in Heinrich Graetz, *The Structure of Jewish History and Other Essays* (New York: Jewish Theological Seminary, 1975), esp. pp. 46–50.

105. Abraham Geiger, *Urschrift und Übersetzungen der Bibel in ihrer Abhängigkeit von der innern Entwicklung des Judenthums* (Breslau, 1857), p. 154.

106. Ibid., pp. 101–58, 170–99, 434–50.

107. Ibid., pp. 157–58.

108. See Heschel, "Geiger on Christianity," chap. 2.

109. For the unusually respectful criticism of Krochmal, see *Ma'amar ha-Ishut*, pp. 76–83; for the more acerbic critique of Rapoport, pp. 22–25; of Frankel, p. 75; of Graetz, pp. 81–82, to which compare 62–64. In general, the work of Samuel David Luzzatto is favorably received by Holdheim, for he ackowledged the inferior quality of rabbinic exegesis, and relied explicitly on tradition for his conservatism. Holdheim saw this as honest, if wrong, as opposed to the others, Rapoport in particular, whose work was not; see below.

110. See Schorsch, "Scholarship in the Service of Reform," pp. 95–97.

111. Samuel Holdheim, *Ma'amar ha-Ishut* (Berlin, 1861), p. 3.

112. Ibid., p. 58.

113. Ibid., p. 86.

114. Ibid., pp. 85–86.

115. Ibid., pp. 156–60.

116. Ibid., pp. 23–26.

117. One can find arguments that overlap with Holdheim's in the work of the Galician scholar Yehoshua Heshel Schorr, and the otherwise unknown Jacob Kittseer, Jr. of Pressburg. Theirs, too, were lonely voices. Most modern-

izing Jews recognized that a complete divorce between modern and rabbinic forms of Judaism could not be achieved.

118.   In the end, there is something rather sad about Holdheim's book. For all its antirabbinic animus, it is a work infused with the language and thought processes of talmudic learning. It is fitting that the book ends with a lengthy *pilpul* designed to show that the rabbis did not know what they were talking about when they said that the slaughtering of the Passover sacrifice may be done on the Sabbath when it falls on the fourteenth of the month of Nisan. The Sadducees, who must have opposed this ruling, of course knew better.

I will leave it to the Freudians to decide what to make of the fact that this work of cultural parricide was written in rabbinic Hebrew. It is, to my knowledge, the only work he was to write in that language, the medium of discourse of his youth. It may well be, of course, that he wanted to keep this work private, "within the family" as it were.

119.   A case in point here is Jost; as noted previously and by others, Jost's work in the 1830s and after was considerably less hostile to rabbinic Judaism. This moderation of hostility has not been adequately explained. In my view, the impetus for Jost's partial turnaround was the publication of Chiarini's work. The latter attacked the very notion of a rabbinic tradition, citing in support the work of Jost. Jost wrote a lengthy response, entitled *Was hat Herr Chiarini in Angelegenheiten der Europäischen Juden geleistet? Eine freimüthige und unparteische Beleuchtung des Werkes: Théorie du Judaïsme* (Berlin, 1830). Here he tries to show that while the rabbis' claims to be the recipients of a long-standing tradition cannot be affirmed by the modern historian, they do not in any way betray dishonesty or fraudulence. Rather, looking at the world the way they did, it was quite reasonable for them to think that laws of recent vintage were far older. They were wrong, but not frauds. From this time forward, Jost was more circumspect in dealing with rabbinic Judaism, even as he makes clear that a purified Mosaism would suit his personal religious taste more fully. It seems to me that Jost, who, for whatever the reason, was committed to remaining Jewish, saw that he could not enhance Jewish survival while presenting the ancient rabbis as morally and religiously inferior.

120.   In my view, it is recognition of this fact—and the need to combat it— that led some Reformers, with Geiger in the vanguard, to attack Christianity and diminish its claim to a truly monotheistic, prophetic heritage. (See Heschel, above, n. 73).

121.   A case in point is an essay by the Galician, Yehoshua Heschel Schorr, written in 1853, which begins with the usual accusation of exegetical turbidity. After but a page and a half, Schorr abandons his diatribe, noting that this has all been said before. See *He-Ḥaluṣ* 1:95–96.

122.   See especially Leopold Löw's *Praktische Einleitung in die Heilige Schrift* (Gross-Kanischa, 1855), pp. 59–68, 89–99.

123.   See e.g., Isaac Mayer Wise's *History of the Hebrews' Second Commonwealth with Special Reference to Its Literature, Culture, and the Origin of Rabbinism and Christianity* (Cincinnati, 1880), pp. 215–21, 246–48; Kaufmann Kohler, *Jewish Theology* (New York: Macmillan, 1918), pp. 7–14 and passim;

idem, *Origins of the Synagogue and the Church* (New York: Macmillan, 1929), pp. 134–45 and passim; Hermann Cohen, *Religion of Reason out of the Sources of Judaism* (New York: Ungar, 1972), pp. 24–34, esp. 28–29, and passim. I have focused on subsequent Reformers, but Geiger's negative work was rejected by contemporary Reformers as well. See especially Leopold Löw's *Praktische Einleitung.*

124. This does not, of course, imply that the Reform reclamation of the rabbinic past was in any sense compatible with traditional sensibilities. While these reclamations were clearly not culturally parricidal in the way in which the work of Maimon and Holdheim may be so characterized, they were very selective in their determination of what continues to speak to modern Jews. Thus, traditionalists felt the need to reject these works and respond to them.

125. In the interests of time and space, I have limited my discussion to certain central figures in Germany. There were other lesser figures there, and, more importantly, central figures in Eastern Europe and Hungary who also were involved with the issues under discussion here. Such figures would include Yehoshua Heschel Schorr, Leopold Löw, Moshe Leib Lilienblum, Yehudah Leib Gordon, and Micha Yosef Berdichevski, inter alia.

Chapter 7. The Traditionalists Strike Back

1. This is not to suggest that such simple restatements were not forthcoming. I merely intend to suggest that they were thoroughly ineffective in persuading those not in the choir. Those who wished to genuinely *respond* to the challenges had to seek other means than those that had worked in the past.

2. See Yovel, *Spinoza and Other Heretics*, pp. 57–73.

3. For an interesting if long-winded and tendentious contemporary account, see Eliezer Ha-Cohen Zweifel, *Shalom al Yisrael* (Zhitomir, 1873), pt. 4. See also Leopold Löw, *Gesammelte Schriften* (Szegedin, 1889; repr., Hildesheim: Georg Olms, 1979), 1:241–317.

4. My omission of Zunz and Steinschneider from this list is justified by their differing existential commitments, and by the fact that the foci of their historical work differed considerably from those of the scholars listed here.

5. Reuven Michael, ed., *Heinrich Graetz: Tagebuch und Briefe* (Tübingen: J. C. B. Mohr, 1977), pp. 135–36 (diary entry for 15 September 1844) .

6. He uses the Greek "ἄνθρωπος."

7. Michael, *Tagebuch*, p. 135.

8. Ibid., p. 140.

9. Ibid., p. 135. See also Ismar Schorsch, "Ideology and History," pp. 33–37.

10. See J. Eschelbacher, "Michael Sachs," *Monatschrift für Geschichte und Wissenschaft des Judentums* 52 (1908); Monika Richarz, *Der Eintritt der Juden in akademischen Berufe* (Tübingen: J. C. B. Mohr, 1974), 99, 101; Schorsch, "Ideology and History," p. 25. On his religio-historical views, see Max Wiener, *Jüdische Religion im Zeitalter der Emanzipation* (Berlin, 1933), pp. 85ff. See

now Franz D. Lucas and Heike Frank, *Michael Sachs: Der konservative Mittelweg* (Tübingen, 1992). My thanks to Prof. Michael Meyer for this reference.

11. Michael Sachs, *Die religiöse Poesie der Juden in Spanien* (1845) (Berlin, 1901; repr., New York: Arno Press, 1980), p. 146.

12. Ibid., pp. 162–63.

13. *Literaturblatt des Orients*, 6:635. This was part of a lengthy review of Geiger's works on the Mishnah; for discussion, see Schorsch, "Ideology and History," pp. 35–36.

14. *Literaturblatt des Orients*, p. 795.

15. He had, to be sure, already formulated a competing vision of Jewish history generally. In his essay "The Structure of Jewish History" he laid out his view of the inner dynamic of Jewish history, which was formulated in contradistinction to the animating historical visions of the Reformers. See Heinrich Graetz, *The Structure of Jewish History and Other Essays* (New York: Jewish Theological Seminary, 1975), pp. 63–124; see also Ismar Schorsch's introduction to that volume.

16. He did of course publish many scholarly articles and monographs along the way, however.

17. As early as 1846, Graetz had expressed his sensitivity to this matter; see Graetz, *The Structure of Jewish History*, pp. 93–94.

18. For discussion, see Harris, *Nachman Krochmal*, chap. 3.

19. For discussion regarding all of this, see Schorsch, "History and Ideology."

20. Graetz's reading of rabbinic sources tends to be naïvely credulous, like that of many like-minded scholars. We should note, though, that he was not unaware of the difficulties of using rabbinic sources for historical purposes. In the preface to an article to be discussed below, Graetz notes that one needs to establish criteria before one accepts the historical veracity of a talmudic statement. As a rule, he suggests that something reported in two documents that could not have influenced one another, such as the Bavli and Yerushalmi, should be treated as an objective report on which one can rely. See his "Jüdisch-geschichtliche Studien," *Monatschrift für Geschichte und Wissenschaft des Judentums* 1 (1852): 114. A similar methodological claim regarding attributions was recently made by David Kraemer in his *Mind of the Talmud* (New York: Oxford University Press, 1990), pp. 22–25.

21. *Monatschrift für Geschichte und Wissenschaft des Judentums* 1 (1852): 156. By *Forschung* Graetz intends midrash, as will become clear presently.

22. This claim is based on a number of reports in rabbinic literature of the encounter between Hillel and the "Bene Bateira," whoever they were. The story goes that the day of the Passover sacrifice coincided with the Sabbath, and it was not clear to the Bene Bateira, who were charged with making the decision, whether it was permissible to prepare the sacrifice on the Sabbath. They turned to Hillel, who, according to one version, introduced seven hermeneutical rules, a number of which could provide the answer in the affirmative. In Graetz's reading, the Bene Bateira rejected all the rules in principle, for the rules were new and not part of the tradition. His other "proof" of Hillel's innovation is the

existence of the thirteen principles of R. Ishmael, which are clearly to be seen as a further development and refinement of these rules. Thus, the seven rules of Hillel are the beginning of a process that, as we shall see in greater detail below, went through parallel development in the schools of Rabbis Aqiba and Ishmael.

23.   Graetz's imaginary tale has led him into difficulties, in that in the rabbinic sources the Bene Bateira are depicted as accepting Hillel's claim that he received the law from his teachers; they are further depicted as abdicating their leadership position in favor Hillel, the great sage who was their superior. Graetz could not give any credence to this version, for in his telling of the tale, the Bene Bateira would not have accepted the notion of traditional law; that was the bone of contention in the first place. It is for this reason that Graetz depicts the Bene Bateira not as having abdicated but as having been dismissed from their position. They stood in Hillel's way, and were sent packing.

24.   Heinrich Graetz, *Geschichte der Juden* (Berlin, 1853), 4:18.

25.   Ibid., p. 23.

26.   Ibid., p. 34.

27.   Ibid., p. 49.

28.   Ibid., pp. 49–56.

29.   Ibid., pp. 58–59.

30.   Referring to Joshua's rejection of a heavenly voice in a famous talmudic story; see Bavli, Baba Mezia 59b.

31.   See above, chapter 1.

32.   See Graetz, *Geschichte*, 4:496–499 n. 7.

33.   Ibid., p. 62.

34.   Ibid., p. 63.

35.   Ibid., 68–69.

36.   Ibid., p. 71.

37.   Ibid., p. 69.

38.   See above, chapter 2, pp. 44–45.

39.   Ibid.

40.   Also evident is Graetz's other historiographical passion, the political history of the Jews.

41.   The ability to effect this compromise is critical to Graetz as I understand him. By means of this compromise rabbinic Judaism incorporated the means to respond as creatively as necessary to new circumstances, while still possessing the means to reign in excess. It is interesting to note that Graetz's contemporary, the Orthodox rabbi Samson Raphael Hirsch, sees Graetz as pleading for a return to Ishmaelian principles (see below), while Ismar Schorsch sees Graetz as suggesting that it was Aqiba who was most responsible for "securely [laying] the foundation of rabbinic Judaism" ("Ideology and History," p. 38). The former sees Graetz as too much of a Reformer; see below.

42.   Samson Raphael Hirsch, *Gesammelte Schriften*; English translation: *Collected Writings of Rabbi Samson Raphael Hirsch*, vol. 5 (Spring Valley, N.Y.: Feldheim, 1988), pp. 3–206.

43.   Hirsch, *Collected Writings*, 5:39–42.

44.   Ibid., p. 77.

45. Ibid., pp. 161–89. Hirsch saw Graetz as a champion of Ishmael, precisely because he assumed that Graetz's description of Ishmael's exegesis would logically lead to an easing of the halakhic burden. He thus focuses his refutation on, inter alia, the many severities attributed to R. Ishmael in rabbinic literature. Most of his comments miss the point, but they tell us much about Hirsch himself, particularly his assumption that what Graetz considered "healthy" exegesis—were it creative, and were there any within rabbinic literature—would naturally lead to reform.

46. Zvi Menaḥem Pineles, *Darkah shel Torah* (Vienna, 1861), p. 179. Pineles challenges the whole conception, calling attention to Hirsch's review and his counterevidence. He understands that since it is based on the give-and-take of the Bavli, it may be dismissed as reconstructive and secondary, but he argues that the other midreshe halakhah and the Tosefta make the whole matter untenable. See further pp. 16–19.

47. For discussion of these influences, see Hans Liebeschütz, *Das Judentum in deutschen Geschichtsbild vom Hegel bis Max Weber* (Tübingen, 1967), pp. 113–25, and S. Heschel (chapter 6, n. 73).

48. See chapter 6, n. 123.

49. Geiger, *Urschrift*, pp. 434–50.

50. See Meyer, *Response to Modernity*, pp. 105–7.

51. Ibid., pp. 84–89.

52. See Ismar Schorsch, "Zacharias Frankel and the European Origins of Conservative Judaism," *Judaism* 30 (1981): 344–54.

53. Zechariah Frankel, *Vorstudien zu der Septuaginta* (Leipzig, 1841), p. xii. The translation is from Ismar Schorsch, "The Ethos of Modern Jewish Scholarship," *Leo Baeck Institute Yearbook*, 1990, 67.

54. Frankel, *Vorstudien*, p. xii.

55. Ibid., p. xiii.

56. Ibid.

57. Ibid., p. xiv.

58. Ibid., pp. 180–81.

59. For discussion, see James Q. Whitman, *The Legacy of Roman Law in the German Romantic Era* (Princeton: Princeton University Press, 1990), pp. 92–199, esp. pp. 102–31. Consider what we have seen in Frankel and the following comments of Puchta: "Alongside what was written, a great part of the law existed unwritten, living and evolving in the consciousness of the people as customary law. Both written and unwritten law were perfectly equivalent, both were the property of the people. The twelve tables were intended to present the fundamental principles of the entire legal system, the rest of Roman law appeared as an extension of it, as twigs that shot forth from its trunk and branches. The newly developing and growing law that existed undelineated in the conviction of the people was put in the context of the twelve tables. This was the business of the legal specialist of the age" (G. F. Puchta, *Cursus der Institutionen* [Leipzig, 1845], p. 281, cited in Whitman, *Legacy*, p. 127).

60. For discussion, see Rivka Horowitz, *Zechariah Frankel ve-Reshit ha-Yahadut ha-Positivit-historit* (Jerusalem: Shazar Institute, 1984), pp. 18–19;

Schorsch, "Zacharias Frankel," pp. 348–52; for more general discussion of Savigny and Jewish law, see Harris, *Nachman Krochmal*, pp. 226–32. As far as I am aware, Frankel never refers to them directly, perhaps because of Savigny's anti-Semitism, perhaps because he did not think the cause of his argument would be advanced in any way by such reference. See also, Meyer, *Response to Modernity*, pp. 414–15 n. 98.

61. Zechariah Frankel, *Der gerichtliche Beweis nach mosaisch- talmudischen Rechte* (Berlin, 1846), p. 100. See also pp. 55–62.

62. See Friedrich Karl von Savigny, *Of the Vocation of Our Age for Legislation and Jurisprudence* (London, 1831), pp. 20–30; on the legal importance of *gemeinsame Überzeugung* and the role of scholars in determing what it is in Puchta's work, see Whitman, *Legacy*, pp. 122–24.

63. Frankel, *Der gerichtliche Beweis,* p. 6. We should note that Frankel identifies Eduard Gans as representative of the opposite point of view. Gans, a convert from Judaism, was an ardent disciple of Hegel, and an inveterate opponent of Savigny.

64. As Hegel (and Kant and many others) would see it from one perspective, and as Samson Raphael Hirsch would see it from another.

65. Frankel, *Der gerichtliche Beweis,* p. 43.

66. Ibid., p. 101. Compare his treatment of the matter some seven years later in his article, "Geist der palästinischen und babylonischen Hagada," *Monatschrift für Geschichte und Wissenschaft des Judentums* 2 (1853): 396.

67. In my opinion, this argument is not as weak as arguments ex silentio usually are. There is the support of the work as a whole which repeatedly stresses the response to life, not to text; and there is the fact that every other document that one would expect to find in this list, down to the *responsa* of Yoel Sirkes (the *Bach*), is mentioned.

68. Zechariah Frankel, *Über den Einfluss der palästinischen Exegese auf die alexandrinische Hermeneutik* (Leipzig, 1851), pp. 1–2.

69. See esp., ibid., pp. 89–99, 133–60.

70. As is well known, Frankel attended the second of these conferences in 1845, and there sought to impress upon the participants the importance of "positive-historical" Judaism. He failed and bolted from the conference.

71. The proximity of Frankel's views to those of Krochmal is unmistakable, and suggests that he learned much from the Galician sage. See Harris, *Nachman Krochmal,* pp. 235–40.

72. Zechariah Frankel, "Über palästinische und alexandrinische Schriftforschung," in *Programm zur Eröffnung des jüdisch-theologischen Seminars zu Breslau* (Breslau, 1854), p. 7. Again here, the influence of Krochmal's work is unmistakable. See Harris, *Nachman Krochmal,* pp. 240–42.

73. Frankel, "Über palästinische," p. 19.

74. Ibid.

75. Zechariah Frankel, *Darkhe ha-Mishnah* (Breslau, 1859), pp. 2–3.

76. In addition to the enactments of the *Soferim* that had a connection to Scripture, extrabiblical Jewish law contained another category, namely, the *halakhah le-Moshe mi-Sinai,* the law given to Moses at Sinai. Frankel explains

that these laws did not really originate at Sinai, but do extend back into antiquity, have no scriptural support, and in general are seen as so authoritative that they are "as if they were given to Moses at Sinai" (*Darkhe ha-Mishnah,* pp. 20–21). This statement, more than any thing else he wrote in the work, engendered great controversy. See above, note 3, and see Hirsch, *Collected Writings,* 5:209–330. It is interesting to note that it was precisely the *Darkhe ha-Mishnah,* which in many respects is far more traditional than Frankel's earlier works, that led to controversy. Clearly, Frankel's status from 1854 as the head of the seminary in Breslau lent greater urgency to opposing him.

77. Frankel, *Darke ha-Mishnah,* pp. 16–17.

78. Ibid., pp. 18–19.

79. He diverges from Graetz significantly, though, regarding the emergence of Jewish exegetical activity, and also in his description of the approaches of the Shammaites and Eliezer ben Hyrkanus; see ibid., pp. 47–57, 78–87.

80. Frankel, however, insists that Elazar ben Azariah also followed the basic principles of Ishmael. Ibid., p. 113.

81. Ibid., p. 122.

82. Ibid., pp. 112–22.

83. See *Darkhe ha-Mishnah,* p. 113.

84. Ibid., pp. 120–21.

85. The first volume appeared in 1871, the fifth and last in 1891. For useful summary and appreciation of this work, see Solomon Schechter, "The History of Jewish Tradition," in his *Studies in Judaism: First Series* (Philadelphia: Jewish Publication Society, 1907).

86. Entitled, *Di Grinder un Boyer fun Yidntum Dor Dor Vedorshav: oder di Geshikhte fun der Toyre Shebalpe,* 2 vols. (New York, 1922).

87. Although Ahad Ha-am, writing in 1893, seemed to feel that it was both read and honored. See his "Ha-Lashon ve-Sifrutah," in his *'Al Parashat Derakhim,* 4 vols. (Berlin, 1921), 1:192.

88. Isaac Hirsh Weiss, *Zikhronotai me-Yalduti 'ad Mil'ot li Shemonim Shanah* (Warsaw, 1895), pp. 3–83; quotation on p. 8.

89. Isaac Hirsh Weiss, ed., *Sifra de-Be Rav* (Vienna, 1862), pp. iii–iv.

90. See Mordechai Breuer, *Jüdische Orthodoxie im deutschen Reich, 1871–1981: Die Sozialsgeschichte einer religiösen Minderheit* (Frankfurt am Main: Jüdischer Verlag, 1986), pp. 120–33.

91. See his explanation of the title; Isaac Hirsh Weiss, *Mekhilta . . . im Peirush Midot Soferim* (Vienna, 1865), p. 2. The description of the work on the German title page speaks volumes about the editor; it reads: "nebst einer Einleitung über die historische Entwicklung der Halacha und Hagada in den ältesten Zeiten."

92. The memoirs skip over many more important things, such as the suicide of a son who described him as a monster. Important and rather unflattering information regarding Weiss in Vienna may be drawn from Freud's letters; see Robert Wistrich, *The Jews of Vienna in the Age of Franz Joseph* (Oxford: Oxford University Press for the Littman Library, 1990), pp. 556–58.

93. On this institution, see N. M. Gelber, "Beit ha-Midrash le Rabbanim

be-Vina," in S. K. Mirsky, ed., *Mosedot Torah be-Eiropa be-Vinyanam u-ve-Ḥurbanam* (New York, 1956), pp. 715–30.

94.   It is possible that the shift was occasioned by a reading of the second edition of Krochmal's *Guide,* which appeared in 1863; his introduction to the *Mekhilta* refers to it, whereas the earlier introduction does not. This is, of course, pure speculation, although there is no denying the enormous influence that Krochmal's work exercised on Weiss, even if it did not play a critical role in his personal transformation.

95.   See his article "Iyyun Tefillah," *Bikkurim* 1 (1864): 85. In this article published just months before the introduction to the *Mekhilta,* Weiss set out to evaluate Zunz's claim that the eighteen-blessing prayer could not have been developed in the days of the men of the Great Assembly. He writes, "Since this claim goes against the thinking to which we have been accustomed from our youth, and against what has been received from our sages, may their memory be for a blessing, who taught us . . . it is difficult for me to separate myself from their tradition in any matter; on the other hand, it is incumbent upon us to critically evaluate the judgment of its opponents, lest they say that our love for the tradition of our sages, may their memory be for a blessing, has distorted our judgment, such that we make darkness light and light darkness."

96.   Weiss, *Mekhilta,* pp. ii–iii.

97.   See inter alia Wilhelm Bacher, *Die Bibelexegese der jüdischen Religionsphilosophen des Mittelalters vor Maimûni* (Budapest, 1892; repr., Gregg International, 1972), p. 72 n. 1; and idem, *Die Bibelexegese Moses Maimunis* (Budapest, 1896; repr., Farnborough: Gregg International, 1972), pp. 19–22.

98.   Isaac Hirsh Weiss, *Dor Dor ve-Dorshav* (Berlin: Platt and Minkus, 1924), 2:127.

99.   This is not meant to suggest that Aqiba did not think that his *derashot* truly represented what the Torah intended. A study of his *derashot* would lead inevitably to the opposite conclusion. Thus, while most of the Aqiban exegeses did not generate laws previously unknown, neither can they be seen as playful connections that were not designed to elucidate the text. See ibid., p. 115.

100.   See in general, ibid., pp. 101–27. See esp. p. 106.

101.   Even among those committed liberal Jews who may be offended by rabbinic Judaism's patriarchy argue that abandoning this patriarchy is consistent with the vital, progressive possibilities inherent in rabbinism.

102.   See the recent collection of his writings on Volozhin entitled *Pirqe Volozhin* (Holon, 1984), pp. 17, 20, 28. As Berdichevski correctly notes, the yeshiva student who clandestinely read from the works of the historical school was a clearly identifiable "type" in Volozhin (and, he could have noted, other yeshivot), although, to be sure, such a student was in the minority (see *Pirqe Volozhin,* p. 51).

103.   Elḥanan Wasserman, "Mikhtav she-Nishlaḥ le-"Yisrael ha-Ṣa'ir," in idem, *Qoveṣ Ma'amarim* (Tel Aviv, 1986), pp. 71–72.

104.   See Samuel Joseph Fuenn, *Divre ha-Yamin le-Vene Yisrael* (Vilna, 1871, 1877), esp. 1:71ff., 2:189–20. See also his polemic against Geiger in the "Notes to Chapter Three," pp. 29–38. See also Zweifel, *Shalom 'al Yisrael,* pt. 4, pp. 50–51.

Chapter 8. Midrash and Orthodoxy

1. The phrase is Klaus Epstein's in *The Genesis of German Conservatism* (Princeton: Princeton University Press, 1966), p. 66.

2. Following the procedure of the previous chapters regarding the term reform, when used as a generic term, "orthodoxy" will not be capitalized; when used to refer to a specific variety of Jewish religion, it will be.

3. The German lands include Posen and other Polish areas that came under Prussian rule with the partitions of Poland; the Lithuanian Jewish Kulturbereich includes the Baltics generally, western Belarus and northern Poland. We should note that in all these areas the newly emergent patterns of orthodoxy coexisted with communities—generally in rural and semirural areas— that should more properly be called traditionalist than orthodox.

Germany and Lithuania were not the only areas that saw the emergence of distinctive Orthodox communities. Important Hasidic courts in Poland, Ukraine, Galicia, and Belarus became self-consciously orthodox throughout the nineteenth century; Hungary and Galicia, in particular, were home to a non-Hasidic Orthodoxy as well. I have focused on Germany and Lithuania because, in my judgment, these Orthodox communities most directly engaged the issues dealt with in this book. Even though more distinctive patterns of religious adjustment are manifest in Hungary than Lithuania, for the most part Hungarian Orthodoxy eschewed responding directly to the historical and ideological claims of reformers, as opposed to their practical consequences. Their leading scholars stressed the authority of the *Shulḥan Arukh*—indeed, in some ways apotheosized this authority—and rarely felt threatened by the Reformers' efforts to portray themselves as emulating the ancient rabbis nor by their claim that the *derashot* of the rabbis represent distortions of the Torah (if indeed they were even aware of them). The efforts of the historical school to deal with the issues of this book elicited little reaction as well. Gottlieb Fischer took part in the controversy surrounding Frankel (see previous chapter); the far more learned Yiṣhaq Zvi Margareten wrote a response to Pinḥas Menaḥem Heilperin's response to Holdheim entitled *Sefer Toqef ha-Talmud*. One can find other such efforts, but nothing comparable to what was produced in Germany and Lithuania.

4. See Mordechai Breuer, *Jüdische Orthodoxie*. While Breuer's central focus is on a later period, he sets the events of that period within the context of the earlier emergence of Orthodoxy. See also, Robert Liberles, *Religious Conflict in Social Context: The Resurgence of Orthodox Judaism in Frankfurt am Main, 1838–1877* (Westport, Conn.: Greenwood Press, 1985).

5. For discussion, see Harris, *Nachman Krochmal*, pp. 221–23.

6. See H. Jolowicz, *Geschichte der Juden in Königsberg* (Posen, 1867), pp. 107–41.

7. Ibid., pp. 140–41.

8. J. L. Saalschütz, *Das Mosaische Recht nebst den vervollständigenden thalmudisch-rabbinischen Bestimmungen* (Berlin, 1846). The title makes his orientation clear. In his introduction he stated, "Unumgänglich nothwendig aber schien es, die Haupt Bestimmungen des spätern Jüdischen Rechts, die

Michaelis gänzlich vernachlässigte, auch hier auf die Quellen selbst eingehend, zu berücksichtigen. Eine vollständige Darstellung des gesammten Thalmudischen Rechtes, nach allen seinen Einzelheiten, würde die Grenze unserer Aufgabe bei Weitem überschritten haben und schien auch nicht in dem Bedürfnisse der Leser dieses Buches zu liegen. Aber die Mittheilung des Betreffenden aus dem Rechte der Mischnah, mit Eingehung auf die Entscheidungen welche, für die dort unentschiedene Controverse, die Gemara und die Commentatoren darbieten, so wie die theilweise Berucksichtigung der noch spätern Quellen wird, als gesondert unter dem Texte beiherfolgend, wohl nicht unwillkommen seyn" (ibid., p. iv).

9. Jacob Katz, *Out of the Ghetto*, pp. 121–22.

10. See Abraham Berliner, "Davar 'el ha-Kore," in *Ha-Ketav ve-ha-Kabbalah,* 4th ed. (Berlin, 1880), pp. v–vi. See also Yehudah Cooperman, *Pirke Mavo le-Feirush ha-Ketav ve-ha-Kabbalah al ha-Torah* (Jerusalem: Haskel, 1986), p. 9.

11. See Mordechai Breuer, *Jüdische Orthodoxie,* p. 170.

12. As he put it in the description of the work that appeared on the "shar-blatt," the work's intent was to "explain the verses according to the method of *peshat,* to unify them with the oral law."

13. This is an old rabbinic topos, given new meaning by Meklenburg. See his *Ha-Ketav ve-ha-Kabbalah,* vol. 1, pp. vii–ix.

14. Ibid., pp. vii–x, note 2.

15. Ibid., pp. xiv–xv, note 3.

16. Obviously, the English terms are my own, and their respective uses to distinguish different forms of multiple meanings is arbitrary.

17. Meklenburg, *Ha-Ketav ve-ha-Kabbalah,* p. ix and xiv–xv. See also, Cooperman, *Pirke Mavo,* p. 12.

18. Cf. the remarks of the Gaon of Vilna in Moshe Philip, ed., *Sefer Mishle 'im Be'ur ha-GRA* (Petah Tiqvah, 1985), p. 35 (ad Prov. 2:3) .

19. Meklenburg, *Ha-Ketav ve-ha-Kabbalah* ad Lev. 1 : 2, s .v. "min ha-şon." Compare the comments of the Gaon of Vilna to Proverbs 2: 3 (see previous note).

20. For further discussion, see Yehudah Cooperman, *Pirqe Mavo,* pp. 26–38.

21. Unlike Wessely and Meklenburg, Mendelssohn refused to collapse the distinction between *peshat* and *derash.*

22. See Meklenburg, *Ha-Ketav ve-ha-Kabbalah,* pp. xv–xxii (= note 4) .

23. See Cooperman, *Pirke Mavo,* pp. 13–16. Cooperman makes no effort to identify who Meklenburg's targets were, other than the obvious, the translation of Mendelssohn.

24. Compare *Ha-Ketav ve-ha-Kabbalah* to Lev. 15:28, s.v. "ve-aḥar tithar," and Michael Creizenach, *Thariag oder Inbegriff der mosaischen Vorschriften nach talmudischer Interpretation* (= *Schulchan Aruch,* vol. 1) (Frankfurt am Main, 1833), p. 194 (= *Gebot,* no. 248); and *Ha-Ketav ve-ha-Kabbalah* to Deut. 6:7, s.v. "ve-shinantam le-vanekha and Thariag," pp. 114–16 (= *Gebot,* 12).

25. Compare Meklenburg, *Ha-Ketav ve-ha-Kabbalah,* to Exod. 20:13, s.v. "lo tin'af" and Mendelssohn's translation to that verse. The German translation produced under the editorship of Zunz, published in 1837, follows Mendelssohn. We should note that actually it is Meklenburg who diverges from the traditional interpretation here.

26. Jacob Katz, "Pulmus ha-'Hekhal' ve-Asifat Braunschweig," in his *Ha-Halakhah ba-Meṣar* (Jerusalem: Magnes Press, 1992), pp. 43–72; quotation, p. 56.

27. See Noah H. Rosenbloom, *Ha-Malbim* (Jerusalem: Mossad ha-Rav Kook, 1986), pp. 1–87.

28. For discussion of Malbim's years in Kempen, see Rosenbloom, *Malbim,* pp. 31–43.

29. Meir Leibush Malbim, *Ha-Torah ve-ha-Mitzvah* to Leviticus, p. 2a.

30. Ibid.

31. I do not mean to suggest that Malbim denied the traditional basis of rabbinic Judaism. Like all rabbinic Jews, he affirmed that some laws were received traditions, and, like most rabbinic Jews since the early Middle Ages, he affirmed that the hermeneutic (and grammatical) principles, whose number he greatly increased, were received from Sinai. He could not, however, accept the notion that the entire network of practices and observances were received from Sinai, because this was at odds with talmudic discourse. At the same time, he does not claim that everything attached to a *derashah* necessarily originated through midrash. In some cases, as with the constellation of marriage and divorce laws, it is clear to Malbim that the rules were transmitted by means of an unbroken tradition from Moses; this does not in any way diminish the need to explain rabbinic midrash as *peshat.* See his comments to Deut. 24:1.

32. The phrase is from Exod. 24:12; in light of the discussion in the Bavli, Berakhot 5a, it can be translated as "The Torah and Tradition." The commentary was first published in 1860, when Malbim was serving as a rabbi in Bucharest.

33. We should note, however, that Yiṣḥak Ya'aqob Reines, the most modern voice within the Lithuanian rabbinate, found the *Ayelet ha-Shahar* to be the most compelling part of Malbim's work, because it was systematic rather than ad hoc. See his *Ḥotam Tokhnit* (1880; Jerusalem, 1934), p. 10. In general Reines deprecated the approach of those who would claim that the *derash* is the *peshat,* because they had to make up rules as they went along to make the theory work. For Reines's own views on our issues, see pp. 45–262, and the discussion below. David Zvi Hoffmann also found some of Malbim's rules useful, although he too went his own way in dealing with the matter. See below.

34. For the significance of these numbers, see, most conveniently, the opening lines of this book.

35. The tabernacle, i.e., the place where God's presence is manifest.

36. See Malbim, *Ha-Torah ve-ha-Mitzvah,* p. 2b, s.v. "ve-hine batarti."

37. To be sure, Hirsch had his predecessors, among them his own two teachers, Jacob Ettlinger and Isaac Bernays. For a broader discussion of the "new rabbinate" in Germany, see Ismar Schorsch, "Emancipation and the

Crisis of Religious Authority: The Emergence of the Modern Rabbinate," in Werner Mosse, et al., eds., *Revolution and Evolution: 1848 in German-Jewish History* (Tübingen: J. C. B. Mohr, 1981).

38. For biographical information, see Noah H. Rosenbloom, *Tradition in an Age of Reform: The Religious Philosophy of Samson Raphael Hirsch* (Philadelphia: Jewish Publication Society, 1976), 3–120.

39. See Rosenbloom, *Tradition in an Age of Reform,* pp. 68–70.

40. Particularly his review of Creizenach's *Schulchan Aruch.*

41. See, e.g., Hirsch's responses to those who refused to circumcise their children in his recently published collection of *responsa,* letters and other writings, *Shemesh Mirpa* (Brooklyn: Mesorah Publications, 1992), pp. 187–88 (from 1843) and pp. 199–200 (from 1850). See also his response to the Braunschweig conference, pp. 188–96. For background, see Jacob Katz, *Ha-Halakhah be-Meṣar,* pp. 123–49.

42. See above, chapter 7, notes 42–45.

43. The English translation is by Hirsch's grandson, Isaac Levy, in Samson Raphael Hirsch, *The Pentateuch: Translation and Commentary* (Gateshead: Judaica Press, 1973).

44. Ibid.

45. The fact that Hirsch, in his polemics against Graetz and Frankel, acknowledges that occasionally a law is created or restored by means of midrash in no way mitigates the difficulty of talmudic discourse, as the latter suggests that the recourse to midrash was not merely occasional. For discussion and sources, see Kalman Kahana, "Torah shebekhtav ve-Torah shebe'al peh bemishnato" in Yonah Emanuel, ed., *Harav Shimshon Rafael Hirsch: Mishnato ve-Shitato* (Jerusalem: Feldheim, 1989), pp. 75–84.

46. See, e.g., his comments to Exod. 22:11. It is instructive that he there deals with but one of the three midrashic responses to the source of a compensated bailee's liability for a lost object.

47. As we have seen, there are many who argue for a comprehensive tradition who nevertheless insist that the written Torah contains enough allusions to the oral that one could reconstruct the latter in the event that it is forgotten (in addition to what has been cited here, such as Nieto, see the comments of the Maharsha to Gittin 60b; I am grateful to Prof. Yaakov Elman for this reference). Hirsch is, to my knowledge, the only one to suggest that the written Torah is *nothing more than* a means of calling attention to a comprehensive, antecedent oral revelation.

48. See also his comments to Exod. 21:6.

49. In addition to the Bible commentary, see also his translation of and commentary on the Prayer Book, *The Hirsch Siddur* (Jerusalem: Feldheim, 1969), p. 38 (= comments to the thirteen exegetical principles).

50. Hirsch's commentary to Psalm 119 also provides interesting insight into his attitude to religious praxis.

51. I will leave it to the psychohistorians to determine the significance of Hirsch's likening of divinely imposed religious norms to incurable illness; each represents a condition one must bear without hope for a reprieve.

52. See Breuer, *Jüdische Orthodoxie*, pp. 160–87; idem, "Ḥokhmat Yisrael: Shalosh Gishot Ortodoxiot," in *Sefer Yovel Likhvod Moreinu ha-Gaon Rabbi Yosef Dov Halevi Soloveitchik*, 2 vols. (Jerusalem, 1984), 2:856–65.

53. First published in 1878 as *Geschichte Israels;* known as *Prolegomena,* etc., in all subsequent editions, beginning with the second in 1883.

54. For a sympathetic portrait of Hoffmann's scholarly work, see Chaim Tchernowitz, "Rabbi David Hoffmann," in idem, *Masekhet Zikhronot: Parṣufim ve-ha-'Arakhot* (New York, 1945), pp. 244–64. See also David Ellenson and Richard Jacobs, "Scholarship and Faith: David Hoffmann and His Relation to *Wissenschaft des Judentums,*" *Modern Judaism* 8, no. 1 (February 1988): 27–40; Alexander Marx, *Essays in Jewish Biography* (Philadelphia: Jewish Publication Society, 1947), pp. 185–222.

55. For discussion, see John Rogerson, *Old Testament Criticism in the Nineteenth Century: England and Germany* (Philadelphia: Fortress Press, 1985), pp. 79–140, 257–72, and passim; Hans-Joachim Kraus, *Geschichte der historisch-kritischen Erforschung des Alten Testaments* (Neukirchener Verlag, 1982), pp. 133–274.

56. He wrote "Wie wir schon vorher bemerkt haben, sind uns sehr viele Bestimmungen der göttlichen Gesetze nicht durch die Schrift, sondern nur durch mündliche Überlieferung mitgetheilt worden. Nun aber haben sich unsere Weisen bemüht, für diese traditionellen Bestimmungen Anhaltspunkte in der Schrift zu finden. Dies gelang ihnen durch ein tieferes Eindringen in den Sinn der Schriftworte oder durch ein tieferes Forschen in der Schrift. . . . Diese Ansicht über den *midrasch,* welche auch Rambam und viele Andere ausgesprochen haben, wollen wir unsere Schrifterklärung zu Grunde legen. Nach dieser sind die halakhot, die im midrasch aus der Schrift hergeleitet werden nicht erst in Folge dieser derash entstanden, sondern sie sind traditionelle Lehren, fur die man nur durch diese derashah einen Anhaltspunkt suchte, entweder um sie besser zu begründen, oder um sie vor vergessenheit zu bewahren." *Das Buch Leviticus, übersetzt und erklärt von Dr. D. Hoffmann,* erster halbband (Berlin: Verlag M. Poppelauer, 1905), pp. 3–4.

57. See David Zvi Hoffmann, *Die wichtigsten Instanzen gegen die Graf-Wellhausensche Hypothese,* 2 vols. (Berlin, 1904, 1916). This work is devoted to showing the implausibility of the Wellhausen hypothesis by displaying its many inconsistencies. Clearly, its intended audience went well beyond the Orthodox community of Germany. In this work Hoffmann is content to try to refute the hypothesis, and he sees little need to resolve the textual difficulties fueling the critical theories. That task he reserved for his Leviticus commentary, which, as he noted in the *Vorwort* to volume 2 of *Die wichtigsten Instanzen,* carried forward his program of challenging Wellhausen, but this time positively, and with extensive citation of rabbinic sources, which are conspicuously absent from *Instanzen.*

58. See his *Das erste Mishna.*

59. David Zvi Hoffmann, *Zur Einleitung in halakischen Midrasch* (Berlin, 1886), p. 4.

60. He wrote, "Oft gewinnt R. Akiba eine Lehre vermittels tiefer Deutungs-

regeln aus dem Schrifttexte, während R. Ismael dieselbe Lehre durch einen einfachen logischen Schluss folgert oder aus deutlichen Schriftwort ableitet" (*Zur Einleitung*, p. 6). At times Hoffmann's claim that R. Ishmael was committed to *peshat* itself involves a "midrashic" reading of his teaching. For example, at Yerushalmi, Shabbat 9d, Hoffmann sees R. Ishmael's reliance on the word *niddah* as affirming the simple meaning of this word. Actually, R. Ishmael is learning a *gezerah shavah,* since, viewed philologically, the word *niddah* does not connote temporary disqualification. Only by virtue of its application to one menstruating does it achieve that legal significance.

61. Hoffmann, to his credit, recognized that this claim required some justification. See *Zur Einleitung,* p. 10.

62. Ibid., esp. pp. 5–12.

63. See his *Untersuchungen über die halakischen Midraschim* (Berlin, 1927), esp. pp. 126–39.

64. Hoffmann, in this book and in subsequent publications, energetically went about identifying Ishmaelian midreshe halakhah to Leviticus and Deuteronomy to complement the already known, allegedly Aqiban, *Sifre Zutta* to Numbers; in addition he became the first to try to reconstruct the Aqiban midrash to Exodus, *Mekhilta de-Rabbi Shim'on bar Yoḥai.*

65. For discussion, see Breuer, *Jüdische Orthodoxie,* pp. 178–87.

66. See ibid., pp. 184–85; Kahane, "Torah she-bekhtav," pp. 81–84.

67. Breuer, *Jüdische Orthodoxie,* p. 183; English translation *Modernity Within Tradition* (New York: Columbia University Press, 1992), pp. 198–99 (emphasis added).

68. See Immanuel Etkes, *Rabbi Israel Salanter ve-Reshita shel Tenu'at ha-Musar* (Jerusalem: Magnes Press, 1982), pp. 147–52; idem, "Pareshat ha'haskalah mi-Ta'am' ve-ha-Temurah be-Ma'amad Tenu'at ha-Haskalah be-Rusya," *Zion* 43 (1978): 264–313, reprinted now in Etkes, *Ha-Dat veha-Ḥayyim* (Jerusalem: Mercaz Zalman Shazar, 1993), pp. 167–216; Michael Stanislawski, *Tsar Nicholas I and the Jews* (Philadelphia: Jewish Publication Society, 1983), pp. 49–122. Etkes and Stanislawski rightly emphasize the role of the state in eliciting this perception; Stanislawski in particular emphasizes the role of the state in the emergence of a distinct Orthodox identity. It is worthy of note that the state's education minister, Serge Uvarov, defined the role of *haskalah* to be to aid in the mitigation of the influence of the Talmud on Russian Jewry. (See Etkes, *Ha-Dat veha-Ḥayyim,* pp. 170–71.)

69. For discussion and refinement of this point, see Michael A. Meyer, "The German Model of Religious Reform and Russian Jewry," in Isadore Twersky, ed., *Danzig, Between East and West: Aspects of Modern Jewish History* (Cambridge: Harvard University Press, 1985), pp. 67–91

70. See Mordecai Zalkin, "Haskalat Vilna (1835–60): Kavim le Demuto" (M.A. thesis, Hebrew University, 1992), esp. pp. 92–140.

71. See Yitzḥaq Baer Levinsohn, *Beit Yehudah* (Vilna, 1839), pt. 1, pp. 93, 140ff.; pt. 2, pp. 36–37, 45–50. The whole work, while providing some "modern" interpretations of rabbinic institutions, contains an apologia for rabbinic religion. Although Levinsohn was not himself a Lithuanian, he was the "father"

of the Lithuanian *haskalah* all the same, as has been noted by many; see most recently, Zalkin, "Haskalat Vilna," pp. 94–95. We should also note that both the first and second editions of *Beit Yehudah* were published in Vilna by the Romm family press; the role of the Romm Press in Lithuanian Jewish culture remains unappreciated.

72. For list of some of these, see Yehoshua Heshel Levin, *Ma'alot ha-Sulam* (Jerusalem, 1989), pp. 54–57 n. 13.

73. For a study of important aspects of this social substratum, see Immanuel Etkes, *Lita biRushalayim* (Jerusalem: Yad Yitzḥaq ben Zvi, 1991), pp. 17–84.

74. In some cases this meant refining the efforts of earlier correctors who had made mistakes. For example in the *Sifra*'s discussion to Lev. 20:14, discussed in chapter 1, the printed texts of the *Sifra* reflect the conclusion of the Bavli. As the Gaon realized, though, such a correction made the Bavli's argumentation that produced the conclusion incomprehensible. He thus restored the "original" text, so that the Bavli's transmutation of its meaning would make sense. In this case, the Gaon's restoration is supported by mss., and obviously undid the damage done by an earlier hand. Still, it is often the case that the Gaon's emendations are motivated by a desire to harmonize the different rabbinic texts; this tendency of the Gaon led Abraham Geiger to express his gratification that someone like the Gaon did not come along until the eighteenth century, and that his glosses on the *Mekhilta* were not published until 1844, long after printed editions of the midreshe halakhah were available. Had such a person lived earlier, his emendations might have been accepted by printers as the authoritative text, which would have made a reconstruction of the history of halakhah impossible. See Geiger, *Urschrift*, appendix 1. As for the Gaon's own rationalization of emending texts, see Israel of Skhlov, *Pe'at ha-Shulḥan* (Jerusalem: Yad Binyamin, 1968), p. 5d.

75. E.g., his deletion of two phrases from Horowitz-Rabin, ed., *Mekhilta*, Mishpatim, 7, pp. 272–73; see note 14 beginning on p. 272.

76. This is particularly evident from the claim advanced by his student, Ḥayyim of Volozhin, that the Gaon explained to him that he would only emend a text if he could find fifteen witnesses from elsewhere in the oral Torah to support it. Hyperbolic or otherwise, the statement plainly indicates the extent to which the Gaon considered the entire rabbinic literature to be of one piece. (See Israel of Skhlov, *Peat ha-Shulḥan*).

77. See Bezalel Landau, *Ha-Gaon he-Ḥasid mi-Vilna* (Jerusalem, 1965), pp. 70–85; Maimon (below, n. 81), pp. 92–97.

78. For a description of its contents, see Landau, *Ha-Gaon*, pp. 299–300 n. 4.

79. According to an oft-repeated story, the Gaon did all his own writing, producing seventy works, until the age of forty. After this he wrote no more himself, but produced works only through his students. The *Aderet Eliyahu* certainly seems to fit the latter type, although those responsible for its publication claim to have a manuscript of the Gaon. It was not one of the seven works whose authenticity was assured by the *beit din* in Vilna soon after the Gaon's death. If a remark by Menasseh of Ilya, to the effect that the Gaon opposed

those who would collapse the distinction between *peshat* and *derash,* is accurate (see *Ma'alot ha-Sulam,* note 11), there is reason to think that the Gaon "wrote" the work after becoming acquainted with Wessely's Leviticus commentary (1783), since the *Aderet Eliyahu* opposes the primary tendency of Wessely's work, although this is far from certain, not least because Wessely already gave voice to his views on *peshat* in his *Gan Na'ul* (1755). If all this conjecture were right, the work could be dated to the last fourteen years of the Gaon's life.

80.   Ben Zion Katz emphasized the kabbalistic thrust of the Gaon's commentary. See Ben Zion Katz, *Ḥasidut Rabbanut Haskalah,* 2 vols. (Tel Aviv: Devir, 1959), 2:28–31.

81.   See Y. L. Ha-Kohen Maimon, *Toledot ha-Gra* (Jerusalem: Mossad ha-Rav Kook, 1970), pp. 83–90. Maimon also identifies the Frankist movement as a source of the Gaon's anxiety regarding the future of traditional Judaism.

82.   Although I see the Gaon's work as standing in partial opposition to Wessely's, there was a report to the effect that the Gaon praised the latter's work; see Sandler, *Ha-Be'ur la-Torah,* p. 138. In note 8 on this page Sandler provides an external reason to question the reliability of this report; I do not find this reason at all convincing (cf. Israel Klausner, *Vilna be-Tequfat ha-GRA* [Jerusalem: Sinai, 1942], p. 46). A comparison of the scholars' approaches to the Bible, however, leads me to the conclusion that they are quite distinct. If the Gaon did indeed praise Wessely's work, I suspect it must have been rather faintly.

83.   See Halivni, *Peshat and Derash,* pp. 30–31, who discusses the Gaon's seminal comment to Exod. 21:6. In addition to the source he cites there, attention should be directed to *Aderet Eliyahu* to Gen. 1:1, s.v. "et." It is true that in the passage quoted by Halivni, the Gaon contrasts the *peshat* with a *halakhah le-Moshe mi-Sinai,* which uproots the former; it is difficult to know how literally to take this, as throughout the commentary the Gaon refers to the *derashot* of the sages as determining meaning. See, e.g., his comments to Exod. 21:8, 22 and Lev. 7:18. See also the Gaon's comments to Prov. 1:6, 8:6, and 8:9, the last to be cited below. See Yeshayahu Wolfsberg, "Ha-Gaon mi-Vilna ke-'Ishiut u-khe-farshan," in J. L. Hacohen Maimon, *Qoveṣ Ma'amarim ve-Ha'arot 'al Mishnat ha-GRA ve-Talmidav* (= *Sefer ha-GRA,* pt. 4) (Jerusalem: Mossad ha-Rav Kook, 1954), pp. 163–69; and see now Avia Hacohen, "Be-'Ikve Be'ur ha GRA le-Farashat 'Amah 'Ivriah," in *Sefer ha-Yovel le-Rav Mordechai Breuer: 'Asufat Ma'amarim be-Mada'e ha-Yahadut,* 2 vols. (Jerusalem: Akademon, 1992), 1:77–87.

84.   See Ḥayyim Hillel Ben-Sasson, "'Ishiuto shel ha-GRA ve hashpa'ato ha-historit," *Zion* 31 (1966): 53–73.

85.   This work was the first of the Gaon's to be published, apparently in accord with his wishes.

86.   See *Sefer Mishle 'im Be'ur ha-GRA* ad 8:6–11, esp. 8:6. On the reliability of this commentary as a reflection of the Gaon's thinking, see Ben Sasson, "'Ishiuto shel ha-GRA," note 28.

87.   On the meaning of this phrase, see the Gaon's comments to Prov. 2:3.

88.   See the Gaon's comments to Prov. 2:3, and the many sources cited by Ben Sasson, "'Ishiuto shel ha-GRA," pp. 53–73.

89. See also his comments to Deut. 17:11.

90. On the significance of these terms in the Gaon's commentary, see his remarks to Prov. 1:2. *Ḥokhmah* refers to the theoretical mind, whereas *binah* concerns the practical mind, specifically how to observe the Torah properly. In the example here, the practical mind leads to the exclusion of the gorer; the discerning practical mind understands precisely why the *vav* leads to this exclusion, as opposed to any other,

91. See, e.g., *Aderet Eliyahu* ad Deut. 11:32.

92. For further explanation, see his *Qiṣur Mekhilta* included in the Warsaw 1887 edition of *Aderet Eliyahu* (and subsequent editions) ad Exod. 21:24; see also the actual commentary of the Gaon on this verse. Here, as in a number of other cases, he invokes the talmudic saying "halakhah 'oqeret miqra." It seems to me that "halakhah" here means midrash.

93. Of course, this intellectual effort must be guided every step of the way by Scripture's language; otherwise it would lead one astray. See his comments to Deut. 11:32.

94. Dov Ber Treves, *Revid ha-Zahav* (Bene Brak, 1967), title page. I have little to say regarding this work, as the complete first edition (1797) is unavailable to me, and only the volumes to Genesis and Exodus have appeared in the ongoing second edition. A comparison of his lengthy treatment of Exodus 21–22 with the laconic treatment of the Gaon is instructive. It seems to me that Treves certainly saw exegesis as generating law. However, it also seems to me that he conceptualized the matter differently than did the Gaon, as he saw the teachings of the rabbis as more fully embedded within the *peshat* than did the Gaon. Information regarding Treves is hard to come by; he is referred to briefly in Fuenn's *Qiryah Ne'emanah*, p. 200; Steinschneider's *'Ir Vilna*, p. 19; and Israel Klausner's *Vilna be-Tequfat ha-Gra*, index. A brief discussion of the work may be found in Yehudah Cooperman's *Li-feshuto shel Miqra* (Jerusalem: Haskel, 1974), pp. 86–93.

95. See Shaul Stampfer, "Three Lithuanian Yeshivot in the Nineteenth Century" (diss., Hebrew University, 1981), pp. 1–30.

96. See Abraham Menes, "Patterns of Jewish Scholarship in Eastern Europe," in Louis Finkelstein, ed., *The Jews: Their Religion and Culture* (New York: Schocken, 1971), pp. 177–227; Samuel K. Mirsky, ed., *Mosedot Torah be-Airopah be-Vinvanam u-ve-Hurbanam* (New York: Histadrut ha-Ivrit be-Amerikah, 1956).

97. The existence of the commentary was widely known, as it was noted by Berlin in the introduction to his commentary on the *She'iltot*; see below.

98. Berlin, "Kidmat ha-emek," p. 11.

99. See, e.g., Berlin, *Ha-'Amek Davar* to Lev. 18:5, and Deut. 32:47. To insist that the *derash* is *peshat* is to denigrate the *pilpula shel Torah* that is the most fundamental requirement of the Jew, and which is so obviously manifest in Jewish intellectual history. Further, to collapse the distinction means that, theoretically, the text and its full range of meanings are as available to Gentiles as to Jews.

100. Berlin, "Kidmat ha-'Emek," par. 7.

101. See ibid., par. 3, and comments to Deut. 31:19.

102. See especially his comments to Num. 21:20.

103. Berlin, *Ha-'Amek Davar* ad Lev. 25:18.

104. See Berlin, "Kidmat ha-'Emek" to *Ha-'Amek Davar*, par. 5 and idem, "Kidmat ha-'Emek" to *Ha-'Amek She'elah* (= *She'iltot* commentary), 1:10; compare his comments at Deut. 1:3, where he contradicts this and says that the hermeneutic principles were part of the tradition handed down by Moses. In all these places, and many others, he acknowledges that by means of these principles the sages added laws and explanations in every generation.

105. Similar claims are advanced in his comments to Lev. 1:2, 18:5, Num. 15:23, Deut. 4:1.

106. See, e.g., his comments to Lev. 26:3 and Deut. 4:1; 4:6.

107. See Immanuel Etkes, *Rabbi Israel Salanter ve-Reshita shel Tenu'at ha-Musar* (Jerusalem: Magnes, 1982), pp. 147–52; idem, "Pareshat ha'haskalah mi-Ta'am' ve-ha-Temurah be-Ma'amad Tenu'at ha-Haskalah be-Rusya," *Zion* 43 (1978): 264–313 (reprinted now in Etkes, *Ha-Dat veha-Hayyim* (Jerusalem: Mercaz Zalman Shazar, 1993), pp. 167–216; Michael Stanislawski, *Tsar Nicholas I and the Jews* (Philadelphia: Jewish Publication Society, 1983), pp. 49–122.

108. See Gideon Katzenelson, *Ha-Milhamah ha-Sifrutit bein ha-Haredim la-Maskilim* (Tel Aviv, 1954); Svia Nardeni, "Temurot be Tenu'at ha-Haskalah be-Rusya be-Shenot ha-Shishim ve-ha-Shiv'im shel ha-Me'ah ha-tesha' 'esreh," in Etkes, *Ha-Dat ve-ha-Hayyim*, pp. 300–327; Azriel Shohat, *Mosad "ha-Rabbanut mi-Ta'am" be-Rusya: Parashah be-Ma'avaq ha-Tarbut bein Haredim levein Maskilim* (Haifa, 1976); Michael Stanislawski, *For Whom Do I Toil?* (New York: Oxford University Press, 1988), pp. 68–105.

109. Compare Cooperman, *Li-Feshuto shel Miqra*, pp. 76–86. See, e.g., Berlin's snide comments in "Kidmat ha-Emek" to *Ha-'Amek She'elah* 2:2 and 2:4; see also his responsa *Meshiv Davar*, 1:9, 1:15 and 1:44.

110. See Berlin, "Kidmat ha-Emek" to *Ha-Amek She'elah* 2:2 and 2:4.

111. This is most evident in his introduction to *Ha-Amek Davar* on Leviticus.

112. "Kidmat ha-'Emek" to *Ha-'Amek She'elah* (= *She'iltot* commentary) (Jerusalem: Mossad ha-Rav Kook, 1975), 1:14, p. 10.

113. I do not mean to suggest that Berlin's work is informed by some modern historical sense. Certainly, he is willing to quickly invoke "tradition" as the answer to all kinds of problems. In noting the simultaneous existence of relatively apodictic and casuistic styles in different periods of talmudic commentary and halakhic *responsa*, he suggests that there were those who had traditions and thus did not need to resort to casuistry, while there were those in other locations who did not have these traditions (ibid., 1:10–14.) This is scarcely impressive historical explanation, but that is beside the point. What I am suggesting is that within his frame of reference, Berlin's work is informed by a more honest and bold apprehension of the nature of talmudic tradition.

114. This position is doubtlessly influenced by the comments found in the Yerushalmi, Pe'ah 2:6 and Hagigah 1:8. A similar attitude underlies the Hatam Sofer's objections to biblical translations; see his *Derashot*, 1:102a.

115. Some have argued that the development of new methods of Talmud study—methods that were far less interested in explicating the wide range of

rabbinic literature, and which were based on penetrating analyses of the Babylonian Talmud and especially its medieval interpreters—in the 1870s should be understood as a response to the *haskalah*. See now Norman Solomon, *The Analytic Movement in Rabbinic Jurisprudence* (Atlanta: Scholars Press, 1993). This may well be; these methods certainly represented a retreat from the more potentially subversive aspects of traditional Lithuanian scholarship. They did not, however, address the challenges of the *haskalah* head-on.

116. See, e.g., *Ha-Levanon* (1873), pp. 202–6.

117. First published in 1901.

118. A good example of Epstein's approach to our issues, and the limitations of the work, may be found in his comments to Exod. 28:9, note 30. Much of Epstein's concern revolved around Maimonides' idiosyncratic citation of rabbinic prooftexts that did not correspond to those of the Talmud; see also his comments to Lev. 22:19, note 112.

119. See Micha Yosef Bin Gorion (= Berdichevski), *Ma'amarim*, pt. 3 in *Kitve Micha Yosef Bin Gorion: Ḥadashim gam Yeshanim* (Leipzig, 1921), pp. 14–17.

120. We yet await a full scholarly biography of Reines; for now see Geulah Bat-Yehudah, *'Ish ha-Me-'orot* (Jerusalem: Mossad ha-Rav Kook, 1985) and Joseph Wanefsky, *Rabbi Isaac Jacob Reines: His Life and Thought* (New York, 1970). Most work on Reines has focused on his Zionist activities and thought; see most recently, Eliezer Schweid, "Te'ologia Leumit-Ṣionit be-Reshitah: 'al Mishnato shel Harav Y"Y Reines," in *Meḥqarim be-Kabbalah be-Filosofia Yehudit u-ve-Sifrut ha-Musar ve-ha-Hagut Mugashim le-Yeshayahu Tishby* (Jerusalem, 1986), pp. 689–720. For bibliography on the yeshiva in Lida, see Bat-Yehudah, *'Ish ha-Me-'orot*, p. 288 n. 16.

121. See Bat-Yehudah, *'Ish ha-Me-'orot*, p. 24.

122. Yiṣḥaq Ya'aqob Reines, *Ḥotam Tokhnit* (Jerusalem, 1934), p. 14.

123. Ibid., p. 15

124. Ibid., p. 17.

125. Ibid., pp. 10–11.

126. Ibid., pp. 45–49. Obviously, Reines has some familiarity with popularizations of Kantian thought, if not with Kant's work directly. While such popularizations certainly existed in Hebrew, it is beyond the scope of this study to try to determine precisely where Reines got his ideas and vocabulary.

127. Pages 156–85 are particularly helpful important in this regard.

128. See Bat-Yehudah, *'Ish ha-Me-'orot*, pp. 28–32.

129. See the revised edition of Berlin's *Meshiv Davar* (Jerusalem, 1993), 5:44. This source contains sharp and nasty comments regarding Reines's work.

130. Again here, it is worthwhile recalling the work of Berdichevsky (although it should be noted that at an early and moderate stage of his career, Berdichevsky reacted to Reines's book with measured appreciation; see Bat-Yehudah, *'Ish ha-Me-'orot*).

131. I am certainly aware that there is an asymmetry in my treatment of the German and Lithuanian approaches. The fact is that there were many more significant Lithuanian scholars than have been treated here, whereas, in my

view, far less is lacking in my discussion of the Germans. I can only justify this by stating that the influence of the Gaon of Vilna was so vast in this culture, and the ideal of creative Torah study so pervasive, that broader discussion of the ideological structure of this Orthodoxy here would be largely repetitive. I would like to call attention to one aspect of the work of Abraham Isaac Kook. His oeuvre is by far the most studied of all rabbinic scholars originating in Lithuania, but one aspect of his thinking on our subject has gone unnoted as far as I am aware. In his biography of his father-in-law Eliahu David Rabonowitz-Teomim (known as ADeReT), Kook addressed the matter of contemporary heresy. Kook insists that the oral Torah rests on its acceptance by the nation as a whole more than anything else. He explains that many have thought that the oral Torah rests on the greatness of the sages, and for this reason have undertaken to attack their reputation. However, while the sages are indeed great, the "eternal foundation [of the oral law] is simply the acceptance of its way of life by the nation throughout the generations." The various injunctions of the medieval sage Rabbenu Gershom are invoked as evidence. He goes on to explain, in a characteristic manner, that the nation is suffused by divinity, and thus its historical, defining culture is valid, no matter how critically one may approach even the Bible. There is simply no basis for the practical negation of halakhah. See his *'Eder ha-Yeqar* (1906; Jerusalem: Mossad ha-Rav Kook, 1985), pp. 38–40. On Kook's thought in general, see Zvi Yaron, *Mishnato shel ha-Rav Kook* (Jerusalem, 1979).

132. The ideal was manifest not only in the yeshivot, some of which enjoyed substantial financial support from the broader community, but in the various learning circles centered in the Lithuanian synagogues. Groups existed for the study of Mishnah, *'Ein Ya'aqob*, and Talmud; at times these groups brought together people of the same trade, at other times people of different trades but of the same intellectual caliber. The point is that even among those who did not devote themselves fully to Torah study, study was not relegated to professionals, but was part of the cultural lifeblood of traditional life in Lithuania.

133. To be sure, they identified textual supports for this fixed orally transmitted material, but this is a legally secondary phenomenon, despite Meklenburg's efforts to claim otherwise.

134. I do not in any way mean to deny the halakhic expertise of people like Hildesheimer and Hoffmann. I simply mean to suggest that as German Orthodoxy had no hope of developing a talmudically learned laity, its leaders had good reason to underemphasize the centrality of Torah study as a religious activity and as a central element in the emergence of defining religious norms.

Chapter 9. Conclusion

1. See above, chapter 1, p. 23.

2. Michael Chernick's forthcoming work on the use of the *gezerah shavah* shows that in tannaitic literature there is a far higher level of discipline involved in the use of this technique, which had a high potential for abuse, than had previously been supposed.

3. I must stress again here that I am not interested in the historical question of whether laws really were created this way. I am addressing the internal systemic understanding of how laws were extrapolated from the biblical text; whether historians would endorse this understanding is of very limited importance for the understanding of Jewish cultural history.

4. See, for example, Naḥmanides' commentary to Exod. 21:24.

5. See Ḥ. Merḥaviah, *Ha-Talmud be-Re'i ha-Naṣrut* (Jerusalem: Mossad Bialik, 1970); and Amos Funkenstein, *Perceptions of Jewish History* (Berkeley: University of California Press, 1993), pp. 189–96.

6. It is worth noting that at least one rabbinic scholar, Moses of Coucy, who was aware of Christian polemics against the Talmud, adopted the comprehensive tradition position; see his *Sefer Miṣvot Gadol*, prohibitions 140–41.

7. Funkenstein, *Perceptions,* pp. 196–201.

8. One need only compare the East European intellectuals who found their way to Reform Judaism in America with the early German Reformers to illustrate the point.

9. This process took place, with very different dynamics, to be sure, in Germany and among the transplanted Eastern European Jews in the United States. Certainly, in the Jewish community of Palestine/Israel the battles between the Orthodox and modernists of various types went (and goes) on. Yet this battle revolves around very practical matters of state politics and power, and no longer addresses the broader cultural questions I have been addressing. Similarly, the Orthodox in the United States do battle with liberal forms of Judaism with regard to specific issues that affect the broader community, such as conversion and patrilineal descent. This community takes the existence and illegitimacy of these forms of Judaism for granted and rarely feels the need to polemicize against them except when such public issues emerge. For recent discussion of this triumphalist Orthodoxy in the United States, see Jack Wertheimer, *A People Divided: Judaism in Contemporary America* (New York: Basic Books, 1993), pp. 114–36. As Wertheimer correctly notes, the battles in the Orthodox community are primarily internal ones between those Orthodox elements who cautiously embrace modern culture and those who reject it outright.

10. See, e.g., Moshe Ostrowsky, *Ha-Middot she-ha-Torah Nidreshet ba-hen* (Jerusalem, 1924); Moshe Avigdor Amiel, *Sefer ha-Middot le-Ḥeqer ha-Halakhah* (Jerusalem, 1929), a work more interested in the principles underlying halakhic discussion, but that sheds light nonetheless on rabbinic exegetical principles. As for the German Orthodox, their culture underwent a number of changes, in which, as far as I can see, the issues of the previous century were submerged. See Breuer, *Modernity Within Tradition,* chap. 7.

Attention should also be directed to Joseph B. Soloveitchik's "Shne Suge Masoret," in his *Shi'urim le-Zekher Aba Mari Z "L* (Jerusalem, 1983), pp. 220–39.

11. See many of his articles collected in volume 5 of his *Sifra* (Jerusalem: Jewish Theological Seminary, 1991), and his introduction to this work in his volume 1 (1989).

12. Arnold Eisen, "Re-reading Heschel on the Commandments," *Modern*

Judaism 9, no. 1:15. Heschel's *Theology* (= *Torah min ha-Shamayim be-'Aspaqlariah shel ha-Dorot*) has, in recent times, received some attention. In addition to Eisen's work, Gordon Tucker delivered a paper on it at the Association for Jewish Studies conference in December 1992.

13. See, for example, his note to line 20 on his p. 161.

14. See his *Mavo'ot le-Sifrut ha-Tannaim* (Jerusalem: Magnes Press, 1957), pp. 521–746.

15. It is worth noting that these scholars were drawn to the Aqiba/Ishmael divide posited by Graetz, but rejected the—to Graetz—yet more important Hillel/Shammai divide. As far as I know, only one scholar followed Graetz on this, and that was Adolph Schwarz in his *Die Controversen der Schammaiten und Hilleliten* (Vienna, 1893).

16. See his *Peshat and Derash* and his earlier *Midrash, Mishnah and Gemara* (Cambridge: Harvard University Press, 1986). See also his "On Man's Role in Revelation," in Jacob Neusner et al., eds., *From Ancient Israel to Modern Judaism: Intellect in Quest of Understanding: Essays in Honor of Marvin Fox,* 4 vols. (Atlanta: Scholars Press, 1989), 3:29–49. Jacob Neusner also denies the exegetical seriousness of the rabbis, apparently as part of his apologetic construction of philosophical rabbis.

17. See his *Carnal Israel: Reading Sex in Talmudic Culture* (Berkeley: University of California Press, 1993), p. ix; in addition to this work he is referring to his earlier *Intertextuality and the Reading of Midrash* (Bloomington: Indiana University Press, 1990). See also Steven Fraade, *From Tradition to Commentary: Torah and Its Interpretation in the Midrash Sifre to Deuteronomy* (Albany: SUNY Press, 1991); José Faur, *Golden Doves with Silver Dots* (Bloomington: Indiana University Press, 1986); and Susan A. Handelman, *The Slayers of Moses: The Emergence of Rabbinic Tradition in Modern Literary Theory* (Albany: SUNY Press, 1982).

Abraham ben David of Posquières (Rabad). *Commentary on Sifre Bamidbar.* Vienna, 1862.

———. *Sifra de-Ve Rav.* With commentaries of Rabad and Samson of Sens. Jerusalem, 1969.

Abraham Ibn Ezra. *Kitve R. Avraham Ibn Ezra.* Jerusalem: Makor, 1970.

———. *Perush al ha-Torah.* Edited by Asher Weisser. 3 vols. Jerusalem: Mossad ha-Rav Kook, 1977.

Abraham Maimonides. *Perush al Bereshit Shemot.* London, 1958.

Abramson, Shraga. *'Inyanot be-Sifrut ha-Geonim.* Jerusalem: Mossad ha-Rav Kook, 1974.

———, ed. *Peraqim min Sefer Mevo ha-Talmud: ha-Makor ha-Aravi ve-Targum Ivri.* Jerusalem: Mekitze Nirdamim, 1990.

Abravanel, Isaac. *Pirqe Avot im Perush Mosheh bar Maimon ve-Yitzhak Abrabanel, Naalot Avot.* Brooklyn, N.Y.: Hayim Elazar Raikh, 1992.

Acosta, Uriel. *A Specimen of Human Life.* New York: Bergman Publishers, 1967.

———. *Die Schriften.* Amsterdam, 1922.

Ages, Arnold. *French Enlightenment and Rabbinic Tradition.* Heft 26. Frankfurt am Main: Analecta Romanica, 1970.

Ahad Ha-am. *'Al Parashat Derakhim.* 4 vols. Berlin, 1921.

Aicher, Gerog. *Das alte Testament in der Mischna.* Freiburg im Breisgau: Herder, 1906.

Albeck, Ḥanokh. *Das Buch der Jubilaen und die Halacha.* Berlin: Siegfried Scholem, 1930.

———. *Mavo' La-Talmudim.* Tel Aviv: Devir, 1969.

———. *Untersuchungen über die halakischen Midraschim.* Berlin, 1927.

———. ed. *Shishah Sidre Mishnah.* Jerusalem and Tel Aviv: Mossad Bialik and Devir, 1957–59.

Albo, Joseph. *Sefer ha-'Iqqarim.* Standard editions.

Altmann, Alexander. *Moses Mendelssohn: A Biographical Study.* Philadelphia: Jewish Publication Society, 1973.

Amar, Reuven. "Yafeh le-Besamim." Introduction to *Besamim Rosh.* Jerusalem, 1984.

Amiel, Moshe Avigdor. *Sefer ha-Middot le-Heqer ha-Halakhah.* Jerusalem, 1929.

Amir, Abraham Shaul. *Mosadot u-Tearim be-Sifrut ha-Talmud.* Jerusalem: Mossad ha-Rav Kook, 1977.

Anushiski, Shneur Zalman Dober. *Maṣav ha-Yosher*. Vilna: A. T. Katsenelenboygen, 1881–87.

Armogathe, Jean Robert. ed. *Le grand siècle et la Bible* (= *Bible de tous les temps*, vol. 6). Paris: Beauchesne, 1989.

Ashkenazi, Bezalel. *Shitah Mekubeṣet*. Standard editions.

Ateret Tzvi: le-R. Tzvi Hirsh Grets be-yom melot lo shivim shanah. Breslau, 1887.

Auwers, Jean-Marie. "L'interpretation de la Bible chez Spinoza; ses presupposes philosophiques." *Revue Théologique de Louvain* 21, no. 2 (1990).

Avital, Moshe. "The Yeshivah and Traditional Education in the Literature of the Hebrew Enlightenment Period." Diss., Yeshiva University, 1977.

Azulai, Hayim David. *Shem ha-Gedolim*. Standard editions.

Bacharach, Yair. *Havvot Yair*. Standard editions.

———. *Yair Netiv. Bikkurim* 1 (1864).

Bacher, Wilhelm. *Die Bibelexegese der jüdischen Religionsphilosophen des Mittelalters vor Maimûni*. Budapest, 1892.

———. *Die Bibelexegese Moses Maimûnis*. Budapest, 1896. Reprint, Gregg International, 1974.

———. *Die exegetische Terminologie der jüdischen Traditionsliteratur*. 1899. Reprint, Hildesheim: Georg Olms, 1965.

Bar-Ilan, Meir. *Raban shel Yisrael: Rabbenu Naftali Tzevi Yehudah Berlin ha-Natziv, Toldotav, Korotav, ve-Hashkefotav*. New York: Histadrut ha-Mizrahi ba-Amerikah, 1943.

Baron, Salo. *A Social and Religious History of the Jews*. Vol. 6. New York: Columbia University Press, 1973.

Bartal, Yisrael, et al., eds. *Ke-Minhag Ashkenaz u-Folin: Sefer Yovel le-Chone Shmeruk*. Jerusalem: Zalman Shazar, 1993.

Barzilay, Isaac Eisenstein. *Between Reason and Faith*. The Hague, 1967.

———. *Yoseph Shlomo Delmedigo: His Life, Works and Times*. Leiden: E. J. Brill, 1974.

Bashyatchi, Eliyahu. *Sefer ha-Miṣvot Aderet Eliyahu*. Ramlah (Israel), 1966.

Basnage, Jacques. *L'histoire et la religion des juifs depuis Jesus Christ jusqu'à présent*. 1709.

Bat-Yehudah, Geulah. *'Ish ha-Me'orot*. Jerusalem: Mossad ha-Rav Kook, 1985.

Becker, Hans-Jurgen, and Peter, Schäfer. *Synopse zum Talmud Yerushalmi*. Tübingen: J. C. B. Mohr, 1991.

Beer, Hayim. *Gam Ahavatam gam Sin'atam: Byalik, Brenner, Agnon, Ma'arkhot Yaasim*. Tel Aviv: Am Oved, 1992.

Beer, Hayim, Yaakov Goldshtain, and Yaakov Shavit, eds. *Leksikon ha-Ishim shel Eretz-Yisrael, 1799–1948*. Tel Aviv: Am Oved, 1983.

Behr, Meshullam Fischel. *Divre Meshullam: Koveṣ Ma'amarim ve-He'arot*. Frankfurt a.M.: D. Droller, 1925.

Belavel, Yvon, and Dominique Bourel, eds. *Le siècle des lumières et la Bible* (= *Bible de tous les temps*, vol. 7). Paris: Beauchesne, 1986.

Belke, Hans-Jurgen. *Die preussische Regierung zu Königsberg, 1808–1850.* Köln: Grote, 1976.

Bell, David. *Spinoza in Germany from 1670 to the Age of Goethe.* London: University of London, 1984.

Benin, Stephen D. *The Footprints of God: Divine Accommodation in Jewish and Christian Thought.* Albany: SUNY Press, 1993.

Ben-Sasson, Haim Hillel. *Hagut ve-Hanhagah.* Jerusalem: Mossad Bialik, 1959.

———. "'Ishiuto shel ha-GRA ve-Hashpa'ato ha-Historit." *Zion* 31 (1966).

———. *Perakim be-Toldot ha-Yehudim Bime ha-Beinaim.* Tel Aviv: Am Oved, 1977.

Ben-Sasson, Yonah. *Mishnato ha-'Iyyunit shel ha-Rema.* Jerusalem: Israel Academy of Sciences and Humanities, 1984.

Ben-Shammai, Haggai. "Between Ananites and Karaites: Observations on Early Medieval Jewish Sectarianism." In *Studies in Muslim-Jewish Relations,* vol. 1, edited by Ronald L. Nettler. Chur, Switzerland: Harwood Academic, 1993.

Benveniste, Hayyim ben Israel. *Kenesset ha-Gedolah Orah Hayyim.* Jerusalem, 1965.

Benvenisti, Joshua. *Sedeh Yehoshua.* Brooklyn, 1991.

Ben-Yehudah, Eliezer. *Dictionary of the Hebrew Language.* 8 vols. New York: Thomas Yoseloff, 1960.

Benzeeb, Judah Loeb. *Talmud Leshon Ivri.* Vilna: Ha-Almanah ve-ha-Ahim Rom, 1879.

Berdichevski, Micah Josef bin Gorion. *Halifat Igrot.* Edited by Shelomoh Bertonov. Holon and Tel Aviv: Bet Devorah ve-Immanuel, 1984.

———. *Kitve Micha Yosef Bin Gorion: Hadashim gam Yeshanim.* Leipzig, 1921.

———. *Kol Maamre Mikhah Yosef bin Goryon.* Tel Aviv: Am Oved, 1952.

———. *Ma'amarim: Inyene Mehqar.* Warsaw: Tushiyah, 1902.

———. *Mi-Shene Olamot.* Tel Aviv: Devir, 1988.

———. *Pirqe Volozin.* Holon: Bet Devorah ve-Immanuel, 1984.

———. *Yisrael ve-Oraita be-Sifre Shadal über Juden und Judenthum.* Krakow: Y. Fisher, 1892.

Berkovitz, Jay. *The Shaping of Jewish Identity in Nineteenth-Century France.* Detroit: Wayne State University Press, 1989.

Berlin, Naftali Zvi Yehudah. *Birkat ha-Neziv.* Jerusalem, 1980.

———. *Ha-'Amek Davar.* Standard editions.

———. *Ha-'Amek She'elah* (= *She'iltot* commentary). Jeruslaem: Mossad ha-rav Kook, 1975.

———. *Meshiv Davar.* Jerusalem, 1993

Berlin, Shaul. *Sheelot u-teshuvot Besamim Rosh*. Edited by Reuven Amar. Jerusalem, 1984.

———. *Sheelot u-teshuvot Besamim Rosh*. Krakow, 1881.

Berliner, Abraham. "Davar 'el ha-Kore." In *Ha-Ketav ve-ha-Kabbalah*. 4th edition. Berlin, 1880.

Bernus, Auguste. *Richard Simon et son histoire critique du Vieux Testament: la critique biblique au siècle de Louis XIV*. Lausanne, 1869. Reprint, Geneva: Slatkine Reprints, 1969.

Bickerman, Elias Joseph. *The Maccabees: An Account of Their History from the Beginnings to the Fall of the House of the Hasmoneans*. Translated by Moses Hadas. New York: Schocken, 1947.

Blair, Ann, and Anthony Grafton, eds. *The Transmission of Culture in Early Modern Europe*. Philadelphia: University of Pennsylvania Press, 1990.

Blidstein, J. "Where Do We Stand in the Study of Maimonidean Halakhah?" In *Studies in Maimonides*, edited by Isadore Twersky. Cambridge: Harvard University Press, 1991.

Bornkamm, Heinrich. *Luther and the Old Testament*. Translated by Eric Gritsch and Ruth Gritsch. Edited by Victor Gruhn. Philadelphia: Fortress Press, 1969.

Boyarin, Daniel. *Carnal Israel: Reading Sex in Talmudic Culture*. Berkeley: University of California Press, 1993.

———. *Ha-Iyyun ha-Sephardi*. Jerusalem: Makhon Ben-Zvi, 1989.

———. *Intertextuality and the Reading of Midrash*. Bloomington: Indiana University Press, 1990.

Brann, Marcus. *Geschichte des jüdische-theologischen Seminars*. Breslau, 1904.

———. *Heinrich Graetz: Abhandlungen zu seinem 100. Geburtstage, 31 Oktober 1917*. Vienna, 1917.

Breuer, Edward. "In Defense of Tradition: The Masoretic Text and Its Rabbinic Interpretation in Early German Haskalah." Diss., Harvard University, 1990.

Breuer, Mordechai. "Ḥokhmat Yisrael: Shalosh Gishot Ortodoxiot." In *Sefer Yovel Likhvod Moreinu ha-Gaon Rabbi Yosef Dov Halevi Soloveitchik*. 2 vols. Jerusalem, 1984.

———. *Jüdische Orthodoxie im deutschen Reich, 1871–1981: Die Sozialsgeschichte einer religiösen Minderheit*. Frankfurt a.M.: Jüdischer Verlag, 1986.

———. *Modernity Within Tradition*. New York: Columbia University Press, 1992.

———, ed. *Torah im Derekh Eretz: Ha-Tenuah, Isheha, Rayonoteha*. Ramat Gan: Bar-Ilan University, 1987.

Brinker, Menahem. *Ad ha-Simtah ha-Tveryanit: Maamar al Sippur u-Maḥashavah bi-Yeṣirat Brener*. Tel Aviv: Am Oved, 1990.

————. ed. *Barukh Shpinozah: Qoveṣ Ma'amarim al Mishnato*. Tel Aviv: Mif'alim ha-Univeritaim le-Hoṣa'ah le-'Or, 1979.

Buchner, A. *Der Talmud in seiner Nichtigkeit*. Warsaw: Missions-Druckerei, 1848.

Carlebach, Elisheva. *The Pursuit of Heresy: Rabbi Moses Hagiz and the Sabbatian Controversies*. New York: Columbia University Press, 1990.

Charlesworth, James H., ed. *Jubilees, Book of*. In *The Old Testament Pseudepigrapha*. 2 vols. Garden City, N.Y.: Doubleday, 1985.

Chernick, Michael. *Hermeneutical Studies in Talmudic and Midrashic Literature* (in Hebrew). N.p.: Haberman Institute, 1984.

Chiarini, Luigi. *Théorie du Judaïsme*. 2 vols. Paris, 1830.

Chorin, Aaron. *Iggeret Elasaf: oder Zendshrayben Aynes Afrikanishen Rabian zaynen kollegen in Eyropa*. Prague, 1826.

————. *Tzir Ne'eman*. Prague, 1831.

Christfels, Peter. *Gespräch in dem Reiche der Todten über die Bibel u. Talmud zwischen dem seeligen Herrn Doctor Luther u. dem berühmten jüdischen Ausleger, namens Raschi*. Schwabach, 1737–39.

Cohen, Hermann. *Religion of Reason out of the Sources of Judaism*. New York: Ungar, 1972.

Cooperman, Yehudah. *Li-Feshuto shel Miqra*. Jerusalem: Haskel, 1974.

————. *Pirqe Mavo le-Feirush ha-Ketav ve-ha-Kabbalah al ha-Torah*. Jerusalem: Haskel, 1986.

————. *Pirqe Mavo le-Feirush Meshekh Ḥokhmah la-Torah*. In *Meshekh Ḥokhmah*, 3 vols., edited by Yehudah Cooperman. Jerusalem, 1986.

Creizenach, Michael. *Thariag oder Inbegriff der mosaischen Vorschriften nach talmudischer Interpretation* (= *Schulchan Aruch*, vol. 1). Frankfurt am Main, 1833.

David ben Solomon ibn Abi Zimra (Radbaz). *Metzudat David*. Jerusalem, 1989.

Delitzsch, Franz. *Jewish Artisan Life in the Time of Our Lord, to Which is Appended a Critical Comparison between Jesus and Hillel*. Translated by Mrs. Philip Monkhouse. London, 1877.

"Der Mangel an Glaubensinnigkeit in der jetzigen Judenheit: Bedenken eines Laien." *Wissenschaftliche Zeitschrift für jüdische Theologie* 1 (1835).

Deutsch, Gotthard. *Hainrikh Grets: Tequfat Meah Shanah*. Translated by A. Schmerler. New York, 1921.

Diderot, Denis. *Oeuvres complètes*. Edited by J. Assezat. Paris: Garnier, 1876.

Dubois, Marcel. *Yahadut ve-Yehudim be-'Eine Maskilim Nokhrim vi-Yehudim*. Jerusalem: Hebrew University, Jewish History Faculty, 1987.

Edelmann, Simhah Reuben. *Doresh Reshumot*. Warsaw, 1893.

Einhorn, David. *Ausgewählte Predigten und Reden*. New York, 1881.

————. *Das Princip des Mosaismus und dessen Verhältnis zum Heidenthum und rabbinischen Judenthum.* Leipzig, 1854.

————. *David Einhorn Memorial Volume: Selected Sermons and Addresses.* Edited by Kaufmann Kohler. New York: Bloch, 1911.

————. "Stellung des neueren Judenthums zum Thalmud." *Sinai* 1, nos. 1–3 (1856).

Einhorn, Zeeb Wolf, ed. *Midrash Tannaim.* Vilna, 1838.

Eisen, Arnold. "Re-Reading Heschel on the Commandments." *Modern Judaism* 9, no. 1 (1989).

Eisenstein-Barzilay, Isaac. "The Treatment of the Jewish Religion in the Literature of the Berlin Haskalah." *Proceedings of the American Academy for Jewish Research* 24 (1955).

Elbaum, Jacob. *Petiḥut ve-Histagrut.* Jerusalem: Magnes Press, 1990.

Elbogen, Ismar. "Der Streit um die 'positiv-historische Reform.'" In *Festgabe für Claude G. Montefiore.* Berlin, 1928.

Eliakh, Dov. *Avi ha-Yeshivot: Toldot Ḥayyav u-Mishnato shel Ḥayyim mi-Volozin.* Jerusalem: Makhon Moreshet ha-Yeshivot, 1991.

Elijah ben Loeb Foulda. *Commentary on the Yerushalmi.* Standard editions.

Elijah ben Solomon, Gaon of Vilna. *'Aderet 'Eliyahu.* Warsaw, 1887.

————. *Liqqute ha-GRA.* Edited by Isaak Eizik Haver. Jerusalem, 1976.

————. *Qiṣur Mekhilta.* In *'Aderet 'Eliyahu.* Warsaw, 1887.

————. *Sefer Mishle 'im Be'ur ha-GRA.* Edited by Moshe Philip. Petah Tiqvah, 1985.

Ellenson, David and Jacobs, Richard. "Scholarship and Faith: David Hoffmann and his Relation to *Wissenschaft des Judentums.*" *Modern Judaism* 8, no. 1 (February 1988).

Elon, Menahem. *Ha-Mishpat ha-'Ivri.* 2 vols. Jerusalem: Magnes Press, 1978.

Epstein, Klaus. *The Genesis of German Conservatism.* Princeton: Princeton University Press, 1966.

Epstein, Yaaqob Nahum. *Mavo le-Nusaḥ ha-Mishnah.* Jerusalem, 1948.

————. *Mavo'ot le-Sifrut ha-Amoraim.* Jerusalem: Magnes Press, 1962.

————. *Mavo'ot le-Sifrut ha-Tannaim.* Jerusalem: Magnes Press, 1957.

Epstein and Melamed, eds. *Mekhilta de-Rabbi Shim'on bar Yohai.* Jerusalem, n.d.

Erik, Max. *Etudn tsu der geshikte fun der Haskole: 1789–1881.* Minsk, 1934.

Eschelbacher, J. "Michael Sachs." *Monatsschrift für Geschichte und Wissenschaft des Judentums* 52 (1908).

Etkes, Immanuel. *Lita biRushalayim.* Jerusalem: Yad Yitzhaq ben Zvi, 1991

————. "Pareshat ha-'haskalah mi-Ta'am' ve-ha-Temurah be-Ma'amad Tenu'at ha-Haskalah be-Rusya." *Zion* 43 (1978).

————. *Rabbi Israel Salanter ve-Reshita shel Tenu'at ha-Musar.* Jerusalem: Magnes Press, 1982.

————, ed. *Ha-Dat ve-ha-Ḥayyim.* Jerusalem: Merkaz Zalman Shazar, 1993.

Ettinger, Samuel. *Historyah ve-Historyonim.* Jerusalem: Merkaz Zalmen Shazar, 1992.

Fahn, Rubin. *Tequfat ha-Haskalah be-Vienah: Tziyur Toldoti-Tarbuti.* Vienna, 1919.

Fano, Menahem Azariah da. *'Asarah Ma'amarot. im Perush Yehudah Leb ben Shimon.* Jerusalem, 1973.

Faur, José. *Golden Doves with Silver Dots.* Bloomington: Indiana University Press, 1986.

———. *In the Shadow of History: Jews and Conversos at the Dawn of Modernity.* Albany: SUNY Press, 1992.

Faust, Ulrich. *Mythologien und Religionen des Ostens bei Johann Gottfried Herder.* Munster: Aschendorff, 1977.

Faybush, Shneur. *Mishnayot, im targum ashkenazi . . . ve-im perush.* Vienna: Menorah, 1927.

Federbush, S. *Ha-Rambam, Torato ve-'Ishiyuto: Qoveṣ le-regel mel'ot sheva me'ot ve-ḥamishim shanah le-fetirato.* New York, 1956.

Feigensohn, Samuel Shraga. *Elbonah shel Torah.* Berlin: T. H. Ittskovski, 1928.

Feiner, Shmuel. *Ha-Haskalah be-Yaḥasah la-Historyah: Hakarat he-'Avar ve-Tifqudav bi-Tenuat ha-Haskalah ha-Yehudit (1782–1881).* Diss., Jerusalem, Hebrew University, 1990.

Feldblum, Meyer S. "Criteria for Designating Laws." In *Maimonides as Codifier of Jewish Law,* edited by N. Rakover. Jerusalem, 1987.

Finkelstein, Louis. "Ha-De'ah ki 13 ha-Middot hen Halakhah le-Moshe mi-Sinai." In *Sefer ha-Zikaron le-Rabbi Shaul Liebermann,* edited by Shama Friedman. New York: Jewish Theological Seminary, 1993.

———, ed. *The Jews: Their Religion and Culture.* New York: Schocken Books, 1971.

———, ed. *Sifra.* 5 vols. Jerusalem/New York: Jewish Theological Seminary, 1989–91.

———, ed. *Sifre on Deuteronomy.* New York, 1969.

Fischer, Jedidiah Gottlieb. *Delatayim u-Veriah le-Me ha-Shiloaḥ.* Vienna, 1855.

Fishbane, Michael. *Biblical Interpretation in Ancient Israel.* Oxford: Clarendon Press, 1985.

———. *The Garments of Torah: Essays in Biblical Hermeneutics.* Bloomington: Indiana University Press, 1989.

———. "Use, Authority and Interpretation of Mikra at Qumran." In *Mikra: Text, Translation, Reading and Interpretation of the Hebrew Bible in Ancient Judaism and Early Christianity,* edited by Martin J. Mulder, 339–77. Assen, The Netherlands: Van Gorcum, 1988.

———, ed. *The Midrashic Imagination: Jewish Exegesis, Thought, and History.* Albany: SUNY Press, 1993.

Fishman, Talya. "*Kol Sachal*'s Critique of Rabbinic Tradition: A Solution to the Problem of Galut." Diss., Harvard University, 1986.

Fraade, Steven D. *From Tradition to Commentary: Torah and Its Interpretation in the Midrash Sifre to Deuteronomy.* Albany: SUNY Press, 1991.

————. "Interpretive Authority in the Studying Community at Qumran." *JJS* 44 (Spring 1993).

Frankel, David. *Qorban ha-'Edah* and *Shi'are Qorban.* Standard editions of the Yerushalmi.

Frankel, Israel. *Peshat (Plain Exegesis) in Talmudic and Midrashic Literature.* New York: Sepher-Hermon Press, 1956.

Frankel, Zechariah. *Darkhe ha-Mishnah.* Breslau, 1859.

————. *Der gerichtliche Beweis nach mosaisch-talmudischen Rechte.* Berlin, 1846.

————. "Geist der palästinischen und babylonischen Hagada." *Monatsschrift für Geschichte und Wissenschaft des Judentums* 2 (1853).

————. *Mevo ha-Yerushalmi.* Breslau, 1870.

————. *Über den Einfluss der palästinischen Exegese auf die alexandrische Hermeneutik.* Leipzig, 1851.

————. "Über palästinischen und alexandrinische Schiftforschung." In *Programm zur Eröffnung des jüdisch-theologischen Seminars zu Breslau.* Breslau, 1854.

————. *Vorstudien zu der Septuaginta.* Leipzig: F. C. W. Vogel, 1841.

Freimark, Peter, and Arno Herzig, eds. *Die Hamburger Juden in der Emanzipationsphase (1780–1870).* Hamburg: Hans Christians, 1989.

Freudenthal, J. *Spinoza: Leben und Lehre.* 2 vols. Heidelberg, 1927.

Freund, Roman. *Karaites and Dejudaization: A Historical Review of an Endogenous Paradigm.* Stockholm: Almqvist & Wiksell International, 1991.

Friedman,Shama. ed. *Sefer ha-Zikaron le-Rabbi Shaul Liebermann.* New York: Jewish Theological Seminary, 1993.

Fromer, Jakob. *Der Organismus des Judenthums.* Charlottenberg, 1909.

————. *Der Talmud: Geschichte, Wesen und Zukunft.* Berlin: P. Cassirer, 1920.

Fuenn, Samuel Joseph. *Divre ha-Yamim le-vene Yisrael.* Vilna, 1871–77.

————. *Ha-Otzar: Otzar Leshon ha-Miqra ve-ha-Mishnah.* 4 vols. Warsaw: Ahiasaf, 1903–13.

————. *Kenesset Yisrael.* Warsaw, 1886.

————. *Nidḥe Yisrael.* Vilna: Y.R. Rom, 1850.

————. *Qiryah Ne'emanah.* Jerusalem, 1968.

————. *Sofre Yisrael.* Vilna, 1871.

Funkenstein, Amos. *Perceptions of Jewish History.* Berkeley: University of California Press, 1993.

————. *Theology and the Scientific Imagination in the Seventeenth Century.* Princeton: Princeton University Press, 1986.

————. *Signonot be-Farshanut ha-Miqra bime ha-Benayim.* Tel Aviv: Gale Tzahal, Misrad ha-Bitahon, 1990.

————. *Tadmit ve-Toda'ah Historit ba-Yahadut u-vi-Sevivatah ha-Tarbutit.* Tel Aviv: Am Oved, 1991.

Gaier, Ulrich. *Herders Sprachphilosophie und Erkenntniskritik.* Stuttgart-Bad Cannstatt, 1988.

Gafni, Yeshayahu. *Yehude Bavel be-Tequfat ha-Talmud.* Jerusalem: Mercaz Zalman Shazar, 1991.

Gay, Peter. *The Enlightenment.* New York: Norton, 1966.

Gebhardt, Carl. *Die Schriften des Uriel da Costa.* Amsterdam, 1922.

Geiger, Abraham. "Das Verhältnis des natürlichen Schriftsinnes zur thalmudischen Schriftdeutung." *Wissenschaftliche Zeitschrift für jüdische Theologie* 5 (1844).

————. "Der Formglaube in seinem Unwerth und in seinem Folgen." *Wissenschaftliche Zeitschrift für jüdische Theologie,* 1839.

————. "Der Kampf christlicher Theologen gegen die bürgerliche Gleichstellung der Juden, namentlich mit Bezug auf Anton Theodor Hartmann." *Wissenschaftliche Zeitschrift für jüdische Theologie* 1 (1835).

————. "Die nordfranzösische Exegeten-Schule im 12 Jahrhundert." In *Nit'e Na'amanim,* edited by S. L. Heilberg. Breslau, 1847.

————. "Die wissenschaftliche Ausbildung des Judenthums in den zwei ersten Jahrhunderten des zweiten Jahrtausends bis zum Auftreten des Maimonides." *Wissenschaftliche Zeitschrift für jüdische Theologie* 1 (1835).

————. *Leon da Modena.* Breslau, 1856.

————. *Nachgelassene Schriften.* Berlin, 1878.

————. *Parshandata.* Breslau, 1855. Reprint, Jerusalem: Makor, 1971.

————. *Urschrift und Übersetzungen der Bibel in ihrer Abhängigkeit von der innern Entwicklung des Judenthums.* Breslau, 1857.

————, ed. *Magen ve-Tzinnah.* Breslau, 1856.

Geiger, Ludwig. *Abraham Geiger: Leben und Lebenswerk.* Berlin, 1910.

Gelber, N. M. "Beit ha-Midrash le-Rabbanim be Vina." In *Mosedot Torah be-Eiropa be-Vinyanam u-ve-Ḥurbanam,* edited by S. K. Mirsky. New York, 1956.

Gersonides (Levi ben Gerson, Ralbag). *Peirush ha-Torah.* Jerusalem: ha-Rav Kook, 1992.

Gilat, Yiṣḥaq D. *Peraqim be-Hishtalshelut ha-Halakhah.* Ramat Gan: Bar-Ilan University Press, 1992.

Gilon, Meir. *Kohelet Musar le-Mendelssohn 'al Reqa' Tequfato.* Jerusalem: Israel National Academy of Sciences, 1979.

Glatzer, Mordechai. *'Ittur Sofrim (Sefer ha-'Ittur) le-Rav Yishaq ben Rav Abba Mari: Pirqe Mavo.* Jerusalem: Hebrew University, 1985.

Glinski, Gerhard von, and Peter Worster. *Königsberg: Die ostpreussische Hauptstadt in Geschichte und Gegenwart.* Berlin: Westkreuz, 1990.

Goitein, S. D., ed. *Religion in a Religious Age.* Cambridge, Mass., 1974.

Goldberg, Jacob. *Ha-Mumarim be-Mamlekhet Polin-Lita*. Jerusalem, 1985.

Goldscheider C., and A. Zuckerman. *The Transformation of the Jews*. Chicago: University of Chicago Press, 1984.

Goshen-Gottstein, Moshe H. "Bible et judaisme." In *Le grand siècle et la Bible* (= *Bible de tous les temps*, vol. 6), edited by Jean Robert Armogathe. Paris: Beauchesne, 1989.

Gottlober, Abraham Baer. *Bikoret le-toldot ha-Karaim*. . . . Vilna: Fin and Rosenkrantz, 1865.

Grab, Walter, and Julius H. Scoeps. *Juden im Vormärz und in der Revolution von 1848*. Stuttgart: Burg Verlag, 1983.

Graetz, Heinrich. *Geschichte der Juden*. 11 vols. Berlin, 1853.

———. *Gnosticismus und Judenthum*. Krotoschin: B. L. Monasch, 1846.

———. *Heinrich Graetz: Tagebuch und Briefer*. Edited by Reuven Michael. Tübingen, J. C. B. Mohr, 1977.

———. "Jüdisch-geschichtliche Studien." *Monatsschrift für Geschichte und Wissenschaft des Judentums* 1 (1852).

———. *The Structure of Jewish History and Other Essays*. New York: Jewish Theological Seminary, 1975.

Grafton, Anthony. *Defenders of the Text: The Traditions of Scholarship in an Age of Science, 1450–1800*. Cambridge: Harvard University Press, 1991.

Grafton, Anthony, and Ann Blair, eds. *The Transmission of Culture in Early Modern Europe*. Philadelphia: University of Pennsylvania Press, 1990.

Granot, Moshe. *Demuyot Miqraiyot be-Sifrut ha-Haskalah ba-Shanim, 1789–1829*. Ramat Gan: Bar-Ilan University, 1979.

Green, William Scott, ed. *Approaches to Ancient Judaism: Theory and Practice*. Missoula, Mont.: Scholars Press, 1978.

Greenberg, Gershon. "Mendelssohn in America: David Einhorn's Radical Reform Judaism." *Leo Baeck Institute Yearbook* 27 (1982).

Greenberg, Moshe. "Some Postulates of Biblical Criminal Law." In *The Jewish Expression,* edited by Judah Goldin, 29–34. New Haven: Yale University Press, 1976.

Groner, Zvi. *The Legal Methodology of Hai Gaon*. Chico, Calif.: Scholars Press, 1985.

Grossman, Avraham. *Ḥakhme Ashkenaz ha-Rishonim*. Jerusalem: Magnes Press, 1981.

Grunewald, Pinchas Paul. *Eine jüdische Offenbarungslehre: Samson Raphael Hirsch*. Bern: P. Lang, 1977.

Güdemann, Moritz. *Das Judentum in seinem Grundzugen*. Vienna, 1902.

———. *Judaische Apologetik*. Glogau: C. Flemming, 1906.

———. *Wie sollen wir die Bibel lesen?* Vienna, 1909.

Gunter, Arnold. *Johann Gottfried Herder*. Leipzig, 1988.

Guterman, Alexander. *Hatzaotehem shel Yehude Polin le-Tiqqunim be-*

Ma'amadam ha-Huqi, ha-Kalkali, ha-Hevrati ve-ha-Tarbuti bi-Tequfat ha-Seym ha-Gadol (1788–1792). Jerusalem, 1975.

Guthe, Hermann. *Luther und die Bibelforschung der Gegenwart*. Tübingen, J. C. B. Mohr, 1917.

Hacohen, Avia. "Be-'Ikve be'ur ha-Gra le-Farashat 'Amah 'Ivriah." In *Sefer ha-Yovel le-Rav Mordechai Breuer: 'Asufat Ma'amarim be-Mada'e ha-Yahadut*. 2 vols. Jerusalem: Akademon, 1992.

Hadassi, Judah ben Elijah. *Eshkol ha-Kofer*. 1836. Reprint, Jerusalem: Makor, 1968.

Hagiz, Moses. *Eleh ha-Miṣvot*. Jerusalem, 1963.

———. *Mishnat Ḥakhamim*. Brooklyn, N.Y., 1979.

Halevi, Judah. *Kuzari*. Translated by Judah ibn Tibbon. Edited by A. Zifroni. Israel, 1964.

———. *Kuzari*. Translated by Yehudah Even-Shemuel. Tel Aviv: Mossad Bialik, 1972.

Halivni, David Weiss. *Meqorot u-Mesorot*. 5 vols. Vol. 1, Tel Aviv: Devir, 1968. Vol. 2, Jerusalem: Jewish Theological Seminary, 1975. Vols. 3 and 4, Jerusalem: Jewish Theological Seminary, 1982. Vol. 5, Jerusalem: Magnes Press, 1993.

———. *Midrash, Mishnah and Gemara*. Cambridge: Harvard University Press, 1986.

———. "On Man's Role in Revelation." In *From Ancient Israel to Modern Judaism: Essays in Honor of Marvin Fox.*, vol. 3, edited by Jacob Neusner et al. Atlanta: Scholars Press, 1989.

———. *Peshat and Derash: Plain and Applied Meaning in Rabbinic Exegesis*. New York: Oxford University Press, 1991.

Halkin, Abraham. "Mi-Petiḥat Rav Saadia Gaon le-Ferush ha-Torah." In *Sefer ha-Yovel likhvod Levi Ginzberg*. New York, 1946.

Handelman, Susan A. *The Slayers of Moses: The Emergence of Rabbinic Interpretation in Modern Literary Theory*. Albany: SUNY Press, 1982.

Harkavy, Albert. *Sefer ha-Miṣvot le-Anan ha-Nasi*. St. Petersberg, 1903.

——— *Zikhron ha-Gaon Rav Shemuel ben Ḥofni u-Sefarav*. St. Petersberg, 1880.

Harris, Jay M. "Between Tradition and Wissenschaft: Modern Students of Midrash Halakhah." In *The Uses of Tradition: Jewish Continuity in the Modern Era*, edited by Jack Wertheimer. New York: Jewish Theological Seminary, 1992.

———. "Ibn Ezra in Modern Jewish Perspective." In *Rabbi Abraham Ibn Ezra: Studies in the Writings of a Twelfth-Century Jewish Polymath*, edited by Isadore Twersky and Jay M. Harris. Cambridge: Harvard University Press, 1993

———. *Nachman Krochmal: Guiding the Perplexed of the Modern Age*. New York: New York University Press, 1991.

Havlin, S. Z. "'Al 'ha-Ḥatimah ha-Sifrutit' ke-Yesod ha-Ḥalukah le-Tequfot be-Halakhah." In *Meḥqarim be-Sifrut ha-Talmudit*. Jerusalem: Israel National Academy of Sciences, 1983.

Hazard, Paul. *The European Mind: The Critical Years 1680–1715*. New York: Fordham University Press, 1990.

Heilberg, S. L., ed., *Nit'e Na'amanim*. Breslau, 1847.

Heilpern, Pinḥas Menaḥem. *'Even Boḥan*. Frankfurt a.M., 1846.

———. *Teshuvot be-'Anshe 'On*. Frankfurt a.M., 1845.

Heinemann, Yitzhak. *Darkhe ha-Agada*. Jerusalem: Magnes Press, 1974.

Herder, Johann Gottfried. *Herders Sämtliche Werke*. Edited by Bernhard Suphan. Berlin: Weidmann, 1877–1913.

Hermann, Rudolf. *Die Gestalt Simsons bei Luther: Eine Studie zu Bibelauslegung*. Berlin: A. Topelmann, 1952.

Herzig, Arno, and Peter Freimark. *Die Hamburger Juden in der Emanzipationsphase (1780–1870)*. Hamburg: Hans Christians, 1989.

Heschel, Abraham Joshua. *Torah min ha-Shamayim be-Aspaklaria shel ha-Dorot*. 3 vols. London, Soncino Press, 1962–65 (vols. 1 and 2). New York: Jewish Theological Seminary, 1990 (vol. 3).

Heschel, Susannah. "Abraham Geiger on the Origins of Christianity." Diss., University of Pennsylvania, 1989.

Heymann, Claude. "Le rabbin S. R. Hirsch, un romantique?" *Nouveaux Cahiers* 99 (1989–90).

Hirsch, Salomon Zebi. *Korot Yisrael ve-Emunato*. Vienna, 1873–79.

Hirsch, Samson Raphael. *Collected Writings of Rabbi Samson Raphael Hirsch*. Spring Valley, N.Y.: Feldheim, 1988.

———. *The Pentateuch: Translation and Commentary*. Translated by Isaac Levy. Gateshead: Judaica Press, 1973.

———. *Shemesh Mirpa*. Brooklyn, N.Y.: Mesorah Publications, 1992.

———. *Siddur: Translation and Commentary*. Jerusalem: Feldheim, 1969.

———. *Über die Beziehung des Talmuds zum Judenthum und zu der sozialen Stellung seiner Bekenner*. Frankfort am Main, 1884.

Hobbes, Thomas. *Leviathan*. New York: Penguin Books, 1968.

Hoffmann, David Zvi. *Abhandlungen über die pentateuchischen Gesetze*. Berlin: M. Driesner, 1880s.

———. *Das Buch Deuteronomium, übersetzt und erklärt von Dr. D. Hoffmann*. Berlin: Verlag M. Poppelauer, 1913–22.

———. *Das Buch Leviticus, übersetzt und erklärt von Dr. D. Hoffmann*. Berlin: Verlag M. Poppelauer, 1905–6.

———. *Das erste Mishna*. Berlin, 1883

———. *Die wichtigsten Instanzen gegen die Graf-Wellhausensche Hypothese*. 2 vols. Berlin, 1904, 1916.

———. *Mar Samuel*. Leipzig, 1873.

————. *Melamed Le-Ho'il*, 3 vols. Frankfurt am Main, 1926–32.

————. *Untersuchungen über die halakischen Midraschim*. Berlin, 1927.

————. *Zur Einleitung in die halachischen Midraschim*. Berlin, 1886–87.

————, ed. *Mekhilta de-Rabbi Shim'on bar Yohai*. Frankfurt am Main, 1905.

Holdheim, Samuel. *Das religiöse und politische im Judenthum: Eine Antwort auf Dr. Frankel's Kritik der Autonomie der Rabbinen und der Protocolle der ersten Rabbiner-Versammlung in Betreff der gemischten Ehen*. Schwerin, 1845.

————. *Der religiöse Fortschritt im deutschen Judenthume: Ein friedliches Wort in einer aufgeregten Zeit*. Leipzig, 1840.

————. *Die erste Rabbinerversammlung und Herr Dr. Frankel*. Schwerin, 1845.

————. *Geschichte der entstehung und entwicklung der jüdischen reform-gemeinde in Berlin. Im zusammenhang mit den judischreformatorischen gesammtbestrebungen der neuzeit*. Berlin: J. Springer, 1857.

————. *Ma'amar ha-Ishut*. Berlin, 1861.

————. *Verketzerung und Gewissensfreiheit*. Schwerin, 1842.

Horowitz, Rivka. *Zechariah Frankel ve-Reshit ha-Yahadut ha-Positivit-historit*. Jerusalem: Shazar Institute, 1984.

Horowitz, ed. *Sifre al Bamidbar*. Jerusalem: Wahrmann, 1966.

Horowitz and Rabin, eds. *Mekhilta de-Rabbi Ishmael*. Frankfurt am Main, 1931.

Hutner, Yitzhaq. *Quntres 'Osef ha-Halakhot ha-mehudashot ha-nimsaot ba-Sifra asher lo ba Zakhran ba-Taklmud Bavli*. Appended to Shachna Koloditzky's edition of the Sifra in *Peirush Rabbenu Hillel* Jerusalem, 1961..

Ibn Habib, Jacob ben Solomon. *'En Yaakov: 'im Kol ha-Mefarshim*. Vilna, 1883–90.

Ibn Hayyim, Aaron ben Abraham. *Midot Aharon*. Venice, 1609.

————. *Qorban Aharon ve-hu Perush le-Sefer Sifra*. Venice, 1609–11.

Ibn Hayyim, Aaron ben Abraham, with Naftali Tzevi Yehudah Berlin. *Qorban Aharon*. Jerusalem, 1969, 1987.

Ibn Shuaib, Joshua. *Derashot 'al ha-Torah*. Jerusalem: Makor, 1969.

Idel, Moshe. *Language, Torah and Hermeneutics in Abraham Abulafia*. Albany: State University of New York Press, 1989.

————. "Midrashic versus Other Forms of Jewish Hermeneutics: Some Comparative Reflections." In *The Midrashic Imagination: Jewish Exegesis, Thought, and History*, edited by Michael Fishbane. Albany: SUNY Press, 1993.

Immanuel, Yonah ed. *Ha-Rav Shimshon Refael Hirsh: Mishnato ve-Shitato*. Jerusalem and New York: Feldheim, 1988.

Israel of Skhlov. *Pe'at ha-Shulhan*. Jerusalem: Yad Binyamin, 1968.

Jacobs, Louis. *Jewish Biblical Exegesis*. New York, Behrman House, 1973.

————. *Theology in the Responsa*. London: Routledge and Kegan Paul, 1975.

Jellinek, Adolphe. *Aus der Zeit: Tagesfragen und Tagesbegebenheiten*. Budapest, 1884.

————. *Kuntres Taryag: Sofer u-Moneh Shirim u-Sefarim u-Maamarim al Taryag Mitzvot*. Vienna, 1878.

Johlson, J., trans. *Die Bibel. Die fünf Bücher Mose, nach dem masoretischen Texte*. Frankfurt a.M., 1831.

Jolowicz, H. *Geschichte der Juden in Königsburg*. Posen, 1867.

————. *Zwei Bücher Bluthen rabbinischer Weisheit*. Thorn, 1849.

Jost, I. M. *Geschichte der Israeliten*. 10 vols. Berlin, 1821–45.

————. *Was hat Herr Chiarini in Angelegenheiten der Europäischen Juden geleistet? Eine freimüthige und unparteische Beleuchtung des Werkes: Théorie du Judaïsme*. Berlin, 1830.

Judah Aryeh mi-Modena [?]. *Behinat ha-Kabbalah*. Goritiae, 1852.

Judah ibn Tibbon. *Ruah Hen*. With commentary by Israel ha-Levi, author of *Netzah Yisrael*. Jerusalem: Makor, 1969.

Kadushin, Max. *The Rabbinic Mind*. New York: Bloch, 1972.

Kahana, David. *Yehudim ve-Yahadut ba-Sifrut ha-Polanit shel ha-meah ha-tesha-esreh: Le-Toldot beayat ha-Yehudim be-Polin*. Tel Aviv, 1980.

Kahana, Kalman. *Ha-Ish va-Hazono*. Tel Aviv, 1964.

————. *Ha-Torah ha-Mesurah le-Shitat ha-Rambam*. Tel Aviv, 1953

————. *Heqer ve-'Iyyun: Qoves Ma'amarim*. Tel Aviv, 1960–67.

————. *Le-Heqer Be'ure ha-GRA la-Yerushalmi ve-la-Tosefta*. Tel Aviv, 1957.

————. "Torah she-be-Khtav ve-Torah she-Be'al Peh be-Mishnato." In *Ha-Rav Shimshon Rafael Hirsch: Mishnato ve-Shitato*, edited by Yonah Immanuel. Jerusalem: Feldheim, 1989.

Kalmin, Richard. *The Redaction of the Babylonian Talmud: Amoraic or Saboraic?* Cincinnati: Hebrew Union College Press, 1989.

Kamin, Sarah. *Bein Yehudim le-Nosrim be-Parshanut ha-Miqra*. Jerusalem: Magnes Press, 1992.

————. *Rashi: Peshuto shel Miqra u-Midrasho shel Miqra*. Jerusalem: Magnes Press, 1986.

Kaplan, Lawrence Jay. "Rationalism and Rabbinic Culture in Sixteenth-Century Eastern Europe: R. Mordecai Jaffe's *Levush Pinat Yikrat*." Diss., Harvard University, 1976.

Kaplan, Yosef. *Mi-Nasrut le-Yahadut: Hayyav u-Fa'alo shel ha-Anus Yitzhaq Orobio de Castro*. Jerusalem: Magnes Press, 1983.

Kaplan, Yosef, Henry Méchoulan, and Richard H. Popkin, eds. *Menasseh Ben Israel and His World*. Leiden and New York: E. J. Brill, 1989.

Karo, Joseph. *Kessef Mishneh*. Printed in standard editions of Maimonides' *Mishneh Torah*.

Kashani, Reuben. *Ha-Karaim: Korot Mesorot u-Minhagim*. Jerusalem, 1978.

Kasher, Menhaem. *Ha-Rambam ve-ha-Mekhilta de-Rashbi*. Jerusalem, 1980.

————. *Humash Torah Shlemah*. 43 vols. to date. New York: American Biblical Encyclopedia Society, 1938–.

Katchen, Aaron L. *Christian Hebraists and Dutch Rabbis*. Cambridge: Harvard University Press, 1984.

Katz, Ben-Zion. *Ḥasidut, Rabbanut, Haskalah*. 2 vols. Tel Aviv: Devir, 1959.

Katz, Jacob. *Exclusiveness and Tolerance*. New York: Schocken Books, 1962

———. *Ha-Halakhah ba-Meṣar*. Jerusalem: Magnes Press, 1992.

———. *Halakhah ve-Qabbalah*. Jerusalem: Magnes Press, 1984.

———. *Mesoret u-Mashber*. Jerusalem: Mossad Bialik, 1958.

———. *Out of the Ghetto*. New York: Schocken Books, 1973.

Katzenelson, Gideon. *Ha-Milḥamah ha-Sifrutit bein ha-Ḥaredim la-Maskilim*. Tel Aviv, 1954.

Keshet, Yeshurun. *M.Y. Berdichevski (Bin-Guryon): Ḥayav u-Fo'alo*.

Kisch, Guido. *Das Breslauer Seminar*. Tübingen, 1963.

Kittseer, Jakob. *Inhalt des Talmuds und seine Autorität*. Pressburg, 1857.

Klausner, Israel. *Toldot ha-Agudah Nes Tziyonah be-Volozin: Teudot u-Mismakhim*. Jerusalem: Mossad ha-Rav Kook, 1953.

———. *Vilna: Yerushalayim de Lita*. Lohame ha-Getaot, Bet Lohame ha-Getaot, ha-Kibbutz ha-Meuḥad, 1983.

———. *Vilna be-Tequfat ha-GRA*. Jerusalem: Sinai, 1942.

Klausner, Joseph. *Historyah shel ha-Sifrut ha-'Ivrit ha-Ḥadashah*, 6 vols., Jerusalem, 1952.

Klein, Salomon. *Mi-Pene Kosht: Bikoret Sefer Darkhe ha-Mishnah asher Ḥiber ha-Rav Frankel*. Frankfurt, 1861.

———. *Le Judaïsme; ou, La verité sur la Talmud*. Mulhouse: J. P. Risler, 1859.

Koepke, Wulf, ed. *Johann Gottfried Herder: Innovator through the Ages*. Bonn: Bouvier, 1982.

———, ed. *Johann Gottfried Herder: Language, History, and the Enlightenment*. Columbia, S.C.: Camden House, 1990.

Kohler, Kaufmann, ed. *David Einhorn Memorial Volume: Selected Sermons and Addresses*. New York: Bloch, 1911.

———. *Jewish Theology*. New York: Macmillan, 1918.

———. *Origins of the Synagogue and the Church*. New York: Macmillan, 1929.

Kohut, Alexander. *Arukh ha-Shalem*. 6 vols. Jerusalem, 1970.

———. *The Ethics of the Fathers*. Edited. and revised by Barnett Elzas. New York, 1920.

Kokhavi, David ben Samuel. *Sefer ha-Batim al ha-Rambam*. New York: M. Bloi, 1978–79.

Kondylis, Panajotis. *Die Aufklärung*. Stuttgart: Klett-Cotta, 1981.

Kooiman, Willem Jan. *Luther and the Bible*. Translated by John Schmidt. Philadelphia: Muhlenberg Press, 1961.

Kook, Abraham Isaac. *'Eder ha-Yeqar*. 1906. Reprint, Jerusalem: Mossad ha-Rav Kook, 1985.

———. *Ma'amre ha-Reayah*. Jerusalem, 1983.

———. *'En Ayah: 'al Aggadot Ḥazal she-be-En Yaaqov*. Jerusalem, 1987.

Kraemer, David. *The Mind of the Talmud*. New York: Oxford University Press, 1990.

Kraus, Hans-Joachim. *Geschichte der historisch-kritischen Erforschung des Alten Testaments*. Neukirchener Verlag, 1982.

Kriwitski, David. *Keshet u-magen*. Berdichev, 1911.

Krochmal, Nahman. *Moreh Nevukhe ha-Zeman*. Waltham, Mass., 1961.

Kugel, James L. *The Idea of Biblical Poetry*. New Haven: Yale University Press, 1979.

———. *In Potiphar's House: The Interpretive Life of Biblical Texts*. San Francisco: Harper Collins, 1990.

Lagree, Jacqueline. "La lecture de la Bible dans le cercle de Spinoza." In *Le grand siècle et la Bible* (= *Bible de tous les temps*, vol. 6), edited by Jean Robert Armogathe. Paris: Beauchesne, 1989.

Landau, Beṣalel. *Ha-Gaon he-Hasid mi-Vilna*. Jerusalem, 1965.

Landau, Yeḥezkel. *Ḥiddushe ha-Ṣelaḥ*. Standard editions.

Lang, Berel. "The Politics of Interpretation: Spinoza's Modernist Turn." *Review of Metaphysics* 43, no. 2 (1989).

La Peyrere, Isaac de. *Men Before Adam*. London, 1656.

Lazarus-Yafeh, Hava. *Intertwined Worlds: Medieval Islam and Bible Criticism*. Princeton: Princeton University Press, 1992.

Lerner, Hayyim Zevi. *Moreh la-Lashon*. Vilna: Ha-Almanah ve-ha-Ahim Rom, 1896.

Lessing, G. E. *Lessing's Theological Writings*. Edited and translated by Henry Chadwick. Palo Alto, Calif.: Stanford University Press, 1956.

Levin, Sabina. "Beit ha-Sefer le-Rabbanim be-Varshe, 1826–1863." *Gal-Ed* 11 (1990).

Levin, Yehoshua Heshel. *'Aliyot Eliyahu*. Jerusalem, 1989.

Levine, Baruch. *The JPS Torah Commentary: Leviticus*. Philadelphia, 1990.

Levinger, Ya'aqob. *Darkhe ha-Maḥashavah ha-Hilkhatit shel ha-Rambam*. Jerusalem, 1965.

———. *Ha-Rambam ke-Filosof u-khe-Foseq*. Jerusalem: Mossad Bialik, 1989.

Levinsohn, Yiṣḥaq Baer. *Beit Yehudah*. Vilna, 1839.

———. *Zerubavel*. Warsaw, 1901.

Levitats, Isaac. *The Jewish Community in Russia, 1772–1844*. New York: Columbia University Press, 1943.

Levy, Ze'ev. *Baruch or Benedict?: On Some Jewish Aspects of Spinoza's Philosophy*. New York: Peter Lang, 1989.

———. "The Problem of Normativity in Spinoza's 'Hebrew Grammar.'" *Studia Spinozana* 3 (1987).

Lewin, B. M. *Oṣar ha-Ge'onim*. 12 vols. Haifa, 1928.

Liberles, Robert. *Religious Conflict in Social Context: The Resurgence of Orthodox Judaism in Frankfurt am Main, 1838–1877.* Westport, Conn.: Greenwood Press, 1985.

Lieberman, Saul. *Ha-Yerushalmi Ke-feshuto.* Jerusalem, 1935

———. *Hellenism in Jewish Palestine.* New York: Jewish Theological Seminary, 1962.

Liebermann, Eliezer. *Or Nagah.* Dessau, 1818.

Liebeschütz, Hans. *Das Judentum in deutschen Geschichtsbild vom Hegel bis Max Weber.* Tübingen, 1967.

Lipschitz, Jacob Lipmann. *Maḥaziqe ha-Dat.* Piotrkow Trybunalski: M. Tsederboym, 1903.

———. *Zikhron Yaakov: Historyah Yehudit be-Rusya u-Folin shenot 520–656, 1760–1896.* 2d ed. Bene Berak, 1967.

Livné-Freudenthal, Rachel. "Der 'Verein für Cultur und Wissenschaft der Juden' (1819–1824) zwischen Staatkonformismus und Staatskritik." *Tel Aviver Jahrbuch für deutsche Geschichte* 20 (1991).

Loewenich, Walther von. *Luther und Lessing.* Tübingen: J. C. B. Mohr, 1960.

Loewenstamm, Abraham ben Aryeh. *Der Talmudist wie er ist; oder, Wir sind alle Menschen.* Emden, 1822.

———. *Tzeror ha-Ḥayyim.* Amsterdam, 1820.

Löw, Leopold. *Gesammelte Schriften.* Szegedin, 1889. Reprint, Hildesheim: Georg Olms, 1979.

———. *Praktische Einleitung in die Heilige Schrift.* Gross-Kanischa, 1855.

Lowenstein, S. M. "The Readership of Mendelssohn's Bible Translation." *Hebrew Union College Annual* 53 (1982).

Lowy, S., *The Principles of Samaritan Bible Exegesis.* Leiden: E. J. Brill, 1977.

Lucas, Franz D., and Heike, Frank. *Michael Sachs: Der konservative Mittelweg.* Tübingen, 1992.

Luria, David. *She'elot u-Teshuvot Radal.* Tel Aviv: Y. D. Land, 1967.

———, ed. *Sha'are Teshuvah: 753 Teshuvot ha-Geonim.* Leipzig, 1858.

Luria, Solomon. *Yam shel Shelomo.* Standard editions.

Luzzatto, Samuel David. *Beit ha-Oṣar.* Leopoli, 1847

Mahler, Raphael. *Divre Yeme Yisrael: Dorot Aḥaronim.* Merḥaviah, 1954.

———. *Hasidism and the Jewish Enlightenment: Their Confrontation in Galicia and Poland in the First Half of the Nineteenth Century.* Philadelphia: Jewish Publication Society, 1985.

Maimon, Solomon. *Lebensgeschichte.* 1792. Frankfurt am Main: Insel Verlag, 1984.

Maimon, Y. L. Ha-Kohen. *Toldot ha-Gra.* Jerusalem: Mossad ha-Rav Kook, 1970.

———, ed., *Qoveṣ Ma'amarim ve-Ha'arot 'al Mishnat ha-GRA ve-Talmidav* (= *Sefer ha-GRA,* pt. 4). Jerusalem: Mossad ha-Rav Kook, 1954.

Maimonides, Moses (Moshe ben Maimon, Rambam). *Commentary on the Mishnah.* Edited and translated by Yosef Kafih. 3 vols. Jerusalem: Mossad ha-Rav Kook, 1976.

———. *The Guide of the Perplexed.* Translated by Shlomo Pines. Chicago: University of Chicago Press, 1963.

———. *Mishneh Torah.* Standard editions.

———. *Sefer ha-Miṣvot.* Edited by Ḥ. Chavel. Jerusalem: Mossad ha-Rav Kook, 1981.

Malakhi ben Yaʻakov ha-Kohen. *Yad Malakhi.* N.p., n.d.

Malbim, Meir Leibush. *Ha-Torah ve-ha-Mitsvah.* Jerusalem, 1969.

Manuel, Frank. *The Broken Staff.* Cambridge: Harvard University Press, 1992.

Margareten, Yiṣḥaq Zvi. *Sefer Toqef ha-Talmud.* Brooklyn, N.Y., 1983.

Margolies, Moses. *Pene Moshe* and *Marʼeh Penim.* Standard editions of the Yerushalmi.

Margoliot, Mordecai, ed. *Sefer Hilkhot ha-Nagid.* Jerusalem, 1962.

Marx, Alexander. *Essays in Jewish Biography.* Philadelphia: Jewish Publication Society, 1947.

Mauthner, Fritz. *Der Atheismus und seine Geschichte im Abendlande.* Stuttgart, 1922.

McCaul, Alexander. *Israel Avenged, by Don Isaac Orobio: Translated and Answered.* London, 1839.

———. *The Old Paths; or, A Comparison of the Principles of Modern Judaism with the Religion of Moses and the Prophets.* London: London Society's Office, 1837.

———. *Sketches of Judaism and the Jews.* London: B. Wertheim, 1838.

Méchoulan, Henry, and Gérard Nahon. *Menassah ben Israel: The Hope of Israel.* Oxford: Oxford University Press for the Littman Library of Jewish Civilization, 1987.

Méchoulan, Henry, Yosef Kaplan, and Richard H. Popkin, eds. *Menasseh Ben Israel and His World.* Leiden and New York: E. J. Brill, 1989.

Medini, Ḥayyim Hizkiah. *Sedeh Ḥemed.* 10 vols. Warsaw, 1896–1911.

Meklenburg. *Ha-Ketav ve-ha-Kabbalah.* 4th ed. Berlin, 1880.

Mekhilta. meet Rabbi Yishmael ve-Rabbi Akiba, im beʼur berure ha-middot . . . meet Yiṣḥaq Eliyahu Landa. Vilna, 1844.

Melamed, Ezra Zion. *Mefarshe ha-Miqra.* Jerusalem, Magnes Press, 1975

———. *Midreshe Halakhah shel ha-Tannaim be-Talmud Bavli.* 1943. Jerusalem: Magnes Press, 1988.

Menahem ha-Meiri. *Beit ha-Beirah ʻal Masekhet Avot.* Jerusalem: Makhon ha-Talmud ha-Yisraeli ha-Shalem, 1964.

Menasseh ben Israel. *The Conciliator: Reconcilement of the Apparent Contradictions in Holy Scripture.* London, 1842.

———. *Mishnayot im Hagahot Menassah ben Yisrael.* Amsterdam, 1643–44.

————. *Nishmat Hayyim*. Reprint, New York, 1984.

Mendelssohn, Moses. *Jerusalem; or, On the Religious Power and Judaism*. Hanover, N.H.: University Press of New England, 1983.

————. *Netivot ha-Shalom*. Vienna, 1846.

Menes, Abraham. "Patterns of Jewish Scholarship in Eastern Europe." In *The Jews: Their Religion and Culture*, edited by Louis Finkelstein. New York: Schocken Books, 1971.

Merhaviah, *Ha-Talmud be-Re'i ha-Narut*. Jerusalem: Mossad Bialik, 1970.

"Mevo ha-Talmud." In Vilna ed. of BT Berakhot.

Mevorakh, Barukh. *Reshit ha-Haskalah be-Germanyah, 1769–1799: Meqorot le-targil*. Jerusalem: Hebrew University, Jewish History Faculty, 1966.

Meyer, Michael. "The German Model of Religious Reform and Russian Jewry." In *Danzig, Between East and West: Aspects of Modern Jewish History*, edited by Isadore Twersky. Cambridge: Harvard University Press, 1985.

————. "Jewish Religious Reform and Wissenschaft des Judentums." *Leo Baeck Institute Yearbook* 16 (1971).

————. "Ob Schrift? Ob Geist? Die Offenbarungsfrage im deutschen Judentum des neunzehnten Jahrhundert." In *Offenbarung im jüdischen und christlichen Glaubensverständnis*, edited by Jakob J. Petuchowski and Walter Strolz. Freiburg, 1981.

————. *The Origins of the Modern Jew*. Detroit: Wayne State University Press, 1967.

————. *Response to Modernity*. New York: Oxford University Press, 1988.

Michael, Reuven. *Ha-Ketivah ha-Historit ha-Yehudit meha-Renasans 'ad ha-'Et ha-Ḥadashah*. Jerusalem: Mossad Bialik, 1993.

————. *I. M. Jost*. Jerusalem, 1983.

————, ed. *Heinrich Graetz: Tagebuch und Briefe*. Tübingen: J. C. B. Mohr, 1977.

Michaelis, Johann David. *Mosaisches Recht*. Biehl, 1777.

Midrash ha-Gadol. 5 vols. Jerusalem: Mossad ha-Rav Kook, 1975.

Midrash Rabbah. 2 vols. Vilna, 1887.

Milikowsky, Chaim Joseph. *Seder Olam: A Rabbinic Chronography*. Ann Arbor, Mich., 1981.

Mirsky, Samuel K., ed. *Mosedot Torah be-Eiropah be-Vinyanam u-ve-Ḥurbanam*. New York: Histadrut ha-'Ivrit be-Amerikah, 1956.

Mishnayot im Hagahot Menassah ben Yisrael. Amsterdam, 1643–44.

Mishnayot im targum ashkenazi . . . ve-im perush . . . meet Shneur Faybush. Vienna: Menorah, 1927.

Morell, Samuel. *Precedent and Judicial Discretion: The Case of Joseph ibn Lev*. Atlanta: Scholars Press, 1991.

Morton, Michael. *Herder and the Poetics of Thought*. University Park: Pennsylvania State University Press, 1989.

Moses of Coucy. *Sefer Miṣvot Gadol.* Standard editions.

Mosse, Werner, et al. eds., *Revolution and Evolution: 1848 in German-Jewish History.* Tübingen, J. C. B. Mohr, 1981.

Naḥmanides, Moses. "Hassagot" to Maimonides' *Sefer ha-Mitzvot.* Edited by Ḥ. Chavel. Jerusalem: Mossad ha-Rav Kook, 1981.

———. *Kitve Ramban.* 2 vols. Edited by Ḥ. Chavel. Jerusalem: Mossad ha-Rav Kook, 1964.

———. *Peirush 'al ha-Torah.*. Edited by Ḥ. Chavel. Jerusalem: Mossad ha-Rav Kook, 1966–67.

Nardeni, Ṣvia. "Temurot be-Tenuʻat ha-Haskalah be-Rusya be-Shenot ha-Shishim ve-ha-Shivʻim shel ha-Meʼah ha-Teshaʻ ʻEsreh." In *Ha-Dat ve-ha-Ḥayyim,* edited by Immanuel Etkes. Jerusalem: Merkaz Zalman Shazar, 1993.

Nemoy, Leon. *Karaite Anthology.* New Haven: Yale University Press, 1952.

Nettler, Ronald L. ed., *Studies in Muslim-Jewish Relations.* Vol.1. Chur, Switzerland: Harwood Academic, 1993.

Neubauer, Jacob. *Ha-Rambam 'al Divre Soferim.* Jerusalem: Mossad ha-Rav Kook, 1954.

Neusner, Jacob. *Midrash in Context.* Philadelphia: Fortress Press, 1983.

———. *Sifra: An Analytical Translation.* Atlanta: Scholars Press, 1988.

———. *The Talmud of the Land of Israel.* Vol. 35: *Introduction: Taxonomy.* Chicago: University of Chicago Press, 1983.

Neusner, Jacob, et al., eds. *From Ancient Israel to Modern Judaism: Essays in Honor of Marvin Fox.* 4 vols. Atlanta: Scholars Press, 1989.

Nieto, David. *Esh Dat.* London, Tomas Aylif, 1715.

———. *Matteh Dan.* Jerusalem: Mossad ha-Rav Kook, 1958.

Orobio de Castro, Isaac. *Israël Avengé.* London, 1770.

———. *Israel Avenged: Translated and Answered by the Reverend Alexander McCaul.* 2 parts. London, 1839.

———. *La observancia de la divina de Mosseh.* Coimbra, 1925.

Olender, Maurice. *The Languages of Paradise.* Cambridge: Harvard University Press, 1992.

Osier, Jean-Pierre. *D'Uriel da Costa à Spinoza.* Paris: Autre Rive, 1983.

Ostrowsky, Moshe. *Ha-Middot she-ha-Torah Nidreshet ba-hen.* Jerusalem, 1924.

Pelli, Moshe. "The Attitude of the First Maskilim in Germany towards the Talmud." *Leo Baeck Institute Yearbook* 27 (1982).

Perla, Yeruham Fischel. *Sefer ha-Mitzvot le-Rasag.* New York, 1962.

Petuchowski, Jacob J. "Abraham Geiger and Samuel Holdheim—Their Difference in Germany and Repercussions in America." *Leo Baeck Institute Yearbook* 22 (1977).

———. *The Theology of Haham David Nieto: An Eighteenth-Century Defense of the Jewish Tradition.* New York: Ktav, 1970.

Petuchowski, Marcus. *Der Tanna Rabbi Ismael*. Halle, 1892.

Philipson, David. *The Reform Movement in Judaism*. New York: Macmillan, 1907.

Pick, H. "Aktenstücke zur Geschichte der Talmudausgaben Berlin-Frankfurt an der Oder." In *Festschrift zum siebigsten Geburstage David Hoffmanns,* edited by Simon Eppenstein et al. Berlin, 1914.

Pineles, Zvi Menaḥem. *Darkah shel Torah*. Vienna, 1861.

Pinto, Isaac de. *Apologie pour la nation juive*. Amsterdam, 1762.

Plaut, Gunther W. "German-Jewish Bible Translations: Linguistic Theology as a Political Phenomenon." *The Leo Baeck Memorial Lecture #36*. Leo Baeck Institute. New York, 1992.

———. *The Rise of Reform Judaism: A Sourcebook of Its European Origins*. New York: World Union for Progressive Judaism, 1969.

Plessner, Salomon. *Rechtfertigung des jüdischen Religion und des jüdischen Charakters*. Leipzig, 1832.

Popkin, Richard H. *The History of Scepticism from Erasmus to Spinoza*. Berkeley: University of California Press, 1979.

———. *Isaac La Peyrere 1596–1676: His Life, Work and Influence*. Leiden and New York: E. J. Brill, 1987.

Popkin, Richard H., Yosef Kaplan, and Henry Mechoulan, eds. *Menasseh Ben Israel and His World*. Leiden and New York: E. J. Brill, 1989.

Porton, Gary G. "According to Rabbi Y: A Palestinian Amoraic Form." In *Approaches to Ancient Judaism: Theory and Practice,* edited by William Scott Green. Missoula, Mont.: Scholars Press, 1978.

Poznanski, S. "Anti-Karaite Writings of Saadia Gaon." *Jewish Quarterly Review,* o.s. 10 (1898).

Preus, James Samuel. *From Shadow to Promise: Old Testament Interpretation from Augustine to the Young Luther*. Cambridge: Harvard University Press, 1969.

Pritzker, Asher. *Ha-Meilah: Hitboleleut, Hamarah, Reformah*. Tel Aviv, 1957.

Puchta, G. F. *Cursus der Institutionen*. Leipzig, 1845.

Pummer, Reinhard. "Einführung in den Stand der Samaritanerforschung." In *Die Samaritaner,* edited by Ferdinand Dexinger and Reinhard Pummer. Darmstadt: Wissenschaftliche Buchgesellschaft, 1992.

Rabinovits, Natan David ben Yehudah Leyb. *Binu Shenot Dor va-Dor*. Jerusalem: Feldheim, 1984.

Rabinowitz, R. N. *Ma'amar al hadpasat ha-Talmud: Toldot hadpasat ha-Talmud*. Jerusalem: Mossad ha-Rav Kook, 1952.

Rabinowitz. Z. W. *Sha'are Torat Eretz Yisrael*. 1941.

Raeder, Siegried. *Die Benützung des masoretischen Textes bei Luther in der Zeit zwischen der ersten und zweiten Psalmenvorlesung (1515–1518)*. Tübingen: J. C. B. Mohr, 1967.

Ragoler, Abraham ben Solomon. *Ma'alot ha-Torah*. Brooklyn, 1978.

Rakover, Nahum, ed. *Maimonides as Codifier of Jewish Law.* Jerusalem: Library of Jewish Law. 1987.

Rapoport, Solomon Judah Leib. *Naḥalat Yehudah.* Krakow, 1868; Lvov, 1873.

Rappel, David. *Ha-Vikuah 'al ha-Pilpul.* Jerusalem: Devir, 1980.

Reggio, Isaac Samuel. *Beḥinat ha-Kabbalah.* Gorizia, Italy, 1852.

————. *Ha-Torah ve-ha-Pilosofia.* Vienna, 1828.

————. *Sefer Torat Elohim kollel Ḥamishah Ḥumshe Torah Meturgemanim Italkit u-Mevu'arim Be'ur ḥadash ke-fi Pashte ha-Ketuvim u-khellale ha-Lashon.* 5 vols. Vienna, 1821.

Reifmann, Jacob. *Iyyunim be-Mishnat ha-Ra'ava.* Collected and annotated by Naftali ben Menahem. Jerusalem: Maḥbarot le-Sifrut, 1961.

————. *Maamar Teudat Yisrael.* Berlin, 1868.

————. *Meshiv Davar.* Vienna, 1866.

Reiner, Elhanan. "Temurot bishivot Polin ve-Ashkenaz be-Me'ot ha-16-17 ve-ha-Vikuah 'al ha-Pilpul." In *Ke-Minhag Ashkenaz u-Folin: Sefer Yovel le-Chone Shmeruk,* edited by Yisrael Bartal et al. Jerusalem: Zalman Shazar, 1993.

Reines, Yiṣḥaq Ya'aqob. *Ḥotam Tokhnit.* 1880. Jerusalem, 1934.

————. *Kol Yaakov: 'al devar ha-yeshivah ha-kedoshah be-Lida.* Lida, 1907/8.

————. *Me'orot Gedolot.* 1886

Reissner, Hanns Günther. *Eduard Gans: Ein Leben in Vormärz.* Tübingen, J. C. B. Mohr, 1965.

Revah, I. S. *Spinoza et Juan de Prado.* Paris: Mouton, 1959.

Reventlow, Henning Graf. *The Authority of the Bible and the Rise of the Modern World.* Philadelphia: Fortress Press, 1985.

Reventlow, Henning Graf, and Benjamin Uffenheimer, eds. *Creative Biblical Exegesis: Christian and Jewish Hermeneutics through the Centuries.* Sheffield, England: JSOT Press, 1988.

Reventlow, Henning Graf, et al., eds., *Historische Kritik und biblischer Kanon in der deutschen Aufklärung.* Wiesbaden, 1988.

Reynolds, Frank E., and David Tracy, eds. *Myth and Philosophy.* Albany: State University of New York Press, 1990.

Richardson, Peter. *Law in Religious Communities in the Roman Period: The Debate over Torah and Nomos in Post-Biblical Judaism and Early Christianity.* Waterloo, Ont.: Wilfrid Laurier University Press, 1991.

Richarz, Monika. *Der Eintritt der Juden in akademischen Berufe.* Tübingen: J. C. B. Mohr, 1974.

Ritter, Immanuel Heinrich. *Geschichte der jüdischen Reformation.* 4 vols. Berlin: Steinhal, 1858–1902.

————. *Mendelssohn und Lessing.* Berlin, 1886.

Rivkind, Isaac. *Ha-Netziv ve-Yiḥuso le-Ḥibbat Ṣion: Pereq mi-Toldot Ḥayav u-Feulotav.* Lodz, 1918.

Robertson, Ritchie. "From the Ghetto to Modern Culture: The Autobiographies of Salomon Maimon and Jakob Fromer." *Polin* 7 (1992).

Robinson, John A. T. *The Priority of John.* Edited by J. F. Coakley. London: SCM Press, 1985.

Robinson, Thomas A. *The Bauer Thesis Examined: The Geography of Heresy in the Early Christian Church.* Lewiston, N.Y: Edwin Mellen Press, 1988.

Rogerson, John. *Old Testament Criticism in the Nineteenth-Century: England and Germany.* Philadelphia: Fortress Press, 1985.

Rosenberg, Shalom. "Emunat Ḥakhamim." In *Jewish Thought in the Seventeenth Century,* edited by Isadore Twersky and Bernard Septimus. Cambridge: Harvard University Press, 1987.

Rosenbloom, Noah H. "Discreet Theological Polemics in Menassah ben Israel's *Conciliador.*" *Proceedings of the American Society for Jewish Research* 58 (1992).

———. *Ha-Malbim.* Jerusalem: Mossad ha-Rav Kook, 1986.

———. *Tradition in an Age of Reform: The Religious Philosophy of Samson Raphael Hirsch.* Philadelphia: Jewish Publication Society, 1976.

Rosenthal, David, and Yaakov Sussmann, eds. *Meḥqere Talmud.* Jerusalem: Magnes Press, 1990.

Rosenthal, Erwin I. J., ed. *Saadya Studies.* New York: Arno Press, 1980.

Rousseau, Jean-Jacques. *The Social Contract.* Baltimore: Penguin, 1979.

Ruderman, David B. "Jewish Thought in Newtonian England: The Career and Writings of David Nieto." *Proceedings of the American Society for Jewish Research* 58 (1992).

Saadia Gaon. *The Book of Beliefs and Opinions.* Translated into English by Samuel Rosenblatt. New Haven: Yale University Press, 1948.

———. *'Esa Meshali: Sefer milḥemet ha-Rishon neged ha-Karaim.* Edited by Binyamin Menasheh Levin. Jerusalem: Mossad ha-Rav Kook, 1942.

———. *Sefer ha-Emunot ve-ha-Deot.* Edited and translated by Joseph Kafih. Jerusalem, 1970.

Saalschütz, J. L. *Das Mosaische Recht, nebst den vervollständigenden thalmudisch-rabbinischen Bestimmungen.* Berlin, 1846.

Sachs, Michael. *Die religiöse Poesie der Juden in Spanien* (1845). Berlin, 1901. Reprint, New York: Arno Press, 1980.

Saenz-Badillos, Angel. "The Biblical Foundation of Jewish Law According to Maimonides." In *Maimonides as Codifier of Jewish Law,* edited by Nahum Rakover. Jerusalem: Library of Jewish Law, 1987.

Safrai, Shmuel. "Halakhah le-Moshe mi-Sinai—Historia 'o Teologia." In *Meḥqere Talmud,* edited by Yaakov Sussmann and David Rosenthal. Jerusalem: Magnes Press, 1990.

Salant, Nathan N. *Zikhron Rabenu Shemuel Salant.* New York, 1919.

Salmon ben Yeruim. *Sefer Milḥamot Hashem.* Edited by Israel Davidson. New York: Jewish Theological Seminary, 1934.

Salomon, H. P. *Saul Levi Mortera en zihn "Traktaat Betreffende de Waarhied van de Wet van Mozes."* Braga, 1988.

Salvador, Joseph. *Histoire des Institutions de Moïse et du peuple Hébreu.* Paris, 1828.

Samet, Moshe. *"Besamim Rosh* shel R. Shaul Berlin: Bibliografyah, Historiyografyah, ve-Ideologyah." *Kiryat Sefer* 50 (1973).

Samson ben Isaac of Qinon. *Sefer ha-Keritot.* Amsterdam, 1709.

Samson of Sens. *Sifra de-Ve Rav.* With commentaries of Rabad and Samson of Sens. Jerusalem, 1969.

———. *Sifre al Ba-Midbar.* With commentary by Rabad and Samson of Sens.

Samuel ben Meir (Rashbam). *Perush ha-Rashbam ha-Shalem 'al ha-Torah.* Edited by David Rosen. Breslau, 1882.

Sandler, Peretz. *Ha-Biur la-Torah shel Moshe Mendelssohn ve-Siyyato: Hithavuto ve-Hashpa'ato.* Jerusalem: Reuven Mass, 1984.

Schäfer, Peter. *Studien zur Geschichte und Theologie des rabbinischen Judentums.* Leiden: E. J. Brill, 1978.

——— and Hans-Jurgen Becker. *Synopse zum Talmud Yerushalmi.* Tübingen, J. C. B. Mohr, 1991.

Scharzbach, Bertram Eugene. "La fortune de Richard Simon au 18ᵉ siècle." *Revue des Études Juives* 146, nos. 1–2 (1987).

Schechter, Solomon. *Studies in Judaism: First Series.* Philadelphia: Jewish Publication Society.

Schick, Moses ben Joseph. *Maharam Shik ha-shalem al ha-Torah.* 3 vols. Jerusalem, 1990–92.

Schiffman, Lawrence H. *The Halakhah at Qumran.* Leiden: E. J. Brill, 1975.

———. "The Sadduceean Origins of the Dead Sea Scrolls." In *Understanding the Dead Sea Scrolls,* edited by Hershel Shanks. New York: Random House, 1992.

———. *Sectarian Law in the Dead Sea Scrolls: Courts, Testimony and the Penal Code.* Chico, Calif.: Scholars Press, 1983.

Schlesinger, Akiva Joseph. *Lev ha-'Ivri.* Jerusalem: S. Tzukerman, 1923.

Schlueter, Margarete. "Jüdische Geschichtskonzeptionen der Neuzeit; die Entwürfe von Nachman Krochmal und Heinrich Graetz." *Frankfurter Judaistische Beiträge* 18 (1990).

Schmelzer, Menahem. "Hebrew Printing and Publishing in Germany." *Leo Baeck Institute Yearbook* 33 (1988).

Schoeps, Hans Joachim. *Israel und Christenheit: Jüdisch-christliches Religionsgespräch in neunzehn Jahrhunderten.* Munich: Ner-Tamid Verlag, 1961.

Schoeps, Julius H., and Walter Grab. *Juden im Vormärz und in der Revolution von 1848.* Stuttgart: Burg Verlag, 1983.

Scholder, Klaus. *The Birth of Modern Critical Theology.* London: Trinity Press International, 1990.

———. *Ursprunge und Probleme der Bibelkritik im 17. Jahrhundert: Ein Beitrag zur Entstehung der historisch-kritischen Theologie.* Munich: Kaiser, 1966.

Scholem, Gershom. *On The Kabbalah and Its Symbolism.* New York: Schocken Books, 1969.

———. *The Messianic Idea in Judaism.* New York: Schocken Books, 1971.

———. *Sabbatai Sevi.* Princeton: Princeton University Press, 1973.

Schorr, Yehoshua Heshel. "Halakhah le-Moshe mi-Sinai." *He-Ḥaluṣ* 3 (1857).

Schorsch, Ismar. "Breakthrough into the Past: The Verein für Kultur und Wissenschaft der Juden." *Leo Baeck Institute Yearbook* 33 (1988).

———. "Emancipation and the Crisis of Religious Authority: The Emergence of the Modern Rabbinate." In *Revolution and Evolution: 1848 in German-Jewish History,* edited by Werner Mosse et al. Tübingen: J. C. B. Mohr, 1981.

———. "The Ethos of Modern Jewish Scholarship." *Leo Baeck Institute Yearbook* 35 (1990).

———. "From Wolfenbüttel to Wissenschaft—The Divergent Paths of Isaak Markus Jost and Leopold Zunz." *Leo Baeck Institute Yearbook* 22 (1977).

———. "Ideology and History in the Age of Emancipation." In *The Structure of Jewish History and Other Essays,* by Heinrich Graetz. New York: Jewish Theological Seminary, 1975.

———. "Scholarship in the Service of Reform." *Leo Baeck Institute Yearbook* 35 (1990).

———. "Zacharias Frankel and the European Origins of Conservative Judaism." *Judaism* 30 (1981).

Schott, Heinrich August. *Geschichte der deutschen Bibelübersetzung D. Martin Luthers und der fortdauernde Werth derselben, aus den Quellen ausführlich dargestellt und wider alte und neue Gegner vertheidiget.* Leipzig: K. F. Kohler, 1835.

Schreiber, Emanuel. *Abraham Geiger, the Greatest Reform-Rabbi of the Nineteenth Century.* Spokane, Wash., 1892.

———. *Abraham Geiger als Reformator des Judenthums.* Loebau, 1879.

———. *Reformed Judaism and its Pioneers: A Contribution to Its History.* Spokane, Wash.: Spokane Publishing Co., 1892.

Schröter, Robert, ed. *Sefer Teshuvot Dunash Halevi ben Labrat al Rabbi Saadia Gaon.* Reprint, Jerusalem, 1971.

Schutze, Jochen. *Die Objektivität der Sprache: Einige systematische Perspektiven auf das Werk des jungen Herder.* Köln: Pahl-Rugenstein Verlag, 1983.

Schwartz, Daniel R. *Studies in the Jewish Background of Christianity.* Tübingen, J. C. B. Mohr, 1992.

Schwarz, Adolph. *Die Controversen der Schammaiten und Hilleliten.* Vienna, 1893.

Schweid, Eliezer. "Te'ologia Leumit-Ṣionit be-Reshitah: 'al Mishnato shel Harav Y"Y Reines." In *Meḥqarim be-Kabbalah, be-Filosofia Yehudit, u-ve-Sifrut ha-Musar ve-ha-Hagut Mugashim le-Yeshayahu Tishby*. Jerusalem, 1986.

Sefer ha-Malbim: meah shanah li-fetirato. Bene Beral, 1979.

Sefer Volozin: Sifrah shel ha-Ir ve-shel Yeshivat "Etz Hayyim." Tel Aviv, 1970

Seforno, Ovadiah. *Commentary on the Torah*. Standard edition.

Septimus, Bernard. "'Open Rebuke and Concealed Love': Nahmanides and the Andalusian Tradition." In *Rabbi Moses Nahmanides (Ramban): Explorations in His Religious and Literary Virtuosity*, edited by Isadore Twersky. Cambridge, Harvard University Press, 1983.

Septimus, Bernard, and Isadore Twersky, eds. *Jewish Thought in the Seventeenth Century*. Cambridge: Harvard University Press, 1987.

Shanks, Hershel, ed. *Understanding the Dead Sea Scrolls*. New York: Random House, 1992.

Shatzky, Jacob. *Kultur-geshikhte fun der Haskole in Lite*. Buenos Aires, 1950.

————. *Yiddishe Bildungs-palitik in Poilin fun 1806 biz 1866*. New York: YIVO, 1943.

Sherira Gaon. *Iggeret Rav Sherira Gaon*. Edited by B. M. Lewin. Haifa, 1921.

Shmueli, Ephraim. *Bein Emunah li-Khefirah: Rabbi Yehudah Aryeh Modina ve-Uriel Akostah, Parashah be-Toldot ha-Apikorsut be-Yisrael*. Tel Aviv: Masadah, 1961.

————. *Masoret u-Mahapekhah*. New York, 1942.

Shneor Phoebus ben Menahem of Bolechow. *Hiddushim me-Arba asar Shorashim shel . . . ha-Rambam ve-ha-Ramban*. Istanbul, 1749.

Shoḥet, Azriel. *'Im Hilufe Tekufot*. Jerusalem: Mossad Bialik, 1960.

————. *Mossad "ha-Rabbanut mi-Ta'am" be-Rusya: Parashah be-Ma'avaq ha-Tarbut bein Ḥaredim le-vein Maskilim*. Haifa, 1976.

Shvarts, Yehudah, ed. *Moreshet Rabbane Hungaryah*. Haderah: Yad le-Kehilot Transilvanyah, 1987.

Sifra de-ve Rav. Mevuar al yade Meir Ish Shalom. Jerusalem, 1966.

Sifre de-ve Rav Mevuar 'al yede Meir Ish Shalom. Jerusalem, 1966.

Sillman, Yoḥanan. "Torat Yisrael le-'Or Ḥiddusheha—Beirur Phenomenologi." *Proceedings of the American Academy for Jewish Research* 57 (1990–91).

Simon-Nahum, Perrine. *La cité investie: La "Science du judaïsme" français et la République*. Paris, Cerf, 1991.

Simon, Richard. *Apologie pour l'auteur de l'Histoire critique du Vieux Testament contre les faussetés d'un libelle publié par Michel le Vassor, prêtre de l'Oratoire*. Rotterdam: R. Leers, 1689.

————. *Histoire critique du Vieux Testament*. Rotterdam, 1685. Reprint, Geneva: Slatkine Reprints, 1971.

Sofer, Moses. *Ḥatam Sofer: Hamesh Shitot*. Jerusalem: Makhon le-Hotza'at Seferim ve-Heker 'al Shem ha-Hatam Sofer, 1967.

——. *Ḥatam Sofer: Ḥidushim u-Ve'urim 'al ha-Mitzvot.* Jerusalem: Makhon le-Hotza'at Seferim ve-Heker 'al Shem ha-Hatam Sofer, 1975.

——. *Ḥatam Sofer: Kelalim be-Sugyot ha-Shas.* Jerusalem: Makhon le-Hotza'at Seferim ve-Heker 'al Shem ha-Hatam Sofer, 1981.

——. *Ḥatam Sofer 'al ha-Torah.* Jerusalem: Makhon le-Hotza'at Seferim ve-Heker 'al Shem ha-Hatam Sofer, 1977.

——. *Ḥatam Sofer he-Ḥadash 'al ha-Torah.* Jerusalem: Hotza'at Makhon Da'at Sofer, 1989.

——. *Ḥiddushe Ḥatam Sofer 'al ha-Torah he-Ḥadash.* Mekhon Da'at Sofer, 1986.

——. *Ḥut ha-Shani.* Jerusalem: Mekhon Hatam Sofer, 1969.

——. *Mishle ha-Ḥatam Sofer: Tokheḥat Musar.* Edited by Yuda ha-Kohen Shtrasser and Aharon Perl. Brooklyn, N.Y.: Makhon Shem mi-Shemuel, 1990.

——. *Torat Mosheh.* Vienna, 1893–1906.

——. *Torat Mosheh: 'al Ḥamishe Ḥumshe ha-Torah.* New York: Hotza'at Grosman, 1960.

——. *Torat Moshe ha-Shalem.* Jerusalem: Makhon le-Hotza'at Seferim ve-Heker 'al Shem ha-Hatam Sofer, 1990

——. *Tzavaat Mosheh.* Brooklyn, N.Y., 1982.

Solomon, Norman. *The Analytic Movement in Rabbinic Jurisprudence.* Atlanta: Scholars Press, 1993.

Solomon ben Abraham ibn Adret (Rashba). *Responsa.* 7 vols. Bene Berak, Tel-Aviv, Jerusalem, 1965–70.

——. *Teshuvot ha-Rashba ha-Meyuḥasot la-Ramban.* Tel Aviv, 1989.

Soloveitchik, Joseph B. *Shi'urim le-Zekher Aba Mari Z"L.* Jerusalem, 1983.

Sorkin, David. "From Context to Comparison: The German Haskalah and Reform Catholicism." *Tel Aviver Jahrbuch für deutsche Geschichte* 20 (1991).

——. "Jews, the Enlightenment, and Religious Toleration—Some Reflections" *Leo Baeck Institute Yearbook* 37 (1992).

——. *The Transformation of German Jewry, 1780–1840.* New York: Oxford University Press, 1987.

Spektor, Isaac Elhanan. *Eṣ Peri: 'al haḥzakat limude ha-Torah ve-lomdeha.* Vilna, 1881.

Spinoza, Benedict de. *The Collected Works of Spinoza.* Edited and translated by Edwin Curley. Princeton: Princeton University Press, 1985.

——. *Ethics.* In vol. 1 of *The Collected Works of Spinoza,* edited and translated by Edwin Curley. Princeton: Princeton University Press, 1985.

——. *Hebrew Grammar* [*Compendium Grammatices Linguae Hebraeae*]. Translated by Maurice J. Bloom. New York: Philosophical Library, 1962.

———. *Spinoza Briefwechsel.* Edited and translated by Carl Gebhardt. Leipzig: Verlag von Felix Meiner, 1914.

———. *A Theologico-Political Treatise.* Translated by R. H. M. Elwes. New York: Dover Publications, 1951.

Staerk, Willy. *Die jüdisch-deutschen Bibelübersetzungen.* Frankfurt a.M.: Kauffmann, 1923.

Stampfer, Shaul. "Three Lithuanian Yeshivot in the Nineteenth Century." Diss., Hebrew University, 1981.

Stanislawski, Michael. *Tsar Nicholas I and the Jews.* Philadelphia: Jewish Publication Society, 1983.

———. *For Whom Do I Toil?* New York: Oxford University Press, 1988.

Steinmann, Jean. *Richard Simon et les origines de l'exégèse biblique.* Paris: Desclée de Brouwer, 1960.

Steinmetz, David C., ed. *The Bible in the Sixteenth Century.* Durham, N.C.: Duke University Press, 1990.

Steinschneider, Hillel Noaḥ Magid. *'Ir Vilna.* Jerusalem, 1969.

Stemberger, Gunter. "Die Datierung der Mekhilta." *Kairos* 21 (1979).

Stork, Theophilus. *Luther and the Bible.* Philadelphia: Lutheran Board of Publication, 1873.

Strack, H. L., and Stemberger, Gunter. *Einleitung in Talmud und Midrasch.* Munich: C. H. Beck, 1982.

———. *Introduction to the Talmud and Midrash.* Minneapolis: Fortress Press, 1992.

Sussmann, Ya'aqob. "History of *Halakhah* and the Dead Sea Scrolls—Preliminary Observations on *Miqṣat Ma'aseh ha-Torah* (4QMMT)." *Tarbiz* 59 (1989–90).

———. "Ve-Shuv le-Yerushalmi Neziqin." In *Meḥqere Talmud*, edited by Yaakov Sussmann and David Rosenthal. Jerusalem: Magnes Press, 1990.

Tannenbaum, M. *Der Talmud in seiner Wichtigkeit.* Magdeberg, 1849.

Tchernowitz, Chaim. *Ha-Talmud: sekirah kelalit al mahut ha-torah she-baal peh, yisud ha-halakhah ve-hishtalshelut yetziratah ad hatimat ha-Mishnah.* Warsaw, Hotzaat ha-Sefer, 1912.

———. *Masekhet Zikhronot: Parṣufim ve-ha-'Arakhot.* New York, 1945.

———. *Pirqe Ḥaim.* New York:. Bisaron, 1954.

———. *Toledot ha-Halakhah.* 4 vols. New York, 1934–50.

———. *Toledot ha-Poskim.* 3 vols. New York, 1946–47.

Terquem, Olry. *Première [-neuvième] lettre d'un Israelite français à ses correligionnaires.* Paris, 1821–37.

Theodor, J., and Ch. Albeck, eds. *Bereshit Rabbah.* Jerusalem: Wahrmann, 1965.

Tiktin, Salomon. *Darstellung des Sachverhältnisses in seiner hiessigen Rabbinats-Angelegenheit.* Breslau, 1842.

Tov, Emanuel. *Textual Criticism of the Hebrew Bible.* Minneapolis: Fortress Press, 1992.

Tracy, David, and Reynolds, Frank E., eds. *Myth and Philosophy.* Albany: State University of New York Press, 1990.

Treves, Dov Ber. *Revid ha-Zahav.* 1797. Bene Brak, 1967.

Twersky, Isadore. *Introduction to the Code of Maimonides (Mishneh Torah).* New Haven: Yale University Press, 1980.

———. *Rabad of Posquières: A Twelfth-Century Talmudist.* Cambridge: Harvard University Press, 1962.

———, ed. *Danzig, Between East and West: Aspects of Modern Jewish History.* Cambridge: Harvard University Press, 1985.

———, ed. *Rabbi Moses Nahmanides (Ramban): Explorations in His Religious and Literary Virtuosity.* Cambridge: Harvard University Press, 1983.

Twersky, Isadore, and Septimus, Bernard, eds. *Jewish Thought in the Seventeenth Century.* Cambridge: Harvard University Press, 1987.

Twersky, Yohanan. *Me-en Eliyahu: Haye ha-Gaon R. Eliyahu mi-Vilnah ve-Torato.* Ramat Gan: Masadah, 1960.

Ucko, Sinai. "Geistesgeschichtliche Grundlagen der Wissenschaft des Judentums." Reprinted in *Wissenschaft des Judentums in deutschen Sprachbereich: Ein Querschnitt,* edited by Kurt Wilhelm. Tübingen: J. C. B. Mohr, 1967.

Uffenheimer, Benjamin, and Reventlow, Henning Graf, eds. *Creative Biblical Exegesis: Christian and Jewish Hermeneutics through the Centuries.* Sheffield, England: JSOT Press, 1988.

Urbach, Efraim. *Ba'ale ha-Tosafot.* 2 vols. Jerusalem: Mossad Bialik, 1980.

———. "Ha-Derashah ki-yesod ha-halakhah u-va'ayat ha-Soferim." *Tarbiz* 27 (1958): 166–82.

———. *Hazal Pirqe Emunot ve-De'ot.* Jerusalem: Magnes Press, 1969.

Valdberg, Mosheh. *Kakh hi darkhah shel Torah.* 2 vols. Jassy, 1864–68.

Van Bunge, Wiep. "On the Early Dutch Reception of the *Tractacus Theologico-Politicus.*" *Studia Spinozana* 5 (1989).

Vermes, Geza. *Post-Biblical Jewish Studies.* Leiden: E. J. Brill, 1975.

Von Dohm, Christian Wilhelm. *Über die bürgerliche Verbesserung der Juden.* Berlin, 1781. Reprint, Hildesheim: Georg Olms, 1973.

Von Savigny, Friedrich Karl. *Of the Vocation of Our Age for Legislation and Jurisprudence.* London, 1831.

Wacholder, ben Zion. "The Date of the Mekhilta de-Rabbi Ishmael." *HUCA* 39 (1968), 81–118.

Wanefsky, Joseph. *Rabbi Isaac Jacob Reines: His Life and Thought.* New York, 1970.

Wasserman, Elhanan. *Qoves Ma'amarim.* Tel Aviv, 1986.

Weber, Ferdinand Wilhelm. *Jüdische Theologie auf Grund des Talmud und verwandter Schriften, gemeinfasslich dargestellt.* Leipzig: Dorffling & Franke, 1897.

Weinberg, Werner. "Les traductions et commentaires de Mendelssohn." In *Le siècle des lumières et la Bible* (= *Bible de tous les temps*, vol. 7), edited by Yvon Belavel and Dominique Bourel. Paris: Beauchesne, 1986.

Weinryb, Bernard D. *The Jews of Poland*. Philadelphia: Jewish Publication Society, 1972.

Weiss, Isaac Hirsh. *Di Grinder un Boyer fun Yidntum Dor Dor Vedorshav: oder di Geshikhte fun der Toyre Shebalpe*. 2 vols. New York, 1922.

———. *Dor Dor ve-Dorshav (Zur Geschichte der jüdischen Tradition)*. Berlin: Platt and Minkus, 1924.

———. "Iyyun Tefillah." *Bikkurim* 1 (1864).

———. "Mavo'ot ha-Talmud ve-Toldotehem." In *Beit Talmud* 1 (1881).

———. *Netzaḥ Yisrael*. Vienna, 1864.

———. *Zikhronotai me-Yalduti 'ad Mil'ot li Shemonim Shanah*. Warsaw, 1895.

———, ed. *Mekhilta. im Peirush Midot Soferim*. Vienna, 1865.

———, ed. *Sifra de-Be Rav*. Vienna, 1862.

Wellhausen, Julius. *Prolegomena zur Geschichte Israels*. 1878.

Werses, Samuel. *Haskalah ve-Shabtaut: Toldotav shel Maavak*. Jerusalem: Merkaz Zalman Shazar, 1988.

———. *Megamot ve-Ṣurot be-Sifrut ha-Haskalah*. Jerusalem: Magnes Press, 1990.

Wertheimer, Jack. *A People Divided: Judaism in Contemporary America*. New York: Basic Books, 1993.

———, ed. *The Uses of Tradition: Jewish Continuity in the Modern Era*. New York: Jewish Theological Seminary, 1992.

Wessely, Naftali Herz. *Divre Shalom ve-Emet*. Berlin, 1782.

———. *Gan Naul*. Vienna, 1829.

———. *Imre Shefer. Be'ur al sefer Bereshit*. Edited by S. Reggio. Goritiae, 1854.

———. *Levanon*. Amsterdam, 1765–66.

———. *Masekhet Avot im Peirush Yen ha-Levanon*. Warsaw, 1898.

Whitman, James Q. *The Legacy of Roman Law in the German Romantic Era*. Princeton: Princeton University Press, 1990.

Wieder, Naftali. *The Judean Scrolls and Karaism*. London: East-West Library, 1962.

Wiener, Max. *Abraham Geiger and Liberal Judaism*. Philadelphia: Jewish Publication Society, 1962.

———. *Jüdische Religion im Zeitalter der Emanzipation*. Berlin, 1933.

Wilhelm, Kurt. ed. *Wissenschaft des Judentums in deutschen Sprachbereich: Ein Querschnitt*. Tübingen: J. C. B. Mohr, 1967.

Willi, Thomas. *Herders Beitrag zum Verstehen des Alten Testaments*. Tübingen, J. C. B. Mohr, 1971.

Wise, Isaac Meyer. *History of the Hebrews' Second Commonwealth with Special Reference to Its Literature, Culture, and the Origin of Rabbinism and Christianity.* Cincinnati, 1880.

―――. *History of the Israelitish Nation: From Abraham to the Present Time.* Albany, N.Y.: J. Munsell, 1854.

Wistrich, Robert. *The Jews of Vienna in the Age of Franz Joseph.* Oxford: Oxford University Press for the Littman Library, 1990.

Wolfsberg, Yeshayahu. "Ha-Gaon mi-Vilna ke-Ishiut u-khe-Farshan." In *Qoveṣ Ma'amarim ve-Ha'arot 'al Mishnat ha-GRA ve-Talmidav* (= *Sefer ha-GRA*, pt. 4), edited by Y. L. Ha-Kohen Maimon. Jerusalem: Mossad ha-Rav Kook, 1954.

Wolfson, Elliot R. "Beautiful Maiden Without Eyes: *Peshat* and *Sod* in Zoharitic Hermeneutics." In *The Midrashic Imagination: Jewish Exegesis, Thought, and History,* edited by Michael Fishbane, 155–203. Albany: State University of New York Press, 1993.

―――. "By Way of Truth: Aspects of Naḥmanides' Kabbalistic Hermeneutic." *AJS Review* 14, no. 2 (Fall 1989).

Wolfssohn, Aaron. *Kalut daat u-ṣeviut: Rav Hanokh ve-Rav Yosefkhi.* Tel Aviv: Mifalim Universitaiyim le-hotzaat le-or, 1977.

Wood, Arthur Skevington. *Luther's Principles of Biblical Interpretation.* London: Tyndale Press, 1960.

Woodbridge, John D. "German Responses to the Biblical Critic Richard Simon: From Leibniz to J. S. Semler." In *Historische Kritik und biblischer Kanon in der deutschen Aufklärung,* edited by Henning Graf Reventlow et al. Wiesbaden, 1988.

Worster, Peter, and Gerhard von Glinski. *Königsberg: Die ostpreussische Hauptstadt in Geschichte und Gegenwart.* Berlin: Westkreuz, 1990.

Wurzburger, Walter S. "Samson Raphael Hirsch's Doctrine of Inner Revelation." In *From Ancient Israel to Modern Judaism: Essays in Honor of Marvin Fox.*, vol. 4, edited by Jacob Neusner et al. Atlanta: Scholars Press, 1989.

Yaari, A., ed. *Yahadut Lita.* Tel Aviv: Am ha-Sefer, 1959–66.

Yalkut Shim'oni. Editio princeps. Reprint, Jerusalem, 1968.

Yaron, Baruch. *Hitbolelut Yehudim ve-Radikalizm Hungari.* Jerusalem: Magnes Press, 1985.

Yaron, Zvi. *Mishnato shel ha-Rav Kook.* Jerusalem, 1979.

Yerushalmi, Yosef Hayim. *From Spanish Court to Italian Ghetto.* New York: Columbia University Press, 1971.

―――. *Zakhor.* Seattle: Washington University Press, 1982.

Yiṣḥaq ben Abba Mari. *Sefer ha-'Ittur.* Vilna, 1874.

Yom Tov ben Abraham al Ishbili. *Ḥiddushe ha-Ritba: Masekhet Yebamot.* Jerusalem: Mossad ha-Rav Kook, 1992.

Yovel, Yirmiyahu. *Spinoza and Other Heretics.* Princeton: Princeton University Press, 1989.

Zac, Sylvain. *Spinoza et l'interprétation de l'écriture.* Paris: Presses Universitaires de France, 1965.

Zacuto, Abraham. *Sefer Yuḥasin.* Edited by H. Filipowski. Frankfurt a.M., 1924.

Zalkin, Mordekhai. "Haskalat Vilna [1835–60]: Kavim le-Demutah." M.A. thesis, Hebrew University, 1992.

Zeitlin, Solomon. *Studies in the Early History of Judaism.* 4 vols. New York: Ktav, 1978.

Zevin, Shelomoh Yosef. *Ishim ve-Shitot.* Tel Aviv, 1966.

Zimmels. Hirsch Jacob. *Leopold Zunz.* London, 1955.

———. *Rabbi David ibn Abi Zimra.* Breslau, 1932.

Zimmer, Eric. *Rabbi Hayim ben R. Betzalel me-Fridberg: Aḥi ha-Maharal mi-Prag.* Jerusalem: Mossad ha-Rav Kook, 1987.

Zucker, Moshe. *Perushe Rav Saadia Gaon le-Vereshit.* Jerusalem: Jewish Theological Seminary, 1984.

Zuckermandel, Moses Samuel. *Zur Halachakritik: Ein Beitrag zur Kritik und Geschichte der Halacha.* Frankfurt a.M.: J. Kauffmann, 1911–13.

Zunz, Leopold. *Der Ritus des synagogalen Gottesdienstes.* Berlin, 1859.

———, ed. *Die Bibel. Die vierundzwanzig Bücher der Heiligen Schrift, nach dem masoretischen Texte.* Translated by H. Arnheim, Julius Furst, and M. Sachs. Frankfurt a.M.: Kaufmann, 1885.

Zweifel, Eliezer ha-Cohen. *Shalom 'al Yisrael.* Zhitomir, 1873.

Printed in Great Britain
by Amazon

32151273R00225